The Educated Child

A Parent's Guide
from
Preschool through Eighth Grade

WILLIAM J. BENNETT
CHESTER E. FINN, JR.
JOHN T. E. CRIBB, JR.

A TOUCHSTONE BOOK
Published by Simon & Schuster
New York   London   Toronto   Sydney   Singapore

TOUCHSTONE
Rockefeller Center
1230 Avenue of the Americas
New York, NY 10020

TOUCHSTONE and colophon are registered trademarks of Simon & Schuster, Inc.

Credits for the National Assessment of Education Progress (NAEP) reports
are listed following the Index.

Manufactured in the United States of America

1 3 5 7 9 10 8 6 4 2

The Library of Congress has cataloged the Free Press edition as follows:

Bennett, William J. (William John)
　　The educated child : a parent's guide / William J. Bennett,
Chester E. Finn, Jr., and John T. E. Cribb, Jr.
　　　p.　cm.
　　Includes bibliographical references and index.
　　　1. Education, Elementary—Parent participation—United States
Handbooks, manuals, etc.　2. Early childhood education—Parent
participation—United States Handbooks, manuals, etc.　3. Home and
school—United States Handbooks, manuals, etc.　I. Finn, Chester E.
II. Cribb, John T. E.　III. Title.
　　LB1048.5.B45　1999
　　　371.19'2—dc21　　　　　　　　　　　　　　　　　99-40335
　　　　　　　　　　　　　　　　　　　　　　　　　　　　CIP

ISBN 0-684-83349-2
　　　0-684-87272-2 (Pbk)

For our children—and yours

Contents

Contents

Acknowledgments

THIS BOOK WOULD NOT EXIST WITHOUT THE GENEROUS assistance of a great many people—mothers, fathers, teachers, principals, coaches, counselors, scholars, curriculum developers, and more. No one could have asked for wiser or more dedicated advisors. Collectively, they represent hundreds of years of experience in the twin arts of parenting and educating. They reviewed drafts, gave commentary, made suggestions, corrected mistakes, supplied information, and offered remarkable insights. While they do not necessarily agree with everything we think—and are not fairly held responsible for what we've written—their judgment and expertise profoundly influenced our work for the better on nearly every page.

We would like to thank the following individuals in particular for reviewing portions of the evolving manuscript at various stages and providing invaluable feedback: Rachel Abrams, Phyllis Aldrich, Joanne Anderson, Debi Backes, Elayne Bennett, Mark Boyea, Larry Braden, Ed Brann, Mary Butz, Nelson Cooney, Kaki Cribb, Dennis Denenberg, Ann Dobbs, Diane Fisher, Danielle Crittenden Frum, Karen Ghrist, Kevin Giblin, Olympia Glaros-Fafoutis, Peter Greer, Paul Gross, Bonnie Hedrick, Ann Hingston, Linda Hoekstra, Wade Horn, Mary Beth Klee, Kate and Les Lenkowsky, Robert Lillie, Joe McIlhaney, Debra Mentzer, Ginny Miller, Peter Perretti, Victoria Ann Price, Diane Ravitch, Sue Reiter, Jennifer Royall, Peggy Sapp, David Saxe, Trish Scalia, Patricia Scott, Linda Stark, Sandra Stotsky, Nancy Strother, Hope Taft, Mary Thompson, Leah Vukmir, Christiana Whittington and Ned Williams. Stephanie Lee and Madeleine Will were extra patient with Chapter 11, where their knowledge of resources helpful to parents of disabled children yielded many worthy additions.

We are greatly indebted to E. D. Hirsch, John Holdren, Connie Jones, and the Core Knowledge Foundation for generous permission to summarize portions of the Core Knowledge Sequence, which is as good a curriculum as we know—and is being successfully taught today to thousands of children in hundreds of U.S. schools. Don Hirsch and his colleagues also steered us toward needed experts and veteran educators.

Mater Dei School in Bethesda, Maryland, kindly gave permission to reprint its admirable character code. Likewise, South Boston Academy Charter School in Massachusetts made available its exemplary "Contract of Mutual Responsibilities."

This book benefited enormously from the sound advice, genuine enthusiasm, and fine editorial skills of our terrific editor, Chad Conway, and from the tireless efforts of the entire team at The Free Press. Bob Barnett, agent extraordinaire, provided his usual astute counsel. Our colleagues Noreen Burns, Kevin Cherry, Steve Coleman, Michele Hyde, Marci Kanstoroom, Monica Lee, Manon McKinnon, Tracey Nicholas, Mike Petrilli, Jake Phillips, and Irmela Vontillius gave invaluable aid in all sorts of ways, from research to logistical support, and helped keep this complicated project on track.

One of the wonders of modern technology is that those who embark on a project such as this can tap into ideas and opinions of people all over the country via the Internet, which hums with education discussions among parents and teachers alike. We wish especially to recognize the good work of the Education Consumers ClearingHouse, where we often found intelligent conversation, lively debate, and quotable comments.

In a sense, this book has been a work in progress for some fifteen years. Many of its ideas began to take form when we worked together at the Department of Education in the 1980s. Some reports, speeches, and articles of that era continue to influence our thinking and our words. Likewise, the authors have had various ties over the years with myriad groups and organizations that influenced our thinking and added to our knowledge and experience. We wish to acknowledge our affiliation with three mentioned in these pages, the Center for Education Reform, the Educational Excellence Network, and the Thomas B. Fordham Foundation.

Families never get enough recognition for what they tolerate and what they add in the course of book writing. Suffice it to say that Elayne Bennett, Renu Virmani Finn, and Kirsten Cribb have ample reason to be glad that we're finally finished, and to feel more than a little pride in a product that they have helped immeasurably to bring about. As for our children—four so far, and counting—they were and continue to be our beloved "beta sites" for most of what we know, and more that we still have to learn, about what it means to be parents and to be educated. We trust that *their* children will benefit from this accumulating knowledge.

Before You Begin

THIS BOOK CAN HELP YOU SECURE A GOOD EDUCATION for your child. Before you begin, please take a moment to read these few guidelines and caveats.

The Educated Child is organized into three main parts. Part I is for parents of preschoolers. It will help you get your child ready for school and do your vital job as his "home room" teacher in the years before kindergarten.

Part II addresses the academic curriculum from kindergarten through eighth grade. (Throughout this book, we use the term "elementary school" to refer to these grades.) These chapters outline important knowledge and skills your child should learn. They give tips for appraising his progress, as well as tools to help you decide whether your school is doing a good job. You'll also find plenty of ideas about ways to supplement the school's efforts at home.

Part III moves outside the formal curriculum and takes up important matters such as character education and teaching children with special needs. These chapters discuss how to help your child succeed in elementary school. They alert you to some issues, problems, and puzzles you may encounter, and suggest ways to stay involved in your child's education.

It is not necessary to read this book straight through, from cover to cover. Treat it as a resource to consult during your child's passage from the earliest years to the threshold of high school. Keep it on a handy shelf. Pick it up and browse from time to time. Check to see what sorts of lessons good schools teach. If your child needs to improve his homework habits, turn to that section. If you have doubts about your school's social studies curriculum, spend some time with the chapter on history and geography. This book can be a tool to help you stay a step ahead of the game and spot problems before they have a chance to hinder your child's education.

It is not necessary to take every action suggested in this book. In the coming chapters, while reminding you of basic parental responsibilities, we also offer many different ideas about how to fulfill those duties—activities you might try, questions you might ask teachers, books you might share with your child. We do not mean that you should attempt all, or even most of, the specifics! That is unnecessary and for most parents not possible. You don't have that much time. The activities in this book come recommended by a wide variety of parents, teachers, and principals whose judgment we trust, but the authors certainly have not done every one of them with their own children. The many examples, strategies, and ideas we offer are meant as helpful suggestions. Some will be better suited than others for your particular child and your particular school. We leave it to you to choose among them.

Your child does not have to know every item listed in this book to be considered "educated." He does not have to read every book recommended, try every activity, and master every fact. The authors do not know every single thing that a good elementary school might teach. Nor, probably, do you. The point is that good schools introduce children to most of the topics outlined here, and they do it in an organized, sustained fashion. Not every lesson your child studies will stay in his head. But a great deal of it will remain and have a defining impact on his education.

The authors drew on the experience of many good parents and fine teachers in assembling this book. Their advice informs virtually every page. Nothing in this book is revolutionary, however. You will find no magic bullets or profound secrets. You will find a measure of common sense, which in our time is very much needed in education. Sometimes we need to reaffirm common sense in order to focus on what is important, reinforce our confidence, and speed our efforts along.

It also helps to reaffirm common sense because there are more than a few "experts" in this field who act as though education is an arcane science that only highly trained professionals (like themselves) can really fathom. Sometimes they make parents feel unqualified to judge what is happening in their schools and their children's lives. They spout jargon and invoke theories to justify low expectations and achievement. This book will fortify you against such excuses. Degrees, certificates, credentials, fancy terms—none of these guarantees a good education, and you should not be intimidated by them.

In truth, it takes no special expertise to judge a school. You don't have to be a shoemaker to know that the shoe doesn't fit. You don't have to be a curriculum developer or district superintendent to know that your child's education isn't going right. You may not feel comfortable judging a specific lesson or teaching method. But if you pay attention to what your child is learning, you can get an accurate sense of whether the school is doing a good job overall.

Think of this book, then, as common sense plus. It can reaffirm your own prudent judgment, plus give you some solid ideas about what a good education looks and feels like.

The ideas, strategies, and suggestions included here are intended as education equalizers. They don't depend on how much money you have, the color of your skin, or your own educational background. Your attitudes and efforts are more important to your child's academic success than family income or the number of diplomas hanging on your wall. A parent who dropped out of high school but now has a strong commitment to education is much more valuable than a Ph.D. parent with an attitude of indifference toward his child's learning. One of the great American ideals is that *all* parents should be able to secure a good education for their children. We believe in that ideal and offer this book in that spirit.

A Note to Single Parents

We all know that raising a child alone is tough. We recognize that it's also harder for a single parent to help his or her child get the best possible education. You are stretched thinner on time, energy, and resources. Nevertheless, you *can* do it. You may need to call in allies—brothers, sisters, grandparents, neighbors, pastors, friends. Your first job may be to round up people you trust to help make sure homework gets done, to read with your child, or just to keep an eye on him and give him someone to talk with while you are away. One of the authors grew up in a home without a father. He and his brother were raised by their mother, with help from a grandmother. With effort, they made it work. Millions of other Americans are doing the same. All kids don't get equal starts, but the relevant adults in a child's life still make the defining difference in his education.

A Note to Home Schoolers

Parents who school their children at home will find many parts of this book valuable. Read through the discussions of what good schools do. You'll want to provide most of the same benefits. Many questions that we suggest parents ask of their schools are ones you will want to ask of yourself.

The core curriculum described in this book can provide a framework for decisions about what is most important for you to teach. In sections such as "Teaching Your Child Good Study Habits" and "Tests and Testing," you'll find pointers to help your child become a good student. You may gain useful insights from discussions of such topics as television, physical fitness, sex education, and drugs and alcohol. We also furnish numerous suggestions for parents who wish to supplement their child's education, lists that may be even more beneficial for moms and dads who are shouldering the burden of schooling at home. (Our hats are off to you!)

A Note to New Americans

Many people newly arrived on these shores encounter an education system that is very different from the one they grew up with. They are deeply concerned about the quality of American schools but not sure how to approach them. If you are new to this country, this book will provide an orientation to American schooling—its troubles as well as its strengths. It can help you learn to take part in school life, as well as judge what you must do to make the system work well for your child.

This country, perhaps more than any other, draws strength from the coming together of people from all over the world. Amid that diversity there exists a common culture—the ideas, knowledge, and beliefs we all share as Americans. One of the main jobs of an elementary school is to welcome *all* children to the best of that common culture. This book will help you decide whether your school is doing that job well. It will help you determine whether your school is getting your child ready to succeed in this land of opportunity.

A Note to Teachers

Although this book is written primarily for parents, teachers and other educators can also benefit from it. You may or may not discover anything new about schools, but you will likely gain a clearer understanding of what your "clients" seek. As will be evident, we urge parents to hold high expectations for their children and their schools. First, however, parents must take their own educational responsibilities very seriously. You will find that we, too, have scant patience for parents who expect you to do the entire job. In these pages, you will see some ways that parents can lend a hand—indeed, ways that you can reasonably expect them to involve themselves with their children's education.

This book alternates (by chapter) between masculine and feminine pronouns when referring to children. We have adopted this convention since America has approximately equal numbers of girls and boys. Because the majority of U.S. educators at the elementary school level are women, we use feminine pronouns to refer to teachers.

Nobody is perfect. No parent can do a flawless job. The authors, and the people whose advice we have incorporated, are all mistake-making adults who do not always practice what we preach. (We approach this subject, by the way, with diverse perspectives: one of us has finished seeing his children through school, another is in the process, the third has yet to begin.) The most any of us can do is try our hardest for our kids. The higher we aim, the better off they will be. Children—and schools—rise with parents' expectations. The only way to lift our young people is to lift our own sights and standards. We wish you well. Your kids are counting on you.

Introduction

THE PURPOSE OF THIS BOOK IS TO HELP YOU SECURE A good education for your child from early childhood through the eighth grade. As far as learning goes, these years are far and away the most important. They are the time when children acquire the bricks and mortar of a solid education—the knowledge, skills, habits, and ideals that will serve as the foundation of learning and character throughout their lives. If that edifice is solid by the end of eighth grade, then a student's future is bright indeed. If poorly constructed, the outlook is much dimmer.

Our aim is three-fold. First, we hope to remind parents of their own responsibilities in educating their children. There are few secrets to raising good students. What needs to be done is mostly a matter of common sense. But there is much you can do, and a few things that you must do, to see that your child learns well.

Second, this book will help you determine whether your school is doing a good job. Many parents assume that their children's schools maintain high expectations and offer a quality education. They naturally want to believe that the academic program is strong. Our message to you is: "Trust but verify." The reality is that too many American schools are *not* doing right by their pupils. In the coming chapters, you'll find some tools you can use to figure out whether your child is truly getting a good education, and some suggestions about how to correct problems at school.

Third, this book paints a fairly detailed picture of what a well-educated child knows and can do. For much of American history, there existed the idea of a "good education." It meant possessing certain knowledge and skills, and behaving in a certain way. Today, regrettably, such a vision is missing from many schools. They are reluctant to specify the lessons that all children should learn. This is a shame, because some things *are* more important to know than others.

This book helps you know what to look for in a good education. It reminds you of what to stand for as a parent, and what you should not stand for. It draws on common sense, the experience of many teachers and parents, the wisdom of the ages, and much of the best available research. We can all use allies in our efforts to raise children. Think of this book as an ally to help you keep yourself, your child, and your school on track.

You Are Your Child's Most Important Teacher

There is an old saying that a parent's heart is the child's schoolroom. Your dreams, your efforts, your examples and loving exhortations—these set the boundaries of your child's education. The seminal lessons taught in the home stay with children as they make their way through school and life, shaping their interests, ideals, and enthusiasm for learning. Parents are children's first and most important teachers. Raising your child is your number one job. Seeing that he gets a good education is, in many respects, the crux of that task.

The pressures of time, work, and competing interests tempt us to hand more and more of our educational responsibilities to others. Parents often get a subtle, alluring, but deeply damaging message from today's culture: your role is not quite so important after all. You can delegate. You can outsource. Children will suffer no harm—in fact, they may reap some benefits—when they get more of their care and guidance from others. Specialists and experts can fill in for you, pay attention for you, make decisions for you, give guidance where you cannot. Let others take charge of education: curriculum directors, counselors, child care professionals, even children themselves. It is a seductive siren song. It gives the green light for surrendering part of a sacred duty.

You must resist these temptations. For good or ill, you are always your child's most influential teacher. Even when he reaches school age, you are still the dean-at-home, the chief academic officer. The more involved you are, the better your child's chances of getting a good education. If you begin to remove yourself from the learning process, those chances start to plummet. If you turn over your most important responsibilities to others, you may doom his school career. That amounts to educational abandonment, a pernicious form of child neglect. You need to be in charge of your child's education. So take charge.

Several critical elements can come only from you. First among these is your love. The psychologist Urie Bronfenbrenner says that the one indispensable condition for a child's successful upbringing is that at least one adult must have a deep and irrational attachment to him. In other words, someone must be absolutely crazy about that child. Children are put on this earth to be loved. They need unconditional devotion (*not* unconditional approval). When they grow up knowing that an adult is always there as guardian angel and guide, they thrive. When they sense that such devotion is missing, things can begin to go terribly wrong with their educations and their lives.

Your attitude about education is another key predictor of academic success. Your child looks to you for cues about what is important in life. He is always watching for your approval or disapproval, for your interest or indifference. If you care, he cares. If he sees that you value learning, he will probably do the same. If he observes you putting education second or third, he may not take his schoolwork seriously. Consistent reinforcement means everything. The messages you send determine in no small way how well your child reads, writes, and thinks. Every morning, you must send him off to school with a good night's sleep, a decent breakfast, and a positive attitude toward learning.

Instilling the highest ideals is crucial: Belief in the value of hard work. A strong sense of responsibility. A willingness to keep trying until success finally comes. Respect for legitimate authority. Such traits are the engines that power learning at school, in college, and in life. Academic success depends on them. Transmission of these virtues is more than just part of the territory of parenthood. It is a fundamental obligation.

Your expectations are all important. Children strive to clear the bars that their parents set. So long as those standards are fair and reasonable, they help kids flourish. Parents' expectations determine whether children finish homework on time and study for tests. They separate good students from bad. They help set the course of life. It is said that Abraham Lincoln's mother told him over and over again what kind of good, hardworking man she hoped he would become. Many years later Lincoln observed, "All that I am, and all that I hope to be, I owe to my angel mother." Setting standards for children is not placing a burden on them. It is an expression of love and confidence.

Good students usually come from homes where moms and dads have tried to create a rich learning environment. They've stimulated their children's curiosity by showing them that the world is a fascinating place and helping them explore it. This does not require you to spend lots of money or have a degree in education. It mostly consists of seeing that your child grows up with interesting things to do. It means reading aloud to him, and listening to him read aloud. It means playing games, asking and answering questions, explaining things as best you can. It means exposing him to varied experiences and visiting places together—taking walks in the woods, working in the garden, occasionally going to a museum or monument. Such activities turn children into curious students.

Education success comes from putting enough time into the right work. What one spends time on is what one ends up knowing. If your child spends endless hours playing video games, he will know all the ins and outs of video games. If he spends time on math and science, then that's what he will know. Academic achievement also hinges, to no small degree, on the time *you* devote to education. If you spend time helping your loved one learn to read, master those multiplication tables, and listen carefully when others are talking, his chances of doing well in school are much better.

Know what your child is doing—where he is, who his friends are, what books he reads, what movies he sees. Keep track of schoolwork— what he is learning, whether he's finishing his assignments, if he's prepared for that upcoming test. The parents of good students keep an eye on what the school teaches. They have a sense of the expectations it maintains, the discipline it requires. Your child's education demands your vigilance. You must stay alert. No one else will do it for you. When a parent's attention wanders, a child may quickly veer off the learning track. It may be harder than you think to get him back on.

You teach by example. Aesop tells a wonderful fable about a crab and his son scurrying over the sand. The father chastised his child: "Stop walking sideways! It's much more becoming to stroll straightforward." The young crab replied: "I will, father dear, just as soon as I see how. Show me the straight way, and I'll walk in it behind you." There is nothing like the quiet power of intellectual example and moral example. Parents teach in everything they do. More often than not, your child will walk it the way you walk it.

For most moms and dads, faith is a crucial part of education. Believing that children are moral and spiritual beings, they want their loved ones to be educated in a way that reflects those beliefs. Public schools, by law, cannot be of help in the inculcation of faith. But there are other institutions—churches, synagogues, mosques, and of course religious schools—that can be critical teachers. Bear in mind that religious training can help young people become better students, and there is ample evidence that faith safeguards children from threats that wreck educations at an early age, such as drugs, alcohol, and sexual experimentation.

The rules you maintain lie at the foundations of a good education—rules such as "All schoolwork must be finished before you talk to your friends on the phone," and "Always speak politely to teachers." Without clear direction from parents, most students do not know how to conduct themselves.

Rules about television are *especially* critical to academic success. In this country, television has become an enemy of education. In many homes, it is a constant interference with learning. Television is not only a distraction and sometimes a cesspool, but watching it also means your child is losing the opportunity to do something more valuable. Almost anything else—reading, exercising, playing a game, talking with parents, even sleeping—is a better use of your child's time. The research is clear: excessive television hurts a youngster's school achievement. A TV set on all the time is a sign of parental indifference. Yes, there is some good TV, but if you care about education, your youngster cannot sit slack-jawed hour after hour in front of the tube.

These, then, are the fundamentals. Your love. Your attitude about education. Your efforts to stimulate your child's curiosity. Your ideals, rules, and expectations. The time and attention you pay, and the examples you set. These themes are at the core of this book. They are necessary ingredients on your end. They do not guarantee academic achievement, but they make it much more likely. They put your child's education in the hands best able to direct it: yours.

Lessons That Good Schools Teach

Parents often attach the most importance to higher education, yet elementary school has a far greater impact. Except for family and church, no institution is so influential. We ask elementary schools to help shape our students' first and lasting ideas about themselves, their country, and the world. We expect them to teach basic knowledge and nourish the appetite for learning. In the K–8 years, children gain—or fail to gain—skills they will need throughout their educations and careers. They develop habits and values they will carry the rest of their days. Elementary school is an invitation and encouragement to a fulfilled life. In educational significance, its mission dwarfs all others.

The authors have visited hundreds of schools across the country. We have learned that good elementary schools share a certain character or ethos. They teach certain lessons and uphold certain ideals. It takes no expertise to recognize whether a school is doing right by its students. You can begin to get a good sense of it just by spending a little time in its classrooms and corridors.

Good schools attend to the basic subjects: English, history, geography, math, science, art, and music. They focus on these academic fundamentals. They don't clutter the curriculum with so many other topics that the basics get pushed aside. Students know that learning this core curriculum is serious business.

Good elementary schools concentrate on essential skills. Perhaps most of all, that means teaching students how to comprehend the written word. Reading is the heart and soul of elementary education. If a child goes on to high school unable to read fluently, his chances for academic success are in great peril. Other vital skills also need to be mastered before eighth grade. We expect elementary schools to teach children to speak and write well; to add, subtract, multiply, divide, and measure things; to think logically and clearly; to ask good questions, analyze problems, and search for correct answers.

Knowledge is just as important as skills. Good elementary schools recognize that there are some facts and ideas that all American students should know. For example, they teach students what a right triangle is, what happened in 1776, where the earth is in our solar system, what a Trojan horse is. Good schools spell out for parents the fundamental knowledge they intend to transmit. Teaching it is serious work, not a chance by-product of learning skills.

Elementary schools hold the responsibility of transmitting to each new generation what may be called our "common culture," the things that bind Americans together as one people. In its highest form, this common culture is the sum of our intellectual inheritance, our legacy from all the ages that have gone before us. It is the knowledge, ideas, and aspirations that shape our understanding of who we are as a people. Our common culture is found in documents such as the Constitution and the Declaration of Independence; in principles such as the belief that all men are created equal; and in events from our past, such as the landings of the *Mayflower* at Plymouth and the *Eagle* on the moon. It lies in great stories and poems, such as Charles Dickens's A *Christmas Carol* and Emma Lazarus's "The New Colossus." Americans of all backgrounds want schools to acquaint children with our common legacy. As the journalist Walter Lippmann once observed, no culture can survive that is ignorant of its own traditions.

Teaching cultural literacy is part of the effort of raising good citizens. This task, too, belongs in considerable part to the elementary school: to help lay the groundwork for young people's eventual entry into the democratic community of responsible adults. Teachers acquaint pupils with their rights as well as their duties to their fellow citizens and their country. Teddy Roosevelt once said that "the first requisite of a good citizen in this republic of ours is that he shall be able and willing to pull his own weight." Good schools teach such civic virtues. They help children learn to live up to their obligations, not to shrink from toil, and to give others the respect they are due. They teach them to recognize America's faults, but also to offer this country the great honor it deserves. They help children become, in Madison's words, "loving critics."

In that vein, good elementary schools help parents develop character in children. They never lose sight of the fact that the formation of intellect and character go hand in hand. In training young hearts and minds toward the good, they make conscious efforts to inculcate virtues such as self-discipline, diligence, perseverance, and honesty. Teachers cultivate these traits largely through the formation of habits: getting to class on time, being thorough about assignments, saying "Yes, Ma'am" and "Yes, Sir" to teachers, cleaning up after oneself. They offer lessons that appeal to children's moral imaginations. They help students come to know virtue.

These are lessons that good elementary schools must teach. Our system of education is like a pyramid. Success at each level—high school, college, and beyond—depends on earlier preparation. Mediocrity at any stage will diminish possibilities for the next. A cracked foundation threatens the whole.

Will Your School Educate Your Child Well?

It is well documented that many U.S. schools are not meeting today's challenges. Surveys and test scores are disheartening. The National Assessment of Educational Progress reports that fewer than one third of fourth graders are "proficient" readers. Nearly 40 percent read below the "basic" level, which means they can barely read at all. In math, nearly

40 percent of eighth graders score below basic. Americans are now sadly accustomed to newspaper reports that fewer than one in five American children knows the purpose of the Declaration of Independence, or that one third of high school seniors can't identify the countries we fought during World War II.

Employers complain that many job applicants lack the basic reading and math skills they need to perform the jobs they are seeking. They say that many students come out of school with poor work habits, including disorganization, irresponsibility, and an inability to get to work on time. College officials voice similar concerns. Nationwide, about three in ten first-time college freshmen now have to take remedial courses in reading, writing, or mathematics. As Steven Sample, president of the University of Southern California, has observed, "A country that has the best universities in the world has among the worst elementary and secondary schools."

There are some bright spots in the academic record, particularly in the lower grades. In international math and science tests, for example, American fourth graders fare well compared with students in other nations. By the eighth grade, however, their performance is middling. By twelfth grade, they occupy the international cellar. In math and science, American seniors are among *the worst in the industrialized world*.

Clearly something is going wrong, particularly in the middle and high school grades. Unlike students in other countries, our kids seem to do worse the longer they stay in school. By the end of eighth grade, many are ill-prepared for the kind of high school education we want them to have.

The U.S. has been "reforming" its schools for the better part of two decades. We've tried a hundred different programs and a thousand gimmicks. We've poured in countless billions of dollars. Yet it's clearer than ever that none of these nostrums has worked—and some have made matters worse. It is deeply disturbing that in the most prosperous country in the world, our education system is failing so many of our children.

Low academic standards afflict many schools. Textbooks, tests, and assignments are watered down. "We're just demanding less and less, all the time," says a veteran North Carolina teacher. "I'm teaching lessons in the eighth grade that I used to teach in the sixth." Students learn to get by with less than their best. "No one corrects bad spelling or punctuation—and we're talking about third grade," says one worried mom. "Everyone gets a gold star." Some schools seem to have forgotten that there is a difference between making a lesson interesting and making it easy. "My seventh grader spent the last two weeks of social studies class cutting pictures out of magazines," another parent reports. "What is he learning? He's getting real handy with the scissors."

Some schools do not focus enough on basic subjects. Judging by their students' assignments, learning to cherish the rain forests, recognize ethnic foods, and feel good about oneself have become more important than mastering the three Rs. It's not that matters like respecting the environment are not important. They are. But too often they are used as an excuse not to tackle the tough academic fundamentals. Remember, education is largely time on task. We learn what we do. If a child does not work many math problems, we ought not be surprised that he doesn't know much math.

In many places, educators no longer take responsibility for stating which facts and lessons are most important to know. They no longer say: "Here is what we will teach your child before he leaves us. This is what a good education looks like." Instead, they talk about teaching students to "learn how to learn," and remain vague about exactly *what* they should learn. Some schools look largely to children's preferences, instincts, and feelings as teaching guides. For example, in one school saluted for its progressive attitude, the principal proudly announced that he uses "the smile gauge"—if students are smiling, they are doing their jobs. This is a questionable approach to teaching and learning, to say the least.

The poet Samuel Taylor Coleridge once invited a friend with such notions of education to view his garden. "But it is covered with weeds," his friend said in surprise. Coleridge explained that he was letting the garden make up its own mind about what to produce. "The weeds, you see, have taken the liberty to grow," the poet explained, "and I thought it unfair of me to prejudice the soil towards roses and strawberries." If schools do not spell out what a student should learn, you can count on his education being choked with weeds.

In some schools you find an unruly atmosphere. Kids act up, use foul language, talk rudely to teachers—and get away with it. The adults in charge are unwilling to tell them to sit down, be quiet, and get down to work. In some places, we've forgotten that self-discipline is not the enemy of learning—or of happiness. It is, rather, a necessary condition. We act as if young people cannot develop the self-control to pay attention, do what the teacher says, and stick with assignments until they get them right. We've given up the notion of insisting on studious, respectful children.

Many schools no longer possess a moral center. Their teachers have been discouraged from taking up character training in a direct fashion. They are reluctant to "impose their values" on students. Their overriding concern is to demonstrate how tolerant they are of others' behavior and choices. Saying to children "What you are doing is bad and wrong" might trample their rights, inflict feelings of shame, or damage their self-esteem. Meanwhile, more and more young Americans graduate with a shaky sense of right and wrong.

Let us be clear. The United States is blessed with a number of excellent elementary schools. Many, however, are mediocre, and there are some that we would not wish on any child. Here is the bottom line: you cannot automatically assume that your school is doing a good job teaching your child—even if it assures you that it is. You must pay attention and look to see exactly what sort of education your child is getting.

Our Schools and Our Culture

It would be easy to point fingers at the schools and say, "There lie all our problems." There is no doubt that the school system is the source of many of its own shortcomings. But the truth is that U.S. schools are filled with dedicated teachers and principals who want more than anything else for American schoolchildren to succeed. These people are on the front lines. They see firsthand what's right and what's wrong in our classrooms. They are heartbroken that so many of their schools get mediocre results.

Talk to these women and men, and you begin to sense deeper problems at play, problems larger than the schools themselves. The disturbing news is that many teachers feel as though they are working with little help from parents. They express dissatisfaction, worry, even bitterness over their circumstances. They are convinced that many schools struggle partly because parents are not holding up their end of the bargain. These educators are right.

According to the research organization Public Agenda, more than four out of five public school teachers say many parents fail to set limits and create structure at home, fail to control how much time their kids spend with TV, computers, and video games, and refuse to hold their kids accountable for their behavior or academic performance. Too many moms and dads are failing to get their children interested in learning. They are not making sure that assignments get done. They are not teaching the self-discipline, perseverance, and respect that enable students to succeed.

This lack of supervision yields real classroom consequences. Nearly seven in ten teachers say they face a serious problem because so many students try to get by doing as little work as possible. More than half say they have serious problems with students failing to do homework. And more than four teachers in ten point to kids who are disruptive in class. "Very few students bring good habits to class," says an Indiana teacher. A Nebraska teacher agrees: "Parents are not sending them to school prepared. Simple things like basic manners, but lots of parents don't do this anymore—'please, thank you, close your mouth when you chew.' The parent hasn't taught the child: 'Get your things together the night before, leave them in front of the door.' . . . Today's kids need more than what they're getting."

To be sure, many youngsters still come from homes where the message from parents is: "We care about what you are doing, we want to be involved, and we're with you every step of the way." But in other homes the signal to the school is: "Here are our children. They're in your hands now. Let us know how it turns out." As Diane Ravitch of New York University observes, too many mothers and fathers have the attitude that school is like a car wash where you drop the child off at one end and pick him up at the other. They do not realize that, to get a good student, you have to be involved in the washing.

More and more, America has asked schools to fill in the gaps and pick up the slack where families leave off. We've tried to turn schools into the first line of defense against problems far beyond their competence to handle successfully. Teachers today tell us that much of their time is spent "raising children"—teaching them the basics of hygiene, manners, and rudimentary respect for the rights and property of others. They counsel children of divorce, teach kids the facts of life, and train them in "conflict resolution." Meanwhile, we also expect them to make sure students learn to read, write, multiply, and divide. More than four out of five teachers say that many parents expect the school to do their job for them. Half of parents surveyed say schools should be able to do a good job with students whose moms and dads pay little attention to discipline and supervising behavior![1]

Such expectations are unreasonable. We should not ask schools to take on basic socialization *and* basic academics. There simply is not enough time. Even with perfect school attendance, American children spend less than 10 percent of their time from birth to age eighteen in school. There is no way that 10 percent can overcome what is happening—or not happening—in the other 90 percent. When schools stray too far from teaching basics like English, science, and history, they take time away from what they can do best.

We can't expect teachers to produce good students if we don't send them the right sort of raw material—youngsters who are well behaved and eager to learn. If parents don't spend enough time with their kids, don't try to get them interested in reading, don't pay attention to homework, and don't see that children are prepared for tests, the school's job is next to impossible. When students come to class with a cavalier attitude about education, poor work habits, little self-control, and no respect for authority, a good education is already out of reach.

If we've learned anything in the last three decades, it is this: schools cannot take the place of moms and dads. When parents are distracted from their most important responsibilities, it is exceedingly difficult for teachers to fill the breach.

In the end, it is hard to escape the conclusion that what we see in our classrooms is a reflection of the larger culture, and that the mediocrity of our schools is part of a general lowering of standards. We have teachers who shy away from teaching right and wrong because they've been made to feel that the greatest sin is to be "judgmental." We have administrators who fear strict discipline because they don't want to get sued by parents. We have kids coming to class who've spent thousands of hours in the company of TV shows, movies, video games, and music which celebrate trash: profanity, violence, promiscuity, foul language, and rebellious attitudes. We have parents who rarely complain when their kids get lots of As in "fun" courses but turn plaintive when teachers try to give more homework or raise standards. If this is the world in which our schools have to operate, no wonder the education system has problems.

We repeat: many schools do a fine job. Likewise, millions of devoted parents want to do everything in their power to see that their children get good educations. Still, when we look at the cultural and educational landscape that our children are growing up in, like many Americans we find that things are not as they should be. This country is able to offer most of its young people a great deal materially, but is not necessarily giving them some of the things they need most. We are tolerating mediocrity on the hard, important lessons and trying to compensate with a kind of material lavishness that cannot plug the gap. We are doing well in many ways, but not nearly as well as we might in others. For all of this nation's greatness, it is not giving many students an education worthy of our ideals.

The good news is that it does not have to be this way. You can make a difference—all the difference—if you take certain steps and keep your eyes on certain goals. Education is not an enigmatic enterprise. There is no mystery about what makes good students and good schools. We spell out the basics in this book, together with steps you can take at home with your child, ways to see if your school is doing a good job, and strategies to adopt when things go wrong. James Madison said that "a people who mean to be their own governors must arm themselves with the power which knowledge gives." If you arm yourself with a little knowledge about what works in education, and take some of the actions described in these pages, the power is yours to help your loved one learn to his potential.

Please remember that, so long as you remain at the center of the education process, good things are likely to happen. Countless American parents prove it every school year, including those newly arrived on our shores. There will be bumps in the road, but your child is growing up in an amazing country and in an astonishing time. Despite our problems, the opportunities for education are more than plentiful. We hope this book is both informing and encouraging. We hope it bolsters your determination. We hope it helps you raise an educated child.

TEN PRINCIPLES FOR PARENTS OF EDUCATED CHILDREN

These are ten critical propositions will help you raise an educated child. Please take them to heart.

1. **Parents are the first and most important teachers.** The more involved you are, the better your child's chances of getting a good education. You can make the difference.

2. **Your teaching must not stop when schooling starts.** Some parents withdraw from involvement in education once their children reach school age. This is a mistake. Teachers cannot do a good job without your aid, support, and interest.

3. **The early years build the foundation for all later learning.** Make it sturdy. The first few years of life and then the first few years of school are critical. A solid education by eighth grade is a necessity or there will be trouble in high school and beyond.

4. **American schools are underperforming.** Many schools don't pay enough attention to academic basics, and standards are often too low. Trust but verify. Do not just assume that your school is doing a good job.

5. **Learning requires discipline; discipline requires values.** Too many classrooms are disrupted by disrespectful, unruly children. Too many kids have not been taught the virtues necessary to succeed in school.

6. **Follow your common sense.** Some people act as though it takes a special degree to know if a school is doing a good job. Wrong. You are the expert on your own child. Pay attention, talk to teachers and other parents, and trust your instincts.

7. **Content matters: what children study determines how well they learn.** Many schools are unwilling to say exactly which facts and ideas their students should know. This is a fundamental problem in American education. Some things are more important to learn in elementary school than others.

8. **Television is an enemy of good education.** In many homes, TV is the greatest obstacle to learning. We urge you to shut it off from Sunday evening until Friday evening during the school year.

9. **Education reform is possible.** You can change the system. If you are interested and engaged, there is much you can do to ensure that your child receives an excellent education. There are ways to improve your child's school, especially if you join forces with other parents.

10. **Aim high, expect much and children will prosper.** No parent, school, or child is perfect, but we all rise toward the level of expectations. The surest way to learn more is to raise standards.

PART I

THE
PRESCHOOL
YEARS

THE FIRST THREE TO FIVE YEARS OF LIFE ARE, IN MANY WAYS, the most critical period in a child's education. Observers of human nature have long recognized the profound importance of early learning. "Train up a child in the way he should go, and when he is old he will not depart from it," advises the Book of Proverbs. "The most important part of education is right training in the nursery," Plato observed. Consider a few of the physical, intellectual, and emotional developments that mark the preschool years:

- **Growth of curiosity.** Children are born to learn. All healthy infants exhibit an innate desire to investigate in the first weeks and months of life. It is crucial to fan those early sparks of curiosity throughout the preschool years. If they are dampened, a child's academic future is jeopardized. Teachers rank curiosity as a vital quality for a child to possess when entering kindergarten—more important than knowing the alphabet or how to count.

- **Development of interests.** The interests children find early in life can be powerful predictors of later academic success. For example, teachers know that youngsters are more likely to become good readers if they develop a fondness for hearing stories read aloud during the preschool years. They learn to write more easily if they acquire an interest in drawing and scribbling before they reach school age.

- **Formation of character.** Students who have been taught the importance of hard work and responsibility are much more likely to get good grades. Such ideals and habits take root *before* the school years. They settle into young minds and hearts through the standards that parents set, the exhortations they offer, the expectations they establish, and the examples they place before their children.

- **Shaping of personality.** Most students of human development agree that the foundations of an individual's personality are laid early. Attitudes and dispositions may change in later life, but early childhood experiences are crucial contributors to the complex mix of thoughts, feelings, and behaviors that make up each person.

- **Social development.** Modern psychology tells us that childhood experiences have an enormous impact on the ability to form close emotional ties with others. In their earliest relationships with parents, in particular, children gain understandings of how others will treat them and how they should treat others. These expectations are long lasting, helping to shape social behavior throughout adulthood.

- **Brain development.** A child's brain structure continues to develop after birth. Cells are growing. Microscopic nerve connections are being formed. Some research suggests that early childhood experiences—the images a youngster sees, the language he hears, the books he's exposed to—may affect the actual wiring of the brain.

- **Language development.** The amount of language learned during the first few years is awe-inspiring. By the time a child is three years old, he should be able to understand most of the words he will use in everyday conversation for the rest of his life. Language skills honed in the preschool years have a heavy bearing on whether or not a child gets off to a good start in school.

In some respects, the chances of your child's doing well in school are determined *before* he reaches kindergarten. Likewise, your greatest contribution to what you hope will be a lifetime of learning comes now, in the preschool years. If you do your job well at the beginning, your child is likely to thrive when he comes into contact with other teachers. If you provide a loving and safe home; if you give him the feeling that he is cared about and cared for; if you provide a stimulating environment and ample chances for him to explore it; if you set sensible limits and the right examples; if you read to him, play with him, talk to him, and answer his questions—if you do all these things, schoolteachers should be able to serve him well. If you do not do these things, it will be immensely difficult for professional educators to save your child from academic mediocrity.

You may find that assertion disconcerting. Of course there are exceptions. But the weight of a vast body of education research, as well as the experience of countless teachers and parents, stands behind this statement: much of your child's learning potential is set for life at a very early age.

It is important to understand that early developments are under considerable genetic control. We all come into the world with some inborn abilities, limitations, and predispositions. Youngsters are malleable, but not infinitely malleable. To some extent, parents must work with the unique faculties that nature has given their children. Still, nurture—your nurture—has a great deal to say about how your child's natural gifts will unfold and grow.

CHAPTER 1

Fostering a Love of Learning

GETTING YOUR CHILD'S EDUCATION OFF TO A GOOD START does *not* take extraordinary efforts or extravagant stimulation. You do *not* need a degree in child psychology. Raising a child does *not* require "trained caregivers" to supply expertise that parents lack. On the contrary, you are the most qualified person to teach and guide your young child, because he is a part of you and loves you.

You should supply five basic ingredients in these years before school: your love, protection, and care; your time; a positive learning environment; an attitude that values learning; and strong moral training.

Your Love, Protection, and Care

All children come into the world fragile and helpless. In order to survive even a few hours, they need adults to supply food, shelter, warmth, and care. But meeting their physical needs is just the start. To develop well, from the very beginning children need a family. A deep commitment from at least one responsible, caring adult is crucial. (Obviously, having both a mother and a father in the home is the best arrangement.) Every child needs someone who gives uncompromising love and boundless devotion, someone whom that child can learn to love back. This is a basic fact of human growth and emotional development. *Nothing is more crucial than giving your young child the feeling of being loved and cared for, and instilling a basic sense of trust that he can depend on you for nurture and protection.*

24

The emotional bond between parent and child has powerful effects on education. Preschoolers who feel loved are more likely to be confident, and confidence makes exploring a new world much easier. A strong, loving relationship increases youngsters' eagerness to learn new things. For example, a child wants to learn how to read in part because he wants to please his parents, whom he sees reading and who encourage his own efforts to read. Children like to learn because they love their parents, and know their parents love them back!

Forming a close bond with children is a natural part of the parenting process. Most moms and dads need no urging and little guidance here; these manifestations of love spring from the heart. The kinds of actions and gestures you instinctively want to offer your child are exactly the kinds he needs to gain a sense of nurture and protection. Holding and cuddling him from the day he is born, talking to him, playing with him, setting rules that are good for him, telling him over and over again that you love him—such actions and expressions have a profound impact on his development now, and on the kind of student he'll be later. Children thrive when they have parents who are loving and dependable, when they know that, no matter what may happen in their lives, someone will look after them, keep them safe, and show them the limits of good behavior. When it comes to young children, loving and learning go hand in hand.

Your Time

The best way to show your love and help your child learn is to spend *time* with him. Shaping good attitudes and habits takes time. Setting good examples takes time. The encouragement your youngster craves— whether it's for learning how to climb the stairs, how to read his first word, or how to write his name—requires your time and presence. You have to be available, perhaps more than you imagined.

It has become popular in recent years to distinguish between "quality time" and "quantity time." Some parents want to believe that they can spend fewer hours with their children so long as they put that shared time to good use. The fact is that children do not flourish on small, concentrated doses of attention from mothers and fathers. They need your frequent company if they are to learn from you. This may be a hard truth to accept in these modern days, but it is reality. For children, quality time is quantity time. When it comes to teaching and learning, there is no substitute for lots of time together—and children know it.

In the eyes of your child, your presence in his life is proof that you are interested and that you care. It shows that he comes first—not your work, or your friends, or a ball game on TV. In his book *The Hurried Child*, Professor David Elkind tells this anecdote about a conversation he overheard when visiting his son's nursery school class:

Child A: "My daddy is a doctor and he makes a lot of money and we have a swimming pool."
Child B: "My daddy is a lawyer and he flies to Washington and talks to the President."
Child C: "My daddy owns a company and we have our own airplane."
My son (with aplomb, of course): "My daddy is here!" with a proud look in my direction.[1]

Keep in mind that one reason the preschool years are unique is that, in all likelihood, this is the period when your child wants your company more than he wants anyone else's. He's interested in what you have to say (most of the time, anyway). You're his best pal. Later, he'll often be elsewhere: in class, with his friends, or in his room, away from mom and dad. The preschool years offer the most opportunities to be together. Don't neglect them.

Chore Time Is Teaching Time

If you're like most parents, much time with your child is also chore time. Sure, you'd like nothing more than to spend most of the day reading aloud, taking trips to the zoo, and playing "educational" games that will help him grow. Unfortunately, you've also got to get an oil change, rake the backyard, take out the trash, and clean the spare bedroom before Uncle George comes to visit.

The good news is that those pesky chores also have teaching value. With a little effort, you can turn many household routines into good learning opportunities for your child. He learns an enormous amount in your company if you simply talk to him as you work. Never mind feeling slightly foolish. Explain what you are doing. Tell him why you are doing it. He'll pick up all sorts of vocabulary and absorb knowledge about what things are and how they work.

Almost any household activity can become an informal lesson. Writing a grocery list can be a perfect chance to practice recognizing some letters. ("I'm writing the word *butter*. Do you remember what that first letter is?")

Cooking invariably involves weighing, measuring, counting, and grouping. ("I have to fill this cup until it is half full. Will you tell me when the milk gets to this line right here?") Doing the laundry can be a sorting game. ("Why don't you help me put all the socks in this pile, and the shirts in that pile?") Sprinkle your routines with questions. Running errands in the car: "Who can count the green cars on the road?" In the study: "How many books do I have on my desk?"

Daily routines draw on a whole range of organizational and problem-solving skills, the same skills your child will someday need to complete a school assignment or project at work. He can learn the value of planning ahead, and then executing the plan. He gradually comprehends that every large job is really a series of smaller tasks. He sees that work is a means to an end. When he helps, he learns about teamwork.

Certain character lessons will seep in, too. By watching you, he learns about sticking with a task until it's finished. He sees how to perform a duty thoroughly and responsibly. If given the chance to make even small contributions, he begins to learn the satisfaction of a job well done.

Above all, keep talking. The stimulation, the exchange of ideas, and the responses elicited will all serve to build up a host of skills, making chore time a teaching time, and making it more enjoyable for both of you.

A Positive Learning Environment

One of your fundamental jobs is to give your child some experiences that pique his curiosity and supply fundamental knowledge about the world. This does not mean bombarding him with glitzy, noisy stimuli all day long, going out and buying lots of fancy "educational" gear, or enrolling him in the most expensive preschool in town. It mostly entails making sure he has interesting things to do. Since the world is so novel to him, and he naturally wants to explore it, this is not a difficult task. In fact, for children this age, a "learning environment" often consists of everyday activities—playing with toys, watching a parent do chores, or running around the backyard.

Expose your child to a widening range of experiences as he grows. A baby who has just learned to crawl is a little Marco Polo, anxious to explore all those mysterious corners of your living room and kitchen. Give him the freedom to investigate while you are nearby. (Make sure you've taken precautions to child-proof your home!) As he grows, give him changes of scenery. Take him with you on errands to the bank or hardware store. Take a trip across the street to meet your neighbor's new puppy. Find a hill for your toddler to run up and down. Just about any place you go, there will be something to stimulate his curiosity.

As he grows through the preschool years, organize little "field trips" to check out less familiar bits of the world. Spend an afternoon at the science museum. Take him to the airport to see planes land and take off. Or into the country to get a pumpkin. Lie on your backs to watch the clouds on a summer afternoon. And, of course, read all sorts of books to him.

Introduce your child to different people: extended family members, neighbors, and figures in the community. Point out the police officer, the fireman, the postman. Youngsters who know only their immediate family are less likely to thrive in the larger world and may be either too trusting or too nervous of others.

Choosing Toys That Teach

Toys are the "tools" of learning for kids in the pre-kindergarten years. Keep in mind, though, that rarely does the teaching value of a toy have a direct relation to how many batteries it uses or lights it flashes. A high price tag does not make it better for your child. Expensive toys that claim to teach tykes are often less "educational" than some pots and a big wooden spoon from the kitchen. Computer software is often little better for kids than sitting and watching TV. It certainly isn't as helpful as spending time with a parent reading, counting, playing games, or taking a walk in the park.

Often it's the simple toys that do the best job putting little imaginations and muscles to work. For toddlers, the old standbys you played with in your childhood are still fine: balls, blocks, cups, pans, plastic rings, simple puzzles, a sand box. A well-stocked box of construction paper, crayons, washable markers, glue, buttons, felt, and safety scissors is a treasure chest for preschoolers. A big basket filled with grown-up clothes and costumes (dime store crowns, plastic armor, discarded necklaces) is a big draw for most children.

There is no need to keep adding toy after toy to the mix. Most parents eventually learn that the more toys they buy, the more toys they see sitting untouched in the back of the closet. Children who possess several chests full of playthings often flit from one to another without really appreciating any of them. Ironically, too many toys can lead to boredom—or worse, to a spoiled and ungrateful child who constantly thinks he's entitled to another present.

An Attitude That Values Learning

How do you teach that you value learning? First, and perhaps most important, by your good example. Your actions always speak volumes to your child. Your own reading, wondering out loud, pointing things out, and showing a general interest in the world are powerful signs of your attitude about learning.

You also instill ideals about education with your excitement over your child's discoveries and achievements. Enthusiasm is contagious with preschoolers. If he sees you responding warmly to his attempts to learn, he'll take pleasure in them, too. Ask questions about what he's doing, and answer any questions he has. Take part in his activities by introducing him to a new book or game, or helping him with something that's giving him trouble. Even just playing with your child will be interpreted as a sign that you care about what he's learning.

Keep in mind that it is difficult for anyone else to take a parent's place when a young child looks for reinforcement about learning. Chances are, no one else (except perhaps grandpa and grandma) will get as excited as you when your child takes his first step, or speaks his first word, or counts to ten for the first time. No one else is going to be able to muster quite as much interest in that misshapen piece of clay he says is an elephant. The more you are there to encourage his efforts, the more he'll want to learn.

Adult responses can mean everything. Imagine three children, each frequently receiving a particular message:

Scene 1:

Little Girl: "Daddy! Look what I found!"
Dad: "What have you got there? That's a beautiful leaf. Where did you find it?"
Little Girl: "In the yard."
Dad: "Where do you think it came from?"
Little Girl: "That tree."
Dad: "I bet it did. What does it feel like?"
Little Girl: "Like paper."

Scene 2:

Little Girl: "Daddy! Look what I found!"
Dad: "We need to go, honey. Leave that here."
Little Girl: "It's a red leaf."
Dad: "I told you to put it down. It might have bugs on it. Now come on, we don't have time for that."
Little Girl (dropping the leaf): "Yuck. Leaves have bugs on them."

Scene 3:

Little Girl: "Look what I found!"
Baby-sitter: "That's nice."
Little Girl: "It's a leaf."
Baby-sitter: "I see that. Why don't you go play with your toys?"
Little Girl: "I want to show Daddy my leaf."
Baby-sitter: "Daddy won't be home until after you've gone to bed. You
    know that. You can show him on the weekend, OK?"

It's not difficult, is it, to tell which child's curiosity is being encouraged,
and which ones' inquisitiveness is being dampened?

Early Moral Training

A child who is already learning about traits such as responsibility, self-
discipline, and perseverance before he begins school has a good shot at
doing well at his studies. Conversely, if he shows up in class with bad
habits such as laziness and disrespect for elders, there is little that teachers can do. An education disaster is already in the works.

This is not to say that your preschooler must always be an angel. All
children test boundaries and stray from model behavior. In the end,
however, despite some who will tell you that peers or the popular culture have more influence than nurturing parents on how a child acts,
the buck stops squarely with you. You are responsible for the way your
young child behaves.

You teach your child good character in several ways. (See Chapter 3,
"Teaching Character in the Early Years.") You do it by your good example. Little eyes are watching. As you do, so will your child do. You teach
virtue through high expectations and clear, consistent rules. You also
form character in children by talking to them about good and bad behavior. There is much unwarranted cynicism and embarrassment today about
"moralizing." Little children need to be told about right and wrong, and
when adults stand silent, then we shouldn't be surprised if young people
grow up with muddled notions of how to conduct themselves. Parents
can talk about good character in the context of everyday actions, as well
as in stories they read to children. They can talk about it in the context of
their faith—which for most of us serves as the bedrock of morality.

Teachers say that many moms and dads are falling down on the job
of character training. They are not sending to school children who are

well behaved, ready to work hard, and respectful of adults. Says a Texas teacher, "Some kids come to class with an attitude that they don't have to listen to you, that just because you're an adult, you don't have the right to tell them what to do. They think they're in charge, because they don't have that structure at home."[2] Frequent among educators, these exceedingly sad commentaries explain much that is wrong with our schools.

How Young Children Learn

Here are some critical points about how little children learn, as well as some reminders about what they need—and don't need—to be ready for school.

- **Children need to be healthy, rested, and well-nourished.** They need a balanced diet, abundant exercise, and enough sleep. They need regular medical checkups to keep track of their growth and development. This way, developmental delays can be detected and addressed as soon as possible. Children need immunizations to prevent diseases like tetanus and measles that can have dire effects on their development. They need adults constantly watching out for their safety and well-being. Without these basic ingredients, a child's education—and much more—is at risk even before he gets to school.

- **Children come into the world programmed to imitate.** Your child is constantly copying what he sees and hears. He takes careful note of your words, behaviors, attitudes, moods, habits, and priorities. He observes how you treat other people, how you spend your time, how you go about your work and meet your obligations. He watches to see what brings a smile to your face, and what makes you bored or angry. All these things are early and powerful lessons. They shape his own behavior and attitudes, including his attitudes about learning.

  You are *always* teaching by example—not simply with your words, but also by your most ordinary actions. Imitation is perhaps the most important way a young child learns. Teaching by example is probably the most important kind of teaching you do.

  Sometimes you will fall short, of course. When you do, acknowledge it to your child. Explain that "Daddy said something he shouldn't," or "I lost my temper, and that is bad." Help your child learn from your mistakes by being honest about them.

- **Reading to your child is critical.** As a parent, you have many important responsibilities in the preschool years. There are many skills, ideas, facts, and lessons to impart. From an academic standpoint, however, reading aloud reigns supreme. "No man has a right to bring up his children without surrounding them with books, if he can afford it," Horace Mann said. "The love of knowledge comes with reading and grows upon it." If you want your youngster to become a good student when he gets to school, get him excited about books. Read aloud to your child. If you do nothing else with him, read aloud. (See "Getting Ready to Read," page 41.)

- **Too much TV interferes with learning.** Television is one of the most destructive influences on education in America. It saps time from other activities—like reading or talking with mom and dad—that are much more beneficial to children. It often exposes youngsters to images they should not see and language they should not hear. Sitting in front of the set all day breeds intellectual lethargy and a couch-potato physique.

  Establish good habits and firm rules now, in the pre-kindergarten years. Above all, set limits. The American Academy of Pediatrics recommends no TV at all under the age of two. So do we. An hour a day is more than enough for older preschoolers. Television should not become a constant baby-sitter. Remember, these early years are critical. Do not let the TV set gobble them up. (See "Television and Your Child's Education," page 576.)

- **Children need practice and routine.** Doing things over and over again is necessary and fun for young children. They don't get bored with repetition nearly as quickly as you do. In fact, they thrive on it. For example, practice is how your child masters his body. That's why a toddler is so happy picking up pebbles over and over again—he's actually learning how to make his fingers grasp tiny objects.

  Routine is important for little children in part because it provides the repetition necessary for learning. It is crucial in developing good habits. A familiar rhythm in daily life gives children a sense of security in a world they see as strange and unpredictable. Without that sense of security, a child may have a hard time learning. When your child wants to play Hide and Seek one more time, or begs to go down to the pond to see the minnows for the third day in a row, remember that small children need to do things over and over again to learn and to feel confident in their learning.

- **Children need to ask lots of questions and get your answers.** Asking questions is perhaps the most obvious way that children learn. You'll probably decide it's the most exhausting, too, when your preschooler starts to ask "why?" from breakfast till bedtime. As tiresome as these ceaseless queries can be, however, it is important to remember that they are vital signs of his eagerness to learn.

  Children's first "how" and "why" questions generally appear around age three. They indicate that he has an emerging interest in reasoning. He wants to understand the way things work. If you take the time to answer his questions, his sense of curiosity and desire to explore will be heightened. If you ignore them, or act bothered by all those inquiries, you may make him feel guilty about asking and thereby squelch his urge to learn. (Naturally, parents cannot answer *every* question kids ask. Boundaries must be set. Sometimes kids need to be told, "Mommy is busy right now—let's save that question until later.")

- **Little children don't think like you do.** Everyone knows that babies don't think rationally at all. Once children gain a fair command of language, however, some parents mistakenly assume they can reason like adults. In fact, the power to think logically unfolds much more slowly than the ability to use words. A preschooler's conversation may *sound* amazingly precocious, but the thoughts underlying those words are actually quite childlike and illogical. His reasoning is still primitive. Much of his thinking is based on surface appearances, and his conclusions about things he sees are frequently wrong.

  Teaching very young children therefore calls for a great deal of patience and understanding. Sometimes it requires firmly telling a child "No" and realizing that there is no point in trying to reason with him about it, because he cannot understand your logical explanations!

- **Direct experience is critical.** Adults have all sorts of abilities we take for granted when facing a new situation. We can rely on past experiences, reason out an answer to a problem, picture a solution in our minds, or grasp new ideas through print. For very young children, though, these mental abilities don't exist or aren't fully formed.

Preschoolers rely much more heavily on direct experience to gather knowledge. They learn through their bodies—by seeing, hearing, touching, tasting, and smelling things that are physically present.

- **Trial and error are a big part of learning.** A young child's day is full of mistakes. That's one of the chief ways he learns, since he's trying so many things for the first time. Each time he fails, he learns something new.

    One of your jobs is to show your child the right way to do things. It is also important, however, to give him chances to try on his own, even when you know he's not going about something the correct way (unless, of course, what he's doing is unsafe or harmful). As he grows older, urge him to keep trying when things don't go right the first or second or even third time—because perseverance is the key to a great deal of living and learning.

- **Play is the business of childhood.** Just as lion cubs romp and play at stalking one another to build the skills they'll need for survival, childhood play is how human beings ready themselves for the adult world. It's the way children gather rudimentary knowledge about things such as colors and numbers. It gives practice in a host of skills that adults take for granted—abilities as basic as running or heeding directions.

    Play encourages exploration. It exercises growing bodies and imaginations. It offers chances to interact with parents and other children, and gives practice using words. Play makes learning fun, and that's important. When a child gets to school, studying should become a more formal and serious endeavor. In the preschool years, a great deal of learning comes through just having a good time.

- **No two children grow exactly in the same way.** In any group of preschoolers, even among siblings, there is wide variation in the rates at which individuals develop and learn fundamental lessons. It is possible to say that, *on average*, children begin to walk alone at about twelve to fourteen months. Yet it's perfectly *normal* for a child to start walking at ten months or fifteen months. Likewise, some children are using short sentences by age two, while others use only simple words. As long as your child is in good health and you provide lots of attention, care, and stimulating activities, he should come along just fine.

Don't be too pushy. Some moms and dads become obsessed with the idea of making sure their preschool kids "get ahead." They buy picture book after picture book. They pull their hair when they hear that little Jane down the street is already reading *Green Eggs and Ham* by herself, and sit down to the next story time with drill sergeant determination. They purchase lots of expensive "educational" toys, shuffle their kids from activity to activity to make sure they're always "learning" something, and pay big bucks to enroll their three-year-olds in "schools" where they can hone that academic edge.

If you recognize these signs in yourself, lighten up. You could be on the verge of doing more harm than good. Very young children generally do not thrive under that kind of pressure. We do not say it is wrong to set high expectations for your child. Little children should be engaged, stimulated, and encouraged—but not rushed. Don't try to hurry your preschooler to become a scholar before he's had a chance to be a little kid. After all, innocence and youthfulness are treasures that last only so long, and then they're gone.

CHAPTER 2

Getting Ready for School

CHILDREN ARE APT TO GET OFF TO A BETTER START IN school if they enter kindergarten with certain basic skills and attitudes, as well as some general knowledge about the world. The following list, though not exhaustive, indicates the sorts of things they should be learning during the preschool years. This chapter and the next explain how you can teach such lessons. You need no special training or elaborate equipment. Preschoolers can learn everything they need to know through everyday experiences with you.

It is unlikely that your child will master all of the items on this list before kindergarten—especially since, in some communities, children begin school as early as age four. Do not worry if she cannot do some of these things by the time she starts kindergarten. If she has a good many of them under her belt, and is making progress on others, she's probably ready to begin a successful learning experience at school.

Bear in mind that being "ready" for kindergarten depends partly on what your child's new school or teacher expects. One teacher may like incoming children to know a few letters and numbers. Another may believe it's more important for them to know how to behave, dress, and go to the bathroom by themselves. It's a good idea to call your school several months before your child begins and inquire about expectations. Your kindergarten may provide its own list of recommended skills and behavior for parents to teach in the preschool years.

You ought not view this as a punch list that you must tackle item by item! Your child will reach most of these goals naturally as you play, read, talk, and do chores together.

KINDERGARTEN READINESS LIST

General Knowledge

Is curious and eager to learn
Names familiar objects and their uses (e.g., chair, spoon, soap)
Identifies some common animals (e.g., dogs, cows)
Identifies some zoo animals (e.g., monkeys, elephants)
Names familiar places and explains their uses (e.g., store, playground)
Knows and identifies familiar people by name
Recognizes primary colors
Understands position concepts (e.g., up, down; in, out)
Understands basic size words (e.g., big, little; long, short)
Understands words for when things happen (e.g., now, later; never, always)
Understands words for how things feel (e.g., hard, soft; hot, cold)
Understands words for how things move (e.g., fast, slow; stop, go)

Self-Knowledge

Knows own full name .
Knows own age
Knows own gender
Knows parents' and siblings' full names
Knows home address
Knows telephone number
Names basic parts of body (e.g., head, hands, toes)

Reading and Writing Readiness Skills

Enjoys listening to stories and poems
Recalls basic facts about stories
Looks at picture books
Tells what is happening in pictures
Knows what an alphabet letter is
Understands that words are written using letters

Recognizes own first name in print
Learning to print own first name
Shows an interest in what words on a page say (for example, by pretending to read)
Understands that print communicates information
Scribbles and draws

Speaking and Listening Skills

Communicates needs, feelings, and thoughts verbally
Speaks clearly enough for nonfamily members to understand
Takes part in everyday conversation with other children and adults
Relates simple accounts of personal experiences
Asks questions to gain information
Answers easy questions
Follows simple (two- or three-step) directions
Listens to a story being told or read
Retells little stories
Answers simple questions about stories
Places a short series of events in correct order
Makes up "pretend" stories
Recognizes common sounds (e.g., dog barking, car horn honking)
Recognizes differences in dissimilar sounds (e.g., loud or soft, high or low)
Recognizes rhyming sounds
Repeats nursery rhymes
Repeats a short sentence
Completes a sentence with the proper word
Tells the meaning of common words
Enjoys listening to music

Math and Science Readiness Skills

Counts aloud to ten
Counts a few objects
Likes to play counting games
Understands concept of more or less
Understands concept of same or different
Understands concept of empty or full
Understands concept of all or none
Tells if two objects are similar or different in color, shape, and size
Matches like objects by color, shape, or size

Tells which of three objects is biggest or smallest, longest or shortest
Arranges objects (such as blocks or balls) in order by size
Sorts objects into groups whose members are alike in some way
Recognizes basic shapes (e.g., circles, squares, triangles)
Has general understanding of time (e.g., day, night; yesterday, today, to-
  morrow)
Understands that money buys things

Large Motor Skills

Runs
Walks in a straight line
Walks backward a few steps
Walks up and down stairs, one foot after the other
Jumps on both feet, forward and backward
Hops on one foot a few times
Stands on one foot a few seconds
Throws, bounces, catches, and kicks a ball
Climbs, swings, and slides on outdoor toys
Pedals a tricycle
Claps hands

Fine Motor Skills

Pastes things on paper
Molds with clay
Opens and closes buttons, snaps, and zippers
Stacks and builds with blocks
Puts together easy puzzles
Draws with a pencil, colors with a crayon, paints with a brush
Copies a simple shape or letter
Cuts with blunt scissors
Picks up small items, such as beads or dimes
Screws jar lids on and off
Laces shoes, or threads string through large beads

Character Formation

Respects adult authority
Follows rules
Learning to use good manners

Learning to control temper
Learning to be patient
Learning to work independently and do some tasks for self
Learning to concentrate on a task
Learning to stick with and finish tasks
Helps parents with chores
Understands that others have rights and feelings
Learning to take responsibility for own belongings
Respects others' property
Knows it is important to tell the truth

Social Skills

Leaves home and parents for a few hours without being upset
Becoming confident enough to explore and try new things
Plays quietly alone for a while
Plays with other children
Generally gets along with peers
Learning to work with others on a task
Learning to take part in group activities
Learning to share
Learning to take turns
Learning to sit quietly and pay attention

Self-Reliance Skills

Handles toilet needs without help
Washes hands and face
Dresses and undresses self
Handles spoon and fork satisfactorily
Helps care for own belongings
Learning to pick up after self
Carries food on a plate, and liquid in a cup
Pours water into glass without spilling much
Stirs mixture in bowl without spilling much
Spreads peanut butter or jam on bread
Turns faucets on and off
Knows how to use tissue or handkerchief
Knows key safety rules (e.g., looking both ways before crossing street)
Asks for help when needed

GETTING READY TO READ

Teachers don't expect your child to show up on the first day of school already knowing how to read. They do hope she shows up eager to learn how and in possession of some pre-reading skills. Children get the most out of reading instruction when they come to school already interested in books. *Therefore one of your most important goals in the preschool years—from an academic standpoint, your most important goal bar none—is to get your child excited about reading.*

Reading is the heart of education. The school curriculum is based on it. Better readers get better grades. Reading enriches the imagination and provides core knowledge. It builds vocabulary, teaches grammar, and makes students better spellers and writers. It will give your child years of pleasure. So the groundwork you lay now is critical.

You can begin encouraging a love for books and stories in three ways. Make sure your home is a place where books are ubiquitous and cherished. Offer yourself as a good reading role model. Above all, read to and with your child.

Making Your House a Book House

Oliver Wendell Holmes once said: "I like books. I was born and bred among them, and have the easy feeling when I get in their presence, that a stable-boy has among horses." That's exactly how you want your child to feel. You want her to grow up in the presence of books and to think of them as things that make her home every bit as warm and comfortable as her favorite blanket or pet puppy. One of your first steps is to make sure books are plentiful.

- **Let babies play with books.** The sooner little children get their hands on books, the sooner they'll begin to think of them as companions. Board books (ones with stiff pages) make good "toys" for tiny children who need practice grasping and manipulating things. Try putting one or two in your child's crib after she falls asleep. You may get a few extra winks in the morning when she wakes up and finds them.

- **Make books available around the house.** Make sure your child can pick one up and look at it just about anywhere. Put books and magazines on coffee tables, on nightstands, in the kitchen.

- **Give your child's books a special place.** It is important that your child have some books of her very own, with her name proudly inscribed inside. Set aside a place where she can keep them, in her room or some other place she frequents. If you can, give her books their own little shelf in a location that communicates importance and respect, such as the family room or study.

- **Remember the classics.** You'll want to expose your child to a wide variety of books. Some books, though, are better than others. Be sure to include children's classics in the mix at your house—timeless stories children adore like *Mother Goose*, *The Three Little Pigs*, and *The Runaway Bunny*. Raise your child on wonderful tales and poems with rich language and unforgettable characters, stories that have the power to stimulate the imagination and make youngsters fall in love with reading.

- **Bring books home from the library.** If your child spends lots of wonderful time snuggled up with you and library books, she'll probably turn into a library fan. So make sure there are a few borrowed books to enjoy.

- **Make story characters a part of your home.** When you decorate the bedroom or playroom, consider wallpaper, posters, curtains, or bedspreads that contain characters from favorite books. Keep your eye out for toys and games based on stories she likes. For example, a stuffed Peter Rabbit that becomes a best friend will entice your child toward Beatrix Potter's tales.

- **Subscribe to one or two children's magazines.** Consider ordering a periodical such as *Ladybug* or *Highlights for Children*. In good children's magazines you'll find read-aloud stories, accessible articles, poems, craft projects, games, and puzzles. Ask other parents, a librarian, or a veteran preschool teacher for recommendations. Your child will look forward to receiving her very own magazine in the mail, just like mom and dad.

Choosing Books for Children

The good news is that there are literally thousands of children's books out there. The bad news is that many of them will not be suitable for your child, for one reason or another, so you are going to have to spend some time picking and choosing. Remember, those words and pictures will be shaping your little one's view of her world. Devote the same kind of time and attention to finding the right books for your child as you do to choosing her clothes, food, toys, and playmates.

Once you start asking, you'll find plenty of people eager to give advice about which books to try. Friends with children are often good guides. Booksellers, librarians, and preschool teachers can recommend specific books and steer you toward lists of children's titles. Your minister or rabbi may have some good ideas. Consult your own parents, too. They probably remember the books you liked as a tot, and some will still be in print. (Some may still be on their shelves.)

After getting advice, you must still use your own judgment. Just because a friend or a list recommends a book does not mean it's appropriate for your purposes. (Friends have all kinds of tastes, and books can end up on lists for all sorts of reasons, often political.) You know your child's interests, needs, and abilities better than anyone else, so you need to decide what is right for her.

Then, of course, *your* picks will be evaluated by your child, who will inevitably be the final judge. If she likes a book, it's usually the "right" choice, especially if you've pre-screened it. As she gets older, encourage her to take part in choosing books—a trip to the library or bookstore to pick a new book together will probably make her all the more excited about reading it.

Thirty Great Books Every Preschooler Should Meet

Here are thirty "preschool classics" to share with your child. They are just some of the many wonderful books to enjoy together in the early years.

Make sure your home library contains a book or two about your faith. (such as a child's book of Bible stories), a good collection of folk and fairy tales, and at least one volume of nursery rhymes and children's poetry.

Alexander and the Terrible, Horrible, No Good, Very Bad Day, Judith Viorst
Are You My Mother?, P.D. Eastman
Ask Mr. Bear, Marjorie Flack
Caps For Sale, Esphyr Slobodkina
The Carrot Seed, Ruth Krauss
The Cat in the Hat, and other books by Dr. Seuss
A Child's Garden of Verses, Robert Louis Stevenson
Corduroy, Don Freeman
Curious George, Hans Rey
Danny and the Dinosaur, Syd Hoff
Frog and Toad Are Friends, Arnold Lobel
Goodnight Moon, Margaret Wise Brown
Harry the Dirty Dog, Gene Zion
If You Give A Mouse A Cookie, Laura J. Numeroff

Little Bear, Else Holmelund Minarik
The Little Engine That Could, Watty Piper
The Snowy Day, Ezra Jack Keats
Madeline, Ludwig Bemelmans
Make Way For Ducklings, Robert McCloskey
The Polar Express, Chris Van Allsburg
Richard Scarry's Best Storybook Ever, Richard Scarry
The Runaway Bunny, Margaret Wise Brown
The Story of Babar, Jean de Brunhoff
The Tale of Peter Rabbit, Beatrix Potter
The Very Hungry Caterpillar, Eric Carle
There's a Nightmare in My Closet, Mercer Mayer
There Was an Old Lady Who Swallowed a Fly, Simms Taback
Where The Wild Things Are, Maurice Sendak
Where's Spot?, Eric Hill
Winnie-the-Pooh, A. A. Milne

Setting a Good Reading Example

You send precisely the wrong message if you have lots of books lying around your house but your child observes that *no one ever touches them*. Remember, young children are imitation machines. Readers raise readers.

- **Make sure your child sees you reading.** If she notices that you're in the habit of curling up with a good book or magazine, she'll likely want to do the same. If you haven't picked up a good one lately, here's the perfect reason to rediscover the joys of reading for yourself. Of course, on many days your schedule may not permit you to spend time alone with a book until *after* children are in bed! Still, it is important to set a good reading example whenever you can.

- **Talk to your child about what you're reading.** Tell her why you read different things, and what you learn from them: "I just got this letter from Aunt Gloria; she says she's coming to see us next month." Tell her how much you enjoy personal reading: "I just finished reading a wonderful story about some people who climbed the highest mountain in the world. It makes me want to put on my boots and take a hike."

- **Read ordinary things aloud.** Read short, simple things from magazines, newspapers, signs, and so on to let your child know you are constantly gathering information from print. With the sports section: "This headline says 'Panthers Win in Overtime.' That's Daddy's team." At the zoo: "This sign says 'Monkey House.' Do you want to go in and see the monkeys?"

- **Demonstrate how print gives directions.** Cookbooks offer a great opportunity to demonstrate to children that printed words carry information and instructions. You can use your own, or one of the many cookbooks written especially for children. Show your child how the book tells you to mix "two eggs," "two cups of milk," etc.

- **Look things up together.** When your child asks a question (particularly one you don't know the answer to) occasionally say, "Let's find out," and reach for a dictionary, atlas, or encyclopedia. Or boot up the computer. You'll be showing that you consider her question important, that you like to learn things, and that printed words supply answers.

What Does My Child Read into My Behavior?

- Does my child ever see me with a book, newspaper, or magazine in my hands?
- Does she hear me sound enthusiastic about reading? When was the last time she heard me ask a friend, "Have you read any good books lately?" or tell my spouse, "I just couldn't put it down!"
- Where are my own books—in a prominent place where I can reach for them easily, or down in the basement on a dusty shelf?
- Do I have a library card? When was the last time I checked out a book for myself?
- What was my favorite book when I was little? Have I shared it with my child?
- How many times in the last month did my child see me reach for a dictionary, almanac, or encyclopedia to look something up?
- My child is likely to conclude that what I spend my time doing is what I value. Does she see me more with my hands on a book or my eyes on the TV?

READING TO YOUR CHILD

The best way to start turning your child into a reader is the old-fashioned way: reading aloud to her. Studies show that children learn to read more easily when they've heard books read aloud at home. That's why kindergarten teachers list reading aloud as one of the most important things parents can do to help children prepare for school. Educators say they can usually tell which children have parents who read aloud, because they come to school eager to read and convinced that books are enjoyable.

There lies the key to why reading to your child sets her on the road to becoming a good reader herself. From the beginning, you are showing her that *reading is fun*. If your reading aloud brings her pleasure, she's likely to want to take up the habit herself.

All sorts of things happen when you sit and read a story to a child.

- **Good example.** Reading to your child is a great way to offer yourself as a reading role model. It won't take long for her to develop a yearning to open a book and make all those wonderful words and stories come out just like you do.

- **Knowledge of how books work.** With time and repeated readings, your child begins to grasp the basic mechanics of books. She sees that these squiggly patterns on the page give information. She learns which way to hold a book and which direction to turn the pages. She becomes aware that English words are read from left to right, that they are made up of letters, and that the sound of a word has something to do with the sequence of its letters.

- **The alphabet.** Reading out loud is a good way to introduce your child to the alphabet. The more you read together, the more she'll begin to recognize some letters. After a while, she may begin to recognize a few short words, too.

- **Attention span.** Your child must be able sit still and listen to the teacher in school. Reading aloud is an excellent way to slowly stretch her attention span. Your first sessions may last only a minute or two. By kindergarten age, your child will probably be able to listen for ten or fifteen minutes—maybe longer, if the story's a great one.

- **Comprehension.** The more practice your child gets listening to you read, the better she becomes at grasping information she hears.

- **Vocabulary, grammar, and more.** Many of the same benefits your child will someday gain from reading by herself begin to accumulate now, as you read for her. Her vocabulary grows. Her ear for grammar develops. Her imagination stirs. Her curiosity sparks.

- **Knowledge about the world.** Reading aloud helps your child gather all sorts of fundamental information about the bewildering world in which she finds herself: that fires are hot, that airplanes take you places, that saying "please" and "thank you" helps you get along with people. It also lays a foundation of cultural literacy, the knowledge of the beliefs, ideas, and heritage that define the community she lives in.

- **Moral literacy.** Literature teaches not only about the world, but also about the heart and soul. If you choose stories carefully, reading aloud is a way to help your child learn about right and wrong. Many tales offer timeless examples of virtues and vices—"The Tortoise and the Hare" for perseverance, "King Midas and the Golden Touch" for greed.

- **Story components.** Reading stories to your child makes her familiar with basic elements of fiction such as characters, setting, plot, action, sequence, and point of view. Reading simple poetry introduces her to meter and rhyme.

- **Time with each other.** Of the many activities you'll share with your child, few will offer more opportunity to draw closer together. Story time tends to be a time when your child has you all to herself. She can put her head on your shoulder, listen to your voice, ask questions, and whisper in your ear. As you talk about what you've read, you'll discover some of your child's own thoughts, dreams, worries, and hopes.

    Sharing a good book or story does something to link hearts and minds. Years from now, when she's grown and gone, you'll probably think back on those quiet moments when the two of you snuggled up with a picture book, and you'll cherish those memories like few others.

Reading Rules of Thumb

It's never too early to start reading to your child. It's never too late, either, but the longer you wait, the more difficult it may be to establish the habit. Start as soon as you can. Here are some pointers about reading aloud:

- Pick a quiet place that is free of interruptions and distractions. Get cozy. Invite your child into your lap. She'll grow fonder of books if she associates them with cuddling up with you. Make reading together an invitation to safety, security, and love.

- Children usually operate best following predictable schedules. Try to establish a set routine for reading every day—after lunch or dinner, or before nap time or bedtime, for example.

- Make sure you read (or at least glance through) a book to see if it's appropriate before sharing it with your child.

- Choose stories that generally keep pace with your child's intellectual and emotional growth. Ask yourself questions such as: Is my child going to be able to understand the words and the plot? Is there too much description to hold her attention? Are there so many characters, she'll be confused? Start with simple picture books and slowly work your way to longer and more complex stories.

- Take advantage of your child's interests and experiences. If she's fascinated by squirrels, for example, try to find a storybook with a squirrel as a main character. If you've just returned from a trip to the beach, you might choose a book that involves seagulls or boats.

  Conversely, give your child some real-world exposure to things you've read about together. If she particularly likes a story about clowns, take her to a circus and show her the real thing. She'll be all the more excited about reading that book again.

- Don't ignore poetry! Read books with catchy rhymes and refrains that your child can repeat with you. After a while, she'll be able to say some verses all by herself. There is nothing like poetry to help nurture one's love of words.

- Ham it up. Use a gruff, growly voice when the Father Bear says, "Someone's been eating my porridge!" and a high, tiny voice when the Baby Bear cries, "Someone's sleeping in my bed!" Make sound effects. If a giant is coming, stomp with your feet or thump the table with your hand—or lumber across the room yourself. She'll love it.

- Occasionally run your finger under the words as you read. Such casual pointing helps your child grasp the connection between what you are saying and all those strange marks she sees on the page. She'll also learn that you read from left to right.

- Invite little ones to turn the page when it's time. They often feel more involved in the reading process if they get to "help" that way.

- Don't hesitate to edit. You don't have to read every word on the page. When reading to babies, you may want to simply point to pictures and talk about them. With toddlers, shorten or skip long parts of a story that will lose their interest. Make up your own story about the pictures. Or substitute your child's name for the name of one of the characters.

- Don't just read a story: talk with your child about it. This is important. When you get your child to talk about what you read together, you prompt her to think, and she gets more out of it.

- Pause at appropriate places and ask questions: "What kind of sound does the tiger make?" or, "Do you remember what happens next?" Ask older preschoolers questions that require a bit more thinking, such as "Why do you think the little girl gave her mittens to her friend?" or, "What caused Pinocchio's nose to grow?"

- Encourage your child to repeat familiar lines from time to time. Stop right before the end of a phrase or sentence and let her say the next word. Or invite her to finish the rhyme of a poem you've read again and again. These kinds of activities get her involved with the language printed on the page. They also stimulate her use of memory.

- Children benefit most from reading aloud when they talk about the meaning of words. The first time you read a story, take a moment to explain words your child is not familiar with: "Do you know what a camel is? It's like a horse with a big hump on its back. See the hump?" The next time you read it, you might point to the picture and ask, "Do you remember what this animal is called?"

- Don't be put off if your child interrupts a story to ask questions. Don't balk if she asks the same questions every time you read it. Answer patiently and thoroughly, then pick up where you left off. Remember, questions are her way of gathering knowledge.

- Your child will probably want to hear the same story over and over again. Don't say, "No, we've already read that one." Endure the repetitiveness of that umpteenth-plus-one reading. In a big world that's mostly run by big people and full of unpredictable situations, a familiar story is something your child can depend on. Also remember that she learns about language (and life) in increments. She discovers brand new things each time she hears that story.

- There is no rule for how long you should read to your child at a sitting; as long as she enjoys it is as good a guideline as any. Don't worry if she grows restless as you read. All preschoolers have short attention spans. With practice, you can gradually help her increase it. If she can sit and listen intently for fifteen minutes at a stretch by the time she's four or five years old, you're both doing just fine.

Many parents stop reading aloud when their children start to read on their own. They think the youngsters are getting "too old for story hour" and should spend the time practicing by themselves. This is a mistake. Young readers enjoy listening to books and stories that they can't yet handle on their own. Suddenly halting the practice of reading to your child will limit her to simple books that may not be very satisfying. Naturally, you should encourage her to read to herself as soon as she knows how. Invite her to read simple stories to you. But also keep reading aloud to her, throughout the early grades, so long as she enjoys it.

At this point, you may be thinking to yourself, "Wait a minute—I don't have time to read to my child every day. I work for a living, and when I'm not working, I'm cooking, cleaning, running to the store for diapers, or taking my kid to the dentist."

As tough as it may sound, the only answer to that kind of objection is: *make time somehow*. Reading to your child is that important.

Checking Out the Library

How many times in the past month did you take your child to the video store to rent a movie? How many times did you take her to the bookstore or library? If she knows the Blockbuster aisles better than the bookshelves, consider a change of scenery for your next outing together.

The local library can be one of your best teaching tools. If it's a good one, you'll find hundreds, sometimes thousands, of fine children's books there. It offers the ability to feed your child a steady, economical diet of wonderful stories, adventures, pictures, ideas, and answers to questions, all by simply walking through the doors.

As soon as possible, begin to visit the library with your child. You'll probably find a section devoted entirely to books for children. Familiarize yourself with the way the collection is organized (where the picture books are, where the poetry books are, etc.). If there is a children's librarian, get to know her, and introduce your child to her. She can give you a little tour of the collection and may be full of helpful suggestions. She should be able to tell you about special library programs such as story hours for preschoolers.

When she's old enough, give your child time to explore the rows of titles herself. Ask her to help you choose books to take home. She'll be more interested in a story she helped pick.

Your library probably has a place where you can sit and quietly read to your child. You may want to do that every so often. It will help her understand that the library is a place where you enjoy learning.

Playing with Sounds in Words

You can help your child understand that words are comprised of a string of sounds—an important concept for future success in learning to read. Dr. Barbara Foorman of the University of Houston suggests that parents help their three- to five-year olds recognize that there are beginning, middle, and ending sounds in words.

You might play a game with your child in which you say a short word slowly and ask her to repeat the first, middle, and last sound she hears. For example, say the word *ccc-aaa-ttt*. Point out that the first sound is *ccc*, the middle sound is *aaa*, and the last sound is *ttt*. Ask your child to say the sounds, too. Then try it with word *hhh-aaa-ttt*. This is a game that can be played while driving in the car, taking a walk, or waiting at the doctor's office.

Many three-year-olds will not be able to recognize letters, but they will be able to imitate sounds their parents are making. Playing with sounds and listening to words as you read aloud provides an important base for the systematic phonics that your child will take up when she gets to school.

Learning About Letters

Most children still learn their ABCs the old-fashioned way—the alphabet song. Almost all youngsters love it. So sing the ABCs to your baby, and when she's old enough to join in, teach her to sing along with you. At first she'll have no idea that the "lyrics" are really letters. (Listening to toddlers and preschoolers butcher the alphabet song is one of the amusements of parenthood. One of the authors reached first grade before realizing there is no such letter as *elemento* between *k* and *p*.) No matter; down the road, when your child begins to comprehend that we use the alphabet to read and write, knowing the song will help her feel like those letters are old friends.

Reciting the alphabet does not mean your child can recognize individual letters in print. That takes more practice and different skills. Most kindergarten teachers don't expect children to know all the letters before they get to school. If your child is ready and willing, however, go ahead and teach them to her. It will get the reading show on the road faster.

ABC books (such as Kathleen and Michael Hague's wonderful *Alphabears*) are a time-honored way to learn the letters. Alphabet blocks, too, are still a fine way to help your child literally get her hands around the letters. Get some magnetic letters for the refrigerator door. Children like to move them around and learn to arrange them into their own names. The kitchen is a great place to hunt for letters together. Challenge your preschooler to find two *T*'s on a box of spaghetti, or three *F*'s on the cans in the cupboard.

Story hour may be the best time of all to teach some letters and the sounds they make. Point to letters as you read aloud. "Look, here's the word BAT. Do you remember what this first letter is? What sound does it make?" Repeat the word two or three times to help her associate the letter with its sound.

Whether it's letters on traffic signs, labels on a cereal box, comics in the Sunday paper, or—above all—books off the bookshelf, make sure you read! Read to your child, read with your child, read before your child. As Saint Augustine reminded us: "Take up and read, take up and read."

GETTING READY TO WRITE

Even toddlers who can hardly hold a crayon love to "write" all over a blank piece of paper. (If you're not careful, they may use the wall instead.) They take great joy in the movement and in watching each stroke leave a magical record behind. You should nourish this natural love for drawing. The more your preschooler uses crayons and markers, the more comfortable she'll be with the idea of communicating on paper. Research shows that children who are encouraged to draw and scribble stories at an early age will later learn to write more easily, effectively, and confidently. Drawing helps develop motor control and hand-eye coordination. It encourages creativity. It helps forge language skills such as reading.

To make your home an environment that encourages the desire to write, the first step is to set a good example. If your child sees you writing and reading, she'll become eager to put her own marks on paper.

Call her attention to the act of writing whenever possible. Explain to her why you are using pen and paper. Let her know when you're composing e-mail, sending a birthday card, or paying the bills. Ask her to "help" when you make a list of things to do or when you leave a note for your spouse. She'll come to see that it is possible to set down marks that have meaning. She'll eventually realize that these are the same kinds of symbols she sees in books. She'll understand that writing allows you to convey information to others, that it helps you organize and complete your tasks.

Here are some other things you can do:

- **Supply writing materials.** Keep a good supply of crayons, markers, and paper on hand. Older preschoolers will enjoy using pencils with erasers, colored pencils, ballpoint pens, watercolors, finger paints, and chalk. Keep a drawer or art box for such supplies.

- **Encourage drawing and "writing" projects.** Your child might like to draw pictures of favorite characters or scenes from stories you've read aloud. Fold a piece of construction paper and ask her to decorate a homemade greeting card for a relative. Tape a big piece of butcher paper on a wall and let her make a mural. Draw pictures on the driveway with colored chalk.

  If you have a computer at home, occasionally let your youngster peck away at the keys. She'll be thrilled when her gibberish magically slides out of the printer. When she learns to spell her own name, she'll love finding the right keys and making it appear on the screen right before her eyes.

- **Talk about her work.** Be sure to respond to the ideas your child is trying to express in her scribbles and drawings. By holding a conversation with her about what she's created, you award her work the highest prize: your interest.

- **Show it off.** It's important to have at least one location in your home where you display the fruits of her labors. Find a prominent place on a wall for a bulletin board, or use magnets to hang drawings on the refrigerator door.

- **Take dictation.** This is a technique used by preschool and kindergarten teachers to get children interested in writing. Encourage your child to tell you a story. As she dictates, print her words on paper.

She'll be excited to find that she's "written" something and at hearing her very own words read back to her.

- **Keep a family diary.** Show it to your child. Explain that you are keeping a record of some things she does and says. You'll both get a big kick out of reading it in the coming years and rediscovering how clever or silly she was.

At some point—particularly if you've made a practice of reading aloud and encouraging your child to draw and scribble—your preschooler may show an interest in learning how to print some letters on her own. One word she'll probably yearn to write is her own name.

Teachers don't expect children to know how to print by the time they begin kindergarten, but if she is eager to try now, by all means encourage her. Show her how to make the different letters. Give her models to copy. Let her use some wide-lined paper if she enjoys that (the kind she'll use in primary school); it will probably make it easier for her to form the letter shapes. Spend time "writing" together, talking about what sounds the letters make, and looking for them in words.

At this stage, do not be overly concerned about penmanship. Her A's may be lopsided, her *K*'s twice as tall as her *T*'s, and the tails of her *Y*'s may run out of room. That's normal. Few preschoolers possess the motor control to form nice-looking letters. Later, during the school years, neatness *should* be emphasized. Right now, you want her to be excited about the fact that she's learning to write.

She'll probably reverse a few letters here and there, and spell her name a dozen different ways when she begins writing it on her own. That's normal, too. Gently show her the right way, being careful to offer praise all the time. As with learning to balance a bicycle, she'll get there, but only after a lot of time, many tries—and much cheerleading by you.

PRESCHOOL ART

Drawing gets preschoolers on the road to writing. Why else are art activities important? They foster creativity, stimulate the imagination, awaken the senses, and aid the development of fine motor skills. They give little children opportunities to experiment, solve problems, and make some decisions by themselves. Those lumpy sculptures and scribbly pictures are among the most joyful expressions of the prekindergarten years.

Keep some basic supplies in the house: paints, brushes, paste, Play-Doh, yarn, lots of colored paper. Your kitchen is probably a serviceable studio for finger painting, making collages, creating costumes, and building mobiles. Ask at your bookstore or library for books containing simple art projects. Look around for art "classes" that parents and little kids can take together. You might want to make occasional visits to museums to acquaint your child with different types of art.

LEARNING TO SPEAK AND LISTEN WELL

Teachers say that being able to communicate thoughts and needs verbally is one of the most important skills your child should possess when entering kindergarten. Listening carefully is also a big part of learning in school. Research shows a strong connection between speaking and listening skills and the ability to read and write. For example, students who are good listeners in kindergarten and first grade are likely to become successful readers by third grade.

Considering its complexity, mastering language may be the greatest intellectual accomplishment of early childhood. Yet once they get going, little children pick up the meanings of words and develop an understanding of grammar at an astonishing rate. In truth, so long as she is exposed to spoken language, your child would eventually learn to talk with fairly little effort on your part. *How well* she ends up speaking and listening, however, has much to do with your efforts. Your main responsibility is to talk with your child a great deal. Here are several points to keep in mind.

- **Begin early.** Start talking regularly to your infant. She won't understand what you're saying for quite a while, but she will get familiar with the rhythms and intonations of speech. Hearing your voice will make her feel good, too!

- **Talk about the here and now.** For the first two years of life in particular, babies are geared toward objects they can see and touch at that moment. So talk to your little one about what is going on in front of her.

- **Be specific.** The more concrete you are with your language, the faster your child's vocabulary will grow. Identify things by their names ("Pick up the shell" instead of "Pick that up"). Use descriptive adjectives ("Let's put the blue socks on your feet").

- **Speak clearly and correctly.** Remember, you are her most important language model. If she hears you say "I don't got nothing to wear," she may end up speaking that way, too. If you often use bad grammar or profanity, now is the time to clean up your act. Assume that whatever you say will eventually come out of her mouth as well.

- **Build vocabulary through experience.** Your child is more apt to understand and use new words if she has some concrete experience with the things those words stand for. Try to expose her to a range of sights and sounds. Take little trips around your town to see and talk about different things. Picture books are great, but seeing a real bus or train or cow will mean more to her than a drawing of one.

- **Show how to listen.** You are your child's best audience as well as her best model of how to pay attention. Show her your interest when she speaks. One good way is to look her in the eye when she talks to you. That way she'll know she has your ear.

- **Ask and answer questions.** The questions and answers you share with your child give her practice speaking and listening. They show her that conversation is one of the best ways to learn—and that you want to talk with her.

- **Discuss the meaning of words.** Take the time to talk about words your child is learning, particularly those that stand for abstractions. Demonstrate what words mean, if possible. For example: "We're driving very *slowly* now—those people on the sidewalk are keeping up with us. Now look, we're driving *faster*—we're leaving those people behind."

- **Read aloud.** Preschool children who are read to daily have higher than average verbal skills. Reading to a child is perhaps the best way to help her learn to listen. It builds vocabulary and increases comprehension.

- **Tell stories.** Telling stories is a great way to engage the imagination and practice language skills. Most children love it when their parents tell stories, both true stories from their own childhood ("When I was a little girl, my daddy and I built a . . .") and make-believe tales. Invite your preschooler to tell you a tale. Act out favorite stories together.

- **Give your child practice talking with others.** You may be so used to your preschooler's speech that you can easily decipher her words, even when they're unclear. When she gets to school, though, she must enunciate well enough for strangers to understand her. She'll be hearing lots of unfamiliar voices, too. So give your preschooler the chance to talk with children and adults outside your family.

Some parents worry when their toddler does not begin to speak as quickly as other children, but it's normal for youngsters to develop speaking skills at different rates. In fact, progress in the ability to *understand* words is a better indication of language development in the first two or three years of life. As long as they are gaining the ability to comprehend language at a healthy rate, "slow talkers" will likely catch up with their more verbose friends.

If you suspect a problem with your child's language development, however, by all means see a physician. He may want to test for a hearing problem, which if left untreated can impede learning skills. (See "Children with Disabilities," page 466.)

Family Music

Music "wakes the soul and lifts it high," the essayist Joseph Addison observed. Could any sound call children to good sentiments more than a parent's lullaby? We urge you to make music a part of your loved one's life from the cradle onward.

Hearing music helps your preschooler learn about different sounds and gives practice listening closely. Singing lyrics expands vocabulary. Dancing and playing simple instruments help develop muscle coordination and offer creative ways for your child to express herself. Best of all, music is something for families to share. It helps make childhood a happy time.

Nurture your youngster's appreciation by playing a variety of recordings: children's songs, classical music, hymns, gospel, folk music, rock. (This is a chance to expand your own listening horizons.) Sing together. Encourage her to dance and play toy instruments—drums, bells, tambourines, keyboards. Keep a basket of instruments near the family stereo for "parades" and "concerts." Occasionally take her to a performance for children. These early efforts within the family are perhaps the most valuable musical instruction a child can receive.

GETTING READY FOR ARITHMETIC

"One, two, three, four, five . . ."

Making it all the way to ten is a great source of pride and excitement for many preschoolers. Learning to count is a time-tested, natural introduction to the world of arithmetic. There are other basic math concepts your child will need to grasp in school as well, such as comparing, matching, grouping, and ordering things. These concepts take children quite a while to master—years, in fact. Teachers will work on them when your child goes off to school, but you can get started in the preschool years.

The best way for children to move toward understanding basic math principles is through simple activities that engage those concepts. It's easy to expose your child to mathematics in her play and in your everyday routines. For example, when she counts with you while she stacks blocks—"One, two, three blocks!"—she slowly comes to realize that adding one to two makes three. When she plays with you in the sandbox, and hears you say, "Let's put more sand on the pile," she gradually understands, as she sees the pile grow, that "more" involves a greater quantity than "less." When she helps you measure a piece of wood in the workshop by running her finger along the tape measure while she counts off the numbers—"two, three, four inches"—she gains tangible evidence that four inches is longer than two inches. Someday, it will dawn on her that four is more than two. She is laying the foundation for that understanding.

Here are some ways to build good pre-kindergarten math skills. Go slowly. Make it fun. Remember, children acquire these abilities very gradually.

- **Comparing things.** More, less, small, large, taller, shorter, empty, full: all these terms involve basic mathematical comparisons. In your daily routines, practice comparing things with your preschooler. Who has more milk in her glass, Megan or Julie? Which cereal box is fuller? Which book is thicker? Even comparisons that don't involve quantities (Which ball do you want, the red one or the green one?) are valuable, because recognizing when two things are "same" or "different" (i.e., equal or unequal) is a fundamental activity in math.

- **Matching things.** Matching things develops the concept of one-to-one correspondences. Invite your child to practice around the house. Ask her to help you put one stamp on each envelope, one straw in each glass, or one hot dog in each bun. Setting the table is a great way to teach about one-to-one correspondences, too. Ask your child to put one spoon with each plate, one fork with each napkin, etc.

Match things in picture books: "There's a purple penguin. Do you see another purple penguin?" Match sizes: "I've got a long block. Can you hand me another one just like it?" Simple board and card games like Bingo, Lotto, and Go Fish are also great for learning to match.

- **Grouping things.** Introduce your child to the notion of sets by helping her see how different groups of things have common characteristics. Picture books are a natural way to practice. ("All the elephants have long trunks, don't they? And all the giraffes have long necks.") Sorting activities are invaluable. In the workshop, ask her to put the screws into one box, the screwdrivers into another. Keep four jars handy for pennies, nickels, dimes, and quarters, and ask your child to help you sort your change when you empty your pockets or purse. Practice sorting things by color, size, or shape.

- **Ordering things.** Putting things in order teaches about sequences. This concept is often difficult for preschoolers (it may not fully develop until age five or six) because it involves comparing several items and sorting them into their proper relationships. Reading favorite stories is a good way to help children learn about sequences, because it gives them practice anticipating the order of events in familiar plots. Singing songs and reading poems help, too, since they can recognize a progression in the verses and stanzas.

Help preschoolers practice ordering things by size. For example, stack blocks on top of each other, largest on the bottom, smallest on top. Or cut drinking straws into different lengths, and practice arranging them side by side, from shortest to longest. Order by amount: pour different quantities of juice into identical glasses, and let your child line them up from emptiest to fullest. Practice making patterns. For example, string some colored beads in a simple sequence (red, blue, red, blue).

- **Noticing shapes.** By exposing your child to a few basic shapes (circles, squares, and triangles) and teaching her their names, you introduce her to geometry. Point to different shapes around you. ("Look, the top of this can is round, just like a circle.") You might want to cut out and practice sorting cardboard shapes. ("Let's put all the triangles in one pile, the squares in another.")

Beginner-style jigsaw puzzles are a great way to explore concepts such as space, size, shapes, lines, and positions. Even two- and three-piece puzzles encourage little minds and hands to manipulate, sort, compare, and match. A good set of building blocks containing a variety of forms is also excellent for hands-on exploring of shapes.

- **Counting things.** Kindergarten teachers say that playing counting games is one of the best ways parents can prepare their children for school. Start giving your child a familiarity with numbers by counting out loud yourself. In the kitchen, count as you cook: "This recipe calls for two cups of flour—one, two. Now I'm going to add three eggs—one, two, three." Count letters as you drop them into the mailbox, snaps as you fasten your child's shirt, stairs as you climb together. Before you know it, your child will be chanting those numbers right along with you.

  Once your child reaches the stage of being able to say the numbers herself, invite her to count all sorts of things with you. At the store: "Let's get four apples." At the park: "How many ducks are on the pond?" Board games are great for beginning counters because they get to roll the die, count the dots, and then count the spaces as they move their piece.

- **Recognizing the numerals.** Most kindergarten teachers don't expect children to know their numerals before coming to school. But if you play lots of counting games with your preschooler, she'll probably take an early interest in those squiggly marks. You can certainly go ahead and introduce the written 1, 2, 3's. Ask at the library or bookstore for good picture books that involve numerals. Get a set of blocks with raised numerals. Make up simple card games. ("I found a card with a three on it. Can you find another?") Practice spotting numerals together in the newspaper or on price tags at the store.

PRESCHOOL SCIENCE

In the annals of scientific discovery, there is a famous tale about how James Watt let a giant out of a teakettle. The story goes that the little Scottish boy was sitting in the kitchen one day, wondering about the causes of things, when his gaze fell upon the kettle sitting on the stove. A cloud of vapor was rising from its spout, and the lid began to rattle.

"What's in the teakettle?" he asked.

"Just a little water," his mother answered.

"But there must be something else in there. It lifts the lid and makes it shake."

"That's only the steam. The fire makes the water hot, and it turns into steam."

"The steam must be very strong, to lift the iron lid," James marveled. "If just a little bit of water is so strong, why can't a great deal of water be a great deal stronger? Couldn't it make enough steam to turn big wheels, and lift heavy weights, and draw our wagons, and do all sorts of work for us?"

We cannot know whether that long-ago conversation is fact or fable. But this much is certain: the Scottish lad, who was a delicate child, received much of his early education at home from his mother. His father also let him spend a great deal of time in his carpentry shop. He made a special set of small tools for young Jamie, and gave him his own little workbench and forge, so the boy grew up thinking about things mechanical. Not so many years later, James Watt—whose name we still honor when we measure power in "watts" or "kilowatts"— helped spark the Industrial Revolution by inventing the first practical steam engine.

You, too, have a natural little scientist on your hands. The world is fresh and unexplained, and your child is filled with a longing to discover how it all works. She's a botanist in the backyard, a chemist in the kitchen, an engineer among her pile of blocks. Your job is to sustain that childlike impulse to investigate so the inner scientist doesn't disappear when the brand-newness of the world wears off.

Getting your child interested in easy playtime science takes no special scientific knowledge on your part. It's not essential that you still remember precisely how photosynthesis works. What's critical is your *attitude* about science. If your preschooler sees that you are excited about watching, testing, exploring, and understanding, she will reflect that enthusiasm.

Even if you grasp the principles behind the science, your child almost certainly won't. That's okay. The concepts can come later. There is an old saying that "experience is the mother of science." Right now, your child is building a foundation out of experience. A few years later, when teachers introduce her to the laws and axioms behind the phenomena, her simple preschool science experiences will provide a base for learning.

Some of the scientific activities you and your child can practice together are:

- **Investigating and exploring.** Preschoolers are natural investigators. Turn over some rocks to see what's living underneath. Put an ice cube on the hot sidewalk and watch it melt. Put up a bird feeder and watch the birds come. What time of day do they like to eat? Follow a parade of ants down the sidewalk. Where are they coming from? Where are they going? Why do you think they are traveling?

- **Observing.** Talk to your child about how things look, sound, feel, taste, and smell. Get a magnifying glass and take a close-up look at the world of the park: leaves, rocks, tree bark, insects. Plant a garden and watch it grow. Touch some pavement in the sun, then pavement under a shady tree. Which feels warmer? Many children love to watch changes in themselves; find a wall where you can mark your little one's height with a pencil every month or so.

- **Collecting.** Gathering "specimens" is a fundamental scientific activity your child can enjoy. It's also a good way to encourage math skills like sorting and counting. Catch some bugs in a jar. Help your child start a collection of rocks, shells, trading cards, plastic dinosaurs— whatever interests her.

- **Organizing.** Scientists make studying the world more manageable by classifying natural phenomena. You can give your child practice classifying by asking her to sort the spoons into one pile and forks into another when you empty the dishwasher. An older preschooler might enjoy picking up leaves when you walk around your neighborhood, and then organizing them by size and shape. Give your child a magnet, and sort the items it will pick up into one pile, those it won't pick up into another.

- **Measuring and comparing.** Your child does not even have to know how to count to do some simple measuring and comparing. Which of those dogs is bigger? Which plate has more mashed potatoes on it? Older preschoolers learning to count may enjoy using straws or popsickle sticks to "measure" things by laying them end to end. How many straws do you have to lay down to get from one side of the kitchen table to the other? How about the sandbox?

- **Thinking about cause and effect.** Little children are intensely interested in how and why things happen. Talk to your preschooler about simple causal relationships in the world around her. Help her notice how, when it rains, the ground gets soft and squishy. When the wind blows hard, the trees all shake and bend in the same direction. When the kettle boils, steam rises.

- **Predicting.** One of the best ways to prepare your child for science is to help her get into the habit of asking, "What will happen if . . . ?" Making the right prediction isn't important right now—just wondering and having fun guessing is enough. What will happen if we put this rock into a basin full of water? Will it sink, or float? How about this piece of wood? What will happen if we mix these two colors in our paint set together? When we hold a rubber ball close to the floor and let it drop, it bounces just a little. What will happen if we hold it up over our heads and let it fall: Will it bounce more or less?

BUILDING MOTOR SKILLS

Running. Climbing. Pushing. Building. Early childhood is a very physical time. Preschoolers devote much of their days to these kinds of actions for a simple reason: they must practice using their arms, legs, hands, and fingers. Scientists and educators refer to the process by which children slowly gain control over their bodies as "motor development." They generally divide motor skills into two broad categories. Large motor skills involve muscle activities such as walking or moving one's arms. Fine motor skills require the use of smaller muscles and involve more precise movements, such as using the fingers to draw.

Good motor skills are important to your child's physical fitness and ability to conduct everyday activities like brushing her teeth, or getting the cereal from her bowl to her mouth. Other reasons they are crucial include:

- **Early intellectual development.** Activities that build good physical skills are intimately connected with a young child's intellectual development. The better a young child's motor skills, the more she can explore. The more she can explore, the more she will learn.

- **Social and emotional development.** Competent motor skills give young children a greater sense of being in control and able to do things for themselves. This helps to build confidence and independence. It also enables children to take part in social interactions (like playing patty-cake with big brother). Simply put, good motor skills bring great happiness to small children.

- **Success in school.** When your child gets to school, her teachers will expect her to be able to do certain basic things, such as hang up her coat, and carry things without dropping them. Many group activities will involve various motor skills, from joining hands and dancing in a circle to finger painting, cutting, and pasting.

- **Writing.** This critical academic activity requires a lot of fine motor skill. No one expects your child to be able to write neatly when she reaches school, but if she does not have the skills that enable her to hold and manipulate a crayon or pencil, she will have difficulty learning to print letters and numbers.

Generally speaking, two things must happen for a child to acquire good motor skills. First, she must do lots of physical growing. Her muscular, skeletal, and nervous systems must all develop and strengthen. Second, she must gain coordination. She must learn to orchestrate the movements of her muscles to achieve a desired result. She must also learn to gauge distances and direct her hand movements under the guidance of her eyes. This is a matter of practice—lots of it. One big reason children so enjoy scribbling, coloring, building with blocks, taking things apart and putting them back together is that such games turn clumsy hands into deft fingers.

Nature seems to have programmed little kids to enjoy doing things that help them develop. Even babies do a seemingly endless amount of reaching, grabbing, fingering, and dropping of objects in order to exercise the body and develop coordination. During the toddler and preschool years, children spend a great deal of time catching and throwing balls, hopping up and down, pushing and pulling wagons—all activities that aid motor development.

The process of gaining motor skills by no means flows at an even pace. It's common for a young child to make rapid advances in a particular ability, suddenly stall for several weeks, or even seem to regress, and then just as suddenly zoom ahead again. Furthermore, different children gain control over their bodies at slightly different speeds. For example, it's normal for one child to begin walking at fourteen months when his older sister took her first step at age one. In any group of preschoolers, some kids will be a bit further along than others at throwing and catching, jumping rope, drawing, and such.

Since they naturally spend so much time using their arms, legs, and hands, children don't need any special classes or exercises to help them develop competent motor skills. So long as they have proper nourishment, adequate health care, plenty of physical activity, opportunities to play, and encouragement from adults, most do just fine in learning to control their bodies.

The key thing to remember is that early childhood should be an active time. That means less time in front of the TV, and lots of playing and exploring the world. Physical activity in the preschool years helps your child grow up happy and strong, and is an important part of getting ready for school.

Resources to Help Your Preschooler Learn

Here are a few good resources where you can find ideas and activities to help your preschooler learn. Ask parents you trust for their recommendations as well.

Books

Active Learning Series, Debby Cryer (Addison-Wesley, 1987–88)—A collection of five books, each containing simple activities to stimulate children's motor skills, imaginative play, language, and number concepts.

The New Read-Aloud Handbook, Jim Trelease (Penguin, 1995)—Explains the virtues of reading aloud and lists over 1200 titles suitable for preschoolers and older children.

Oppenheim Toy Portfolio Baby and Toddler Play Book, Stephanie and Joanne Oppenheim (Oppenheim Toy Portfolio, 1999)—Practical advice on which games to play, books to read, songs to sing, and toys to explore with children, ages 1 to 3.

Parents Are Teachers, Too: Enriching Your Child's First Six Years, Claudia Jones (Williamson Publishing, Charlotte, Vermont, 1988)—Suggests creative ways for parents to help preschoolers learn, including games that foster reading, writing, and math concepts.

Playtime Learning Games for Young Children, Alice S. Honig (Syracuse University Press, Syracuse, New York, 1982)—Contains 24 fun games to teach thinking skills to children age two to kindergarten.

Things to Do with Toddlers and Twos (1984) and *More Things to Do with Toddlers and Twos* (1990), Karen Miller (Telshare Publishing, Chelsea, Massachusetts)—Full of excellent ideas for teaching and playing with young children (18 months–3years).

Magazines

Children's Software Revue (Active Learning Associates)—Reviews software for schoolage children and preschoolers. Maintains a Web site at www.childrensoftware.com.

Chirp Magazine (Bayard Press)—Filled with puzzles, crafts, colorful illustrations of favorite songs and rhymes, and original poems and stories.

Highlights for Children (Highlights for Children, Inc.)—A monthly magazine with a mix of stories, articles, puzzles, poetry, riddles, jokes, and cartoons.

Ladybug (The Cricket Magazine Group)—A monthly read-aloud magazine that features fiction, nonfiction, poems, songs, and activities.

Web Sites

FunSchool (www.funschool.com)—Contains over 150 educational games for children from preschool to fourth grade.

ParentSoup (www.parentsoup.com)—Helpful parenting tips and advice, as well as activities, games, and articles geared toward educating very young children.

ReadyWeb (http://readyweb.crc.uiuc.edu)—Contains helpful articles and pamphlets on school readiness.

CHAPTER 3

Character Education in the Early Years

CULTIVATING THE INTELLECT IS A VERY IMPORTANT PART OF a good education. It is incomplete, however, without another critical component: moral training.

Intellectual and character development go hand in hand. Certain qualities of good character are necessary for academic achievement; if your child goes through school without such personal traits as responsibility, self-discipline, and perseverance, his grades almost certainly will suffer. Other virtues—such as compassion, courage, and loyalty—may not be quite so crucial to studying and testing well, but if your child graduates without them, it really doesn't mean a great deal that he's at the top of his class. He'll likely end up failing in more important ways.

Children don't come into the world knowing the difference between right and wrong. They must learn how to be honest, brave, and kind, just as they must learn how to lace their shoes and add two and two. The transmission of virtues is one of a parent's most critical jobs, and attention to the virtues is one of the most important ties that bind a family together. As Aristotle observed, "It is the peculiarity of man, in comparison with the rest of the animal world, that he alone possesses a perception of good and evil, of the just and the unjust, and of other similar qualities; and it is association in these things which makes a family."

Moral education—conditioning the heart and mind toward the good—starts at home, and you are probably the most important teacher of the virtues that your child will ever have. The lessons you offer during the first years of life will remain in his affections and memories, becoming moral compass points, guiding him throughout adulthood.

Character development takes place in many ways. (We do well to recall that the Greek word *charakter* means "enduring marks," traits that can be formed in a person by an almost infinite number of influences.) With young children, it invariably involves *training in good habits*. Again, we can draw on Aristotle, who reminded us that habits formed in youth make all the difference. In time, of course, you want your child to understand the meaning of ideals such as justice, fairness, and self-control, and why it is important to live up to them. It's going to be a while before he's mature enough to comprehend these concepts, though, and if you put off teaching them until he's old enough to participate in a Socratic dialogue, it will be too late.

At the beginning, therefore, teaching character largely involves inviting and expecting your child to exercise the virtues over and over again, even before he understands or can explain why. A child learns how to be thorough and responsible the same way he learns to catch a ball or recognize vowels—through practice. With enough repetition and reinforcement, good behavior becomes natural.

The ingredients for learning virtuous habits are:

- **Good example.** There is nothing more influential in a child's life than the moral power of quiet example. Yours is the most influential and lasting of all. It is the most powerful tool you have in teaching character. For children to take morality seriously, they must, with their own eyes, see adults taking it seriously. If they witness their parents working hard, treating others kindly, and taking responsibility for their own actions, they will fashion their own behavior similarly. On the other hand, children cannot learn about honesty if they observe their parents lying or cheating. We can't hope that a teenager will speak civilly if he has grown up listening to the adults in his house cursing and yelling.

  Parents aren't perfect. Sometimes mom and dad do things that are wrong. Explain to your child that we all fail sometimes, but we can admit our failures, learn from them, and try harder the next time.

- **High expectations.** Young children enjoy living up to their parents' expectations. It makes them feel proud and good about their own actions. Make standards clear. "It is wrong to hit your baby brother." "You must not yell at Mommy or Daddy or other grown-ups." If you ask for reasonable standards of behavior (taking into account your child's age and capabilities), and provide lots of love and encouragement, your young one will thrive on the challenge of measuring up to your expectations.

- **Sensible rules.** Rules of good behavior are not simply devices by which adults control children's actions. They are crucial tools in molding character. For example, the child who learns to follow the precept "When we get through drawing with our crayons, we always put them back into the box" is learning to practice responsibility and self-discipline. He is also getting ready for school, because schools by necessity are institutions of rules—rules like "Raise your hand if you want to ask a question" and "The first word in a sentence is always capitalized."

    We don't want to suggest that childhood should be like the army. Little children should have plenty of fun and freedom to explore the world around them, but they also need and want clear, consistent limits. Rules are part of life, and the longer you wait to break that essential piece of news, the harder it's going to be for your child to cope with it. If he is going to do well in school and beyond, it is vital that you begin teaching him to respect and follow rules in the preschool years.

- **Good manners.** The rules of conduct that we call manners have been called "little morals." They are important teachers of character that help turn children into civil human beings. "Politeness," Thomas Jefferson noted to his grandson, "is artificial good humor, it covers the natural want of it, and ends by rendering habitual a substitute nearly equivalent to the real virtue." In other words, by following good manners in daily life, we learn to control our passions, and we become mindful of how our actions and words affect others. At some point, with enough practice, the learned formalities become second nature.

    Some veteran teachers say they can no longer count on students coming to school with decent manners. This is bad news for schools, because it makes it infinitely harder for educators to teach and for students to learn. (It can also mean that school becomes a place where kids pick up bad habits from each other.) Training children in good manners is a duty no parent should take lightly. It requires lots of prompting, reminding, and good example setting. Give your child plenty of opportunity to practice with playmates and strangers—the waitress in a restaurant, the taxi driver, the cashier at the store.

- **Practicing the virtues together.** Daily routines and projects can become exercises in good behavior. You teach compassion when you encourage your child to make a drawing for a sick aunt. You teach friendship and generosity when you ask him if he wants to decorate an extra cupcake to take to a neighbor. You teach about work when the two of you wipe the table together after dinner. Character lessons are like any other kind of learning: little children often take more delight in them when they can share them with you.

- **Talking about right and wrong.** Children know that parents discuss things that are important to them. A preschooler who hears his father talk enthusiastically about football all autumn long, but never once hears any comparable gusto about people treating each other fairly, or the importance of telling the truth, may get wrong impressions about life's priorities.

  Talking with children about virtues does not mean preaching to them. Rather, it means patiently explaining the way the world works and the way people ought to live. It means helping your child understand what the virtues mean: "We have two pieces of cake, so let's give one to Robert. That way he'll have one, too. If Robert had two pieces of cake, would you like it if he gave you one? You see, sharing is part of being a good friend." It means calling little children's attention to examples of good (and bad) character around them.

- **Reading about the virtues.** Harvard president Charles W. Eliot once observed that "in the campaign for character, no auxiliaries are to be refused." The stories and poems you read to your child are important allies. They can help you introduce the virtues. (How many of us first learned about perseverance, even though we would not have understood that word, by following the efforts of "The Little Engine That Could"?) Stories can give children specific reference points, so that they have a stock of examples illustrating what we see to be right and wrong. Heroes and heroines of literature give little children ideals for which to strive. They help children come to admire and love the good.

- **Going to the house of God.** For most people, faith in God is the anchor of morality. It furnishes a context in which the virtues and their practice make sense. For many families, going to church or temple, attending religious training, and praying at mealtimes and bedtimes are the kinds of activities that lay the most solid foundations for ethical behavior. Make no mistake about it: early religious training is also peerless preparation for the coming school years. Faith helps youngsters stay away from troubles like alcohol and drugs. It can help them be better students, and become young people of good conscience and good habits.

In the end, moral training is arguably the central task of education, more central even than the three Rs. Nothing more powerfully shapes a child's life than his values, his beliefs, his sense of right and wrong. Since time immemorial, it is the obligation of parents, preeminently, to provide these things. For parents, there is no more important, or rewarding, task.

Forming Character for School Success

Some virtues usually associated with moral development are also essential for academic success. Children who practice them are more likely to have higher grades and fewer discipline problems. Here are six key ideals you should begin instilling in your child during the preschool years:

- **Work.** Schoolwork, homework, and teamwork all involve very real work for young people. Your preschooler is too young to labor tirelessly at any task, physical or mental, but it's not too early to start teaching what diligence is all about. It is important to give your child little jobs that he can handle—raking a corner of the yard, rinsing the grapes before lunchtime, washing part of the car with you. Carefully show him—several times, if necessary—how to do each task. Demonstrate how it can be done cheerfully and with pride. As he grows, teach him about planning a job, being thorough about it, dividing big projects into smaller pieces, working patiently, cooperating with others to get a task done, and finishing what he's started. All these efforts mark successful work, in school and in life.

- **Responsibility.** Instill responsibility in your preschooler by giving him routine chores (which will require some reminding by you): putting food in the dog's bowl once a day, bringing the newspaper inside before breakfast, watering a plant every Sunday. Raise him to know he is responsible for following certain rules: dirty clothes must go into the laundry hamper, toys must be put back into the chest at the end of the day, teeth must be brushed before getting into bed.

  These activities may seem far removed from the world of school, but showing up for class on time, handing in the right assignments, and taking care of computer equipment are all activities that call for a degree of responsibility. They require some maturity. By giving your preschooler little duties and teaching him to fulfill them, you help him toward that maturity.

- **Perseverance.** In school, your child will run into math and science problems that he won't understand at first. In English and history, he'll sometimes get long reading assignments. He'll need to know how to stick with a task and complete what he's started. Begin teaching your preschooler stick-to-itiveness by gently steering him into activities that give him the chance to say, "I did it!" These need not be momentous endeavors. Small trials and triumphs have great value. Turning a screw in the workshop just like daddy does. Finally being able to get dressed all by himself. Climbing the hill before sledding down. All these experiences teach your child that he can succeed if he keeps trying.

  Keep in mind that most younger preschoolers do not possess attention spans that allow them to stick with activities for very long. They also don't yet have a strong sense of goal-oriented behavior. It's natural for them to want to stop in the middle of a story, or wander off to do something else even though that block tower is only half built. As your child gets closer to kindergarten age, however, you can encourage him to complete the games and activities he starts. At times, that may mean putting a task aside for a while and coming back to finish it later.

- **Self-Discipline.** Little children come without the ability to govern many things about themselves—their tempers, their appetites, their bladders, their impulse to rush out the door to play in the snow without a stitch of clothing on. Since they do not have much self-control, it is parents' job to put limits in place for them. Ultimately, the point is to instill self-discipline. Parents do this largely through repeated practice of appropriate behaviors, until good habits are formed. (See "Discipline in the Preschool Years," page 74.)

Study after study has shown that good behavior and academic success go hand in hand. Possessing self-discipline leads to higher grades. Researchers have also found that young children develop best and are *happier* when parents run the home with a firm but loving hand.

- **Respect.** Teach respect for authority, including teachers and other parents. That includes training your child in some basic rules of civility such as being quiet when others are talking, and never being sarcastic to adults. Raise your youngster to live by the Golden Rule and to remember that others have rights and feelings, too.

  Teach respect for property, such as how to take care of your own things, and how to take special care with others' belongings. Show your child how to treat the environment with care (no littering, no wasting).

  Teach that some ideals deserve esteem. Most parents will want to teach reverence for the teachings of their religion and respect for the religious beliefs of others. You can also plant the seeds of respect for country. Take your child to a Fourth of July parade. Fly the flag together. Recite the Pledge of Allegiance—you will probably be surprised how quickly preschoolers learn it if they hear it on a regular basis. Talk to him about how America is a wonderful place, and how lucky he is to live here. It's also very important to demonstrate respect for education and for school as a place of learning.

- **Honesty.** We live in an age when many adult Americans say there are no absolute standards for morals and ethics, a time when many schoolchildren admit in surveys to shoplifting, cheating, and lying—and yet say they are "satisfied" with their behavior. Often the message from the culture seems to be that truthfulness is old-fashioned. You can replace it with whatever you want, whatever you crave or think you need.

  All of this is deadening to the souls of the young. It is harmful to their intellects, for one simple reason: in the end, truth is the aim of learning. "The man who is really a lover of learning," Socrates told his students, "must from youth on strive as intensely as possible for every kind of truth." If education is to be of any real value at all to your child, you must teach him how to recognize the truth, and raise him to love it.

Discipline in the Preschool Years

Too many parents in this country are unwilling to discipline their children. They demand too little in the way of good conduct and don't hold kids accountable for bad behavior. They've been convinced by mental health professionals and early childhood development experts that children need to feel good about themselves above all. Building self-esteem has taken the place of forming good character.

Some moms and dads have come to believe that it is their duty to erase frustration, disappointment, and boredom from their children's lives, and help them be happy at all times. Others feel guilty because neither parent is around for most of the day. They don't want to spoil what little time they have together by punishing when kids misbehave. They fear that discipline may be misunderstood as withholding affection. Embarrassed about their own authority, they act like they are not sure how to accept the responsibility of being an adult in charge of a child—as if they're more comfortable being a pal than a parent. This sets the stage for ongoing issues of control in the home.

We should not be surprised if these parents' children grow into students who don't want assignments that call for hard work, who have to be entertained as they are educated, and who complain when they are asked to meet high standards. After all, they are used to something else. We should not be surprised to hear teachers remark that their classrooms are full of young people who think of little but themselves. We should not be shocked if young adults don't understand that self-gratification is not the goal of life, and that there are real-world consequences for bad behavior.

If you do not discipline your child in the early years, you are inculcating some awful habits, attitudes, and expectations that are likely to carry into the school years and beyond. You are denying your child a critical part of a good education. If you want him to turn into a good student and a morally strong person, you cannot be reluctant to correct bad conduct. A child's self-esteem is far more resilient than many parents think and many experts imply. In the long run, a child's self-respect will be greater if he has developed a solid sense of self-control.

There is no single right way to discipline. Different approaches—scolding, time-outs, spanking, removal of privileges—work with different children, ages, and circumstances. Yet effective methods share some common traits: Parents are firm about maintaining limits. They set clear rules so children have no doubts about the boundaries of acceptable behavior. They make sure kids know the consequences of unacceptable conduct, and they remain consistent about enforcing the rules. They leave no question about who has the final say when disagreements arise.

Parents punish when necessary, but they also praise and reward good behavior. They try to live up to the standards they set for their children. When parents do wrong themselves, they set an example by apologizing and accepting responsibility. It is important that children see adults facing up to their own mistakes. It is also important for them to understand that grown-ups' shortcomings are not an excuse for kids to misbehave.

It is critical that parents agree on the boundaries of acceptable behavior and the type of discipline to be used. Make sure regular baby-sitters and day care providers follow the same line. It is a recipe for trouble when a child gets mixed signals from the various adults who are supposed to be in charge.

As in most successful activities, effective discipline involves moderation and common sense. Parents must be realistic about the abilities of young children. Obviously, the younger the child, the less adults can expect in the way of self-control. Effective disciplinarians set reasonable rules, manageable limits, and fair punishments. They do not govern for the sake of control. Rather, they recognize their children's individuality, and allow them to exercise as much autonomy as possible. They leave room for mistakes, knowing that children are not angels, and that forgiving is part of a parent's job.

Finally, effective discipline includes one essential ingredient: parents let their daughters and sons know over and over that they care more than anything else about their children's well-being, and that they discipline out of love.

Social Skills

Social skills enable children to get along with others, work as part of a group, follow rules, make and keep friends, and act with confidence. All of these abilities are important at school. They also build good character.

As in all areas of growing and learning, the family exerts a profound influence on the early development of social skills. Through warm, loving relationships with parents and siblings, children gain a safe base from which to form ties with other people. They build an understanding of how other people will treat them and how they should treat others. They learn basic social behavior through the expectations and rules that parents set, the rewards and punishments associated with those rules, and, perhaps most important, the examples placed before them. Your preschooler watches closely how you treat your spouse, other children, friends, and strangers. As he begins to interact with people outside the family, he will model his behavior on actions he has witnessed at home.

Little children also develop social skills through play. Babies and toddlers, of course, are mainly interested in playing with their parents and other familiar adults, as well as older siblings. Gradually, as they grow through the preschool years, children develop more interest in the company of friends. It's important to give your preschooler some chances to be with other kids. Kindergarten teachers don't expect their charges to possess polished social skills. But your child will get off to an easier start in school if you've spent time working on these areas:

- **Recognizing rules.** Children need to know that certain rules of social behavior (such as no biting, no hitting, and no pushing to the head of the line) must always be followed.

- **Learning that others have their own views and feelings.** Only very slowly do children come to realize that others' points of view may be different from their own. Then they can begin to develop empathy—the ability to discern and share another person's feelings or ideas. It is this capacity to put oneself in another's place that makes children willing to share, take turns, cooperate, and treat playmates with kindness and respect. Preschoolers do not have a clear sense of empathy, but you can help them begin to understand by talking about other people's thoughts and feelings. ("How do you think he feels now? Does he look sad?")

- **Understanding that others have rights.** Children gradually learn about rights and obligations by the rules you set ("You cannot use mom's computer if you have jelly on your fingers"), by your explanations ("We have to be quiet in the library, because the other people are trying to read"), and by the examples you offer (doing unto others as you would have them do unto you).

- **Sharing.** Sharing does not come automatically to most little children. You must routinely demonstrate it ("I found two shiny pebbles.

Would you like one?"), invite it ("May I look at your book while you play with my hat?"), and at times require it ("We need to let Jimmy play with the bear for a while now").

- **Taking turns.** This is a form of sharing that requires little children to do something hard: wait. It's important to practice because there is plenty of turn taking in school—waiting to answer until the teacher calls, waiting your turn to touch the turtle in the science corner, waiting your turn to kick the soccer ball.

- **Respecting others' property.** When your child gets to school, he'll be surrounded by dozens of other little kids with their own books, crayons, lunch boxes, and toys. He needs to know how to treat his classmates' property, as well as the school's.

- **Learning to be a part of the group.** Becoming part of a group is not automatic for small children. It requires them to suspend the expectation that everything revolves around them. Playing simple games with rules is a good way to practice.

- **Working with others.** Pitching in with family chores and routines is probably the best way for preschoolers to learn about teamwork and helping others.

- **Sitting quietly.** Your child will spend a good portion of his school career sitting quietly at a desk or table, paying attention to the teacher or his own work. He needs to know how *not* to interact with children around him at times.

- **Recognizing adult authority.** Teaching and learning are virtually impossible at school without this ingredient. Instill in your child respect for all adults.

- **Being polite.** Children are more apt to get off to a good start in school—and be more confident of their own social skills—if they've learned to treat others with courtesy. Train your child to say "please," "thank you," "yes, Sir," and "yes, Ma'am."

- **Leaving home and family for a few hours without being upset.** Going off to school might be scary if your child isn't used to being separated from you. Give him some experience being away from home in the care of other adults, perhaps at a playmate's house or a preschool.

Social skills emerge slowly in children. Throughout these early years, you will need to persevere. You'll have to go over rules again and again, talk to your child many times about the right way to treat others, and stand ready to step in when tempers erupt or feelings get hurt. As Dr. Spock has said, "Children do need to be guided and reminded and corrected—no matter how well disposed they are."

Helping Your Child Learn Self-Reliance

A big part of the curriculum of the home during the preschool years is helping your child learn to do some things for himself. It's important that he be able to handle certain everyday tasks by the time he goes to kindergarten.

- **Classroom learning depends on children helping themselves.** If a teacher has to spend much of the day wiping noses, taking children to the bathroom, and struggling with jackets, there'll be little time for teaching and learning.

- **Children are embarrassed when they can't do things for themselves at school.** They're sensitive about "looking like babies" in front of their classmates. If your child constantly needs the teacher's help with tasks like putting on gloves or going to the toilet, he may be teased for it and start to dislike school.

- **Self-help brings confidence and independence.** You don't think twice about a simple act such as pouring yourself a glass of milk. For little children, being able to do that kind of thing on their own is immensely important. It makes them feel like they have some control over their lives and surroundings.

- **Self-reliance fosters responsibility.** As your preschooler comes to depend on himself and take care of his possessions, he gradually learns to answer for his own behavior. Practicing self-reliance now prepares him for the responsibilities he'll have in school later: keeping track of school assignments, taking care of his books, handing in homework on time.

- **Self-reliance also teaches perseverance and thoroughness.** Learning to button a shirt isn't easy. Children usually have to try again and again before getting it right. Likewise, seeing a task through to the end—hanging up the washcloth and putting the cap back on the toothpaste before rushing outdoors to play—takes practice. The persistence and thoroughness your child learns by helping himself at home will give him a leg up on academic challenges when he gets to school.

As much as possible, let your child try to zip that zipper, hang up his jacket, or put away his toys by himself. Don't always give in when he says "Do it for me." That spoils children. Invite him to begin doing a task on his own, and tell him you'll be there to help when he can't get any futher. Don't forget to say, "You can do it!"

You'll find no shortage of ways to work on independence. When he's old enough, teach your child to carry his own plate away from the table after dinner, to hang up the towel after his bath, to get a tissue and blow his nose all by himself. Asking him to give you a hand as you fix breakfast ("Can you open this box for me?") hastens the day when he can fix that bowl of cereal on his own. Since making decisions is a big part of self-relience, give him practice by offering limited choices ("One of us can wash these cups, and the other can dry them. Which do you want to do today?") A weekend with grandpa and grandma helps him realize that he can cope with some of life's vicissitudes even when you're not around.

Stand ready with patience and encouragement. Mastering the basic tasks of everyday living is a road fraught with peril—soap in the eyes, juice spilled down clean shirts, arms stuck inside sweaters. There will be frustrations and disappointments along the way. Be prepared to cheer the little successes and come to the rescue in times of trouble.

CHAPTER 4

Day Care and Preschool

MORE THAN HALF OF U.S. PRESCHOOL CHILDREN ARE NOW cared for by someone other than their parents—often for a good chunk of their little lives. Millions of Americans drop their infants and toddlers off at day care as they head to work. Millions more enroll their children in preschools to give them a taste of the school experience.

If you are considering day care or preschool, you are in essence asking someone else to take your place for part of the day during this most formative phase of your child's life. That means you must tread cautiously, make wise decisions, and always be vigilant about your child's best interests.

DAY CARE

For many reasons—some laudable, some unavoidable, some selfish, some tragic—a great many parents now rely on someone else to care for their young children during the day. Some can count on a grandparent or other relative for care. A small percentage of families employ their own nanny, baby-sitter, or au pair. Many find a "home care" provider, someone in the business of looking after a small group of youngsters in her own home. Still other parents rely on day care centers, which often handle large numbers of children.

No matter what the arrangement, many parents fret: How will day care affect my child? Am I doing the right thing?

These are hard questions without simple answers. We believe that any honest consideration of day care starts with an undeniable truth: in caring for a child, nobody can take the place of a loving parent. No one else can give the same devotion and understanding. No one else—except perhaps grandparents—harbors such hopes and dreams. No one else has the patience and single-minded attentiveness to this particular child among all children.

Still, some form of day care may be necessary in your circumstances. In that case, you want to find a place that comes as close as possible to giving the kind of attention and affection you shower on your child. You want a place where someone helps satisfy her growing curiosity. If your child is an infant, you want a place where someone is always there to pick her up, rock her, talk to her, smile back when she smiles, watch her while she crawls about, and help her feel that the world is warm and friendly. If your child is a toddler or older preschooler, you want day care that offers a stimulating environment for her to explore, a place where an adult genuinely wants to help her learn. You want someone who patiently asks and answers questions, reads stories aloud, sings songs, plays games, helps her stack those blocks, and shows excitement over her scribbles.

That kind of high-quality substitute care is not easy to come by. Much day care is little more than custodial care—someone who feeds and watches over children, diapers or wipes their noses when necessary, perhaps plays with them some, but basically just keeps them safe and reasonably comfortable until it's time to go home. In many cases, the quality of care that children get is not what it should be. A 1995 study, for example, found that most children in day care centers receive "poor to mediocre" care which does not meet their needs for health, safety, warm relationships, and learning. Dr. Stanley Greenspan, professor of pediatrics and psychiatry at George Washington University, puts it bluntly: "Much of the child care available for infants and toddlers in this country simply isn't good for them."

Even in places where the care is "adequate," the question still arises: What are the effects on children who are separated from their parents for much of their young lives? You hear conflicting arguments. Day care proponents say that if the quality of care is good, it doesn't really affect children at all. Critics warn that too much time spent in day care can cause psychological, social, and behavior problems. As we read the research, the bottom line is that there are few solid conclusions right now. Widespread use of day care is still a relatively recent phenomenon, and social scientists have not had enough time to measure its lasting effects. The best that can be said is not very comforting: no one knows for sure.

Parents must therefore rely on their common sense (which is often what social science ends up confirming, anyway). Common sense tells us that, since youngsters are not all alike, and since the quality of day care varies tremendously from place to place, the effects are going to differ from child to child. Some children will be fine spending a few hours a day away from both parents and being well looked after in excellent day care. For others, though, the separation may pose developmental risks, risks apt to be deepened in a sub-par day care center. Parents know their own children best, and that makes them the best judges of what is safe and right.

Ask yourself some important questions. First of all, is it necessary to put your child in full-time day care? We believe "necessary" is the true standard you should use. Come up with another option if you can. Some parents set up home offices so they can be near their kids at least part of the week. Some moms and dads work alternate shifts to ensure that one parent is always home. Still others find weekend work to help with expenses and allow continual parental care.

Many parents (such as single moms) have no choice but to use day care. They may not like it, but they have no viable alternative. Let's be honest, though. There are some moms and dads in this country who place their children in day care forty or more hours a week—almost from the time they are born—when they don't really have to. They often do it for the sake of a high-status position, a fancier home, or expensive vacations. Here in the wealthiest country in the world, many of us now send our kids off to be raised by others. That should give us all pause. If turning your little one over to someone else all day long is avoidable, we advise against it.

If your decision is to use day care, ask yourself: How is this particular arrangement affecting my child? Is it *good* for her? Would I want to be left in that place each day if I were her? Can I work out a better arrangement? What is she missing by not being with me? What am I missing by being away from her?

No one but you can truly assess whether your child is happy, secure, and developing well in these crucial early years. To you falls the duty of remaining vigilant and monitoring how well your loved one is doing in someone else's care. If you don't, you are asking for problems down the road. (See "Looking for a Good Preschool," page 85. Many of the questions suggested there are ones you may also want to ask when considering day care.)

A Word About Day Care Licensing

One of the first things parents searching for day care discover is that much of it is unregulated by government. That's especially true in the case of private homes where someone is looking after just two or three children. Many such home care providers are not licensed, even though in most jurisdictions they are supposed to be. On the other hand, child care centers with staffs that serve larger numbers of children are almost always inspected and licensed by the state or municipality.

Licensing criteria vary quite a bit from locale to locale. They usually address such health and safety matters as proper ventilation, the height of toilets, and the presence of enough fire exits. Many regions set limits on how many children someone can care for. Some require certain kinds of teacher training.

These are all important concerns, but the truth is that government licensing or certification, where it exists, may mean very little as far as ensuring that your child receives high-quality care. A license may give you some comfort about basic safety and hygiene concerns, but you ought not take it to represent any guarantee of a sound curriculum or decent learning experience. It's more or less like the inspection sticker some states require you to get for your car each year. It tells you the windshield wipers and brake lights are working, but really says nothing about how good the engine is, or what kind of ride you can expect.

If you're considering a larger child care center and no one there is able to show you a license, by all means find out why not. On the other hand, if you're thinking of making arrangements with a friend down the street who has an excellent track record of caring for children, is great with kids, and has many satisfied former clients, that may be all you need to know. What's most important is that you do some due diligence, carefully judge whether a place is right for your child, and give it your seal of approval.

PRESCHOOL

Many parents want to give their children a taste of school in the prekindergarten years. Some make considerable sacrifices to put their four-, three-, or even two-year-olds into the best preschool programs they can find, perhaps for only a couple of hours a day. A generation ago, preschools for barely toilet trained youngsters were relatively rare. Today they are sprouting up all over.

A universe of options has emerged. They go by different names: preschool, play school, nursery school, pre-kindergarten program, Head Start (a government-sponsored preschool program), early childhood development center, and so forth. They may be run by churches, synagogues, or community organizations such as the YMCA. Some are provided by employers. Some are operated by the local public school system, attached to a private school, even run by a university. Others are commercial enterprises. In large child care centers, the line between "day care" and "preschool" is often blurred.

To confuse the picture further, you'll hear all sorts of terms used to describe the different types of education philosophy or teaching methods these places use: Montessori, progressive, traditional, whole child, total child, child-centered, and structured, to name a few. (Most of these terms are impossible to define with any precision, because what they actually mean in practice may vary from place to place, even from one educator to the next.)

Having some choices is great. It means you have a better chance of finding the right fit for your family and child. It also means you need to do some diligent searching and sifting.

Is Preschool Necessary?

Your child will be grown and gone before you know it. Like many other parents, you probably yearn to spend as much of this precious time together as you can. What if you decide to keep your child at home during the preschool years? Will you be depriving her of crucial skills and knowledge that only others can provide? Are you predestining her to lag behind all her little peers when kindergarten starts?

Absolutely not. A child fortunate enough to have a parent or other caring adult at home, in a setting that supplies intellectual stimulation, love, and interaction with others, is likely to be just fine without any formal "early childhood school." This is even more apt to be the case when the choice is between a loving, attentive atmosphere at home and a mediocre preschool, which may be all that some parents can find, or perhaps afford.

Many parents feel compelled to put their children in preschool because "everyone else is doing it." You are the best judge of what's right for your child and what's possible in your situation. If your instincts and knowledge of your child tell you that home is best, then by all means keep her there as long as you can. You'll want to see that she gets opportunities to be around other children—perhaps through a weekly play group, a dance or gymnastics class, a church group, or activities like story hour at the local bookstore. Talk to her, read to her, draw with her. Offer chances to play different games, see different sights, explore different places, and try different experiences. Give her all the loving guidance that only you, her parent, can offer, and she will flourish at home.

Looking for a Good Preschool

The first rule of looking for a preschool is to start early. There are lots of other parents out there just like you, trying to locate the best people to teach and watch over their children. The supply of excellent preschools is limited. The best programs may have waiting lists, even selective admissions, so don't delay.

Naturally, you'll have to consider some practical matters: Must the preschool be near my home or workplace? How much time will I have to transport my child to and from preschool? How much can I afford to spend? (As you probably know, good preschooling is sometimes very expensive.)

These are important factors. Sometimes parents' decisions turn on them. But you also have larger considerations to weigh: your child's needs. How many hours per day or week can she handle being away from home? How much structure does she need? Would she flourish more in a busy or quiet environment? What kinds of activities interest her the most? (For example, if she loves to sing and dance, you might look for a preschool teacher who emphasizes music.) What activities worry her or make her insecure? Do you need to locate a place that accepts children who are not fully toilet trained?

You'll want to find a preschool where small children feel secure and loved. You're looking for a place that will foster joy in learning and work hand in hand with you to give your child the same kind of experiences you would provide were she in your charge during those same hours.

A good preschool offers a wide range of stimulating activities that call on children to learn about themselves and their world. There is plenty of play, some of it structured but still with ample opportunities for children to choose activities on their own. Youngsters listen to stories, play games, talk and sing and get chances to ask questions.

Good preschools give children a sense of self-reliance by helping them adapt to a setting outside the home, try new things, and make some decisions on their own. They help children learn to follow rules and directions. Youngsters learn something about responsibility by helping with easy chores.

Preschool is a good place to begin learning about companionship— getting along with playmates, joining in group projects and games, taking turns, sharing, and settling disputes without hitting, biting, or pulling each other's hair. It's a good setting for little children to learn about respect for adults, as well as other people's property.

Usually, the best way to begin a search is through the parent grapevine. Ask your friends with children about their preschools. Find out whether they like the teachers, and why. Ask people you trust for recommendations, including your pediatrician or clergyman.

Plan to spend at least a couple of hours at a prospective preschool. It's not too much time for such a big decision. For part of that visit, just be a "fly on the wall." Observe how the teacher deals with children, how they react to her, and how they treat each other. Take a complete tour of the classroom, playground, bathroom, kitchen, and any other areas used by children.

Interview the teacher or director. Ask questions about the qualifications, experience, and education philosophies of the adults who will be helping you raise your child. Try to get a sense of what they're like as people. Ask yourself: Is this someone I want to leave my child with every day? Take your child to the school for an hour or so, and see how she reacts to the surroundings.

Here are some points to consider (many of these questions apply to day care centers as well):

- **Is this place safe?** Any preschool's first responsibility is to ensure your child's security and well-being. Is the facility in good repair? Are floors, walls, bathrooms, and equipment clean? Are the toys you see suitable for your child's age? Is playground equipment sturdy? Do the teachers keep an eye on their charges and set reasonable limits on activities? Do children seem well behaved for their age? Is there a policy to ensure that parents don't bring children to preschool when they are sick and may infect others?

- **Is it a cheerful, pleasant place?** Are children smiling? Do you hear mostly sounds of youngsters singing, laughing, playing, and chattering? Or mostly crying, hitting, throwing, and screaming? Are the walls decorated with colorful pictures, perhaps with artwork by the children? Do the kids seem secure and trusting? Are they comfortable asking the teacher questions? Do they smile at her, hug her hello, and wave goodbye? Ask yourself: If I were a child, would I want to spend a lot of time here?

- **What is the teacher like?** This is the person who will be standing in for you. Does she seem full of energy and happy to be in this job? Is she patient and affectionate with children? Does she spend a good deal of time talking with them, and listening carefully when they talk to her? Does she praise children for accomplishments and good behavior? Does she resolve disputes quickly, calmly, and fairly? Ask about the child-to-teacher ratio. Are there enough adults to supervise all the children here, and help each child learn?

  Ask the teacher how much experience she has. You might also ask about credentials. Does she have any training in early childhood education, and if so, what kind? Good training can make a big difference in the kind of teaching and care someone can offer. Do not assume, however, that a certificate or degree guarantees that your child will be in good hands. A degree from a well-known institution may sound impressive, but it's sometimes hard to know what kind of education it really represents. Furthermore, experience can more than make up for a lack of paper credentials.

- **What do parents say?** This is key. If you don't already know others whose children attend (or recently attended) this preschool, ask the director to give you the names of two or three parents you can call as references. She'll probably put you in touch with her happiest customers, so you may want to track down one or two other parents you can talk to as well. Ask what they like and dislike about the preschool experience their kids are getting. Their answers may provide your best insights into the strengths and weaknesses of a place you're considering.

- **What is this preschool's education philosophy?** Find out what kinds of things the director or teacher thinks children should learn in the first few years of life, and how she thinks adults can best help them learn. For example, you might ask: What skills will my child be working on? What are your favorite games to help teach those skills? How do you know how well a child is learning? (If there is a handbook, you may find the school's philosophy described there as well.)

If you are examining a preschool that uses a specific method of instruction, such as Montessori, make sure you understand what the teachers there mean by that term. Don't be afraid to ask about terms you don't know. If the school is affiliated with a religious organization, find out whether that relationship influences teaching methods. Talk with the teacher about any particularly strong child-rearing opinions you hold. Do the two of you agree about important things? Be sure to find out her views about discipline. How are tantrums handled? Can she state the rules she expects children to follow? Are these compatible with your rules at home?

The bottom line is that you want a clear understanding of the teacher's goals. You want to make sure they are goals you share for your child, and that you agree on the methods for reaching them. You want to find a place where you and the teacher will work together, not against each other.

- **How do children spend their time?** Ask the teacher to describe the daily routines. Does it sound like they will provide the right amount of structure for your child? You're looking for a program that exposes children to a wide range of activities, one that encourages plenty of imaginative play and creative expression. It should encourage children to move about and explore things in a stimulating environment. There should be opportunities to play with other children in small groups, as well as chances to play and practice skills alone at times. You probably also want an underlying "curriculum," i.e. explicit cognitive goals—knowledge and skills—that the preschool imparts to children of this age.

   You might ask questions such as: How often would you read to my child? What kinds of activities would you encourage to help her learn colors and shapes? When do children get to sing and dance? Do children get any chores to help them learn about work and responsibility? What if a child does not want to participate in a group activity?

- **What equipment and facilities are on hand?** Is there enough room for all the children to move around and play? Is the outdoor playground inviting? Is there a suitable indoor alternative for a rainy day? Is there a well-stocked bookcase? Are there games and puzzles appropriate for children like yours? Are there drawing, painting, and coloring supplies on hand? Building blocks? Simple musical instruments, like bells and tambourines? Is there a place for science activities, such as growing plants? How about a pet (hamster, fish, rabbit) for children to watch and care for?

- **Are parents involved?** You want a place where parents and teachers constantly give each other feedback and reinforce each other's efforts. Ask questions such as: How do parents and teachers stay in touch? How often does the teacher discuss a child's experiences, accomplishments, and problems with the parents? Are there individual parent-teacher conferences on a regular basis? Are parents allowed to drop by at any time? Are they invited to help in the classroom, or join in special events such as field trips? In the end, you're looking for a teacher who enjoys not only being with your child, but who wants to spend a little time with you as well.

One final word of advice about your search. Don't fall into the trap of thinking that a higher price tag automatically means a better preschool. Spending a ton of money to send your child to that elite, trendy learning center where Mr. and Mrs. Important send their progeny does not mean that school will do any better job teaching and caring for your child than the cheaper one down the street. Money never ensures a good learning experience for children.

Staying Involved

Once you've found the right preschool, your job is to work in partnership with the teacher and director.

- Touch base frequently. Ask the teacher how she prefers to stay in contact with moms and dads. Some parents build a couple of minutes into their daily schedule so they can have a quick word with the teacher when they pick up their child. Be sure to attend parent meetings and teacher-parent conferences. Don't hesitate to use voice mail and e-mail. (Your child's little backpack may or may not be a secure place for written notes.)

- Let the teacher know what you and your child are doing at home, and ask her to work in tandem with you. For example: "We're trying to teach Margaret to say 'please' and 'thank you'—can you remind her, too?"

- Conversely, try to integrate your child's experiences at preschool into your activities at home. For example, ask the teacher: "What books have you been reading out loud lately? We'll read them at bedtime."

- Let the teacher know of any experiences at home that might affect your child's mood or behavior—the death of a pet, a grandparent's illness, and so on. Be sure to let her know about any special events that have excited your child's interest: "We watched a robin build a nest outside our kitchen window this weekend. Jack is really fascinated by birds now."

- Get to know other parents, so that you can compare your children's experiences. Work with them to get your children together once in a while outside the school setting.

- When you can make the time, spend a half hour visiting the preschool. It's a great way to see how your child is getting along, watch the teacher in action, and show your interest. Be wary of preschools that want parents around only at drop-off and pick-up times.

- If possible, volunteer to help out. Read aloud to the children, or take turns driving on a field trip. If you can't ever get free during the day, volunteer to make treats for a class party, or to phone other parents about an upcoming event.

- Talk to your child every day about her experiences "at school." Ask which toys she played with, what games she liked best, whether she had a good time. Let her know you like talking about what she does while you're apart. Let her know you care what happens at school.

- If your child resists going back to "school," pay attention. Find out why. There may be a good reason you will want to know about.

Putting your little one in preschool creates a whole new set of responsibilities for you. Look at those obligations as an opportunity: you can begin training yourself to stay involved in your child's schooling. Establish that habit now, and you may well keep it up, all the way through high school (and perhaps into college). On the other hand, if you pay scant attention to her preschool experiences, you may be forming a different pattern, one you'll probably regret on a distant graduation day.

PART II

THE CORE CURRICULUM

THE FOLLOWING FIVE CHAPTERS ADDRESS THE ACADEMIC curriculum. Essentially, they answer the question: What should children study from kindergarten through eighth grade? Elementary school should be primarily about the basics. They are what matter most and schools must attend to them. This part of the book covers the academic core in five subjects: English; history and geography; the arts; math; and science.

It is imperative that you find out whether your child's school has a coherent and demanding course of study centered on these essential subjects. If teachers are not focused on them, the students won't be either, and that means hard times ahead in high school and college. The first eight or nine years of formal education lay the foundation on which all further study and habits of mind rest. Without a well-defined sequence of academic goals centered on the basics, and teachers committed to helping youngsters reach them, your child's education is at grave risk.

THE IMPORTANCE OF A SOLID
CORE CURRICULUM

Most parents assume that their school follows a well-planned curriculum. They trust professional educators to know what is important for students to learn. They take for granted that school officials have devised a careful course of study to teach those lessons in a purposeful way over several years. *The disconcerting reality is that in many American schools, there is no clearly defined curriculum that spells out exactly what all children should know and be able to do before they graduate.* In some schools, written guidelines simply are not there. In other schools they may exist, but no one really follows them. Often the guidelines are so nebulous that they offer little real guidance (e.g., "Students should read a wide range of print and nonprint text" or "Students are expected to make decisions using information"). Recently, a number of schools, districts, and states have been moving to address this fundamental problem by setting academic standards. The results, so far, are uneven. Although some standards are quite good, in many places mediocrity and vagueness prevail.

The education establishment offers plenty of excuses as to why schools have such a hard time spelling out what students should learn. Some assert that Americans no longer agree on what children should know. ("Since there's no consensus on a core body of knowledge, teachers can't be expected to teach it.") Some argue that a core curriculum is an elitist idea. ("We don't want to impose our views on others.") Others insist that "rigid" curricular demands stifle children's individual interests and rob teachers of their creative freedom. Further, goes this reasoning, knowledge is changing so fast, who can tell what children will need to know by the time they get out of school? Better to concentrate on teaching them durable skills. ("Giving people tools is probably more important than all that information—which they can always look up.")

All of these excuses defy common sense and show a profound underestimation of children's abilities to learn. They also show contempt for knowledge itself. The vast majority of U.S. parents realize that some things are more important to know than others, and can agree on what most of those things are. Rich, rewarding curricula excite children's interests in learning, not dampen them. Students *do* respond to high expectations. But if they are to achieve ambitious goals, schools must first spell them out.

When schools neglect to prescribe what's academically important and hold out a structured plan for learning it, the results are predictable and painful. Large gaps appear in children's knowledge. They may, for example, make it all the way through school without ever reading the Gettysburg Address or learning where the Mississippi River flows. Conversely, they may cover the exact same ground two or three times. A second grade teacher, for example, may spend a few days on the rain forests, a popular topic; in the same school, a third grade teacher is also keen on the subject, so the children study it again the following year; meanwhile, a fifth grade teacher has worked up a unit on rain forests to satisfy the district's "environmental awareness" requirement.[1]

In a good school, the principal and teachers share a common vision of what students should know. That vision is spelled out in a clear, specific curriculum that states what children are expected to learn each year. The curriculum puts academics first. It sets high but attainable standards. It teaches fundamental skills and general knowledge about important people, ideas, events, and terms—knowledge that becomes a foundation for deeper, more sophisticated studies in high school and college.

Learning focuses on the basics: reading and writing, math and science, history and literature, and an introduction to the arts. A good school also teaches children how to think for themselves, to respond to questions, to solve problems, to pursue an argument, to weigh alternatives. It helps them develop those habits of mind and traits of character that are prized by our society, preparing them for entry into the community of responsible adults.

None of this is to say that all schools should teach exactly the same things. No single curriculum is appropriate in all parts of a country as big and diverse as ours. Nevertheless, all communities require some common ground. When schools manage time wisely and concentrate on academics, they should be able to provide students with a solid education in core knowledge and skills, while leaving time to address different priorities and individual interests.

The point is that every good school has a clearly conceived and articulated sense of itself. Each institution must decide—and tell parents—what it considers an educated child to be and what knowledge he should possess. While doing so, no school should act as if it were operating in a vacuum. Some things *are* more important to know than others. A good plan of study marks the points of significance so that children are not wandering aimlessly over the academic terrain.

CHECKING ON YOUR SCHOOL'S
STANDARDS OF LEARNING

You must look with sharp eyes at the curriculum of your child's school. Do not assume it is sound. One of the authors' children moved between two elementary schools and ended up repeating the first grade because of the first school's faulty curriculum.

Here are some things you can do to check on your school's learning goals. You'll need to ask questions, scrutinize what's being taught, and use your judgment as to whether this school is teaching what children should know. Be forewarned: in some schools, posing a question as simple as "What do you expect my child to learn?" meets stonewalling. "I got this 'Well, I don't really know' attitude," says a mom who called her elementary school to find out what the third grade curriculum is. "It seems to be an attitude of 'I really don't want you to know.' I feel like I must be the only one who's ever requested this information. When I tried to make an appointment with the principal they hedged, saying she was real busy." Schools without coherent curricula are like emperors without clothes. The people in charge may not like it when you start wondering aloud if something important is missing.

You probably won't have to take all the steps listed below. You will have to invest some quality time in this investigation, though.

- **Ask to see the school's plan of study for each grade.** Your child's teacher or the front office should be able to give you a copy of the school's learning goals. (If nobody can produce one, it's a bad sign.) Does the curriculum provide specific information about what students should learn at each grade level? Is it written in clear, understandable language—or jargon that leaves you scratching your head? Does it stress the academic core, focusing mainly on English, math, history, geography, science, and the arts? Do learning goals seem reasonably high?

- **Compare your school's curriculum to the one in this book.** The chapters that follow outline an excellent, tested core curriculum for elementary school. Look to see if your school's learning goals measure up to it. (See the section below, "How to Use This Book to Examine Your School's Curriculum.") You might also call a school in your area that enjoys a good reputation, ask to see an outline of its curriculum, and compare it to your school's own.

- **Ask your child's teacher what she plans to teach.** Talk to her about the specific topics and lessons she will cover over the course of a marking period or semester. Get her to describe learning goals for the coming weeks. Ask what she expects your child to know and be able to do by the end of this period.

- **Look carefully at textbooks, assignments, and other material.** Take the time to go through the books your child is using, particularly at the beginning of the year or semester. Do assignments teach important lessons? Are they sufficiently demanding? Scanning textbooks will also help you plan ways to supplement your child's education at home.

- **Talk to your child.** Make it a habit to discuss what he's learning. This is critical. Does he seem to be learning what the school's curricular guidelines say he will? Does he find his lessons challenging and interesting? Is he getting much homework? If you only inquire occasionally, you'll probably get an answer such as "Oh, it's going okay." Get into the routine of talking with him almost every day about what's happening in school so he gets used to keeping you up to date on academic progress.

- **Serve on a curriculum committee.** If you want an even closer look at what your school teaches, offer to serve as a parent representative on a group such as a textbook selection committee, curriculum review committee, or teacher evaluation committee. It won't necessarily mean that you'll get your way in choosing books and lessons, much less teachers, but it will give you a greater voice and an inside view of your school's standards of learning.

HOW TO USE THIS BOOK TO EXAMINE YOUR SCHOOL'S CURRICULUM

One main purpose of this book is to help you appraise the job your school does in teaching English, history, geography, math, science, and the arts. The coming chapters discuss why it's important for schools to give students a solid foundation in these basic subjects. They go over some knowledge and skills that all children should acquire. They alert you to potential problems and suggest questions you might ask at parent-teacher conferences or parents' nights.

For convenience of discussion, we have grouped grades into three clusters: primary grades (K–3), intermediate grades (4–6), and junior high grades (7 and 8). We do this because some issues are not specific to any one grade, but may be pertinent to a certain age group. Your school may or may not reflect this same grouping of grade levels. It may, for example, be a "middle school" serving grades five through eight. More and more schools are dropping the "junior high" terminology, but for the purposes of this book, we find it a useful phrase to encompass seventh and eighth grades.

Within each of those three broad clusters, you will find grade-by-grade outlines of a model curriculum. These outlines are excerpted from the Core Knowledge Sequence, an excellent curriculum used in hundreds of schools with real results. (See "The Core Knowledge Sequence," page 100.) You'll also find examples of activities that children may pursue in good classrooms, homework problems they might get, and some important knowledge they should learn. All of this information represents the kind of rigorous, ambitious curriculum you would find in a good school preparing students for eventual college study.

Why include so much detail? Many parents assume that their schools maintain high standards. It's natural, after all, to want to believe that your child is in good academic hands. You may have taken pains to get your child into that particular school, either by moving to its neighborhood or by applying for admission. The problem is that parents often have no yardstick by which to judge their school's learning goals. The purpose of framing a good curriculum in this book is to give you such a tool.

Compare what you see here with what your school teaches. Decide for yourself how the school measures up. Your hopes may be affirmed across the board. You may find that your school is demanding in some subjects but not in others. Or you may realize that it isn't providing a sound education at all. As we discuss in the coming pages, many institutions do not do a good job teaching basic academic subjects. If your school is inflicting a mediocre education on your child, the sooner you know it the better.

Before you use this part of the book, a few important explanations and caveats are in order.

First, we repeat an earlier warning: you may find that in fact your school has no written, coherent standards that specify exactly what children should learn in each grade. Or you may find that the school's written goals are so nebulous that they're practically useless. Sadly, this isn't uncommon in American education. It means you may have to look very closely at your child's course work to discern exactly what the school is (or isn't) teaching.

Some parents (particularly those with kids in weaker schools) may be surprised at how ambitious the lists in this book are. Can third graders really learn about ancient Rome, and seventh graders learn about chemical bonds? Indeed they can. And they do—in good schools across this country (including Core Knowledge schools) and in schools in foreign nations whose students routinely trounce American kids in international tests. When schools hold and enforce high expectations, children respond.

This is not to imply that children or their parents have to know every item listed in the coming sections to be considered "educated." (Certainly we, the authors, cannot define every term, solve every problem, or recall every fact cited in these pages—nor have we read every single book listed and recommended.) But good schools expose children to most of these topics. They plant seeds of knowledge in a wide range of topics, seeds that will grow in later grades when students tackle those topics again in greater depth. As E.D. Hirsch and John Holdren of the Core Knowledge Foundation point out, a critical goal is for elementary pupils to become broadly familiar with important people, terms, and ideas so that later, when they hear or read about them, they have a frame of reference, a satisfying sense that "I *know* something about that!"[2]

The following chapters do *not* list everything children study in elementary school (there is not room for that here). Nor do they reprint the entire Core Knowledge Sequence. This book should not be taken as a complete menu of learning, or as an outline of the only lessons worth studying. You should not take the lists you find here as an argument for excluding other topics, ideas, and resources. (We do not, for example, address the important issue of foreign language study during the elementary years.)

Please understand that, in all likelihood, your own school's course of study will *not* look exactly like this outline. Curricular content varies to some degree from school to school, even among very good institutions. Different schools and teachers emphasize different topics according to state standards, community wishes, student interests, and teacher strengths. Schools in Texas, for example, may teach more Mexican history than schools in Maine or Michigan, where students are likely to learn more Canadian history. A second grade teacher who speaks fluent

French may put that expertise to use by teaching children a few French words. At a science magnet school, the curriculum obviously will be weighted heavily toward science.

The order in which topics are taught also varies. Two equally good schools may sequence their content and skills somewhat differently. For example, this model suggests that children learn something about how sound travels in third grade; if your own school teaches that in fourth grade, there is no reason for alarm. (If, on the other hand, your school doesn't introduce that topic until seventh or eighth grade—or doesn't seem to cover it at all—you may have grounds for worry.)

Do not, therefore, insist that your school's curriculum line up grade by grade with what follows. Rather, use this book to give you a *general* sense of the knowledge and skills that should lie at the heart of a solid elementary school curriculum. Over time, with some attention on your part, you should get a good idea of whether the education your child is receiving is on a par with the one outlined here.

In looking through these pages, you may find some terms and concepts that you don't recall or understand, particularly when your child reaches the junior high math and science years. (How many of us, for example, really remember what "supplementary angles" are?) Even when you don't understand a term, you can still ask your child if he has come across it in school. Also, you can go over these lists with your child's teacher, and ask her whether she covers particular topics. If she says no, ask when (that is, at what grade level) your child will be learning about them.

For the most part, the next few chapters focus on *what* your child should be learning in school, not on *how* teachers should teach those lessons. Although we weigh in on a few prominent debates about instructional methods, such as the phonics versus whole language argument in reading, this book is mostly concerned with results, not with how they are produced. This is a concern that you probably share. After all, when you order dinner in a restaurant, you expect the food to taste good, but you don't tell the chef how to cook it. He knows his craft and that's best left to his expertise. He also knows that, if he dishes up bad food, his customers will not return. In that spirit, this book does not often presume to instruct teachers about specific methods. Good teachers use a variety of ways to teach. They find the techniques that work best for them and their students. That's their job, their supposed expertise. Our suggestion is that you be fairly flexible about the educational methods that your school uses, but firm and insistent about results.

Finally, a word about your own role. The following chapters suggest many specific things that you can do to enrich your child's education—books to read together, activities to try at home, places to visit. You should by no means feel as though you have to try all these suggestions. Pick out the ideas that seem most appropriate and try one now and again. (If your child is most interested in science, you may find more suitable activities in that chapter. If your school is particularly weak in history, you may find yourself turning to that part of the book more often.) Use this book for perspective and general guidance, not as a giant punch list that you and your child must complete.

Ten Signs of a Good School

Most good schools display these qualities:

1. **A Safe and Orderly Atmosphere.** Discipline and academic success go hand-in-hand. Where there is chaos or fear, little learning occurs. Good schools are havens of sound conduct and mutual respect. The building is clean. The rules are clear—and enforced.

2. **A Clear Academic Mission.** Good schools spell out the knowledge and skills that children must acquire. They have a coherent course of study focused on English, math, science, history, geography, and the arts. Most of the day is devoted to these core subjects.

3. **Attention to Character.** Good schools treat children as moral beings. They teach about right and wrong. Teachers help train children in habits that lead to better lives. Beware of schools that are "value neutral" zones.

4. **Fine Teachers.** Teachers are the heart of any educational enterprise. Good schools are full of adults of sound character who like children, know the material, and effectively impart knowledge and skills. Good schools reward greatness in teaching and refuse to tolerate mediocrity.

5. **Strong Leadership.** It is rare to find a good school without a strong principal. The vision she holds has much to do with how well pupils will learn. She puts academics first. She protects the school day for teaching and learning.

6. **High Expectations.** Attitudes toward learning often become self-fulfilling prophecies. Schools that maintain high standards get greater academic achievement from children. Schools that offer dumbed-down lessons, trivial books, and slipshod standards get little in return.

7. **Homework.** Achievement rises when teachers give homework and children conscientiously do it. Little homework indicates a school that doesn't take academics seriously.

8. **Evaluation and Feedback.** Good schools hold all their students accountable for meeting standards. They monitor how children are performing. They provide feedback to teachers, and pupils. Teachers give honest grades. They recognize and reward success. They intervene in the event of failure.

9. **Parent Involvement.** Good schools are surrounded by moms and dads who monitor and assist with academics, stay in touch with teachers, and raise children who are well-behaved and ready to learn. Good teachers view parents as allies and invite them to join the education enterprise.

10. **A Sense of Community.** A good school is a welcoming place where youngsters know that adults care deeply about them. All its participants—grownups and children alike—share enthusiasm, pride, and a sense of common purpose. There is much seriousness about learning, and also much joy.

The Core Knowledge Sequence

Our grade-by-grade curriculum guides are excerpted from *The Core Knowledge Sequence: Content Guidelines for Grades K–8*, copyright by the Core Knowledge Foundation, a nonprofit, nonpartisan organization dedicated to excellence and fairness in early education. Our excerpts are presented with the generous permission of the foundation, which takes no position either on our selection of excerpts or on the views expressed in this book. The Core Knowledge Sequence is the best content guide for the elementary grades that we have seen. It is meant by its authors to occupy at least 50 percent of the whole school curriculum. Today the well-tested Sequence is being used in several hundred U.S. schools, and in those that we have visited it engages and stimulates the children while supplying them with important knowledge and valuable skills. The excerpts we offer from the Sequence are meant to give readers a clear idea of what a good elementary curriculum looks like. The complete Sequence, a document of some 200 pages, is available from the Core Knowledge Foundation, 801 East High Street, Charlottesville, VA 22902 (804-977-7550). A full exposition of the contents of the Sequence is set forth in the book series edited by E.D. Hirsch, Jr., with the titles *What Your Kindergartner—Sixth Grader Needs to Know,* available in bookstores, or from the Core Knowledge Foundation. (For more information, visit the Core Knowledge Web site at www.coreknowledge.org.)

CHAPTER 5

English

LEARNING TO READ, WRITE, AND SPEAK WELL IS THE MAIN order of business in the early years of instruction in English. No matter how good your school is, you must work on these critical skills with your child to ensure that he masters them. In addition, English studies should open your child's eyes to the world of great literature. It is not enough to monitor how well he can read; you must also pay attention to the particular books and stories he comes across.

In the following pages, we outline some of the knowledge and skills that your child should gain in his studies and summarize a model English curriculum you can compare to your own school's courses. We address some of the debates about teaching the language arts and suggest some things to do at home to buttress your child's education.

WHAT GOOD SCHOOLS TEACH—AND WHY

Reading

Good schools assume as their sublime and most solemn responsibility the task of teaching every child to read. Make no mistake, this is *the* critical business of education in the early years. When an elementary school sends a child to high school unable to read fluently, his chances for later academic success are in grave jeopardy.

Schools meet this solemn responsibility, in part, by taking the advice of the philosopher Epictetus: "If you wish to be a good reader, read." There is no other way. In good elementary classrooms, children read stories, poems, novels, biographies, essays, drama, magazines, and newspaper articles. They read every day at school, and they read at home.

Good teachers know that teaching children *how* to read is only half the job. *What* they read is equally important. After all, the books, stories, and poems of childhood teach lasting lessons. As Howard Pyle, an outstanding author and illustrator of young people's literature, once observed, "In one's mature years one forgets the books that one reads, but the stories of childhood leave an indelible impression, and their author always has a niche in the temple of memory from which the image is never cast out to be thrown into the rubbish-heap of things that are outgrown and outlived." Schools—and parents—must choose their children's reading materials with great care.

What kind of lessons should literature teach young students?

Books and stories should instruct youngsters about the ways of the wide and unfamiliar world they are entering. In reading "The Wolf in Sheep's Clothing" or "The Ugly Duckling," children learn that things (and people) aren't always what they seem. In the myth of Phaeton, they learn about the dangers of recklessness and overreaching. With *Tom Sawyer* or *Alice in Wonderland,* they learn about different shades of human behavior. By offering students such works, we sharpen their visions and give them glimpses of universal truths about the human condition. We help them to know themselves and awaken in their hearts a kinship with others.

Good literature not only tells young people about life; it also offers lessons about how to live a *good* life. In the pages of books, youngsters can see what virtues such as compassion, courage, and responsibility look like in action. In *Pinocchio,* children uncover the pitfalls of dishonesty. In the story of Queen Esther, they discover the risks and rewards of loyalty. Such literature reinforces the examples and exhortations of adults and clarifies notions of right and wrong for young people. It can supply cogent reminders of ideals that last a lifetime. Many great men and women at a critical instant have recalled a simple fable, familiar verse, or tale of a childhood hero first encountered in school.

Reading should also teach children about the history, beliefs, and aspirations that we Americans hold as a people. In biographies of Abigail Adams or Frederick Douglass, students learn about this nation's struggles for liberty. In stories about Henry Ford or Cyrus McCormick, they see why America is known as the land of opportunity. Reading about the Wright brothers and George Washington Carver, they learn about that national trait known the world over as "American ingenuity." Good schools do not hesitate to steep children in such ideals and traditions, and to explain why they deserve both admiration and allegiance.

It is also largely through reading that children come to know images, symbols, and expressions that Americans hold in common. Students learn what an "Achilles heel" or "Trojan horse" is by reading stories from Homer. They find out what "Camelot" means by reading Arthurian legends, what "Mount Vernon" is through stories of George Washington. On the surface, these may seem like trivial lessons, but those little things add up to something grand: a collective vocabulary that helps bind us together as a civilization. These images and terms fill our literature, our newspapers, even our daily discourse. An educated person possesses enough background knowledge to know what they mean when he runs across them. More to the point, knowing stories of Huck Finn and John Henry means claiming a legacy. Such tales have inspired generations of Americans. As part of our national memory, they help tell us who we are as a people. Reading these works helps children from every sort of background enter into our common culture.

Such knowledge is indispensable to a rich intellectual life. You want your child to be exposed to and appreciate truly great books and art at various stages of his education. Many of these works assume that the audience is already acquainted with certain images, stories, and subjects. When your child reads *Moby-Dick* in high school or college, for example, the first words he'll run across will be "Call me Ishmael." Herman Melville wrote that opening line for a reader already familiar with the biblical story of Abraham's elder son. Likewise, Botticelli painted his famous *Birth of Venus* for an audience versed in classical mythology; for the modern student with no inkling of who Venus was, this masterpiece may be reduced to a strange picture of an unclad lady standing in a seashell.

These allusions are not cultural frills. Those who miss them miss something important. The philosopher Descartes remarked that reading great books is like having careful conversations with the noblest thinkers of past centuries through which they reveal their best thoughts to us. In fact, great books, poems, works of art and music are all part of a long conversation that echoes through the ages, embodying mankind's greatest ideas and achievements. Like any conversation, this discourse of civilization uses a common vocabulary of themes, images, and stories. For your child to be able to participate in that great conversation—to penetrate it, to appreciate the magnificence of its ideas, the grandeur of achievement, the rich legacy of human endeavor—he must have a familiarity with the references and metaphors that make up the common language. Elementary school reading should begin equipping children with knowledge of their literary heritage so that, over the course of a lifetime, they can reap the full benefits of the great tradition that precedes them.

Perhaps above all, reading assignments should draw on the power of good literature to lift children up, intellectually and spiritually. By this, we do not mean raising their "self-esteem." In too many schools, the drive to make sure children "feel good about themselves" has contributed to the dumbing down of reading selections with infantile vocabulary and prose so simple it's deadening. This cheats our students. When schools undershoot the mark, they not only produce poor readers, but they undermine children's respect for English as a subject and trivialize their sense of language as an art form. Good schools do the opposite. They expect much from students when it comes to reading. They invite them to enter a world of ideas, language, and beliefs with which they are not familiar but which can raise them up, encourage them, stimulate their minds, and improve their sensibilities.

This notion of using schoolbooks to uplift and improve is especially important today, when so much of what children encounter in the popular culture is crude, ugly, mindless, or amoral. Too often the sounds young people hear on radio, the images they see on TV, and the language they hear at the mall or playground take aim at their coarser sensibilities and pull down their standards. English class should be a haven where they encounter a richer, more elevating diet.

We should offer all our children, in the words of Matthew Arnold, the "best which has been thought and said." That is why, in good schools, students spend significant time with the classics—Aesop's fables, Hans Christian Andersen's tales, *Treasure Island*, *The Jungle Book*, *The Secret Garden*, *Little Women*—and others on the long list of books that have delighted and fascinated generations of children. The student who learns to read but never gets the chance to experience the classics is being shortchanged. They carry powerful images, unforgettable characters, compelling lessons. They offer examples of rich language and vocabulary more demanding than most stories written for children today. They have the ability to fire the imagination, stir the emotions, and move the soul. They have stood the test of time and captured hearts because they speak to childhood as its own special time, with its own delights, dreams, uncertainties, and wonder. Taken together, these shared experiences put students into contact with that great conversation and make them heirs to a grand tradition.

This is not to say that elementary school students should read only "classics." There are many fine contemporary works, and children should spend time with them as well. There are also many wonderful stories, both new and old, from cultures all over the world. In the last few decades, U.S. publishers have devoted much energy to bringing these stories to life for youngsters. If schools manage their time wisely, and require enough at-home reading, there should be enough time for classics as well as multicultural and modern literature.

The ultimate goal is to make sure that young children are exposed to inspiring, demanding works of literature. Good schools don't focus solely on teaching the skill of reading, but also pay attention to what children read and the knowledge that they draw from their books. Keep this thought in mind: education is the architecture of the soul, the leading of children to what is good and fine. Expect your child's English teachers to lead him to truly good and fine works of literature.

Writing

Along with reading, students should spend a great deal of time learning to write. The age of telephones and video conferences is also the age of e-mail. The written word is still the primary, indispensable form of communication. Résumés, formal letters, reports, minutes, and other standard paperwork require no less skill on a word processor than with a quill pen. More than ever, successful careers call for good writing skills.

There are other reasons to spend time with pen and paper in school. Learning to write helps reading development and influences how effectively we speak. Writing practice also brings discipline to the thoughts behind our words. To put together a coherent composition, we must first organize our ideas. To fashion a paragraph, we must bring order to a narrative or argument. To choose the right word, we must dispel inexact notions. In short, writing is good mental exercise. It sharpens the intellect. "Whenever, on account of its vagueness, I am dissatisfied with a conception of the brain, I resort forthwith to the pen, for the purpose of obtaining, through its aid, the necessary form, consequence, and precision," wrote Edgar Allan Poe.

For many people, writing becomes an immensely enjoyable habit. They find fulfillment and self-discovery in retiring to a quiet place with a pen and their thoughts—to write in a journal, compose a letter, or fashion a poem. "The incurable itch of writing possesses many," the Roman satirist Juvenal observed. Every good English teacher longs to help children acquire that itch.

It is a fact of life that some older children (and adults) break into a sweat at the thought of picking up a pen or sitting down at a word processor. They do not like to write because it is a struggle for them. More often than not, their anxiety arises from lack of practice. Writing is like any other craft: skill comes from training and experience. The key to turning children into fluent writers who derive real pleasure from composition is lots of practice.

Therefore elementary school students should get frequent writing assignments. This does not mean filling in blanks in workbooks, or scribbling a sentence here and there. One sign of a good school is that children do plenty of extended writing. They write stories, poems, letters, essays, book reports, and research papers. In many schools, they keep daily journals. Writing is part of every subject, not just English. Students produce reports about science projects. They answer essay questions in history class. Students write and write and write some more, until it becomes second nature to put pencil to paper (or fingers to keyboard) and produce something coherent and expressive.

In good elementary schools, children study the nuts and bolts of writing. They learn about nouns, adjectives, direct objects, and other parts of speech. Teachers grade spelling, punctuation, and word usage. They give regular lessons in vocabulary enrichment. They demand neatness and good penmanship. Children learn how to structure sentences and organize paragraphs. They learn the conventions for composing letters. They practice outlining their thoughts before they begin longer assignments. They learn to revise their work and proofread for errors.

Learning about adverbs and taking spelling tests may sound old-fashioned. In fact, you'll find some educators who neglect or scoff at such exercises. "No communicative purpose is served when children are asked to identify parts of speech," some educational materials claim. "I don't like grammar," some teachers have been known to announce to their own classes. But those who insist on their students' knowing grammar aren't being fuddy-duddies. They know from experience what works in turning children into coherent, fluent writers. Grammar, spelling, and usage rules are to writing what the multiplication tables, rules of addition, and subtraction are to math. They are not always fun, but they are necessary. Look to see if the study of writing mechanics is part of your school's curriculum.

Speaking

Speaking, too, is a language art. Learning to speak properly requires a good deal of training, and children must get it in school. It is a critical part of the curriculum and cannot be taken for granted. Standard English is the language of business and commerce in this country. All students need to speak it well.

Good schools take up this task in several ways. First and foremost, teachers set strong examples themselves. They are careful about the language they use because they know that children imitate the sounds they hear from adults. Good teachers don't ignore bad habits in the classroom. They gently correct children when they hear them using incorrect grammar or muddling their speech with "like" and "you know" every fifth or sixth word. They have children practice speaking clearly and insist on correct speech in all answers and presentations.

Attention is paid to good manners. Children learn to ask questions nicely, talk to elders respectfully, and greet people warmly. (Abraham Lincoln long remembered how the teacher in his one-room schoolhouse had students practice introducing themselves by opening the door, walking in, and politely asking, "Howdy do?") Teachers don't allow unattractive slang in the classroom, and don't let students chew gum while speaking. They insist that children listen quietly and attentively to others.

Good schools recognize that vocabulary enrichment makes students more articulate. Learning new words should be emphasized, both through reading and vocabulary exercises. Children practice choosing the right words when they speak. The study of grammar helps them know why they ought not use double negatives, and why verbs should agree with their subjects.

Younger students practice telling stories, describing things they've seen or heard, and participating in classroom discussions. You'll hear much conversation in good English classes—not just blabbing the first things that come to mind, but focused conversation, guided by the teacher. Children practice asking thoughtful questions in class and making comments on what others have said. As they get older, they give oral reports and short talks. They recite poems, portions of famous speeches, or passages from dramas they've memorized. They practice giving speeches they've written themselves and may engage in formal arguments, following rules of debate.

Again, some of these methods and rules may sound old-fashioned, but good schools know they work. These are important lessons for young people to learn. If not in English class, and not at home, it is hard to imagine just where young people will learn to speak well.

How Do You Recognize "Great" Literature?

The only way to be sure your school is exposing your child to good books and stories is to read some of them yourself. As often as possible, pick up one of your child's reading assignments and ask yourself these questions:

- Do *you* find it interesting? Great children's literature has the capacity to intrigue adults, too. It transcends age by appealing to the childlike wonder in all of us. Is the language rich? Is the story powerful? Are there characters or actions or lessons that can lodge in the heart? (Who can ever forget the image of William Tell taking careful aim? Or Robinson Crusoe coming upon that mysterious, lone footprint in the sand?)

- What will your child discover in this book? Can it teach him something important? William Faulkner reminded us that really good literature speaks to us about "the old verities and truths of the human heart, the old universal truths lacking which any story is ephemeral and doomed—love and honor and pity and pride and compassion and sacrifice."

- Is this a book that has been around for some time, that generations have read and enjoyed? There are many fine new books, and your child should have plenty of opportunities to read them, but he should also spend time with "old" books. Most books written in any given year are merely average, or worse. Time has a way of testing literature. It weeds out the mediocre and preserves the best. Schools should take advantage of time's filter. A fair portion of what students read should fall into the category of "the classics."

- Is this a book you loved in your own childhood? Is it one the teacher has loved? One of our responsibilities as parents and teachers is to share with children the works we have cherished ourselves. Wordsworth wrote, "What we have loved, others will love, but we must teach them how."

Not everything your child reads will ascend to this level, especially in the earliest grades, when he is laboring to discern the difference between "the" and "they." But *some* of the stories that you and the teachers read aloud, even to very young children, should meet that high standard. As your child moves through the intermediate grades, more and more of the books he reads in school should be works whose contents merit knowing. A good education is largely defined by what you know. The choice of books matters.

How Are Schools Doing?

Today, unfortunately, many girls and boys are not learning English nearly well enough. The National Assessment of Educational Progress (NAEP) reported in 1998 that fewer than one third of fourth graders and eighth graders are "proficient" readers, and just a few percent at each grade can be considered "advanced." Even more troubling, nearly 40 percent of fourth graders and more than a quarter of eighth graders are reading at levels below what NAEP considers "basic," which is to say they can barely read at all.

Other measures are equally alarming. The Scholastic Assessment Test (SAT) average verbal score has never recovered from the long slump that began in the mid-1960s. Nor do U.S. schools fare particularly well in international comparisons. Among economically advanced countries, our students come in dead last in terms of reading progress made between the ages of nine and fourteen. Much of the problem lies in the low expectations that schools hold for children. A recent study of state English standards by the Thomas B. Fordham Foundation found that most states don't even have well-formulated goals in this subject. It's no surprise that children are left deficient.

Warning signs abound that fundamental skills and knowledge are not being learned. "Students are not required to write in cursive," says one discouraged mom of a third grader. "When I questioned the principal about this, she stated that it was not necessary for them to master cursive or spelling, because they don't need either in order to use a computer!" "Reading is so difficult for them," reports a high school teacher of her students. "Not only are they unable to sound out new words, but they have low levels of vocabulary knowledge. The public would be aghast if they knew the common, everyday words that today's teenagers simply do not know."

Professors complain of having to dumb down the college curriculum. University officials find themselves assigning more and more freshmen to remedial English classes. According to one survey, nearly seven out of ten employers say that high school graduates are not ready to succeed in the workplace. "They can't spell. . . . Tenses are not consistent. . . . It all goes back to the schools," complains one New York City employer.[1] One test found that only 20 percent of seventeen-year-old American kids could write a simple one-paragraph letter applying for a job in a supermarket.

Although some schools do a fine job of teaching English, it's not hard to see that the present state of language arts education in much of the U.S. is far from what it ought to be. This is a situation that you must take seriously. No other subject matters as much for your child's success in education and in life. One can imagine doing well enough in some careers without knowing much science or history or even math, but success in today's America without proficiency in English is virtually unthinkable.

THE ENGLISH CURRICULUM

The following pages outline what thorough, comprehensive language arts instruction looks like from kindergarten through the eighth grade. Your school should teach your child to read, write, and speak well. This will require systematic work in several different areas—phonics, reading comprehension, grammar, vocabulary, spelling, handwriting, etc. Another critical objective is to expose your child to wonderful works of fiction, nonfiction, and poetry. We cannot stress enough the idea that *what* your child reads is as important as how well he learns to read.

To that end, this section includes three lists of excellent literary works for children. You may wish to see how many of them your child's school includes in its curriculum, and how many are readily accessible on classroom shelves or in the school library. Obviously, these lists are not exhaustive; they represent only a fraction of the fine works available for children. Furthermore, no single syllabus of readings can or should be established for all schools. Each has its own character, its own community, and its own pupils; each must choose books accordingly. Still, you *should* expect your school to teach the kind of high-quality literature cited in the following pages. You should see many of these classics included on your school's reading lists.

Keep in mind that the organization of the language arts curriculum varies quite a bit between institutions. For example, some schools do a good deal of systematic phonics work in kindergarten, while others wait until first grade. One good school may concentrate on ancient Greek mythology in the intermediate grades, another in junior high. Therefore, do not expect your school's course of study to look exactly like the outline here, which is summarized from the Core Knowledge Sequence, an excellent curriculum used in hundreds of schools (see page 100). Do, however, compare the two in a general sense. If you find that many of the elements on this outline are missing from the education your child is getting, have a talk with the English teacher, curriculum director, or principal.

The Primary Grades—Kindergarten Through Third Grade

Learning to read is by far the most important task for children to accomplish in the primary grades. If it does not happen during these first few years, it will be very difficult to make up the lost ground later on. Children who experience school failure often begin to have serious problems around fourth grade, when they must start applying their reading skills in earnest to other academic subjects. Therefore your goal is to make certain your child is reading at grade level and with interest by the end of the third grade.

Most primary teachers start the year expecting to find a room full of kids reading at many different levels. This is partly due to the fact that, just as children don't all start to walk at the same age, they catch on to reading at varying rates. It's also partly because some children (almost always the more "advanced" readers) are fortunate enough to have parents who read with them at home. It takes a skillful teacher to keep everyone moving along, bringing some children up to speed even as she helps the faster readers zip ahead. It's a good idea to talk to her and watch her in action to find out how she manages this difficult job.

You should see a good deal of explicit, systematic phonics work going on. (See "Phonics Versus Whole Language: How Should Children Learn to Read?" page 149.) Expect to pitch in at home to help your child with word identification strategies—sounding out words, breaking longer words into smaller pieces, and blending letter sounds together, for example. Since children learn to read at different rates, some will finish most of the necessary phonics work during first grade, others by grade two or the beginning of grade three. By the end of the primary grades, phonics work should be complete for the class as a whole, which means that these vital reading skills and strategies have been internalized—automated, really—by all children in the class.

You should also see a great deal of emphasis on reading comprehension. The aim of reading, after all, is not simply to figure out the words, but also to understand and appreciate the content. At the outset of a reading lesson, you'll often see good teachers going over the meaning of new words that youngsters will encounter. Teachers also may lead a brief discussion to supply the background knowledge required to understand the selection. ("Today we are going to read a story about a king of England named King Alfred. Who can tell me where England is? Who knows what a king is?") After reading the story, teachers ask questions to help children understand the plot and central ideas. ("Why did King Alfred disguise himself as a shepherd? Why wasn't he angry with the old woman when she scolded him?") This kind of work is essential to advance reading comprehension.

Students who go through all the hard work of learning to read will lose their appetite if the books they're given are dull or dumbed down. Schools should offer first-rate, exciting stories that feature fresh vocabulary, worthwhile knowledge, and the sense that reading is fun.

Classics of children's literature—*The Littlest Angel, The Cat in the Hat, The Just So Stories*—should hold a prominent place in the curriculum. Primary school students can even enjoy wonderful stories such as *The Scarlet Pimpernel* and *Journey to the Center of the Earth* if these works have been adapted for children in imaginative, challenging ways. Ask the teacher to show you the program of study and a list of stories the class will read. Look to see if the classroom has a mini-library or reading corner. Take a few moments to see what is there—and how much it is used.

Making sure that children learn the basics of writing is another absolute in the primary grades. Students learn the fundamentals of putting letters, words, sentences, and paragraphs onto paper. Once they begin formal writing lessons, you should see much regular practice. Skill sheets and workbooks can help children practice basic lessons, but most writing should be in the form of brief compositions corrected by the teacher—stories, letters, short descriptions of things seen, regular journal entries, and so forth. Studying fundamental rules of grammar, language usage, and writing mechanics is critical; if children don't know the rules of writing, it is hard to expect them to write well. Attention to good handwriting habits should also be evident. By the end of the third grade, students should be comfortable coming up with ideas and expressing them legibly with their pencils.

Spelling and vocabulary should be learned in several ways. Children pick up spellings and meanings of words by frequent exposure to them in the context of reading assignments. New words should also be learned through noncontextual approaches, such as studying word lists, mastering spelling rules, working with analogies, and providing synonyms and antonyms.

Children should spend much time practicing oral language—learning to express their thoughts clearly, to describe things vividly, to take part in conversations, and to speak before groups. They learn these skills in several ways: reading aloud, explaining topics, telling the class about things they've seen and done, or recounting familiar stories. Habits of speaking are being formed during these early school years. They are a bit like table manners. There are proper, polite ways to eat, and there are correct, civil ways to speak. English class—and parents—should address speaking etiquette and proper usage.

Learning how to listen closely and politely is also critical. Throughout his academic career, much of your child's classroom time will be spent listening. Listening to directions, listening to the teacher explain ideas, listening to what fellow classmates have to say. A tremendous amount of learning depends on this basic skill. Do not ignore it. Watch to see if your child is sharpening his abilities to pay attention when you and others talk. One of the authors had a teacher who said, "You have two ears and one mouth. Use them in that proportion."

Many study and research skills are taught in the context of English lessons. In the primary grades, children get an introduction to the library, learn its layout and rules, and practice finding books there. They visit the library regularly to borrow books for independent reading. Students practice skills such as alphabetizing words and looking up topics in an index. They learn to use basic reference resources like dictionaries, encyclopedias, atlases, and the Internet.

Given that nothing else is half so important to learn in these first years, don't be surprised to see "language arts" consume at least half the learning time of the average school day. Reading and writing should be embedded in every facet of the school's curriculum. History lessons should involve reading biographies and stories about the past; science lessons should include writing reports on experiments. Everywhere you turn, no matter what the subject, there should be books, books, books.

KINDERGARTEN

Kindergarten introduces children to reading and writing. Students begin phonics. They spend a good deal of classroom time with books; a significant part of each day is devoted to teacher-led story time. Youngsters have many chances to take part in conversations, ask questions, talk about stories, tell their own stories, and describe things. During class activities, they begin learning some rules of conversation such as taking turns speaking, and listening politely. Among other things, kindergartners:

Reading and Comprehension

- learn how print works (e.g., we read English print from left to right, top to bottom)
- recognize and name the letters of the alphabet (upper case and lower case)
- begin phonics: learn that letters represent sounds; identify letter sounds; identify words that rhyme; orally blend sounds to make words; break words into syllables; identify the beginning and ending sounds of short spoken words, etc.
- begin to read some short words (e.g., cat, sit, milk, frog)
- begin to recognize common words by sight (e.g., a, the, I, my, you, is, are)
- read some simple phrases or sentences (e.g., "cat ran up," "Sam sat.")
- tell what happened after listening to stories; predict what will happen next
- practice distinguishing reality from fantasy in stories
- listen to and follow oral directions
- read aloud with someone outside of school at least ten minutes daily

Writing and Spelling

- learn to write own name (first and last)
- write all letters of the alphabet (upper case and lower case)
- use letter-sound knowledge to write simple words and messages

Literature

- learn basic story parts (e.g., title, beginning, end)
- listen to and join in saying short poems (e.g., Mother Goose poems)
- listen to stories, fables, and legends (e.g., "Chicken Little," "Johnny Appleseed," Aesop's "The Hare and the Tortoise")

- listen to nonfiction prose (e.g., short biographies, books about dinosaurs)
- tell and "write" their own stories (by drawing pictures, telling stories to teacher while she writes them down, etc.)
- learn some basic literary terms (e.g., author, illustrator)

(drawn from the Core Knowledge Sequence)

In a good kindergarten classroom, you might see children:

- sitting on the floor around the teacher while she reads "The Indian Cinderella" (a Native American tale from Canada) from a big picture book
- helping the teacher make a list of words that begin with the *b* sound
- picking out words that rhyme as the teacher reads poems such as "Twinkle, Twinkle Little Star" or Eliza Lee Follen's "Three Little Kittens"
- filling in words or finishing sentences as they listen to the teacher read a familiar story
- dressing up as favorite characters in stories the teacher has read aloud
- reading or looking at picture books on their own

FIRST GRADE

First Grade is devoted largely to learning to read. The goal is to be able to read (aloud and silently) texts written for first grade, such as E.H. Minarik's *Little Bear* books, Syd Hoff's *Danny and the Dinosaur,* and Arnold Lobel's *Frog and Toad* books. Phonics work is critical here, as is immersing children in a literature-rich environment. Students continue hearing stories read aloud by the teacher (as they will for the next few years). They get lots of time to ask and answer questions about readings. They practice using basic grammar correctly when they speak. With teachers' and parents' help, they write simple words, sentences, and passages. Among other things, first graders do the following:

Reading and Comprehension

- continue phonics work: count the syllables in a word, identify letter sounds in words, blend letter sounds to make words, etc.
- sound out short words (e.g., mop, boat, cake, feet, chin, boot, kite)
- sound out unfamiliar words when reading

- recognize some common "sight words": (e.g., have, says, one, where)
- read simple stories and beginning reader books (silently and aloud)
- predict what will happen in stories and later discuss whether prediction was right
- discuss what, when, where, how, why, and what-if questions about readings
- read and understand simple instructions
- read aloud with someone outside of school at least ten minutes daily

Writing

- practice writing brief compositions (e.g., stories, descriptions, letters, journal entries)

Spelling

- spell words dictated by teacher
- correctly spell short words (e.g., cat, pig, tent)
- learn simple spelling rules reflected in phonics (e.g., *a-consonant-e* makes the long *a* sound, as in "gate")

Grammar and Usage

- capitalize the first word of a sentence, names of people, and pronoun "I"
- use periods, question marks, and exclamation points at ends of sentences
- make words plural by adding *s*

Literature

- read and listen to poems (e.g., "Solomon Grundy," Gelett Burgess's "The Purple Cow," Eugene Field's "Wynken, Blynken, and Nod")
- read and listen to stories, including fables, fairy tales, and legends (e.g., "Jack and the Beanstalk," "Hansel and Gretel," "Puss-in-Boots")
- learn some folk tales from around the world (e.g., China's "Lon Po Po," Japan's "One-Inch Boy," Spain's "Medio Pollito")
- learn some basic literary terms (e.g., character, hero, heroine)

- read and listen to nonfiction prose (e.g., history books, books about art)
- take part in a class play
- learn some conventions and terms of drama (e.g., actors, scenery, props, stage)
- practice telling and writing their own stories

(drawn from the Core Knowledge Sequence)

In a good first grade classroom, you might see children:

- hearing stories such as "The Pied Piper " and "The Honest Woodman," and then talking about why it is important to tell the truth

- after listening to some Beatrix Potter tales, working with the teacher to compose their own animal story

- keeping lists of "Things I Can Do" to record progress in writing (e.g. write my name; write all the letters; write my address; use periods)

- identifying the long vowel sounds in words such as "cake," "eat," and "hello," and the short vowel sounds in words such as "rock," "little," and "happen"

- listening to the teacher as she explains the rules for a class discussion and the reason for each rule

- taking turns explaining why something they brought from home is important to their families

---

SECOND GRADE

Second Grade students continue learning how to read. They may need to do more explicit phonics work, reviewing what they learned in first grade and practicing with new letter-sound patterns. By the end of this year, decoding (i.e., turning letters into speech sounds) should be almost automatic for most children, allowing them to focus on meaning. The overall goal is to be able to read (aloud and silently) texts written for second grade, such as Peggy Parish's *Amelia Bedelia* books, Lillian Hoban's *Arthur* books, and second-grade-level volumes in such nonfiction series as *I Can Read* and *Let's Read and Find Out*. Second graders also get plenty of practice writing. They build speaking skills by telling stories aloud, taking part in dramatic activities, and participating in class discussions. Among other things, second graders do the following:

Reading and Comprehension

- continue to sound out words (e.g., rabbit, caterpillar, motorcycle)
- accurately read single-syllable and most two-syllable words (e.g., boy, tough, night, apple, riddle, basket)
- recall incidents, characters, facts, and details of texts
- answer what, how, why, and what-if questions about readings
- discuss similarities in characters and events from different stories
- retell stories and explain information learned from a text in their own words
- read outside of school at least fifteen minutes daily

Writing

- write brief stories, poems, letters, descriptions, and reports
- with help, write compositions with a beginning, middle, and end
- practice using paragraphs
- with help, revise work for clarity and edit for spelling and mechanics
- practice writing neatly

Spelling and Vocabulary

- correctly spell words containing spelling patterns studied so far
- learn and review spelling rules (e.g., the *f* sound is sometimes spelled *ph*, as in "phone")
- begin using dictionary to check spelling and word meanings
- learn some common contractions (e.g., can't, I'm) and abbreviations (e.g., Mr., Ms.)
- provide synonyms (e.g., happy, glad) and antonyms (e.g., hot, cold) for given words

Grammar and Usage

- identify subjects and predicates in simple sentences
- learn what nouns are; how to make singular nouns plural
- study correct usage of verbs; how to change from present to past tense
- learn what adjectives are; use adjectives to compare by adding *er* and *est*

- practice using capital letters, periods, question marks, exclamation points
- learn to use commas in dates and addresses

Literature

- read and listen to poems such as Christina Rossetti's "Hurt No Living Thing," Nancy Byrd Turner's "Lincoln," Clement C. Moore's "The Night Before Christmas"
- read and listen to stories such as "Beauty and the Beast," "The Emperor's New Clothes," and the African tale "Talk"
- read nonfiction prose (e.g., accounts of real-life heroes)
- read Greek myths (e.g., "How Prometheus Brought Fire," "Oedipus and the Sphinx")
- read American tall tales (e.g., Paul Bunyan, Pecos Bill, Casey Jones)
- learn more basic literary terms (e.g., myth, limerick)
- tell and write their own stories

(drawn from the Core Knowledge Sequence)

In a good second grade classroom, you might see children:

- reading a tall tale about Stormalong and then discussing how the author exaggerated actions and characters
- reading "The Blind Men and the Elephant" (a fable from India) and writing a moral for the story
- reading sets of words and choosing the ones that don't belong (e.g., milk, ham, paper, cake)
- writing letters to first graders telling them what they enjoyed learning in the first grade and what they're doing in second grade
- reading stories they've written to the class, then revising their drafts after hearing classmates' comments about what is unclear or missing
- researching and writing labels for specimens the class has collected outside (e.g., leaves, insects, nests)

THIRD GRADE

Third grade students should be competent at decoding (i.e., turning letters into speech sounds) most one- and two-syllable words, and increasingly able to decode multisyllable words. The overall goal this year is to be able to read (aloud and silently) texts written for third grade, such as Beverly Cleary's *Ramona* books, Laura Ingalls Wilder's *Little House in the Big Woods*, and third-grade-level volumes in such nonfiction series as *Let's Read and Find Out* and *New True Books*. Students get frequent chances to write. Attention to spelling and penmanship continues; children routinely proofread and correct their own work. Among other things, third graders do the following:

Reading and Comprehension

- independently read longer works of fiction ("chapter books") and nonfiction
- orally summarize main points from readings
- ask and answer what, how, why, and what-if questions about texts
- use a dictionary to look up unfamiliar words
- learn to use a table of contents and index
- read outside of school at least twenty minutes daily

Writing

- write brief stories, reports, poems, letters, descriptions, etc.
- find information in basic sources (e.g., children's encyclopedia) to write reports
- learn letter-writing conventions (e.g., heading, salutation, closing, signature)
- practice writing paragraphs with topic sentence, central idea, supporting details
- practice organizing, drafting, revising, and proofreading their writings

Spelling and Vocabulary

- get regular practice at spelling and vocabulary enrichment
- spell most words correctly when writing; use dictionary to check spellings
- study use of prefixes (e.g., *re, un, dis*) and suffixes (e.g., *er, less, ly*)
- practice using homophones correctly (e.g., by, buy; to, too, two)
- recognize common abbreviations (e.g., St., U.S.A., ft.)

Grammar and Usage

- distinguish complete sentences from fragments; identify subjects and predicates

- identify and use declarative, interrogative, imperative, and exclamatory sentences
- study use of nouns, pronouns (singular and plural), verbs (action and helping), adjectives (including articles a, an, the), and adverbs
- know how to use: period, question mark, exclamation point, comma (in dates; addresses; in a series; after *yes* and *no*), apostrophe (in contractions and possessive nouns)
- recognize and avoid the double negative

Literature

- read and listen to poems such as Isaac Watts's "The Bee," Lewis Carroll's "The Crocodile," Ogden Nash's "Adventures of Isabel"
- read and listen to stories such as "Aladdin and the Wonderful Lamp," Hans Christian Andersen's "The Little Match Girl," "The People Could Fly" (African-American tale)
- read and listen to nonfiction prose (e.g., books about famous scientists)
- read myths from Greek, Roman, and Norse mythology (e.g., "Cupid and Psyche," "Horatius at the Bridge," "The Death of Balder")
- learn more literary terms (e.g., biography, autobiography, fiction, nonfiction)
- tell and write their own stories

(drawn from the Core Knowledge Sequence)

In a good third grade classroom, you might see children:

- after hearing the legend of "Androcles and the Lion," taking turns telling about a time when they were a good friend to someone
- writing reports on a recent field trip to an aquarium, and then reading them to the class
- writing their own endings to the African tale of Makulu after the teacher reads the first part aloud
- pointing out the subjects and predicates in sentences they've written
- rewriting sentences by substituting pronouns for nouns ("When Jim saw the ball, Jim reached and caught the ball.")
- listening to a local poet talk to the class about how she writes poems

Good Books for the Primary Grades

Here are the kinds of books you see in a good language arts program during the K–3 years. Students will be able to read some of these books themselves, depending on the age and reading ability of the child. Other titles lend themselves well to reading aloud to children.

Aesop for Children, Aesop
Hans Christian Andersen's Fairy Tales, Hans Christian Andersen
Anno's Alphabet and *Anno's Counting Book,* Mitsumasa Anno
Wiley and the Hairy Man, Molly Bang
Madeline books, Ludwig Bemelmans
The Three Billy Goats Gruff, Susan Blair
Freddy the Detective, Walter R. Brooks
The Pied Piper of Hamelin, Robert Browning
The Story of Babar, the Little Elephant, Jean de Brunhoff
Mike Mulligan and His Steam Shovel and *The Little House,* Virginia Lee
   Burton
Jack and the Three Sillies, Richard Case
The Ramona and Henry Huggins books, Beverly Cleary
Adventures of Pinocchio, Carlo Collodi
Chanticleer and the Fox, Barbara Cooney
The Courage of Sarah Noble, Alice Dalgliesh
Book of Nursery and Mother Goose Rhymes, Marguerite de Angeli,
   editor
Drummer Hoff, Barbara Emberley
The Three Bears, retold by Paul Galdone
Grimm's Fairy Tales, Jacob and Wilhelm Grimm
The Wonder Book, Nathaniel Hawthorne
One Fine Day, Nonny Hogrogrian
Little Red Riding Hood, retold by Trina Schart Hyman
John Henry: An American Legend and *The Snowy Day,* Ezra Jack Keats
Pecos Bill, Steven Kellog
Just So Stories, Rudyard Kipling
The Arabian Nights and *Aladdin and the Wonderful Lamp,* Andrew Lang
Piping Down the Valleys Wild, Nancy Larrick
The Story of Ferdinand, Munro Leaf
How Many Spots Does a Leopard Have? And Other Tales, Julius Lester
Pippi Longstocking books, Astrid Lindgren
Frog and Toad Together, Arnold Lobel
Mrs. Piggle-Wiggle, Betty MacDonald
Make Way for Ducklings and *Blueberries for Sal,* Robert McCloskey
Every Time I Climb a Tree, poems by David McCord
Anansi the Spider: A Tale from the Ashanti, retold by Gerald McDermott
When We Were Very Young and *Winnie-the-Pooh,* A.A. Milne
Amelia Bedelia, Peggy Parish

Cinderella, Charles Perrault
The Tale of Peter Rabbit, Beatrix Potter
Ride a Purple Pelican and *Read-Aloud Rhymes for the Very Young*, Jack Pre-
    lutsky, editor
Curious George books, H.A. Rey
The Dancing Stars: An Iroquois Legend, Anne Rockwell
Where the Wild Things Are and *Chicken Soup with Rice*, Maurice
    Sendak
The Cat in the Hat, Green Eggs and Ham, Horton Hatches the Egg, and
    others by Dr. Seuss
Caps for Sale, Esphyr Slobodkina
Noah's Ark, Peter Spier
Abel's Island and *Sylvester and the Magic Pebble*, William Steig
Mufaro's Beautiful Daughters: An African Tale, John Steptoe
A Child's Garden of Verses, Robert Louis Stevenson
East O' the Sun and West O' the Moon, Gudrun Thorne-Thomsen
Brian Wildsmith's Illustrated Bible Stories, Philip Turner
Alexander and the Terrible, Horrible, No Good, Very Bad Day, Judith
    Viorst
Ira Sleeps Over, Bernard Waber
The Trumpet of the Swan, E.B. White
The Velveteen Rabbit, Margery Williams
Crow Boy, Taro Yashima
Owl Moon and *The Seeing Stick*, Jane Yolen
Lon Po Po: A Red-Riding Hood Story from China, Ed Young
Rumplestiltskin, retold by Paul O. Zelinsky

How Well Read Is Your Primary School Child?

By the end of the third grade, your child should be familiar with many of the
following, through books he has read and stories you've read to him:

• The Boy Who Cried Wolf—Aesop fable

• The Goose That Laid the Golden Egg—Aesop fable

• The Ugly Duckling—Hans Christian Andersen story

• "God bless us, every one!"—Tiny Tim's prayer in Dickens's *A Christmas
  Carol*

• Babe the Blue Ox—Paul Bunyan's companion

• "Open, Sesame"—Ali Baba's magical password in *Arabian Nights* tale

• The Yellow Brick Road—path to the Emerald City in Oz

• Anansi the Spider—trickster of African folktales

• Goldilocks—little girl who explored the Three Bears' house

- The Boy and the Dike—stuck his finger in a hole to keep back the sea
- Christopher Robin—Winnie-the-Pooh's owner in A. A. Milne tales
- Brer Fox and Brer Rabbit—animal foes in *Uncle Remus* stories
- "Do unto others as you would have them do unto you."—Golden Rule
- King Midas—greedy king with the golden touch
- Zeus and Hera—also known as Jupiter and Juno; king and queen of the Greek and Roman gods
- Unicorn—mythical horselike beast with a single horn on forehead
- Trolls—mythical dwarves who live in caves or under bridges
- William Tell—Swiss archer who shot an apple off his son's head
- Pocahontas—Indian maiden who saved Captain John Smith
- Noah's Ark—carried the animals in biblical flood
- Glass slipper—footwear Cinderella left at the ball
- The Owl and the Pussycat—sea-goers of Edward Lear's poem
- "But he's wearing no clothes!"—observation of child in Hans Christian Andersen's "The Emperor's New Clothes"
- Sherwood Forest—Robin Hood's home

Questions to Ask the Teacher

In the primary grades, you may want to ask your child's teacher questions such as:

- How much time do you spend reading aloud to children in class?
- What books, stories, poems, and other reading selections will my child be reading or listening to in your class?
- Do you teach reading through both systematic phonics and real literature?
- How do you manage working with different levels of reading proficiency in class? Do you group children according to reading ability? How does my child read compared to his classmates?
- How do you deal with children who are advanced readers? With those who are lagging behind?
- What percentage of this school's third graders read and write at grade level?
- If children misspell words, do you correct them? If not now, when does this school begin to do so? How do you teach spelling? Do you have new vocabulary words each week? Do you send word lists home?
- On average, how much daily classroom time is spent on writing instruction?

- Can you show me a book or a list of words you expect my child to be able to read by the end of the marking period? A sample composition or list of words you expect him to be able to write by that time?
- Do you have a list of books you recommend for home reading?
- How often do children in your class visit the school library?

What If My Child Has a Reading Problem?

Sometimes it's hard to tell if "slow" readers are just late bloomers or if there is a real problem. If you are worried about your child's reading skills, it's better to be safe than sorry. Between the ages of five and eight, learning to read has to be at the top of your child's educational priority list. Nothing is more important to later academic success, so don't hesitate to secure all the help you think he needs. Here are some steps to take (you may only need to take one or two):

- **Talk to the teacher to see if she thinks there is a problem.** Tell her your concerns. Find out how your child is doing in her classroom. The teacher may feel there is no cause for worry. Remember, it is normal for children to pick up reading skills at different rates. It may be that your child will catch up without extra help. (One reason it's important for you to get to know the teacher is that you'll have to decide whether or not to trust her if she tells you "everything is fine.")

- **If there is a problem, talk to the teacher about what to do next.** There may also be a school counselor available. Discuss the value of having your child tested or evaluated by a specialist to find out what's wrong. Part of the school's job is to devise a strategy to help your child catch up. The teacher should explain that plan and work with you in putting it into effect. There are any number of options: assign more or different homework; change the reading program or materials the teacher is using; move your child to a different reading group; get extra tutoring; consider a remedial reading program; or even have your child repeat a grade. Whatever the plan, make sure to ask which parts you can do at home.

- **Consider getting a second opinion.** Sometimes schools simply don't recognize reading problems until they're acute, or they misdiagnose problems. If you feel you're not getting satisfactory advice, you will find in many communities private consultants who work with concerned families. These people can provide additional evaluation and make a recommendation. They're often listed in the Yellow Pages under "Educational Consultants." The best way to choose one, though, is to ask around and find other parents who can supply references.

- **Consider having your child tested.** It may be that he would benefit from some expert diagnostic testing. The education consultants mentioned above can lead you to such professionals. In many communities, there are well-established centers and individual psychologists who specialize in precisely this kind of help for families. Your school may have been in touch with them for other children over the years. Chances are, some parents you know have relevant experience, too. Do not be embarrassed to ask. Your child's learning challenges and the necessary corrective actions may be clearer once an expert has looked closely at the problem.

- **Make sure the school is doing a good job.** There is always the possibility that the problem lies not with your child but with the teacher or school. Talk to other parents about their children's progress. Are they satisfied? Ask to see the school's reading test scores. Where does it rank in the district and state? Ask about the particular teaching method the instructor is using. Is there evidence that it has a proven track record? Do other teachers in the school use different methods?

- **Arrange for tutoring.** You may need to find someone who can give your child extra one-on-one instruction. The school may be able to supply a tutor or help you find one. Look for someone experienced working with young readers. If your child has a specific reading problem, you want someone trained to deal with it. Other children, however, blossom with a college or high school student who spends extra time reading with them.

  When you find a tutor, don't simply hand your child over. Get to know her and make sure she understands what you want. Get her to explain the method of instruction and ask how you should supplement it.

- **Do more at home.** Don't leave the whole burden of helping your child catch up on the school or a tutor. Remember, it's quite possible that *you* are the best reading coach for your child. If the teacher says he needs an extra thirty minutes of reading practice per day, or an extra twenty minutes of phonics, take it seriously.

  Remember that even in the best of classrooms and schools—and the best of households—there are children who would benefit from extra help, more time, or a different approach. If your daughter or son is one of those youngsters, don't be ashamed. Instead, start looking for the best approach to fix the situation. As with most problems, the earlier it is addressed, the more readily it is solved.

The Intermediate Grades—Fourth Through Sixth Grades

Success in the intermediate grades depends on whether the basics have already been mastered. More than anything else, that means being a comfortable reader and reasonably fluent writer. From here on, these are the main tools on which success in school depends. If your child is behind in these two critical areas going into the fourth grade, take immediate action. Make sure he gets extra help and spends time reading and writing.

Now that your child can read, school should expose him to all sorts of selections worth reading, everything from folktales to biographies to magazine articles. In English class itself, the focus should turn more toward literary readings. As your child moves through the intermediate grades, less class time should be spent reading practical or informational texts, and more time devoted to literature such as stories, poems, novels, plays, literary prose, and great speeches. Students should read many fine works: ancient mythology, famous folktales from around the world, children's classics such as *The Lion, the Witch, and the Wardrobe* or *Where the Red Fern Grows,* and some children's versions of great literary classics (such as good retellings of Dickens's masterpieces). As always, you must ask the teacher what the class will be reading, and satisfy yourself that most of those assignments rely on high-quality, demanding literature.

Part of the teacher's job is to show your child how to get the most from the material. The rewards of good literature depend largely on the ability of the reader to find the intended meaning. To do this, not only must students be able to grasp increasingly complicated language and plots, they must learn to interpret literary devices such as imagery and flashbacks. They must understand the different elements in a story or poem and how they work. Developing this skill takes practice. This is why good English teachers spend considerable time asking questions such as "What do you think of when the poet describes a tree wearing 'a nest of robins in her hair'?" This is why they teach children to analyze stories for setting, plot, and character, and why they require students to know figures of speech such as alliteration and simile. It's one reason good teachers have students memorize some quality poetry and prose. Although sometimes wrongly criticized for pushing "rote" assignments, they recognize that the full benefits of good literature usually don't come with the first reading, but require work, time, and thought. As Edmund Burke observed, reading without reflecting is like eating without digesting.

Writing assignments should also be frequent during these years. Children should be encouraged to write creatively, but you should also see an increasing emphasis on expository writing, such as book reports, descriptive essays, summaries, and brief biographies. Expository writing trains children to think and write analytically. Students learn how to plan and organize papers, revise, and proofread. They refine their penmanship in the process. By the end of sixth grade, your child should be able to write a clear, well-organized three- or four-page paper.

Students should visit the library frequently and learn to use reference works such as glossaries, thesauruses, bibliographies, and electronic databases. They should work on basic research skills such as formulating questions, analyzing information, and developing conclusions.

Learning rules of grammar and writing mechanics will make your child a better writer. Therefore you should see youngsters studying such topics as subjects and predicates, verb tenses, and punctuation. Vocabulary and spelling work should continue. Children learn word meanings and spellings in the context of their reading (particularly if they are encouraged to look up unfamiliar words in the dictionary) but exercises such as learning assigned word lists, making analogies, taking dictation from the teacher, and studying word origins are also important. You should see frequent spelling and vocabulary tests (at least once a week) in the intermediate grades.

Development of oral language skills continues. Your child should get experience making "formal" presentations to the class, such as reciting a poem, reading a book report, or giving a talk on a topic he's researched. Children practice using standard English, enunciating clearly, maintaining good posture, and making eye contact with listeners. They work on listening to what others have to say, asking thoughtful questions, and making relevant observations. They practice distinguishing fact from opinion when listening to others, and using evidence to support their assertions. You can't expect your child to be a polished public speaker by the end of the sixth grade, but with enough training, he should be able to take part in group discussions and make short presentations to his classmates without much difficulty.

By the intermediate grades, English is apt to be one subject among half a dozen, yet it permeates all the others. You may hear a teacher use the phrase "writing across the curriculum." That means writing takes place in every subject area. Once your child starts learning various subjects from different teachers, the writing involved in history, science, math, and other classes should be linked to the goals of the English curriculum.

FOURTH GRADE

Fourth grade students should be fluent, competent readers. They should be able to focus on the meaning and details of texts. They read selections from children's classics and contemporary works, both fiction and nonfiction. They also read a variety of poetry. They get many opportunities for writing, both imaginative and expository, with an increased emphasis on the latter including summaries, book reports, and descriptive essays. Children are given more responsibility for organizing, editing, and proofreading their work. Among other things, fourth graders do the following:

Writing and Research

- write reports, summaries, descriptions, letters, stories, and poems
- practice organizing, drafting, revising, and proofreading writings
- practice identifying the purpose and audience of the writing; defining a main idea and sticking to it; providing an introduction and conclusion; using clear, organized paragraphs
- use different resources (e.g., encyclopedias, magazines, interviews) to write short reports
- learn to document sources in a rudimentary bibliography

Spelling and Vocabulary

- get regular practice in spelling and vocabulary enrichment
- spell most words correctly when writing; use dictionary to check spellings
- practice using synonyms and antonyms
- study more prefixes (e.g., *im, non, mis, pre*) and suffixes (e.g., *ily, ful, able, ment*)
- review homophones that often cause problems (e.g., there, their, they're; its, it's)

Grammar and Usage

- distinguish complete sentences, sentence fragments, and run-ons
- identify subjects and predicates; study subject-verb agreement
- use declarative, interrogative, imperative, and exclamatory sentences
- know the following parts of speech and how they are used: nouns, pronouns, verbs, adjectives, adverbs, conjunctions, interjections

- know how to use the following punctuation: period, question mark, exclamation point, comma, apostrophe, quotation marks

Literature

- read poems such as Edna St. Vincent Millay's "Afternoon on a Hill," Ralph Waldo Emerson's "Concord Hymn," Langston Hughes's "Dreams"
- learn basic poetry terms (e.g., stanza, line)
- read stories such as Jonathan Swift's *Gulliver's Travels* (adapted for young readers) and "The Magic Brocade" (Chinese folktale)
- read famous myths and legends (e.g., stories of King Arthur and the Round Table)
- learn more literary terms and characteristics (e.g., novel, short story, plot, setting)
- read nonfiction prose (e.g., magazine articles, books about nature)
- read famous passages from speeches (e.g., Patrick Henry's "Give me liberty or give me death" and Sojourner Truth's "Ain't I a Woman?")
- take part in dramatic activities
- read outside of school at least twenty minutes daily

(drawn from the Core Knowledge Sequence)

In a good fourth grade English class, students get assignments such as:

- After reading several poems such as "April" by Sara Teasdale, "A Summer Morning" by Rachel Field, and "The Garden Year" by Sara Coleridge, write a short rhymed poem about the seasons or the weather.

- Read "Fog" by Carl Sandburg and participate in a classroom discussion about the uses of imagery in that poem.

- Write a brief report about a class trip to view an art exhibit.

- Write the following words as the teacher calls them out and uses them in sentences: quickly, wonderful, wrap, hear, here.

- Write sentences using the present and past tenses of the following verbs: sing, find, buy, think, rise, give, lie.

- Choose an animal and, using the library's reference books or computer to research information, write a short report on it for a guide to local fauna that the class is putting together.

FIFTH GRADE

Fifth grade readings should fan students' love of literature and build a storehouse of literary knowledge. Children sample all sorts of genres: short novels and stories, poetry, plays, essays, biographies, great speeches, and documents from American history. They discuss how the details of a text and the writer's use of language affect meaning. Students continue imaginative writing but also get much practice in expository writing (book reports, essays that explain a process, descriptive essays). They should be able to revise and edit to produce a finished product that is thoughtful, well organized, and generally correct in grammar, mechanics, and spelling. Among other things, fifth graders do the following:

Writing and Research

- write reports, summaries, letters, descriptions, essays, stories, poems, etc.
- use different resources (e.g., atlases, glossaries, the Internet) to write reports
- practice organizing, drafting, revising, and proofreading
- write reports that address a specific audience; define a main idea; provide an introduction and conclusion; use organized paragraphs; illustrate points with good examples; document sources in a simple bibliography

Spelling and Vocabulary

- get regular practice in spelling and vocabulary enrichment
- spell most words correctly when writing; use dictionary to check spellings
- study more prefixes (e.g., *anti, co, inter, semi*) and suffixes (e.g., *ist, ish, ness, tion*)

Grammar and Usage

- correct sentence fragments and run-ons
- identify subjects and predicates; use correct subject-verb agreement
- know the following parts of speech and how they are used: nouns, pronouns, verbs, adjectives, adverbs, conjunctions, interjections
- study pronoun agreement with antecedents
- correctly use punctuation studied in earlier grades and expand on it (e.g., use a colon before a list; commas with an appositive)

Literature

- read poems such as Julia Ward Howe's "The Battle Hymn of The Republic," Emily Dickinson's "I Like to See It Lap the Miles," William Blake's "The Tiger"
- study literary terms and devices (e.g., alliteration, onomatopoeia, metaphor, simile)
- read stories such as Laura Ingalls Wilder's *Little House on the Prairie* or excerpts from Cervantes's *Don Quixote* (adapted for young readers)
- read plays such as Shakespeare's *A Midsummer Night's Dream* (adapted for young readers)
- learn dramatic terms and characteristics (e.g., tragedy, comedy, act, scene)
- read myths and legends such as "The Samurai's Daughter" (from Japan) and "Scarface" (a Plains Indian legend)
- read nonfiction prose (e.g., articles about history and geography)
- read great speeches such as Lincoln's Gettysburg Address and Chief Joseph's "I will fight no more forever"
- read outside of school at least twenty-five minutes daily

(drawn from the Core Knowledge Sequence)

In a good fifth grade English class, students get assignments such as:

- Before writing a short biographical essay about Amelia Earhart, write down the five main points you want to convey.

- Take dictation from the teacher as she reads a short paragraph from a ghost story.

- Write and then perform with classmates a brief play based on one of the stories in Virginia Hamilton's *The People Could Fly: American Black Folk Tales*.

- Tell what's wrong with the following sentence: "Becky and Susan are going with Dana and I to the game."

- After reading some tales about Sherlock Holmes, work with classmates to write your own mystery, which other students will try to solve.

- Pick a hero from history, read about his or her life, and give a brief talk to the class about why you admire this person.

SIXTH GRADE

Sixth grade is a year for developing deeper reading skills and a more so-phisticated understanding of literature. Students are exposed to broader and more complex material. They explore, for example, how imagery and style affect the reader. Children get many opportunities for imagi-native writing of stories and poems but also hone the necessary skills for producing polished reports and essays. They should be able to express themselves with increasing confidence, technical correctness, and fluid-ity. Among other things, sixth graders do the following:

Writing and Research

- write essays, reports, summaries, letters, descriptions, stories, poems, etc.
- practice organizing, drafting, revising, and proofreading their writings
- write a persuasive essay: practice defining and supporting a thesis; distinguishing evidence from opinion; anticipating counterargu-ments; using reasonable tone
- write a research essay: gather information; take notes; organize out-line; acknowledge sources; prepare bibliography
- write a standard business letter

Speaking and Listening

- participate civilly and productively in group discussions
- give a short speech to the class
- use standard English when presenting in class

Spelling and Vocabulary

- continue regular spelling practice and vocabulary enrichment
- review spelling rules (e.g., rules for use of *ie* and *ei*)
- work on commonly misspelled words (e.g., conscious, minimum, separate)
- study Latin and Greek words that form common roots (e.g., *ante*, *bios*, *magnus*)

Grammar and Usage

- identify independent and dependent clauses
- identify and use simple, compound, complex, and compound-complex sentences

- correctly use punctuation studied in earlier grades
- learn to use a semicolon or comma in compound sentences
- study the active and passive voices
- practice using troublesome verbs (e.g., sit, set; rise, raise; lie, lay)
- study correct use of troublesome words (e.g., good, well; like, as; who, whom)

Literature

- read poems such as Rudyard Kipling's "If," Paul Laurence Dunbar's "Sympathy," Edgar Allan Poe's "The Raven"
- study poetry terms and characteristics (e.g., meter, couplet, rhyme scheme)
- read stories such as *The Odyssey* (adapted for young readers) and Frances Hodgson Burnett's *The Secret Garden*
- read plays such as Shakespeare's *Julius Caesar* (adapted for young readers)
- read classical mythology such as the stories of Apollo and Daphne, Narcissus and Echo, Pygmalion and Galatea
- study literary terms and devices (e.g., epic, imagery, symbol, personification)

(drawn from the Core Knowledge Sequence)

In a good sixth grade English class, students get assignments such as:

- After reading several myths about the Greek goddess Artemis (Diana), answer the following questions: What was Diana's favorite pastime? What kind of people regarded her as their protector? Who was her twin brother? How is Diana usually identified in art?

- Read Henry Wadsworth Longfellow's "A Psalm of Life" and find places where the poet uses simile or personification.

- Interview two adults to find out the greatest examples of perseverance they have witnessed; then write an essay exploring the theme of perseverance, drawing on both the interviews and fictional stories read in class.

- Write a formal letter to the principal telling how you have personally benefited from school this year.

- Memorize and recite the poem "I Wandered Lonely as a Cloud" by William Wordsworth before the class.

- In a classroom discussion, practice summarizing the previous speaker's main point before responding to it.

Good Books for the Intermediate Grades

Here are the kinds of books you see in a good language arts curriculum in grades four through six:

Little Women, Louisa May Alcott
Sounder, William H. Armstrong
Mr. Popper's Penguins, Richard Atwater
Tuck Everlasting, Natalie Babbitt
Peter Pan, J.M. Barrie
Crickets and Bullfrogs and Whispers of Thunder: Poems and Pictures,
    Harry Behn
Stories of the Gods and Heroes, Sally Benson
Sundiata: The Epic of the Lion King, Roland Bertol
Doctor Coyote: A Native American Aesop's Fables, retold by John Bier-
    horst
The Secret Garden, Frances Hodgson Burnett
Sadako and the Thousand Paper Cranes, Eleanor Coerr
A New Treasury of Children's Poetry: Old Favorites and New Discoveries,
    edited by Joanna Cole
Prairie Songs, Pamela Conrad
James and the Giant Peach and *Charlie and the Chocolate Factory,* Roald
    Dahl
The Black Stallion, Walter Farley
Thor and the Giants, Anita Feagles
Great Brain books, John D. Fitzgerald
The Whipping Boy, Sid Fleischman
Johnny Tremain, Esther Forbes
Selections from *Poor Richard's Almanack,* Benjamin Franklin
*And Then What Happened, Paul Revere?; What's the Big Idea, Ben
    Franklin?;* and *Where Was Patrick Henry on the 29th of May?,* Jean
    Fritz
A Swinger of Birches: Poems of Robert Frost for Young People, Robert Frost
Julie of the Wolves, Jean Craighead George
The Wind in the Willows, Kenneth Grahame
Mythology, Edith Hamilton
The People Could Fly: American Black Folk Tales, Virginia Hamilton
Misty of Chincoteague and *Brighty of the Grand Canyon,* Marguerite
    Henry
The Phantom Tollbooth, Norton Juster
The Trumpeter of Krakow, Eric Kelly
The Jungle Book and *Captains Courageous,* Rudyard Kipling
Lassie Come Home, Eric Knight
From the Mixed-up Files of Mrs. Basil E. Frankweiler, E.L. Konigsburg
Tales from Shakespeare, Charles and Mary Lamb
A Wrinkle in Time, Madeleine L'Engle

The Lion, the Witch, and the Wardrobe, C.S. Lewis
Castle and *Cathedral*, David Macaulay
Sarah, Plain and Tall, Patricia MacLachlan
Paul Bunyan Swings His Axe, Dell J. McCormick
Snow Treasure, Marie McSwigan
The Borrowers, Mary Norton
Hailstones and Halibut Bones, poems by Mary O'Neill
Bridge to Terabithia and *The Great Gilly Hopkins*, Katherine Paterson
Tales of Mystery and Imagination, Edgar Allan Poe
The Merry Adventures of Robin Hood, Howard Pyle
The Westing Game, Ellen Raskin
Where the Red Fern Grows, Wilson Rawls
The *Harry Potter* series, J. K. Rowling
Bambi, Felix Salten
Abe Lincoln Grows Up and *Rootabaga Stories*, Carl Sandburg
Black Beauty, Anna Sewell
A Day of Pleasure: Stories of a Boy Growing Up in Warsaw, Isaac Bashevis Singer
Call It Courage, Armstrong Sperry
Heidi, Johanna Spyri
Treasure Island, Robert Louis Stevenson
The Nutcracker: A Story and a Ballet, Ellen Switzer
Charlotte's Web and *Stuart Little*, E.B. White
Little House on the Prairie, Laura Ingalls Wilder
Swiss Family Robinson, Johann Wyss

How Well Read Is Your Intermediate Grade Child?

By the end of the sixth grade, a well-read child should be able to identify many of the following:

- Long John Silver—peg-legged pirate of Stevenson's *Treasure Island*
- Judas Iscariot—apostle who betrayed Jesus
- "A penny saved is a penny earned"—maxim from Franklin's *Poor Richard's Almanack*
- Tinker Bell—fairy in *Peter Pan*
- Mary Lennox—heroine of Frances Hodgson Burnett's *The Secret Garden*
- Toad, Mole, Rat, and Badger—animal friends in Kenneth Grahame's *Wind in the Willows*
- Thor and Freya—god of thunder and goddess of love in Norse mythology
- Mount Olympus—home of the Greek gods
- Helen of Troy—beautiful Greek woman whose kidnapping led to Trojan War

- Pecos Bill—tall-tale cowboy

- "Let there be light"—Genesis 1:3

- "Mine eyes have seen the glory of the coming of the Lord"—opening line of Julia Ward Howe's "The Battle Hymn of the Republic"

- John Henry—hero who raced the drilling machine

- Lilliputians—tiny people in Jonathan Swift's *Gulliver's Travels*

- Excalibur—King Arthur's sword

- King Solomon—wise king of ancient Israel

- "One, if by land, and two, if by sea"—signal in the North Church tower in Longfellow's poem "Paul Revere's Ride"

- Cheshire cat—grinning cat in Lewis Carroll's *Alice in Wonderland*

- Meg, Jo, Beth, and Amy—sisters in Louisa May Alcott's *Little Women*

- Wilbur the pig, Templeton the rat, and Charlotte the spider—animals in E.B. White's *Charlotte's Web*

- "Four score and seven years ago . . ."—opening words of Gettysburg Address

- setting—the time and place of a story

- rhyme scheme—the pattern of rhyming words in a poem

- simile—a comparison of two unlike things using the word "like" or "as" (e.g., "a nose like a cherry")

Wellsprings of Western Literature

The two greatest literary sources in the Western tradition are the Bible and classical mythology. For centuries, the archetypal stories contained in these works have influenced thinkers and writers. Throughout school, your child will encounter biblical and mythological references time and again—in Shakespeare's plays, in the Founding Fathers' writings, in modern newspaper editorials, even in science class. (All of the other planets in the solar system, for example, are named for Roman gods and goddesses.)

In many places, however, the Greek and Roman myths have been squeezed out of the curriculum. You should talk to your child's teachers and find out when the school introduces children to classical mythology.

Many public schools are unnecessarily shy about exposing students to timeless Bible stories. Therefore, if your child does not meet these wonderful tales in church or synagogue, you may need to take care of this part of his education at home. Regardless of your faith, your child's cultural literacy will be deficient without at least a passing knowledge of some famous Bible stories.

Here are some (but not all!) of the stories a well-educated child should read:

Great Classical Myths

Theseus and the Minotaur
The Trojan Horse
Odysseus and the Cyclops
Perseus and Medusa
The Labors of Hercules
Arachne's Tapestry
Icarus and Daedalus
Phaeton and the Chariot of the Sun
Persephone and Hades
Orpheus and Eurydice
King Midas and the Golden Touch
The Quest for the Golden Fleece

Twelve Great Bible Stories

Adam and Eve in the Garden of Eden
Noah and the Ark
The Story of Moses
David and Goliath
Ruth and Naomi
Joseph and the Coat of Many Colors
Daniel in the Lion's Den
The Story of Queen Esther
The Birth of Jesus
The Parable of the Good Samaritan
The Parable of the Prodigal Son
The Sermon on the Mount

Questions to Ask the Teacher

In the intermediate grades, you may want to ask the teacher questions such as:

- What books, stories, poems, and other selections will my child be reading in your class? What writing assignments will he get in the coming weeks?

- What is my child's reading level? How is it measured? How often is it monitored?

- How much time do you expect children to spend reading at home every day? How much time writing?

- Can you show me examples of excellent writing from children at this grade level? What areas of my child's writing skills need the most work? What can I do to help him improve?

- How do you teach vocabulary? How do you test children's vocabulary?
- What rules of grammar will my child be studying this year?
- Do you ever require children to memorize fine poetry or prose? Could you give me an example of something they will memorize this year?
- Does my child participate in discussions about books and stories the class has read?
- What kinds of assignments do you give to practice using reference works such as dictionaries, encyclopedias, thesauruses, and bibliographies?
- What are your goals for my child with respect to reading and writing by the end of the marking period (or term)?

Junior High—Grades Seven And Eight

At this stage of a youngster's schooling, he should have mastered the fundamentals of English. Your child should now be a capable reader, writer, and speaker. With those basics in place, this subject is now a versatile, often enjoyable tool for advancing his education.

Generally speaking, junior high students should read the equivalent of "a short book a week" suitable to their grade level. It's fine for some of those books to be lighter works of the student's own choosing, plus magazines and newspapers. Teachers and parents should make sure, however, that a significant portion of reading time is spent with increasingly rich and complex literature. Take a look at the reading list for your child's English class. At this point, it should include some selections that you recognize as works of fine literature. Your child should have the pleasure of meeting unforgettable characters such as Ichabod Crane and Captain Nemo, stories such as *The Three Musketeers* and "The Pit and the Pendulum," poets and authors such as Emily Dickinson and Ray Bradbury. A syllabus that does not include this kind of material is shortchanging your child and skimping on his education. Teachers should help students develop the ability to draw meaning from great reading. Assignments should require students to examine texts closely. Good literature will broaden, deepen, and sharpen your child's awareness of life.

Frequent writing experience is also necessary for students to polish mechanics and develop individual style. Assignments should be varied: essays analyzing literature; reports that convey factual information; papers that lay out logical, persuasive arguments; compositions describing personal experiences; and stories and poems of the students' own creation. Your child should get better at writing papers that capture and hold the reader's attention. He should learn to be concise and specific as well as mechanically correct. Some assignments should be multipage ones, long enough to show an understanding of the complexities of a given topic. Junior high papers should include some research reports that require a student to collect information, analyze and organize it, write lucidly about what he's found, and document his sources and findings. Your child should practice revising and proofreading his written work.

Children become good writers by applying the rules of grammar, language usage, and writing mechanics. There is so much to remember that junior high students should review conventions learned in the intermediate grades, as well as tackle trickier topics such as adjectival and adverbial clauses. Diagramming sentences helps students understand rules, internalize skills, and use language skillfully. Vocabulary and spelling work continues. The more your child reads, the more words he will learn. Students also benefit from exercises such as learning word lists, writing the definitions of assigned words, and studying etymology (the roots of words and where they come from). As in earlier grades, junior high schoolers should get frequent vocabulary and spelling tests.

One goal of English class is to turn students into courteous, confident, and effective speakers. This is an age when some children seem to forget all the manners they've ever been taught about acceptable modes of conversation. The popular culture, to which adolescents naturally look for cues, is no help. The classroom, however, *every* classroom, should be a bastion of civil language. Children should practice the art of speaking well. They should take part in orderly, respectful discussions in which students ask questions that are to the point, make thoughtful comments, give persuasive arguments, and show respect for their teachers and fellow pupils. They should have regular opportunities to stand and deliver interesting oral presentations. These lessons will serve them well in later life.

SEVENTH GRADE

Seventh grade assignments include some demanding titles and authors that students might not read on their own. Frequent writing exercises should allow students to write their own fiction and poetry, but instruction should emphasize expository writing such as essays and reports. Essays should have a main point and coherent structure. Paragraphs should have a focus, be developed with evidence and examples, and have transitions between them. Essays should employ appropriate tone and diction, as well as correct spelling and grammar. Among other things, seventh graders do the following:

Writing and Research

- get frequent, varied writing assignments: book reports, summaries, descriptive essays, stories, poems, etc.
- write nonfiction essays that describe, narrate, persuade, compare and contrast
- write clear, organized, documented research essays
- practice organizing, drafting, revising, and proofreading writings

Speaking and Listening

- participate civilly and productively in group discussions
- give a short speech to the class
- use standard English when presenting in class

Spelling and Vocabulary

- continue regular spelling practice and vocabulary enrichment
- work on commonly misspelled words (e.g., beginning, doesn't, responsibility)
- study more Latin and Greek words that form common roots (e.g., *audio*, *polis*, *super*)

Grammar and Usage

- study prepositional phrases (e.g., adjectival and adverbial; object of preposition)
- study subjects and verbs (e.g., subject-verb agreement with compound subjects)
- study complements (e.g., direct and indirect objects; predicate nouns and predicate adjectives)
- study participles and participial phrases, gerunds and gerund phrases, infinitives and infinitive phrases
- study clauses (independent, dependent, adjective, adverb, and noun clauses)

Literature

- read poems such as Tennyson's "The Charge of the Light Brigade," Robert Service's "The Cremation of Sam McGee," T.S. Eliot's "Macavity: The Mystery Cat"
- study poetry forms (e.g., sonnet, lyric, limerick, haiku)
- read short stories such as Guy de Maupassant's "The Necklace" and Poe's "The Tell-Tale Heart"
- read novels such as Jack London's *The Call of the Wild* and Mark Twain's *The Prince and the Pauper*
- study elements of fiction (e.g., point of view, internal and external conflict)
- read essays and speeches such as George Orwell's "Shooting an Elephant" and Franklin D. Roosevelt's "Declaration of War on Japan"
- read biographies and autobiographies such as Anne Frank's *Diary of a Young Girl*
- read and watch plays such as Edmond Rostand's *Cyrano de Bergerac*
- study elements of drama (e.g., soliloquies and asides)
- study literary terms and devices (e.g., irony, flashback, foreshadowing)

(drawn from the Core Knowledge Sequence)

In a good seventh grade English class, students get assignments such as:

- Read "The Lottery" by Shirley Jackson and write answers to the following questions: What is a scapegoat, and who is the scapegoat here? What are the first signs that something sinister is taking place? What does the story suggest about mass psychology?

- Look for examples of alliteration, assonance, and consonance in Robert Frost's "Nothing Gold Can Stay."

- Diagram this sentence: "Elizabeth gave Maria some extra money."

- In coordination with a study of World War II in history class, interview a veteran or other senior citizen, and write a paper about his or her memories of the war.

- Write an article about an art exhibit for the school's Internet home page.

- Write an essay about someone you know or someone from history who has overcome great obstacles to reach a goal.

EIGHTH GRADE

Eighth grade students continue to study high-quality literature in reading assignments. They closely analyze works in class and in their homework. In their own writing efforts, they should be able to focus on style, reasoning, persuasiveness, and other qualities of the maturing writer. By now, they should be comfortable using "pre-writing" techniques (e.g., outlines to organize ideas); examining their work for clarity and unity; editing or rewriting when necessary; and proofreading the final product. They should be able to put together well-crafted, expressive essays with correct spelling and grammar. Among other things, eighth graders do the following:

Writing and Research

- get frequent, varied writing assignments: book reports, summaries, descriptive essays, stories, poems, etc.
- write nonfiction essays that describe, narrate, persuade, compare and contrast
- write clear, organized, documented research essays
- practice organizing, drafting, revising, and proofreading writings

Speaking and Listening

- participate civilly and productively in group discussions
- give a short speech to the class
- use standard English when presenting in class

Spelling and Vocabulary

- continue regular spelling practice and vocabulary enrichment
- work on commonly misspelled words (e.g., dessert, occurrence, whether)
- study more Latin and Greek words that form common roots (e.g., *locus, phobos, scio*)

Grammar and Usage

- review and practice using punctuation such as colons; semicolons; commas with phrases and clauses; parentheses; hyphens; dashes; italics; apostrophes
- identify misplaced modifiers (e.g., dangling modifiers)
- study parallelism and practice using parallel structure in sentences

- practice using sentence variety (e.g., varying length and structure to avoid monotony)

Literature

- read poems such as e.e. cummings's "Buffalo Bill's," William B. Yeats's "The Lake Isle of Innisfree," Elizabeth Barrett Browning's "How Do I Love Thee?"
- study elements of poetry (e.g., extended and mixed metaphors, allusion)
- read short stories such as Hawthorne's "Dr. Heidegger's Experiment," Tolstoy's "God Sees the Truth but Waits," Stephen Crane's "The Open Boat"
- read novels such as George Orwell's *Animal Farm*, Pearl S. Buck's *The Good Earth*
- study elements of fiction (e.g., characterization, tone, and diction)
- read essays and speeches such as John F. Kennedy's Inaugural Address ("Ask not what your country can do for you")
- read and watch plays such as Shakespeare's *As You Like It*
- study elements of drama (e.g., farce and satire)
- study literary terms and devices (e.g., hyperbole, oxymoron, parody)

(drawn from the Core Knowledge Sequence)

In a good eighth grade English class, students get assignments such as:

- Read the short story "The Open Window" by Saki and point out some places where the author uses foreshadowing.
- Write an original short story that has a beginning, middle, and end.
- After reading Harper Lee's *To Kill a Mockingbird*, choose one scene and compare it to the way it is portrayed in the film by the same name.
- Read "A Noiseless Patient Spider" by Walt Whitman and participate in a class discussion about the poet's use of symbolism. In what ways are the spider and the soul compared and contrasted?
- In cooperation with the science teacher, prepare an oral presentation about a science project for parents' night.
- Using a list of proofreader's marks, read and correct the final draft of a composition about the play *A Man for All Seasons*, which the class attended.

Good Books for Junior High

Here are the kinds of books you see in a good language arts program during the junior high years. Good readers may be ready to tackle some of these titles before seventh and eighth grades. High schoolers—and adults!—will enjoy many of these selections, too.

National Velvet, Enid Bagnold
A Gathering of Days: A New England Girl's Journal, 1830–32, Joan W. Blos
The Moves Make the Man, Bruce Brooks
The Good Earth, Pearl S. Buck
Alice's Adventures in Wonderland and *Through the Looking-Glass*, Lewis Carroll
Neighbor Rosicky, Willa Cather
The Dark Is Rising, Susan Cooper
The Red Badge of Courage, Stephen Crane
Madame Curie: A Biography, Eve Curie
Robinson Crusoe, Daniel Defoe
Great Expectations, Charles Dickens
I'm Nobody! Who Are You?, Emily Dickinson
Narrative of the Life of Frederick Douglass, Frederick Douglass
Adventures of Sherlock Holmes and *The Lost World*, Arthur Conan Doyle
The Count of Monte Cristo and *The Three Musketeers*, Alexandre Dumas
My Family and Other Animals, Gerald Durrell
The Fun of It: Random Records of My Own Flying and of Women in Aviation, Amelia Earhart
Washington: The Indispensable Man, James Thomas Flexner
Diary of a Young Girl, Anne Frank
You Come Too, Robert Frost
A Raisin in the Sun, Lorraine Hansberry
The House of Seven Gables, Nathaniel Hawthorne
The Old Man and the Sea, Ernest Hemingway
The Gift of the Magi and Other Stories, O. Henry
Kon-Tiki, Thor Heyerdahl
The Legend of Sleepy Hollow and *Rip Van Winkle*, Washington Irving
A Boy of Old Prague, Shulamith Ish-Kishor
Story of My Life, Helen Keller
Kim, Rudyard Kipling
To Kill a Mockingbird, Harper Lee
The Call of the Wild, Jack London
Good Night, Mr. Tom, Michelle Magorian
The Crucible, Arthur Miller
Mutiny on the Bounty, Charles Nordhof and J.N. Hall
Island of the Blue Dolphins, Scott O'Dell
The Scarlet Pimpernel, Baroness Emma Orczy

Animal Farm, George Orwell
Harriet Tubman: Conductor on the Underground Railroad, Ann Petry
The Complete Tales and Poems, Edgar Allan Poe
The Chosen, Chaim Potok
The Yearling, Marjorie Kinnan Rawlings
The Light in the Forest, Conrad Richter
The Little Prince, Antoine de Saint-Exupéry
Early Moon, Carl Sandburg
Ivanhoe, Sir Walter Scott
Selected plays and sonnets, William Shakespeare
Frankenstein, Mary Shelley
A Tree Grows in Brooklyn, Betty Smith
The Red Pony and *The Pearl*, John Steinbeck
The Strange Case of Dr. Jekyll and Mr. Hyde, Robert Louis Stevenson
Roll of Thunder, Hear My Cry, Mildred Taylor
A Connecticut Yankee in King Arthur's Court and *The Adventures of Tom Sawyer*, Mark Twain
Journey Home, Yoshiko Uchida
20,000 Leagues Under the Sea, and *Around the World in Eighty Days*, Jules Verne
Up From Slavery, Booker T. Washington
The Time Machine, H.G. Wells
Ethan Frome, Edith Wharton
The Sword in the Stone and *The Once and Future King*, T.H. White
The Bridge of San Luis Rey, Thornton Wilder
The Virginian, Owen Wister

How Well Read Is Your Junior High Schooler?

By the end of the eighth grade, a well-read child should be able to identify many of the following:

- "Elementary, my dear Watson!"—Sherlock Holmes's refrain

- Romeo and Juliet—protagonists in Shakespeare's play

- Mr. Christian and Captain Bligh—first mate and captain in *Mutiny on the Bounty*

- Romulus and Remus—legendary founders of Rome

- "Some animals are more equal than others"—pigs' proclamation in George Orwell's *Animal Farm*

- Aunt Polly and the Widow Douglass—Tom Sawyer's and Huck Finn's guardians

- "O Captain! my Captain! our fearful trip is done . . ."—opening line of Walt Whitman's poem about the fallen Abraham Lincoln

- "All for one and one for all!"—creed of the Three Musketeers
- "But I have promises to keep, and miles to go before I sleep"—from Robert Frost's "Stopping by Woods on a Snowy Evening"
- Friday—Robinson Crusoe's friend
- Isis—ancient Egyptian goddess
- Hermes—also known as Mercury; messenger of the Greek and Roman gods
- The Golden Fleece—object of Jason and the Argonauts' quest
- Damon and Pythias—legendary loyal friends
- Sodom and Gomorrah—Biblical cities destroyed because their citizens were evil
- "To every thing there is a season, and a time for every purpose under the heaven . . ."—Ecclesiastes 3:1
- Sleepy Hollow—Headless Horseman's haunt
- "Friends, Romans, countrymen, lend me your ears"—Mark Antony's speech in Shakespeare's *Julius Caesar*
- "But there is no joy in Mudville—mighty Casey has struck out."—last line of Ernest Lawrence Thayer's "Casey at the Bat"
- "The Pit and the Pendulum"—Edgar Allan Poe tale
- Buck and John Thornton—dog and master in Jack London's *The Call of the Wild*
- foreshadowing—hints during a story about what will happen later
- hyperbole—extravagant exaggeration (e.g., "a mile-wide smile")
- protagonist—the main character in a story, novel, or play

Memorizing Poems and Prose

A junior high textbook of classical myths that was in use about twenty-five years ago contains occasional "Lines to be Memorized," such as this verse about Zeus from the *Iliad*.

> He whose all-conscious eyes the world behold,
> The eternal Thunderer sat, enthroned in gold.
> High heaven the footstool of his feet he makes,
> And wide beneath him all Olympus shakes.

Requiring students to commit poetry and fine prose to memory is not very popular in many schools these days. Modern educators often scorn it as autocratic "rote" learning that wastes time and stifles children's creativity. Once upon a time, some exceptionally creative people took a different view. Homer and the ancient Greeks thought of memory and imagination as going hand in hand. In their mythology, the nine Muses—goddesses who presided over literature, art, music, dance, and learning in general—inspired intellectual and artistic endeavors. The Muses were the daughters of Zeus, the king of the gods, and Mnemosyne, the goddess of Memory. To the Greeks, memory *was* the parent of creativity and wisdom.

Many good teachers still have students occasionally memorize great poetry and prose. They do so for several reasons. First, it's solid, demanding mental work, and that is good for children. Second, reciting works before others makes for excellent practice at public speaking. Third, memorizing beautiful language helps children come to know it well. They listen closely to the rhythms and sounds of the words as they say them again and again. They find layers of meaning they would surely overlook with only one reading.

Finally, memorizing a few poems and passages (such as the Gettysburg Address or part of the Declaration of Independence) actually attracts many children to literature. When students commit a beautiful work to memory, they make it their own. They discover that to know it is to love it, and often carry it with them for life. Long after leaving school, many adults cherish the lines they learned in class. Their creativity remains intact, the Muses alive and well.

Questions to Ask the Teacher

In the junior high grades, you may want to ask the English teacher questions such as:

- What books, stories, poems, and other reading selections will my child be reading in your class?

- What literary classics will the class be studying?

- What writing assignments will my child get in the coming weeks? What are the goals of these assignments?

- Will he follow a writing process (i.e., pre-write, write a first draft, edit, revise, rewrite, proof final copy)?

- What kinds of exercises do your students do to learn rules of grammar and language usage?

- Will my child be writing any papers that involve research in the library or on the computer?

- How are students honored for excellent writing?

- How often do you give essay-style tests that require students to write out thoughtful answers in paragraph form?

- How often do you give assignments that require classroom speaking, such as oral reports or organized debates?
- What kind of practice will my child get analyzing literature (for character motivation, figurative language, etc.)?
- What should I be doing at home to help?
- What are your goals for my child with respect to reading and writing by the end of the marking period? (Ask to see samples of the work she expects children to be able to do.)

ISSUES IN LANGUAGE ARTS EDUCATION

This section takes up a few questions parents naturally have about the language arts curriculum and addresses some shortcomings in the teaching of English in U.S. schools. While some institutions do a great job, and you may find few of these problems in your own school, you certainly won't be alone if much of what follows sounds discouragingly familiar. Either way, these discussions should help you become a more informed education consumer.

Phonics Versus Whole Language: How Should Children Learn to Read?

Nothing stirs stronger passions among educators—or parents and policymakers—than the issue of how children should be taught to read. Which is better for your child: phonics, or the "whole language" approach?

In phonics, children begin by learning the basic sounds represented by letters and combinations of letters; they are then taught to "decode" written words by "sounding them out," letter by letter and combination by combination (e.g. the difference between *th* and *ch*). Phonics teachers usually emphasize the single accurate spelling of any word. Lessons often include games, drills, and skill sheets that help youngsters associate the letters with sounds. Students read "decodable" stories containing only words they can sound out using the phonics lessons they've learned.

Whole language teachers, on the other hand, generally take the view that phonics drills and stories with phonetically controlled vocabulary turn students off. They hold that children acquire reading skills naturally, much the way they learn to speak. In their view, understanding the relationships between sounds and letters is only one of many ways students can learn to recognize new words, and sound-letter relationships do not necessarily need to be formally taught. Whole language theory says that children learn to read and write best by being immersed in interesting literature, where they learn words in a context they enjoy and understand. Students are encouraged to figure out the meaning of new words using a variety of cues, such as by associating them with accompanying pictures, or looking at the ways they are used in sentences along with more familiar words.

The argument between phonics and whole language advocates has been raging for decades. ("I have seen the devastating effects of whole language instruction on older students," a Colorado teacher writes, for example. "These students cannot spell or write properly because of years of learning bad habits encouraged by whole language.") It's come to be known by some as the "Reading Wars." Yet many years of experience as well as research by scholars such as Jeanne Chall, Marilyn Adams, and Sandra Stotsky tell us that there really should be no debate at all. The evidence is clear: an effective reading program combines explicit phonics instruction with an immersion in high-quality, interesting reading materials.

This is an important topic, so we want to be clear. Most children get off to a better start learning to read with early, systematic phonics instruction. Therefore the teaching of these skills should be a vital part of beginning reading programs for most youngsters, and should be in the instructional kit of every primary school teacher. If your child's teacher doesn't believe in using—or does not know how to use—phonics instruction as part of reading class, your child may have trouble learning to read proficiently.

Whole language proponents, however, do make a good point. Schools should also offer children intriguing books and wonderful stories. The *love* of reading, after all, arises not from mastery of decoding techniques but from being able to apply those newly acquired methods to engaging material. Phonics exercises are necessary to help most young children master the letter sounds, but drills and worksheets are not enough. They do nothing to capture the child's imagination as literature can. All readers, even the youngest, should be given entertaining stories geared to their level.

In this respect, a healthy blend of phonics and whole language makes the most sense. The best primary teachers make phonics a fundamental part of their classrooms, but have at their disposal a whole arsenal of other techniques—and plenty of terrific reading materials. They use both interesting decodable texts and great children's literature containing vocabulary that is not phonetically controlled.

Some phonics advocates are so enthusiastic that you might erroneously get the impression that phonics is supposed to remain part of English class throughout one's education. As an explicit part of reading instruction, however, it is something to be taken up very seriously in the earliest years; for most children, it gradually fades into the background by the end of third grade. Learning phonics should be like learning to balance on a bicycle—at first it takes lots of conscious practice, but once mastered is virtually effortless. You want the act of decoding words to become automatic as quickly as possible, freeing your child to focus on meaning and the pleasure of reading.

How do you know if your child's teacher is paying the right amount of attention to phonics in the earliest grades? Simply put the question to her: Do you teach phonics? If she responds, "No, we don't stress that," you may very well have a problem. You need to find out exactly what her instructional philosophy is, and what kind of track record it has.

Even if she nods and says, "Yes, we teach phonics," it does not tell you how effective a job she'll do. Outrageous though it is, some primary school teachers have a shaky grip on effective methods of teaching reading. This is rarely because they're stupid or uncaring, but rather because they've passed through a teacher training program or college of education that didn't do the job properly, or where the professors frown upon the whole notion of phonics. ("I was told by the 'professionals' that they didn't teach phonics because 'English is not a phonetic language,'" one disconcerted mom reports.)

Furthermore, hearing a teacher say "We teach phonics" does not tell you *how much* phonics she puts into the mix, or how it's done. On the one hand, it may mean so much work with the *bah, beh, bih, boh, buh* sounds that reading turns into a dreary chore. On the other extreme, there are some schools that throw a few token sound-letter games into the lesson plans just so parents will feel assured that their children are "learning phonics." Schools have discovered that most parents "believe in" phonics—but sometimes teachers are perfunctory about it.

The best strategy is to keep an eye on your child's progress when the school begins to teach reading, whether in kindergarten or first grade. Take a good look at the materials and assignments. Visit the class one day and observe a reading session. Is there an emphasis on making sure children learn the connections between letters and sounds, through drills, worksheets, word games, questions from the teachers, and entertaining stories that children read?

Even more important, though, is to sit down with your beginning reader on a routine basis to see how and what he's reading. If he can read more words this week than the week before, if he tries to sound out new words, and if he seems to enjoy spending time with his books, the balance is probably right.

When Should Students Start to Read?

Kindergarten, rather than first grade, is increasingly viewed as the place where children should begin learning to "read." This shift has caused debate among educators who specialize in "early childhood." Many worry that a move toward early reading will bring pressures and burdens that many five-year-olds are not ready to handle. The trend can also lead to questions among parents, who hear that more and more kindergarten classes are taking up reading instruction. Will our children be left behind, they wonder, if our school waits until first grade?

In reality, most kindergarten—and first grade—teachers face classes that read at almost as many different levels as there are children in the room. The number of youngsters who enroll in kindergarten already knowing their letters and eager to begin learning words seems to be growing, thanks to the spread of preschool programs, certain computer software programs, a few reading-friendly television shows, and, far and away the most important, parents who read aloud during their little ones' preschool years. Other children, especially those from disadvantaged backgrounds, may arrive in kindergarten without even the rudiments of reading. Bear in mind, also, that it is natural for little children to develop at different physical, emotional, and intellectual paces. In this respect, asking "When should my child start to read?" is like asking "When should my child start to walk?" There is no universal answer. It depends on the child.

Given all these variables, a kindergarten teacher faces a difficult challenge. She must help the reading-ready children forge ahead while at the same time pay extra attention to children who need more basic help. Some youngsters will be able to read quite a few words, phrases, and sentences by the end of kindergarten; others need a bit more time.

This is normal and acceptable. There is no rule that says every child must start reading in kindergarten.

The best idea is to talk to your kindergarten teacher at the beginning of the year to make sure that her plans will accommodate your child's present reading abilities. Let her know exactly what you've been doing at home during the last few months—how much time you and your child have been spending with books, which books he likes best, how many letters and letter sounds he knows, which words (if any) he already recognizes. Tell her what your expectations are for the coming months. Ask what kinds of activities she can offer to keep stimulating his interest and help him move forward. Keep in mind (and make sure she agrees) that it makes no sense to hold back kindergartners who are highly motivated to read—or pester those who aren't. Talk to the teacher about how you can best do your part at home, and then of course make sure you do it.

Don't fret if your daughter or son does not really start reading during kindergarten, so long as you can see a solid foundation for later fluency being laid. Remember that America has seen generations of successful doctors, lawyers, teachers, scientists, and business executives who did not begin reading until first grade—sometimes even later.

If, however, your child gets very far into first grade and has not begun to show considerable signs of progress in this department, you probably have grounds for worry. At that point, you should sit down with the teacher and talk about what steps the two of you need to take together. It will probably involve more work at home.

Should Schools Group Children According to Reading Ability?

When formal reading instruction begins, many teachers divide their classes into small reading groups. Students are assigned to groups based on their reading skill and language development. The groups may be reading different books, or they may be reading the same book at different rates. The teacher moves from group to group, working with one set of children while the other groups keep reading and discussing stories among themselves.

This kind of "ability grouping" invariably offends some parents—most often those with children in the "slower" reading groups. They worry that, once placed in a slower group, their child will be stuck with the label and have a tough time moving out. Many education theorists have become critics of ability grouping and point out, for example, that students in slower groups often get less interesting reading material. Despite the best efforts of teachers to de-emphasize the levels of groups by using cute names such as "bluebirds" and "redbirds," kids are pretty quick to figure out where their group ranks. The result, some educators argue, is damaged self-esteem.

Tracking that permanently and completely separates youngsters is certainly to be avoided. But the reality is that a primary grade classroom is naturally full of children who read at different levels and it's absurd to expect the whole class to proceed at the same pace. If you teach that way, you either have to hold some readers back, or give others material they can't yet handle.

If handled skillfully, putting students into different reading groups helps children work at a level and pace suited to their abilities. The faster readers can swing right along; slower readers can be given additional time and help. This is not to say that young readers should always be divided, but neither does it make sense to expect the whole class to always read in lockstep.

Talk to your child's teacher about how she intends to work with youngsters at different levels of proficiency in reading. Ask questions such as: Do all children in the class read the same books at the same time, or are there opportunities for students to read different books according to their various reading levels? How do you make it possible for the better readers to keep moving ahead at their own pace? What strategies do you use to help the slower readers catch up with the rest of the class, rather than staying stuck in the "slow" group? How often do groups change? How much time are you able to spend with each group? With individual children?

Sometimes teachers enlist better readers to assist slower readers. Up to a point, this kind of "buddy system" can be good for everyone concerned: the stronger reader solidifies his skills by explaining them to someone else, and the slower reader benefits from the extra help. This technique should be used in moderation—not as a substitute for teachers who help all their pupils to advance in reading as rapidly as they are able.

If your child starts first grade in a slower group, there is no cause for panic or embarrassment, given that children pick up reading skills at different rates. Students in slower groups often catch up with the early readers. If your child is still lagging in reading proficiency in second grade, however, you should talk with the teacher.

Any number of things could be going awry. It may be the school is not doing justice to youngsters who need extra help—or who are ready to forge ahead more quickly. If you hear the teacher talk about "mixed ability grouping" or "whole class instruction," inquire further. That jargon may in fact mean the whole class is held to the pace of its slowest pupils or those in the "middle." Take a good, hard look at the schoolbooks your child is being given. If they seem too easy, it's a pretty good sign that the reading curriculum is being geared toward less accomplished pupils. In that case, talk to the teacher about how your child can keep moving ahead at his own pace. If, on the other hand, reading assignments are consistently too tough for your child, he will likely benefit from an arrangement that gives extra time and attention to those who need it.

In either case, don't feel the least bit guilty lobbying for an approach that's friendlier to both students and teacher (as well as more compatible with common sense): flexible groupings of youngsters for reading lessons according to how far they've come and how well they're doing. Never forget that by far the most important reading "group" is the one that consists of parent and child. That group of two will help your loved one zoom ahead or, if necessary, work a little harder to catch up with his classmates.

When Should Children Learn to Write?

Many preschools and kindergartens teach children about the concept of "writing" through activities such as moving magnetic letters around, drawing pictures that tell stories, and dictating stories to the teacher. Most kindergartens help boys and girls learn how to print their own names, and many introduce children to the concept of printing letters and even a few words and phrases. Then in first grade, students really get down to the business of using pencils and paper to write.

This is a general schedule only. Keep in mind that, as in learning to read, there is no exact timetable as to when a particular child should start writing letters, words, and sentences. That's partly due to the different rates at which youngsters develop in the years leading up to first grade. After all, keeping those *a*'s and *b*'s between those lines requires no small amount of motor skill. Some children are able to maneuver a pencil with dexterity a bit sooner than others. The amount of encouragement that little ones receive in the company of family members also has a great deal to say about when kids start to write. And that varies tremendously from home to home. Do not be surprised to find a wide range of skill levels in a kindergarten or first grade class. Some children will come to school barely able to print a few letters or words, while others are already busy writing sentences and even simple stories.

If you've given your child lots of opportunities to use crayons, pencils, and pens during the pre-K years, chances are good that he'll be eager and able to start writing letters and easy words by kindergarten or even sooner. There is no reason in the world to hold him back. As soon as he shows an inclination, get him started. Give him lots of inspiration and praise. To repeat: his passion for writing in school will probably reflect the signals he's receiving at home. Just as young students who love reading are likely to have parents who share books and stories, children who like to write usually developed that taste in the company of mom and dad.

Talk regularly with the teacher about your child's progress. Keep tabs on exactly what kinds of writing activities he's doing in class, and let the teacher know what sort of practice he gets at home. Make sure he's meeting her expectations. If he's behind in this skill, extra work at home may well be the answer. Likewise, if he's moving ahead of the class, see that the school offers assignments and activities that will challenge him and keep him going.

What If the Teacher Does Not Correct My Child's Spelling?

Little Susan comes home from school proudly bearing her latest composition.

"My dogs nam is Hapyy. He likes to brk. My dad covrs his eers when he brks."

The top of the page is adorned with a big gold star and the teacher's comment: "Good work!"

Meet "invented spelling." This approach holds that rigorous rules inhibit creativity and stifle a first or second grader's urge to write. Learning to spell "should ultimately be as natural, unconscious, effortless, and pleasant as learning to speak," says one proponent. If you sense that this concept of writing resembles the "whole language" theory of reading, you're not wrong. Both derive from a deeply ingrained view of education that is commonly dispensed by teachers' colleges: the view that learning should bloom naturally, like wildflowers, rather than be cultivated like a formal garden.

Teachers who subscribe to this view are inclined to let young children write words the way they hear them ("elfunt" for "elephant") and rarely correct misspellings. The theory is that gradually students will learn to recognize and correct their own mistakes through such activities as reading, discussing possible spellings with peers, editing their classmates' writings as well as their own, and gauging their audiences' responses when they read their writings aloud. Eventually (usually by second grade), teachers decipher and untangle the spelling systems children have invented for themselves.

In the opinion of some teachers and many parents, however, invented spelling is just another name for misspelling—and one more reason so many students have little command over the written language. "My fourth grader's papers are full of misspelled words—no one seems to be correcting her, and she never has spelling tests," one parent moans. A California mom reports that in her twin sons' fifth grade spelling bee, nobody in the class was able to make it past the first round.[2]

Few people deny that beginning writers need some latitude. A main goal is to get them excited about writing and accustomed to getting their ideas set down on paper. Nit-picking about spelling may intimidate early efforts and bruise a child's pride in early authorship. Most parents know this as a matter of common sense. When your kindergartner comes running to you with her very first letter that reads 'I luv yu Momi' you don't grab a red pen and start circling mistakes. You pretend it's Nobel Prize material and proudly mount it on the refrigerator.

The problem is that all too often in the world of professional education, common sense gets stretched way out of shape. Clearly, in some schools, invented spelling goes too far. Whether it's for fear of "stifling independence" or aversion to "rote memorization," poor spelling is tolerated well past the beginning writer stage. Spelling lists go out the window; tests are rare or nonexistent; children's mistakes cease to be taken seriously. More than one educator has told parents that students don't need to worry too much about spelling nowadays because computers can fix their mistakes for them. "They started laughing," reports one mother who questioned administrators as to why there were no spelling books or lessons. "I'm not kidding! I felt like a very young dinosaur!" The result? Students become rotten spellers, of course.

Encouraging youngsters and nurturing their confidence is one thing. Allowing bad habits to take root is another. Anyone who has been around little children knows that the longer bad habits go on, the harder they are to change. The last thing your child needs is to absorb an early lesson in relativism: doing something the right way doesn't really matter so long as the intention is honorable and the effort sincere. Sadly, this *is* the message communicated in many places.

Sensible ground needs to be occupied here. While children are first learning to write, correct spelling should not be turned into a be-all, end-all concern. Good teachers know they must strike a balance between nurturing creativity and teaching correct conventions. They also remember that when a little one is trying his hand at putting words on paper, he needs (and most likely *wants*) an adult to show him the right way. Talk to your child's primary school teacher and ask her how she deals with writing mistakes, particularly misspellings. If she says it is too early to correct them, ask her when she will begin. If you feel your child is ready to begin receiving gentle, sensible corrections, let the teacher know.

If you find that your child is getting the message that there is no "right" or "wrong" way to spell, you have a problem in the making. Keep a careful eye on his writing. If he's making lots of spelling mistakes in his compositions, and you see no signs that the teacher is trying to reverse the trend, speak up.

By the end of first grade or beginning of second, you should see evidence of formal spelling lessons. You should also see teachers beginning to hold youngsters accountable for their spelling. Look for regular spelling exercises and quizzes that assess spelling progress, as well as signs that children are being taught to find and correct their own spelling mistakes. Keep an eye out for events such as spelling bees, essay contests, or writing awards that confer special status and accolades on pupils who do an especially good job of getting these things right.

Keep up your guard for the kind of attitude that deems spelling bees too "competitive," or insists that tests only hurt children's self-esteem. "Our child's teachers and principal believe that spelling tests do not work," report the parents of a third grader in a small town in New York. "They were bringing in an 'educational specialist' who could prove to all the parents that there are only three types of children: those who already know how to spell the words; those who will study the words, pass the test, and forget the words by Monday; and those who will never learn the words, ever." If you run into that kind of attitude, you may want to start hunting for a different school.

How Important Is Penmanship in an Age of Word Processors?

"Students today can't write," observes Edward Ericson, who teaches English at Calvin College in Grand Rapids, Michigan. "No, I don't mean they can't string words together into sentences and string sentences together into paragraphs. That's old news. I mean they can't *write*. I mean cursive, handwriting, penmanship—that little skill kids used to learn in the second and third grades, as soon as their motor skills developed. . . . Kids today can't string letters together into words. They can't form ovals, loops, and humps. They don't know how to get from an *o* to an *s* or an *r* without lifting the pencil off the paper."[3] Many teachers agree with Ericson's assessment but say that they're asked to do so much nowadays, there just isn't enough time to practice writing legibly. "We're pretty hard-pressed to get everything in," explains a fourth grade teacher in Oklahoma. "Something has to be sacrificed, and usually it's penmanship."[4]

If we're raising a generation of messy scribblers, it's possible that computers are part of the problem. In many elementary schools, children learn to type at keyboards before they write in cursive. Some educators take the view that most writing is now done on word processors, so that is what students should use. Just as calculators make us less dependent on knowing how to add and subtract on paper, they argue, computers make it less important to know how to write legibly. Furthermore, many kids would rather type than use pen and paper, and if keyboards encourage writing, so much the better.

It is our view that children still need plenty of practice learning to write deftly with pencils and pens. They should learn how to print because it is part and parcel of learning what letters and words and reading are all about, and because youngsters like to reproduce what they're seeing. Students need to practice writing in cursive script because the world we inhabit is still not fully "keyboarded," and plenty of occasions still arise—thank-you notes, love letters, college "bluebook" exams—when it is necessary or desirable to write things out. As far as we can tell, handwriting isn't going away any time soon.

But there is another point that parents and schools should not overlook: learning to write neatly teaches lessons that extend beyond penmanship itself. The attitude that the appearance of the marks one leaves behind doesn't matter because a child can always type when legibility is important is an attitude that fosters slovenliness. Good penmanship requires discipline, attention to detail, and pride in work—all things that are good for young students. If lessons in penmanship are being squeezed out of the curriculum at school, we urge you to work on neatness and legibility with your child at home.

What Is the Place of Western Literature in the English Classroom?

In your school's learning objectives for language arts, you will probably see statements such as "Students will read texts by authors of diverse ethnic, racial, socioeconomic, and gender backgrounds" or "Students will be introduced to significant literary works from a variety of cultures and perspectives." You'll have to look closely at the reading lists and your child's assignments to find out exactly what this means.

Today's American students read a much broader range of literature than did schoolchildren in past generations. They're exposed to many wonderful stories from countries and groups whose literature was largely ignored by schools until the last few decades. Inclusion of such works is obviously good for our students. Learning about other cultures strengthens and enriches any education. Americans are a people with worldwide roots, and our diversity is a great asset that should be explored and celebrated.

In some classrooms, however, this trend goes too far. Teachers bend over backward to develop a rainbow of authors; a writer's skin color, gender, or homeland seems to carry more weight than what's actually between a book's covers. The reading curriculum lunges madly from celebrating one culture to saluting the next, informed by no coherent vision of what children need to know and why they should know it. Reading lists spark race-based debates. In 1998, for example, two San Francisco school board members proposed mandating that seven of ten books on the required high school reading list be by nonwhite authors. "A lot of folks say they're tired of the white, European establishment," one of them explained.

This approach is detrimental to your child's education. The test of good literature has nothing to do with an author's color or gender. Fine writing is fine writing, no matter who wrote it. Furthermore, turning Western literature into a side dish in a long buffet of multicultural morsels to be sampled is a misguided policy. In this country, a good elementary and secondary school reading curriculum is anchored firmly in the literature of Western civilization, for some very good reasons.

We live in a Western nation and culture. Most of our children will live in it when they leave school. The best stories, tales, and writings of Western civilization are a repository of our highest shared ideals and aspirations. Reading this body of literature helps us understand ourselves as a people. We should be inviting our students to self-knowledge. Avoiding Western literature breeds self-ignorance.

Images and allusions from centuries of Western writings pervade our American tradition and public discourse. The youngster who reads Martin Luther King and comes across the phrase "I have been to the mountaintop, and I have seen the promised land" cannot grasp the full beauty and tragedy of those words if he has never read the story of Moses. Even some of our language's most common phrases such as "sour grapes" and "don't be a Scrooge" hark back to the likes of Aesop and Dickens. In the United States, you simply cannot be considered literate without some knowledge of the Western canon. If we want our children to be truly educated, we must lay the groundwork in the early grades by giving them access to their literary heritage.

The great books and stories of Western literature are unsurpassed in offering guidance to those who seek serious answers to the great questions, the questions we surely hope all students will ask, such as: What can I know? What should I do? What should I hope for? How should I live? They are unsurpassed in their capacity to teach youngsters about virtues such as courage, honor, justice, and compassion. They speak directly to children, appealing to their imaginations and their capacity for wonder, mystery, and love. The deep, rich well of Western literature for children is an astonishing reservoir. Teachers should draw from it often.

Different parents are comfortable with different mixes of multiculturalism in the English curriculum. Generally speaking, however, literature with Western origins should constitute most of the reading assignments in elementary schools. "Western" literature, it should be remembered, does not mean only books by "dead white males." The Western tradition includes many wonderful works by women and minorities, fine writers such as Edith Wharton, Christina Rossetti, James Baldwin, Ralph Ellison, and Emily Dickinson.

The idea, in the end, is to make sure that "multiculturalism" is really that—drawing upon wonderful literature from several different cultures. Multiculturalism should *not* promote the very kind of exclusivity the movement professes to abhor. That is, it should not be a means to limit readings so that a group learns only about its own distinct culture while ignoring the rich legacy of Western literature all American students deserve to know.

One test you can perform is this: in addition to talking about exposure to "authors of diverse ethnic, racial, socioeconomic, and gender backgrounds," do your school's written standards of learning mention anything about our children's "common literary heritage"? Do they explicitly state that students should acquire a knowledge of American literature and some outstanding works of Western civilization? If not, it is fair to wonder: Why leave that tradition out of a list of stated goals?

Pay close attention to your child's reading assignments, and ask yourself: Do the selections seem to be driven primarily by the quality of the literature? Is the teacher choosing outstanding stories written in rich, demanding language, regardless of their authorship or origins? Or do books and stories appear to be chosen to cover all possible cultures and countries, even if particular readings don't inspire and challenge? Read some of the selections yourself. Children's literature, if it's really good, should be able to capture an adult's attention and imagination to some degree. If time and again, after reading from your child's schoolbooks, you find yourself thinking, "That wasn't all that interesting a story—but at least it's from overseas," then the school is probably more concerned with representing a lot of different peoples and places than with finding quality material from those cultures.

Are Children's Classics Being Slighted?

Most elementary teachers are eager to teach the stories and books they loved in their own childhoods. In some classrooms, however, classic children's literature is slighted. Yes, there are those who would expel *Pinocchio*, tear down *The Little House on the Prairie*, and take Greek mythology off the shelves.

For example, educator and author Herbert Kohl, in his book *Shall We Burn Babar?*, takes a disgruntled look at the elephant who grew up to be king and tells us all that is wrong with this tale: Babar finds himself in a city where "power is with people and not animals"; he is "putty in the hands of the Rich Lady" who tries to help him ("the source of her power is her money—we know little else about her," Kohl observes); by putting on clothes and eating goodies at a pastry shop, Babar "loses his elephant nature." His later return to the forest, where he becomes king, is "the triumph of the Europeanized male." *The Story of Babar,* Kohl concludes, is propaganda for colonialism, racism, and sexism—and so is most of classic children's literature, it seems. A "sensitivity to bias and a vision of equality" are "thoroughly absent in almost all the books written for children in the past." In fact, these works are "written from the perspective of the virtues of individualism, competition, and capitalism." Our youngsters should be protected from such influences, Kohl declares.

What should we give them instead? Kohl longs for works that "question the economic and social structure of our society and the values of capitalism." What we need are stories that encourage thinking about "solidarity, cooperation, group struggle, and belonging to a caring group." He calls for children's literature in which the major force in stories is "the community or some natural social group larger than the family." The characters should "participate in some collective activity" centered on issues of social or economic justice. "This could range from a group of girls at a high school organizing to protest sexism to a story about young resistance fighters in Southern Africa to one about Native American youngsters involved in a struggle to keep a toxic dump off tribal land."[5]

It becomes clear why such critics do not much like classic literature for children: it is a product of Western civilization. There are some educators who have great disdain for the Western tradition in general and American achievement in particular. In their view, Western civilization and America are corrupted by sexism, racism, oppression, capitalism, and treachery toward the environment. To help change society, the children's literature should be changed. In the words of one English teacher, "the Eurocentric dominance must be displaced."

Toward that end, children's classics are pushed out of the curriculum in some schools. In others, the "critical reading" of such works is really nothing more than classroom discussions of racism, sexism, or environmental issues. Students are told to hunt for stereotypes and gender bias in old stories, or the classics are used as launch pads to criticize American society. For example, one lesson plan from a Texas school uses "The Three Little Pigs" and "Cinderella" to prompt student discussions of "the various types of intolerance that exist in our multicultural society." It's one thing to help children examine our world through the prism of literature, but if schools routinely use wonderful stories as tools to high-light America's flaws, they are cheating children of something precious.

The argument that we should jettison many classics because they lack, in Kohl's words, "sensitivity to bias and a vision of equality" is ridiculously overblown. But we should recognize—as most teachers and parents do—that some old favorites, because they come from other times, do in fact contain messages that we don't want today's children to absorb. In some, for example, little girls are not accorded the same status as little boys. This is true not just of Western literature; viewed through modern eyes, old tales from *all* cultures often come with problems. Some works have to be discarded, but the vast majority can be amended when necessary for contemporary readers. There is nothing wrong with taking some of the violence out of the Brothers Grimm when reading their works to young children, or changing the brave prince to a princess when telling a fairy tale to a group of kindergartners. Folk tales in particular have a way of evolving over time—that is their nature. Our aim should be to pass on great stories, updating when necessary, not to purge from the curriculum so many classics that our children will surely love as much as earlier generations have.

Is My Child Really Learning to Understand Literature?

Part of an English teacher's job is to help students learn how to understand and appreciate writing. In some classrooms, however, you may run into trends that interfere with these lessons.

One tendency is to ask pupils to read mainly with an eye toward contemporary social issues. Students are told to read books or find articles which the class then uses to discuss topics like the environment, AIDS, child abuse, drugs, or crime. Certainly, developing informed and responsible citizens is part of every teacher's job, but as reading expert Sandra Stotsky points out, if kids spend most of English class talking about hot-button issues, they necessarily spend little time learning to understand and love literature itself. There is also the danger that, since teachers can't always find good, challenging books about the social issue du jour, they may resort to works of lower quality (as in the kindergarten class that spent several weeks "exploring gender bias and manipulation" in advertisements).

Another practice that interferes with the genuine study of literature is using books as springboards for students to think and write about their own personal experiences. ("I liked this story because it reminds me of my grandmother's house. She has an old porch swing where I like to sit all by myself . . .") A great deal of this kind of self-expression goes on in some classrooms today. It can be very useful for primary grade students because it helps them make a connection between themselves and the stories they read. It can also be interesting, up to a point, for older children. But overdoing personal allusion fosters self-centered thinking rather than real thinking about literature and the beauty of language. Children should learn to use literature to look beyond themselves.

A third tendency is to teach youngsters that all interpretations of readings are equally valid. Signs of this attitude are English teachers praising students for just about any meaning they find in readings, and the constant use of the slogan "There is really no right or wrong answer here." The trendy theory that any text is susceptible to many interpretations flourishes in American education. One person's point of view is just as valid as another's, so who am I to tell you what you should get out of a story or poem? This notion is not very helpful to children who are learning to interpret literature. Obviously, reading is a subjective experience, but if the idea is to teach young people how to look closely at a text, then students should be required to cite evidence to support their interpretations.[6]

Educations suffer when children aren't encouraged to read with care and think seriously about wonderful books. Learning to understand good literature takes time and practice. That learning isn't likely to take place if debates about current events and explorations of personal experiences dominate English class.

Should Children Study Much Grammar?

"Matriarchys v. pratiarchys"

The different between Matriarchys and patriarchys is that when the mother is in charge of the house. sometime the children do whatever they want. But sometimes the mother can do both roll as a mother and as a father too and they can do it very good.
—from the journal of a New York City high school student[7]

It's not hard to find parents pulling their hair over what they perceive as lack of attention to grammar, language usage, and writing mechanics in schools. Many teachers, too, lament the downfall of grammar. "Their writing appears to be more a foreign language than English," sighs one seventh grade teacher from suburban Washington, D.C. "Some students don't know proper nouns and common nouns. We are in a very sad state."[8]

The reluctance to hold students accountable to language conventions is yet another sign of an aversion to structure, order, and tradition in many schools. Showing children the right way and expecting them to do it, we are told, stifles creativity and natural wisdom. Reports one father of his son's school in Manhattan: "Parents of children who were less 'natural' writers than others, who still couldn't compose a correct sentence by third or fourth grade, were still hearing assurances that all children develop at their own pace and that there really is no single 'correct' way to write."[9]

Part of the problem is that teachers and schools are getting some terrible signals from the professional education establishment. Only 55 percent of education school professors (that is, the people who train our teachers) say they would require students to demonstrate that they know proper grammar, punctuation, and spelling before getting a high school diploma. The National Council of Teachers of English says "the power of language and the rules that it follows are discovered, not invoked. . . . Language instruction is developmental rather than remedial." The dictionary definition of remedial, by the way, is "concerned with the correction of faulty study habits and the raising of a pupil's general competence." In plain English, holding students to demanding standards of grammar and usage—and giving them bad grades when they don't live up to those standards—is not to be done.

This is a woeful trend. Learning how to punctuate compound sentences and construct coherent paragraphs may not be the favorite part of English class for many pupils, but such lessons are vital, and elementary schools should spend plenty of time teaching them. At the start, when youngsters are first learning to write, there is no need to obsess about language conventions. After all, children can't possibly be expected to learn all the rules at once. Even in first grade, however, they can begin to follow a few simple procedures such as capitalizing the first word of a sentence. By the time they get out of the primary grades, students should be competent writers who are held to basic conventions of standard English. In succeeding years, the study of grammar should be one way they hone their writing ability.

Just as an artist must learn how to handle his paintbrushes and mix his colors before applying them with precision to his canvas, students need to understand how language is put together and how it works before they can use it skillfully and exactly. The excellent exercise of diagramming sentences is not an end in itself, but a way of internalizing valuable skills and knowledge for later use. Those funny crooked lines on the blackboard of a sixth grade classroom may have vanished from one's memory well before college, but if they were done correctly they will leave behind a solid understanding of the differences between subjects and predicates, direct and indirect objects. Systematic study of the rules of usage helps children write correctly, speak fluently, and read with understanding.

There is one other reason that studying language conventions is good for students. Learning it—*really* learning it—is one of the best intellectual exercises a child can undergo. It means absorbing certain standards and then applying them correctly again and again. This takes discipline. It takes attention to detail. It requires logic and analysis. It involves a good bit of perseverance, too. In short, it not only leads to a competent command of language, it also represents good, rigorous mental training. Parents should insist on thorough instruction in grammar, language usage, and writing mechanics.

Should Schools Be Sticklers About Speaking Proper English?

Marilynn Bland, a school board member in Prince George's County, Maryland, grew concerned that the schools aren't doing enough to teach language skills. One morning, for example, she listened in an elementary school hallway as student after student greeted teachers with improper English and no one said a thing to them about it. "I heard so much improper grammar," she said. "It disturbed me that a teacher would not take a moment to correct the children." So she proposed a rule: teachers would be required to correct students each time they used bad English, whether in classrooms, cafeterias, or hallways. Her idea was immediately deemed "controversial." Other school board members objected. Newspaper articles and editorials appeared. Critics raised the specter of a "language police" and the awful "humiliation of being corrected in public." It seems that good grammar was a threat to children's self-esteem.[10]

You, too, may run across schools where students are not required to speak standard English, where adults do not always bother to correct children when they hear them saying "This pencil don't have no eraser" or "He went through them doors." One of two notions is probably lurking behind such a failure to enforce language conventions.

The first is a "throw-in-the-towel" attitude, as in "these kids have grown up speaking this way, and are always going to speak this way, and I'm not going to be able to change it, so why try?" In which case it's fair to ask: Then why bother being a teacher?

The second notion is a "who's-to-say?" philosophy, as in "no one group of people has any business deciding what is standard or telling another group how to talk." Furthermore, teachers aren't "culturally respectful" (in the words of an Oakland, California, school board member) when they correct students. Other critics are more blunt. They assert, for example, that requiring students to "sound white" is really just an attack on the way some ethnic groups speak. All of this is tragic for the youngsters themselves. It puts political correctness before children's well-being and ignores one undeniable fact: if you want to be successful in this country, the odds are much better if you know how to use standard English.

Standard English (what we used to call "proper" English or "the King's English") is what we use in our wider communications with each other. It is the ticket to achievement. It is a vehicle of commerce. Young people stand little chance of getting into fine colleges or making good livings if they can't speak and write it. *It is the obligation of U.S. schools—one of their greatest academic obligations—to ensure that every child becomes fluent in standard English as rapidly as possible.*

That doesn't mean families and friends can't speak however they like around their dinner table, in church, or in the backyard. Everyone knows that in different parts of America you find variations of the English tongue, from Brooklyn to the hills of east Tennessee to the inner city neighborhoods of Los Angeles. All this is part of the cultural richness of our nation.

Nor does it mean that every teacher should be a Professor Henry Higgins, badgering kids about regional accents and ethnic pronunciations. Different policies fit different places. Some good schools let children use informal language among themselves as long as it is polite. At the same time, they make sure students get lots of classroom time using standard English. Children need practice in order to speak properly, and they need to be corrected when their grammar runs afoul of the rules. Obviously, teachers should correct with sensitivity. But correct they should. After all, how are children going to know when they are making mistakes if adults fail to tell them?

Warning Signs of a Weak Language Arts Program

Be on the lookout for the following signals that something is wrong at your school:

- little or no evidence of phonics instruction in the primary grades
- reading assignments that are easy, uninspiring, or chosen for reasons of political correctness; few classics of children's literature assigned
- bad grammar (or offensive language) goes uncorrected in the classroom
- misspelled words routinely uncorrected
- no explicit goals set for spelling and vocabulary; few spelling or vocabulary tests
- students rarely required to write more than a few words or sentences at a time
- no special recognition of good readers or writers
- few books in the classrooms; school library always looks deserted
- little homework that requires reading and writing
- discussions of literature center on political issues or students' personal experiences
- students often told "there are no right or wrong answers" when analyzing literature
- school-wide reading scores lag behind the district or state averages (given the weakness of most tests, you want your school's scores to be above average; being below average is usually a sign of serious reading failure)

TEACHING READING, WRITING, AND LITERATURE AT HOME

If you want to gamble with your child's academic career, here's one sure way: let his school alone shoulder the teaching of English. Leave it totally in the hands of his teachers. Maybe he'll learn to read and write well. More likely, he won't.

This warning is not an indictment of your child's school. It may be fine. Be aware, however, that even terrific teachers have a tough time teaching these crucial skills all by themselves. This is one area where all teachers need your time and help. If you want your child to do well in school, you *have* to assist him in learning to read and write.

This is not to say you must assume the lead in teaching language arts. That is the teachers' job. What you need to do at home is reinforce their efforts. You must keep track of lessons being taught in class and work on them with your child. If he's learning the letters of the alphabet at school, for example, you need to teach them at home, too, perhaps by occasionally pausing to ask about different letters as you read aloud, or perhaps by making flash cards. If he's learning to sound out words, sit with him for a while every day and give encouragement as he practices decoding, letter by letter and sound by sound. If he has a spelling test coming up, call out the word list while he spells each word. Read over his writing assignments. Make sure he is doing his homework.

As your child gets older, you may begin to feel intimidated by lessons you've forgotten yourself—terms such as "past participle" and "onomatopoeia." If possible, read through his lessons and relearn as he learns. It probably won't be as hard as you think to refresh your own memory. Most important, though, is to keep showing interest and enthusiasm. So long as your child knows you're watching carefully, he'll be more likely to learn his lessons.

One of your main goals is to raise your child to *enjoy* reading. The best way to do this is to share engaging books and stories with him. An adult looking back on his childhood once wrote: "Some people there are who, being grown, forget the horrible task of learning to read. It is perhaps the greatest effort that the human undertakes, and he must do it as a child. . . . I remember that words—written or printed—were devils, and books, because they gave me pain, were my enemies." Then an aunt stepped forward with the gift of a book of Arthurian legends, and John Steinbeck fell under the spell of literature. Books became his friends.

Share wonderful books and stories with your child—as many as you can find. Chances are he will not grow up to be a great novelist, but he may find a passion for reading. That will work magic on his education and his life.

Helping Your Child Learn to Read

Children learn to read by reading. It takes lots of practice. Many American schoolchildren, however, read ten or fewer pages a day for school and homework combined. That is simply not enough experience to turn your child into a really strong reader. He needs to be reading at home, every day. Especially if his homework reading load is light, he needs to spend some additional time with books.

There are a few things we know about home reading in this country. First, the good news. The more reading children do at home, the more likely they are to do well in school. The amount of leisure time spent reading is directly related to children's comprehension, the size of their vocabularies, and gains in their reading ability. Parents count in this equation, too. When they get involved with their children's reading at home, reading scores go up.

Now the bad news. Many American children just don't read much at home. Fewer than half of fourth graders—and barely one fifth of eighth graders—read for fun on their own time, on a daily or almost-daily basis. Among eighth graders, fewer than half read for fun even once or twice a week. Students do, however, watch a lot of TV. Children in the United States watch on average more than three hours a day. This is a disastrous misallocation of time.

These worrisome trends suggest a simple formula that every parent should follow: limit TV watching, get good books into the house, and get yourself involved in reading with your child. With your guidance, enthusiasm, and attention, your child will probably develop good reading habits. That will lead to better grades, and there is a very good chance he will actually look forward to spending time with books. There are few richer gifts that he could carry through life.

Here are some things you can do to help turn your child into a capable and eager reader. (For more tips on encouraging pre-readers and beginning readers, see page 41.)

- **Keep reading aloud.** One of the most important things you can do for your child's education is to set aside a few minutes each day to read to him. Hopefully, you established this habit in the preschool years. Do not stop once your child is in school. A youngster's listening vocabulary runs at least two years ahead of his reading level. If you abruptly stop reading aloud, your child will be left with relatively simple books—simpler, almost certainly, than his thoughts.

That may dampen his interest in learning to read. Many teachers recommend that parents continue to do some reading aloud into the intermediate grades (four to six). Some families enjoy doing it even longer.

While your child is young, it's a good idea to find out what books the teacher is reading aloud, so you can also read them to your child. Hearing the same story more than once helps beginning readers' comprehension. Besides, most young children love to hear favorite stories and poems repeated.

- **Listen to your child read—every single day.** While he's learning to read, your child needs an audience. He needs to show off for you and see you excited about his efforts. He needs your encouragement when he gets stuck, your hints when he's trying to sound out words, your pat on the back when he finally makes it to the end of the sentence. This is another critical few moments you must set aside each day. Make sure your child has your undivided attention while he's practicing this all-important skill.

  Some parents find that, with beginning readers, it helps to take turns reading to each other. First you read a section, then your child reads one. This will keep the story moving along, since the parts he reads may be slow going.

- **Set aside time for children to read by themselves.** Once your child can comfortably read some books on his own, it is important that he get practice reading silently to himself. Not once a month or once a week but nearly every day. If possible, schedule a regular quiet time when everyone at home, including parents, reads their own books, magazines, or newspapers (preferably instead of watching TV). This will both build the vital habit of leisure-time reading and provide a chance to model good reading habits in front of your child.

- **Work on phonics at home.** During the first two or three years of learning to read, you should help your child learn the letter-to-sound relationships, recognize different consonant blends, divide words into syllables, sound out words, etc. Talk with the teacher about the phonics instruction she's giving so you can supplement it at home. She should be able to give you some good charts of letter sounds or manuals about phonics instruction. If you find there is little or no phonics instruction at school, you'll have to step in and do it yourself—do not trust your child's education to a reading program with no phonics component.

Help with Phonics

Here are some resources that can help you teach phonics. Talk with your child's teacher. She may suggest other material suitable for your child.

Hooked on Phonics: Learn to Read (Gateway Learning Company, 1998)—A new version of an old classic, this program is designed for readers ages 4–9. The program works on five different levels that students master with the help of books, workbooks, games, and activities.

Open Court Phonics (SRA Phonics/McGraw-Hill, 2000)—Although designed for school use, parents can purchase any of these three kits (kindergarten, first grade, and second/third grade) for use at home. Each package includes age-appropriate readers as well as workbooks, posters, flashcards, and teaching guides.

Primary Phonics: Workbooks and Phonetic Storybooks, Barbara W. Makar (Educational Publishing Service)—A comprehensive phonics program that guides children from first vowel sounds to the third grade level with worksheets and stories.

- **Supply good books outside of school.** It is a mistake to tell yourself, "The school will assign all the books my child needs to read." Many elementary classes read only a handful of books during a school year. Besides, you don't want your child to equate reading with school assignments, a task to be taken up only when the teacher requires it. Really good students, those who are excited about learning, are usually the ones whose parents take an active role in helping them find books they enjoy.

- **Monitor and supplement the school's reading lists.** Look for books that will complement schoolwork. For example, if the class is studying American Indians, find a book of Native American myths to read together. (Ask your teacher or school librarian if they have lists of suggested readings.) You should also try to fill gaps in the school reading curriculum. This is important. If your child's reading assignments are not challenging enough, or there simply are not enough of them, try to take up the slack at home. You can begin by checking the lists in this chapter. Choose one or two books that aren't on the school's reading list and encourage your child to read them.

- **Expose your child to some classics.** Remember, pay attention not only to how well your child reads, but also to what he reads. You want him to have the opportunity to read some books that millions of other children have loved, perhaps including some that you loved in your own childhood—books like *The Jungle Book*, *Black Beauty*, and *Old Yeller*.

- **Read books and stories about your family's own heritage.** American classrooms are more ethnically diverse than ever. With limited time, teachers cannot be expected to spend much time on every culture. So this is a perfect chance for parents to supplement the school curriculum at home. If your family is of Vietnamese descent, for example, read the folklore and history of Vietnam. Your child may be able to use such readings for elective school assignments. Exploring your family's background and literary heritage will enrich his education immeasurably.

- **Capitalize on your child's interests.** One good way to encourage independent reading is to find materials related to your child's interests. If he loves being outdoors, introduce him to *The Call of the Wild*, or a magazine like *Ranger Rick*. The more interested he is in the subject matter, the more likely he is to pick it up and read it.

- **Talk to your child about what he is reading.** More than one third of fourth graders and three fifths of eighth graders say they talk about reading with family members or friends no more than once or twice a month. This is a mistake. Talking about books helps young readers build vocabulary, make sense of stories, and relate printed words to the world around them. It also lets children know their parents are interested. Frequently ask your child to tell you about what he is reading. What is his favorite story? What does he like about it? Who is his favorite hero?

- **Read what he's reading.** After your child has begun to read on his own, it's a good idea to read some of his books and stories yourself, or at least skim through them. This will make your conversations about literature much more helpful to him. There's a benefit for you, too: you'll probably rediscover some wonderful old childhood characters and tales. You can occasionally invite older children to read and talk about something interesting that *you've* read lately—a newspaper editorial, magazine article, or a page or two from a good book.

- **Visit the library.** If you haven't already started your child on regular trips to the library, begin as soon as possible. Get to know your school's library. Ask the librarian about getting a parent's card so you can check out books.

- **Try book clubs or magazine subscriptions.** Many classrooms offer monthly book selections from *Scholastic, Troll,* or *Weekly Reader;* students can select one or more books per month and purchase them through the school. Ask your teacher about such programs. You may also want to subscribe to one of the several excellent magazines written especially for children, such as *Cricket* or *Boys' Life.*

- **Keep him reading during the summer.** Parents (and teachers) often despair at the amount of learning students lose over summer vacation. Yet children who read during their break often *gain* reading skills. So it's important not to drop the ball when school's out.

  Some schools give summer reading assignments. If your school doesn't, or if its book list is too short, come up with your own reading plan. Ask your child's teacher for book recommendations. You might also check with your local public library—it may have a summer reading program featuring small prizes for children who read a certain number of books. Or you and your child can keep your own chart of how many books he reads, and award your own prize.

- **Start your own book club.** Think about getting together a few of your child's friends and their parents for a book club that meets every few weeks. Youngsters can help choose books and lead discussions. This is a great social activity that can help parents connect with preteens and teens, and foster a love of reading to boot. "Most of our girls will now willingly choose books over television," says Shireen Dodson, who founded a mother-daughter book club in Washington, D.C.[11]

- **Use reference works.** Keep a few reference books in the home—a dictionary, thesaurus, almanac, atlas, and, if you can afford it, an encyclopedia. You can also find all sorts of reference software at your local computer store. Show your child how to turn to these sources for answers. If he's reading L. Frank Baum's *The Wonderful Wizard of Oz*, for example, look up tornadoes in the encyclopedia or on the Internet, and locate Kansas in the atlas. If he's collected shells on the beach, get a field guide and help him identify his finds. When it comes to reading, it's important that you help him learn how to look up words he doesn't know. A child's illustrated dictionary is one of the best books you can give a young reader.

- **Play word and letter games.** Good teachers use all sorts of games to build young readers' skills, and you can do the same. Play Hangman or Scrabble with your child, or any board game that involves reading. Work crossword and word-search puzzles together. Ask your teacher and other parents to recommend good computer games or activity books that help children learn to read, write, and spell. Make up your own activities: find a list of baseball teams in the newspaper and put them in alphabetical order; rearrange the letter magnets on the refrigerator each morning to spell a new "word for the day"; write simple words on index cards, and take turns laying them side by side to make funny sentences. Time spent playing with words will make your child a better reader and writer.

- **Learn where words come from.** The study of word origins, or etymology, is a fascinating subject. Many good dictionaries trace the histories of the words they define. The word "democracy," for example, comes from the Greek words *demos* (people) and *kratia* (power). Learning Greek and Latin roots in particular is an excellent way to build vocabulary. Help your child start a list of words and their origins.

Give your child some latitude about what he reads. Not every book he lays his eyes on has to be a "classic," or one you judge to be "educational." That kind of force-feeding can discourage young readers. A case can be made that parents should welcome just about any material that encourages children's interest in reading, whether it's *Sports Illustrated for Kids* or even some comic books. (That great man of letters, Samuel Johnson, argued that he would let a child "read any English book which happens to engage his attention, because you have done a great deal when you have brought him to have entertainment from a book. He'll get better books afterward.") Books such as the *Hardy Boys* and *Nancy Drew* series are not great literature, but they have delighted countless boys and girls, and helped lead them to a lifetime of reading for pleasure.

It's probably best to let your child explore all kinds of reading material, provided a couple of conditions exist. First, always keep an eye on the books he spends time with. Look through some of them yourself.

Discuss them with your child and correct any dubious ideas or values they impart. (If they're too dubious, explain that you don't want him reading that kind of stuff.) Second, try to make sure your child is exposed to superior books, in and out of school. Comics, celebrity magazines, and other "junk reading" should not completely take over one's literary diet.

Building Reading Comprehension

Youngsters get much more out of books and stories when they talk about them with adults. When reading aloud to your child, or listening to him read, you can use the same strategy that teachers use in the classroom.

• **Prepare your child for the story.** Before reading with your child, introduce any new words and concepts. (This obviously requires your reading or skimming the story beforehand.) "We're going to read a story called 'The Little Hero of Holland.' The land is so low in Holland, they have to keep the sea out. Do you know how they do that?" Providing such background information about main ideas and characters keeps young children from becoming confused during the reading. Studies show that with such preparation, children understand stories more fully and remember their ideas better.

• **Discuss the story.** After reading the story (or, if appropriate, every few paragraphs or pages), ask a few questions about the plot, characters, or theme. "Why was Peter walking alongside the dike? What would have happened if he had pulled his finger out? Why do you think Peter said he wasn't a hero?" Often, young children need explicit prompting to think about aspects of a story before they really grasp what has happened. Talking about stories will help your child realize that the purpose of reading is to get information and insight, not simply to recognize printed words.

   Even with older children who are reading on their own, it will help if you read the same selection and then ask a few thought-provoking questions: "Why do you think Poe's Raven keeps saying 'Nevermore'?" "What do you think the author of this story was trying to say about life?" This will sharpen comprehension and build appreciation for elements of literature such as theme and style. Talking with older children about reading assignments takes some consistency on your part. If you sporadically ask a seventh grader what he's reading, you'll probably get a "just some story" kind of response. Discussing literature, like reading itself, is a habit that must be cultivated, the earlier the better.

Resources That Help Your Child Learn to Read

Here are some good resources that can help your child learn to read. Your child's teacher may be able to suggest other suitable books and materials.

Books

Books to Build On, John Holdren and E. D. Hirsch, Jr. (Delta Trade Books, 1996)—A guide to excellent children's books in various subjects.

The New Read-Aloud Handbook, Jim Trelease (Penguin, 1995)—Explains the virtues of reading aloud and suggests numerous good titles.

The New York Times Parent's Guide to the Best Books for Children, Eden Ross Lipson (Times Books, 1991, Revised and Updated)—An extensive listing of children's classics, organized by topic and age.

Straight Talk about Reading, Susan L. Hall and Louisa C. Moats (Contemporary Books, 1999)—Offers parents excellent practical advice and a fine overview of available resources.

Magazines

Ladybird (Cricket Magazine Group)—A monthly magazine with good read-aloud stories, plus simple texts and poems for beginning readers.

Spider (Cricket Magazine Group)—This monthly magazine offers 6-to-8-year-olds more challenging material as well as games and other projects.

Parent Talk (www.kidscanlearn.com/parental/partalk/menu-pt.html)—An online magazine that provides parents with education research findings and practical advice on reading and other topics.

Web Sites

American Library Association (www.ala.org/parents)—A diversified site that offers comprehensive lists of award-winning books, videos, software.

Children's Literature Web Guide (www.acs.ucalgary.ca/~dkbrown/index.html)—A good resource for parents who want easy access to quality literature Web sites.

Blue Web'n (www.kn.pacbell.com/wired/bluewebn)—Contains a library of learning sites grouped by subject and activity.

The "Prince and I" Web site (www.nfb.ca/kids)—Young children can solve mysteries, write a story, or play games while practicing reading skills.

Software

Arthur's Reading Race (Broderbund, 1997)—Beginning readers will get practice as they walk around this animated town with Arthur, reading signs that say "keep off the grass," etc.

Electronic Storybooks (The Learning Company–Parson's Company, 1995)—Kids can hear children's stories, read aloud on the computer, highlight words for pronunciation, and activate animated skits. (Similar storybooks are available from other children's publishers.)

Reader Rabbit's Interactive Reading Journey (The Learning Company, 1995)—In this game, children help Reader Rabbit turn words and phrases into sentences and then into stories for the Wordville newspaper (which they can later print with their own bylines).

techlearning.com (www.techlearning.com)—Web site for reviews of software in reading, English and other fields.

Helping Your Child Learn to Write

There is an ancient Latin proverb: *Scribendo disces scribere*—By writing you learn to write. In other words, writing, like reading, takes lots of practice.

In many elementary classrooms, opportunities to write more than a few sentences at a time are infrequent, so it is critical that you create an environment that encourages writing at home. Several elements need to be present. First, make sure there are plenty of pencils, pens, and paper around the house. If you have a computer, give your child access to its word processing program (or purchase a program designed for youngsters). If possible, give your child his own table or desk where he can write, away from TVs, radios, stereos, and other distractions. Offer encouragement and praise for his efforts. A place where you make a proud display of his writings—on the refrigerator door or a bulletin board—is a must.

Most important of all, make sure your child spends time writing every day. Homework obviously represents one opportunity. Chances are good in the first few years of school, however, that homework assignments won't be enough, especially if they consist mainly of worksheets that take only minutes to complete. Beginning writers need more sustained efforts.

With a little effort, you'll have no trouble coming up with different ways to give your budding writer additional practice. Have him send letters, notes, and cards to relatives. (Some lined stationery with your child's name printed across the top may provide inspiration.) He can make labels, name tags, and place cards for use in the house. When the kids put on a play or gymnastics show, suggest that they make invitations and write out a program. Ask your child to help you write down the grocery list. He can also write telephone messages or other notes while you dictate. (A bulletin board where family members leave messages for each other is a great aid for reading and writing.)

The older your child gets, the more opportunities there are for him to put his thoughts on paper in lucid, creative ways. Urge him to take part in elective school activities such as writing for the student newspaper, yearbook, or literary magazine. Look for writing contests that feature children's work. Groups that your child belongs to (an astronomy club, soccer league, scouts, etc.) may have writing needs—everything from invitations to meeting minutes to newsletters. Look around for publications to which you and your child can contribute together, such as your church bulletin or neighborhood association newsletter. Local charities sometimes need volunteer writers, too.

Here are some ways to sharpen writing skills:

- **Encourage your child to write stories.** Without a doubt, this is one of the best ways to practice writing and nurture creativity. Initially, you may need to suggest some topics. Ask your child to pretend he is a mountain, or his favorite toy, or a tree blowing in the wind, and write about it. Or suggest an imaginary dialogue, such as a skyscraper talking to passing airplanes. If your child is reading fables in school, make up one together. With practice, your child will begin to come up with his own ideas, and that's when he'll get truly excited about authoring his own stories.

- **Encourage some poetry writing.** Abraham Lincoln, a lifelong lover of poetry, began writing verse when he was young. (Among his early products: "Abraham Lincoln his hand and pen/he will be good but God knows When.") Abe posed no threat to Milton, but the boy who liked to play with words grew up to compose some of the most beautiful speeches in the English language. Composing even silly limericks will aid your child's prowess with the pen.

- **Give spelling lessons.** It is hard to write well if you cannot spell. Keep up with the lists of spelling words your child is supposed to know. Call the words out for him to write down or spell out loud until he knows them. Spelling lessons usually are not a favorite activity. They often call for raw concentration, phonics work, and memorization, but all of those things are good for children.

- **Work on vocabulary.** Learning word meanings helps writing, reading, and speaking skills. Keep tabs on the vocabulary your child is assigned in school. (If he comes home with no word lists, talk with the teacher about how vocabulary is learned and tested.) You may want to call out the words so he can use them in sentences and write definitions. Make flash cards with a word on one side and its definition on the other, if that helps.

Bring new words to your child's attention. Some families choose a "word for the day" or "word for the week" to practice using. Encourage your child to look up unfamiliar words he encounters while reading.

- **Practice good grammar, mechanics, and composition.** Keep up with the writing rules and grammar studied at school and occasionally go over them at home. If the class is learning about modifiers, for example, ask your child to pick out the adjectives in the sentence he has just written. If he's learning to use commas, check his latest letter to grandma and talk with him about its punctuation.

- **Keep a writing folder.** Keep a box or folder where you put samples of your child's writings. Comparing them over several weeks and months will help you gauge his progress. Keeping such a "portfolio" is a strategy that many teachers use.

- **Encourage your child to keep a journal.** Some children enjoy keeping a family diary, in which each member of the family takes turns writing one or two paragraphs about something memorable. Such journals almost always end up being family treasures.

- **Write to your child.** Occasional notes left inside lunch boxes or on pillows may inspire your child to write. There was once a young girl whose parents made a habit of giving little notes of guidance, encouragement, and love. Their simple missives touched her heart; Louisa May Alcott grew up to write books beloved by children everywhere.

- **Help your child find a pen pal.** Ask some out-of-town relatives or friends to correspond with your child, either by letter or e-mail. There are also organizations that help youngsters find pen pals. Ask the teacher if she can recommend one.

- **Help your child write his own books.** Keep the stories he writes and put them in a ring binder. Or encourage him to "publish" them on the computer; he can print out several copies of his stories, staple them together, and mail his book to relatives and friends. Some youngsters also enjoy making their own recipe books, or putting together collections of jokes and riddles that they hear. Blank books, available in bookstores, motivate many to write.

- **Encourage writing related to your child's interests.** Sending away for information about a hobby is a great way to practice writing and build research skills. For example, if your child is intrigued by rockets and outer space, help him write to NASA.

- **Cultivate the habit of writing thank-you notes.** Although getting this done turns out to be a struggle in some families, it is important to do. In addition to honing writing skills, it aids in the development of manners and good reputation.

Helping Your Child Become a Better Writer

Most youngsters approach writing as a one-step process. Even many high school and college students begin writing their papers with scant thought as to what they will say, and hand in their assignments with little or no revision. We shouldn't be surprised that their work is disorganized, artless, and full of mistakes.

Around the time your child starts getting assignments that involve more than a paragraph or two, you can help him learn the different stages that lead to a polished product. Although good English teachers train students to organize, draft, and revise papers, there is rarely time for enough practice in class. It will help to go through the following steps at home. The older the child, the more thorough this process can be.

- **Priming the pump.** Teach your child to take a few minutes and brainstorm before beginning any writing task. This is a time to define the project, nurture inspiration, and decide on a general direction. Encourage him to use you as a sounding board for ideas. If the writing is for school, make sure he can explain the assignment clearly. Help him learn to ask such questions as: What are the main points I want to make? Who will the reader be? What are the most interesting aspects of this subject? Encourage him to jot down random thoughts, words, and ideas. They don't need to be complete sentences or come in any particular order. At this stage, the object is to think imaginatively about the project.

- **Doing research.** For some assignments, your child will need to do some reading before he begins writing. Help him use an encyclopedia, locate books and magazine articles in the library, or go online to find out more about his topic. If he's writing a story with a colt as a character, he may want to look through a book about horses. If he's reporting on a family trip, he may want to consult some leftover brochures, maps, travel guides, or family photos.

- **Making an outline.** Teach your child to organize his thoughts by writing down the main points he wants to make and arranging them in the order he wants to make them. As he begins writing, remind him to refer to this outline from time to time.

- **Writing a rough draft.** Explain to your child that the rough draft is just that—rough. It is a work in progress, and isn't supposed to look polished. In fact, for many writers, the first draft bears little resemblance to the final copy. At this stage, the object is to take a first stab at getting what he wants to say down on paper. Spelling and writing mistakes aren't crucial—he'll fix them in a later draft. Let him know it's fine to change words, cross out sentences, and add new ideas as he goes along.

- **Revising the draft.** Once the first draft is on paper (or computer screen), your child is ready to start editing and rewriting. He should read it over—it may help to read it aloud—to decide whether the writing is clear, and says what he wants it to say. Encourage him to add and delete where necessary, move sentences, think of more descriptive words, fill out incomplete thoughts, and weed out extraneous ones. If necessary, he may want to write a second draft. The older the child, the more drafting and editing you can encourage. For the kind of questions your child should learn to ask himself when revising, see "Revising a Draft," below.

Many children do not like to edit and rewrite because they think it is an admission of failure. (It also takes more effort.) Teach your child that, quite the opposite, good writing requires plenty of rewriting. As Samuel Johnson observed, "What is written without effort is in general read without pleasure."

- **Producing a finished copy.** Once he is satisfied with his draft, your child should make a careful, final copy. Students using a computer need to finalize their writing by making formatting choices such as fonts, margins, and line spacing. Finally, no writing assignment is complete until your child has double-checked his work for errors (see "Proofreading a Paper," below). Teach your child that it's usually easier to spot those pesky mistakes if he puts the paper aside for a while and comes back to it with a fresh eye.

Revising a Draft

Revising a draft is a complex step, because the writer is usually looking at several different aspects of his work. He must consider whether his narrative or argument makes sense as a whole, as well as whether his mechanics are in order. Are ideas missing? Should the wording be simplified? The French novelist Anatole France said that "you become a good writer as you become a good joiner: by planing down your sentences."

It is often a good idea to ask others to look at a draft to get their ideas and opinions on what can make it better. Many children are reluctant to share their work before it is "finished." They may be embarrassed for others to see something that is imperfect, but getting used to constructive criticism is an important part of learning to write.

Here are the kinds of questions your child should apply to his papers at the revision stage:

- Does it say what I meant?

- Will it make sense to someone else?

- Did I stick to my topic?

- Did I leave any important ideas or information out?

- Did I organize information so that the ideas and arguments flow in a logical sequence?

- Did I use reliable sources for my information, and double-check my facts?

- Is there enough detail and description?

- Have I written with a consistent point of view?

- How do my paragraphs and sentences sound?

- Do they all make sense?

- Can I make any changes that will make the writing smoother?

Proofreading a Paper

Every English teacher knows that good proofreading often separates the A papers from the B and C efforts. Homework assignments offer excellent chances for you to help your child develop this habit. Teach him that when he's finished writing, he's not done—he needs to go back and look over his work for mistakes.

Proofreading takes practice. To find errors, your child must focus on each word and sentence at a time. Encourage him to read out loud slowly, listening for words and phrases that don't sound right. It may help if he uses a ruler or blank piece of paper to cover the writing below the line he is examining. Children should learn to ask these kinds of questions about their work:

- Is every sentence a complete thought?
- Does each sentence begin with a capital letter and end with a period, question mark, or exclamation point?
- Did I leave out any vital words?
- Are all the words spelled and used correctly? Are there any I need to check in the dictionary?
- Did I use correct and consistent verb tenses?
- Are all my subjects and verbs in agreement?
- Did I use the right pronouns?
- Did I use the right punctuation marks?
- Is my penmanship neat?
- Did I number my pages?
- Did I remember to put my name, class, date, and, if necessary, a title on my assignment?

Gauging Your Child's Interest and Progress

Throughout your child's school career—but particularly in the first few years, when habits are set—take care to monitor his interest in books, as well as his progress in reading and writing. Ask yourself these questions:

- How much time did he spend reading yesterday? Last week? When was the last time I saw him reading a book or magazine on his own, without urging? When he starts a book, does he usually finish it?
- Does he like to go to the library or bookstore to get new books? Does he pick challenging ones?
- When he reads age-appropriate material aloud, does he read fairly smoothly? Can he sound out unfamiliar words?

- Does he understand what he reads? Can he explain it in his own words?

- When he writes, does he generally spell correctly? Does he follow rules of grammar and punctuation? Does he form his letters neatly, or does his penmanship look sloppy and careless?

- Is his writing cogent for his age? Does he choose words with some care? Are stories written with imagination? Is he learning to write essays that are organized and persuasive?

- How often do I see him turn to reference material—a dictionary, encyclopedia, atlas, or the Internet—to find an answer?

We can't expect young children to develop an interest in reading and writing if they don't witness those activities taking place on a regular basis. But where, outside of school, are they going to see others spending time with books, pencils, and paper? Not on the playground. Not at the mall. Surely not in movie theaters or in front of a TV screen. *It has to be in the home.* Children need to observe family members in the acts of reading and writing—especially reading—if they are going to develop an inclination to do these things, too. Do not underestimate the effect of your example. In these most basic of academic activities, the behavior you model has a direct and lasting impact. (For help in assessing the kind of example you are setting when it comes to reading books, see "What Does My Child Read into My Behavior?" on page 45.)

CHAPTER 6

History
and
Geography

THIS CHAPTER COVERS WHAT IS COMMONLY CALLED "SOCIAL studies" in the school curriculum. We don't call it that, because we're appalled by much of what passes for this subject in many U.S. classrooms: pop psychology, tot sociology, self-esteem exercises, propaganda for particular causes, and other questionable matters. We believe that *history and geography, along with the beginnings of civics and economics,* should comprise the core of what is widely referred to as "social studies." Unfortunately, in many schools these core disciplines do not command the central place that they deserve in the curriculum, so this area may require extra vigilance on your part.

In this chapter, we discuss why history and geography are indispensable. We outline the knowledge and skills your child should gain from their study, and sketch some of the basic civics and economics that should accompany them. We display a model curriculum that you can compare to your own school's courses; address some salient debates in which this field of study is caught up; and alert you to some shortcomings you may encounter at school. We also suggest things you can do at home to round out or shore up your child's education.

WHAT GOOD SCHOOLS TEACH—AND WHY

"Why do I have to study this old stuff? Who cares what happened to a bunch of people who died a long time ago?"

Most likely your child can make it through life without knowing about Julius Caesar or Abigail Adams or Charles Lindbergh, but she will be the poorer for it. Knowing history is the mark of an educated person. At some point, you may need to help your youngster understand why. You may even need to remind yourself. So we begin this chapter by recalling some of the reasons this subject really matters, following a path set down by Professor Walter A. McDougall of the University of Pennsylvania, who has pointed out that studying history helps students grow in three broad areas: the intellectual, civic, and moral spheres.[1]

The Intellectual Function of History

The study of history has the inestimable value of letting us learn from others' experiences. The recorded past is a vast depository of humanity's insights, trials, mistakes, and triumphs. By studying history, we can take this rich accumulation of experience and make it part of our own wisdom. "Not to know what has been transacted in former times is to be always a child," Cicero wrote. "If no use is made of the labors of past ages, the world must remain always in the infancy of knowledge."

When we avail ourselves of others' experiences, history becomes a guide to the present. It does not give us precise directions, of course, but it can be a bright lamp to hang on the bow of our little vessel as we sail forward on what would otherwise be a dark and chartless sea. The student who knows about the Roaring Twenties and Great Depression knows to save for a rainy day because times are not always good. The child who reads about Florence Nightingale battling disease and misery in the Crimea learns that if you're going to tackle a formidable problem, you've got to be organized and determined about it. History's lessons give us practical wisdom about how to handle ourselves in the here and now.

History helps us understand why the world is the way it is. The present, after all, takes its form from the past. Consider this everyday example: when you make a new acquaintance, you don't really "know" him until you've learned something about his background—where he has lived, what he has done, who has influenced him. Know these things, and you understand better what "makes him tick." Similarly, and on a far larger scale, the study of history helps us fathom the world. To understand modern tensions in the Middle East, you need to know something about the long chronicle of the Arab and Jewish peoples, and the creation of Israel as a Jewish homeland in 1948. To have insight into any situation, you need some accurate information about the forces and events that created it.

History is also a great teacher about the vastness and richness of the human condition. Jesse Owens standing up to Nazi racism and going on to win at the 1936 Olympics in Berlin. Anne Sullivan refusing to give up on Helen Keller. Ulysses S. Grant and Robert E. Lee meeting face-to-face at the end of a long and cruel war. These lessons show children how others have acted in different situations. They help youngsters distinguish, as the English historian Thomas Macaulay put it, "what is accidental and transitory in human nature from what is essential and immutable." Studying the beliefs, customs, and institutions of a wide variety of peoples throughout time broadens our own humanity. It awakens students to the almost infinite diversity of human thought and achievement. It helps them appreciate why others may not dress the same way, worship the same way, or have the same priorities. When we see how we resemble and differ from others, we learn something about ourselves, and history becomes a route to self-knowledge for the growing child.

Historical studies provide an organizing framework for several other fields of knowledge. To best understand a work of literature, art, philosophy, or religion, for example, students should know something of the period from which it comes. Reading *A Tale of Two Cities* is much more meaningful if you know something about the French Revolution. Knowledge of history also prepares us for the world of work: professions such as teaching, journalism, and the law all require knowledge of the past.

In fact, studying the past readies us for work in almost any thoughtful endeavor, because it teaches us to think critically and analytically. In the process of reading and contemplating history, a student learns to sort through problems for herself. She gains respect for facts and for proper methods of judging evidence. She practices distinguishing meaningful events from inconsequential ones. She learns to tell truth from falsehood, bias from objectivity, and confusion from lucidity. In short, history is an incubator of critical intelligence.

For those who are willing to open their minds and make the effort, history is a grand adventure. "What could be more agreeable entertainment to the mind, than to be transported to the remotest ages of the world?" asked the Scottish philosopher David Hume. "What spectacle can be imagined so magnificent, so various, so interesting?" Alexander the Great setting out to conquer the world. Joan of Arc being led to the stake. The Lost Colony vanishing forever at Roanoke Island, leaving behind just one mysterious word carved into a tree. If taught properly, history is bound to stir the imagination. This is a subject that both stimulates and entertains the intellect.

The Civic Function of History

Your child may not take a course specifically devoted to "United States Government" or "The Constitution" until high school. Good elementary schools, however, teach "civics" at every grade level—that is, they offer instruction in the knowledge and skills that students will need as responsible Americans. Thomas Jefferson once outlined what this part of your child's education should entail. The author of the Declaration of Independence wrote that schools should teach each student:

> to understand his duties to his neighbors and country, and to discharge with competence the functions confided to him by either. . . . To know his rights . . . and in general, to observe with intelligence and faithfulness all the social relations under which he shall be placed. To instruct the mass of our citizens in these, their rights, interests and duties, as men and citizens are . . . the objects of education.

In good elementary schools, these lessons are taught largely in the context of history. A knowledge of the past makes good citizens on several fronts.

The Founding Fathers knew well that the health of American democracy would depend on individuals making intelligent decisions, both on election day and in the daily conduct of their affairs. Good decisions often require historical intelligence. Citizens cannot comprehend domestic or international issues without some understanding of the train of events leading up to today's questions. Often that train of events leads far into the past. Without such context, voters may not be able to see through the demagoguery of politicians, the sophistry of political commercials, or the harangues of pundits. They may not recognize why a "yea" or "nay" vote was cast in the statehouse or Congress or the United Nations. They may not even understand references to people, places, and events in newspaper articles and television reports. Without historical literacy, there is little hope for the kind of informed citizenry that is needed for successful democracy.

The study of history does more than help make intelligent voters. It also teaches youngsters who we are as a people. It instills a sense that each one of us is part of this common enterprise we call the United States. Consciousness of a shared past is a fundamental basis for social cohesion; it ties together members of any group, whether it be a family, school, town, or nation. The long winter at Valley Forge. The Wright brothers at Kitty Hawk. Neil Armstrong planting his foot on the moon. These events connect us with a common heritage. They are part of the fabric that makes us all Americans.

By studying our past—Philadelphia in the summer of 1787, Gettysburg in the summer of 1863, the March on Washington in the summer of 1963—students gain a basic understanding of the central principles and beliefs that underlie American democracy. They learn how and why our ideals came into being. They learn how hard it has been to protect and preserve them and how long it took to extend them to all citizens. They learn those noble things that make this country so unique and exemplary in the pantheon of nations.

Successful elementary schools teach children to *love their country*. They raise them to be patriots. As the great American lexicographer Noah Webster put it, as soon as a child "opens his lips, he should rehearse the history of his own country; he should lisp the praise of liberty, and of those illustrious heroes and statesmen who have wrought a revolution in her favor."

In some places, teaching patriotism is viewed as something quaint and even embarrassing, an awkward sentiment out of step with modernity. In some classrooms, the explicit teaching of love of country is even regarded with suspicion, as if it were some sort of brainwashing or indoctrination. It is often more fashionable to show children how to be cynical about our civic institutions and heroes of the past. In our view, something is very wrong in such classrooms. There is something pitiful—and dangerous to the health of democracy—about raising children to look with ambivalence or even disdain at this country's history and traditions. Yes, schools should teach students to examine their nation's actions closely, to understand that ours has not been an unblemished saga, and to speak out when they see wrong. Having said this, one hallmark of a good American school should remain: young children leave it understanding—and loving—their country more than they did when they entered.

Good elementary schools have teachers who are versed in democratic ideals, who model them in classroom and corridor, who cherish them, are not afraid to stand up for them, and do not hesitate to instill them in the young. Good schools are full of teachers who love their country and take pride in it. They are eager to instill such pride in their students. They teach children to respect the ways of other nations and cultures. At the same time, they let students know how fortunate they are to be heirs to this country's great political traditions.

The Moral Function of History

The Founders understood that the character of any community ultimately depends on the character of its members, and that the democratic way of life is possible only when individual citizens practice a certain degree of virtue, both in their public and private endeavors. This brings us to the third reason that history lies at the core of the elementary school curriculum: the moral training of the young. The study of the past has long served the function of teaching about right and wrong. "For in history you have a record of the infinite variety of human experience plainly set out for all to see," wrote the Roman historian Livy, "and in that record you can find for yourself and your country both examples and warnings: fine things to take as models, base things, rotten through and through, to avoid." Tacitus, who followed in his footsteps, concurred: "This I regard as history's highest function, to let no worthy action be uncommemorated, and to hold out the reprobation of posterity as a terror to evil words and deeds."

The human record is full of heroes and villains, acts noble and base. Benedict Arnold turning on his countrymen and sullying his name forever. Mother Teresa ministering in the slums of Calcutta. Albert Schweitzer devoting his life to the people of Africa. The chronicles of the ages are, in a sense, a great collection of experiments in how to live. Faraway lives and events are powerful demonstrations. They can help train children's minds and hearts toward the good. They tell what sort of actions, good and ill, we may expect from others, and they defeat notions of moral relativism by demonstrating that some ways of living really are nobler than others.

Here is an excerpt from a book called *Barnes's Elementary History of the United States*, a reader used in American schools a century ago. It says of Abraham Lincoln: "Perhaps the great secret of his success in life lay in the fact that in whatever position he was placed he always did his best." The lesson explains that as a boy he loved to read, and he borrowed every book that he heard of in the neighborhood.

> One book that made a great impression was Weems's *Life of Washington*. He read the story many times. He carried it with him to the field and read it in the intervals of work. Washington was his ideal hero, the one great man whom he admired above all others. Why could not he model his own life after that of the Father of his Country? Why could not he also be a doer of noble deeds and a benefactor of mankind? He might never be President, but he could make himself worthy of that great honor.

In this little lesson about one great American and his affection for the memory of another, the explicit exhortations to good character may sound odd to the modern ear. But they are right on target. Children want to be shown the best way to live. They want responsible adults to teach them. Unfortunately, many schools (and parents) no longer do a good job of using history's heroes and heroines to teach about virtue. "Fad figures and celebrities are everywhere, but the great individuals are hidden away," observes Professor Dennis Denenberg of Millersville State College, Pennsylvania. "How many kids know who Jonas Salk was?" Good schools embrace the moral function of knowing history. They teach the full lessons of the past—which include messages about honesty, courage, perseverance, and work. They call children to listen to the voices of heroes and villains echoing from ages gone by and to adjust their own lives accordingly. Good schools teach history mindful that children are moral beings and should be addressed as such.

History Lessons That Good Schools Teach

What historical knowledge and skills, then, should your child learn in school? An excellent course of study is outlined in more detail in the coming pages, but the first thing to understand is that, in good elementary schools, the history curriculum is about that: history. It is not a grab bag of sociology, psychology, environmentalism, and a host of other "ologies" and "isms"—which is what you find in too many places. It does not mean always talking about current events and controversial issues and "relevant" concerns. It does not mean spending a lot of class time on how students "feel" about the past. Those topics may be worth integrating into the curriculum, *but some pertinent history must come first.*

Centuries of recorded history lie behind us, classroom time is limited, and so choices must be made. In many schools, those choices are made in haphazard fashion. The curriculum becomes a patchwork of readings and lessons following no master pattern. Teachers in one grade are not sure what is taught in other grades. Disorganization may be accompanied by the sense that no one can say with any confidence just what elements of history are really the most important to learn. The result, naturally, is that students' sense of the past is disordered and full of gaps.

Good schools, on the other hand, have a vision of what history lessons are most important for their students to know. They are clear with parents about exactly what body of knowledge they intend to teach youngsters before high school. Generally speaking, that corpus is the basic saga of U.S. and world history—with an emphasis, in world history, on the Western civilization within which the American past is primarily embedded.

By the end of junior high, your child should know about the most salient events in U.S. history (such as the Revolutionary War and civil rights movement), be able to explain their significance, and have a good sense of when and why they occurred. Likewise, she should know something about the most important events in world history (such as the Industrial Revolution and the Holocaust), and be able to place in order and roughly date the major historical periods. She should recognize and place in context some of the important men and women in U.S. and world history. She should have read and studied some pivotal documents (or portions of them) such as the Declaration of Independence and Martin Luther King, Jr.'s, "Letter from Birmingham City Jail." She should be acquainted with some fundamental ideas on which those documents rest, such as the right to "life, liberty and the pursuit of happiness."

In addition to facts, the school should make sure your child understands the concepts that tie them together. Increasingly, as students advance, teachers should link players and scenes to great central themes. In U.S. history, for example, children should come to understand something about the evolution of American democracy, the impact of immigration over the years, and the changing character of family life. In world history, students should examine themes such as the causes of war, the blessings and curses of technological change, and the origins and ideas of the world's great religions. In these contexts, facts convey both knowledge and understanding.

Students should ponder some great questions that go beyond "critical thinking" skills, questions such as: How and why do cultures change? How has the character of great individuals affected the course of history? What kind of role does chance play in human affairs? Thoughtful questions about history should include some that address the moral dimension of life: Why does everyone admire this woman so much? Why was that leader's action so repugnant? Which lives should I remember as guiding stars?

Lest we become complacent about the value of our children learning history, we should recall what C.S. Lewis wrote in *The Screwtape Letters*, as the devil Screwtape urged his nephew and protégé Wormwood to cultivate in men a disdain for the past. "Since we cannot deceive the whole human race all the time," the devil says, "it is important to cut every generation off from all the others; for where learning makes a free commerce between the ages, there is always a danger that the characteristic errors of one may be corrected by the characteristic truths of another." It is to the maintenance of that "free commerce between the ages" that the teaching of history is crucial. Good schools assign this discipline a central place in the curriculum.

The Place of Geography in the Curriculum

Geography is the study of where things are, why they are there, and how they relate to people's lives. It is the study of space and distance and movement, of the interplay between nature and man, between tribe and tribe and nation and nation. It is an important subject that has suffered great neglect in many American schools. You will need to find out if your own school makes it a significant part of elementary education.

History and geography have a special affinity in the curriculum because the human story must be told in terms of both time and place. Students must know some geography to possess even a superficial knowledge of the past—learning about *when* things happened does a child little good if she's fuzzy on *where* they happened. She also needs some knowledge of geography to understand *why* things occurred. For example, students can't really fathom the failures of Napoleon's and Hitler's armies without knowing something about Russia's vast frozen steppes.

There are other important reasons that young people need to learn geography. It provides a context for science lessons they will come across in school. For example, the routes of the great bird migrations in North America are no accident—the lay of the land helps set their course. Geography helps students think more clearly about economic, political, social, and environmental issues. What are the possible consequences when farmlands on a floodplain are replaced by housing developments? Once out of school, young Americans need to know about other people and places to compete successfully in a global economy. It's a pretty good idea to know where Hong Kong is when you interview for a job with a company that does 50 percent of its business there.

In teaching geography, a school's first job is to make children familiar with major features of the earth's surface. Students should learn the names and locations of continents, oceans, countries, large cities, major rivers, mountain ranges, etc. They should get lots of experience reading and using maps. Such foundational knowledge is essential. It's certainly not all there is to know about geography. But having a good sense of the globe orients students when they come across references to the Philippines in their history books, or read in the newspaper that "Pakistan has conducted nuclear tests." Good teachers realize that, if you don't know some basic "map facts," you're lost.

In addition to such knowledge, good schools train students to think about the physical and human characteristics of a place, and the relationships between the two. Geographic inquiry begins with two essential questions: Why are certain things located in particular places, and how do those places influence people's lives?[2] Children study how physical processes shape the land, how natural resources are distributed and used. They learn about the host of ways that the earth's surface affects people's activities, and how humans modify their physical environments. They look at the locations and movements of various human populations; patterns of trade, economic interdependence, and conflict; the way people have divided—and often fought over—control of the land and its resources.

As students progress through school, they examine how geography has had a hand in molding history, and they analyze how it may influence present and future events. Why were the Panama and Suez canals built? How are new national boundaries in Eastern Europe affecting U.S. foreign policy? What effect is a new shopping mall on the west side of town likely to have on local development?

Children should get a thorough dose of geography throughout their years in elementary school. Unfortunately, such sustained curricular commitment is rare. "Here's what happens in too many schools," says one former social studies teacher. "We buy a commercial 'sequenced' map skill program, teach it for seven to nine weeks, and now 'we've done geography.' No wonder we have a nation of geographic illiterates!" Geography deserves to be taken more seriously. We do not say there must be distinct "geography classes" every year, but in good schools, the subject is thoroughly integrated into the curriculum.

When your child is in the primary grades, it is a good idea to ask her teacher what sort of geography she plans to teach in the coming months. When your child is in the intermediate and junior high grades, talk with her history teacher, since history and geography are best studied side by side. Feel free to talk to her English and even science teachers about this, too. In good schools, globes and maps are always at hand, often in view. They're used by teachers and kids on a daily basis to talk about those long-ago stories of Camelot, or why the earth shakes in California, or what kinds of animals live in Australia. There is nearly always an opportunity to work geography into the lesson.

Today's geography teaching tools go way beyond maps, globes, and atlases. This is a subject where technology is more than an "extra"; it can really turn the classroom into a place where students explore foreign lands and unfamiliar cultures. They can piece together on-screen jigsaw puzzles of Asia, watch video footage from the far reaches of the Amazon, or download satellite images of their own hometown. Look to see how your school makes use of technology in its geography curriculum.

Geography is exciting, however, even without the fancy new equipment. A few good books and an inspired teacher are enough to kindle a child's intellectual wanderlust. Back in the 1930s, the adventurer Richard Halliburton wrote about how his lessons made him yearn to explore. "My favorite schoolbook was filled with pictures of the world's most wonderful cities and mountains and temples, and had big maps to show where they were," he said. "I loved that book because it carried me away to all the strange and romantic lands. I read about the Egyptian pyramids, and India's marble towers, about the great cathedrals of France, and the ruins of ancient Babylon. . . . Sometimes I pretended I had a magic carpet, and without bothering about tickets and money and farewells, I'd skyrocket away to New York or to Rome, to the Grand Canyon or to China, across deserts and oceans and mountains . . . then suddenly come back home when the school bell rang for recess."[3] *That* is what this subject should be about for youngsters. In the best elementary schools, geography carries kids away.

What About Economics?

Just as they need to know how our government works and the values undergirding democracy, students should learn something about the structure and principles of America's market economy. Basic economic literacy enables young people to become wise consumers and make sound financial decisions. It turns them into effective workers and perceptive employers, and prepares them for the global marketplace. It helps youngsters understand human nature, since economic motives are often prime movers in people's actions. It allows students to comprehend many events in history, such as the rise of Italian city states during the Renaissance and the great push to settle the American West. Fundamentally, children should learn about the free enterprise system because it lies at the root of the entrepreneurial impulse that gives the American spirit so much of its vigor.

The systematic study of economics will come later in high school or college, but elementary school should lay a foundation. In the lower grades, good schools teach children basic principles in simple terms. Students learn, for example, about division of labor and specialization. The baker makes bread, the carpenter builds houses, the rancher raises sheep. By sticking to one job, people can do it better and more efficiently, and the result is greater good for the whole community. Likewise, youngsters should address practical matters such as that money is used to exchange goods and services, and that the more people want something, the more it may cost. In the upper grades, students should become familiar with terms such as markets, competition, supply and demand. They should learn the difference between public and private ownership, what the stock market is and what banks do. They can grasp the essence of saving and investment. Knowledge of all these things is part of being an informed U.S. citizen.

Unfortunately, in some classrooms (and in much popular media), "economics" lessons are largely about various corporate exploits and misdeeds—giant tankers spilling oil or big tobacco companies peddling cigarettes to kids. Such stories grab headlines and often make for lively classroom discussions. Certainly, the story of capitalism includes a dark side. The marketplace has spawned greed, shortsightedness, carelessness, and even cruelty in pursuit of profit: children working in factories; strip miners ravaging the land; immigrants toiling in sweat shops; sharecroppers falling deeper into debt.

All these episodes are in the history books, and students should know them, but they should also know the bright side of freedom's and capitalism's story. They should learn that ambitious, inspired people once formed companies to explore the New World; founded railroads that helped America grow; and started steel and oil companies that turned it into a great world power. U.S. companies built the rockets that carried men to the moon. They have created medicines to fight countless diseases. The charity of businesspeople has helped to build libraries and parks, to create great universities, to fill museums with works of art, and to preserve vast stretches of wilderness.

Students should know that the American free enterprise system creates the kind of jobs that people in other countries literally risk their lives to get. It gives men and women the opportunity to chase and make real their dreams. In terms of material wealth, it has created a society unparalleled in all of history. This is not propaganda. It is simply the good side of the story. Telling it honestly lets children know what they have inherited, and allows them to appreciate the economic blessings this country has received.

How Are Schools Doing?

Many American students are woefully ignorant of the past. According to the National Assessment of Educational Progress (NAEP), six out of seven eighth graders are less than proficient in their understanding of U.S. history. Approximately six out of ten twelfth graders don't even know the most basic facts about their nation's past. Numerous other studies back up those findings. A recent survey by the Colonial Williamsburg Foundation, for example, found that fewer than one in five American children know the purpose of the Declaration of Independence. Only about a third know that the British Redcoats fought in the Revolutionary War, not the Civil War or World War I.

American students don't learn much about geography, either. According to NAEP, three out of four seniors are less than proficient in the subject; 30 percent don't have even a rudimentary understanding of it. Half of fourth graders can't identify the Atlantic and Pacific oceans on a map. Nor do students know much about civics. The National Constitution Center reports that only about 40 percent of teens can name the three branches of government (although 60 percent can name the Three Stooges). Only one in five knows how many members the United States Senate has; and only 2 percent can name the chief justice of the U.S. Supreme Court (while 95 percent can name the actor who played the Fresh Prince of Bel Air on TV).

One major reason American kids know so little history and geography is that *many schools simply do not teach much about these subjects.* Instead, they teach a hodgepodge of topics called "social studies" which all too often focuses on such things as consumer affairs, ecology, and social action. Schools have been doing this for years and getting away with it. The neglect of history is particularly egregious since it is so central to a good education. "History does not engage the imagination of most elementary school teachers and they, in turn, are not teaching it well," observes one New England educator.

In fact, many elementary teachers don't know much about history, being themselves victims of a school system that treats the subject (disparaged as "pastology" by some education establishment figures) as dead, dull, and irrelevant. "You cannot begin to imagine what they do not know!" moans an education professor who trains future teachers. "They have been so cheated by a social studies curriculum that taught them nothing in the K–3 years, then taught them boring social studies with some history for the next several years. By high school, history is a subject to be avoided. The dire consequence facing us concerning the next generation of elementary teachers can best be recognized in a remark made by the great American humorist Will Rogers: 'You can't teach what you don't know any more than you can come back from where you ain't been.'"

It is dangerous for democracy when self-understanding withers away: the kind of understanding that comes through knowledge of the past, of place, and of basic principles of one's own country and civilization. As Boston University researcher Paul Gagnon has written, American schools are graduating students who are "unarmed for public discourse, their great energy and idealism at the mercy of pop politics and the seven o'clock news." Your own school may do a good job of teaching history and geography, but if it does, it is among the minority of U.S. schools.

THE HISTORY AND GEOGRAPHY CURRICULUM

History lies at the heart of the social studies curriculum in a good elementary school. The following sections will give you an idea of what thorough instruction looks like. You should compare this model curriculum to your own school's course of study, but keep in mind this warning: many American elementary schools simply do not teach children much about the past! Examine your child's lessons closely, and you may find yourself asking, "Where did the history go?" It may have drowned in the "social studies" pond. It may be the victim of the "culture wars" within the field of education. It may be weakened by teachers who simply don't know much history themselves and, therefore, don't teach much of it.

The curriculum outlined here is excerpted from the admirable Core Knowledge Sequence, which is used in hundreds of schools around the country with real results (see page 100). Bear in mind, as you look it over, that different schools arrange their curricula in different ways. In one seventh grade class, you may find children studying the American Revolution, while in the next town their age-mates are reading about ancient Egypt. Many schools work in a unit on state and local history. The point is that even if yours is one of the rare elementary schools that has a solid, history-based program, its curriculum very likely will not match the following model on a grade-by-grade basis.

Ask to see an outline of your school's course of study for the K–8 years. Ask the teachers and principal a few questions: In which grades will my child get a chronological look at the history of the United States? When will she begin systematic study of world history? At what point does she learn the U.S. map? What is the school's plan to teach her how American democracy works? Even if your child is only in kindergarten or first grade, take the time to go over the school's curriculum for the coming years. Otherwise you may discover—when it's too late—that "social studies" has turned out to be an odd jumble of unrelated lessons and activities in which your child has examined the decimation of the rain forest under four different teachers but has never really come to understand what happened in 1776.

A good elementary school gives children fundamental, organized knowledge about the past. It teaches some essentials: Why America broke away from England. Who Abraham Lincoln was. Where Mexico and Canada are. The central principles of the Declaration of Independence. How the federal government is organized. It tells some great stories: Molly Pitcher manning the cannon when her husband falls. Lewis and Clark standing at the forks of the Missouri River, studying its waters intently, knowing that somewhere upstream lies their nation's destiny. There is a great deal to learn. Students will become acquainted in detail with some lives, events, ideas, and places. In the main, however, the idea is to tell youngsters the basic stories of America and Western civilization, and to acquaint them with some non-Western cultures and events. In so doing, good elementary schools build a framework of facts, concepts, and skills on which future studies can hang.

The Primary Grades—Kindergarten Through Third Grade

In many schools, primary grade children study aspects of the world around them: the home, the neighborhood, the school, the community. This approach, known as "expanding environments" or "expanding horizons," is well meaning but often not very stimulating. The following guidelines are meant to broaden the focus, to stretch children's knowledge to encompass many things beyond their immediate world, to fill them with wonder by exposing them to unfamiliar people, far-off places, amazing events and distant times.

The earliest years should introduce exciting highlights of both world and American history—the building of the great pyramids of Egypt, the days of gladiators and chariot races in ancient Rome, the first daring voyages to the New World. Students will return to these subjects for a closer look in the intermediate and junior high grades. For now, the curriculum should pique their interest, focus on key historical issues, and begin to give them some points of reference.

In these first few years, history should be taught as a great story, with myths, legends, folktales, biographies of famous men and women, and thrilling episodes from the past. Since very young children do not have a developed sense of chronology, it makes little sense to insist that they memorize lots of dates. By the end of third grade, however, they should have gained a familiarity with some different eras and begun to develop a basic chronological sense of events. They should get a feel for "what life was like" and "who did what" through stories and activities that let them "visit" people in other times and places. They should learn basic lessons about the traditions of our own and other societies. They should be capable of posing questions about different aspects of human life, and finding answers in their forays into the past: What have different peoples believed about fairness and justice? What did they consider beautiful? Noble? Disgraceful? How have ideas about what makes a hero changed, or stayed the same, over time?

In good schools, children get ample experience working with maps, globes, and other tools of geography. They study maps of the United States and foreign lands as they learn their history lessons. They learn basic terms such as "peninsula," "equator," and "delta," as well as "map facts"—where Washington, D.C., and the Atlantic Ocean are located, for example. They learn concepts such as location, direction, and distance. Teachers prod them to think about ideas such as how the physical environment affects the way people live, and how human activity, in turn, shapes the land.

Learning geography doesn't mean students spend all day memorizing lists of rivers and mountain ranges, although some memory work is fine. Good teachers draw on a variety of techniques to impart knowledge about the planet. For very young children, geography should be a hands-on activity—coloring and drawing maps, and playing games that involve connecting names and places. Good teachers also know that one of the best ways to help a child remember a place is to associate it with an interesting person or exciting story.

Civics education teaches youngsters about being good citizens of the class and school. Children learn how to follow rules and the consequences of breaking them. They practice simple civic virtues such as taking turns and sharing, assuming responsibility for classroom chores, being careful of others' belongings, and respecting the truth. Students also begin to learn what being an American citizen is all about. They learn about some national symbols and stories that tie us together—Plymouth Rock, the White House, Ben Franklin flying his kite, the legend of Betsy Ross sewing the first flag. In good schools, young children study some basics about American democracy. They find out, for example, what "voting" and "elections" are, and begin to develop a sense of why democracy is good. All of these lessons are important. Whether or not they are taught well can have much to do with what kind of citizen your child will grow up to be.

KINDERGARTEN

Kindergarten introduces students to some interesting people and exciting events from history. Using simple maps and globes, children encounter basic geographic terms and concepts. They discuss questions about our system of government such as "What is a president?" and "Why would people want to rule themselves instead of being ruled by a faraway king?" They are introduced to some American symbols and customs. Kindergartners learn about topics such as:

World History and Geography

- what rivers, lakes, and mountains are, and how they are represented on maps
- locations of the Atlantic and Pacific oceans, the North and South poles
- the seven continents and some landmarks, wildlife, etc., on each (e.g., penguins in Antarctica, Eiffel Tower in Europe)

American History and Geography

Geography
- names and locations of hometown and state
- location of the United States

Native Americans
- people and ways of at least one tribe (e.g., Apache, Shoshone, Cherokee)

Early Exploration and Settlement
- voyage of Columbus in 1492
- Pilgrims and Thanksgiving Day celebration
- Independence Day as the birthday of our nation
- slavery in early America

Presidents, Past and Present
- George Washington as "Father of His Country"
- Thomas Jefferson as author of Declaration of Independence
- Abraham Lincoln as "Honest Abe"
- Teddy Roosevelt
- current U.S. president

Symbols and Figures
- some famous symbols (e.g., American flag, Mount Rushmore, the White House)

(drawn from the Core Knowledge Sequence)

In a good kindergarten classroom, you might see children:

- drawing pictures about stories of George Washington and Abraham Lincoln to decorate the classroom for Presidents' Day

- passing around an arrowhead as the teacher asks questions: Who do you think made this? How do you think it was made? What could it have been used for?

- looking at illustrations of the United States flag (e.g., at Iwo Jima, at the first moon landing, in front of the school) and talking about ways it has inspired people

- helping the teacher mark on a map the homes of famous people she reads about

- looking in magazines to find pictures of animals that live in Africa

- holding a "Kids'" Congress" in which children nominate and then vote on "the class animal," "the class color," "the class ice cream," etc.

FIRST GRADE

First grade students read and listen to fascinating stories about the past. In world history, they are introduced to early civilizations, addressing questions such as "What is a civilization?" and "Why are rules and laws important to the growth of civilizations?" Since religion is a shaping force in the story of civilization, children are introduced to some of the major world faiths. In American history, children learn highlights of the story of how we went from colonies to a new, vibrant nation. They get regular work with maps and study geography that relates to historical topics. First graders study topics such as:

World History and Geography

Geography
- map keys, symbols, and terms (e.g., peninsula, island)
- directions on a map: north, south, east, west
- locations of the major oceans
- locations of Canada, United States, Mexico, Central America
- more features of maps and globes (e.g., equator, North and South poles)

Early Civilizations
- Mesopotamia as the "Cradle of Civilization" (e.g., Code of Hammurabi)
- ancient Egypt (e.g., pyramids, hieroglyphics)

History of World Religions
- Judaism (e.g., story of the Exodus, symbol of Star of David)
- Christianity (e.g., story of Jesus, symbol of the cross)
- Islam (e.g., story of Muhammad, symbol of crescent and star)

Modern Civilization and Culture: Mexico
- geography of Mexico (e.g., Yucatan Peninsula, Mexico City)
- culture of Mexico (e.g., Indian and Spanish heritage)

American History and Geography

Early People and Civilizations
- hunters and nomads (e.g., gradual development of villages and cities)
- Maya, Inca, and Aztec civilizations

Early Exploration and Settlement
- Spanish conquistadors (e.g., Cortés, Pizarro)
- early English settlements (e.g., Jamestown, Plymouth colony)
- plantations and slavery in the Southern colonies
- Puritans in New England

The American Revolution
- famous episodes (e.g., Paul Revere's ride, Boston Tea Party)
- famous people (e.g., Ben Franklin, Martha Washington)
- signing of the Declaration of Independence

Early Exploration of the American West
- Daniel Boone and the Wilderness Road
- Lewis and Clark, Sacajawea
- geography (e.g., Appalachians, Mississippi River, Rockies)

Symbols and Figures
- famous symbols (e.g., Liberty Bell, eagle)

(drawn from the Core Knowledge Sequence)

In a good first grade classroom, you might see children:

- examining how the Golden Rule has been expressed by various religions and cultures, and talking about how to treat others

- painting a mural of Egyptian pyramid construction
- making a clay map of Mexico
- learning which famous Americans' faces appear on coins and bills
- helping the teacher keep a time line showing the different stories she has read to the class
- making a simple map of the community with correct labels

SECOND GRADE

Second grade continues the work of introducing students to great civilizations and major religions, as well as significant events in U.S. history. Students learn that immigrants have come to this land for many reasons, and that many people have struggled to make sure that the proposition that "all men are created equal" applies to all citizens. They talk about such questions as "What are some basic functions of American government?" Children build map skills and think about geography as they study historical topics. Second graders study topics such as:

World History and Geography

World Geography
- geography of Asia (e.g., location of Himalaya mountains)
- more geographic terms (e.g., coast, valley, desert)

Early Civilizations: Asia
- India (e.g., Hinduism, Buddhism, Ganges River)
- China (e.g., teachings of Confucius, Great Wall, invention of paper)

Modern Civilization and Culture: Japan
- geography of Japan (e.g., Tokyo, Mount Fuji)
- traditional customs and modern ways (e.g., kimonos, life in cities today)

Ancient Greece
- geography (e.g., Aegean Sea, Crete)
- famous stories (e.g., race from Marathon, conquests of Alexander)
- Athens and the beginnings of democracy
- famous thinkers (e.g., Socrates, Plato)

American History and Geography

American Government: The Constitution
- the Constitution as basis of our government
- James Madison, "Father of the Constitution"
- government by consent of the governed

War of 1812
- causes of war (e.g., impressment of American sailors)
- famous battles and events (e.g., Dolley Madison and Washington's portrait)

Westward Expansion
- pioneers heading west (e.g., Oregon Trail, Pony Express)
- new means of travel (e.g., canals, railroads)
- Native Americans (e.g., Sequoyah, Trail of Tears)

The Civil War
- controversy over slavery, North versus South
- famous figures of the war (e.g., Grant and Lee, Clara Barton)
- Lincoln and keeping the union together
- Emancipation Proclamation and the end of slavery

Immigration and Citizenship
- why immigrants come to America (e.g., freedom, opportunity)
- Ellis Island and the Statue of Liberty
- what it means to be an American citizen (e.g., right to vote and hold public office)

Civil Rights: Famous Events and People
- Jackie Robinson in major league baseball
- Rosa Parks and the Montgomery bus boycott
- Martin Luther King, Jr., and the dream of equal rights for all

Geography of the Americas
- North American geography (e.g., Gulf of Mexico, Great Lakes)
- the fifty states
- South American geography (e.g., Brazil, Andes mountains)

(drawn from the Core Knowledge Sequence)

In a good second grade classroom, you might see children:

- illustrating some sayings of Confucius
- dramatizing the death of Socrates
- reading a simple biography of Francis Scott Key, and then telling the class how he came to write "The Star-Spangled Banner"
- writing an imaginary journal entry of a girl or boy on a wagon train headed to California
- practicing the difference between direct democracy (the whole class voting on some rules for the day) and representative democracy (the class electing a smaller group to make rules)
- putting together little books about their own family backgrounds, including interviews with older family members, family photos, and maps of countries their ancestors came from

THIRD GRADE

Third grade students build on their earlier study of Greece to learn about ancient Rome. They also study the Vikings, including their early explorations of North America. In this grade, children begin a more detailed, chronological study of U.S. history. They learn about the thirteen colonies before the Revolution, including some differences between the Southern, New England, and Mid-Atlantic colonies. Children use maps frequently and learn about the geography of historical topics covered. Third graders study topics such as:

World History and Geography

World Geography
- more geographic terms (e.g., boundary, delta, strait)
- how to measure distances on a map with a bar scale
- use of atlas and online resources to find geographic information
- geography of Canada (e.g., Montreal, Hudson Bay)
- important world rivers (e.g., Amazon, Indus, Rhine)

Ancient Rome
- geography of Mediterranean region (e.g., Asia Minor, Persian Gulf)
- exciting stories of Rome (e.g., legend of Romulus and Remus, destruction of Pompeii)

- famous figures (e.g., Julius Caesar, Cleopatra)
- "decline and fall" (e.g., legend of Nero fiddling as Rome burns)
- rise of Byzantine Empire (e.g., Constantinople, Justinian's Code)

The Vikings
- Viking life (e.g., sailing, trading, raiding)
- Viking explorers (e.g., Erik the Red, Leif Eriksson)

American History and Geography

Earliest Americans
- crossing the Bering Strait land bridge
- early Native Americans (e.g., Pueblos, Cherokee Confederacy)

Early Exploration of North America
- Spanish explorers (e.g., Ponce de León, Hernando de Soto)
- founding of St. Augustine
- Spanish settlement of Southwest (e.g., legend of the "Seven Cities of Gold")
- search for the Northwest Passage (e.g., John Cabot, Henry Hudson)

The Thirteen Colonies Before the Revolution
- geography of the colonies (e.g., differences in climate, agricultural systems)
- Southern colonies (e.g., tobacco in Virginia; rice and indigo plantations in South Carolina)
- New England colonies (e.g., Pilgrims and Puritans in Massachusetts; Roger Williams and Anne Hutchinson in Rhode Island)
- Mid-Atlantic colonies (e.g., Dutch settlement in New York; William Penn and Quakers in Pennsylvania)

(drawn from the Core Knowledge Sequence)

In a good third grade classroom, you might see children:

- acting out a brief play they've written about the assassination of Julius Caesar
- building cardboard models of Viking ships, based on readings the class has done
- marking on maps the routes of the early explorers of America such as Verrazano and Coronado
- discussing the different reasons that early settlers came to America

- reading aloud brief essays on a day in the life of a Puritan child, and talking about how it was different from life today
- identifying some differences among the Southern, New England, and Mid-Atlantic colonies (such as the use of slavery in the South and the growth of maritime trade in New England)

Is Your School Teaching Historical Literacy?

Here are examples of names, places, events, and phrases that children should learn about in the primary grades. If your school is doing a good job teaching history and geography, your child should be able to identify most of them by the time she finishes third grade.

- Pharaohs—rulers of ancient Egypt
- Alexander the Great—empire-building king of Macedonia
- Parthenon—great temple in Athens
- Roman Forum—center of public business in ancient Rome
- Julius Caesar—great Roman general and statesman
- Great Wall of China—longest wall in the world, built to keep out invaders
- Leif Eriksson—Viking explorer who reached North America
- *Niña, Pinta, Santa María*—Christopher Columbus's ships
- Pocahontas—friend of Jamestown settlement; saved Captain John Smith's life
- Plymouth Colony—the Pilgrims' settlement
- "Author of the Declaration of Independence"—Thomas Jefferson
- "Father of his country"—George Washington, first president
- Minutemen—citizen-soldiers ready to fight at a moment's notice in Revolutionary War
- Lewis and Clark and Sacajawea—explored the continent to the Pacific Ocean
- Trail of Tears—path of Cherokee Indians when they were forced west
- The Alamo—old mission where Texans fought the Mexican army for independence
- Harriet Tubman—heroine of the Underground Railroad
- "Honest Abe"—Abraham Lincoln, president during Civil War
- Susan B. Anthony—fought for women's right to vote

- Thomas Edison—great American inventor (phonograph, electric light)
- "I have a dream"—words of Martin Luther King, Jr., during the March on Washington
- Democracy—government by the people
- Pledge of Allegiance—your child should know by heart
- "The Star-Spangled Banner—your child should be able to sing it
- "E Pluribus Unum"—national motto: Out of many, one
- The White House—home of the president in Washington, D.C.

Questions to Ask the Teacher

In the primary grades, you may want to ask the teacher questions such as:

- What is the main purpose in social studies lessons? How much attention is paid to history and geography?
- What famous stories, myths, and legends about the past will my child learn this year?
- Which heroes from history will she learn about?
- How do you help children begin to get a feel for the chronological sequence of historical eras and events?
- Can you help me understand the school's history curriculum for the coming years? (For example, in which grades will my child get a chronological look at U.S. history?)
- What geography lessons will my child learn in the coming months? What maps will she study? What terms and skills will she learn?
- How do you teach children about democracy? What will my child learn about how government works in America?
- What lessons will help my child learn about the rights and responsibilities of a good citizen?
- What can I do at home to interest my child in history and to reinforce what you're doing in class?

The Intermediate Grades—Fourth
Through Sixth Grades

In the intermediate grades, good teachers still use exciting stories to capture children's imaginations, while supplementing with more analysis and reflection. Students can also be expected to gain more detailed knowledge—such as what happened at Yorktown, what the Articles of Confederation were, and how checks and balances work. They should be ready to interpret specifics in light of broader themes and concepts, and to develop a more nuanced understanding of why things happen—how the surface of the earth has affected where cities have sprung up, or what factors led Columbus to set sail for the unknown. They should develop increasingly sophisticated habits of thought and inquiry—looking for clues, weighing evidence, comparing different perspectives.

As in the primary years, this model curriculum is broken into two broad strands in each grade: world history and geography, and American history and geography. In world history, students (having been introduced to ancient civilizations in the K–3 years) examine the legacy of enduring ideas from these cultures. That includes some ideas of Judaism and Christianity that have had profound influences on the shaping of this country—concepts about law and social responsibility, for example. The aim is not to preach but rather to understand the pivotal place of religion and religious ideas in history.

Children study the history of Western civilization in chronological fashion. They look at the Middle Ages, the Renaissance and Reformation, the Enlightenment, and the Industrial Revolution. World history topics include China's dynasties, early and medieval African kingdoms, Mesoamerican civilizations, and feudal Japan. Children address such questions as: How do we know about these past civilizations? What made their cultures flourish? What made them change? What do their art and literature tell us about them? How did they interact? In addition to important historical events and figures, students examine the everyday lives of people in different times and places.

In American history, intermediate grade students continue the chronological investigation that began in the third grade. Along the way, they take up questions such as: What made the "American experiment" unique? Why did so many Americans keep moving west? How does the Civil War relate to the ideals expressed by our Founding Fathers? They examine basic principles of American democracy, both in historical context and in terms of today's issues—ideas such as the rule of law and that "all men are created equal." They look at some documents, such as the Preamble to the Constitution, that laid the foundations of American ideals. They revisit questions such as: Why does a society need laws? Who makes the laws in the United States? Where do they get the authority to make those laws?

By end of the intermediate grades, children should be comfortable reading and using maps. They should know some specific map facts—such as the name of each state's capital. They should be familiar with terms such as "elevation," "topography," and "tributary." During these years, children learn to ask questions such as: How has that river affected political boundaries? What has it meant to the economy of the region? What responsibilities do the people upstream have to those downstream? In this respect, geography draws in history, civics, and some informal economics.

FOURTH GRADE

Fourth grade students learn about Europe in the Middle Ages. Building on their introduction to Islam in first grade, they read and hear more about Islamic civilization. They study some early and medieval African kingdoms. In U.S. history, children explore the American Revolution. They take a closer look at the Declaration of Independence, the Constitution, the difficult task of establishing democratic government, and some basic principles of American democracy. Fourth graders study topics such as:

World History and Geography

World Geography
- how to read maps using longitude and latitude
- more map features (e.g., time zones, International Date Line)
- relief maps
- major mountains and ranges (e.g., Mount Everest, Alps)

Europe in the Middle Ages
- geography of Western Europe (e.g., English Channel, Danube River)
- invasions after the fall of Rome (e.g., Visigoths, Attila the Hun)
- role of the Christian Church (e.g., rise of monasteries, Charlemagne)
- feudalism (e.g., lords and vassals; code of chivalry)
- growth of towns (e.g., guilds and apprentices)
- England (e.g., Magna Carta, beginnings of Parliament)

The Spread of Islam and the "Holy Wars"
- Muhammad the Prophet; Allah; the Koran
- Islamic culture (e.g., the "Five Pillars," Arabic numerals)

- wars between Muslims and Christians (e.g., Crusades, Saladin, Richard the Lion-Hearted)

Early and Medieval African Kingdoms
- early African kingdoms (e.g., Kush, Axum)
- medieval kingdoms of the Sudan (e.g., Ghana, Mali, Songhai)
- geography of Africa (e.g., Sahara desert, Congo River)

China: Dynasties and Conquerors
- early dynasties (e.g., Han, Tang, Song dynasties)
- Mongol invasions and rule (e.g., Genghis Khan, Kublai Khan, Marco Polo)
- Ming dynasty (e.g., the "Forbidden City," explorations of Zheng He)

American History and Geography

The Revolution
- French and Indian War
- causes and provocations of Revolution (e.g., British taxes, Boston Massacre)
- famous events (e.g., Valley Forge, Yorktown)
- famous figures (e.g., Nathan Hale, Lafayette)

Making a Constitutional Government
- main ideas of Declaration of Independence (e.g., "all men are created equal")
- making a new government (e.g., Constitutional Convention)
- principles of the Constitution (e.g., separation of powers, checks and balances, Bill of Rights)
- basic functions of government (at local, state, and national levels)

Early Presidents and Politics
- Washington as first president
- establishment of national capital
- growth of political parties (e.g., Jefferson versus Hamilton; modern-day system)
- highlights of presidencies through Andrew Jackson (e.g., Louisiana Purchase, Monroe Doctrine)

Reformers
- abolitionists (e.g., Frederick Douglass, William Lloyd Garrison)
- women's rights (e.g., Seneca Falls convention, Lucretia Mott)
- Dorothea Dix and the mentally ill

Symbols and Figures
- famous symbols (e.g., Great Seal of the United States, U.S. Capitol building)

(drawn from the Core Knowledge Sequence)

In a good fourth grade history class, students get assignments such as:

- Participate in a class discussion comparing the role of religion and faith in medieval Europe, Africa, and China.

- Describe some of the obligations of lords and vassals under feudalism in Europe.

- Write an "eyewitness report" about the Boston Tea Party from the perspective of a patriot.

- Write a report about the same event from the viewpoint of a loyalist.

- Take part in a mock Constitutional Convention, with students taking the roles of various delegates and explaining their states' positions on key issues.

- Following a field trip to city hall and the county courthouse, write a report on how some of the functions of government studied in class are put into actual practice.

- Find the point 20° N 80° E on world maps centered on the equator, the North Pole, and the South Pole.

How Are American Fourth Graders Doing?

Here are two examples of U.S. history questions given to fourth graders on the National Assessment of Educational Progress in 1994:

1. Which of these was one of the thirteen colonies that fought the American Revolution against the British?

A. Illinois	C. New York
B. California	D. Texas

National result: 32 percent of fourth graders chose the correct answer, C.

2. *I have a dream that one day this nation will rise up and live out the true meaning of its creed: "We hold these truths to be self-evident; that all men are created equal."*

I have a dream that one day on the red hills of Georgia the sons of former slaves and the sons of former slaveowners will be able to sit down together at the table of brotherhood.

I have a dream that my four little children will one day live in a nation where they will never be judged by the color of their skin but by the content of their character.

I have a dream that one day . . . little black boys and black girls will be able to join hands with little white boys and girls and walk together as sisters and brothers.

The speech was given by:

A. Abraham Lincoln   C. George Bush
B. Gloria Steinem   D. Martin Luther King, Jr.

National result: 87 percent of fourth graders chose the correct answer, D.

FIFTH GRADE

Fifth grade students, having been introduced to ancient Mesoamerican civilizations in the first grade, now take a closer look at their achievements and ways of life. They continue the chronological study of European history, beginning with the Age of Exploration. They learn about the Renaissance as the "rebirth" of ideas from classical civilizations; the Reformation; and some highlights of English and Russian history. They also study feudal Japan. In U.S. history, students learn about Westward Expansion, the Civil War, and Reconstruction. As always, children acquire geographic knowledge and skills as they study historical topics. Fifth graders study topics such as:

World History and Geography

World Geography
- climate zones: Arctic, Temperate, Tropical
- great lakes of the world (e.g., Caspian Sea, Lake Victoria)

Mesoamerican Civilizations
- geography of Central and South America (e.g., Amazon River, Argentina)

- Maya, Inca, and Aztec civilizations (e.g., Mayan calendar, Machu Picchu)
- Spanish conquerors (e.g., effects of diseases on native peoples)

European Exploration, Trade, and the Clash of Cultures
- motivations for exploration and trade (e.g., spices and silk, spread of Christianity)
- explorations and colonization (e.g., Vasco da Gama, Magellan)
- trade and slavery (e.g., Dutch East India Company, "triangular trade")

The Renaissance and the Reformation
- rise of Italian city-states (e.g., Florence and the Medici family)
- great artists (e.g., Leonardo da Vinci, Michelangelo)
- values of the Renaissance (such as found in Machiavelli's *The Prince*)
- Protestant Reformation (e.g., Martin Luther and the Ninety-five Theses)

England from the Golden Age to the Glorious Revolution
- reigns of Henry VIII and Elizabeth I
- naval dominance (e.g., defeat of the Spanish Armada)
- the English Revolution and the Glorious Revolution
- Cromwell, the Puritans, and the Restoration

Russia: Early Growth and Expansion
- Russia as successor to Byzantine Empire and culture
- great Russian rulers (e.g., Peter the Great, Catherine the Great)
- geography of Russia (e.g., Ural mountains, Siberia)

Feudal Japan
- shoguns and samurai
- Buddhism and Shintoism
- geography of Japan (e.g., Sea of Japan, four main islands)

American History and Geography

Westward Expansion Before the Civil War
- early explorations and pioneers (e.g., Daniel Boone, Santa Fe Trail)
- Indian resistance (e.g., Battle of Tippecanoe)
- Conflict with Mexico (e.g., the Alamo and the Mexican War)
- Manifest Destiny

The Civil War: Causes, Conflicts, Consequences
- causes and precursors (e.g., slavery, John Brown's raid, Lincoln-Douglas debates)
- key leaders, events of the war (e.g., Robert E. Lee, Gettysburg, Sherman's march)
- Reconstruction of the South (e.g., carpetbaggers, rise of Ku Klux Klan)
- Thirteenth, Fourteenth, and Fifteenth Amendments to the Constitution

Westward Expansion After the Civil War
- moving west (e.g., homesteaders, Transcontinental Railroad)
- the Wild West (e.g., cowboys, Jesse James, Annie Oakley)
- Indian cultures and conflicts (e.g., Little Big Horn, Wounded Knee)

U.S. Geography
- major geographic features (e.g., Gulf Stream's effect on climate)
- U.S. regions and their characteristics (e.g., New England, Midwest, Southwest)
- the fifty state capitals

(drawn from the Core Knowledge Sequence)

In a good fifth grade history class, students get assignments such as:

- Explain why the Aztecs, who greatly outnumbered the Spanish, were nevertheless conquered by them.
- After reading brief biographies of Copernicus and Galileo, write a brief essay about what can happen when people challenge traditional views.
- Join a class discussion about how the classical world's regard for balance and order is reflected in Renaissance art.
- Read two articles from 1859 about John Brown's Raid, one from a Northern newspaper and the other from a Southern newspaper, and write a brief essay contrasting these accounts.
- Examine some Mathew Brady photographs and use them to give a short report on consequences of the Civil War.
- Compile a first-person journal of an immigrant laborer helping to build the Transcontinental Railroad.

Does My Child Know the Map?

Knowing where things are isn't all there is to geography, but it's important. By the time your child finishes elementary school, she should be able to locate most of these places:

Bodies of Water

Pacific, Atlantic, Indian, and
    Arctic oceans
Caribbean Sea
Mediterranean Sea
Red Sea

Mountain Ranges

Alps
Andes
Himalayas
Rockies

Deserts

Sahara
Gobi
Mojave
Great Arabian

Rivers

Amazon
Nile
Mississippi
Tigris and Euphrates

Islands

Cuba
Great Britain
Greenland
Hawaii

Countries

Brazil
China
Italy
South Africa

Cities	Man-made Landmarks
London	Eiffel Tower
Mexico City	Egyptian pyramids
Tokyo	Panama Canal
Washington, D.C.	Statue of Liberty

SIXTH GRADE

Sixth grade students deepen their knowledge of some topics to which they were introduced in earlier grades. They examine our legacy from some ancient civilizations, including durable ideas about democracy, government, right and wrong. World history then picks up the chronological thread (from fifth grade) with a look at the Enlightenment, the French Revolution, Romanticism, and Latin American independence movements. The story continues in U.S. history with studies of industrialism and its consequences. As in all grades, history and geography lessons go hand in hand, and civics frequently reappears. Sixth graders study topics such as:

World History and Geography

World Geography
- more map features (e.g., Prime Meridian, Arctic and Antarctic circles)
- great deserts of the world (e.g., Gobi, Mojave)

Lasting Ideas from Ancient Civilizations
- Judaism (e.g., concepts of law, justice, and social responsibility)
- Christianity (e.g., ideas from the Sermon on the Mount)
- Greek democracy and philosophy (e.g., the *polis* and Athenian assembly)
- classical ideals of life and work (e.g., the "Golden Age" of Pericles)
- Roman Republic (e.g., consuls, tribunes, and senators)
- Roman Empire (e.g., rule of law, Julius Caesar)

The Enlightenment
- faith in science and reason (e.g., Newton and the laws of nature)
- views of human nature (e.g., Thomas Hobbes, John Locke)
- influences on beginnings of U.S. (e.g., idea of "natural rights")

The French Revolution
- causes and precursors (e.g., the three estates, Versailles)
- major figures and events (e.g., Marie Antoinette, fall of the Bastille)
- reign of Napoleon (e.g., invasion of Russia, Waterloo)

Romanticism
- main ideas and figures (e.g., Jean-Jacques Rousseau)
- Romanticism in literature, art, and music

Industrialism, Capitalism, and Socialism
- the Industrial Revolution (e.g., factory system and its effects)
- capitalism (e.g., Adam Smith, law of supply and demand)
- socialism (e.g., Marx's theory of class struggle, denial of private property)

Latin American Independence Movements
- key revolutions and figures (e.g., Benito Juárez, Simón Bolívar, José de San Martín)
- geography of Central and South America (e.g., rain forests, major cities)

American History and Geography

Immigration, Industrialization, and Urbanization
- nineteenth century migrations (e.g., Irish potato famine, "The New Colossus," "melting pot")
- America as the "land of opportunity" versus resistance to immigrants
- the Gilded Age (e.g., Horatio Alger, industrial cities, political bosses)
- growth of organized labor (e.g., sweat shops, Haymarket Square)
- rise of big business (e.g., Andrew Carnegie, J.P. Morgan)
- free enterprise versus government regulation (e.g., Sherman Antitrust Act)

Reform Movements
- Progressive era (e.g., muckraking, Jane Addams)
- reform for African-Americans (e.g., Booker T. Washington, W.E.B. Du Bois)

- women's suffrage (e.g., Susan B. Anthony, Nineteenth Amendment)

(drawn from the Core Knowledge Sequence)

In a good sixth grade history class, students get assignments such as:

- Tell how some of the main ideas from Judaism, Christianity, ancient Greece, and ancient Rome have influenced American ideals and our system of government.

- Participate in a class debate about what lessons we might draw for modern society from Rome's decline and fall.

- Write a biographical sketch of Simón Bolívar and his contribution to history.

- Research and write a paper about life around 1900 in a Chinese community in San Francisco.

- Using copies of newspaper articles and editorials from the early twentieth century, list some arguments given at that time for and against women's suffrage.

- Play a role in a panel discussion in which some "great thinkers" (e.g., Plato, Locke, Marx) discuss their philosophies of human nature.

Is My Child Geographically Literate?

This is a challenging list of geography terms. If your child can explain what most of them mean by the end of elementary school, her teachers have done a good job of making her geographically literate.

- bay—an inlet from the sea or other large body of water
- canal—a man-made waterway built to carry goods or water
- canyon—a deep, narrow valley with steep sides
- delta—a fan-shaped deposit of sand, mud, silt, or other material at the mouth of a river
- equator—imaginary line encircling the earth halfway between the North and South poles
- floodplain—level land that may be submerged during flood times
- glacier—a large, long-lasting body of ice that advances slowly down a slope
- gulf—a large part of an ocean or sea extending into the land

- isthmus—a narrow strip of land between two bodies of water, joining two larger land areas
- oasis—a fertile spot in the desert
- peninsula—a piece of land sticking into the water
- plain—a large area of level or gently rolling land
- plateau—an area of generally level land that is elevated above the land around it
- reef—a chain of rocks or coral lying near the surface of the water
- reservoir—an artificial lake where water is stored
- strait—a narrow body of water connecting two larger bodies of water
- swamp—saturated, low-lying land where trees and shrubs grow; surface water is present at least part of the year
- tributary—a stream that feeds a larger stream or a lake

Is Your School Teaching Basic Economics?

Your child probably won't take a class on economics until high school or even college. Nevertheless, good elementary schools teach some fundamental terms and principles. Here are some basic lessons that children should learn in elementary school:

- different kinds of work people do and the names of their jobs
- using money as a way to exchange goods and services
- difference between money and barter economies
- difference between paying by cash, check, and credit
- difference between consumers and producers
- limited resources means that people must make choices
- money can increase in value by investing
- illustrations of supply and demand (e.g., when an item is plentiful or unpopular, it is often cheap)
- prices influence people's buying decisions (e.g., if the cost of something goes up, people may be less willing to buy it)
- if someone concentrates on making just one thing, he can produce it more efficiently
- difference between human resources (people working), natural resources (coal deposits, forests, etc.), and capital resources (machines, tools, etc.)
- prices of goods are influenced by factors such as the cost of raw materials, labor, tools, and transportation

- competition often makes goods cheaper and better
- role of unions
- ways governments can affect economies (e.g., taxation, regulation)
- economic incentives often have powerful effects on human behavior
- entrepreneurship and hard work have been crucial to America's economic success

---

Questions to Ask the Teacher

In the intermediate grades, you may want to ask the teacher questions such as:

- What parts of American or world history will my child study this year?
- What cultures and traditions will she learn about?
- When will my child learn the history of this state?
- Will there be any field trips to learn about local history?
- What are some examples of basic historical knowledge (important dates, names, events, etc.) that my child will be expected to recall?
- What important figures from U.S. history will the class study?
- What primary sources (documents, music, art, artifacts, etc.) will my child be using?
- What countries, cities, rivers, etc., should she be able to identify on the map by the term's end? What geographic concepts and skills will you be teaching?
- Will students be responsible for knowing the names and locations of the fifty states and the names of their capitals? Names and locations of major cities?
- Will my child be taught the basic stories of American and Western civilization in this school? Will she get some exposure to some non-Western cultures, too?
- How will the school help teach my child to be proud of her country?
- What can we do at home to deepen her understanding of history and geography and to reinforce what you're doing in class?

Junior High—Seventh and Eighth Grades

In the primary and intermediate grades, this model history curriculum is divided into distinct world and American strands. By the junior high years, these strands have merged. Generally speaking, studies in seventh and eighth grades cover the twentieth century, beginning around the time America became a world power and moving through post–Cold War challenges. Central themes include growth and change in American democracy, and interactions with world forces, particularly nationalism and totalitarianism.

In grade eight, students get a unit on civics. They review what they've learned about the principles of American democracy, then take a closer look at the Constitution and at how government functions in this country.

As children study events that have taken place beyond our borders, they become familiar with America's role in the unfolding of world affairs. They also study the history, geography, and achievements of other nations and cultures.

One overarching goal of studying world history should be to come to know the grand story of mankind's age-old endeavors: the struggle of people to survive, to dominate others or gain freedom, to build or tear down, to better themselves, to find spiritual meaning. History should help students see how people in other times and places have faced profound questions of truth, justice, and personal responsibility; what they have judged to be worth striving and even dying for; how they have persevered or succumbed when severely tested. Students should come to see that, in the course of human events, ideas have had real consequences, as have the efforts of individuals. Children should have the chance to ponder some of the great questions that history poses: What makes societies last or fall apart? What are the causes of economic success? What roles do religious beliefs play in the affairs of men? From all of this, students should gain a knowledge of the many differences that exist among the world's peoples, as well as the shared humanity that transcends time and place.

SEVENTH GRADE

Seventh grade continues the chronological study of world and American history. The curriculum begins with the emergence of the U.S. as a world power around the turn of the twentieth century. Students then learn about World War I, the Russian Revolution, America in the 1920s, the New Deal, and World War II. In concert with these topics, children learn the geography of Europe, Japan, and the United States. Seventh graders study topics such as:

America Becomes a World Power

- Spanish-American War (e.g., Teddy Roosevelt and the Rough Riders)
- Complications of imperialism (e.g., war with the Philippines)
- Building the Panama Canal

Geography of Western and Central Europe

- main physical features, national boundaries, major cities and capitals, peoples, languages, religions, natural resources, industries, and transportation routes

World War I

- causes and antecedents (e.g., European nationalism and colonialism)
- key events (e.g., Gallipoli, trench warfare)
- Treaty of Versailles, Wilson's Fourteen Points and the League of Nations

The Russian Revolution

- causes and antecedents (e.g., "Bloody Sunday," economic strains of World War I)
- Revolutions of 1917 and civil war (e.g., Nicholas II and Alexandra, Lenin)
- geography of Russia (e.g., Caspian Sea, Moscow)

America from the 1920s to the New Deal

- Roaring Twenties (e.g., flappers, Prohibition, Lost Generation)
- Culture and technology (e.g., Jazz Age, Lindbergh, motion pictures)
- Great Depression (e.g., Crash of '29, Dust Bowl)
- Roosevelt and the New Deal (e.g., Social Security, growth of unions)

World War II

- rise of totalitarianism (e.g., Mussolini, Stalin, Hitler)
- war in Europe and Pacific (e.g., Pearl Harbor, Battle of Midway, D-Day)

- war at home (e.g., rationing, "Rosie the Riveter")
- the Holocaust (e.g., Dachau, Anne Frank)
- the atomic bomb (e.g., Manhattan Project, Hiroshima)
- end of the war (e.g., Nuremberg trials, creation of United Nations)

Geography of the United States

- physical features (e.g., Atlantic coastal plain, Death Valley)
- population distributions and major cities
- regional characteristics (e.g., Sun Belt, West Coast, Mason-Dixon line)

(drawn from the Core Knowledge Sequence)

In a good seventh grade history class, students get assignments such as:

- Write an editorial either favoring or opposing United States participation in the League of Nations.

- Do a "radio broadcast" ("Live from Harlem") on the Harlem Renaissance in the 1920s, including samples of literature and music.

- Using the stock market pages from the newspaper, think of two good questions to ask a stockbroker who is coming to talk with the class about how the market works.

- Name three New Deal agencies and explain their roles in FDR's attempt to revitalize the American economy.

- Research and debate with a classmate the following proposition: "The United States was right to drop the atomic bomb in 1945."

- On a map of the Eastern United States, give examples of how physical features have affected the location of cities, political boundaries, and transportation routes.

EIGHTH GRADE

Eighth grade continues the chronological study of world and American history and brings it nearly to the present. The curriculum begins with the decline of European colonialism and moves through the post–Cold War world. In this grade, students also delve deeper into the principles of the U.S. Constitution and structure of American democracy. In concert with historical subjects, children learn about the geography of several foreign lands. Eighth graders study topics such as:

The Decline of European Colonialism

- breakup of the British Empire (e.g., Gandhi, Indian independence)
- geography of India and South Asia (e.g., Indus and Ganges rivers, monsoons)
- creation of People's Republic of China (e.g., Mao Zedong, the Long March)
- geography of China (e.g., Tibetan plateau, Gobi desert, Hong Kong)

The Cold War

- origins of Cold War (e.g., Berlin Airlift, communist expansion)
- Korean War (e.g., MacArthur, 38th Parallel)
- America in the Cold War (e.g., McCarthyism, Cuban Missile Crisis, moon race)

The Civil Rights Movement

- segregation (e.g., Jim Crow, "separate but equal")
- key events and figures (e.g., March on Washington, Little Rock school integration)
- the Great Society (e.g., War on Poverty, Civil Rights Act of 1964)
- assassinations of Martin Luther King, Jr., and Robert F. Kennedy

The Vietnam War and Rise of Social Activism

- war in Vietnam (e.g., domino theory, antiwar protests)
- Watergate
- social activism (e.g., feminist movement, environmentalist movement)

The Middle East and Oil Politics

- Arab-Israeli tensions (e.g., creation of Israel, Six Day War, Camp David treaty)
- geography of Middle East (e.g., oil fields, West Bank)

The End of the Cold War and Continuing Challenges

- Détente (e.g., diplomatic opening to China)
- breakup of U.S.S.R. (e.g., Solidarity movement, fall of Berlin Wall)

- China under communism (e.g., Cultural Revolution, Tiananmen Square)
- contemporary Europe (e.g., Common Market, new nations of Eastern Europe)
- changes in South Africa (e.g., end of apartheid, Nelson Mandela)

Civics: The Constitution and American Democracy

- principles of democracy (e.g., rule of law, popular sovereignty)
- overview of the Constitution (e.g., separation of powers)
- Bill of Rights (e.g., freedom of speech and religion)
- legislative branch (e.g., how a bill is passed)
- executive branch (e.g., role of the Cabinet)
- judiciary (e.g., role of Supreme Court)

Geography of Canada and Mexico

- geography of Canada (e.g., two official languages, provinces and territories)
- geography of Mexico (e.g., Mexico City, oil and gas fields)

(drawn from the Core Knowledge Sequence)

In a good eighth grade history class, students get assignments such as:

- Fill in the names of the major countries on an unlabeled map of the Middle East.
- "Korea points like a dagger at Japan." Explain how this thinking led to a foreign policy of "containment" and U.S. involvement in the Korean War.
- Read excerpts from Martin Luther King's "Letter from Birmingham City Jail" and talk about why he thought he must break unjust laws "openly, lovingly, and with a willingness to accept the penalty."
- In the late 1970s, toward the end of the Cold War, some politicians talked about the shift from a "bipolar" to a "multipolar" world. Write a persuasive essay explaining what was meant and affirming or denying that this has happened.
- Explain the basic steps in how a bill becomes law.
- Write and perform with classmates a "newscast" on the fall of the Berlin Wall.

How Are American Eighth Graders Doing?

Here are two examples of history questions given to eighth graders on the National Assessment of Educational Progress in 1994:

1. The Lend-Lease Act, the Yalta Conference, and the dropping of the atomic bomb on Hiroshima are all associated with the:

    A. First World War
    B. Second World War

    C. Korean War
    D. Vietnam War

    National result: 41 percent of eighth graders chose the correct answer, B.

The Destruction of Tea at Boston Harbor, N. Currier, 1846. Museum of the City of New York, The Harry T. Peters Collection.

2. Identify the event that is portrayed in the picture above. Why is the event important in United States history?

    National result: 19 percent of eighth graders were able to give an appropriate response by identifying the event as the Boston Tea Party and explaining that it showed colonial resistance to British policies, which in turn led to the American Revolution.

Is Your School Teaching Literacy in American History?

Here are examples of names, places, events, and phrases from American history that children should learn during elementary school. If your school is doing a good job teaching history, your child should be able to identify many of the items on this list by the time she finishes eighth grade.

- Amerigo Vespucci—Italian explorer for whom America is named
- Mayflower Compact—Pilgrims' written agreement about how to govern themselves
- Iroquois Confederacy—powerful alliance of Indian tribes in upper New York
- Lexington and Concord—first skirmishes of Revolutionary War
- "We hold these truths to be self-evident, that all men are created equal . . ." — words of the Declaration of Independence
- Marquis de Lafayette—French nobleman who aided American cause in Revolution
- "We the people of the United States, in order to form a more perfect union . . ."—beginning of Preamble to the U.S. Constitution
- Manifest Destiny—idea that the U.S. was meant to expand west to the Pacific Ocean
- Middle Passage—voyage of slave ships from Africa to America
- '49ers—those who took part in the California gold rush in 1849
- Frederick Douglass—great spokesman for abolitionist cause
- Lincoln-Douglas debates—pre–Civil War debates between Abraham Lincoln and Stephen Douglas about slavery
- Clara Barton—nurse on Civil War battlefields, founder of American Red Cross
- Appomattox, Virginia—scene of Robert E. Lee's surrender to Ulysses S. Grant
- Sitting Bull—chief who called for the Sioux to fight for their land
- Ellis Island—island in New York harbor, historical gateway for immigrants
- Jane Addams—ran Hull House in Chicago to aid the poor and immigrants
- San Juan Hill—battle in Cuba fought by Teddy Roosevelt and his Rough Riders
- Model T—affordable automobile built by Henry Ford
- Kitty Hawk, North Carolina—scene of the Wright brothers' first powered flight
- Suffragists—people who supported women's right to vote

- Pearl Harbor—U.S. naval base in Hawaii attacked by Japanese at outset of World War II
- *Brown v. Board of Education*—1954 Supreme Court decision ending segregation in schools
- "That's one small step for [a] man, one giant leap for mankind"—Neil Armstrong's first words on the moon's surface

Is Your School Teaching Literacy in World History?

Here are some names, places, events, and phrases from world history that children should learn about during elementary school. If your school is doing a good job teaching history, your child should be able to identify many of the items on this list by the end of eighth grade.

- Code of Hammurabi—ancient Babylonian set of laws
- Aristotle—great Greek philosopher
- Rig Veda—ancient, sacred Hindu book of hymns and sayings
- "Land of the Rising Sun"—Japan
- "Et tu, Brute?" ("And you, too, Brutus?")—Julius Caesar's words upon his assassination
- Cleopatra—queen of ancient Egypt
- Mecca—birthplace of Muhammod in Arabia; holiest city in Islam
- Battle of Hastings—key victory of William the Conqueror during Norman Conquest of England
- Magna Carta ("Great Charter")—pledge signed by King John, guaranteeing certain rights and liberties
- Mansa Musa—ruler of the kingdom of Mali
- Black Death—devastating plague that swept Europe in Middle Ages
- Marco Polo—Venetian adventurer who traveled to the court of Kublai Khan in China
- Gutenberg Bible—book printed by Johannes Gutenberg, inventor of the printing press in Europe
- Northwest Passage—much sought after sea route over North America to Asia
- Tenochtitlán—grand Aztec city
- Queen Elizabeth I—great ruler of England during the Renaissance
- "Let them eat cake"—words of Marie Antoinette during French Revolution

- James Watt—inventor of practical steam engine, which helped spark the Industrial Revolution

- José de San Martín—great revolutionary leader of South America

- Florence Nightingale—nurse who treated the British wounded during Crimean War

- Assassination of Archduke Francis Ferdinand—killing that helped trigger World War I

- Bolsheviks—communist revolutionaries of the Russian Revolution

- Third Reich—name that Hitler gave to the era of Nazi rule in Germany

- "We shall fight on the beaches, we shall fight on the landing grounds, we shall fight in the fields and in the streets . . ."—pledge of Winston Churchill during World War II

- Berlin Airlift—relief operation to West Berlin during the Cold War

Is Your Child Learning How American Democracy Works?

The following twenty questions are the type that immigrants must answer to become U.S. citizens. By the time she leaves eighth grade, your child should know enough about the governing principles and institutions of the United States to pass such a "citizenship test."

- What are the three branches of government?

- What are the basic duties of Congress?

- How many senators are there in the U.S. Senate?

- Who are the two senators from your state?

- For how long do we elect representatives to the U.S. House of Representatives?

- What are the basic duties of the Supreme Court?

- Who selects the Supreme Court justices?

- Who is your current state governor?

- How many terms can a president serve?

- What is the minimum voting age in the United States?

- Who signs bills into law?

- Name three rights or freedoms guaranteed by the Bill of Rights.

- What are the first ten amendments to the Constitution called?

- What is the introduction to the Constitution called?

- Who is the commander in chief of the U.S. military?

- Explain the principle of "the rule of law."

- What does "checks and balances" mean?
- What is the Cabinet?
- What do the stars on the flag mean?
- What do the stripes on the flag mean?

Questions to Ask the Teacher

You may want to ask your child's junior high school history teacher questions such as:

- What significant events and individuals from history will my child study this year?
- What important documents (e.g., the Constitution, Gettysburg Address) will she study this year?
- What biographies will she read for history class?
- What important dates do you require students to know?
- Will my child study the ideas of the Founding Fathers, principles of American democracy, and the structure of government in the United States?
- Will my child be learning any fundamental lessons about economics and the free enterprise system?
- How do you balance the need to learn both U.S. and world history? In world history, how do you apportion time and attention among various cultures and civilizations?
- Are you able to use technology to teach about history and geography (for example, by touring famous historical sites via computer)?
- Will this course help my child find some heroes from the past and present, exemplary lives that teach about virtue and how to live a good life?

ISSUES IN THE TEACHING OF HISTORY

The following pages take up some controversies and shortcomings in the teaching of history in American schools. The main problem you may face is that many elementary schools simply don't teach much history at all! Textbook writer Joy Hakim tells of visiting a fourth grade class in Norfolk, Virginia, asking the nine-year-olds what they knew about George Washington, and looking out at a sea of blank faces. "Don't you teach history in the fourth grade?" she asked. "Yes, and there are the books," the teacher answered, pointing to a stack in the corner.

"I've been meaning to get to them, but I have to stick to the important subjects."[4]

The anecdote represents (one hopes) an extreme example, but the sad fact is that a lackadaisical attitude about history is not rare. A 1998 appraisal of state history standards conducted by the Thomas B. Fordham Foundation concludes that "the vast majority of young Americans are attending schools in states that do not consider the study of history to be especially important." It is therefore imperative that you check on how much time and attention your school is devoting to this core subject, and find out exactly what your child is studying.

What Happened to the Story in History?

If your child shows scant interest in her history lessons, do a little investigating. Start by taking a close look at the schoolbooks. Many of today's texts manage to squeeze every last ounce of excitement out of history. They're often badly written and impersonal, full of simplistic language and wooden treatments of what should be exciting events. Lots of photos, colors, and charts crowd the pages; the strategy seems to be to entertain students not with fascinating history but with books that resemble computer games. "We've lost a lot of literary quality as we've replaced the core text with pictures, white space, and all sorts of glossy graphics," says Gilbert Sewall of the American Textbook Council. "Not so long ago there were passages of narrative designed to tell some sort of story of the past. But those seem to have disappeared."[5]

Therein lies a big problem. Once upon a time, school history books told history as a fascinating *story* full of intrigue, struggle, pathos, and triumph. In far too many texts today, that great story is gone. No wonder kids think this subject is boring!

Dull texts are a symptom of what has happened to the teaching of history in many schools. What was once a subject of high drama has morphed into that interdisciplinary tangle called social studies. Many of the great episodes of the past that excite youngsters about history are neglected—or retold in a critical voice that knocks old heroes off their pedestals.

Too often, today's education frowns on history tainted by "romance"—that is, accounts telling of adventure, heroism, and idealism. This shortchanges our young, because the truth is that history is often filled to the brim with romance, particularly when it comes to the great story that is America. As the historian Bernard DeVoto wrote, "If the mad, impossible voyage of Columbus or Cartier or La Salle or Coronado or John Ledyard is not romantic, if the stars did not dance in the sky when our Constitutional Convention met . . . well, I don't know what romance is. Ours is a story mad with the impossible, it is by chaos out of a dream, it began as dream and it has continued as dream down to the last headlines you read in a newspaper. . . . The simplest truth you can ever write about our history will be charged and surcharged with romanticism."[6]

In a sense, history is one great big story made up, like the Arabian Nights, of countless smaller stories, tales of adventure and suspense that transport youngsters across oceans and ages. Especially in the early years of elementary school, that's the way it should be told. This does not mean abandoning facts. It merely means putting the facts in narrative form. It means combining concepts with lively episodes and biographies that capture the imagination of children. The destruction of Pompeii. Washington crossing the Delaware. The mysterious last flight of Amelia Earhart. John Paul Jones hurling his famous reply from the deck of his burning ship: "I have not yet begun to fight!" If great stories like these are missing from your child's education, you can hardly be surprised if she seems uninterested.

Good elementary school teachers make the past come alive in all sorts of ways. They use literature and primary sources—the diary of a nineteenth-century immigrant, or newspapers from the day after John F. Kennedy was shot. They use music and art to teach history, and spice up lessons with field trips to local museums and historical sites. They stage class reenactments of famous events—the surrender at Appomattox, Sally Ride's trip into space, or the death of Mary, Queen of Scots. They invite guest speakers—someone who lived through the Great Depression or landed on the beaches of Normandy. They have children read good biographies and help them find heroes from the past. They get students to focus on key historical issues and to ask themselves questions such as "Why did they think and act the way they did?" Above all, they strive to get the drama and romance—the story—back into history. When lessons are full of lively, challenging accounts, elementary school children aren't likely to be bored.

"Expanding Environments": Will They Expand—or Narrow—Your Child's Education?

For decades, many American elementary schools have followed a social studies sequence in the early grades known as "expanding environments" or "expanding horizons." This approach places less emphasis on stories of long ago and far away and instead concentrates on the close-to-home aspects of students' lives. Basically, it places the child at the center of the universe. Kindergartners typically learn about "myself" (in courses with titles such as "Awareness of Self in a Social Setting"). First graders might study "schools and families" (e.g., "The Individual in Primary Social Groups: Understanding School and Family Life"); second graders might study "my neighborhood"; third graders "my community"; and fourth graders "my state." Children get assignments such as "Take a walk in the neighborhood and tell about it," or "Write about some ways that people depend on others in our community."

This kind of sequence dominates social studies in the early years in many U.S. schools. The consequence, of course, is far less time for stories about the past. As the distinguished education historian Diane Ravitch points out, most American schoolchildren get very little history in the early grades. What they get is tot sociology.[7]

Expanding horizons dates from the 1930s, when educators became convinced that the pain and suffering of the Depression made early study of the distant past less relevant, and that young students should instead be taught about the complex societal forces that had produced their families' plights. The original rationale evaporated long ago, but the sequence held on in the schools and persists to this day. Advocates argue that, by studying themselves and their own world, children build their sense of self and prepare to become members of the community. Furthermore, they insist, young children are not "developmentally" ready to learn about times and places far beyond their immediate perceptions. It's pointless, according to that reasoning, to expect them to absorb lessons about ancient Rome or colonial America.

Many educators will tell you that expanding horizons is based on years of research, but they're stumped when asked to point to any convincing studies. "I asked a dozen leading scholars in the fields of cognitive psychology, child development, and curriculum theory about the matter," Dr. Ravitch reports. "None knew of any research justifying the expanding environments approach; none defended it. All deplored the absence of historical and cultural content in the early grades." While it's true that, in general, learning proceeds from the familiar to the un-familiar, that is no reason to assume young children's interests are con-fined to their immediate surroundings. On the contrary, just watch a child's eye's light up when she hears a story beginning "A long time ago, in a faraway land . . ."

In fact, if anything deadens learning, it's the type of sterile, vapid, nonhistory so many youngsters get nowadays under the heading "social studies." Take this lesson entitled "Our Needs and Wants" from a recent second grade textbook:

Needs are things people must have to live. We all need food to eat. We need clothes to wear. We need shelter, or cover, for pro-tection. We also need love and friendship. Needs are the same for everyone all over the world.

Wants are important, too. Wants are things we would like to have. Different people have different wants. What do you want?[8]

What would you rather read if you were a second grader, that kind of drab prose, or stories of lost cities, brave explorers, daring patriots, and heroes who never quit?

Certainly, youngsters should learn about their schools, neighbor-hoods, and communities. But those topics should not push history and geography aside. In some primary classrooms, teachers have become dis-satisfied with the expanding environments approach and have begun to supplement it with history stories from long ago, folktales from around the world, thrilling biographies, poetry, and songs from different cul-tures. They explore exciting myths and legends, and teach about our nation's past. They spend more time with engaging books that give ba-sic introductions to complex topics such as ancient Egyptian religious beliefs or explorations of the American West. These kinds of activities capture children's attention, stretch their imaginations, and supply foundational knowledge that will support later studies in history. In the first few years of school, talk to your child's teachers, examine the mate-rial they use, and make sure they are truly enhancing—not limiting—your child's chances to glimpse other times and places.

What Is "Social Studies"?

When your child gets to the age at which core subjects are taught in dif-ferent class periods by different teachers (usually in the intermediate grades), one of her courses is likely to be "social studies." You might assume that means studying lots of history along with some geography and civics. Far too often, that isn't the case. Social studies has been called the Great Dismal Swamp of today's school curriculum, a morass of trendy topics, education fads, and political correctness, a place to shape children's attitudes rather than teach them history. Sociology, political science, psychology, sensitivity training, critical thinking, values clarification, decision making, diversity education, environmental education, consumer education—you name it, and it probably comes under the broad umbrella of social studies.

A class in Kansas practices conflict resolution techniques, with students deciding if they are "sharks" (competing), "teddy bears" (accommodating), or "owls" (collaborating). In a Texas schoolroom, children are asked to give "several incidences [sic] in which they have been the recipients or the perpetrators of racial, cultural and/or socioeconomic intolerance." In an Oklahoma school, children play a "post–nuclear war survival" game: there are twelve people in a fallout shelter, but food and water are sufficient for just seven, so students must decide who lives and who dies.

Sometimes social studies activities become chances for educators to grind political axes. In one North Carolina school, fifth graders were given election worksheets that said Democrats "stand up for the poor, factory workers, farmers, women, and minorities," while Republicans "watch out for owners of large businesses . . . and wealthy people." Even when social studies actually means history, it may turn out to be history lite. In some classrooms, children spend much time expressing their personal interpretations of the past (for example, by painting an abstract of how they "feel about" the slave trade). "Hands-on" projects sometimes look suspiciously like busywork; students might glue Popsicle sticks onto milk cartons to make "log cabins" but do little reading about what pioneer life was really like.

Some of the various subjects taken up under the rubric of social studies are, in themselves, instructive and worthwhile. We have no quarrel with children learning how to care for the environment, respect other cultures, and get along with others. Yet, the question arises: Are these subjects crowding out the real study of history? You need to be aware that when your child passes into a class called social studies, she's entering a room in which all sorts of things can go on, some good and some bad. Over the course of elementary school, lessons should consist mostly of history, geography, and civics, with most time and attention given to history. If time is spent on a lot of other stuff instead, your child's education in this area probably resembles the social studies curricula in many American schools: basically a mess.

How Important Are Facts in History?

"Why should students have to identify the Southern Christian Leadership Conference?" a teacher asked a state school board member.

"Because that was Dr. King's organization," the board member replied.

"They can find that in the library," the teacher countered.[9]

This exchange illustrates an attitude, all too common among educators, that disparages the learning of facts, including facts about the past. It's much more important, according to this view, for students to learn to "think critically" and grasp larger lessons about society. "I'd rather they understand the concept of colonialism and imperialism," says a New York education professor, "than to know when Columbus discovered America."[10] The same attitude extends to geography. Just one third of education professors say that kids should be required to know the names and locations of the fifty states before getting a diploma. "Why should they know that?" asks a Los Angeles professor. "When I need to know that, I can go look it up."[11] This approach helps explain why barely one third of our seventeen-year-olds can place the Civil War in the correct half-century, and why so many American young people can't even find the United States on the world map.

Of course teachers should teach thinking skills. Children should learn, for example, how to find places in an atlas, how to make connections among different episodes in history, how to come up with their own thoughtful questions about events that took place long ago. Likewise, they must come to understand important concepts and significant ideas: what freedom of speech means, what institutions such as capitalism and socialism are all about, the various causes of war, and so forth.

None of this should be taken to mean, however, that teachers can't or shouldn't hold children responsible for knowing facts as well. There is no conflict between acquiring knowledge and developing analytic skills. On the contrary: facts, concepts, and thinking are inseparable. Students can scarcely think seriously about history or grasp larger themes if they have no background knowledge to support their reasoning. How can they analyze a 1945 newspaper report about the Yalta conference if they're not sure who Stalin was, or where the Soviet

Union was? Facts are indispensable to real insights and "critical thinking." They inform children's understanding of history and geography.

There is no need to turn history into a grand game of Trivial Pursuit and require students to memorize the population of Mexico or the latitude of Singapore. But there is nothing demeaning about having children learn key dates and names and even memorize a few lists, so long as the point is to help them see how these facts fit into the bigger picture.

You should not be shy about asking your child's teacher what basic information she expects students to acquire and retain. Does she answer in vague terms, or show you fuzzy written standards such as "students will demonstrate how significant events have influenced the past and present in United States history"? Or can she produce some specific goals that spell out just what students are expected to know? Take a look at textbooks, homework, and other materials. Do tests and assignments ever require students to demonstrate a command of specific names, dates, terms, or map locations? Or are they loaded with questions that don't call for factual responses, such as "construct a dialogue between a pioneer and an Indian chief"? These inspections are worth making. They may tell you how much history your child will actually know at the end of the year.

Dates Your Child Should Learn

One specific question you might pose to your child's teacher is: What important dates do you require children to know? You may get a reply such as: "We teach children how to understand history, not just memorize a list of times and places." Translation: "We don't require students to learn any dates at all."

The problem is that history is a story—a complicated one—and to understand the narrative you need some concept of the order and timing of events. Teaching a handful of important dates is an excellent way to help a child get the story line straight. As she meets new characters and subplots in her studies, she'll be able to peg them against a few chronological markers.

Here are some key dates your child should learn as she studies U.S. history. If she can tell you what most of them signify (or, conversely, tell you approximately when the following events occurred), she's probably got a good chronological grasp of the nation's past.

1492—Columbus reaches America
1607, 1620—Jamestown, Plymouth colonies founded

July 4, 1776—Declaration of Independence
1787—Constitutional Convention
1803—Louisiana Purchase
1849—California Gold Rush
1861–65—Civil War
1917—America enters World War I
October 1929—Stock Market Crash
December 7, 1941—Pearl Harbor
Summer of 1963—March on Washington
1989—end of the Cold War (fall of the Berlin Wall)

What Is the Place of Multiculturalism in History Class?

The past few decades have seen a great broadening of history studies in the classroom. Today's children are likely to read about women, minorities, and cultures that were once given less attention or ignored entirely. Overall, this is a healthy development for our schools. Our cultural and ancestral diversity is an important part of our national heritage. It should be studied and celebrated. This should not, however, keep us from teaching students about the common inheritance that binds Americans together.

There are two kinds of "multiculturalism" in the curriculum. One, which we favor, is inclusive; it seeks to incorporate many strands into the fabric of the past, leaving out nobody's part of "the story." All children are expected to learn the whole story, not just their own part. The other kind of multiculturalism, which we believe cheats children and is bad for the nation, encourages students from different backgrounds to learn primarily their own heritage, their own ancestors' part of the story, while slighting or even deprecating everybody else's parts. This brand, in emphasizing what makes us different from one another—as opposed to the history, ideals, and principles that make us one people—is exclusive and divisive. It is worth guarding against.

Another danger in multiculturalism, even the kind we favor, is overcrowding the curriculum, which can lead to some truly important people and events being given short shrift. One recent American history textbook, for example, reduces Thomas Edison's contributions to these four words: "Edison invented electric light." Another disposes of the Wright brothers with a single caption: "U.S. Army buys first airplane from the Wright brothers."[12] In their accounts of the Boston Massacre, several texts now focus on Crispus Attucks, a runaway slave, rather than people such as Samuel Adams, Paul Revere, and John Adams. It is definitely good to teach students that an African-American was among the first to shed blood in the Revolution, but the heavy emphasis often seems to push other pivotal figures to the perimeters of the story.[13]

Nowadays, history textbooks are usually the work of committees that pour tremendous energy into making sure everyone is represented and no one offended. "Social studies is ripe for pressure from a multitude of special interest groups," says Anthony Lucki, president of Harcourt Brace. "It's the most difficult area to publish in, no question about it."[14] Each paragraph is carefully sifted, negotiated, and sanitized. Lists of taboos are drawn up. In some books, for example, "slaves" have become "enslaved persons" on the grounds that slavery was a condition imposed on people, not a part of their essence as human beings. References to "Halloween" are stricken to avoid connotations of witchcraft or satanic practices. "Before, we used to send the books out to scholars," an editor explained to the New York Review of Books. "Now we also send them to one reader for the Islamic point of view, to a feminist, an African-American, an Asian-American, a Native American, and a Christian fundamentalist so that they are carefully screened."

By the time a book makes it through all those strainers, we should not be surprised that it's a bland mishmash. "It is a process that is destined to produce a dumbed-down product," says Byron Hollinshead, head of American Historical Publications and former president of American Heritage. "Textbooks are not written for children, they are written for textbook committees who flip through them to make sure they have the right ethnic balance and the proper buzz words."[15]

Yet another problem is that in some classrooms, if history is not "multicultural" enough, it's banished as politically incorrect. Remembering the Pilgrims' first Thanksgiving, for example, is out of favor in many elementary schools. Harvest festivals and multicultural feasts are in. At times, the scramble to "include" one particular group or another leads to distortions or even rewritings of history with little or no factual basis. One publisher revised an eighth grade textbook to teach children that a "Spanish" explorer named Bartolomeo Gomez, not the English explorer Henry Hudson, was the first European to discover the Hudson River. The author of the book (who was not consulted about the change) points out that Gomez was in fact Portuguese, and although he sailed along the Atlantic Coast, there is only slender evidence that he even sighted the Hudson and none to indicate that he sailed into the river.[16] Some Afrocentric curricula, meanwhile, have taught students that Socrates was black, that Aristotle looted the library of Alexandria, and that the ancient Greeks stole their philosophy from Africa and passed it off as their own achievement. This is multiculturalism run so amuck that it is embarrassing to all concerned.

There is no single best multicultural formula for every American classroom. Each teacher must use her skill to find the right balance of lessons from various sources and cultures, taking into account the heritages of her students. Here are a few questions to ask yourself as you watch over your child's lessons: Are history studies inclusive enough so that she can learn about different peoples and cultures? Or are they narrow and limiting, concentrating on just one or two cultures—be they European or some "neglected" groups—to the exclusion of others? Is the curriculum well ordered, or is the teacher skipping from culture to culture in a politically correct attempt to touch every corner of the globe?

Is the textbook interesting, or has the drive to please everyone turned it into mush? Does the class spend so much time studying what makes us different from one another that children aren't learning about the history, principles, and ideals that make us all Americans? Watch to see that history lessons are broad enough for students to learn something about different peoples and cultures, but not spread so thin as to ignore many of the important topics and concepts outlined in this chapter.

How Much of History Should Be Devoted to Western Civilization?

Closely related to the issue of multiculturalism is the matter of Western civilization's place in the history curriculum. In world history, should teachers spend more time on Western Europe or offer a "world cultures" program that gives equal attention to Africa, Central and South America, and other regions? In American history, should the legacy of Western civilization be emphasized, or should non-Western contributions be given equal footing?

Among some historians and social studies teachers, there is fairly strong sentiment for de-emphasizing the legacy of the West. This bias is most pronounced on college campuses. For example, the historian Stephen Ambrose tells of attending a university panel on political correctness in the teaching of history. The woman sitting next to him, a teacher of American political thought, remarked that she'd dropped Thomas Jefferson from her class's reading list. The author of the Declaration of Independence had been replaced with the book *God Is Red*. "And I said, 'Excuse me?'" Ambrose relates. "'You're teaching the young people of Wisconsin. Their parents are taxpayers who pay your salary. And you leave out Thomas Jefferson?' And she said, defiantly, 'Yes. I want them to get the view of Native Americans.' And the audience cheered and applauded."[17]

Since universities often set the curricular tone, it's no surprise that this attitude filters down to secondary and even some elementary schools. Many students make it to graduation learning little or nothing about Western contributions such as Athenian democracy or the Magna Carta. Some textbooks seem to make conscious efforts to slight achievements of the West, particularly those associated with white males. In one 700-page world history text designed for sixth or seventh grade use, for example, the Renaissance merits all of six pages. Children meet Isabella D'Este and Christine de Pizan, who get about the same amount of space as Nicolaus Copernicus. Galileo is nowhere to be found. The unit on African history, by comparison, is more generous: Mali, Ghana, and South Africa get sixty-four pages.[18]

Many lessons and texts tout the "three worlds meet" concept of American history, which teaches that Native American, Western European, and African cultures came together to found this country. Certainly, people from all three continents and cultures contributed to the new nation, and all have played significant roles in the course of American history. To suggest, however, that the Western European tradition is simply one leg in a three-legged stool is to deceive children about their nation's past.

In elementary school world history classes, the emphasis should be on Western civilization. The reason is simple: we study the West because it is ours. It is the culture in which Americans live. It is the water, and we are the fish. We live in a society governed by precepts that are fruits of Western civilization, and that bear witness to its moral and intellectual development. The institutions that inform our conduct and the ideas that bind us as a people acquired their shape in the course of Western history. To understand their own legacy, young Americans need to know from whence it comes.

Western civilization is not, of course, the whole story. The East and other cultures boast immense achievements of their own and are well worth studying. Learning about other cultures acquaints us with the fascinating world that we inhabit. It broadens our sensibilities, and helps us understand places and values that are different from our own. It helps us appreciate the different heritages of many newly arrived Americans. It aids us to compete in a global economy. By learning about those who are different from us, we learn something about ourselves. Yet as the American philosopher Arthur E. Murphy pointed out, "We do not understand the ideals of other cultures better by misunderstanding our own."

Elementary school children should be given ample opportunity to study non-Western cultures, but the study of the West should be emphasized. Children can then build solid knowledge and understanding of other traditions on that sturdy base. If schools manage their time wisely, and give history and geography the place they deserve in the curriculum, it should be possible for students to come to know Western civilization and also to get a good taste of some non-Western cultures before graduating.

Is It America the Beautiful—or the Bad—in History Class?

A class of fourth graders in New York City learns about the first Thanksgiving by listening to their teacher read a story not about Plymouth Rock and the *Mayflower*, but about a bunch of "strange-looking people" who invade a family's backyard, rob their house, cut down their trees, kill the pets, and plunder the garden.[19] Another group of youngsters is told to walk around the neighborhood for a week and record instances of prejudice they witness. (The teacher "never told my children that the country they lived in was doing better than ever in race relations, and far better than most other countries," a chagrined father notes.)[20] A class of seventh graders studies the atrocities committed by Christopher Columbus, then votes to declare him a villain. In New Orleans, a school board decides to remove George Washington's name from an elementary school because he was a slave owner.

In some places, school lessons not only de-emphasize the achievements of America and Western civilization, they focus on the darker side of their histories. Again, the higher you look in education, the more such sentiment you find. There is a great deal on college campuses, a good amount in high schools, and sometimes, as the above examples illustrate, the censuring starts at the elementary school level.

The cumulative effect is to present the history of the United States and European nations as a saga of greed, racism, sexism, imperialism, paternalism, victimization, and environmental devastation.

This is not to suggest that you should be on a hunt for "un-Americanism" in the classroom, or that your school is trying to turn your child against her country. On the contrary, if your school is like most, it is full of patriotic teachers who have chosen their profession in part because they love their country and want to help the next generation of Americans along. The problem, in general, lies with the political correctness that rules the day within academia and the education establishment from which so many teachers take their cues.

A telling document is the first draft of the National Standards for United States History, which was created in 1994 by a broad alliance of social studies organizations, scholars, and teachers to improve the teaching of history. Not surprisingly, much of the actual drafting was done on a university campus. The result was a lengthy document that suggested many topics for children to study. Senator Joseph McCarthy and McCarthyism, for example, were referenced nineteen times. The Ku Klux Klan was mentioned seventeen times. Yet Americans such as George Washington, Paul Revere, and Alexander Graham Bell got fleeting or no mention. In studying West Africa, students were encouraged to examine the "achievements and grandeur of Mansa Musa's court, and the social customs and wealth of the kingdom of Mali." The study of wealth in the U.S. took a different tone; children were instructed to conduct a trial of John D. Rockefeller for "unethical and amoral" business practices.[21] Europeans, according to the standards, "invade" other countries, while similar actions by non-Westerners were called "expansion."

The standards were revised following a public outcry sparked by many critics, including the United State Senate. Yet the same politically correct attitudes fill much of the curricular material now being produced. In one recent textbook for fifth graders, for example, the entire Jackson era is reduced to 160 lines, 118 of which are devoted to the forced removal of Indians from Georgia and the Trail of Tears.[22] The impulse to see American history through the prism of racism and oppression is due partly to the fact that, in past decades, school lessons often glossed over the injustices of America and the West. Now the pendulum has swung to the other extreme. In making up for past lapses, educators often end up largely recounting our sins and neglecting our virtues.

Accentuating the negative isn't fair to children. It can cause them to become unduly mistrustful of their own country. More important, the vision of America it offers is false. Indeed, there are great blots on the historical record of American and Western civilization. Students should be taught about those failings, but not at the exclusion of the achievements. Balance is needed.

For all its errors, this can be said about the story of Western civilization in general and the United States in particular: it is a mostly good and hopeful story. It is the story of the creation of a fair and honorable form of government, representative democracy. It is the story of undeniable, if uneven, improvement in standards of living and in the quality and value of human life. It is the story of the triumph of the human spirit. "When I read the work of Martin Luther King, Jr.," says history educator Mary Beth Klee, "I am always struck by his tremendous love of country. The one man who has probably made the greatest difference to this nation in the late twentieth century is a black man who loved his country unabashedly and saw not just its dirty underbelly, but its moral strength, its good core, and its enormous potential." When you examine your school's history lessons, look to see that, in the overall telling, this is the story that is told. It is the truth, and your child deserves to know it.

Warning Signs of a Weak History and Geography Program

Watch for the following clues that something is wrong at your school:

- "social studies" classes and textbooks neglect history and geography
- little expectation that children will recall important events, individuals, places, dates
- children not learning the U.S. and world maps; maps rarely displayed or used
- little reading and writing in history class; few original documents studied
- teachers and principal vague about what history lessons are most important for youngsters to learn
- no clear year-to-year written plan that ensures children don't end up with large gaps in their knowledge of history
- boring, uninspired textbooks that leave the "story" out of history
- lessons aim largely at shaping social and political attitudes rather than teaching about the past

- studies focus on just one or two groups' cultures and pasts
- conversely, curriculum leaps dizzily from culture to culture
- U.S. history lessons emphasize differences among groups (rather than history, principles, ideals that make us all Americans)
- history lessons concentrate on failures and mistakes while ignoring ideals and accomplishments
- history and legacy of Western civilization de-emphasized

TEACHING HISTORY AND GEOGRAPHY AT HOME

Your school should take the lead in teaching history and geography, but you can provide important supplements and encouragement. One of your main goals is to get your child excited about the past. A terrific way to do that is to read great books and stories. Raise your child on accessible biographies about great figures such as Madame Curie or Father Damien. Read stories about gripping events like the sinking of the *Titanic*, Chuck Yeager breaking the sound barrier, or Heinrich Schliemann searching for the lost city of Troy. Sample stories from around the world. You'll increase many times over your child's chances of excelling in history and geography.

Talk to your child about history. Help her learn to pose and think about questions such as: What sort of people lived in that time and place? What did they believe in? What was good about the way they acted? What problems did they face? Talk about great history stories together. What do you think happened to little Virginia Dare and the Lost Colony? What made Benedict Arnold betray his country? Such discussions will deepen her understanding, and may make a world of difference in how much she gets from her lessons.

Teaching History at Home

History should be fun. If you were never wild about it yourself, now is the chance to kindle your own interest. Here are some ways for you and your child to have a good time learning about the past together.

- **Talk about personal pasts.** Share your memories about life when you were young. Encourage grandparents and other older family members to do the same. Most of them are walking historians who can pass along a wealth of information about days gone by. Many children enjoy tape-recording interviews with relatives about "long-ago" times. They may not think of it as "oral history," but that's what it is. Help your child learn to ask questions such as: What was school like then? What kind of clothes did you wear? What did you do for entertainment? How was travel different?

- **Look at old things together.** Your parents' attic or cellar may be full of musty relics of your own history that your child can see and touch—old family photographs, letters, clothes, tools, magazines, toys. Flea markets, antique stores, old barns, and storage sheds are also good places to learn how people used to live and how things have changed. So, of course, are museums.

- **Make a "family archive."** Help your child build a collection of "artifacts" that chronicle her own personal history. Start a scrapbook with her. It might contain photos, postcards from places your family visits, tickets from ball games, letters from friends and relatives, etc. Find an old box where your child can store mementos: videotapes of family events, favorite old toys, worn-out Little League uniforms, clay sculptures from art class, etc. Teach your child how to label things, recording their dates and noting their significance.

- **Learn about your family's heritage.** Find stories, music, artwork, and recipes from your ancestors' homeland. Help your child get to know other relatives, including any overseas family. (What fun to find a cousin in another land for a pen pal or e-mail correspondent!) Read books about the country or region from which your family comes.

- **Make a family tree.** Genealogy is a great way for children to learn how to conduct historical research. It's also a fascinating, long-term history project that the family can work on together. You'll probably find books in the library or bookstore that tell how to learn about your ancestors. Watch the newspaper's community calendar for announcements about genealogy classes.

- **Get to know your region's past.** Short field trips are a great way to interest your child in the past as well as in local geography. Look for nearby places to visit such as monuments and battlefields. Even medium-sized communities usually have historical museums of various kinds, sometimes associated with the community itself, sometimes with famous people who once lived in it. If there is a local historical association in the area, its members can probably give good advice on what to see and do.

- **Research the history of something old in town.** Pick out an interesting building or site—an old train station, statue, church, or downtown store—and help your child investigate its past. When was it built? Why? By whom? Has it always looked like that? Find out by visiting the local history section of your library, the town clerk, your newspaper's archives, or people who have lived in town a long time.

- **Turn vacations into history lessons.** Before you go on a family trip, find some books about your destination and help your child learn a little about its past. (How did that beach get its name? When was the lighthouse built? Have there ever been any shipwrecks there?) After the trip, encourage your child to read more about that place. Include visits to historical sites in some of your vacations. If possible, visit our nation's capital sometime. Head for places such as the Alamo in Texas or Colonial Williamsburg in Virginia.

- **Celebrate holidays and anniversaries.** Start your own family traditions. Read part of the Declaration of Independence aloud on the Fourth of July. Put up pictures of Washington and Lincoln on Presidents' Day. Visit a veterans' cemetery or monument to the war dead on Memorial Day. Fly your flag on Flag Day (June 14). Talk to your child about what each anniversary represents and why it is important.

- **Make a time capsule.** This is fun for a young child on her birthday. Take a box or jar and fill it with a few things that make a record of that day: a photograph of your family, a tape-recorded "message to the future," birthday cards received, the front page from that day's newspaper, etc. Have your child write a short letter to whoever opens the time capsule. Seal it up and write the date on top. Store it in the attic or bury it in the backyard.

- **Make time lines.** It takes quite a while—several years of study—for children to bring a sense of chronological order to their understanding of the past. You can help by constructing a time line on a large piece of poster paper. Make it big, colorful, and fun to look at. Your child can paste drawings of heroes or pictures of important events onto it. Whenever she reads a book or story about history, help her mark its place on the time line. Talk about relationships in time: Who traveled first, Marco Polo or Christopher Columbus? How did Marco Polo's journey to the east encourage Columbus to sail west?

- **Help your child find heroes in history.** "What kind of people do I admire the most? Whom do I look up to when I think about people from the past? Why do I admire them?" These are great questions for your child to think about. Encourage her to make a list of her heroes and write down why she admires each one. Help her find pictures or make her own drawings of heroes to hang in her room. Urge her to write stories about them, and look for books to read about favorite heroes.

- **Expose your child to key American documents.** In history class, your child should come into direct contact with some of the writings that underlie our nation's ideals and shape its system of government. These works are important enough to read at home, too. Share with your child highlights from documents such as Thomas Paine's "Common Sense," the preamble of the Constitution, and Lincoln's Second Inaugural Address. Help her puzzle out the meaning of obscure phrases and reflect on why those words were so important to the people living in those times—and their significance for people living today.

- **Teach about current events.** Look through the newspaper and find stories to read together. Invite your child to watch newscasts with you. Help her look up important names she does not recognize, and find places in the news on the map. Talk about current events—explain what they mean and your opinions about what is happening. After your child learns about a subject, encourage her to express her views. Help her learn that there is usually more than one side to an issue.

- **Watch some television and videos about history.** Good documentaries and historical dramas can really help bring history alive. There is some excellent programming that parents and older children can enjoy together, such as *The American Experience* series, many of A&E's *Biography* installments, and some of the very fine shows from the History, Learning, and Discovery Channels.

Resources That Help Your Child Learn History

Here are some good books, magazines, software, and other resources that can help your child learn about history. Your child's teacher may have more suggestions.

Books

The America Reader, edited by Diane Ravitch (HarperCollins, 1990)—A chronological collection of important writings by political leaders, writers, poets, and social reformers. Includes many of the words that shaped our nation. Ages 11 and up.

Childhood of Famous Americans (Simon and Schuster)—Biographies of the childhoods of many famous men and women. Ages 9 to 12.

A History of US, Joy Hakim (Oxford Univ. Press, 1999)—This ten-volume history of the United States reads like a good story. Ages 11 and up.

Hooray for Heroes! Books and Activities Kids Want to Share with Their Parents and Teachers, Dennis Denenberg and Lorraine Roscoe (Scarecrow Press, 1994)—Full of ideas for parents who want to help children learn about great heroes. Includes extensive list of biographies.

If You Lived In . . . (Scholastic)—Describes what it would have been like to live at different times in history. The series includes volumes on colonial times and the Civil War. Ages 7 and up.

My First Book of Biographies: Great Men and Women Every Child Should Know, Jean Marzollo (Scholastic, 1994)—Forty-five short biographies with color drawings appropriate for reading aloud to young children.

Timetables of History, Bernard Grun (Simon and Schuster, 1991)—A chronological linkage of people and events in world history. A useful resource for parents or children 13 years and up.

World Leaders, Past and Present (Chelsea House)—An engaging biography series of over 150 world leaders. Ages 11 to 14.

Magazines

Cobblestone (Cobblestone Publishing)—Each issue focuses on a particular topic in U.S. history. Includes stories and activities. Grades 4 to 9.

Calliope (Cobblestone Publishing)—Similar to *Cobblestone,* but devoted to World history. Grades 5 to 9.

Games and Software

Brain Quest (Workman)—Flash cards that test factual knowledge of history and geography. Ages 9 and up.

Multi-Educator: American History (Computer Vistas Unlimited)—Text and narration of more than 400 major historical events, documents, addresses, and statistics. A reference tool for the whole family.

Oregon Trail (Learning Co.)—Interactive game about life on the Oregon Trail. Ages 10 and up.

Where in Time Is Carmen Sandiego? (Learning Co.)—Interactive game that teaches history. Ages 9 and up.

Web Sites

American Memory (http://lcweb2.loc.gov/ammem/ammemhome.html)—Maintained by the Library of Congress. Includes a learning page with interactive online activities and a variety of primary sources for history.
Helping your Child Learn History (www.ed.gov/pubs/parents/History)—Maintained by U.S. Department of Education. Provides activities and resources, plus suggestions for teaching children about history.
National Council for History Education (www.history.org/nche)—A comprehensive collection of history Web sites.

Teaching Geography at Home

With good books, you can conduct a marvelous, childhood-long tour of strange lands and romantic wonders: stories about climbing Mount Everest, the building of the Taj Mahal, sightings of monsters in Scotland's Loch Ness. Read about the Mayan ruins at Chichén Itzá, the rocky heights of Gibraltar, the desert city of Timbuktu. Along the way, your child will learn a lot about geography.

Here are other good ideas to choose from:

• **Keep an atlas and globe within reach.** For young children, globes are more fun—you can even get inflatable ones that you can toss around the room like beachballs. If you and your child are reading a story about William Tell, find Switzerland together. If your family is going to a Thai restaurant, or renting the movie *Casablanca*, or if a favorite football team is playing in Cleveland this weekend, reach for the atlas. Keep the atlas handy when older children are reading newspapers and magazines.

• **Put maps and pictures of interesting places on the walls.** An eighth grader who won his state's geography bee was asked to account for his curiosity and success. "When I was four, we had all these flags in my room," he said. "That got me interested in maps and books, and it just went from there."[23] Get a bulletin board and pin up magazine pictures of places you and your child have read about. Put a great big U.S. map up in your child's bedroom or rec room. If you or your spouse goes on a business trip, plot your route with your child.

- **Learn the map and globe.** Don't hesitate to do some old-fashioned memory work. Make flashcards and teach your child the names of the states and their capitals. Practice filling in the names of states and countries on outline maps. Challenge your child with geography fact questions: What is the largest ocean? The smallest continent? Does the Western Hemisphere lie north, south, east, or west of the Prime Meridian?

- **Play geography games and puzzles.** Put together puzzles of the United States and world maps. Check at your toy store or computer shop for games and software programs that teach geography.

- **Do some traveling.** Even local travel can be broadening for kids. Go see a dam at a nearby lake, walk through an old forest in a state park, or check out that annual German heritage fair in the next county. Use maps to show your child where you are going, what route you will follow, and why you selected it. Your child can learn to help "navigate" the family's journeys while in the car.

- **Get a taste of other cultures.** Sample foods from around the world: invite your child to help you cook ethnic dishes, or go with you to a foreign-food restaurant. Listen to music from other cultures. Young children enjoy learning about other countries' holidays by dressing up or making decorations. Older children may enjoy a foreign pen pal.

- **Study a map of your town.** It's important that your child see some maps that depict places she knows. Get one of your city and look for familiar streets and areas. Help your child find her home, her school, your office, the family's church, favorite park, etc.

- **Make your own maps.** Help your child make a simple map of your house, showing different rooms, positions of furniture, trees in the yard. Make a map of your neighborhood; label your house and neighbors' houses, streets, stores, parks, etc.

- **Give your child a compass.** Help her learn north, south, east, and west relative to your house. Once she learns how to use the compass, hide a "treasure" and write out simple directions to find it: "Take twenty-five steps east from the mailbox, then ten steps south . . ." Organizations such as the Girl Scouts and Boy Scouts are great ways to learn map-and-compass skills and to practice orienteering with friends.

- **Collect coins or stamps from around the world.** They usually carry images of countries' flags, leaders, animals, etc. Encourage your child to turn to an encyclopedia or the Internet to learn about what's pictured.

Resources That Help Your Child Learn Geography

Here are some good books, magazines, software, and other resources that can help your child learn about geography. Your child's teacher may have more suggestions.

Books

Circling the Globe: A Young People's Guide to Countries and Cultures of the World (Kingfisher Books, 1995)—A reference book and atlas combined. Includes maps, pictures, and information on countries of the world. Ages 9 and up.

Geography From A to Z: A Picture Glossary, Jack Knowlton, illustrated by Harriet Barton (HarperCollins, 1988)—A reference work for younger children that uses pictures to introduce geographic terms.

New True Book Series (Children's Press)—Reliable and informative books in geography, history, and other fields. Written for the beginning reader, but can be read aloud to younger children. Ages 7 and up.

Where on Earth: A Geografunny Guide to the Globe, Paul Rosenthal (Alfred A. Knopf, 1992)—An entertaining book that uses humor to introduce children to geography. Ages 11 and up.

Magazines

Kids Discover (Kids Discover)—Engaging magazine covers geography , science, and history. Each issue is devoted to a single topic. Grades 2–7.

National Geographic World (National Geographic Society)—Lively articles on geographic topics supplemented with pieces of general interest. Ages 8 to 14.

Software

Encarta Virtual Globe 98 Edition (Microsoft)—A good reference tool to help build geographic literacy. Ages 9 and up.

GeoSafari (McNally)—Interactive game format with questions on history, geography, and science. Ages 8 and up.

National Geographic GeoBee (National Geographic Society)—Tests children's geography knowledge in a game format. Ages 10 to adult.

Where in the World Is Carmen Sandiego? (Learning Co.)—Interactive game that teaches geography.

Web Sites

Helping Your Child Learn Geography (www.ed.gov/pubs/parents/Geography)—Maintained by U.S. Department of Education. Provides activities, resources, and suggestions for teaching children about geography.
National Geographic Society (www.nationalgeographic.com)—Contains resources, activities, and information on geography, overlapping into history. For both adults and children

Teaching Civics at Home

The family is the fundamental "body politic" where children learn about the rights and duties of citizens. Here are some questions to ask yourself as you go about teaching civics through your words and example.

- Am I teaching my child that citizenship begins at home? Am I raising her to treat parents and siblings with respect, to take a responsible place in the family, to do her share around the house? Am I conducting myself in the ways I'm encouraging my child to behave?

- Do I know the people who live on my street? When was the last time I did something to help a neighbor?

- Does my child see me living up to basic civic responsibilities—obeying traffic laws, fulfilling my jury duty when called, following the game regulations when fishing or hunting?

- Do I participate in the community? Am I a member of any civic organizations or neighborhood groups? When was the last time I offered my services at my church or temple? Do I participate in school events?

- Do I encourage my child to volunteer at her school, church, or youth group? Have I ever done volunteer work alongside my child?

- Do I vote regularly? Do I encourage my child to vote in school elections? Have I ever taken my child with me to the polls?

- Do I know the names of my elected representatives? Do my children know them?

- Does my child see me reading newspapers and magazines to make informed judgments about current issues and events? Do I encourage my child to read the newspaper and watch the news? How often do I discuss current events with her?

- Have I ever told my child that I love our country? Does she see me stand up for it when it is unfairly criticized?

- Does my family have an American flag? Do we fly it on appropriate occasions? Have I taught my children some rules for taking proper care of it?

- Have I taught my child the words and the meaning behind the Pledge of Allegiance and "The Star-Spangled Banner," and other patriotic songs such as "America"? Does our family pause to honor the meaning of holidays such as the Fourth of July and Memorial Day?

- Have I ever taken my child to see the local government at work by arranging a tour of city hall, the courthouse, the fire station, the police station, or a National Guard unit?

- Have we taken a family trip to see the state capital and tour the statehouse? To meet our legislators? Have we ever visited Washington, D.C.? Have we visited other places that help define America and illustrate its greatness, such as Independence Hall, Mount Rushmore, or the Grand Canyon?

- How often do I talk to my child about the values and behaviors that are part of being a good citizen?

Teaching Basic Economics at Home

Your elementary school should teach some basics about how the free enterprise system works, with more formal study of economics coming in the high school and college years. That said, you should also be aware that the most powerful lessons your child learns about money will come at home. Your child will take a deep interest in how you handle it. She'll pick up on how much you think about it. From your behavior and exhortations, she'll come to conclusions about how to get it (many young children really *do* think it's made inside ATMs), how to save it, and how to spend it—wisely or not.

Here are a few ways to impart knowledge and good habits about money, economics, and personal finance. Choose the ones that are best for your child.

- **Give your child a weekly allowance.** For hands-on experience managing money, nothing beats a regular allowance. To teach responsibility, there are two important points to remember. First, no matter how large or small the amount, the allowance should come at regular intervals. That way your child learns to plan her spending—to make and live within a "budget"—until the next allowance. Second, the allowance should be a set amount (which will probably increase as your child gets older) and unless it is a special occasion, you should not give in and hand your child more cash just because she asks for it.

  Many parents like to give allowances in exchange for household chores because it helps youngsters learn that the way to get money is to work for it. A child is apt to spend a bit more wisely when she's earned the dollar she's holding in her hand.

- **Teach your child how to save.** Saving is not something that comes naturally. Young people need to be shown the merits of delayed gratification with money. Teach them the same way your parents taught you, with a piggy bank or jar where they can watch money grow until they have accumulated enough to buy what they want. When your child is old enough, take her down to the bank to open a savings account. (Today's service charges can easily wipe out any interest earned on accounts with small balances, but some institutions will waive those charges on a child's account. Check with your bank.) Junior high school is not too early for children to start contributing to their own college fund, even if it's only a token amount every month.

- **Teach your child to keep track of where her money goes.** This is a good exercise for junior high students. Over the course of a month, have your child record all money received (lunch money, allowance, odd jobs, gifts, etc.), all money spent (specifying what it went toward—books, CDs, computer games, etc.), and all money saved. At the end of the month, you can sit down with your child to talk about "budget priorities" and how responsibly she's handling her cash.

- **Take some behind-the-scene tours of local businesses.** If you call ahead and ask, you'll find that many business proprietors are happy to give children and parents a walk-through tour during a spare moment. You may want to do this as a school or club field trip. Arrange to go see the production line at a factory, or ask for a tour of a local radio station. Your child may be interested in seeing how food is prepared in your favorite restaurant, how the local newspaper is put together, or how houses are designed at an architect's office. These are all firsthand looks at capitalism at work.

- **Follow a stock on the stock market.** There's no substitute for experience when it comes to learning about the stock market. Buying your child a few shares in a company whose product she knows well—Coca-Cola, Nike, McDonald's—is the best way to get her involved. Make it a habit to check the financial pages together every once in a while. Over time, your child will get a feel for market machinations and learn about price changes, dividends, stock splits, and the like.

- **Encourage entrepreneurship.** The proverbial lemonade stand is an American rite of passage and a great way for little ones to learn about getting money in exchange for goods and services. Family yard sales are also good ways for kids to take part in selling something. As your child gets older, you may want to encourage her to look around the neighborhood and see if there is a service she can provide—pet and plant sitting, lawn care, window washing, tutoring younger students, etc. She may take on a newspaper route, a regular baby-sitting job, or other useful, paid work. As long as they don't interfere with her studies—a problem for some young Americans, especially in high school—such jobs can give a first taste of being "in business" and build good work habits while earning pocket money.

Do remember that money matters can be great opportunities to teach about virtues such as generosity and selflessness. Encourage your child to spend her money occasionally on someone else. She might choose to buy small presents for siblings, parents, or friends. Or you may wish to make your child responsible for buying a minor household item every once in a while—something the whole family can use. You might encourage her to set aside a small portion of her allowance or earnings for charity. This is an important lesson about good stewardship of money: it's not there just to satisfy our own personal wants.

CHAPTER 7

Art and Music

THIS CHAPTER ADDRESSES VISUAL ARTS (DRAWING, PAINTING, sculpture, etc.) and music in the curriculum. Some schools do a fine job of teaching these rich subjects, but in others they are woefully neglected.

The arts deserve serious attention. True, learning about them is not as "essential" as knowing how to read, write, add and subtract when it comes to earning a diploma or landing most jobs. That's why our utilitarian society often neglects the arts. But they are important for *all* our children in other ways. A fully educated person knows something about them because many magnificent expressions of the human intellect and spirit lie in this realm. The great Russian novelist Leo Tolstoy defined art as "a human activity having for its purpose the transmission to others of the highest and best feelings to which men have risen." Children who miss an education in the arts miss something beautiful. They miss an extraordinary means of understanding themselves and the world around them.

In the following pages, we briefly discuss why elementary schools should be earnest about teaching music and art. We touch on the state of arts education today; give examples of the knowledge and skills your child should gain; and suggest some things you can do at home to make sure his education is well rounded in this area. Unfortunately, it is not possible to cover all the arts (such as dance and drama) here.

WHAT GOOD SCHOOLS TEACH—AND WHY

We should teach children about music and art for a host of reasons. They reveal the aesthetic dimension of the human mind. They train young eyes and ears to appreciate the world around us. They help satisfy children's longings to transcend the ordinary, to hear and see what they have not heard and seen before.

Art and music activities nurture creativity. They help children learn to express themselves. Students get practice imagining, experimenting, solving problems, thinking independently, and making their own decisions. They gain pride in accomplishment. Lessons in the arts may even boost overall academic achievement. Music, for example, can train the mind in skills such as organizing complex material and analyzing patterns. Bear in mind that just as some students excel in math or English, others are most gifted in the arts. Surely we want schools to nurture their talents, too.

Experiencing wonderful examples of art and music links students with the past. It teaches them about the traditions and cultures that have shaped our society, and helps them appreciate other people's cultural heritages. When we hold up to students true masterpieces of art and music, we teach them to discriminate between what is fine and what is mediocre, between the sublime and the mundane. We cultivate in their hearts a love for beauty. With attention from adults, that capacity for delight will bloom. With nourishment, it will flourish in the years beyond elementary school. As Wordsworth said, "The music in my heart I bore, long after it was heard no more."

For all of these reasons, the fine arts are part of a good school's curricular architecture, not casual outbuildings thrown up on the periphery. Lessons take place on three different fronts: creative, analytical, and historical.

One way for young children to explore and enjoy the fine arts is to *do* them. At least half of their study in this field should involve creating and performing—painting, drawing, sculpting, singing, playing simple instruments, etc. Active practice is the way to understanding. And it is the way children learn to express themselves. In the words of the great clergyman Henry Ward Beecher, "every artist dips his brush into his own soul, and paints his own nature into his pictures." It is no small thing to be able to communicate one's thoughts and feelings on a canvas, potter's wheel, or keyboard. Students in good schools get the chance to try their own hands at it. The expectation isn't that all children will become fine artists or musicians (although some will). The point is for them to know the challenge, perseverance, and joy of creation.

From an early age, lessons should also include instruction in understanding. In good schools, children are taught how to look and listen closely. They practice thinking, talking, and writing about art and music. They learn to examine a work to discern the meaning that the artist intended, as well as to find meaning for themselves. Students study some basic elements of art and music (such as how painters use balance and symmetry in their works, or what the term "melody" means to the musician). This knowledge of theory helps them analyze and appreciate fine works. It aids their own creative efforts as well.

Children should also explore the arts as part of history. The grand record of human achievement is chronicled in the columns of ancient Greek temples, the caves of Ajanta and Ellora in India, and the compositions of Gershwin. A really good arts program gives students an introduction to that record, its lasting ideas and inspirations. It helps youngsters appreciate the artistic legacy of Western civilization to which they are heirs. It also gives them ample opportunity to sample works of non-European origins—such as Navajo sand paintings, Japanese scrolls, or Ife sculptures from Nigeria. Through a broad study of works from different times and cultures, children find the human spirit revealed.

It follows, then, that schools should put children into the company of some fine music and inspiring art—the *Venus de Milo*, Handel's *Water Music*, the flying buttresses of Notre Dame. Students should learn about the lives of some renowned artists and composers. This is not to say that everything they study has to fall into the category of "the sublime," but schools should treat students to some masterpieces they might not run across elsewhere. Outside of class, children can find plenty of trashy music and what passes for art in the popular culture. Inside the classroom, they should get some of the really "good stuff." There is no reason to limit them to less.

The point is not to turn them into young art critics. Rather, it is to help them appreciate the best we have to offer and set them on the road toward becoming culturally literate. There are some schools, unfortunately, that seem to operate under the assumption that youngsters today can't grapple with great works. That kind of attitude sells children short. Good schools know that a selection from Duke Ellington or a portrait by Rembrandt can stir great interest in the classroom. With encouragement from adults, children respond rapturously when exposed to quality in the arts, and the effects run deep. As Plato reminded us long ago, make color and light, harmony and rhythm a part of education, and they will find their way into the secret places of the soul.

How Are Schools Doing?

Many American schoolchildren draw a blank when it comes to the arts. In 1997, the first extensive assessment of arts education in two decades found that few students could answer in-depth questions or complete challenging tasks in music, theater, or the visual arts. The National Assessment of Educational Progress found that, even though most elementary schools offer some sort of weekly art and music education, few students get the chance to create or perform on a frequent basis. Only about one in four eighth graders say they get the chance to sing or play a musical instrument in class every week. Only about two thirds say they get to paint or draw weekly.

Many educators report that, as schools have been asked to take on more and more responsibilities—both academic and nonacademic—art programs have been squeezed hard. In some schools, the study of the arts is now regarded as a "frill." This is ironic, given that one purpose of a good education in the arts is to put students in touch with some of the highest achievements of civilization.

The extent and quality of arts programs vary widely in American schools. That means many students do not get adequate instruction and are not expected to learn much in these fields. You'll need to look at your own school's program to see what kind of arts education it offers.

THE ART AND MUSIC CURRICULUM

The following sections will give you a sense of what an ambitious art and music curriculum looks like. This outline is excerpted from the excellent Core Knowledge Sequence (see page 100). Your own school's curriculum very likely will not match it on a grade-by-grade basis. Nevertheless, you can look to see if your school has a structured plan that, like this one, offers children a challenging experience in the enjoyment, understanding, and creation of music and art.

These lists do not contain all the topics to be covered in a complete curriculum. They should be considered as highlights from a grand exhibition, not the entire display.

Students learn much by looking at outstanding examples of art; listening to different types of wonderful music; reading about composers and artists; learning about some artistic concepts and terms; and studying the cultures and periods in which works were produced. There is a lot of knowledge to be absorbed. The following lists focus mainly on such knowledge, but keep in mind that, in a good program, children also get many opportunities to practice and engage in the artistic process—to sing, play instruments, paint, make prints and collages, etc. Elementary school studies should place a special emphasis on creativity and active participation.

The Primary Grades—Kindergarten Through Third Grade

The early years introduce children to music and art. In music, children sing, play games that involve songs and tunes, and get the chance to experiment with different instruments. Lessons teach about concepts such as rhythm, pitch, and volume. Students also learn some basics of reading music (e.g., that music is written down as notes on a staff). They grow familiar with different instruments and the sounds they make. They listen to a wide range of recordings—timeless classics such as Bach's *Jesu, Joy of Man's Desiring,* folk songs such as "On Top of Old Smokey," ancient strains such as dance songs of the Southwestern Indians.

Art lessons include activities such as painting, drawing, and craftmaking. Children learn about elements such as shape, color, form, and texture. They look at some famous examples of sculpture, painting, photography, design, and architecture—such as Winslow Homer's *Snap the Whip,* King Tut's mummy case, or the White Heron Castle of Japan. They get to know some different kinds of folk art, such as early American quilts. By examining many works and talking about them, children begin to build a habit of enjoying art in a thoughtful way.

KINDERGARTEN

Kindergarten students get lots of time to "play" with art and music—everything from finger painting to cutting-and-pasting to playing simple instruments. They sing old favorites such as "The Bear Went Over the Mountain" and "Hush Little Baby." They look at all kinds of pictures and listen to much music, and they practice talking about what they see and hear. Among other things, kindergartners learn about topics such as:

- how various colors can create different feelings (e.g., red as "warm," blue as "cold")
- kinds of lines (e.g., straight, zigzag, thick, thin)
- types of sculpture (e.g., Statue of Liberty, totem poles, mobiles)
- how to look closely at pictures (e.g., Diego Rivera's *Mother's Helper*)
- some basic elements of music (e.g., recognizing a steady beat; loud and quiet sounds)
- what some different instruments look and sound like (e.g., guitar, piano, flute)
- how to listen to and enjoy music (e.g., Camille Saint-Saëns's *Carnival of the Animals*)

(drawn from the Core Knowledge Sequence)

FIRST GRADE

First grade students continue to explore the world of art and music through activities such as drawing, molding with clay, and marching to a beat. They are exposed to some wonderful art such as *Whistler's Mother* and Georgia O'Keeffe's *Shell* paintings. They learn of ancient art forms such as mummy cases. They sing both recently composed songs and some that generations of Americans have loved, such as "She'll Be Comin' Round the Mountain." By listening to works such as Prokofiev's *Peter and the Wolf*, they grow familiar with the sounds that different instruments make. First graders learn about topics such as:

- how primary colors can be mixed to make other colors
- use of color in different works (e.g., Monet's *Tulips in Holland*)
- basic shapes (e.g., squares, triangles, circles) in nature and art
- use of textures in different works (e.g., smooth, scratchy, slippery)
- different kinds of pictures, such as portraits (e.g., Leonardo's *Mona Lisa*) and still lifes (e.g., van Gogh's *Irises*)
- art from ancient times (e.g., cave paintings, Great Sphinx)
- basic elements of music (e.g., humming a melody; playing simple rhythms)

- what composers do; what an orchestra is
- different kinds of music and dance, such as jazz (e.g., recordings of Louis Armstrong) and ballet (e.g., Tchaikovsky's *Nutcracker Suite*)

(drawn from the Core Knowledge Sequence)

SECOND GRADE

Second grade students learn more about art and music by painting, making simple prints, playing rhythms and melodies, etc. They learn some traditional songs such as "Home on the Range" and "Swing Low Sweet Chariot." They listen to entrancing music such as selections from Beethoven's *Pastoral* Symphony. Teachers open children's eyes to the world of art through works such as van Gogh's *Starry Night* and Rodin's *The Thinker*. Second graders learn about topics such as:

- the use of line in different works (e.g., Picasso's *Mother and Child*)
- various examples of sculpture (e.g., *Flying Horse* from Wu-Wei, China)
- what landscape painting is (e.g., Thomas Cole's *The Oxbow*)
- differences between lifelike and abstract art (e.g., Albrecht Dürer's *Young Hare* and Matisse's *The Snail*)
- different examples of architecture (e.g., the Parthenon, Great Stupa of Sanchi, India)
- more basic elements of music (e.g., what a scale is)
- instruments in the string family (e.g., violin, viola, cello)
- instruments in the percussion family (e.g., drums, cymbals, maracas)
- keyboard instruments (piano, organ)
- lives and works of different composers (e.g., Vivaldi and *The Four Seasons*)

(drawn from the Core Knowledge Sequence)

THIRD GRADE

Third grade students explore lots of artistic and musical activities such as painting their own murals and singing in rounds. They learn more old favorites such as "Down in the Valley" and "You're a Grand Old Flag." They listen to some timeless music such as the opening of Gershwin's *Rhapsody in Blue* and the finale of Rossini's *William Tell Overture*. They look at wonderful works of art such as Mary Cassatt's *The Bath* and Edward Hicks's *The Peaceable Kingdom*. Third graders learn about topics such as:

- use of light and shadow in paintings (e.g., Vermeer's *Milkmaid*)
- how artists create an illusion of space and depth in paintings (e.g., Jean-François Millet's *The Gleaners*)
- how artists use patterns, balance, and symmetry in their paintings (e.g., Rosa Bonheur's *The Horse Fair*)
- American Indian art (e.g., Navajo blankets, Hopi dolls)
- art of ancient Rome and Byzantine civilization (e.g., Roman aqueducts, Byzantine mosaics)
- basic elements of music (e.g., how to read notes)
- brass instruments (e.g., trumpet, trombone, tuba)
- woodwind instruments (e.g., flute, clarinet, oboe)
- lives and works of different composers (e.g., John Philip Sousa and "The Stars and Stripes Forever")

(drawn from the Core Knowledge Sequence)

The Intermediate Grades—Fourth Through Sixth Grades

In the intermediate grades, students meet more great art and music from various cultures. When studying a work, they learn something about the events, traditions, and ideas of the time within which it was created. Learning to place a work within its historical and cultural context is an important key to appreciating much art and music. A good curriculum helps elementary school children build the necessary background knowledge.

In music, students grow familiar with some famous composers. They sample a wide range of recordings, such as Gregorian chants, piano concertos by Mozart and Schumann, and American folk songs. They get more elementary music theory (e.g., what an octave is) and learn more about reading music (e.g., the difference between sharps and flats). They get a chance to play some instruments (keyboard, recorder, tambourine, etc.) if these are available in school.

Art lessons acquaint students with great painters, sculptors, and architects. By looking at works such as a Rembrandt portrait, the temple art of Southeast Asia, or the abstract sculptures of the Yoruba artists of Africa, children refine their ability to interpret art. They discuss the elements present in the works they view—perspective, proportion, scale, etc. They learn some characteristics of art from different periods (e.g., Renaissance artists often chose classical subjects and placed a new emphasis on humanity). And, of course, they get more chances to do their own drawing, painting, and sculpting.

FOURTH GRADE

Fourth Grade students examine all kinds of art, from Chinese porcelains to antelope headdresses of Mali to the famous picture of *Washington Crossing the Delaware* by Emanuel Leutze. They have some adventures listening to wonderful music—such as finding out what's so surprising about Haydn's *Surprise* Symphony. Selections often relate to topics covered in their history classes. Fourth graders study topics such as:

- art of the Middle Ages in Europe (e.g., tapestries, Gothic cathedrals)
- Islamic art and architecture (e.g., the Dome of the Rock, the Taj Mahal)
- art of Africa (e.g., ceremonial masks, bronze sculptures of Benin)
- art of China (e.g., silk scrolls, calligraphy)
- art of the young United States (e.g., Gilbert Stuart's *George Washington*)
- elements and terms of music (e.g., recognizing theme and variations)
- recognizing different vocal ranges (e.g., soprano, alto, tenor, baritone)
- lives and works of different composers (e.g., George Frideric Handel and the "Hallelujah Chorus" from the *Messiah*)

(drawn from the Core Knowledge Sequence)

FIFTH GRADE

Fifth grade students, as in prior grades, learn about art and music through active practice and by meeting splendid works such as da Vinci's *The Last Supper* and Mussorgsky's *Pictures at an Exhibition*. The examples they examine frequently relate to their history lessons. Fifth graders study topics such as:

- art of the Renaissance: paintings (e.g., Michelangelo's Sistine Chapel); sculpture (e.g., Donatello's *Saint George*); and architecture (e.g., the cathedral of Florence)
- nineteenth-century American art: landscape paintings (e.g., Albert Bierstadt's *Rocky Mountains*) and genre paintings (e.g., George Caleb Bingham's *Fur Traders Descending the Mississippi*)
- art of Japan (e.g., the Great Buddha, landscape gardens)
- elements and terms of music (e.g., crescendo and decrescendo)
- music from the Renaissance (e.g., choral works, lute songs)
- American musical traditions: (e.g., spirituals of African-Americans)
- lives and works of different composers (e.g., Beethoven and Symphony No. 5)

(drawn from the Core Knowledge Sequence)

SIXTH GRADE

Sixth Grade students begin a survey of Western art and music from early to modern times; this year's topics extend to the mid-nineteenth century. Children learn about some major characteristics of each period and school (e.g., how classical art emphasizes balance and proportion). They look at, listen to, and discuss works that illustrate each period. Sixth graders study topics such as:

- Classical art from ancient Greece and Rome (e.g., *The Discus Thrower*, the Pantheon)
- Gothic art (e.g., spires and pointed arches in cathedral architecture)
- Renaissance art (e.g., Raphael's *The School of Athens*)
- Baroque art (e.g., a Rembrandt self-portrait)
- Romantic art (e.g., Delacroix's *Liberty Leading the People*)
- elements of music (e.g., what an octave is)
- Baroque music (e.g., selections from Bach's *Brandenburg Concertos*)
- Classical music (e.g., Beethoven's *Moonlight* Sonata)
- Romantic music (e.g., Chopin's "Minute" Waltz)

(drawn from the Core Knowledge Sequence)

Junior High—Seventh and Eighth Grades

Junior high students try various art forms—painting, pottery, photography, playing instruments, etc. They also learn more about major developments in Western art and music. As in earlier years, they examine reproductions of famous works such as Degas's ballet paintings and Edward Hopper's *Nighthawks*. They listen to recordings of masterpieces such as Antonin Dvorák's *New World Symphony* and Scott Joplin's "Maple Leaf Rag." They grow familiar with more non-Western works, such as Japanese koto music and Indian sitar ragas. Students learn more about the concepts and vocabulary that artists use (such as what "surrealism" means in art, or what "allegro" and "adagio" mean in music). By the time they finish eighth grade, children should be able to examine a great work of art or music closely; think about it; talk a bit about its style and features; draw some meaning from it; and articulate in an intelligent way not only what they like or dislike about it, but also why it is considered a work of excellence.

SEVENTH GRADE

Seventh grade students continue a broad survey of Western art and music, picking up where the sixth grade left off. Children learn about major characteristics of each period and genre (e.g., Impressionist painters were interested in capturing the qualities of light). They have a chance to appreciate a few works from each school. Seventh graders study topics such as:

- Impressionism (e.g., Renoir's *Luncheon of the Boating Party*)
- Post-Impressionism (e.g., Cézanne's *Apples and Oranges*)
- Expressionism and Abstraction (e.g., Edvard Munch's *The Scream*, Paul Klee's *Head of a Man*)
- modern American painting (e.g., Andrew Wyeth's *Christina's World*)
- Romantic music (e.g., Berlioz's *Symphonie Fantastique*)
- how music can depict a nation's identity (e.g., Tchaikovsky's *1812 Overture*)
- American musical traditions: blues and jazz (e.g., twelve-bar blues form; Duke Ellington's "Take the 'A' Train")

(drawn from the Core Knowledge Sequence)

EIGHTH GRADE

Eighth grade lessons complete the broad survey of Western art and music history and sample more non-Western art. As before, children learn some major characteristics of each period and a few terms of each genre (e.g., what "overture" and "aria" mean in opera). They get a chance to learn about some famous works and artists. Eighth graders study topics such as:

- painting since World War II (e.g., works of Jackson Pollock, Roy Lichtenstein)
- photography (e.g., works of Dorothea Lange, Ansel Adams)
- twentieth-century sculpture (e.g., Henry Moore's *Two Forms*)
- architecture since the Industrial Revolution (e.g., Eiffel Tower, Empire State Building)
- non-Western music (e.g., sitar music from India, Caribbean steel drums)
- how music can depict a nation's identity (e.g., Aaron Copland's *Appalachian Spring*)
- modern music (e.g., Debussy's *La Mer*)
- opera (e.g., selections from Rossini's *The Barber of Seville*)
- American musical theater (e.g., selections from Broadway shows such as *Oklahoma!* and *West Side Story*)

(drawn from the Core Knowledge Sequence)

How Strong Is the Fine Arts Program at Your School?

Here are some questions that will help you determine whether your school takes the fine arts seriously.

- Do students get regular chances to sing, play instruments, paint, sculpt, etc.?
- Are they exposed to masterpieces of music and art, great works they might not otherwise experience?
- Do they learn about art and music from different historical periods?
- Do lessons teach basic elements and vocabulary of art and music?
- Are there teachers on staff who are well trained in art and music?
- What kinds of equipment and materials does the school have—textbooks, art supplies, prints of great paintings, music recordings, musical instruments?
- Does the school have a music room and art studio (or space set aside for these activities)?

- Is ample time for art and music built into students' schedules in every grade?
- Is pupil artwork displayed around the school? Does the school ever hold concerts or recitals?
- Do students ever take field trips to art exhibits or concerts?

TEACHING ABOUT ART AND MUSIC AT HOME

You need not turn your house into an art gallery or concert hall, but you should encourage your child to take part in some art and music activities. You can help expose him to some fine works. There is a world of masterpieces out there. It's easy for American youngsters to grow up in ignorance of them since a much larger universe of mediocrity (and worse) competes for their attention. Parents can help young eyes and ears learn to appreciate true artistic achievement.

Don't be bashful about trying to refine your child's sensibilities in a low-key way. Try to broaden his horizons. We know families where art and music offer occasions for wonderful time spent together.

Here are some commonsense things to do, even if you have little training in the visual arts and music. (Activities such as these may open new vistas for you, too.)

- **Look at different kinds of art.** Take an occasional trip to a nearby museum, gallery, or local art center. Sometimes these places put on special exhibits for young people. There may also be a local studio where you can watch artists at work. When your child sees something he really likes, you can help him find out more about the artist.

  Consider joining a museum tour with a knowledgeable guide. Many places have volunteer docents who specialize in explaining the works of art to children. If the museum has an "acoustiguide" (cassette-and-headphone) that's right for children, rent it. If there is an exhibit of the works of a particular artist, learn something about him first from a biography or encyclopedia entry and then go see his paintings.

- **Bring good art into your home.** You may want to hang one or two inexpensive prints. Museum shops sell posters and postcards of art works. Some magazines (such as *Smithsonian*) often include beautiful photos of art that you can clip and tack onto a bulletin board. Encourage your child to pick out something he likes. Hang it in his room. Try to include in your home library a book about art that appeals to your child.

- **Encourage art projects at home.** Make sure you have supplies on hand, especially for young children—water-based paint, brushes, drawing paper, glue, clay, etc. Provide space where your child can work on arts and crafts projects. Find a wall, corner or shelf where you can display the results.

- **Find some extracurricular art classes.** If your child is interested, look for courses given by community organizations or a local college, such as workshops on painting, drawing, pottery, or photography. The art teacher at school will probably know where these classes are given. Many communities have children's museums that organize such programs, or art museums with special children's activities.

- **Play different kinds of music.** Explore different styles with your child—classical, jazz, blues, gospel, country, Broadway musicals. Play a recording in the background while you're eating dinner, doing chores, or running errands in the car. Help him open his ears and discover some music that he won't hear on his favorite Top 40 station. Yes, he may turn his nose up at some pieces you like, but you'll also find some favorites together.

- **Attend musical events together.** Take your child to a concert or outdoor musical performance. (Make sure you choose one that is right for his age. A first grader who is made to sit still and listen for two hours will probably have an unfortunate first concert experience.) Keep an eye out for productions such as *The Sound of Music* or *Peter Pan* at local theaters, or rent a musical at the video store.

- **Make a little music as a family.** Sing together—at church or synagogue, while listening to favorite recordings, or just around the house. March and dance to music with young children; collect a few simple instruments for them to play—a drum, woodblock, bells, recorder, inexpensive keyboard, etc. If you play any instrument—even at a rudimentary level—your child will find it fascinating to watch and listen to you.

- **Sign up for music lessons.** If it's within your budget, learning to play an instrument is a great extracurricular activity. It is part of a truly rounded education. Your kid may be no maestro. He may not stick with it for long, but it will help him understand and appreciate this language called music. At some point, your school may offer instrumental lessons, or you could sign him up with a teacher outside of the school. Be prepared to rent or buy an instrument. Remember that it is your job to make sure your child practices regularly.

Resources That Help Your Child Learn About Art and Music

Here are a few good resources that help children learn about art and music. Your child's teacher may have more suggestions.

Books About Art

Discovering Art History, Gerald F. Brommer (Davis Publications, 1996)—An excellent resource for beginning and intermediate students of the arts.

Getting to Know . . . series (Children's Press, 1994)—A series of short books designed to introduce young children to great artists. Ages 4–8.

History of Art for Young People, H.W. Janson and Anthony F. Janson (Harry N. Abrams, 1997)—The standard in its field, this volume is an excellent compendium of art through the ages. Grades 7–12.

I Spy: An Alphabet in Art, Lucy Micklethwait (Mulberry, 1996)—A great book of art for younger kids (ages 4–8), featuring an artist for each letter of the alphabet. Part of the *I Spy* series.

Let's Meet Famous Artists, Harriet Kinghorn, Lisa Lewis-Spicer, and Jacqueline Badman (T.S. Denison and Company, 1998)—History, projects, and insight for children interested in great works of art.

Books About Music

Go In and Out the Window, Dan Fox and P. Fox (Henry Holt, 1987)—This collection of children's songs is lavishly illustrated with works of art drawn from the collections of The Metropolitan Museum of Art.

Wee Sing (Price Stern Sloan Publishing, 1998)—A series of short books that come with a tape or compact disc. Each book covers a different set of songs, with titles such as *Wee Sing America, Wee Sing Around the World,* etc. For children up to age 10.

Music Tapes and CDs

Beethoven for Babies—Brain Training for Little Ones (Philips, 1998)—A well chosen selection of tunes from Beethoven.

Classical Kids series (Atlantic Records, 1997)—A neat collection of introductory material from our most brilliant composers.

Music for Little People (Atlantic Records—Rhino, 1998)—An extremely diverse series of songs for children of all ages, from folk music to Broadway tunes.

CHAPTER 8

Mathematics

THIS CHAPTER COVERS THE MATHEMATICS CURRICULUM. You should spend some time with it for three reasons. First, this subject is one of the most important that children study. Second, if properly taught it is a rigorous subject, and your child will probably need your help and encouragement. Third, math instruction is mediocre in many schools. It is ironic that in a society so dependent upon and admiring of technology, Americans often tolerate second- and third-rate mathematics education. You'll need to check to make sure your own school is doing a first-rate job.

In the following pages, we discuss why it is vital to learn mathematics in the elementary school years. We outline the knowledge and skills your child should gain, and provide a model curriculum that you can compare to your own school's plan of study. We take up some of the current debates about math education and suggest things you can do at home to help your child succeed.

WHAT GOOD SCHOOLS TEACH—AND WHY

At Plato's famous Academy in Athens, an inscription over the door read: "Let no one enter here who is ignorant of geometry." To the ancient Greeks, no academic subject was more important than mathematics, and that view has predominated throughout most of history. The medieval church taught math as training for theological reasoning. John Adams wrote in his diary that mathematics "proved the extent of the human mind to be more spacious and capable than any other science." As mastering math becomes more important than ever, the need for a solid base in this discipline multiplies.

Mathematics leads to higher education. Students who take rigorous math courses are much more likely to go to college than those who don't. More and more good jobs require math. Even routine demands of life—cooking and shopping, figuring out the household budget, interpreting your mutual fund report—draw on math skills.

Good citizenry involves "numeracy"—the capacity to cope with basic mathematical ideas. Understanding the newspaper requires the ability to digest statements such as: "In 1940, the labor force participation rate for men age 65 was 70 percent. Today it is just 33 percent. Thus we are spending more on Social Security benefits at the same time people are contributing less because of early retirement." Americans love to quantify problems, trends, and solutions. Statistics fill our public arena. Someday your child will step into a voting booth to pull a lever. She, too, will need every bit of numeracy she can muster to make intelligent decisions on election day.

Mathematics plays a profound role in man's quest to understand the universe. It is, in part, a study of patterns and as such reveals the regularity and symmetry that often occur in the world around us. The shape of a snowflake, the height of an ocean wave, the brightness of a distant star—all these are described by mathematics. The ancient Greeks believed that the world itself was ordered according to a grand mathematical pattern. By discovering theorems, they sought to unlock the truths of the universe. (The word "mathematics" comes from a Greek word for "learning.")

Mathematics knows no physical bounds. It allows us to push forever outward in our explorations, taking the measure of bodies and events far removed from our immediate grasp. Using a sundial, a well, and a little geometry, Eratosthenes was able to measure the earth's circumference in 230 B.C.—and come within fifty miles of our modern measurement. Two millennia later, Isaac Newton devised equations to calculate the movement of the planets. In the nineteenth century, the Scottish physicist James Maxwell deduced, by mathematical methods, that electromagnetic waves could exist and must travel at the speed of light. His equations laid the groundwork for the development of radio and television. Today scientists continue the work of exploring our universe with mathematics—decoding secrets of DNA, probing the mechanics of the atom, mapping the trajectories of spacecraft.

Most of us will never develop the sophistication required to fathom the complex equations that drive modern discoveries. A sound education in the basics, however, can give students the ability to glimpse the universe through the prism of mathematics. Since that prism expands our view and reveals truths about our world, it is a perspective every educated child should have.

Mathematics develops several critical habits of mind. It is unsurpassed in its demands for clarity in thought. The expression $2x + 6 = 16$ is a neat and concise way of saying, "Find the value of x such that when x is multiplied by two and six is added to that product, the resulting sum is sixteen." Reading and writing equations trains the mind toward exactness. To solve them, a student must interpret problems correctly, recognize a path to a solution, and carry out calculations in an ordered manner. Practicing this kind of mental accuracy teaches students to look at situations critically. It helps them learn to identify the strengths and weaknesses of statements, to bring method and consistency to their own arguments, to distinguish truth from nonsense. Studying mathematics helps develop clear and steady judgment. It builds the confidence and perseverance that students need to tackle tough intellectual challenges, to stick with an assignment until they find the right answer.

Math is particularly good for developing logic skills. Deductive reasoning—reasoning in which the conclusion follows inexorably from the premises—was developed by those classical Greeks who held mathematics in such high esteem, and it remains an essential method for determining whether an idea is valid. Beginning with a set of axioms or statements that are accepted as true, mathematicians carefully reason their way to others that can also be accepted. If $x = 3$ and $y = 2x$, we can deduce that $x + y = 9$. Or, to take another famous example, if all men are mortal and Socrates is a man, then deductive reasoning tells us that Socrates must be mortal. Mathematics is vital to a good education largely because it instills this kind of logic.

Mathematics trains students to think abstractly. Perfect circles may not exist in our world, but they do in the world of geometry. No one has ever seen or touched a number, yet mathematicians manipulate them all the time. Why should we want our children to work with such abstract notions? Because we want them to be comfortable operating in the world of ideas. Though ideas often have "real-world" consequences, they are in themselves abstract. "The science of mathematics presents the most brilliant example of the extension of the sphere of pure reason without the aid of experience," the philosopher Immanuel Kant observed. Dealing with abstractions can be hard work, but the reward is a fertile, cultivated intellect.

Mathematics teaches self-reliance in thinking. If a child learns and understands that the area of a rectangle is found by multiplying its length times its width, and she comes across one measuring 5 inches by 3 inches, she can find its area with perfect assuredness. (Provided she knows her multiplication tables, too!) She does not have to rely on charts, calculators, or other people for the right answer. She can know that her answer is correct, because the logic she has employed is perfectly clear. To take such responsibility for one's own mental processes, and to gain confidence in one's cognitive powers, are critical lessons for the growing student.

Finally, there is beauty and creativity in mathematics. There is something elegant about the fact that in any plane triangle—no matter its shape or size—the sum of the angles will always add up to 180 degrees. The patterns and shapes of geometry can be as intriguing as painted images on a canvas. In fact, the balanced designs of Rembrandt and Picasso are essentially constructions of lines, curves, and angles.

In the end, it is the sober precision of mathematics that gives it grandeur. "Mathematics possesses not only truth, but supreme beauty," the philosopher-mathematician Bertrand Russell observed, "a beauty cold and austere, like that of sculpture, without appeal to any part of our weaker nature, sublimely pure, and capable of a stern perfection such as only the greatest artist can show." We can't necessarily expect an eighth grader struggling with an equation to be enthralled by such attractions. The beauty of mathematics is there, however, and it is worth beholding. Good teachers try to reveal it to students during the course of their studies.

The Right Road for Teaching and Learning Math

How do good schools offer all of these benefits of mathematics? First, they recognize that there is a definite body of knowledge that students should absorb. Just as English has certain elements that must be learned before a student can write fluently—vocabulary, spelling, grammar—math has certain rules and facts that students must know before they can solve challenging problems. For example, they must be able to recall basic number facts of addition, subtraction, multiplication, and division—such as that $3 + 4 = 7$ and $9 \times 9 = 81$. They must know that a pentagon has five sides; that there are 12 inches to a foot and 3 feet to a yard; that you find the volume of a rectangular prism by the formula $V = lwh$.

There is an attitude in some schools today that goes something like this: "It's not so important that students know theorems, equations, and definitions. They can always look those up. What's important is that they understand the concepts behind them." All too often, this is just an excuse for failing to teach children fundamentals. *Of course* we want students to understand the concepts behind the symbols and equations. We want them to grasp how the Pythagorean theorem works, not just be able to plug numbers into it. But educators who scoff at the notion of requiring children to remember that formula have yet to explain the conflict between understanding a "concept" and being able to recall the relevant math facts. The two are not mutually exclusive. More important, it has yet to be demonstrated that students can do math consistently, correctly, and comfortably without knowing fundamental terms, axioms, definitions. Doing math takes knowledge of math. It's that simple.

In addition to basic knowledge, students in good schools gain proficiency in some fundamental skills. For example, children become practiced at counting, comparing, sorting, and ordering things. They learn to add, subtract, multiply, and divide comfortably—first with positive integers, and later with negative numbers, fractions, and decimals. As they pick up mathematical knowledge and skills, students apply those tools to the work of solving problems. Problem solving lies at the heart of the mathematics curriculum.

Ask Japanese and Chinese parents what single factor best explains success in math class, and they are likely to say "hard work." That means practice—the only proven method for learning math well. If you don't see your child working lots of problems in every grade, something is probably wrong with your school.

Why does math require so much practice? First, because it is a tough subject. There is no denying that. Learning tough lessons takes ample time on task.

Second, children must master basic skills and knowledge before they can go on to more sophisticated math. It's like learning to play the guitar well; you can't play competently until forming the different chords with your fingers becomes second nature. If a student has to slow down (or count on her fingers, or pick up a calculator) to remember what 4×6 is, or can't recall the difference between the radius and diameter of a circle, higher mathematical thinking will be very difficult. Some facts and procedures must be learned so thoroughly that they become virtually automatic. Such competence comes only through practice.

Third, as students advance and math concepts get more complex, practice is usually necessary to master ideas the teacher has just introduced. Anytime you undertake something difficult and new, you may not get it right on the first try—or the second or third. It takes several times doing it yourself, laboring over it, giving it all your attention, before you get the hang of it and really begin to understand what it's about. By working their way through several assigned problems, children gain confidence in their ability to handle that kind of exercise, and they strengthen their understanding of the underlying concepts.

Regular practice does not mean sending second graders home with fifty problems every night. Moderation obviously counts in math, as in other endeavors. Neither does it mean mindless repetition. Good schools give challenging assignments that call for imaginative solutions. Children need to reflect on what they are doing in order to learn, so there must be time to think about concepts, weigh ideas, and talk them over with teachers and peers. Nonetheless, there is no better way to think about a math concept than to actively engage it via a problem. With practice comes enlightenment.

Most students would rather be doing something other than laboring over a set of division problems. Why? Because sometimes those problems are *hard* (or should be). They call for persistence and concentration. They demand self-discipline. Getting the right answer sometimes involves mental perspiration. That is the nature of mathematics. It is not a source of instant gratification. Our children may not always find it "fun," but it is good for them nonetheless.

It is said that when Euclid was teaching geometry in Alexandria, Egypt, in the fourth century B.C., King Ptolemy heard of his fabulous calculations and grew curious to observe a class. The pharaoh spent some time listening intently and, growing more fascinated, asked Euclid to give him instruction. The teacher obliged. Starting at the beginning, he explained some basic theorems. King Ptolemy followed the lesson quietly, but after a while interrupted the demonstration.

"This is fascinating," he said, "but as pharaoh I have many other duties to perform, and I have little time. Is there no easier road to the mastery of this subject?" Euclid gently replied: "Sire, there is no royal road to geometry."

There is no royal road to mathematics, not even in elementary school. There are no shortcuts or labor-saving methods to make it easy or always fun. It takes time and practice and thinking and work. It is a rigorous road. Sometimes it is rocky and children have to work harder to get over the bumps. For some students, it is not their favorite trek, but good schools know it is worth the journey, and good teachers work hard to make sure that children undertake it.

How Are Schools Doing?

America has its fair share of brilliant mathematicians, Nobel Prize–winning scientists, and distinguished engineers. Yet our school system as a whole is way behind many other nations when it comes to offering a quality math education to all students. In international tests, U.S. high school seniors are among the worst in math in the industrialized world. Even our best and brightest twelfth graders perform below their peers in most other countries. The Third International Mathematics and Science Study, released in 1998, showed that in just three countries—Lithuania, Cyprus, and South Africa—did students score lower than American twelfth graders. U.S. fourth graders, to be sure, do well compared to children in other lands. Eighth graders are near the middle. In a sense, however, that's even more alarming: the United States appears to be the only country in the world where children seem to do *worse* in math the older they get and the more time they spend in school.

Domestic data are not much more encouraging. On the bright side, SAT math scores have been edging up in recent years. Yet they remain well below their mid-1960s peak. According to the National Assessment of Educational Progress, only about one out of five fourth graders was "proficient" in math in 1996, and only about one out of four eighth graders. Large numbers of children lack a basic grasp of math.

Why has the U.S. sunk so low in mathematics? No doubt there are several reasons. In many schools, the curriculum is disorganized. Many teachers don't have adequate math training. "Honors" students may benefit from a rich and well-taught curriculum while the majority of their classmates make do with poorly taught, dumbed-down lessons. A lack of clear, tough academic standards is a widespread problem. Some schools simply don't require students to put in the time and practice needed to learn the fundamentals.

In this part of the curriculum, as in others, low expectations seem to rule the day. "The pages are covered with pictures and are very colorful, but contain few problems," says one mom about her district's new textbooks. "Our [school's] math consultant told parents that research has shown that the children learn more from doing basic facts on a calculator than through drill and practice," she adds. A worried educator reports on the math program in her school: "The teachers seem to like it because they say it makes math fun. The problem is that the kids don't seem to be learning any basic arithmetic." If they don't learn the basics in elementary school, no wonder they rank near the bottom in world tests by the time they're in high school.

Overall, American schools are not getting the math job done. Too many youngsters leave eighth grade with a shaky foundation that is exceedingly difficult to compensate for later. If they have not spent the time required to master basic knowledge and skills, they are likely never to be comfortable with mathematics, an education gap that is compounded over the course of a lifetime.

THE MATHEMATICS CURRICULUM

The following sections give you an idea of what a good mathematics curriculum looks like from kindergarten through eighth grade. Your school should lay a solid foundation in arithmetic, geometry, and algebra, as well as related topics such as measurement, probability, and statistics. The knowledge and skills to be learned in these years do not come automatically to most children. They require frequent practice and sustained effort. If you do not see your child consistently practicing the rudiments outlined here—working sets of challenging problems on a daily basis—then do not expect her to be a particularly good math student.

As children learn about numbers and equations, they should gradually develop certain habits of mind. Above all, they should learn to think logically. Children should learn to scrutinize problems carefully; separate relevant from irrelevant information; and break large problems into smaller parts. They practice choosing the best approaches to solve a problem. They get in the habit of making precise calculations and expressing answers clearly in mathematical notation. In good schools, attention is paid not only to getting the right answer, but also to *how* you got it. That is, the aim is to make sure students understand (and can explain) exactly how they arrived at a solution. All of these lessons should be solidly embedded in your school's math program.

Mathematics is a precisely structured field and its teaching should reflect this. Lesson plans should be carefully ordered so that students gradually build a base of knowledge and skills, beginning with the simplest and then moving step by step, topic by topic, to more complex ideas. It's a bit like building a tower. Each new floor rests squarely on what has been constructed before. If the walls in the lower floors are weak, the building can't rise very far. Consequently, math is not a subject that treats students kindly when they fail to master the early lessons.

It is important, therefore, that your school be able to show you a curriculum that indicates goals for each grade and proceeds toward them in orderly fashion. The goals should be specific, spelling out what your child should learn and do at each level. If your school presents only vague objectives such as "formulate and solve a variety of meaningful problems," then you have reason to suspect that there is no coherent plan of study. What you may have, instead, are large gaps in the curriculum and a fair amount of needless repetition. That adds up to trouble.

The curriculum outlined here is excerpted from the estimable Core Knowledge Sequence (see page 100). Your own school's curriculum may not look exactly like it on a grade-by-grade basis. No single "best" sequence fits all circumstances. In one school, students may begin adding and subtracting simple fractions in fifth grade. In another, it might be the sixth. The important thing is to satisfy yourself that your school's curriculum is coherent, demanding, and covers the basic ground indicated here in a systematic way over the course of study.

One more word of advice, in case you are one of those people with "math anxiety." Take a deep breath. Sit back and relax. It's okay that you may not understand all of the terms and concepts that follow. Perhaps you did once but have forgotten some of them. (We're with you.) You need not grasp every word to make use of these grade-by-grade summaries. Even if some of it goes over your head, these lists can still help you determine whether your child's school is offering a quality math curriculum. You can look at her textbooks, tests, and homework assignments to see if topics, lessons, and problems resemble the listings here. You can ask your child questions about some of the terms she's studying and observe whether she responds with confidence or just scratches her head. You can talk to the teacher and simply ask, "Will my child learn to solve basic algebraic equations this year?" even if you're not sure how to do that yourself. Be honest with the teacher. Let her know that even if your own math skills are rusty, you still want to do your best to gauge the quality of your school's program and to help your child succeed with it. She should welcome your efforts.

The Primary Grades—Kindergarten Through Third Grade

In these first years, your child learns the basic skills (such as adding and subtracting) and facts (such as what triangles and fractions are) that will support all mathematical work for the rest of her school career—and the rest of her life! This is a time of frequent games and activities that draw on youngsters' natural interest in counting things, manipulating shapes, and exploring patterns. It is also a time of serious work by which students must acquire a good deal of knowledge and understanding, solve challenging problems, and practice certain procedures until they can perform them with ease. Without enough practice now, the sailing will not be smooth in the intermediate and junior high years.

Students in the primary grades spend much time developing "number sense"—an understanding of just what numbers are and how they work. They must learn, for example, that the numeral 5 can stand for 5 apples; that a group of 5 apples contains one more than a group of 4 apples, and that 5 is one more than 4; that 5 is equal to 4 + 1, as well as 3 + 2, etc. All this takes time for youngsters to absorb, so you should see teachers spending an average of an hour a day on math-related activities. (Bear in mind that "math time" in the primary grades sometimes goes hand in hand with other activities, such as arts and crafts.)

By the end of third grade, your child should be comfortable adding, subtracting, multiplying, and dividing with whole numbers. This means she *must* learn, one way or another, the basic addition, subtraction, multiplication, and division tables. For most children, acquiring these facts takes considerable memory work. Youngsters can learn the fundamentals through a variety of ways: flash cards, games, using numbers in everyday activities, talking to mom or dad about math, etc. It also takes working many problems before students can perform basic operations smoothly and consistently. Practice and effort will be required, much of it at home. (See "Teaching Mathematics at Home," page 333.)

To gain the ability to manipulate numbers, children study place value (that different digits within a number represent the ones' place, the tens' place, the hundreds' place, etc.). They learn symbols such as

÷ and >, and how to make number sentences such as 3 + 11 = 14. They solve not only equations, but also word problems and "real-life" problems (such as how many cars the class will need to go on its picnic if each car can carry four children).

You will see your child sorting objects, working with sets, and studying patterns. She'll get lots of practice measuring things. She'll learn to use money and tell time. She'll meet the basic shapes that fill the world of geometry. She'll practice organizing data and reading simple graphs.

Much learning in these grades makes use of "manipulatives," which can be anything from pictures to blocks to plastic pies with pieces that teach about fractions. These hands-on tools help youngsters visualize and literally get a feel for mathematical concepts. Good teachers know how to use them to gradually introduce children to abstract thought.

KINDERGARTEN

Kindergarten is a time of hands-on games that involve counting, comparing, sorting, and ordering objects. Children learn about numbers, quantities, and shapes. They examine patterns and designs. They learn that objects have properties such as length, weight, and capacity, and that these properties can be measured. As they work and play, children get lots of experience talking about ways to solve simple problems. Among other things, kindergartners are able to do the following:

Patterns and Classification

- sort and classify objects by size, shape, color, function, etc.
- practice recognizing sets of objects
- identify items that belong or do not belong in a given set
- work with simple patterns involving shapes, sizes, colors, etc.

Numbers and Number Sense

- use concepts of "same as," "more than," "less than," "most," and "least"
- count, read, and write numbers from 1 to 31
- count backward from 10; by twos to 10; by fives and tens to 50
- count and write the number of objects in a set
- tell "one more than" and "one less than" a given number
- identify ordinal positions, 1st through 6th
- interpret simple picture graphs
- identify ½ of a region, object, or set of concrete objects

Money

- learn to recognize pennies, nickels, dimes, quarters, and one-dollar bills
- learn the $ and ¢ signs; write money amounts using ¢ sign

Computation

- add and subtract to 10, using concrete objects
- learn meanings of + and − signs

Measurement

- identify familiar instruments of measurement (e.g., ruler, scale, thermometer)
- take part in simple measuring and weighing activities
- tell whether objects are taller or shorter, heavier or lighter, etc.
- practice orienting themselves in time (e.g., morning, afternoon, tomorrow)
- tell time to the hour using a clock face
- learn days of week and months of year

Geometry

- learn left and right hands
- use terms of orientation such as top/bottom, on/under, in front/behind
- identify and compare basic plane figures (e.g., square, triangle, circle)

(drawn from the Core Knowledge Sequence)

In a good kindergarten classroom, you might see children:

- playing simple games (like Bingo) that require them to find the right numbers
- making posters to illustrate numbers and sets (drawing one house for 1, two kittens for 2, three cars for 3, etc.)
- following directions that involve numbers (while making necklaces: "Everyone put three red beads on your string. Now everyone put four green beads on your string.")

- arranging shapes in specified patterns: blue circle, blue triangle, red circle, red triangle, etc.
- solving simple math problems while "shopping" at the classroom "store" ("We have seven pennies here. If we spend five of them to buy a pencil, how many pennies will we have left?")
- weighing objects with a simple balance scale. Which is heavier, the baseball or tennis ball?

FIRST GRADE

First grade students learn basic addition and subtraction facts and practice until they can add and subtract small numbers with ease. They learn about place values, work more with sets, and meet simple fractions. In making measurements, students move from using nonstandard units (such as pencil-lengths) to standard units (such as inches and feet). They also gain greater acquaintance with some two- and three-dimensional shapes. They make decisions about how to solve problems and explain the reasons behind the methods they use. They get into the habit of checking to see that their answers are right. Among other things, first graders are able to do the following:

Patterns and Classification

- get more practice classifying objects by size, shape, function, etc.
- define a set by the shared attributes of its members
- identify items that belong or do not belong in a given set
- recognize and extend simple patterns (e.g., 2, 4, 6, 8 . . .)

Numbers and Number Sense

- read, write, and count numbers 0 to 100
- skip-count by twos, fives, and tens
- count forward and backward
- identify ordinal positions, 1st through 10th
- learn about place value (ones, tens, hundreds)
- practice using "more" and "less" with numbers; count how many more or less
- compare quantities using the signs <, >, and =
- learn what simple fractions represent: ½, ⅓, and ¼
- make and read simple picture graphs and bar graphs

Money

- learn relative values of penny, nickel, dime, and quarter
- recognize and use the $ and ¢ signs
- show how different combinations of coins equal the same amounts of money

Computation

- learn addition facts to 12 and corresponding subtraction facts
- study the inverse relation between addition and subtraction
- add and subtract two-digit numbers without regrouping (e.g., 33 + 4 = 37)
- solve basic one-step story and picture problems
- solve simple equations such as ___ − 2 = 7; 5 + ___ = 7

Measurement

- take simple measurements of length, weight, volume, and temperature
- practice measuring with standard units (e.g., inches, centimeters, pounds)
- measure different objects to tell which is longer, heavier, etc.
- tell time to the half hour

Geometry

- identify and draw basic plane figures: square, rectangle, triangle, circle
- identify basic solid figures: sphere, cube, cone
- use terms describing location (e.g., "put the triangle to the right of the square")

(drawn from the Core Knowledge Sequence)

In a good first grade classroom, you might see children:

- looking at pictures of one set of 4 apples and one set of 8 apples and writing "4 < 8"
- figuring out how many cents are in a pile of coins containing, for example, 7 pennies, 2 nickels, and 4 dimes
- stacking cubes into groups of tens and ones to learn about place value

- manipulating objects to learn about fractions (coloring one side of a circle to learn about "one half," folding a piece of paper into four equal parts to learn about "one fourth," etc.)

- exploring different expressions for a number (e.g., 5 can be represented as 4 + 1, 2 + 2 + 1, 8 − 3, etc.)

- gathering simple data ("How many children have dogs at home? How many have cats?") and displaying findings on a bar graph

SECOND GRADE

Second grade students work more on adding and subtracting, and also begin to multiply. They continue working with patterns and sequences; measure with appropriate units; study properties of some basic shapes; and use simple graphs. As before, children often use drawings, models, and other hands-on tools as they learn. They decide the best approach to take in tackling a problem and then justify their reasoning. Activities involve simple logic. Children practice making precise calculations and double-checking their answers. Among other things, second graders are able to do the following:

Numbers and Number Sense

- read, write, order, and compare whole numbers up to 1,000
- count (forward and backward) by twos, threes, fives, tens, fifties, and hundreds
- use a number line
- identify ordinal positions, 1st through 20th
- identify even and odd numbers
- identify place values in three-digit numerals
- round numbers to the nearest ten
- make and read simple charts and bar graphs
- extend patterns that use numbers, symbols, etc. (e.g., 5, 8, 11, 14 . . .)
- recognize simple fractions: ½, ⅓, ¼, ⅕, ⅙, ⅛, ⅒

Money

- read and write money amounts using the $ and ¢ signs, and the decimal point
- show how different combinations of coins equal the same amounts of money

Computation

- learn addition facts to 18 and corresponding subtraction facts
- add and subtract with two- and three-digit numbers
- estimate sums and differences
- use addition to check subtraction
- practice multiplying single-digit numbers by 1, 2, 3, 4, 5
- solve simple word problems involving addition, subtraction, and multiplication
- solve simple equations in the form of ___ − 9 = 7 and 4 × ___ = 8

Measurement

- measure, estimate, and compare objects by size, weight, capacity, and quantity
- make measurements using standard units (e.g., quarts, degrees Fahrenheit)
- tell time to five-minute intervals
- learn to write the date and find it on a calendar
- solve simple problems about elapsed time (how much time has passed?)

Geometry

- learn properties of basic shapes (e.g., a square has four equal sides)
- measure perimeters of squares and rectangles
- associate solid figures with planar shapes (e.g., sphere with circle, cube with square)
- identify lines of symmetry and create simple symmetric figures

(drawn from the Core Knowledge Sequence)

In a good second grade class, students work homework and classroom assignments such as:

- 798 ? 978 (>, <, or =) Answer: <
- You begin playing basketball at 2:00. You stop playing 25 minutes later. What time is it when you stop playing? Answer: 2:25
- Anna, Sam, and Tim want to buy a Wingwort that costs $1.98. Anna has 55 cents in her pocket, Sam has 84 cents, and Tim has 74 cents. If they pool their money, will they have enough to buy the Wingwort? Answer: Yes

- Find the difference: 181 − 39 = ? Answer: 142
- Tell what happens when you multiply a number by 1. Tell what happens when you multiply a number by 0. Answer: When you multiply by 1, the number remains the same. When you multiply by 0, the product is 0.
- Yesterday, Melinda painted a door, and it took 2 cups of paint. Today, she wants to paint 3 more doors, each the same size as the door she painted yesterday. How many cups of paint will she need today? Answer: 6 cups

THIRD GRADE

Third grade students should already know their basic addition and subtraction facts. During this year, they also learn multiplication facts and corresponding division facts. Children practice adding, subtracting, multiplying, and dividing whole numbers. They continue learning about geometric shapes, measuring things, gathering data, and working with simple graphs. By the end of third grade, students should be competent at telling time from a conventional (face) clock, using a calendar, and handling small quantities of money. They analyze problems to figure out how best to tackle them, and explain the logic behind the strategies they use. They practice making precise calculations and checking the validity of their answers. Among other things, third graders are able to do the following:

Numbers and Number Sense

- read, write, order, and compare whole numbers up to 999,999; recognize place value of each digit
- round numbers to the nearest ten and nearest hundred
- learn the concept of negative numbers
- locate positive and negative whole numbers on number line
- make and read bar graphs and line graphs
- learn Roman numerals from 1 to 20 (I–XX)

Fractions and Decimals

- recognize fractions to $\frac{1}{10}$
- write mixed numbers (e.g., $4\frac{3}{4}$)
- equate and compare simple fractions (e.g., $\frac{1}{2} = \frac{3}{6}$; $\frac{5}{8} > \frac{3}{8}$)
- read and write decimals to the hundredths

Money

- write amounts of money using $ and ¢ signs and the decimal point
- make change, using as few coins as possible

Computation

- find the sum (up to 10,000) of any two whole numbers
- given two whole numbers of 10,000 or less, find the difference between them
- learn multiplication facts to 10 × 10 and corresponding division facts
- understand multiplication and division as opposite operations
- multiply two- and three-digit numbers by one-digit numbers (e.g., $52 \times 8 = \underline{\quad}$)
- divide two- and three-digit numbers by one-digit numbers (e.g., $91 \div 7 = \underline{\quad}$)
- practice mental computations and estimating sums, differences, and products
- solve two-step word problems
- solve problems with more than one operation, as for example $(43 - 32) \times (5 + 3) = \underline{\quad}$

Measurement

- measure, estimate, and compare objects by size, weight, capacity, and quantity
- make measurements using standard units (e.g., ounces, degrees Celsius)
- learn some relationships between units (e.g., 1 yard = 36 inches)
- tell time to the minute; solve problems involving time; practice using calendar

Geometry

- identify various polygons (e.g., regular pentagons, hexagons, octagons)
- study concept of area; measure areas of simple figures
- identify basic solids (e.g., spheres, cubes, pyramids)
- identify lines of symmetry; create symmetric figures

(drawn from the Core Knowledge Sequence)

In a good third grade class, students work homework and classroom assignments such as:

- Jenny has 42 eggs. She puts them into 7 baskets so that the same number of eggs is in each basket. How many eggs do 3 baskets hold? Answer: 18 eggs

- Show and explain what happens when you multiply a number by 10, 100, and 1,000 (e.g., 3 x 10 = 30, 3 x 100 = 300, 3 x 1,000 = 3,000).

- Mr. Palmer went on a long business trip. During the first leg, he drove 143 miles from Washington, D.C., to Philadelphia, Pennsylvania. A few days later, he got on a plane and flew from Philadelphia to Atlanta, Georgia, a distance of about 700 miles. Next he rented another car and drove 246 miles to Nashville, Tennessee. How many miles did he drive in all? Answer: 389 miles

- Draw a line segment 2¾ inches long. Draw a line segment 7 centimeters long.

- On December 17, 1903, at Kitty Hawk, North Carolina, Orville and Wilbur Wright became the first people to fly an airplane successfully. Their little craft made a flight 852 feet long. How many yards did the plane fly? Answer: 284 yards

- Write the Roman number XVII as an Arabic numeral. Write 19 as a Roman numeral. Answers: 17; XIX

Does Your Child Know Basic Math Facts?

Here are some examples of the kinds of math facts your child should learn during the primary years. By the end of the third grade, she should be able to explain and use most of the following terms, concepts, and symbols.

- The signs >, <, and = mean "greater than," "less than," and "equal to."

- The *sum* is the result of addition. The *difference* results from subtraction. The *product* is the result when numbers are multiplied. The *quotient* is the result of division.

- Your child should know the *addition tables* (sums to 20) and corresponding *subtraction tables*. She should also know the *multiplication tables* (up to 10 x 10) and corresponding *division tables*.

- A *pair* = 2; a *dozen* = 12; a *half dozen* = 6; a *score* = 20.

- The *numerator* is the top part of a fraction. The *denominator* is the bottom part.

- A *set* is a collection of objects or numbers that are used together or belong together. A *subset* is a set that is part of a larger set.
- The abbreviations *in, ft, yd, mm, cm,* and *m* stand for inch, foot, yard, millimeter, centimeter, and meter. The abbreviations *oz, lb, g,* and *kg* stand for ounce, pound, gram, and kilogram.
- 1 ft = 12 in
  1 yd = 3 ft = 36 in
  1 meter = 100 centimeters
  1 meter is a little more than one yard
- 1 year = 12 months = 52 weeks = 365 days
  1 month = about 4 weeks
  1 week = 7 days
  1 day = 24 hours
  1 hour = 60 minutes
  1 minute = 60 seconds
- 1 dollar = 100 cents = 100¢ = $1.00
  1 dime = 2 nickels = 10 pennies
  1 dollar = 4 quarters = 10 dimes
  1 twenty-dollar bill = 2 ten-dollar bills = 4 five-dollar bills = 20 one-dollar bills
- The A.M. *hours* are between 12 o'clock midnight and 12 o'clock noon. The P.M. *hours* are between 12 o'clock noon and 12 o'clock midnight.
- An *angle* is a corner. It is a figure formed by two lines extending from the same point.
- *Perimeter* is the distance around a figure.
- *Area* is the number of square units that cover the surface of a figure.
- A *rectangle* has four sides and four right angles. A *square* has four equal sides and four right angles. All squares are rectangles, but not all rectangles are squares.
- A *triangle* has three sides and three angles.
- A *semicircle* is a half circle.
- A *cube* has six equal square sides.
- A *sphere* is a perfectly round ball.

Questions to Ask the Teacher

In the primary grades, you may want to ask the teacher questions such as:

- What facts and skills do you expect my child to learn in the coming weeks?
- Can you show me examples of problems you expect my child to be able to solve by the end of the semester?

- Do you expect children to memorize the addition, subtraction, multiplication, and division tables? When do they start? When should they have that memory work completed?

- If you don't require memorization of tables, how do you make sure that children learn them?

- What is the role of calculators in your class? How do you make sure they don't get in the way of learning the fundamentals?

- How is my child doing compared to others in her grade? What's the evidence you use in forming that judgment?

- On average, how much time does your class spend on math each day?

- Can you help me find out how the students in this school perform in math compared to other schools in the district and state?

- What can we do at home to reinforce the math lessons you're teaching?

What If My Child Is Falling Behind?

If your child is doing poorly on math tests, or can't understand the homework assignments, take corrective action. Do not wait. Math lessons build on each other, and future learning depends on the skills acquired now. Here are some steps to take:

- **Talk to the teacher.** Discuss the situation and see what she recommends. She may have some different approaches to the material to try with your child. Work together on a plan to get your child back on track.

- **Help your child review prior lessons.** If your child has hit a snag in math today, it may be because she hasn't thoroughly learned a lesson the class covered days or even weeks ago. For example, if she is struggling with the addition of fractions, it may be because she did not really learn how to find common denominators and needs to get some extra help with that concept. Help her backtrack, isolate the original trouble spot, and get the fundamentals down pat.

- **Ask for additional homework, if necessary.** It's possible your child needs more time on task, in which case you should be prepared to supervise extra exercises at home.

- **Talk to the teacher about arranging tutorials.** If you can't help with troublesome problems, find someone who can. If the teacher can't give tutorials herself, she should be able to help you find someone (perhaps an older student who is good in math) who can spend extra time with your child.

- **Have your child tested, if necessary.** A small percentage of students have trouble with math because of a learning disability. If your child is encountering significant problems not just in math but also in other subjects, some diagnostic testing may be in order. Consult the teacher or school counselor.

She should be able to put you in touch with a professional whose job it is to identify such problems. (See Chapter 11).

If your child is falling behind in math, be prepared for the fact that both of you will have to do some extra work. Nine times out of ten, better skills, understanding, and grades come from buckling down and going the extra mile.

The Intermediate Grades—Fourth Through Sixth Grades

In the primary grades, the first layer of math skills and knowledge was laid. Now that base grows thicker and, with enough practice, more solid as well.

Be aware, however, that in some U.S. schools the math program is not as strong as it should be in the intermediate grades. Lessons do not prepare children for work that lies ahead in junior high and high school. "Most students who enter my eighth grade Algebra I or Honors Algebra classes in September each year are ill-prepared to learn algebra because most of them have not fully mastered arithmetic," says a Georgia math teacher. Her observation is not uncommon.

One difference between the intermediate and primary years is that students are now better able to handle abstract concepts. At this level, children should not have to rely on hands-on objects such as blocks, beans, cardboard cutouts, or fingers to perform basic skills and work most problems. Teachers may still use physical props to help illustrate some lessons, but as cognitive abilities develop, children should be required to do more abstract thinking. Simple manipulatives should be replaced by more advanced tools such as rulers, compasses, and protractors. Although you should still see plenty of straightforward practice in computation, you'll also see growing emphasis on the kind of problem solving that requires students to really think their way through assignments.

Intermediate grade students take on more challenging multiplication and division problems. They also work with fractions, mixed numbers, decimals, and negative numbers. Children should develop a thorough understanding of these numbers and be comfortable computing them by the end of the sixth grade. You'll also see your child get an introduction to topics such as proportions, ratios, percentages, and exponents.

One goal of the intermediate grades is to get your child ready for the more formal study of algebra. She'll learn things such as how a letter can hold the place of a number in a mathematical expression, and how to solve simple equations such as $28 = 7x$. She'll use formulas such as $S = d/t$ (rate of speed equals distance traveled divided by time) and soon will be doing basic algebra without even knowing it!

Students were introduced to plane figures and solids in the primary grades. Now they are more capable of manipulating those two- and three-dimensional shapes in their heads, so a deeper study of geometry can begin. Students spend time working with all sorts of shapes: circles, triangles, parallelograms, pyramids, etc. They learn the formulas to find perimeter, circumference, area, and volume. They study angles and solve problems that involve them. There is nothing quite like the logic and precision of geometry to exercise children's growing cognitive abilities.

Students now learn to measure things with greater accuracy. Measuring is a skill that comes with practice. It is also a skill that takes knowledge: children must learn which units (inches, meters, pounds, liters, etc.) are appropriate for which kinds of measurements. Good schools require children to know the equivalencies between certain basic units (1 yard = 3 feet; 1 meter = 100 centimeters) and teach them how to convert from one unit to another.

In the intermediate grades, teachers expect more "mathematical reasoning." That is, they teach children to think more logically and clearly. Students get into the habit of approaching problems in an organized manner. They think about which parts to tackle first, how to break hard problems into smaller parts, and which information is most important. They practice making precise calculations. They express solutions clearly and accurately using correct mathematical notation. (Sloppiness is rightly penalized in good schools because it often leads to wrong answers.) Children use estimation to decide if their answers make sense and learn to double-check their calculations.

Students are frequently called upon to explain their reasoning in solving problems. They answer plenty of questions to show they understand the concepts underlying their exercises. They discuss alternative methods for finding solutions. They may also make up their own problems to use the math they've learned.

FOURTH GRADE

Fourth grade students continue to practice multiplying and dividing with whole numbers. They also grow more familiar with fractions and decimals. As in earlier years, students practice making calculations in their heads and estimating. These activities strengthen their number sense and mathematical thinking skills. Children also get much practice making precise computations with pencil and paper. In measuring things, they learn to convert between different units of measurement (e.g., 1 cup = 8 fluid ounces). In geometry, they take a closer look at lines, angles, and plane figures; get an introduction to circles; and practice finding the areas of rectangles. Among other things, fourth graders are able to do the following:

Numbers and Number Sense

- read, write, order, and compare whole numbers up to 999,999,999
- identify perfect squares and square roots to 144 (e.g., $9 \times 9 = 81$, $\sqrt{144} = 12$).
- plot points on a coordinate plane (grid)
- learn Roman numerals from 1 to 1,000 (I–M)

Fractions and Decimals

- recognize the fractions to one twelfth (½, ⅓, ¼, . . . ¹⁄₁₂)
- change improper fractions to mixed numbers (e.g., 5⁄2 = 2½)
- put fractions in lowest terms (e.g., ⅖ = ⅓)
- rename fractions with unlike denominators to fractions with common denominators
- compare fractions with like and unlike denominators (e.g., ⅜ < ¾)
- read, write, and compare decimals to the nearest thousandth
- read and write decimals as fractions (e.g., .39 = ³⁹⁄₁₀₀)
- round decimals to nearest tenth or hundredth
- read and write decimals on a number line

Computation

- identify multiples of a given number; common multiples of two given numbers
- multiply by two- and three-digit numbers
- identify factors of a given number; common factors of two given numbers

- divide by one- and two-digit numbers
- practice mental calculations and estimating sums, differences, products, and quotients
- solve two-step word problems involving multiplication and division
- solve equations involving more than one operation

Measurement

- make measurements using standard units (e.g., grams, tablespoons, milliliters)
- learn equivalencies among U.S. customary units of measurement (e.g., 1 lb = 16 oz, 1 gal = 4 qt) and solve problems involving changing units
- learn equivalencies among metric units of measurement (e.g., 1 m = 100 cm, 1 kg = 1,000 g) and solve problems involving changing units
- solve problems on elapsed time

Geometry

- identify and draw points, segments, rays, lines
- identify and draw horizontal, vertical, perpendicular, parallel, intersecting lines
- identify angles as right, acute, or obtuse
- identify various polygons (e.g., parallelogram, trapezoid)
- identify and draw diagonals of quadrilaterals
- begin study of circles (e.g., radius = ½ diameter)
- recognize similar and congruent figures
- learn and use formula for area of a rectangle

(*drawn from the Core Knowledge Sequence*)

In a good fourth grade class, students work homework and classroom assignments such as:

- In the number 36,724,159, a) which digit represents the ten thousands place? b) Which digit represents the ten millions place? c) Round this number to the nearest thousand.
  Answers: a) 36,7**2**4,159 b) **3**6,724,159 c) 36,724,000
- (147 ÷ 21) x (117 ÷ 9) = _____ Answer: 91
- 2/3 = ?/12 Answer: 2/3 = 8/12

• Place the following numbers on a number line: ¾, 3⁄2, 2.25, 0.25

Answer:

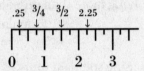

• A rectangle is 7 meters long. Its perimeter is 20 meters. What is the area of the rectangle in square meters? Answer: 21 square meters

How Are American Fourth Graders Doing?

Here are three examples of math problems given to fourth graders on the National Assessment of Educational Progress in 1996:

1. N stands for the number of stamps John had. He gave 12 stamps to his sister. Which expression tells how many stamps John has now?

a. $N + 12$ c. $12 - N$
b. $N - 12$ d. $12 \times N$

67 percent of the national sample gave the correct answer, B.

2. Ms. Hernandez formed teams of 8 students each from the 34 students in her class. She formed as many teams as possible, and the students left over were substitutes. How many students were substitutes?

39 percent of the national sample gave the correct answer, 2.

3. Sam can purchase his lunch at school. Each day he wants to have juice that costs 50¢, a sandwich that costs 90¢, and fruit that costs 35¢. His mother has only $1.00 bills. What is the least number of $1.00 bills that his mother should give him so that he will have enough money to buy lunch for five days?

17 percent of the national sample gave the correct answer, which is 9 dollar bills.

FIFTH GRADE

Fifth grade students practice adding, subtracting, and multiplying with decimals and fractions as they solve problems. They take up ratios and percentages, and learn about these concepts' relationship with fractions and decimals. In geometry, they learn formulas to find areas and volumes of simple figures. They use a protractor and compass to measure angles and construct figures. Youngsters explore the concept of probability as a measure of the likelihood that an event will happen. They practice gathering, analyzing, and recording data using tables, graphs, charts, and grids. They get used to the idea of seeing variables in mathematical expressions. Among other things, fifth graders are able to do the following:

Numbers and Number Sense

- read and write numbers up to the billions
- identify a set and numbers of a set, as indicated by { }
- study prime numbers; identify prime numbers less than 50
- find the greatest common factor and least common multiple of given numbers

Ratio and Percent

- express simple ratios
- make scale drawings
- solve problems regarding speed as a ratio using formula $S = d/t$ (or $D = R \times t$)
- study percentages; find the given percent of a number (e.g., 10% of 50 = ___)
- find fraction, decimal, percent equivalents (e.g., $\frac{3}{5}$ = .6 = 60%)

Fractions and Decimals

- find the least common denominator of fractions with unlike denominators
- compare fractions; put fractions in lowest terms
- add, subtract, and multiply with fractions and mixed numbers

- add, subtract, multiply with decimals; divide decimals by whole numbers
- round decimals; write them in expanded form; place them on number line

Computation

- know commutative and associative properties of addition
- know commutative, associative, and distributive properties of multiplication
- multiply by four-digit numbers; divide by three-digit numbers
- estimate products and quotients; practice mental multiplication and division
- solve multistep word problems and equations with more than one operation

Measurement

- practice measuring with different units (e.g., ft, lb, gal, ml)
- solve problems that involve converting, adding, and subtracting different units

Geometry

- measure and draw various angles, shapes, and line segments
- identify and draw equilateral, right, and isosceles triangles
- identify polygons (e.g., parallelogram, rhombus) and diagonals of polygons
- identify arc, chord, radius, and diameter of a circle
- study concept of pi; compute circumferences of circles
- compute areas of rectangles, triangles, parallelograms
- find areas of irregular figures (such as trapezoids) by dividing into regular figures
- find volume and surface area of rectangular prisms

Probability and Statistics

- understand probability as a measure of likelihood that an event will happen
- solve problems that involve collecting, interpreting, and graphing data

- find the average (mean) of a given set of numbers
- plot ordered pairs (positive and negative whole numbers) on coordinate plane

Pre-Algebra

- solve basic equations using variables (e.g., $39 + x = 75$)
- write and solve equations for word problems

(drawn from the Core Knowledge Sequence)

In a good fifth grade class, students work homework and classroom assignments such as:

- Find the product:

  494

  x 7.3 Answer: 3606.2
- Find the difference:

  $7\frac{5}{12}$

  $-4\frac{5}{6}$ Answer: $3\frac{1}{4}$
- Bob drove for 2½ hours at 60 miles per hour. Susan drove for 2 hours and went 140 miles. Who drove farther? Who drove faster? Answers: Bob drove farther. Sue drove faster.
- 450 ducks were on the lake. Then $\frac{5}{9}$ of them flew away. How many ducks were left on the lake? Answer: 200 ducks
- a) What is the reciprocal of $\frac{5}{27}$? b) What is the product of $\frac{5}{27}$ and its reciprocal? c) What is the product of any number and its reciprocal? Answers: a) $2\frac{7}{5}$ b) 1 c) 1
- Find the area of a right triangle with a base of 3 feet and a height of 48 inches. Express your answer in square inches. Answer: 864 in^2

SIXTH GRADE

Sixth grade students, by the end of the year, should be competent at computing with positive and negative numbers, fractions and decimals. They learn about exponents and do more work with ratios, proportions, and percentages (calculating such things as taxes, tips, and interest). In geometry, they construct various lines, angles, and figures; they get more work using formulas to find the areas, perimeters, and volumes of different figures. Sixth graders also get more experience working with data sets. They prepare for the systematic study of algebra by solving equations containing one variable. Among other things, sixth graders are able to do the following:

Numbers and Number Sense

- read and write numbers up to the trillions
- add and subtract positive and negative integers
- solve problems involving prime numbers; squares and square roots; greatest common factors; least common multiples
- learn to read and use exponents; identify powers of ten up to 10^6

Ratio and Percent

- solve problems involving ratios and proportions; use ratios to read map scales
- practice working with percents
  (e.g., 4 = ___ % of 20; 60% of 1,080 = ___)
- solve problems involving percent increase and decrease

Fractions and Decimals

- learn to divide by a fraction (i.e., multiply by reciprocal)
- add, subtract, multiply, and divide with fractions, mixed numbers, and decimals
- write fractions as decimals, decimals as percents, percents as fractions, etc.

Computation

- multiply and divide multidigit numbers (with and without a calculator)
- solve multistep word problems and equations with more than one operation
- estimate products and quotients

Measurement

- convert units within the U.S. system and within the metric system
- learn prefixes used in metric system (e.g., kilo = thousand, deci = tenth)

Geometry

- construct parallel lines, parallelograms, perpendicular bisectors
- construct, measure, and bisect angles
- draw various shapes when given information about their dimensions
- construct a figure congruent to a given figure
- show what figures would look like if rotated, flipped, reflected, etc.
- identify congruent angles, sides, and axes of symmetry in given figures
- find the perimeters, areas, or missing dimensions of various plane figures
- find the circumferences and areas of circles
- find the volumes or missing dimensions of rectangular solids

Probability and Statistics

- express the probability of an event happening as a fraction or ratio
- solve problems that involve collecting, interpreting, and graphing data
- given a set of data, find the mean, median, range, and mode
- make histograms and tree diagrams
- plot points on a coordinate plane using x-axis and y-axis
- graph simple functions and solve problems using a coordinate plane

Pre-Algebra

- solve equations with one variable (e.g., $4x = 104$)
- write and solve equations for word problems

(drawn from the Core Knowledge Sequence)

In a good sixth grade class, students work homework and classroom assignments such as:

- $6^3 - 3^2 = ?$ Answer: 207

- $(-3\frac{1}{2}) + (-2\frac{1}{3}) = ?$ Answer: $-5\frac{5}{6}$

- A rectangular prism has a width of 4 inches, a height equal to twice its width, and a volume of 288 in^3. What is the length of the prism? Answer: 9 inches

- Express the fraction % as a) a percent b) a decimal numeral.
  Answers: a) 300% b) 3.0

- In Mr. Tardy's clock store, all of the clocks are ticking, but none shows the correct time. There are 24 clocks that are slow, and ¼ are fast. a) How many clocks are fast? b) What percentage of the clocks are slow?
  Answers : a) 8 clocks b) 75%

- Jerry's football team played 9 games this season. The number of points the team scored in those games were 14, 21, 31, 20, 41, 27, 22, 19, and 30. a) What was the team's mean score? b) What was its median score?
  Answers: a) 25 points b) 22 points

Does Your Child Know Basic Math Facts?

Here are some examples of math facts your child should learn during the intermediate grades. By the end of sixth grade, she should be able to explain and use most of the following terms, concepts, and symbols.

- $\leq$, $\geq$ —signs for "less than or equal to" and "greater than or equal to."
- A *prime number* is a whole number greater than 1 whose only divisors are 1 and the number itself (e.g., 2, 3, 5, 7, 11, 13, 17, 19).
- Your child should know common *fraction-decimal-percent equivalencies* (e.g., $\frac{1}{10}$ = .10 = 10%; ¼ = .25 = 25%; ½ = .50 = 50%; ¾ = .75 = 75%).
- The *commutative property of addition* says that A + B = B + A. The *commutative property of multiplication* says that A x B = B x A.
- The *associative property of addition* says that (A + B) + C = A + (B + C). The *associative property of multiplication* says that (A x B) x C = A x (B x C).
- The *distributive property of multiplication* with respect to addition says that (A + B) x C = (A x C) + (B x C).
- A *variable* is a symbol (usually a letter) that stands for numbers in mathematical expressions (e.g., $35 = 7x$).
- 1 m (meter) = 100 cm (centimeters) = 1,000 mm (millimeters).
  1 km (kilometer) = 1,000 m.
- 1 lb = 16 oz.
  1 ton = 2,000 lbs.
- 1 g (gram) = 100 cg (centigrams) = 1,000 mg (milligrams).
  1 kg (kilograms) = 1,000 g (grams).

1 metric ton = 1,000 kg.

- 1 gal = 4 qt.

  1 qt = 2 pt.

  1 pt = 2 cups.

  1 cup = 8 fluid oz.

- 1 liter = 100 cl (centiliters) = 1,000 ml (milliliters).

- *Similar figures* have the same shape, but not necessarily the same size. *Congruent figures* have the same shape and size.

- A *right angle* has a measurement of 90°. An *acute angle* measures between 0° and 90°. An *obtuse angle* measures greater than 90°.

- *Perpendicular lines* are two lines that intersect to form right angles. *Parallel lines* are lines in the same plane that never intersect.

- ~—sign for "is similar to."

  ≅ —sign for "is congruent to."

- A *right triangle* is a triangle that contains a right angle. An *isosceles triangle* is a triangle with at least two sides of equal length. An *equilateral triangle* is a triangle whose sides are all the same length.

- *Pentagons, hexagons, heptagons,* and *octagons* are five-sided, six-sided, seven-sided, and eight-sided polygons.

- The *Greek letter* π (pi) is used to stand for the number of diameter lengths that equal the circumference of a circle. The approximate value of π is 3.14 or $^{22}\!/_7$.

- The formulas for the *circumference of a circle* are $C = \pi d$ (circumference = pi x diameter) and $C = 2\pi r$ (circumference = 2 x pi x radius).

- The formula for the *area of a rectangle* is $A = lw$ (area = length x width).

- The formula for the *area of a triangle* is $A = \frac{1}{2} bh$ (area = ½ x [base x height]).

- The formula for the *area of a circle* is $A = \pi r^2$ (area = pi x the radius squared).

- The formula for the *volume of a rectangular prism or solid* is $V = lwh$ (volume = length x width x height).

- The *mean* is the average of a set of numbers. The *median* is the middle number when a set of numbers is ordered from smallest to largest, or the mean of the two middle numbers if the set has an even number of members. The *mode* is the number in a set of numbers that occurs most often. The *range* is the difference between the largest and smallest numbers in a set.

Why Does My Child Keep Counting on Her Fingers?

Elementary school math is much more of a hands-on experience than it used to be. Math concepts once taught from the blackboard, textbook, or worksheets are now being communicated with concrete objects, known to teachers as "manipulatives." Manipulatives can be anything children can touch—blocks, beans, cardboard cutouts, etc. Teachers use objects because younger children often learn best by touching, holding, and seeing things. Studies show that, in the early grades, manipulatives help students grasp math concepts. For example, first graders can better grasp what fractions are about by cutting a pie into pieces.

In some schools, however, there is excessive reliance on physical activities. Manipulatives crowd out memorizing math facts and practicing basic skills. That leads to trouble. A mother of a fifth grader (who gets As in math) has a common complaint: "I give him $5 to go to McDonald's; the item he wants will cost $2.38, and I ask him how much change he's supposed to bring back," she says. "He can do it if he sits down and figures it out, but a fifth grader should be able to figure that in his head, and he can't. Until last year, I saw him using his fingers for basic subtraction."[1]

In our view (and many teachers agree), relying heavily on manipulatives after the early grades is a mistake. Physical props are valuable teaching tools early on, when children have limited abilities to conceptualize. They can be effective instructional aids in the later grades when a lesson needs to be illustrated. It is essential, however, for children to learn to think abstractly about mathematics. Their prolonged reliance on manipulatives may interfere with that process. Math students should gradually be weaned from dependence on concrete objects. As their cognitive abilities begin to develop, the training wheels need to go.

The routine use of objects to count, add, and subtract should vanish from math classwork and homework around second grade. If your child is still using beans or her fingers beyond that time, count it as clear evidence that "math facts" haven't been automated. Prompt remedial action is called for, even if it is necessary that you handle it at home or engage a tutor.

Questions to Ask the Teacher

In the intermediate grades, you may want to ask your child's teacher questions such as:

- What concepts will my child be studying this term?
- How much do your students practice computation—such as long division and multidigit multiplication?
- What is your policy about calculator use? Are children required to master pencil-and-paper and mental calculation before using calculators?
- At what stage (if ever) do you phase out the use of manipulatives in math class?
- Will you be teaching pre-algebra skills so that my child will be ready to study algebra in junior high?
- What kind of teaching strategy do you use in my child's class? Do you use a traditional teaching of math (such as direct instruction), or a discovery learning approach in which children "construct" concepts, or a mix?
- Does the math program you're using have an established record of success? Could I see some evaluation data on its effectiveness?
- How does a student obtain extra help in math?

Junior High—Seventh and Eighth Grades

Junior high is a critical transition phase in your school's curriculum. It summarizes what has come before and prepares the way for more advanced study. Unfortunately, these years seem to be part of a "weak link" in American mathematics education. Many observers argue that, as students progress into junior high, the typical U.S. math curriculum becomes repetitive and less challenging than it is elsewhere. According to the Department of Education, students in other countries are introduced to algebra and geometry in the years before high school, while relatively few U.S. junior high schools teach these topics.

The following pages outline a challenging model curriculum that gives students strong doses of arithmetic, geometry, and algebra. Remember, your school may not follow this exact sequence. The most important thing is to satisfy yourself that its program is demanding and keeps pupils moving forward.

A healthy dose of algebra in junior high gives students an undeniable advantage. It is the "gateway" to advanced mathematics and science in high school and beyond. Talk to teachers about how much algebra your child will be getting in school, and when it will come.

Another important goal in these years is to teach students logical reasoning, the intellectual heart of mathematics. The math curriculum should stress logic throughout elementary school, but by junior high, students should be ready for reasoning that is both more rigorous and more subtle.

SEVENTH GRADE

Seventh Grade students expand their knowledge of geometry; they take a closer look at three-dimensional objects, study symmetry, learn about angle pairs, and practice finding the perimeters, areas, and volumes of figures. Youngsters get more practice working with whole numbers, fractions, and decimals. They use and solve some simple equations containing a variable. They solve problems involving proportional reasoning (ratios, percentages, etc.). Seventh grade is also a year of refining their abilities to determine probabilities and to work with statistics. Among other things, seventh graders are able to do the following:

Geometry

- construct various three-dimensional objects (e.g., simple right prisms, cones, cylinders, spheres); calculate their surface areas and volumes
- study and construct plane figures that exhibit symmetry
- study angle pairs; understand vertical, congruent, complementary, supplementary, adjacent, corresponding, alternate interior, and alternate exterior angles
- construct parallel lines and a transversal using a compass and straight edge
- demonstrate that the sum of the interior angles of a plane triangle equals 180 degrees
- construct a circle that circumscribes a triangle using compass and straight edge
- know and use formulas to find areas of plane figures (e.g., triangles, circles, parallelograms)

Working with Whole Numbers, Fractions, and Decimals

- know proper order of operations including grouping symbols, and apply to whole number and decimal expressions
- study basic algebraic equations
- apply the distributive and associative properties to numeric expressions
- solve simple equations with one variable (e.g., $12x = 108$)
- add, subtract, multiply, and divide mixed numbers, fractions, and decimals
- compare integers, signed decimals, and fractions using the symbols $<, >, =, \leq, \geq$
- add and subtract integers and signed decimals using parentheses

The Coordinate Plane

- plot points on coordinate plane; identify the coordinates of a given point
- calculate the distance between two points that both lie on the x-axis or y-axis

Proportions and Geometric Proportions

- learn to recognize proportions in tables of numbers and on graphs
- use proportions to complete a set of data and to complete a graph
- solve problems involving percentages, average speeds, and scales on maps
- calculate how the area or volume of a given figure changes when one of its dimensions changes

Probability and Statistics

- interpret statistical data from tables and graphs
- display data on line graphs, bar graphs, histograms, and circle graphs
- determine probabilities of events through experiments and simulations
- given a set of data, find the mean, median, range, and mode

(*drawn from the Core Knowledge Sequence*)

In a good seventh grade class, students work homework and class-room assignments such as:

- <DEF measures 78°. What is the measure of an angle supplementary to <DEF? Answer: 102°

- Find the quotient: 9⅓ ÷ 4⅗. Answer: 2⅘₅

- Find the surface area of a rectangular prism measuring 9 cm long, 6 cm wide, and 2 cm high. Answer: 168 cm²

- The following data show how typical seventh grade girls spend their allowance: Compact disks—40%, Movies—22%, Snacks—9%, Makeup—11%, Magazines—18%. Construct a circle graph to represent these data.

Answer:

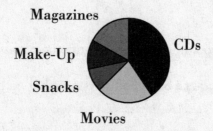

- Kelly's dress shop has been open only six months. Her profits and losses for the first six months of business were: $1,678; −$537; $796; $2,170; −$1,029; $942. What was the average monthly profit?

Answer: $670

EIGHTH GRADE

Eighth grade math is devoted primarily to introductory algebra, a considerable amount of geometry, and the correct handling of linear data. Students continue to use measuring and drawing instruments, to extend their capacity for mental arithmetic and approximation, and to become more familiar with deductive reasoning. Having previously learned to do many computations on paper and in their heads, eighth graders also use a scientific calculator as an aid to problem solving. Among other things, eighth graders are able to do the following:

Geometry

- study the concept of cosine; know that in a right triangle the cosine of an angle is the ratio of the adjacent side to the hypotenuse

- use a calculator to determine the approximate value of an acute angle given the cosine
- study perpendiculars and problems of the shortest distance (e.g., prove that the length of any one side of a triangle is always less than the sum of the other two sides)
- show that the shortest distance from a point to a line is a perpendicular segment
- show that any triangle inscribed in a circle with one side as the diameter is a right triangle
- study properties of triangles (e.g., learn that the medians of a triangle intersect at a point called the center of gravity)
- know and use the Pythagorean theorem to calculate the third side of a right triangle
- study spheres (e.g., know that the section created by the intersection of a plane and a sphere is a circle or a point)
- calculate the surface area of a sphere using the equation $S = 4\pi r^2$ and volume of a sphere using $V = \frac{4}{3}\pi r^3$
- study translations and rotations of plane figures (e.g., construct the image of a point, line segment, and circle through a rotation about a point)
- show that translations of vectors form a parallelogram
- construct an equilateral triangle, a square, and a regular hexagon, given its center and one of its vertices

Working with Numbers

- solve one-step equations of the form $A + x = B$ and $Ax = B$, where A and B are constants
- simplify expressions by using the number properties and combining like terms
- study integer exponents (e.g., know the definition of an exponent n when n is positive or negative; know that a non-zero number to the zero power is one)
- know the multiplication properties of exponents
- convert decimal and whole numbers to and from scientific notation
- work with simple algebraic equations and expressions
- translate word problems into equations and solve them
- factor algebraic expressions
- simplify algebraic expressions by combining like terms
- interpret geometrical problems and put them in equation form

- study numeric comparisons and inequalities (e.g., know that addition or subtraction of the same value from both sides of an inequality maintains the inequality)
- solve one-step inequalities

Organization and Presentation of Linear Data

- study the concept of slope
- understand what a function is and determine the equation of a linear function given its slope and intercepts
- calculate frequencies from data; create charts, graphs, and tables indicating frequencies
- interpret charts or graphs that have been indexed to a particular value

(drawn from the Core Knowledge Sequence)

In a good eighth grade class, students work homework and classroom assignments such as:

- Graph the equation $y = -\frac{1}{2} x + 4$. Find the slope, x-intercept, and the y-intercept. Answer: $x = 8$, $y = 4$, slope $= -\frac{1}{2}$
- Write 37.962×10^{-3} in standard form. Answer: .037962
- Solve the inequality $97 > m + (-15)$. Answer: $m < 112$
- Add the following polynomial and write the answer in simplest form:
  $(y^4 + 3y^2 - y + 1) + (y^4 - 2y^2 + 2y - 9)$. Answer: $2y^4 + y^2 + y - 8$
- This trapezoid was reflected across the y-axis. Find the coordinates of A and B.

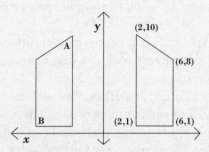

Answer: A $(-2, 10)$; B $(-6, 1)$

Does Your Child Know Basic Math Facts?

Here are examples of the kinds of math facts your child should have learned by the end of the eighth grade. She should be able to explain and use most of the following terms, concepts, and symbols.

- The inverse property of multiplication says that the product of a number and its multiplicative inverse is 1: $\frac{x}{y} \times \frac{y}{x} = 1$
- The addition property of equality states that if $a = b$ then $a + c = b + c$.
- The Pythagorean theorem states that for every right triangle, the sum of the squares of each leg is equal to the square of the hypotenuse: $a^2 + b^2 = c^2$
- The product of two integers with the same sign is positive:

    $(+) \times (+) = (+), (-) \times (-) = (+)$

- The quotient of two integers is negative if the two integers have different signs:

    $(-) \times (+) = (-) ; (+) \times (-) = (-)$

- Order of Operations:

    1. Do all operations inside grouping symbols first.

    2. Simplify all numbers with exponents.

    3. Multiply and divide from left to right.

    4. Add and subtract from left to right.

- The first coordinate, x, of an ordered pair (x,y) is known as the x-coordinate and tells how far left or right to move from the origin along the x-axis. The second coordinate, y, of an ordered pair (x,y) is known as the y-coordinate and tells how far up or down to move from the origin along the y-axis.
- Factorial notation is used to write a product when factors are all consecutive positive integers less than or equal to a number: $6! = 6 \times 5 \times 4 \times 3 \times 2 \times 1$.
- $a{:}b$—symbol for the ratio a to b or a/b
- <ABC—symbol for measure of angle ABC
- $|A|$—symbol for absolute value of A
- $\sqrt{a}$—symbol for the square root of a
- a^n—symbol for the nth power of a

How Are American Eighth Graders Doing?

Here are two examples of math problems included in the eighth grade portion of the National Assessment of Educational Progress in 1996:

1. A car odometer registered 41,256.9 miles when a highway sign warned of a detour 1,200 feet ahead. What will the odometer read when the car reaches the detour?

    a. 42,456.9   d. 41,259.2

    b. 41,279.9   e. 41,257.1

    c. 41,261.3

26 percent of the youngsters in the national sample gave the correct answer, which is E.

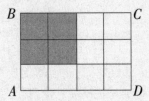

2. In the figure above, what fraction of rectangle ABCD is shaded?

    a. ⅙   d. ⅓

    b. ⅕   e. ½

    c. ¼

65 percent of youngsters in the national sample gave the correct answer, which is D.

Questions to Ask the Teacher

You may want to ask your child's junior high math teacher questions such as:

- What specific knowledge and skills should my child possess by the end of the marking period? (Ask to see examples of the kind of problems she should be able to solve.)

- Will my child be getting a full introductory course in algebra before she reaches high school?

- Can you tell me a bit about your own math training?

- Do students get a good mix of "real-world," practical applications and "pure math" problems that emphasize mathematics' abstract nature?

- Are correct answers to problems emphasized or do you look primarily for the strategies that students use to "tackle" the problems?

- How will you assess my child's progress? How will you determine her course grade?

- About how much time do you expect children to spend on math homework every day?

- What can I do at home to help? (even though I may not understand all the math my child is doing now!)

- How does a student get extra help if her grades begin to fall?

ISSUES IN THE TEACHING OF MATHEMATICS

The following pages discuss some issues and controversies roiling the waters of math education today. In our view, several of the latest trends are not good news, even if they are called "reforms." At some point, you will probably encounter some of these practices. You will have to judge whether they are serving your child well. Whatever conclusions you reach, it is always wise to be on the lookout for strengths and weaknesses in the way your school teaches. This section should help make you more eagle-eyed.

What Is "New" New Math?

The math wars are raging. In one school, an upset mother confronts educators about her first grader's lagging skills—and is advised to get the child a calculator. In another, the teacher who stands at the blackboard and demonstrates how to solve problems is branded "authoritarian." District officials strike certain textbooks from approved lists, even though they raise test scores, because the "experts" say they contain too many formulas or too much "drill and kill." Consultants insist that children do group activities that "reveal" math concepts. One class, the *Los Angeles Times* reports, "grows so frustrated trying to 'discover 1,000 years of math' that the students beg the teacher to explain the material.

So she lectures—but keeps the desks in groups so the principal won't find out."[2]

What's all the fuss about? It's called reform math, "new New Math" (a swipe at the ill-fated New Math movement of the 1960s and 1970s), "whole math" (a pejorative reference to "whole language" reading instruction), or "NCTM math" (after the National Council of Teachers of Mathematics, which has propagated it). You may also hear it called "fuzzy math," "feel-good math," even "rain forest math." With education fads, there's usually a high correlation between the number of nicknames and the level of controversy.

This latest wave of reform began around 1989 when the NCTM, an organization to which many U.S. math teachers belong, released new "standards" for school math. These standards represented a profound change in conventional wisdom about how math should be taught and learned. The traditional method (often called "direct instruction") is that a knowledgeable teacher—usually with the aid of a textbook—introduces a new idea or concept, shows how it works, and then assigns problems that students solve using this new information. Through much practice, students deepen their understanding and accumulate fundamental skills. Teachers expect children to commit basic facts and formulas to memory. In traditional classrooms, partial credit is often given for using reasonable methods to solve test problems, but grades rest largely on finding the right answers.

Things look different in a new New Math classroom. Less emphasis is placed on memorizing basic facts. Instruction "should persistently emphasize 'doing' rather than 'knowing,'" the NCTM says. It also recommends that "decreased attention" be paid to traditional skills such as long division and computations with fractions. New New Math advocates call instead for greater use of calculators to avoid "tedious" pencil-and-paper calculations. Showing kids how to work problems and then assigning practice sets is passé ("drill" turns students off); instead, children should spend more time working in groups to discover important math concepts for themselves. Finding a right answer is often less prized than coming up with interesting strategies to tackle problems and talking them over with classmates.

This new approach to math embraces what educators call the "constructivist" philosophy. Rather than accepting, internalizing, and using knowledge and skills developed by others over the centuries and transmitted by teachers, children are encouraged to try to figure things out for themselves, "constructing" their own meanings and understandings. Teachers thus become "facilitators of learning." Rather than systematically imparting the knowledge they possess, they are supposed to create stimulating environments, encourage youngsters to explore, and guide students as they discover math. Less stress is placed on using deductive logic. Instead, trial-and-error investigations and the "intuitive insights" of children are emphasized. Real-life, practical applications are heralded over math's abstract nature.

The new New Math approach is well intended: to help make math real, vital, and practical, not dull rote learning of uncertain relevance. No one argues with such goals. The approach includes some good ideas that can usefully be *added* to traditional direct instruction in math, but not *substituted*. It's good for children to learn how to solve real-world problems, for example, to select their own strategies to tackle assignments, and to know how to use the latest technology to speed and simplify tasks. In fact, skilled math teachers were giving these kinds of lessons long before the latest reform wave washed upon the education shore.

The problem with the new approach—when it's substituted, rather than added, to time-honored methods of direct instruction—is that it shortchanges students in some very important lessons. These include the need for lots of practice in math; the value of memorization; an emphasis on gradually building basic skills; and proper attention to exactness in answers.

Will the new New Math work? The signs are not particularly encouraging so far, and many moms and dads are troubled. One of the authors, visiting a Colorado school not long ago, heard this from an irked parent: "The kids here are great at solving math problems, only not with numbers." Some educators are also spreading the alarm. "My freshman math students cannot automatically calculate; unless they have a calculator, they are helpless," notes a high school science and mathematics teacher. "Decimals don't make sense to them, and frankly, without basic skills, I don't know that they are capable of learning any of the math or science-related math that I teach."

In California, test scores showed little progress and some deterioration in the years following new New Math's introduction. In 1998, after some rancorous debate, the state turned back toward traditional mathematics programs. As of this writing, the National Council of Teachers of Mathematics is revising its 1989 standards, perhaps partly in response to public outcry. Yet advocates insist that their methods will work and counsel patience. "We knew there needed to be a fair amount of research and teacher training," says one. "We knew it would take 20 or 25 years to pull this off."[3] Those are not soothing words to a parent's ears.

No one single pedagogy fits all lessons and classrooms. A successful educator might use a variety of approaches to teach mathematics to a class of twenty-plus children. Your child's own teacher might employ both old-fashioned drill and newfangled "discovery learning" activities. As long as the children are learning math well, then the more power to her. But *do* take the time to find out how math is being taught in your child's classroom. This important subject can't be taken for granted.

Talk to the teacher about her goals for your child in the coming months. Spend time looking over the textbooks and worksheets. Keep track of homework assignments. Talk to your child and monitor her progress. In other words, get to know the math program. Does it make sense to you? Is it truly challenging? Is it teaching your child the sorts of lessons described in this chapter's curriculum model? The "reforms" that continually reshape American math education make it all the more important that you get satisfactory answers to these questions.

Is Memorization Outdated?

For generations, memorizing the addition, subtraction, multiplication, and division tables has been a rite of passage for elementary school students. Today, however, you may encounter schools where such work is no longer emphasized. An anecdote illustrates the problem. Not long ago, one of the authors was called by two worried dads in the course of a single week. They both reported a problem in almost the same words: "My daughter attends a very good school that we worked very hard to get her into. But in fourth grade she's still counting on her fingers. What's going on?"

What's going on is that some schools have embraced the view that children should not be held responsible for memorizing basic math facts. This attitude usually stems from the conviction that youngsters should "understand" math, not learn it through "rote memorization." You'll hear it said that forcing students to commit those tables to memory takes all the fun out of math and "discourages learning." Some education experts have even concluded that children can proceed without mastering them. "We have for so many years said to kids 'What's 7 + 5?' as if that was the important thing . . ." says a math specialist in

Chicago. "Sure, I think kids should know the multiplication tables, but I wouldn't hold a kid back from doing other stuff if they didn't."[4] Others have gone further and decided that pupils are no longer even capable of mastering those old tables. "Our daughter's teachers and principal told us to our face that a child in the third grade does *not* have the mental ability to memorize addition facts up to ten," one New York mother reports.

The prevailing theory in many classrooms is that fundamental math knowledge should grow naturally in children from the process of exploration and the experience they get solving problems. Rather than memorizing definitions and formulas, children will "develop an understanding and appreciation" of what they need to know. Here's the big problem: no one has provided convincing evidence that this approach works when used as the primary means of teaching math.

Why is it so important that your child know those tables and other basic math facts? Because she needs to be intimately familiar with that information before she can work math problems with ease. Faced with the assignment, "Find the area of a rectangle 40 inches by 90 inches," a student is quickly frustrated if, when she goes to multiply 40 by 90, she cannot remember in a flash that $4 \times 9 = 36$. If she stumbles over a relatively simple problem like that, more sophisticated operations will be virtually impossible.

Learning math involves building a mental storehouse of rules, terms, axioms, and theorems. Doing math well depends on having rapid and accurate recall of that knowledge. Much like internalizing the basic "letter sounds" via phonics-based reading instruction, so that one can automatically use them in tackling an unfamiliar word, getting "$7 \times 9 = 63$" into your mind's hard drive means that this useful bit of information is always there, ready to be used when needed. Says Tom Loveless, a former teacher and Brookings Institution scholar who studies curriculum trends, "I'm not in favor of a dull, drill-and-kill way of teaching math, but there are some elements of math—particularly at the elementary level—where some basic facts simply must be memorized."[5]

Talk to the teacher or principal and find out what the school's expectations are for knowing math facts. Ask whether children are expected to memorize the addition, subtraction, multiplication, and division tables. When do they start memorizing them? When are they expected to have completed them? How are youngsters held accountable for accomplishing this? If the school does not encourage memorizing, how does it go about teaching these basics? If it's a good school, you'll get a straightforward answer that most likely involves starting this process in the first grade and completing it by the end of grade three or grade four. If nobody seems to know the answer to your questions, or you get evasive answers, or you are informed, "We don't do that kind of thing anymore," you should be concerned. It's not only that knowing these tables is important in itself. They are also a reasonable litmus test; a teacher's or principal's view of them is apt to reveal much about how the school approaches mathematics.

Whether or not your child's teacher requires memorizing the basic tables of math facts, you should make it a priority to teach them at home. Don't be afraid to use tried-and-true methods when helping your child learn fundamentals. Write out the tables for study, and have your child practice writing them out, too. Use flash cards as well as oral drills. ("What is 6 times 8? Good. Now, what's 4 times 5?") Be patient. It takes time for children to get this stuff under their belts.

How Important Is Practice?

"We don't plug and chug anymore. We teach them to think." "Repetitious drill-and-kill is a waste. It just teaches rote procedures without fostering mathematical insight." "Too much emphasis on the mechanics of mathematics inhibits learning."

These are the kinds of comments you hear in schools where practice is considered outmoded. In such schools, children aren't as likely to get assignments that involve working a certain kind of problem several times until they master it. Instead, students are given fewer but longer-lasting exercises that often call for group work. They are challenged to put their heads together, figure out how to solve a problem, and articulate the underlying mathematical concepts. Lessons are often of the hands-on type. You might see a group of third graders holding on to a long loop of yarn and moving around to create different geometric shapes. Or sixth graders breaking into small groups with sheets of grid paper and assigned to construct a box that holds the maximum volume.

The quality of such "problem-solving" activities in American schools is uneven, and parents need to ask: Do the assignments successfully challenge children to plumb—and then grasp—key math concepts? A middle school math class studies different ways to get to school. They measure distance and time by walking, riding the bus, and taking carpools. They decide that walking is cheapest and the best exercise, but the bus is safest. Is this really math, or some sort of social science? In another class, students spend several minutes a day expressing their feelings about mathematics in journals. It may help them learn to write (if anyone is correcting their spelling and grammar), but is it eating up time that should be allotted to studying numbers and equations?

The real question is this: Can children get basic math skills without much practice? Or is the approach that says "less drill and computation, more exploring and talking about math concepts" really akin to Harold Hill's "think system" in *The Music Man*? The children of the River City band were given no instruments and no practice. Instead, Professor Hill told them if they would just "think" the Minuet in G, someday they'd be able to play it. "Kids talk about math a lot. They write about math, but they don't actually do it," complains a frustrated California parent.[6] It sounds a lot like River City.

We're all for children engaging in activities designed to illuminate mathematical ideas. The problem comes when the systematic mastery of basic skills is sacrificed. Here is the reality: most children must practice math, and practice a lot, in order to learn it well. If they are going to add, subtract, multiply, divide, find the areas of circles, calculate proportions, and perform an array of other operations with speed and proficiency, they need consistent training. That means working many problems to master fundamental skills. Without such mastery, they'll have a tough time moving forward and tackling more sophisticated problems.

Regular practice, in moderation, is not what drives children away from math. What really makes them dislike and fear math is *not understanding it*. "Math anxiety" arises from not being able to work problems correctly, not understanding important concepts, and not being able to get the right answer when it's your turn at the blackboard. The antidote to such anxiety is greater familiarity with math. And such familiarity comes through repeated exposure. There is no better way for children to gain confidence about working problems and tackling challenges.

Students also need opportunities to reflect about mathematics. Good teachers don't overload kids with pages of problems or rush them for answers. They often tell them to slow down and think. Good classes sometimes spend a whole period on a single problem because the teacher wants the children to develop a deep understanding of the ideas at work. In good schools, there is a balance between in-depth exploration and building proficiency in basic skills. That's important. But if most of the "problem solving" your child does comes in the form of elaborate projects, there's a good chance she won't get enough time on task to master basic skills.

What Is the Role of Calculators in Math Class?

Many American schools now raise students on calculators. Education experts advise that "appropriate calculators should be available to all students at all times." They often recommend "frequent use of calculators" even in the earliest grades.

Calculator proponents argue that technology is doing away with the need to rely on do-it-yourself computation. The National Research Council, an arm of the National Academy of Sciences, asks: "How many scientists or engineers use paper-and-pencil methods to carry out their scientific calculations? Who would trust a bank that kept its records in ledgerbooks?" The National Council of Teachers of Mathematics states flatly, "Valuable class time should not be devoted to developing students' proficiency in calculating 824×689 or 8.24×6.89 with paper and pencil, since these exercises can be done more readily with a calculator."[7]

Such groups assure us that they still believe children should gain "some proficiency" at computing on their own, but clearly, many in the education establishment think that learning to perform basic math operations is passé. In fact, they suggest, these skills aren't really all that critical for learning higher mathematics. So you didn't learn that algebra but you want to do calculus? No problem. We've got calculators. "Weakness in algebraic skills need no longer prevent students from understanding ideas in more advanced mathematics," the National Research Council tells us. "Just as computerized spelling checkers permit writers to express ideas without the psychological block of terrible spelling, so will the new calculators enable motivated students who are weak in algebra or trigonometry to persevere in calculus or statistics."[8]

Many teachers are raising red flags. "That knocks the heck out of trying to motivate them to internalize fundamental numerical relationships," says one. "I've seen seventh graders reach for a calculator to answer questions like 10 minus 4." College professors, too, lament that incoming freshmen now use calculators to do the simplest adding and subtracting. "Things the average students would know backward and forward twelve years ago, these students don't know at all," says Jerry Rosen of Cal State Northridge.[9] Meanwhile, critics note that in nations like Korea and Japan that outscore U.S. students in mathematics, calculator use in the early grades is rare.

It is undeniable that calculators are routinely used in business, science, and throughout the adult world, but that world is not the same as elementary school. There are crucial concepts to absorb and operations to be mastered before children can acquire more advanced mathematical prowess. Students must bring their minds to bear on them. If the calculator is used as a crutch, that process may be impeded.

There definitely is a place for calculators in school, especially in the later grades when students are tackling tougher problems. Nevertheless, calculators should supplement, not replace, important skills. If math beginners are constantly urged to reach for the calculator to do their "nitty-gritty" work, rather than sweating through it themselves, they simply will not get the mental practice they need. They'll never internalize or "automate" any of these basic skills.

Here are a couple of sensible guidelines to keep in mind. First, in elementary school, most mathematics should involve exercises that students work through on their own, without the aid of calculators. Second, calculators should be used only for operations that children have already mastered by hand. Even then, they should not be used so much that youngsters let their skills get rusty or grow dependent on having an electronic device within reach. As a Florida teacher says, "Keeping skills current by using them on a daily basis is essential to higher math processes."

It's a good idea to ask your child's teacher what role calculators play in her classroom. Ask what steps she takes to ensure that they don't get in the way of learning the fundamentals. Watch how your child does her homework. Don't let her get away with punching buttons when she's supposed to be practicing that arithmetic, or using a graphing calculator to find algebraic solutions when the assignment says figure it out yourself. If your child routinely handles assignments with the aid of technology but then struggles when she tries to do the work on her own, something's amiss, and it's time to meet with the teacher.

What Is "Discovery Learning" in Math?

Madalyn McDaniel felt betrayed. Her son had enrolled in a math program where educators promised to teach in a new, more effective way. It wasn't long before she realized that all was not well. Instead of learning rules and formulas, her son and his classmates spent most of their time trying to invent their own methods to solve problems. "He was very frustrated," says McDaniel. "I'd say, 'Look in the book, it will explain.' He'd say, 'Mom, there is no book!'"[10]

In some schools, students spend much time engaged in games and activities that are designed to help them discover math concepts themselves. They often work in groups using hands-on materials. They propose different schemes to find solutions, discuss the merits of alternative approaches, and test their methods through trial and error. The idea behind such "discovery learning" is that if you arrive at knowledge for yourself, it will mean more to you and will last longer in your brain.

The ardor for this approach is fueled by a deep conviction that learning flourishes best when children are allowed to make their own sense out of the world, unhampered by the straitjacket of externally dictated rules and formulas imposed by adults. The pedagogy rests largely on the theory of "constructivism," which, as we noted earlier, holds that knowledge is something that children manufacture for themselves as active participants in the learning process. Each child's understanding is shaped by her own experiences. Thus each individual's knowledge of mathematics is uniquely personal—not something handed down from on high by a teacher or textbook.

Several problems arise when this philosophy occupies the center of elementary school math. When you rely on children to "construct" knowledge or skills—rather than systematically introducing material to them—learning can become a disorganized and time-consuming process. Mathematics is a highly structured body of knowledge and does not lend itself to haphazard learning.

Perhaps the biggest problem with discovery learning in math is that most theorems, conventions, terms, and operations are not "natural" occurrences. As E. D. Hirsch of the Core Knowledge Foundation has pointed out, learning math means mastering an invented system. It is not a process that we can expect young children to develop, "construct," or "discover" on their own. In fact, many mathematical conventions initially puzzle youngsters because they run counter to their natural intuitions—such as fractions getting smaller as the bottom number gets bigger.[11]

Everyone agrees that students should be encouraged to explore new concepts on their own. In good classes, teachers naturally ask some open-ended questions and present problems designed to lead students to fresh insights, but it is not reasonable to expect young children to rediscover the concepts, relationships, and formulas established by brilliant mathematicians over many centuries. Self-discovery cannot be the main avenue of teaching math. Experience (and test scores) shows that students do best when teachers impart mathematical knowledge directly, in an organized and explicit fashion using a variety of proven techniques. To get the job done, math teachers must *teach*.

Look to see whether your child's teacher clearly explains concepts and procedures. Scan the textbook. Are terms defined, procedures demonstrated, and concepts developed thoroughly and directly? If, from visiting the class and talking with the teacher, you find that the philosophy is that students must normally generate their own mathematical understandings, and that an educator should never be the "sage on the stage" who teaches directly, be suspicious. If math class is mostly a series of games, time-consuming projects, and group activities in which children are meant to discover their own way, you probably won't be satisfied with the results.

What Is "Real-World" Math?

Today there is a great emphasis on applying mathematics to "everyday" or "real-world" situations. Word problems are likely to relate to activities such as planning a party or building a doghouse. Peek in a math class and you might see students figuring out how a roller coaster's curves affect its speed, or how to chart classmates' preferences in fast food. Teachers' guides urge educators to give assignments that "have meaning to children" and "relate to their environment."

Showing children real-world applications of math is a good practice. It helps youngsters grasp concepts (problems showing that there are four quarters to a dollar drive home what "¼" is all about) and can make assignments more interesting (for baseball fans, figuring batting averages makes percentages fun). Solving realistic problems demonstrates that math is a practical, useful subject. It helps answer the old question, "Just what good is studying this stuff going to do me, anyway?"

Be aware, however, that the enthusiasm for making math "relevant" can go too far. New York father Sol Stern tells how his son's third grade class spent months building a Japanese garden. "Every day when my son came home, we'd ask him what he did in math. Every day he cheerfully answered, 'We measured the garden.'" The teacher gave assurances that building the garden required "real-life" math skills. "Maybe," Stern wrote, "but my son's conscientious fourth-grade teacher later chafed over having to keep reviewing the multiplication tables that the children were supposed to have mastered in third grade. . . . While it was nice that our children were building Japanese gardens, Japanese kids were leaving our kids in the dust in real math."[12]

Practical applications should augment, not replace, problems and skills that deal with abstractions. "Pure math" exercises such as dividing 3,060 by 36 or finding x for the equation $6x - 19 = -1$ are vital. Why? Because, in the end, math's domain is one of pure thought. For example, the line in geometry embodies an abstract concept. It has no width, no color, no mass. It is composed of points that take up no space. Mathematics *is* an abstract discipline. "It is the activity in which the human mind seems to take the least from the outside world, in which it acts or seems to act only of itself and on itself," the great French mathematician Henri Poincaré observed.

This abstract nature of mathematics is good for young minds. It helps them learn to manipulate ideas. It trains them to think clearly, exactly, and in an organized fashion. Independence of thought is rightly cultivated when students conduct mental operations with the theorems and facts they possess. Math's abstractions make children's thinking more powerful generally and should be valued.

Learning to apply mathematics to the physical world is important, but so is learning to operate in the realm of pure intellect. If your school is so absorbed with making math "relevant" that it shies away from its abstract nature, your child may miss the very benefits that give this subject its place at the heart of the school curriculum.

How Important Is Getting Exact Answers in Math?

Some parts of the education establishment recommend that math teachers de-emphasize the need to find exact answers to problems, and that parents and children adjust their attitudes accordingly. A couple in Illinois, for example, reports that they were urged to send their son to see the school counselor because he "values correct and complete answers too much."[13]

The new New Math philosophy has several beefs with "obsessing" about right answers. It reasons that a correct answer in itself does little to illuminate a child's mathematical reasoning and thinking skills. Computational errors, after all, are less important than understanding the process of solving a problem. Right and wrong answers create "winners" and "losers" and keep kids from feeling good about math. Requiring an exact answer might hinder children's ability to "construct" their own mathematical understandings.

Some educators call for tests that will provide more "authentic" assessments of children's learning, that will allow teachers to gauge "different kinds of knowing" and give "greater insight into students' understanding." More open-ended test questions are encouraged, such as: What are some different ways to solve this problem? What is similar or different about those possible methods? Can you make up some similar problems?

Such assessments work well in some classrooms and not in others. Most good teachers, in fact, use a basket of different criteria and measurements to arrive at a final grade—there is nothing new about that. But all the talk about "authentic assessment" and probing "mathematical understandings" overlooks one simple fact: in math, perhaps more than any other subject, right answers matter. It is a precise discipline that calls for exactitude. That is the nature of mathematics. Changing testing techniques and lowering expectations for children will not do away with that fact. It will just produce more mediocre math students.

The point of a math test (or any test in school) should be to find out what a student knows and does not know. Incorrect answers are valuable clues for teachers. They help zero in on gaps in knowledge, poor understandings of concepts, and sloppy intellectual practices. Used constructively, wrong answers are opportunities to teach children the right way. De-emphasizing correct answers and passing students along, whether or not they've learned the material well enough to find those right answers, is no help to children in the long run. And it's not mathematics.

Does the Teacher Know Enough Math?

There are many excellent math teachers in American schools. Unfortunately, there are also many elementary school teachers who do not have much mathematics education in their backgrounds, particularly in the lower grades. According to the National Science Foundation, only 7 percent of teachers in grades one through four majored or minored in math or math education. In grades five through eight, among those teaching mathematics, only 18 percent majored or minored in math or math education at the undergraduate or graduate level. A good number of teachers (about 40 percent) say they don't feel very well qualified to teach the subjects for which they are responsible. Being afraid that your students will ask questions you can't answer does not make for a great teaching or learning experience.

Schools are in a tough spot. When principals try to recruit people with solid math backgrounds, they find themselves competing against headhunters from high-tech industries. "Those who graduated with a major in math can easily earn much more going into computer-related employment," says the former chair of a high school math department. It's an ironic situation: a healthy demand for math knowledge in the marketplace siphons off the very people we depend upon to impart that knowledge to the next generation.

Given this situation, it is prudent to keep a close eye on the quality of math instruction your child gets. If you think it is subpar, you might tactfully inquire into what kind of math training the teacher has. Don't throw her on the defensive; simply ask her in a gracious way to fill you in on her math background. Remember that, in the primary grades, where one teacher is typically responsible for all subjects, you shouldn't expect a formal math degree. But you might ask what kind of professional classes she's taken to help her teach this particular subject. Generally, around the time of the intermediate grades (and certainly by junior high), your child should have a specialized math teacher. At that point, you hope to see a major in mathematics or some such degree in the teacher's background, but as the statistics cited above show, you're not likely to find it.

Sit in on a class or two, if necessary, to make sure your child is getting the kind of instruction she needs. Keep an open mind about pedagogical styles; math can be taught effectively in many different ways. In general, though, you want to see someone with a command of the facts and procedures who can explain them clearly to students; is not reluctant to dispense knowledge in a straightforward manner; sets clear expectations; constantly asks questions to determine children's present math skill and knowledge levels; gives ample feedback; makes sure students learn basic math facts; offers challenging problems in class and homework assignments; and has students regularly practice the skills being taught.

Finally, you can always ask at the principal's or superintendent's office to see how your school performs on district-wide or state-wide tests. Such scores may not tell you much about your child's own teacher, but they can be revealing about the effectiveness of the school's math program as a whole. Talk with other parents whose children have taken mathematics from this teacher. If most are satisfied, it's a pretty good sign. If you hear several complaints, you may need to watch your child's progress all the more closely. It may help to engage a tutor, or perhaps obtain some suitable computer software to give your child more math practice. You may need to do more teaching at home. You may even decide you need to lobby for a different classroom placement for your child.

Warning Signs of a Weak Mathematics Program

Watch for the following clues that something is wrong at your school:

- little expectation that students memorize math terms, tables, definitions, and formulas
- few practice problems assigned (and teachers who deride worksheets and problem sets as "drill and kill")
- lots of calculator use but few pencil-and-paper calculations
- children adding and subtracting on fingers past the second grade
- textbooks with more pictures and stories about math than equations and problems
- children expected to "discover" or "construct" most math concepts for themselves (or their group)
- heavy use of manipulatives in the intermediate and junior high grades
- imbalance between "real-life" applications of math and problems that involve math's abstract nature
- an attitude that finding exact answers isn't too important so long as the student has an interesting "problem-solving strategy"
- imbalance between group projects and assignments that call for individual problem solving
- teachers who don't clearly and regularly define terms, demonstrate procedures, and explain concepts
- school-wide math scores below district or state averages

TEACHING MATHEMATICS AT HOME

During the preschool years, you spent some time introducing your child to numbers, shapes, sets, and a few other basic math concepts. In elementary school, your encouragement is just as important. Academic success in this subject is directly related to your actions at home. Youngsters whose parents are involved in their schoolwork are more likely to take advanced math courses by the time they hit junior high. Your participation, praise, prodding, and patient explaining can all add up to better grades and higher achievement.

The following pages suggest some good ways to buttress your child's mathematics education. You'll find tips for dealing with homework, as well as ideas for extracurricular math activities. It's a great idea to get advice from the teacher, too. She may have suggestions and materials on hand for parents who want to foster learning at home.

Math Homework Counts

To be a good math student, your child needs to work lots of math problems. The key to success in this subject is simple, but it is time-tested and, frankly, it is the *only* proven method for learning mathematics. Your child must practice and then practice some more.

"Many parents are under the impression that all the math can be done in the classroom," one elementary school teacher notes. The reality is that teachers need most of the daily math period to introduce concepts, check students' comprehension, and help them work through new problems. Often there is little class time left for children to practice what they've learned. Well-designed math homework is the way your child consolidates the knowledge and skills first encountered at school.

As noted earlier, some schools have moved away from the custom of assigning practice sets every night. Requiring children to work a particular type of problem many times is considered "drill"—a dirty word in education circles these days. Drill, it is said, takes the joy away from learning and thus contributes to failure in math. That is certainly true of *too much* drill, but it's also true that, in many cases, it's *lack of drill* that produces poor math grades.

Webster defines "drill" as "a physical or mental exercise aimed at perfecting facility and skill, especially by regular practice." That's why swimmers practice flip-turns and pianists practice Mozart. That's also what your child needs to do with math problems. It is through repeated exposure and practice that students learn to automate skills, solve problems, and come to understand concepts more thoroughly. Practice leads to increased comprehension, competence, and confidence. If your child gets little or no homework, it's probably a symptom of a school that doesn't place much value on regular practice.

When it comes to math education, perhaps the most important thing you can do as a parent is pay attention to homework. At the very least, that means looking to see that your child is getting enough of it to learn the fundamentals and that she's completing the assignments.

To do your job properly, you may need to become more involved. This does not mean you should have to become your child's math teacher. The introduction of concepts and skills should occur in class, by people who can offer expert instruction. But there will be occasions when your child needs clarification, extra help, or encouragement. This will take commitment on your part. It may also mean relearning some basic math so you can help her understand. You may find yourself tackling concepts, formulas, and equations that you haven't thought about since your own school days.

That prospect alarms many parents. They're comfortable sitting down with a child to help her read, or calling out spelling words, or even building a model volcano for a science project. Bring out the math problems, though, and some adults start to feel anxious. Telling themselves they couldn't be much help anyway, they shy away from the math homework. Not surprisingly, this avoidance is infectious; they end up passing along their distaste for the subject to their kids.

If that sounds familiar, you may need to work a bit to overcome your own reluctance. Math is important to your child's future. You'll probably find that you're perfectly capable of understanding and working the homework problems throughout most of the elementary school years.

Here are some guidelines to keep in mind, as well as some strategies you may wish to try with your child:

- **Start overseeing homework early on.** Math concepts are sequential and cumulative. Most of the math studied in the intermediate grades is based on fundamental lessons learned in grades one, two, and three. For example, youngsters must gain a clear notion of what "place value" is all about before they can work with decimals. Failing to learn the early lessons means struggling in later years.

  Another good reason to track math homework from the very beginning is that it will make relearning much easier on *you*. The sooner you begin, the longer you'll be able to keep up with your child. If you wait until fifth grade before you try to help, you may find yourself stumped.

- **Regular, daily practice is essential.** It takes a long time—days, weeks, even months—for some math concepts and applications to sink in. Learning the basics of this subject is a bit like mastering a language. You get to be "numerate" the same way you become "literate." Through regular exposure, terms and rules gradually become second nature. To restate the cardinal rule of learning math: *Practice and more practice is necessary for children to gain fluency with basic operations.* If your child isn't getting enough practice on a particular lesson, don't hesitate to ask the teacher to give you more exercises.

  Especially with younger children, practice in frequent, shorter doses is generally more effective than fewer, longer sessions. Beginning mathematicians will probably learn more (and be frustrated less) from six fifteen-minute study sessions spread out over five days than from an hour and a half all at once.

- **Practice does not just mean rote learning.** It is critical that assignments include problems that are worked from several different angles. This helps students comprehend the concepts underlying mathematical operations. It also sharpens problem-solving skills. Here is an easy example: a first grader might be asked to solve the equations $2 + 3 + 4 = ?$ and $1 + 6 + 2 = ?$ She might also be asked to solve the word problem: "There has been a breakout at the zoo. Jenny found 5 giraffes in her backyard, Henry found 2 rhinos in his tree house, and Alice found 2 monkeys in the kitchen. How many animals did the children find in all?" All these problems help students grasp that there are several ways to get to the sum of 9. Above all, practice sets should be challenging. Homework should routinely include some problems that require a child to think hard.

- **Homework should include some review.** Since each lesson builds on those that came before, students must retain a solid understanding of what was taught previously. Even as new operations and principles are being introduced, children spend time practicing old ones. Homework assignments may consist of three problems like those worked last week, three like the ones worked yesterday, and six more problems dealing with the concept the teacher introduced today.

- **Check your child's understanding.** One useful strategy is to ask your child to explain how she found the solution to a problem. Get her to "teach" you how to do it. Putting the process into words will solidify her own comprehension.

  A verbal explanation can also be a big help to both of you when she's *not* getting the right answer. Ask her to explain how she's approaching that problem and why she picked that particular strategy. When necessary, lead her through the problem one step at a time: "What do you do first? What do you do next?" By checking to see that she understands the reason for each step, you can often isolate the source of trouble.

- **Have your child rework problems she got wrong.** Once your child gets a test back, for example, have her work through any problems she missed. Help her understand what went wrong; go over them until she can work them successfully. She may need more practice working similar problems in the coming days.

- **Read the textbook with your child.** Many students don't read the math textbook very closely—or sometimes at all! They depend on classroom activities and the teacher's explanations. This is a mistake. The textbook (if it is a good one) contains careful presentations of the concepts to be learned. Make sure your child reads each new lesson. Read a few pages with her, if necessary. Don't skip the charts, diagrams, and figures.

- **Keep a portfolio of past work.** Have your child keep old homework and tests in a notebook or folder. It will help you see her progress, and it makes a good resource when it comes to studying for tests.

- **Stay in touch with the teacher.** Her observations will help you know which areas of math need the most practice at home. Ask her what knowledge and skills she plans to teach in the coming weeks. The more you know about her expectations, the easier it is to keep your child on track.

- **Don't go to bed math-mad.** Parent-child math sessions can occasionally get rough. Our own households have known some math-induced tears, some textbooks slamming shut, some cries of "I just don't get it!" and "I can't explain it any better than that!" At that point in the "conversation," take a break. Cool down. Go to your respective corners and try again later. Plutarch writes that in ancient

Greece, the disciples of the mathematician Pythagoras had an iron-clad rule. If, during the day, any members of the society said angry words to each other, they had to shake hands in friendship before the sun went down.

- **Sooner or later, you may get left behind.** It happens to practically every parent. Unless your own work includes a lot of math, the day will likely arrive when you'll no longer be able to answer or explain all those homework problems. Your child suddenly "knows" more than you do—the education is working!

  Most parents hit that wall by the time their children reach junior high, sometimes sooner. At that point, the main thing is to make sure your child is doing her homework problems. Keep an eye on test scores, and talk with both your child and her teacher to make sure she's understanding it all. If not, you'll need to find someone who can help her. (See "What If My Child Is Falling Behind?" page 297.)

Memorizing Math Facts

"Parents often do not help their child with memorization of math facts," says a Florida teacher, "even when we send home letters mentioning their child needs assistance." Neglecting this responsibility can be a big mistake. Children need to be intimately familiar with certain terms, symbols, definitions, and formulas. Often that requires memory work and attention at home. Here are some ideas to choose from:

- Get a set of flash cards. Yes, they're old-fashioned, but they work for many children! You can buy them or have your child make them from blank index cards. Even the process of making them reinforces children's skills.

- Saying something aloud several times is often a good way to focus on it, and therefore begin memorizing.

- With younger children, some sort of physical action—whether it be drawing a picture or stacking blocks—often speeds memorization. "There are five nickels in every quarter. Let's put five nickels in a stack."

- Give your child little oral quizzes: "How many pints are in a gallon?"

- Give short written quizzes: "Write down the formula for finding the perimeter of a circle."

- Look for a good computer program that quizzes children about math facts. Ask the teacher and other parents for recommendations.

- Develop understanding by talking about how math facts are used. When memorizing a rule, write out two or three sample equations and discuss how the rule works. Have your child illustrate terms and definitions. "Can you show me what parallel and perpendicular lines look like?"

- Take it easy. Too much memorization *will* become deadening drill. Go slow. Practice frequently, but in small amounts at a time.

- Review what's already been memorized. Regular review helps move knowledge into long-term memory, makes math facts automatic, and brings better understanding.

Teach Your Child to Check Her Work

Most of the time, there is only one correct answer to a math problem, and getting it requires precision. Carelessness is an enemy. Homework is the perfect time to train your child to be thorough. Teach her that a problem is not finished until she has looked over her work and searched for mistakes. Here are some guidelines your child can practice:

- **Reread the problem.** She should check to see that she's read the question or problem correctly, and has given the answer asked for.

- **Make sure the answer is in the ballpark.** A very useful technique is to eyeball a problem and estimate a reasonable answer. Then work the problem out, and compare the solution to your estimate. Is the final answer in line with the estimate? If not, something may be wrong. This method takes practice, but it aids accuracy and can increase understanding.

- **Check your computation.** For example, double-check addition by adding up the numbers in a different order. Check subtraction by "reversing" the operation and adding. Check multiplying by dividing, and dividing by multiplying. Even when using a calculator, it pays to double-check since it's easy to hit a wrong key.

- **Look for careless work.** "Silly" or "sloppy" mistakes lead to wrong answers in math. Take time to check for little things: Did I put my decimal point in the right place? Did I write "in^2" when I meant to write "in^3"?

- **Work the problem a different way.** Sometimes it pays to rework a problem using a different approach. If the two answers don't agree, one of them is obviously wrong. If they match, you've probably got the right solution.

- **Substitute your answer.** If the problem is $93 = 3(x + 12)$, and you've found that $x = 19$, make sure you plug your answer into the equation and see if it works.

On longer problems with several steps, students should learn to check their work as they go along. The habit of double-checking homework will pay off handsomely when test time comes around. It's also good practice for life.

Resources That Help Your Child Learn Math

Here are some books, magazines, and other resources that can help your child learn mathematics. Your child's teacher may have more suggestions.

Books

Anno's Counting Book, Mitsumasa Anno (Harper Trophy, 1986)—A collection of puzzles, riddles, mazes, etc. Grades K–3.

Everything You Need to Know About Math Homework, Anne Zeman and Kate Kelly (Scholastic, 1994)—Presents mathematics solidly by focusing on basic terms, concepts, and operations.

Family Math, Jean Kerr Stenmark, Virginia Thompson, and Ruth Cossey (Equals, 1986)—A collection of mathematical games and puzzles aimed at introducing basic terms and concepts. (To order, contact Equals at the University of California, 800-897-5036.)

Math Smart Junior: Math You'll Understand, Marcia Lerner and Doug McMullen, Jr. (Random House, 1995)—Offers solid mathematical instruction in units arranged by topic.

Magazines

DynaMath and *Scholastic Math* (Scholastic)—Both magazines present key math concepts using humor, real-life examples, and activities. Grades 3 to 5 and 6 to 9, respectively.

Zillions (Consumers Union)—Shows children how math is useful in the real world.

Web Sites

A+ Math (www.aplusmath.com)—Kids can practice their skills on a wide variety of interactive math games.

Math Archives (http://archives.math.utk.edu)—This site has links to games, instructional sites, and software reviews.

Mathematically Correct (www.mathematicallycorrect.com)—A good site for parents. Dedicated to the debate over "fuzzy math."

SuperKids (www.superkids.com)—An annual "Best Of" software list and the ability to search for good prices make this review site worth checking out.

Through the Glass Wall (www.terc.edu/mathequity/gw/html/gwhome. html)—This site reviews software and gives tips for getting the most out of the software you buy.

Math Activities Around the House

There are all sorts of ways you can reinforce the math lessons being taught at school. You don't need a blackboard and chalk. A math lesson can happen anytime, anywhere. If your child is learning to divide, make up simple division problems: "I have six cookies to give you, your brother, and your sister. How many cookies will each of you get?" When she first learns about place value, you might want to bundle some Popsicle sticks into sets of tens and let her practice writing the numbers for different piles of sticks (3 bundles plus 4 leftover sticks = 34). If she's studying percentages, ask her to figure out the tip when the family eats out.

It is important to show children that this subject has practical uses in everyday living. Home, more than a school classroom, is apt to generate genuine relevance. Point out the ubiquity and utility of numbers to young children—in street addresses, phone numbers, weather reports, sports scores, etc. Make an effort to involve older children in the myriad small calculations you make as you go about chores. If the fertilizer bag says to use 20 pounds for every 5,000 square feet of lawn, ask your child to figure out the area of the yard and let you know how much to spread. Such efforts matter. They solidify knowledge, sharpen skills, and show that math is indeed important. Try a few of these ideas:

- **Practice mental arithmetic.** As your child learns to perform different calculations, ask simple questions that require her to do math "in her head" until she is able to give quick and accurate responses. What number comes between 26 and 28? What's half of 32? What is 6 times 7 plus 14? Count by fives, tens, odds, and evens. Count backward by twenties from 200. Practicing mental arithmetic will enable your child to work school problems more smoothly and automatically.

- **Make up word problems.** It's easy to think of word problems that your child can work, either in her head or with pencil and paper. "Today is September 11. Grandpa will be coming in 4 days. What day will he be here?" Or, "Your book has 116 pages. If you want to read it in one week, how many pages a day will you need to read?"

- **Teach about time.** The concept of time is sometimes difficult to grasp and needs reinforcement at home. You'll have to do plenty of patient explaining, and your child will need lots of practice throughout the primary years. Get a calendar that you can mark together. Practice finding birthdays, holidays, and family vacation dates on it. Ask questions such as: How many Tuesdays are there in April this year? What day of the week is August 9? Help her learn that there are 60 seconds in a minute, 60 minutes in an hour, 7 days in a week, etc.

If all your clocks are digital, get an extra one with a face, hands, and numbers. (You can also make or buy a cardboard "clock" with movable hands to practice telling time.) Maybe get a stopwatch. Ask your child to time all sorts of things. How long does it take dad to cut the grass? How long has big sister been on the phone? As your child progresses through the intermediate grades, make up simple word problems involving elapsed time. If you start playing basketball at 10:15 and play until 11:25, how long have you played?

• **Cook with numbers.** Hopefully, you used the kitchen to teach rudimentary math in the preschool years. Continue that habit through elementary school. It's the perfect place to demonstrate all sorts of weights, measurements, and fractions. "How many cups can we pour into this pint jar? Into this quart jar?" "If there are three eggs left in a carton of twelve, what fraction of the carton have we eaten?"

• **Practice math in the car.** The highway is a good place to come up with math games and problems. Count how many red cars you see in five minutes. Call out the numbers on a passing license plate—who can add them up correctly? If you drove 255 miles today and it took 5 hours, what was your average speed? Pull out the road map and add up how far you have to drive tomorrow. Car rides are a good time to practice basic math facts, too: "What's 5 plus 8? How about 7 times 9?"

• **Play games that use math.** Just about all the card games that children enjoy, such as Go Fish, War, or Gin Rummy, involve numbers and rudimentary arithmetic. Many board games require adding numbers on dice, and counting spaces to be moved. Monopoly gives practice working with money. Battleship teaches about coordinate pairs. Bingo helps young kids learn to identify numbers. Games that involve logic and strategy (like chess) sharpen math skills for older students.

• **Use the computer.** There are many software programs designed to help teach math skills. Talk to the teacher and other parents for recommendations.

• **Teach about money.** Calculations that involve dollars and cents will probably get your child's attention. Ask her to make sure you've received the right amount of change after a purchase. Or add up the cost of items you want to buy from a catalogue. For older children, keeping a checkbook balanced is a great way to practice being mathematically precise. Help your child figure out how much interest is being earned on CDs or savings accounts. Encourage her to develop her own "budget," even if it's just for the few dollars she gets in allowance or earns through chores. Teach her to keep track of how she spends her money.

- **Teach math in the workshop.** If you're the kind who likes to build and fix things at home, you've got ready-made math lessons. Building a rabbit cage? Get your child involved in figuring out how big it should be, how much wire and wood you'll need to buy, how much the material will cost, etc. Do-it-yourself projects are great for putting measuring skills to work. Adding a new deck to the back of the house? Start by making a scale drawing together.

Teaching Your Child to Estimate

Why do you want your child to be able to estimate with numbers? Three reasons. First, when students can make good estimates of an answer, it shows they understand the problem. Second, estimating is valuable in double-checking math problems; it helps students know whether their answers are in the ballpark. Third, estimating is an incredibly practical skill, handy in everything from shopping to leaving a tip.

Estimating is a skill that can be taught, but it requires practice. It is important to give your child experience at home.

Help a primary grade youngster get a feel for what it's all about by asking her to make guesses about items around the house. How long do you think the sofa is? About how much pie is left? How much do you think this potted plant will weigh if we put it on the bathroom scale?

After she's learned to add and subtract double-digit numbers, practice rounding to the nearest five or ten to get approximate answers. (For example, 28 + 39 is close to 30 + 40, or 70.) Later, practice with multiplication. (You know 9 x 43 is close to 10 x 40, so the answer will be somewhere around 400.)

Put estimating to everyday use. If you're going to carpet a room 27 feet wide by 33 feet long, about how many square feet of carpet do you need? If you're buying a shirt for $15.99 and shoes for $43.50, about how much money do you need? The better your child becomes at making reliable estimates in her head, the more comfortable she'll be with arithmetic in general.

Note that before students can become really good at estimating, they must have easy recall of basic math facts (like the addition and multiplication tables) and a good grasp of the place value system (ones, tens, hundreds, etc.). In the end, your child's ability to make "educated guesses" about numbers depends on her command of basic mathematical knowledge.

CHAPTER 9

Science

THIS CHAPTER COVERS THE SCIENCE CURRICULUM. EVERY year, the quality of a child's science education carries greater consequences. Employers say that knowledge of scientific principles will be an important job requirement in the early twenty-first century. Yet they also complain that vast numbers of American students are not learning enough science. Test scores lend support to their concerns. Compared to the rest of the industrialized world, our students lag seriously in science achievement.

In the following sections, we discuss why it is important for your child to get a sound education in this subject, regardless of whether he grows up to work in a science-related field. We outline the knowledge and skills students should gain from their studies. We offer a model curriculum that you can compare to your elementary school's own courses. We address some of the current debates about science education, and alert you to some shortcomings you may encounter at school. Finally, we suggest some things you can do at home to supplement your child's schooling.

WHAT GOOD SCHOOLS TEACH—AND WHY

A healthy chunk of school time should be devoted to exploring plants and animals, rocks and stars, electricity and gravity, and many other science topics. The job of teachers between kindergarten and eighth grade is to give children an understanding of the general laws of nature; make sure they know some important facts and ideas about the universe; train them in some methods scientists use; give them an appreciation of the scien-

345

tific view of the world; and stimulate their desire to ask questions and find answers. This is a big task. There is much ground to cover, and you'll want to pay attention to the emphasis your school places on science.

By the time they leave eighth grade, children should possess a substantial store of knowledge about their world. For example, they should have some idea of how mountains are made and stars are born, what a light-year is, and what makes an igneous rock different from a sedimentary one. They should know what "pollination" and "metamorphosis" mean, and some ways that energy flows through an ecosystem. They should have learned that water boils at 100 degrees centigrade, what happens to light rays when they pass through a lens, and that blood carries oxygen and nutrients to cells in the human body.

This is not to say that schools should just fill children's heads with random factoids and jumbled definitions. Learning is always much more than that, but science class *should* teach plenty of substance. It must teach important facts and concepts. The word "science," after all, comes from the Latin word *scientia*, which means knowledge. Good curricula are exciting, ordered adventures that teach the fundamental information children need in order to think conceptually and creatively about science. They lay a solid foundation of content on which students base more advanced studies in high school and college.

In addition to facts and concepts, your school should teach the basic methods that scientists use in their work. This is imperative. Certain ways of looking at the world lie at the heart of the scientific enterprise. To understand subjects like physics, biology, and astronomy, students must learn these techniques. Scientific inquiry is not easily described (or taught). There is no fixed routine or set of steps that leads a researcher to the answer he's looking for. There are, however, certain features of science that set it apart from other modes of inquiry. It will be useful here to touch on some of the ways scientists think, work, and view the universe, so that you can see whether your child's school teaches these things.

Scientists approach the universe as an ordered place. They don't view it as random but, in a broad sense, as regular and predictable. The earth turns once every twenty-four hours. The tide comes in, and the tide goes out. Scientists aim to recognize such regularities and then uncover the general principles that explain them. That is, they try to attain systematic knowledge that tells us how and why things work the way they do.

Good schools impress on children the idea that in science, for something to be "true," it must be accepted and verified by the worldwide community of scientists. It must be tested or observed again and again, with always the same results. Only then is it regarded as reliable. In other words, to know something in science you have to be able to *prove* it, and so should other people following the same procedures.

This does not mean that scientific knowledge is 100 percent certain. In fact, despite the great lengths scientists go to prove things, they reject the notion of absolute truths (a distinction it takes students a while to grasp). An explanation may seem perfectly sound for years and years—until someone discovers a set of conditions under which it does not apply. The old explanation must then be revised, and occasionally even replaced, to explain more phenomena and answer more questions. This happens repeatedly. It's what scientific progress is all about. For the most part, it is an exceedingly laborious process that requires endless asking, probing, and testing.

Scientists are great observers—they look at things more carefully than other people usually do. They look for the expected *and* the unexpected. Take the example of the Scottish physician Alexander Fleming, who spent years searching for a substance that would fight bacterial diseases. One day in 1928, he picked up a bacteria culture that had been left by an open window and invaded by a mold. He was about to put the ruined specimen into the sink for cleaning, but first he paused to examine it. He noticed that in the area around the mold, the bacteria colonies were transparent. It looked as if the mold was stopping the bacteria's growth. Fleming's taking the time to stop and observe this chance phenomenon led to one of the greatest medical discoveries of all time—penicillin.

Besides being keen observers, scientists are great classifiers. They arrange elements into groups on the periodic table. They organize plants and animals into different species. Why? Because classifying things not only makes knowledge manageable, it also reveals relationships between those things. Scientists are also masters at the art of conducting experiments. In those experiments, they work hard to control all the potential variables. Galileo was one of the first to realize that, by regulating conditions systematically and precisely, he could unveil the laws of nature. In his day, everyone assumed that heavy objects fall to earth faster than light ones. Galileo decided to put it to the test. By rolling balls of different weights down inclined planes (or, as the story goes, dropping them off the Leaning Tower of Pisa), he showed that, excluding the effects of air resistance, all objects fall at the same rate.

Science, more than any other field of inquiry, relies on instruments to attain knowledge—tools ranging from microscopes to atom smashers. One indication of a good elementary school science program is children learning how to observe, measure, and experiment with such basic instruments as rulers, balances, and magnifying glasses. Another indicator is whether children use much math in their science classes. In many ways, math is the language of science. In physics, for example, work is expressed as a mathematical relation between force and distance: $W = F \times d$. Good schools make science lessons an opportunity for students to put the math they've learned to practical use.

Forming hypotheses—proposed explanations—is also a core activity of scientists. Once a scientist has formed a hypothesis based on existing information, he then goes about the business of testing it to see if it holds up. A good hypothesis should be able to predict some facts not already known. For example, the discovery of Neptune, the eighth planet in our solar system, came from a hypothesis formulated in the nineteenth century. Astronomers found that Uranus, then the most distant known planet, did not move exactly the way the laws of gravity and motion said it should. They hypothesized that an unknown planet's gravitational pull was causing this phenomenon. By watching Uranus's orbit, they calculated where the hypothetical planet might be, and eventually they located Neptune.

Scientists are very careful about the ways they think as they work through problems. Their arguments must conform to principles of logical reasoning. They must be adept at employing both deductive logic (using a general principle to reason to a conclusion about a specific question) and inductive logic (forming a general conclusion based on many specific facts, observations, or experiments). Since science thrives on discoveries and new ideas, minds always have to be open to fresh possibilities—even ones at odds with what people generally believe. This can take courage. Galileo was forced by the Roman Catholic Church of his day to renounce what he believed to be true: that the universe did not revolve around the earth. One of his predecessors was burned at the stake for espousing such heresies.

Just as openness to unfamiliar possibilities is a mark of science, so is healthy skepticism. Scientists rarely give new theories widespread acceptance until they are repeatedly tested and proven. Objectivity and intellectual honesty are paramount. Scientists know well that most of our everyday thoughts are affected by preconceived opinions and expectations. This is only human. In science, however, explanations must be based on objective and systematic observations. Thoughtful scientists are constantly checking to weed out biases in the way data are gathered, recorded, and reported. They train themselves to look for anything that might skew the objectivity of their instruments or their methods, and ask how those influences might distort conclusions.

Science is largely a collaborative effort—often on a worldwide basis. The free exchange of ideas is vital for progress. Scientists frequently put their findings on the Internet, give talks and papers at conferences, and publish their work in professional journals. Therefore good science classes help students learn communication skills. They expect children to explain ideas both orally and in writing, as well as to depict information with graphs, charts, and tables.

Important discoveries, inventions, and insights rarely happen overnight. Perseverance is indispensable. Someone once asked Isaac Newton how he had managed to make so many astounding discoveries in physics and astronomy. "By *always* thinking about them," he replied. Even once discoveries or inventions are made, scientists usually have to keep working hard to bring them to the public. When Fleming discovered penicillin, for example, the world showed little interest at first. He patiently continued testing his mold cultures, urging other scientists to study them as well. It was another fifteen years before factories were mass-producing penicillin. Good science teachers nurture that kind of persistence, often by coaxing students to stick with a problem until they eventually find the right answer.

Finally, and perhaps above all, science thrives on a craving to know and understand. Time and time again, breakthroughs happen because someone won't stop asking, "Why?" When Edward Jenner became a doctor in the late eighteenth century, smallpox was rampant. Like many other doctors, he observed that some people seemed to be immune to the disease. He couldn't stop wondering why. Looking into their histories, he found that many of the immune people were dairymaids who had at some point been sick from cowpox. Cowpox was similar to smallpox but was a much milder disease. Jenner's curiosity led to one of the greatest medical breakthroughs in history: people could be vaccinated with a mild, harmless infection to guard against a far more serious illness.

Many children start school burning with the same kind of curiosity that drives scientists. The difference is that they don't yet know how to search for answers to their questions in a systematic way, or to check their answers once they've found them. In good schools, teachers do all they can to keep inquisitiveness alive and make science exciting. Walk into a good science class and you might see the teacher using magnets to make things float before children's eyes, or showing off a five-foot-long snake. Having grabbed their attention, she trains her students in the methods that help them find answers to their questions.

The Value of a Solid Grounding in Science

These, then, are some of the traits that distinguish scientific thought and enterprise: curiosity, careful observation, formulation of testable hypotheses, experimentation, reliance on evidence, adherence to rules of logic, skepticism balanced by openness to new ideas, objectivity, intellectual honesty, and perseverance. Obviously, your child may not grow up to be a scientist. Nevertheless, you should want his school to train him in these modes of scientific inquiry, as well as to teach important facts and concepts. Why should he know these things?

Since science forms the basis of so many businesses and industries, a basic knowledge of subjects such as physics, chemistry, and biology can be important in getting and holding good jobs. There is more at stake here, however, than employment. The modern world is increasingly shaped by scientific discoveries and technological advances. Headlines such as "Fusion Research Effort Draws Fire" and "Gene Therapy for Leukemia Tested" are commonplace. People need a certain amount of fundamental scientific knowledge to understand events that may directly affect their lives.

It's not hard to make the case that today good citizenship requires scientific literacy since so many national debates (global warming, space exploration, cloning experiments, etc.) revolve around science issues. Many newspaper and magazine reports assume some basic scientific background knowledge. Take, for example, these few sentences from a newspaper story about the disappearance of frogs and other amphibians around the world:

> No one knows how many of the world's approximately 4,000 amphibian species may be affected. . . . Nor do scientists yet have conclusive proof as to what may be causing any of the declines. But there are four prime suspects: increasing ultraviolet radiation resulting from ozone depletion, global climate change, pesticides and new diseases—including a recently discovered skin infection caused by a class of aquatic fungi not previously known to affect vertebrates.[1]

This paragraph takes for granted that the reader is familiar with certain terms and ideas: "amphibian," "species," "ultraviolet radiation," "ozone," "global climate change," "infection," "fungi," "vertebrates." Without basic scientific literacy, a reader can't begin to understand what it's about.

A strong education in science helps people think more clearly and logically. As Albert Einstein put it, "The whole of science is nothing more than a refinement of everyday thinking." It is a fine-tuning of common sense and reasoning. By training children in scientific inquiry, we teach them to be systematic, objective, and exact in their thoughts. We teach them to analyze problems carefully, scrutinize evidence, recognize shoddy arguments, and distinguish important facts. A good science education *really does* teach "critical thinking" skills—the kind of skills that come in handy when figuring out a problem on the job, seeing through political and commercial propaganda, or judging the actions and motives of people around us.

Science often has profound—even earthshaking—influences on the way we see ourselves and our universe. From the discovery that the earth moves around the sun to unlocking the secrets of DNA, scientific developments have continually reshaped mankind's political, philosophical, and even religious thought. Each age is defined, in part, by its scientific understandings. Great breakthroughs in research—those taking place today as well as those from history—are part of our cultural identity and heritage. In order to understand ourselves, it is necessary to understand some science.

Finally, knowing science for its own sake is worthy and gratifying. One goal of education is to help us see what is good and beautiful in our world. To paraphrase the English biologist Thomas Henry Huxley, a person ignorant of science goes through life like someone walking through a gallery filled with wonderful works of art, nine tenths of which have their faces turned to the wall. All the events and phenomena your child witnesses during his day—the faucet handle he turns to get the water to brush his teeth, the rain he runs through on the way to the bus, the music he listens to over his radio—operate according to general laws of nature. To possess a fundamental understanding of these concepts is to recognize a marvelous design and unity in the universe. A great satisfaction comes from seeing the connectedness between common specks of dust dancing in a sunbeam and the vast nebulae of outer space. The scientific view of the cosmos can be extraordinarily elegant and aesthetically pleasing. It can lead to a lifelong voyage of exploration and enjoyment. That's reason enough for your child to learn science.

How Are Schools Doing?

At least one third of U.S. students lack a basic grasp of science and more than two thirds lack proficiency in this key subject, according to the National Assessment of Education Progress (NAEP), a test given periodically to schoolchildren across the country. Barely 3 percent of U.S. students perform at the "advanced" level. A recent multi-nation test, the Third International Mathematics and Science Study (TIMSS), paints an equally bleak picture. American youngsters start out strong in their knowledge of science compared to students in other developed countries, but by the eighth grade their scores are mediocre, and by twelfth grade they lag far behind their peers. American high school seniors are among the least prepared in the industrial world when it comes to science skills and understanding.

What is wrong? According to many scientists and educators, American schools simply do not expect students to learn enough science. Goals set for children are often vague and underestimate what they can do. For example, one set of guidelines, the National Science Education Standards, discourages teachers from using models of planets in the K–4 grades because of the "inability of young children to understand that the Earth is approximately spherical." (But those same K–4 kids can "recognize pollution as an environmental issue, scarcity as a resource issue, and crowded classrooms or schools as population problems." Clearly, students are more capable when it comes to building environmental sensitivity.)[2]

Many schools actually seem to expect less of children the older they get. "The U.S. curriculum appears not only to have been unfocused but highly repetitive, lacking coherence, and providing little rigorous challenge during the middle years," report researchers who conducted the TIMSS study. In California, science lessons that were appropriate for seventh graders in 1963 are now taught to ninth graders. In some American classrooms, activities *called* science appear to have little relation to real science. Kids spend time making their own rain sticks so they can "appreciate the sounds of the rain forest," or designing imaginary clothes for insects, or picking up peas with toothpicks to experience how birds eat. In schools that are big on exploring feelings, building self-esteem, and making lessons fun for all, a rational, rigorous subject like science is apt to be discounted.

Some elementary school teachers spend relatively little time on science because they themselves are not comfortable with the subject. One study found that, while seven in ten teachers believe schools should increase the level of science education, only about half that proportion feel "science-literate," and many believe they are less qualified to teach science than other subjects.[3] When teachers lack the necessary training, children may get few opportunities for genuine hands-on investigations. "Often there are little to no scientific endeavors beyond practice reading of passages," says a Texas teacher. Many schools and educators do a fine job teaching this subject, but there is much mediocrity, too, and worse, so you must keep your eyes open.

THE SCIENCE CURRICULUM

Traditionally, the elementary school science curriculum offers a mix of basic life sciences (drawn from biology, botany, zoology, ecology, etc.), physical sciences (physics and chemistry), and earth sciences (geology, oceanography, and meteorology, plus astronomy). Science is a huge field, of course, and time is limited. Good elementary school instruction strives to offer a first look at the natural and physical worlds. The goal is to introduce students to a range of important topics and thought. Lessons supply many facts and concepts that lie at the foundations of science. They also teach some basic skills involved in scientific inquiry.

The following sections will give you an idea of what thorough instruction looks like in grades K through 8. The lists of topics to be covered in each grade are summarized from the Core Knowledge Sequence, an excellent course of study (see page 100). A word of caution is in order, though. The science curriculum is extremely varied in U.S. elementary schools. There is a wide range of topics to cover and no generally agreed "best" order in which to study them. In some good schools, fourth graders might spend a lot of time growing and studying plants, while fourth graders in other schools might devote more attention to studying the earth's resources. One district may introduce genetics in the seventh grade while another waits until eighth. Keep in mind that what follows is meant to be an example of what a very good program looks like, rather than a precise blueprint that every school must follow.

That said, we also emphasize that, for science education to be effective, lessons must come in some sort of carefully ordered sequence—not a random hopping from dinosaurs to stars to ozone holes to maple leaves. Science is, by definition, a system of ordered knowledge, and that calls for a well-structured curriculum. Learning a new concept almost always requires prior knowledge. You can't really understand density, for example, unless you first know something of mass and volume. Each new lesson must build on what has come before.

An ordered sequence also helps avoid big gaps in knowledge (like making it through school without ever having studied light) and needless repetition. To be sure, some repetition helps drive home concepts and gradually increases students' sophistication about topics. A teacher getting ready to teach about plate tectonics may need to go back and remind students of what they learned last year about the earth being divided into concentric spheres of rock and metal. That kind of review is fine. What you don't want to see is children returning again and again to the same topic with no real increase in sophistication. That's the sign of a curriculum in disarray.

Ask to see a summary of your school's science plan for all the grades. Compare it to the model set forth in the next few pages. In all likelihood, the two will not match exactly on a grade-by-grade basis. Your school *should*, however, be able to show you a coherent plan of study that is highly specific about the knowledge and skills children are expected to attain. If no one is able to produce a list of such goals, consider it a bad sign.

You can use this model and your school's plan of study to raise some questions. Are there any major topics that your school's curriculum doesn't cover? Is there a healthy mix of life sciences, physical sciences, and earth sciences? Does your school's curriculum seem about as demanding as the one summarized here—or are children in sixth grade just getting around to learning where the earth is located in the solar system?

Children learn a great deal of science by reading good books and listening to good teachers explain how things work. They also learn by *doing* science, and in a good classroom you'll find students looking through microscopes, digging into dirt samples, poking at specimens, and weighing things. Hands-on explorations are vital. They teach about scientific inquiry, which includes steps like collecting information, forming hypotheses, conducting observations, and making inferences. Children must practice those skills to learn them. Getting their hands dirty in the lab shows students that science is for everyone, not just scientists, and it makes this subject fun. Most teachers will tell you that experiments and demonstrations are great for stimulating curiosity.

There are a few other marks of excellence you should look for. One is lessons and teachers that grab kids' imaginations. The best science teachers often have a streak of the showman in them. They lure their customers into the store with a nifty trick or two. You might see a good teacher mixing up a batch of slime, lifting three students with a lever, or using static electricity to make her own hair stand on end. She might show a video of an astronaut dropping a hammer and a feather side by side on the moon. These kinds of "gee whiz" science lessons spark interest and set the stage for serious learning.

Look to see that the science curriculum is integrated with other core subjects. As your child progresses, you should see him putting math lessons to use in science class by measuring, calculating, graphing, and using equations like $S = d/t$ (average speed is equal to total distance divided by total time). English lessons should be put to use by teachers asking for concise written explanations of the results of experiments. Students should gain historical perspective about scientific endeavors in both their history and their science classes. They should hear and read stories about Copernicus studying the heavens, about Jonas Salk's fight against polio, about Marie Curie's work isolating radium. Such episodes provide concrete examples of how the scientific enterprise works. They are also an important part of our intellectual heritage.

The Primary Grades—Kindergarten Through Third Grade

Good science teachers do everything in their power to encourage curiosity and foster wonder, especially in the primary grades. They know that, in many cases, if children aren't enjoying science by third grade, they're "lost" to this subject; after that, their attitudes may be fixed. A top goal at this age is to fascinate children with neat topics like whales and rockets and rainbows. Good science education really starts with the lesson that *the world is an amazing place.*

When you visit a primary school science class, pay attention to how often the students ask questions. This is a pretty good gauge of whether the teacher is encouraging youngsters' interests. Is this a room full of children eager with inquiries like "Why do bunnies hop?" and "How does the balloon get bigger?" Or is it mostly silence as the teacher drones through the day's lesson? Remember that, at this young age, most children are bursting with "how" and "why" questions. You should be able to hear them. You should witness the teacher respond with straightforward answers and, when appropriate, simple demonstrations.

Obviously, the instruction must suit the age and intellectual development of students. Young grade schoolers can, however, handle a taste of just about any major subject of scientific interest. Take the study of force and motion. Using equations to calculate work or acceleration must wait a few years, but youngsters can build foundational knowledge by experimenting with how much effort it takes to push or pull different objects, and what happens when various things strike each other. The mechanics of photosynthesis should wait for later study of biology and chemistry, but even kindergartners are ready to watch and learn about the development of common flowers from seed to maturity. The point is: first things first, but without delay.

In grades K–3, students start practicing some of the methods that scientists use: making observations, collecting things, comparing and classifying objects, venturing predictions, testing hypotheses, etc. They should get their hands on all sorts of specimens, from leaves and rocks to bugs and fossils. There should be ample opportunity for children to conduct their own simple experiments under the teacher's direction. Students should learn to use some scientific instruments ranging from magnifying glasses to rulers to scales. Through such activities, they begin to grasp the nature of scientific inquiry and the scientific view of the world. They come to understand, for example, that it is important to describe things as accurately as possible so that we can compare our observations with those of others; and that when an experiment is done the same way it was done before, we should expect a similar result.

Students should also learn that much scientific knowledge comes through reading. Scientists routinely turn to the printed word—books, magazines, reference works, Internet sources—to find out what is already known about a subject. Developing that habit is part of good science education. Through reading and classroom discussion, children build a science vocabulary. They learn, for example, what terms such as "predator" and "planet" and "gas" mean. They learn that adult insects have three major body parts and six legs. They come to understand basic concepts, such as that vibrating objects produce sound. Make sure your school is laying this kind of broad foundation of knowledge and skills to support more advanced studies in later years.

KINDERGARTEN

Kindergarten gives youngsters a playful, active introduction to science. Learning comes from listening to the teacher read aloud, but also through direct discovery and simple experiments. Children begin learning how to gather information as they explore objects from pebbles to earthworms to leaves. They practice basic science skills such as looking at things closely, describing objects, and collecting things. They get practice using all five senses and are encouraged to ask lots of "why" and "how" questions. Kindergartners study topics such as:

Plants and Plant Growth

- what plants need to grow (e.g., sufficient warmth, light, water)
- basic parts of plants (seed, root, stem, leaf, flower)
- plants make their own food
- how some food comes from farms as crops

Animals and Their Needs

- what animals need to live (e.g., food, water, space)
- how animals get food (e.g., eating plants or other living things)
- offspring are very much (but not exactly) like their parents
- special needs of animal babies
- taking care of pets

The Human Body

- using the five senses
- taking care of your body (e.g., exercise, cleanliness, healthy foods, rest)

Introduction to Magnetism

- everyday uses of magnets (e.g., cabinet locks, refrigerator magnets)
- classifying materials as attracted or not attracted by magnets

Seasons and Weather

- the four seasons
- observing daily weather changes (e.g., temperature, clouds, rainfall)
- the sun as our source of light and warmth

Taking Care of the Earth

- the need to conserve natural resources
- ways to recycle and save energy (e.g., turning off unnecessary lights)
- examples of pollution (e.g., littering, smog)

Science Biographies

- stories of people such as George Washington Carver and the Wright brothers

(drawn from the Core Knowledge Sequence)

In a good kindergarten classroom, you might see children:

- exploring the schoolyard and identifying things as plant or animal, living or nonliving

- using their five senses to explore different items (under the teacher's supervision!) and talking about questions such as: What does it look like? How does it feel? How does it taste and smell?

- pairing pictures of baby ducks with adult ducks, baby bears with adult bears, etc.

- classifying animals by telling where they live

- taking turns feeding the class's pet rabbit, and helping the teacher chart its weight

- giving some plants sunlight and water, keeping others dark and dry, and comparing the results

---

FIRST GRADE

First grade students conduct simple experiments in which they predict what will happen, test their hypotheses, and record what they find. They draw conclusions about their experiments and practice explaining them. They get used to the idea of working in small teams to investigate and experiment. Children get more experience sorting and classifying things according to their physical properties (e.g., color, shape, texture). They use basic instruments (such as magnifying glasses and rulers) to observe and measure objects. They practice communicating data with simple charts, pictures, and written descriptions. First graders study topics such as:

Living Things and Their Environments

- plants and animals live in environments to which they are suited
- different habitats (e.g., forests, meadows, deserts) and their inhabitants
- the food chain
- classifications of animals (e.g., herbivores, carnivores, omnivores, extinct animals)
- characteristics of oceans (e.g., salt water, currents, landscape of ocean floor)
- great diversity of ocean life (e.g., tiny plankton, giant whales)
- effects of habitat destruction (e.g., water pollution)

The Human Body

- overview of major body systems (e.g., skeletal, digestive, circulatory) and their basic parts (e.g., skull, stomach, heart)
- what germs and diseases are, and preventing illness (e.g., importance of vaccinations)

Matter

- idea that everything is made of matter
- basic concept of atoms; all matter is made up of parts too small to see
- three states of matter: solid, liquid, and gas
- measuring properties of matter (in units such as centimeters, quarts)

Introduction to Electricity

- introduction to static electricity
- basic parts of simple electrical circuits (e.g., battery, wires, bulb, switch)
- difference between conductive and nonconductive materials
- safety rules for electricity (e.g., never touch a switch with wet hands)

Astronomy: Introduction to the Solar System

- basic structure of solar system (the sun and nine planets)
- phases of the moon (e.g., full, half, crescent, new)

- earth's place in solar system (e.g., orbits the sun; rotates every twenty-four hours)

The Earth

- geographical features of earth's surface (e.g., continents, poles, equator)
- inside the earth (e.g., temperatures high enough to melt rocks)
- volcanoes and geysers
- introduction to some different rocks and minerals

Science Biographies

- stories of people such as Rachel Carson, Thomas Edison, and Louis Pasteur

(drawn from the Core Knowledge Sequence)

In a good first grade classroom, you might see children:

- taking apart and reassembling a flashlight, and examining the circuit
- measuring water before freezing it and then after melting the ice to see if the amount stays the same
- drawing diagrams of food chains in a habitat while learning about the plants and animals that live there
- setting up an aquarium for a goldfish (or a terrarium for a snail, a cage for a hamster, etc.), then observing and recording what it does
- making a model of the solar system, using students to represent the sun and planets
- drawing simple diagrams of the layers of the earth

SECOND GRADE

Second grade investigations remain simple but involve slightly more detailed observations and procedures. (For example, children may be asked to classify objects by two or more characteristics.) Students take length, volume, mass, and temperature measurements. They practice describing things accurately. They make models and drawings of the things they investigate, and write short descriptions of what they find. Children practice comparing their observations with those of others.

They put their arithmetic skills to work during science activities. Second graders study topics such as:

Cycles in Nature

- the seasons change as the earth orbits the sun
- how seasons affect living things (e.g., migrations in autumn, hibernation in winter)
- the life cycle: birth, growth, reproduction, death
- basic life cycles of some plants and animals (e.g., oak trees, chickens, frogs)
- the water cycle (e.g., evaporation, condensation, precipitation)

Insects

- ways insects are helpful and harmful to people (e.g., pollination, spreading disease)
- parts of insects (e.g., six legs and three main body parts)
- metamorphosis (e.g., caterpillars changing to butterflies)
- social insects (e.g., ants, honeybees)

The Human Body

- cells: the building blocks of all plants and animals
- idea that cells make up tissues, tissues make up organs, organs work in systems
- the digestive system (e.g., salivary glands, small and large intestines)
- the excretory system (e.g., kidneys, bladder)
- healthy diet (e.g., food pyramid, vitamins and minerals)

Magnetism

- magnetic poles: north-seeking and south-seeking poles
- magnetic fields (strongest at poles)
- law of magnetic attraction: unlike poles attract, like poles repel
- how to use a compass

Simple Machines

- how simple machines make work easier (e.g., lever, inclined plane)
- what friction is, and how to reduce it (e.g., lubricants, rollers)

Science Biographies

- people such as Antonie van Leeuwenhoek and Florence Night-ingale

(*drawn from the Core Knowledge Sequence*)

In a good second grade classroom, you might see children:

- using hand lenses to examine plants at different stages of growth, and drawing the changes they see

- observing and recording activities in an ant farm—how the ants store food, raise their young, build tunnels, etc.

- filling in the class's daily weather chart (temperature, cloud cover, wind, precipitation)

- using a pulley to lift different loads

- sprinkling iron filings on a piece of Plexiglas and moving magnets underneath to observe magnetic fields

- planning a healthy lunch menu, including appropriate servings of food groups

---

THIRD GRADE

Third grade children continue learning how to conduct investigations. Students practice posing questions, making hypotheses, and testing predictions. They use the information they collect to make inferences and draw conclusions. They get experience using a wide variety of equipment—thermometers, rulers, simple balances, etc. They are expected to gather, measure, and record data with greater precision. For example, they may be instructed to measure things to the nearest gram or degree Celsius. Children get more experience working on teams and sharing findings with others. They also practice reaching their own conclusions when working in groups. Third graders study topics such as:

Introduction to Classification of Animals

- how scientists classify animals (e.g., cold-blooded or warm-blooded, vertebrates or invertebrates)
- basic characteristics of fish, amphibians, reptiles, birds, and mammals

The Human Body

- the muscular system (e.g., involuntary and voluntary muscles)
- the skeletal system (e.g., skeleton, spinal column, rib cage)
- the nervous system (e.g., brain, spinal cord, nerves)
- how the eye works (e.g., cornea, iris, pupil)
- how the ear works (e.g., ear canal, eardrum)

Light and Optics

- how light travels (e.g., in straight lines at amazingly high speed)
- difference between transparent and opaque objects
- mirrors, lenses, and their uses (e.g., in telescopes, cameras)
- prisms and the color spectrum

Sound

- how sound is caused by an object vibrating rapidly
- how sound travels in waves; travels through solids, liquids, and gases
- different qualities of sound (e.g., pitch is related to the rate of vibration)
- what causes the human voice (e.g., larynx, vibrating vocal chords)

Ecology

- interdependence of organisms and their environment
- concept of "balance of nature" (not static but constantly changing)
- roles of producers, consumers, and decomposers in the food chain
- how ecosystems can be affected by changes in environment (e.g., rainfall, food supply) and by man-made changes (e.g., industrial waste, run-off from farming)

Astronomy

- what we mean by "the universe"
- our solar system: sun, nine planets and their moons
- how planetary motions cause night and day, seasons, eclipses
- gravity and how the gravitational pull of the moon causes tides
- asteroids, meteors, and comets
- stars and constellations
- space exploration (e.g., telescopes, space probes, space shuttle)

Science Biographies

- people such as Alexander Graham Bell, Copernicus, and John Muir

  (*drawn from the Core Knowledge Sequence*)

In a good third grade classroom, you might see children:

- observing and recording changes in tadpoles
- dividing a nearby field or forest into quadrants and counting populations over a two-week period
- testing several different materials to see how well light passes through them
- making a simple musical instrument using rubber bands, and making it change pitch
- putting together a model of a human skeleton
- taking a field trip to a nearby planetarium or science museum

---

Is Your School Teaching Science Literacy?

Here are examples of science lessons that many good schools teach in the primary school years. By the end of third grade, your child should understand many of these terms, facts, and concepts.

- When two magnets are brought close together, two *like poles* always repel each other, and two *unlike poles* always attract each other.
- Water freezes at 32° Fahrenheit and 0° Centigrade.
- *Evaporate* means to change from a liquid to a gas. *Condense* means to change from a gas to a liquid.
- Sound travels through the air to our ears by way of vibrations in the air.
- Great lightning bolts and the tiny sparks that sometimes shock you when you touch a doorknob both result from the flow of electricity from one place to another.
- *Matter* is the name we give to all the stuff in our physical world, anything that has substance and takes up space. Matter comes in three states: solid, liquid, and gas. Matter can change states.
- *Gravity* is the pull that every object (including the earth) has on other objects.

- A *producer* is a living thing (such as a plant) that makes its own food. A *consumer* is a living thing (such as an owl or elephant) that eats plants, animals, or other living things. A *decomposer* is a living thing (such as a mushroom or mold) that breaks down and feeds on the remains of once-living things.

- An *herbivore* is an animal that eats only plants. A *carnivore* is an animal that eats only other animals. An *omnivore* is an animal that eats both plants and animals.

- When all the living things of a certain kind have permanently disappeared, their kind is *extinct*. When a kind of plant or animal is in danger of becoming extinct, it is *endangered*.

- The ordered stages that occur in a plant's or animal's lifetime are called a *life cycle*. Life cycles involve birth, growth, reproduction, and death.

- A *habitat* is the place where a plant or animal lives.

- *Migration* is the movement of animals from one region to another as the seasons change.

- The job of a plant's *roots* is to hold the plant in place and get water and nutrients from the soil. The *stem* provides support for the leaves, branches, and flowers; it also carries water and nutrients to other parts of the plant. The *leaves* make food for the plant.

- All living things are made of *cells*.

- The five senses are sight, hearing, smell, taste, and touch.

- To prevent illness, you need to take care of your body by exercising, keeping clean, eating healthy foods, and resting.

- The *atmosphere* is the layer of gases surrounding the earth (or another planet).

- Clouds consist of tiny particles of water or ice; the rain, sleet, hail, and snow that fall from clouds are different kinds of *precipitation*.

- *Fossils* are preserved evidence of former life; they give us information about plants and animals that lived long ago, as well as the nature of their environment at that time.

- The earth rotates to the east on its axis once every twenty-four hours, making objects in the sky appear to move from east to west.

- The sun is a star, like the thousands of stars we see in the night sky, but it is the star closest to earth. The earth, one of nine planets in our *solar system*, orbits the sun once a year. It is the third planet from the sun.

- What we call "shooting stars" are really *meteors*—chunks of matter from space that enter the earth's atmosphere and leave trails of light as they burn up.

Questions to Ask the Teacher

In the primary grades, you may want to ask the teacher questions such as:

- What science lessons will my child be studying in the coming weeks?
- About how much time per day do you spend on science?
- What books and stories related to science will the class read?
- Can you tell me about some of the investigations and experiments the class will do?
- What equipment and material (e.g., thermometers, hand lenses, pulleys) will my child get to use?
- Does the school support you with in-service training for science teaching?
- Can you help me get an outline of this school's science curriculum so I'll know what my child will be studying here in the coming years?
- May I volunteer to help when the class is doing experiments or other hands-on activities? May I assist on field trips?
- What can I do at home to reinforce what you're teaching?

The Intermediate Grades—Fourth Through Sixth Grades

Many American schools don't teach enough science in grades four to six. "Students come to junior high with poor and varied backgrounds," explains one science teacher. "You spend so much time catching up on the basics, you can't always cover what is expected." In order to avoid problems later, the school must teach the fundamentals now.

At this stage, students should continue to encounter a mix of physical, life, and earth sciences. Now their studies go a bit deeper. For example, children in grades K–3 should have learned about how plants grow, what they need to survive, and what main structures like roots, stems, and leaves do. Students in grades four to six are ready for a basic introduction to photosynthesis. They also study plant anatomy in more detail, learning about stamens and pistils and such. You'll probably see some review of subjects introduced in earlier grades as students move to deeper levels of understanding.

You should notice other signs of increasing sophistication. Teachers work on bringing greater organization to children's knowledge. For example, students learn about the five kingdoms of living things, and that scientists have organized the earth's geologic history into four major eras. You should see more math creeping into classroom lessons and homework assignments. Teachers should prod children to think about how and why things occur the way they do. They set kids to thinking about questions such as "How does sweating help people cool off?" and "Why is it colder the higher you climb up a mountain?"

During the intermediate grades, children develop a more nuanced understanding of how scientists think. For example, they learn that scientists need a better reason to believe something than "Everybody knows that" or "My brother told me." Claims have to be backed up by evidence. They realize that scientists employ different kinds of investigations (observing things, collecting data, running controlled experiments) to answer their questions, and that those investigations must be repeated several times with consistent results before they are accepted by the scientific community. They get used to the idea that scientists routinely ask questions about the results of other scientists' work, not because they don't trust or respect them, but because close scrutiny is the only way to be sure of the conclusions. These lessons are vital for students learning to take a scientific view of the world.

In the intermediate grades, children develop their abilities to examine things closely, pose thoughtful questions, make predictions, and analyze results. They practice using logic to reason things through. The goal is to build scientific skills so that eventually they can investigate problems on their own and in small teams. This is a lengthy process, and the job will not be complete by sixth grade. It really takes years to hone all the needed skills, but during the intermediate grades, your child should get practice at setting up and conducting simple experiments under a teacher's supervision. He should use basic tools like magnifying glasses, thermometers, balance and spring scales, graduated cylinders, and measuring cups. He should get practice formulating a hypothesis, testing it, recording what he sees, thinking about his results, and taking a stab at figuring out what they mean. If your school is training him in these skills while also teaching concrete facts and knowledge about his world, his education is on the right track.

FOURTH GRADE

Fourth grade students' experiments grow more sophisticated than in the primary school years. With guidance from the teacher, their observations become more systematic; their predictions, hypotheses, and analyses grow more detailed. For example, teachers might ask students to spot contradictory results in their experiments, or make predictions based on data from graphs. Children learn and practice different aspects of scientific inquiry: how to make written descriptions and sketches of observations; keep organized records of investigations; offer reasons for their findings, etc. Fourth graders study topics such as:

The Human Body

- the circulatory system (e.g., structure of heart, role of red and white blood cells)
- the respiratory system (e.g., lungs, oxygen–carbon dioxide exchange)
- effects of smoking on the lungs

Chemistry: Basic Terms and Concepts

- structure of atoms (protons, neutrons, electrons)
- electrical charges of electrons ($-$), protons ($+$), neutrons (neutral)
- basic properties of matter (e.g., concepts of mass, volume, density, vacuum)
- what elements are; some familiar elements (e.g., gold, oxygen)
- how solutions form (e.g., solutes, solvents)

Electricity

- electricity as the flow of electrons
- static electricity
- electric current and circuits (e.g., closed, open, and short circuits)
- conductors and insulators

Geology: The Earth and Its Changes

- earth's layers (e.g., crust, mantle, core)
- earthquakes (e.g., faults, measuring intensity)
- volcanoes (e.g., magma, lava flow)
- theories of how the continents and oceans were formed (e.g., continental drift)
- how mountains are formed (e.g., volcanic mountains, folded mountains)
- formation and characteristics of metamorphic, igneous, sedimentary rocks
- weathering and erosion (e.g., erosion by water, wind, glaciers)

History of the Earth

- fossils as a record of earth's past life
- how fossils are formed; types of fossils (mold, cast, trace, true-form)
- organization of geologic time (Precambrian, Paleozoic, Mesozoic, Cenozoic eras)

Meteorology

- cloud types (cirrus, stratus, cumulus)
- structure of the atmosphere (e.g., troposphere, stratosphere, mesosphere, ionosphere)
- air movement and pressure (e.g., wind direction and speed; low and high pressure)
- cold and warm fronts; thunderstorms, tornadoes, hurricanes
- forecasting the weather (e.g., using barometers, weather maps)

Science Biographies

- people such as Benjamin Banneker, Charles Drew, and Michael Faraday

(drawn from the Core Knowledge Sequence)

In a good fourth grade science class, students get assignments such as:

- Build a basic electrical circuit and explain the role of each part. Use a buzzer to test whether the circuit is open or closed. Test objects with the circuit to determine whether they are conductors or insulators.

- Following the teacher's instructions, build a barometer with a coffee can and balloon, take readings over several days, and explain how the barometer works.

- Record the daily temperature, wind direction, wind speed, air pressure, and types of clouds. Forecast the weather for the next day.

- Following the teacher's instructions, make a mold and a cast fossil of a shell using modeling clay and plaster of Paris.

- Take the pulse of a classmate who is sitting and then again after he runs for one minute. Compare the two readings, and infer why exercise causes a change in heart rate.

- Build models of some simple atoms.

How Are American Fourth Graders Doing?

Here is an example of a science problem given to fourth graders on the National Assessment of Educational Progress in 1996:

You stand on the end of a boat dock and toss a small stone out into a pond of still water. Ripples form on the surface of the water. Which drawing shows what you will see when you look down at the water? (X marks where the stone enters the water.)

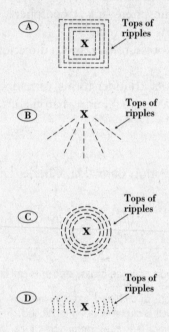

National result: More than two in five fourth graders did not know that the correct answer is C.

FIFTH GRADE

Fifth grade classwork continues training youngsters to conduct investigations. They get practice using the proper instruments to run their experiments. They look closely at the evidence they gather and use it to form conclusions. Children put math lessons to work in science class. For example, they work with simple fractions, decimals, and percentages. They use graphs, charts, and diagrams to report their data. They practice measuring things. Students also put to use the skills they learn in English class. For example, teachers may require them to write reports on their findings, or do library research on science topics. Fifth graders study topics such as:

Classifying Living Things

- the five kingdoms: plant, animal, fungus, protist, moneran
- smaller groupings: kingdom, phylum, class, order, family, genus, species
- how living things are given scientific names (e.g., *Homo sapiens*)
- major characteristics of vertebrates

Cells: Structures and Processes

- parts of cells (e.g., membrane, nucleus, cytoplasm)
- differences in plant and animal cells
- cells without nuclei (e.g., bacteria)
- single-celled organisms (e.g., amoebae, protozoans)
- organization of cells into tissues, organs, and systems

Plant Structures and Processes

- basic structure of nonvascular and vascular plants
- introduction to photosynthesis in plants
- plant reproduction: asexual plants (e.g., algae), spore-bearing plants (e.g., mosses), nonflowering seed plants (e.g., pine trees), and flowering plants (e.g., apple trees)
- main parts of flowers and their functions (e.g., pistil, stamen, pollination)

Life Cycles and Reproduction*

- examples of asexual reproduction (e.g., fission of bacteria, regeneration in starfish)
- sexual reproduction in various animals (e.g., fish, birds, cats)
- reproductive organs in animals: testes (sperm) and ovaries (eggs)
- development of the embryo (e.g., egg, zygote, embryo, fetus, newborn)
- growth stages in organisms (e.g., infancy, childhood, adolescence, adulthood)

The Human Body*

- the endocrine system (e.g., pituitary gland, adrenal glands)
- changes in human adolescence (e.g., release of hormones from glands during puberty)
- the reproductive system (e.g., fertilization, pregnancy)

Chemistry: Matter and Change

- basic atomic structure: nucleus, protons, neutrons, electrons
- how atoms act (e.g., constantly in motion; join to form molecules and compounds)
- common elements and symbols (e.g., H for hydrogen)
- common compounds and their formulas (e.g., H_2O for water)
- what the periodic table is and how it is organized
- two important categories of elements: metals and nonmetals

Chemical and Physical Change

- characteristics and examples of chemical change (e.g., iron rusting, wood burning)
- characteristics and examples of physical change (e.g., glass breaking, water freezing)

Science Biographies

- people such as Galileo, Ernest Just, and Carolus Linnaeus

(drawn from the Core Knowledge Sequence)

*Some schools wait until a later grade to have students study topics relating to sexual reproduction in animals and humans. States and districts have differing requirements.

In a good fifth grade science class, students get assignments such as:

- Examine several types of plants and seeds. Dissect a flower, drawing and identifying its main parts.

- Visit a nearby natural area (wetland, forest, state park, etc.) with a local naturalist. Record observations in your field notebook and, with the naturalist's help, try to classify some things you find.

- Following the teacher's directions, use a mixture of baking soda and vinegar to make a gas and inflate a plastic bag. Record the results; decide whether what you see is a physical change or a chemical reaction, and explain why.

- Research an element: write a short report on its physical and chemical characteristics, who discovered it, where it is found in nature, and its common uses. Make a short presentation about it to the class.
- Draw diagrams of a plant cell and an animal cell, labeling their parts.
- After learning the characteristics of metals, test different materials to determine whether they are metallic or not.

SIXTH GRADE

Sixth grade students, by the end of the year, should be competent at setting up and conducting simple experiments. They practice collecting, recording, analyzing, and reporting their data; stating clear hypotheses; and testing the validity of predictions. They also practice evaluating different explanations of an experiment's result. Sixth graders study topics such as:

Physics: Mechanical Concepts

- concept of speed; use formula Speed = Distance/Time ($S = d/t$)
- concept and examples of force (e.g., gravity, magnetic force)
- concept of work; use equation Work = Force x Distance
  ($W = F \times d$)
- concept of energy as the ability to do work
- difference between kinetic and potential energy
- conservation of energy in a system
- concept of power; use equation Power = Work/Time ($P = W/t$)

Energy, Heat, and Energy Transfer

- different forms of energy (e.g., mechanical, heat, chemical) and their sources
- how energy can change forms (e.g., gas engines, windmills)
- heat and temperature: how vigorously atoms are moving and colliding
- transfer of heat energy by conduction, convection, radiation
- how adding or removing energy can cause physical changes in matter
- what takes place during expansion and contraction of substances

- what takes place during condensation, freezing, melting, and boiling

Astronomy: Gravity, Stars, and Galaxies

- gravity (e.g., how gravity keeps planets in orbit)
- kinds of stars (e.g., red giants, white dwarfs, supernovae)
- major constellations (e.g., Big Dipper, Orion) and galaxies (e.g., Milky Way, Andromeda Galaxy)
- apparent movement of stars caused by rotation of the earth
- deep space objects (e.g., quasars, black holes)

The Forest

- interdependence of life in the forest
- structure of trees (e.g., trunk structure: xylem, cambium, heartwood, bark)
- functions of roots and "crown"; how water gets from ground to treetop
- characteristics of tropical rain forests and temperate hardwood forests
- effects of deforestation (e.g., changes in weather patterns, desertification)

The Human Body

- the lymphatic system (e.g., lymph, lymph nodes, tonsils)
- the immune system (e.g., white cells, antibodies, bacterial and viral diseases)

Science Biographies

- people such as Marie Curie, Albert Einstein, and Isaac Newton

(drawn from the Core Knowledge Sequence)

In a good sixth grade science class, students get assignments such as:

- Test, record, and graph the boiling and freezing points of various substances.
- Attend a viewing of the night sky with local astronomy club members. With their help, observe planets, galaxies, nebulae, etc., through a telescope.

- As part of a class contest, work with a team of students to design and make an insulating container. The prize goes to the team that can keep an ice cube frozen the longest.

- Present a brief report on a common disease, answering questions such as: Is it bacterial or viral? Is it communicable? What are its symptoms?

- Work on a project that demonstrates the transfer of energy from one form to another. (For example, build a waterwheel that powers some other mechanical or electrical motion.)

- Write a short biography of a scientist you admire and read it in class.

Is Your School Teaching Science Literacy?

Here are examples of science lessons that well-educated children have learned by about the time they finish the intermediate grades. By the end of sixth grade, your child should understand many of these terms, facts, and concepts.

- An object that lets light pass through it (such as clear glass) is *transparent*. An object that lets light pass through but scatters it (such as frosted glass or wax paper) is *translucent*. Most objects are *opaque:* they do not let light pass through.

- A *molecule* is a group of atoms tightly bound together. A substance made of only one kind of atom is called an *element*. A *compound* is a substance made up of two or more elements that are chemically combined.

- A *conductor* is any material that transfers heat or electricity. An *insulator* is a material that does not conduct well.

- Most materials expand with increasing temperature and contract with decreasing temperature.

- All objects fall at the same rate in a vacuum. Air resistance affects the rate at which objects fall.

- An *ecosystem* is a community of living things and their environment. Ecosystems vary in size. A maple tree and the organisms that inhabit it can be viewed as a small ecosystem; a rain forest is a large ecosystem.

- In a flower, the *pistil* is the part where seeds form. The *stamen* is the part that contains pollen. The job of the *petals,* which are often the colorful, showy parts of the flower, is to attract birds, bees, and other insects to the flower to help the plant reproduce.

- The *respiratory system* enables us to take oxygen into the body and give off carbon dioxide. Oxygen enters the blood from the lungs and is carried to body cells. Carbon dioxide given off by cells is carried by the blood back to the lungs for removal by exhaling.

- The *cell membrane* is the structure that encloses a cell. It holds the cell together and lets substances pass into and out of the cell.

- *Vertebrates* are animals with backbones (such as humans and fish). *Invertebrates* are animals without backbones (such as worms and insects).

- *Fungi* are a kingdom of organisms that feed on dead organic matter or on living things. Mushrooms, molds, and yeast are different kinds of fungi.

- An *embryo* is an animal or plant in the earliest stages of its development.

- *Erosion* is the gradual wearing away of the earth (or other objects) by forces such as water, wind, or moving ice.

- Clouds are grouped into three main families: cumulus, cirrus, and stratus. *Cumulus* clouds are the large, puffy kind often seen on summer days; they form when warm, moist air rises from the earth's surface and condenses. *Stratus* clouds look like flat, gray blankets covering the sky, and often bring drizzle. They form when a flat layer of warm, moist air rises very slowly and condenses. *Cirrus* clouds are thin, wispy clouds high in the sky; they form when air rises high enough to form ice crystals.

- Tides are caused by the moon's and, to a lesser degree, the sun's gravitational pull on the earth.

- Ocean waves are caused primarily by wind. The harder and longer the wind blows, the larger the waves.

- The earth is made of different layers. The outer layer, called the *crust,* is relatively thin and made mostly of rock. Below the crust is the *mantle,* which is very hot. Below the mantle is the even hotter *core;* it consists of a molten outer core and a solid inner core.

- When rocks form in layers, the oldest layer is usually on the bottom. In an undisturbed sequence of rock strata, fossils embedded in the lower layers are older, and fossils embedded in upper layers are successively younger.

- *Renewable resources* are natural resources—such as wheat or wood—that can be replaced once we use them. *Nonrenewable resources* are ones that can be replaced only very slowly or not at all. Examples include coal and iron ore.

- A *galaxy* is a huge collection of stars held together by gravity. When we see the Milky Way in the night sky, we are looking at the stars and dust clouds of our own galaxy.

Questions to Ask the Teacher

In the intermediate grades, you may want to ask your child's teacher questions such as:

- Will he get a thorough mix of life sciences, physical sciences, and earth sciences this year and next?

- What sorts of experiments and hands-on investigations will he do in your class?

- What sort of skills, techniques, and procedures (e.g., sketching observations, graphing data) do you expect him to learn?

- What kinds of facts, concepts, and science vocabulary do you require him to learn?

- How much math will he use in his science lessons?

- Are there any science-related field trips or class speakers scheduled?

- Can you recommend any good science books for my child as supplementary reading?

- Can you help me find out how the students in this school perform in science compared with other schools in the district and state?

JUNIOR HIGH—SEVENTH AND EIGHTH GRADES

Many American students do not learn as much science as they should in the junior high years. Parents may not know this, though, because students at this age are often uncommunicative about school, and because many parents themselves feel insecure about science. Sometimes terms and concepts (words such as "mitosis" and "refraction") seem a bit daunting to them. That is natural, but do not let it stop you from keeping tabs on the kinds of lessons your child is studying.

As in earlier grades, junior high schoolers get a combination of physical, life, and earth sciences, but now the curriculum aims at more intensive and selective study of topics. For example, youngsters should have learned in earlier grades some basics about sound, such as that it is caused by vibrations, travels in waves, and can move through solids, liquids, and gases. Now students may take a more in-depth look at general properties of sound waves, such as that they can be measured in terms of speed, frequency, wavelength, and amplitude.

Junior high schoolers should glean greater insight into the nature of the scientific enterprise. For example, they should come to understand that scientific knowledge is always backed by solid evidence, yet is still subject to modification if new evidence raises questions about prevailing theories. They should realize that questioning others' ideas, responding to criticism, and debating different theories are all part of the scientific process—so long as it is all done in a cooperative spirit of searching for answers. Students learn that scientists must guard against threats to objectivity because, human nature being what it is, our thinking may be affected by our own biases and hopes. They also come to appreciate that some matters—such as questions of morality or spirituality—cannot be tested in a scientific manner.

Children keep sharpening their skills in scientific inquiry. At this level, investigations should get more ambitious. For example, students take a greater hand in coming up with testable hypotheses. They get practice designing their own experiments. Teachers require children to be more systematic in the ways they make observations, collect evidence, and record their data. They expect their pupils to be precise when presenting results; to use logical reasoning when drawing conclusions; and to accept criticism of their findings.

Good science teachers cultivate certain habits of mind. For example, they train students to be skeptical of claims based on small samples of data or experiments that have not been verified by others. They teach them to watch for faulty reasoning and flawed analogies. Children grow accustomed to thinking of alternative explanations. They learn to be stubborn about finding solutions to problems. If you see such knowledge, skills, and habits emerging in your child, the school is training him well in the ways of scientific thinking.

SEVENTH GRADE

Seventh grade students continue to refine their skills in scientific inquiry. For example, they practice working with dependent variables, independent variables, and constants during investigations. They control variables to test hypotheses. Students learn to look for sources of errors during investigations. They practice explaining their investigations to classmates and answering questions about how they arrived at their conclusions. Seventh graders study topics such as:

Atomic Structure

- early theories of matter (e.g., Greek theory of four elements; alchemy in the Middle Ages)

- start of modern chemistry (e.g., Mendeleyev's work on the periodic table)

Chemical Bonds and Reactions

- how atoms give away, take on, or share electrons
- how chemical bonds are formed during chemical reactions
- how molecules are formed from atoms
- how ionic, metallic, and covalent bonds form
- what happens during oxidation and reduction
- what happens during reactions with acids and bases
- how chemists describe reactions by equations (e.g., HCl + NaOH = NaCl + H_2O)
- the role of a catalyst

Cell Division and Genetics

- cell division in asexual reproduction (e.g., mitosis, diploid cells)
- cell division in sexual reproduction (e.g., meiosis, haploid cells)
- how traits are passed on from one generation to another
- experiments of Gregor Mendel, the "Father of Modern Genetics"
- modern understanding of chromosomes and genes
- DNA codes; how DNA makes new DNA
- genetic engineering and modern researchers (e.g., Barbara McClintock)

Genetics and Evolution

- how genetic changes occur over time (e.g., adaptation, mutation, extinction)
- theory of natural selection (e.g., trait variation, speciation)

Weather

- difference between weather and climate
- composition and general circulation of the atmosphere (e.g., Coriolis effect)
- why trade winds, prevailing westerlies, monsoons, El Niño occur
- how fronts form between areas of higher and lower pressure
- causes and anatomy of storms: thunderstorms, tornadoes, hurricanes, typhoons

Science Biographies

- people such as Charles Darwin and Antoine Lavoisier

(*drawn from the Core Knowledge Sequence*)

In a good seventh grade science class, students get assignments such as:

- Build simple models of some molecules (such as a molecule of NaCl, table salt).
- Test some common substances to see if they are acids or bases.
- Experiment to see how a plant is affected by different levels of acidity in the soil.
- Choose a genetic trait (such as hair color or eye color) and draw a pedigree chart for your family. Include at least two generations.
- Using reference sources like the Internet, plot the positions of hurricanes and tropical storms on a tracking map.
- Participate in a science or invention fair.

EIGHTH GRADE

Eighth grade students strengthen their skills of systematic investigation. They plan, set up, and conduct classroom experiments, and use logic to form conclusions from the results. Math shows up frequently in assignments. For example, students use fractions, percentages, and decimals in their work. They practice using reference books, magazine articles, and the Internet to do research on scientific topics. They share their work in written reports and oral presentations. Eighth graders study topics such as:

Electricity and Magnetism

- electricity as the flow of electrons
- how conductors and insulators work (e.g., conductors easily give up electrons)
- static electricity (e.g., storage in capacitors; grounding; what causes lightning)
- measuring electric potential, current, and resistance (e.g., volts, amps, watts, ohms)

- how movement of charged atoms in planet's molten interior causes earth's magnetism
- connections between electricity and magnetism

Electromagnetic Radiation and Light

- travel of light waves
- the electromagnetic spectrum (e.g., radio waves, light waves, x-rays, gamma rays)
- refraction and reflection (e.g., effects of concave and convex lenses)

Sound Waves

- properties of waves (e.g., speed, frequency, amplitude, wavelength)
- characteristics of transverse and longitudinal waves
- travel of sound waves through different mediums

Chemistry of Food and Respiration

- how living cells get energy (e.g., role of carbohydrates, proteins, enzymes)
- energy in plants: photosynthesis (e.g., use of carbon dioxide, release of oxygen)
- energy in animals: respiration (e.g., use of oxygen, release of carbon dioxide)
- human nutrition and respiration (e.g., role of hemoglobin in the blood)
- human health (e.g., food groups in terms of fats, carbohydrates, proteins, vitamins)

Plate Tectonics, Earthquakes, and Volcanoes

- geological history of earth (e.g., supercontinent Pangaea)
- characteristics of earth's crust, mantle, outer core, and inner core
- how plates move on the earth's surface
- causes and anatomy of earthquakes (e.g., fault, epicenter, Richter scale)
- causes and anatomy of volcanoes (e.g., magma, lava, hot spots)

Science Biographies

- people such as Dorothy Hodgkin and Charles Steinmetz

(*drawn from the Core Knowledge Sequence*)

In a good eighth grade science class, students get assignments such as:

- Make a pinhole camera and take pictures with it.
- Using a wave tank, observe the properties of different waves and how they interact with one another.
- Draw and label the parts of longitudinal and transverse waves.
- Make a map showing the locations of some historic earthquakes and volcanic eruptions. Explain the relationship that tectonic plates have with earthquakes and volcanoes.
- Test some common foods for fat and starch.
- Keep track of what you eat for a day and then determine what percentage of the calories you consumed came from fat.

Is Your School Teaching Science Literacy?

Here are examples of science lessons that well-educated children have learned by about the time they finish junior high. By the end of the eighth grade, your child should understand many of these terms, facts, and concepts.

- The *wavelength* of a sound wave is the distance from one crest of the wave to the next, or from one trough of the wave to the next. The length of light waves is measured the same way.

- Sound travels more quickly through solids than through liquids; it travels more quickly through liquids than through gases.

- *Reflection* is the bouncing of light or sound off a surface. *Refraction* is the bending of light as it passes from one material into another.

- The *atomic number* of an element is the number of protons in an atom of that element. Each element's atomic number is listed on the periodic table of elements.

- A *catalyst* is a substance that starts a chemical reaction.

- An *acid* (such as vinegar) is a compound that has a sour taste and turns litmus paper red. A *base* (such as baking soda) is a compound that has a bitter taste and turns litmus paper blue. When an acid and a base come together, they form water and a salt.

- The *law of conservation of mass* states that matter cannot be created or destroyed by a chemical or physical change; the mass present before and after reactions remains the same.

- A *chromosome* is a stringlike structure in the nucleus of a cell. It carries the genes that determine the traits an offspring inherits from its parents. Most human cells have twenty-three pairs of chromosomes.

- According to the theory of evolution, *natural selection* is the process in which the creatures most fit for their environment live longer and have more offspring. They pass their favorable characteristics on to their offspring. Over time, those characteristics become common, while creatures poorly fitted to the environment die out.

- *Photosynthesis* is the process by which green plants use energy from sunlight to make food. In photosynthesis, plant cells use light energy to make sugars from carbon dioxide and water.

- *Hormones* are chemical messengers that cause changes in tissues and organs in the body.

- *Cartilage* is a flexible tissue that is part of the skeleton and helps protect bones at joints.

- A *neuron* is a nerve cell. Neurons are found throughout the body and carry messages along the nervous system.

- The air in the earth's atmosphere consists largely of nitrogen, oxygen, carbon dioxide, and water vapor.

- *Tectonic plates* are huge slabs that make up the earth's crust and mantle. These plates move on currents of molten rock that flow slowly beneath them. The continents ride atop these plates.

- In geology, a *fault* is a break in rocks along which the rocks have moved. Faults may be caused by the movement of tectonic plates, and earthquakes sometimes occur there.

- *Newton's law of universal gravitation* says that between any two objects in the universe there is an attractive force, gravity, which grows greater as the two objects move closer to each other.

- A *supernova* is the gigantic explosion of a star. A supernova occurs when a massive star uses up all its fuel, collapses on itself, and then explodes.

- The *mid-ocean ridge* is a huge chain of underwater mountains arising from the ocean floor. The longest mountain range in the world, it extends through the Atlantic, Indian, and Pacific oceans.

How Are American Eighth Graders Doing?

Here is an example of a science problem given to eighth graders on the National Assessment of Educational Progress in 1996:

A group of students took potato salad made with mayonnaise to a picnic on a very hot day. Explain how eating the potato salad could cause food poisoning.

Example of a good response: *When the mayonnaise gets too hot it starts growing poisonous bacteria that can give you food poisoning.*

Describe something that could be done to the potato salad to prevent the people who eat it from getting food poisoning.

Example of a good response: *It can be kept in a cooler and stay cool until they want to eat it. Then they should put it back in the cooler.*

National result: 10 percent of eighth graders received a score of Complete, the highest score. (To receive a score of Complete, a student's response needed to explain the cause of food poisoning and describe a method of preventing it, as the above sample responses do.) 61 percent of eighth graders received partial credit for their answers.

Questions to Ask the Teacher

Ask your child's junior high science teacher questions such as:

- What will my child study in the coming weeks and months?
- What are some examples of basic knowledge and concepts that you expect him to learn?
- What lab skills and techniques (e.g., using a microscope, measuring forces) do you expect him to learn?
- Can you describe some experiments he will perform this semester?
- Will there be any writing about science, such as lab reports or research papers? What sorts of math skills will my child need to handle his science lessons?
- What important figures from the history of science will the class study?
- How much time do you expect children to spend on science homework every day?

- How do you assess my child's progress? What weight do experiments and investigations get, and how do you evaluate such activities?

- Is there anything I can do to help, such as line up a guest speaker, or sponsor a science club?

- Are students in this school encouraged to enter science fairs or contests?

ISSUES IN SCIENCE EDUCATION

The following pages take up some of the debates and pitfalls that you should be aware of in science education. Some schools do an excellent job with this subject. In too many places, however, lessons are simply not up to par and schools do not expect enough of students. As the president of the National Science Teachers Association has said, "The students of this nation are not where they should be if we expect them to grow into scientifically literate adults." This section will help you know what questions to ask to make sure your school is serving your child well.

Is Your School Teaching Enough Science?

Many American youngsters just don't get enough instruction in science. In fact, some observers say this is the most neglected major subject in elementary school.

The National Science Foundation reports that, in 1993, the average "self-contained" classroom in grades one to three (i.e., one in which the same teacher teaches all subjects) spent twenty-four minutes a day on science. In grades four to six, the average was thirty-six minutes a day. That may be enough in some schools—if the curriculum is dynamite and the teacher really knows what she's doing—but it's hard to imagine learning a whole lot of science in half an hour or less. In many places, real time on task is actually far less than that. "There are elementary teachers who will pick up a picture book on snails, read [to the students], and consider that their forty-five minutes a week on science," says one California educator.[4]

Unless your child has reached an age at which he's attending a separate science class, it will be hard to assess exactly how much time is spent on this subject. Keep an eye on homework. How much is science-related, compared with other subjects? How often does he get science assignments? Every other day? Once a week? Practically never? Talk to him regularly about class work to get a feel for how much science goes on during the day. Talk to the teacher as well. What science topics will she be covering? Will there be any science-related field trips or guest speakers? How much time per day or week is given to this subject? (You may not get a precise answer to that last question, but the teacher should be able to give you an idea of where science fits into her curricular game plan.)

Learning science well requires some equipment. Students don't need lots of fancy gadgets at the elementary level, but some tools and supplies (magnets, magnifying glasses, thermometers, measuring sticks, etc.) are important. Most school systems have enough money in their budget to provide for such basics, but whether or not they choose to spend it this way is another question. When you visit the school, look to see what kinds of supplies and equipment are on hand. Are they in good repair? You might ask the teacher if she has the necessary materials to teach science lessons well. Is there a science advocate on the school's faculty—someone who looks out for the science program when it comes time to draw up the budget?

Here are a few other clues to look for during school visits. Are there any science-related displays in the classroom—a model of the solar system, for example, or an old hornets' nest? Are there science posters or photos on the walls? Do you see plants, aquariums, ant farms, shell collections, etc.? Is there a place in the room where students can conduct investigations? Do you see any experiments underway? Does the bookshelf or school library contain a decent collection of science books and magazines? Finally, you can ask the principal's office how the school does on state proficiency tests and other such measures of science achievement. Test scores by grade level or even for the whole school can help you gauge how much emphasis the school places on science.

Is the Curriculum Challenging?

The father of a fifth grader reported going to parents' night at school and asking the teacher what his child would be learning in science that year. She said, "We're studying dinosaurs." "Then what?" he asked. "Dinosaurs," she told him. He asked what else. The answer was "dinosaurs."

The students spent the whole year examining dinosaurs from various perspectives, drawing pictures of them, making collages, and writing little stories about them, but they never studied any other science—or for that matter any *real* science. (That child is now in another school.)

Be warned: it's not enough to ask "how much" science your child is getting. You have to find out *what* he's studying. Lightweight science lessons abound in U.S. elementary schools. "Educational content is continually diluted in a failed effort to produce palatable bits of information for progressively less skilled students," lamented the late Nobel Prize winner Glenn T. Seaborg. Many educators worry a great deal about making science entertaining for kids, even if it means low standards and superficial learning. Often the curriculum is so diluted that much of what passes for "science" is really just an array of activities designed to "build student interest" and help them appreciate how enjoyable this subject can be. In some classrooms, students play lots of games. ("Factory pours toxin into a river—everyone loses two green candies.") They conduct investigations that look suspiciously like arts and crafts. ("For an artistic life-science emphasis, we make animal portraits entirely out of once-living things," a fourth grade teacher explains.) They act out little science plays. ("It's hard to figure out how to be a river delta.")

One current enthusiasm is helping students "understand the roles of science" by examining different social issues. Textbooks and teacher guides are full of suggestions such as "Make posters to persuade people to be better caretakers of our natural resources" or "Write a story about a family that lives in the future, at a time when fossil fuels have been used up." Students may spend their time talking about topics like "Do we have an obligation to help developing countries?" They get assignments such as "Debate whether the government has the right to make people wear safety belts" (as part of a study of force and motion). It's all very interesting and makes for lively conversation, but how much of it is really science?

It's fine to help children see science's role in society. There is nothing wrong with spicing up a lesson with a project or demonstration to rouse students' interest; good teachers are masters at that sort of thing. All fluff and no content, however, inevitably leaves students dim on facts, concepts, and skills. Keep track of your child's lessons and make sure you distinguish between the actual study of science (engaging in scientific investigation and acquiring knowledge about atoms, cells, stars, etc.) and activities that are more or less "about" science. If students spend most of their time making portraits of animals out of feathers and shells, watching a lot of neat films about nature, and arguing about pressing social issues, what you're seeing is science fun, or science appreciation, or perhaps some sort of social science. It may have value, but it's not real science.

Does the Teacher Know Enough Science?

Unfortunately, many elementary school teachers are shaky in their own grasp of science. Relatively few have a solid background in the field. Only 3 percent of teachers in grades one through four whose duties include teaching science actually majored or minored in science or science education at the undergraduate or graduate level. The figure is 32 percent for teachers in grades five through eight. Few elementary school teachers say they feel "very well qualified" to teach this subject. "They end up getting a [teaching] job and really have to bone up on the science behind what they are going to teach," observes a Boston education professor.[5] It's no wonder that science often gets less time and attention than other subjects, and that lessons are less than rigorous.

Many schools try hard to recruit instructors trained in the sciences, but that's a tough bill to fill at any grade level. "We're demanding that our kids have more science for graduation when we can't get the teachers," says a Detroit principal. "I can show you classrooms where we've had five or six science teachers because industry keeps hiring them away." Meanwhile, the status quo is tolerated by the bureaucracies and programs that certify teachers, which typically put little emphasis on how deeply educated a person is in a particular subject area, but great emphasis on how many pedagogy classes she's taken. (Critics point out that today, Albert Einstein would not be able to teach physics in America's public school classrooms.)

Given the state of affairs in the science classroom, you may want to find out what kind of background, if any, your child's teacher has in this area. Don't be embarrassed to take the most direct route—tactfully ask her to tell you about her own education. In the primary grades, when children generally have just one teacher, you wouldn't necessarily expect her to have a formal science degree, but you might inquire into the nature of her science background. Ask what kind of pre-service and in-service training she's had to help her teach science to youngsters. Some of these may be courses in which she has studied science per se; others will be "science education" classes which generally focus on classroom methods.

When it comes to an actual science teacher—one who teaches distinct science classes, usually in the intermediate or junior high grades—you can politely inquire whether she has majored in science and, if so, which branch. You can also ask whether the school has a science supervisor, someone with a science background who advises teachers with less academic training in this field.

Finally, don't forget to talk to other parents whose children have studied under this teacher within the last year or two. Do they sing her praises? Or do you hear comments such as, "Michael's really struggling with his seventh grade biology lessons—I don't think the fifth and sixth grade teachers prepared him for the work"? Visit the class sometime to watch the teacher in action. Is she enthusiastic? Does she explain concepts in terms children can grasp? When guiding experiments, does she seem to know how to do them herself? If you're trained in the sciences yourself, see if there is some way the teacher can use your services—she'll probably welcome the help.

What Is the Best Way to Test Students in Science?

The best science programs are guided adventures in which hands-on activities are carefully coordinated with readings from well-chosen books and explanations from knowledgeable teachers. In recent years, many U.S. schools have been expanding the hands-on part of that equation. This means teachers are having to adjust the ways they test students. You may want to look and see how your own child's teacher goes about it.

Tried and true methods are still good for assessing certain kinds of knowledge. Having a student simply explain his understanding of a concept still works. For example, you'll see good teachers asking youngsters to write answers to questions such as "Why do the stars seem to twinkle in the night sky?" Finding out what facts children know is not so difficult: challenging fill-in-the-blank questions, multiple choice tests, true-false quizzes, etc., usually suffice. Some experts get snooty about such "objective" methods and claim that they only test what kids have memorized. That may be true in some cases, but the fact is that acquiring a good amount of factual knowledge is critical. Teachers must find out whether kids are getting it into their brains and holding on to it. In some respects, there is no substitute for a test that says: Tell me what you know—and let me see what you should have learned but as yet have not.

When it comes to actually "doing" science, testing gets trickier. There are all sorts of things a teacher must gauge, and some of them are not easily measured. She must consider a child's competence in setting up and performing experiments; habits of observation; ability to reason scientifically; skill at making inferences and posing hypotheses, etc. Teachers have to take into account that, in classroom experiments, results often vary a bit even when the procedure is performed correctly. Little things like how humid it is that day can throw off students' final answers. Experiments are often conducted in teams, which makes assessing individual performances tougher. Anyone who's ever been to a science fair has a feel for just how hard it can be to "grade" scientific investigations. Judges often struggle to rank criteria such as the difficulty of a chosen topic, the care and planning that went into the project, and the student's perseverance in sticking with it (let alone guessing how much work the parents really did).

In the end, there is no single best method to test learning in science class. Good teachers use a mix of strategies to assess knowledge, understanding, and skills. Short-answer tests; essay questions and written reports; classroom discussions; oral presentations; experiments that students must conduct and explain; and checklists of ability to perform laboratory tasks are all valid. When you meet with your child's teacher, ask her to explain the different assessment methods she uses in science. If nothing else, it should give you a hint of how difficult it can be to appraise learning derived in significant part from hands-on activities.

Should Schools Teach Evolution?

Evolution is one of the most sensitive subjects in the school curriculum. Teachers, state and local school boards, curriculum developers, textbook companies, and legislators have all spent considerable time worrying about how it should be handled. That evolution is taught at all disturbs some parents. Others scoff at anyone who expresses reservations. We know of no solution that will satisfy everyone—other than allowing parents to pick their own schools with their own distinctive emphases and philosophies—but we offer a few thoughts to keep in mind.

First, understand that the theory of evolution is broadly accepted in the scientific community. There is still debate about some of the mechanisms involved, but on the whole, it is considered by scientists to be the soundest explanation for certain patterns and evidence found in nature.

Second, because it is widely regarded as a central organizing theory of biology, most schools do teach evolution. This is a reasonable position for educators to take. Since the worldwide community of scientists views evolution as one of its most important theories, it would be strange indeed if U.S. science classes ignored it.

Third, many religious people have concluded that evolution is itself part of God's creation or design for the universe. Many of the scientists who have contributed to evolutionary theory have been individuals of deep religious faith. Most American parents apparently believe that to accept what science says about evolution is not to deny the existence of God or His role in the creation of earth and life.

You may not share that view of evolution. Like some parents, you may find the theory repugnant to your faith. If so, you must decide how to proceed.

Many parents who do not accept evolution are nonetheless willing to have their children learn what the theory is about in school, while explaining at home why they do not accept it, and what they believe instead. This strategy makes sense to us. Since evolution is accepted scientific theory, and is what much of the world thinks, it seems to us important that educated students know what it is, even if they don't accept it.

It also makes sense, in fact it is essential, for you to instruct your child as to your own religious beliefs. No one, inside or outside the school, should question your right and obligation to do so. The vast majority of American teachers understand that science deals with observable, testable phenomena, while faith reaches far beyond such evidence. Therefore science class is not a good forum in which to debate or test one's religious beliefs. Most teachers recognize that their job is to teach the prevailing scientific theory; the responsibility for relating that theory to one's religious beliefs falls to family and clergy. That approach seems the most workable one to us.

In July 1969, when American astronauts first stood on the moon, they spoke to millions of men, women, and children back home. They read from the Bible. Men of science, men of technology, they read the familiar words of Genesis: "In the beginning God created the heaven and the earth . . ." In that message crackling across the vastness of space itself, there seemed to be an understanding. We will always keep exploring, questioning, and deepening our knowledge of ourselves and the universe. At the same time, for many of us there will always be a deep mystery that lies outside the pale of empirical investigation. Science and faith must exist side by side. That is not a bad lesson for school-children.

Are Science Lessons Getting Too Green?

"Environmental education" is one of the most widely taught subjects in schools today. Children spend a good deal of time on assignments such as "Think of ways you can help future generations have their fair share of metal resources" and "Describe your feelings about forest fires." Teaching materials about the environment flood the schools, from text-book publishers, environmental advocacy organizations, industry groups, and government agencies. Lessons take place across the curriculum, often in science class—so much that, in some places, parents complain about the "greening of science." ("Rain forests *again*? Didn't you study that last year and the year before?") Teaching responsible stewardship of our planet is important, but given the ballooning enthusiasm for this subject in the "science" curriculum, you may need to look closely and ask yourself: Exactly what is my child studying? How much of it is really science?

In 1997, a distinguished panel of scientists, economists, and educators took a close look at environmental education teaching materials used in K–12 classrooms around the nation. This Independent Commission on Environmental Education found some good, but also much that was worrisome. One major finding was that environmental education often involves little or no real science. Frequently, students are encouraged to discuss complicated issues without enough factual knowledge to understand what they're talking about. For example, they get plenty of dire predictions about global warming, but little science about climatic processes. They hear a lot about forests all over the world being in danger, but not so much about natural forest dynamics. Our schools are turning out students who are very concerned about an environment they actually know very little about.

The commission also found that much of the so-called science in the books it examined was misleading or just plain wrong. Exaggerations, partial truths, and distortions abound. One book states that "experts believe that by the year 2000, most of the world's oil may be depleted." Another tells youngsters that "20 million Americans do not have enough food to sustain a normal active life." Lessons tend to over-simplify issues, often suggesting that solutions to problems are obvious, yet failing to inform students about trade-offs. For example, some class-room readings promote recycling without explaining that sometimes it costs more, takes more energy, and creates more pollution to recycle than to make new materials. The commission was troubled to find that "factual errors are common in many environmental education materials and textbooks."

Too often in environmental education, the goal seems to be to cre-ate a nation of eco-activists rather than to present the best available science. Much material has an anti-industry, anti-agriculture bias. Some books even present private property and capitalism as barriers to environmental protection, and call for a more "equitable" distribution of wealth and resources. Students may be urged to send funds to envi-ronmental groups, write legislators in support of solar collectors, and live a "greener" lifestyle. Lessons sometimes resort to scaring kids with apocalyptic visions of the future—pictures of the Statue of Liberty un-derwater, or references to living "in a world without trees." Occasion-ally it gets downright hysterical, such as the textbook that quotes David Foreman, founder of EarthFirst!: "When a chain saw slices into the heartwood of a two-thousand-year-old Coast Redwood, it's slicing into my guts. . . . Madmen and madwomen are wrecking this beautiful, blue-green, living Earth."[6]

Given the varying quality of curricular material in the schools, it is a good idea to ask yourself some questions. Do your child's "environmen-tal education" lessons really teach much about the environment? Are they mostly about scientific knowledge, or about attitudes and be-havior? Do readings present different sides of problems and solutions? Is enthusiasm for teaching responsibility toward the environment sup-planting real science in the curriculum? When that happens, you get graduates who are convinced that the rain forests need saving but don't have the foggiest idea where they are, why they get all that rain, or why trees need water.

Warning Signs of a Weak Science Program

Watch for the following clues that something is wrong at your school:

- little time given to science compared to other subjects
- teachers seem unsure or hesitant about science lessons

- no scientific investigations and experiments visible
- no student work (posters, plants, aquariums, models, etc.) displayed
- few science-related reading assignments; little science homework
- few science books in the school library; outdated books and material
- students rarely required to recall specific terms, facts, formulas, theories, and concepts
- little or no math used in science assignments and lessons
- no space available for experiments and science projects
- little science equipment on hand—or children not taught to use it
- "environmental education" supplants much of the science curriculum
- older students' hands-on "investigations" look like arts and crafts or game time
- much repetition of topics (without deepening sophistication) from year to year

TEACHING SCIENCE AT HOME

About 150 years ago, a mother in Port Huron, Michigan, took her son out of school after a teacher called the youngster "addled." She knew the boy was bright, so she decided to teach him at home. She encouraged his questions, let him set up a lab in the basement with old bottles and wires and parts he'd collected, and gave him a primer on physics called the *School Compendium of Natural and Experimental Philosophy*, which was full of experiments he could perform himself. Many years later, the son told a newspaper reporter, "My mother was the making of me." By that time, Thomas Edison was America's most celebrated inventor and scientist.

There are several lessons to be drawn from Edison's life. One is this: physics, chemistry, and biology aren't just for the school lab. You can learn plenty of science at home.

Perhaps the single best thing you can do is simply foster your child's wonder about the world and teach him to ask: Why is that? What are clouds made of? Where does the water in rivers go? What makes birds fly? (Young Edison asked himself that one. He once talked a playmate into swallowing worms to find out if that was the birds' secret.) This is the beginning of all scientific discovery—the wondering and thinking about what we see and hear. Nurturing your child's curiosity is the first, all-important step.

A second step is to give children—especially younger schoolchildren—hands-on adventures with science at home. As we pointed out earlier, children begin to learn science by *doing* science. Reading about it is critical, too—there is no substitute for it—but it's the hands-on part of science that really gets youngsters excited. It gives them concrete evidence of principles and facts in action. As Edison said, you need to show the child the cocoon unfolding, the butterfly emerging. The knowledge that comes from the actual seeing makes all the difference, so invite your child on little journeys of discovery. Turn over that rock in the backyard and see what's living underneath. Watch together to see how many days it takes that tulip to bloom. When people stand upright with their arms outstretched to either side, which is greater— their width, or their height? Urge your child to grab a measuring tape and find out. Such simple investigations will make all the difference to his science education.

Many parents hesitate when it comes to teaching this subject because they don't have a lot of confidence in their own scientific literacy or their ability to answer questions. (Even a simple query from a child— like, "Dad, why is the sky blue?"—can give most of us trouble.) But children rarely fault their parents for answering, "I don't know, *let's find out!*" It's your *attitude* about science that's going to impress your child and kindle his own fascination. Edison's mom was no scientist—but she was profoundly interested in her son's excitement. Aim to supply that kind of enrichment.

Teaching Your Child to Think Like a Scientist

One of your school's tasks is to train your child in the process of scientific research and thinking (or "scientific inquiry," as it's sometimes called in classrooms today). Scientific inquiry mostly involves being curious about the world, looking at things closely, testing ideas carefully, using common sense, engaging in patient work, and making an occasional leap of the imagination. Both analytical and creative, it's a process that takes several years of training before students get the hang of it. You can make a big contribution by practicing it at home.

Here are some of the ways scientists proceed while conducting an inquiry. They don't always come in the same order, but these steps are almost always involved one way or another. Help your child work through these processes as he thinks about a problem. Drawing his attention to the various stages of investigation will sharpen his science thinking skills.

MAKING OBSERVATIONS

Looking at things closely is one of the oldest and most fundamental scientific methods. Investigations usually begin with observing something and wondering about it. Every step after that—from coming up with a hypothesis to running a test to analyzing the results—involves even more observing. Looking carefully is a trait children develop only with practice.

Start building observation skills by talking with your child about what he sees when you go places together. Draw attention to details— like the fact that all the trees you're hiking past today have moss growing on the same side. Why is that? There are several strategies you can use to encourage children to look more closely. For example, ask your child to write down or draw pictures of what he sees. (Asking youngsters to collect five different leaves and draw colored pictures of them is a great science lesson, because it makes them really *look* at those leaves.) Invite your child to compare things: Which is the brightest star in the sky tonight? Classifying objects often requires close scrutiny: put all the scallop shells in one pile, oyster shells in another. Look for changes in things: What's the difference between that dandelion today and yesterday?

ASKING QUESTIONS

It's fine for younger children to ask "What's that?" but scientific investigation usually requires more precise queries. As your child grows, teach him to refine and focus questions. Break broad questions into sets of smaller ones that will help direct an investigation. Instead of asking, "What's that fuzzy stuff on these leaves?" good science students learn to ask: "What are these tiny hairs on the undersides of these leaves? How do they help the plant live and grow? Why don't I see them on the leaves of this neighboring plant?" Likewise, the question "What do birds eat?" is a great beginning, but to conduct his own investigation, your child may first need to narrow it: "What do the birds in our backyard eat?" Or even further: "Will some of the birds in our backyard eat peanuts? Which birds?" One way to practice formulating clear, thought-ful questions is to write them down before launching an investigation.

FORMING A HYPOTHESIS

Once your child has posed a question, he may want to form a hypothe-sis. A hypothesis is really nothing more than an educated guess about why or how something happens—a possible explanation based on the information you've already observed. After forming a hypothesis, scien-tists then proceed to test it (by gathering data, by doing experiments, etc.) to see how it holds up. Your child may notice the days getting longer in May and wonder how much later the sun sets from day to day. He may guess that it sets about two minutes later than the day before. To test his hypothesis, he'll need to watch and record the time of sunset over the next several days. (Or, to go another route, look up sunset times in the newspaper for a few days.)

Forming a good hypothesis takes some talent, experience, and cre-ativity. At first, your child may offer nothing more than wild guesses or hunches. That's fine; each time he considers a problem, encourage him to come up with as many explanations as possible. With enough prac-tice, he'll learn to think about what he's seeing and propose explana-tions based on the evidence before him, explanations that can somehow be tested. Those are the marks of good hypotheses.

Sometimes children are reluctant to form hypotheses because they're afraid of being wrong. Practice removes that fear. It's important to let children know that not all hypotheses turn out to be correct—sci-entists make "good guesses" that turn out to be wrong all the time. Even incorrect hypotheses are valuable in that they are part of a search for the truth.

PLANNING AND CONDUCTING THE INVESTIGATION

Scientists use different kinds of investigations to answer their questions. The inquiry may involve going to books to get more information. It may involve simply watching closely—to find out what those ants are carrying, you may need to follow their trail back to the source. It might involve collecting and classifying specimens. Do fireflies give off heat when they flash? Your child will have to catch a few to find out. Fre-quently, science involves setting up and running an experiment. What makes bread rise? Leaving out an ingredient and seeing what happens is the experimental part of the inquiry.

Before starting an investigation, it's good practice to talk with your child about how he plans to proceed. What kind of equipment will he need? How long will it take? What are the steps involved? What conditions need to be controlled? In our example of investigating sunset times, your child would need a spot with a clear horizon, otherwise his observations won't be very accurate. In successful experiments (as in many of life's projects), the most effort often goes into planning and preparing. Again, writing down how he intends to proceed may help focus his thoughts.

RECORDING AND ANALYZING WHAT HAPPENS

Gathering measurable data is a vital part of any scientific investigation. Help your child learn to observe carefully, write down what he sees, and organize that information in a way that helps him understand it. For example, if he's investigating what kinds of bugs live in your garden, he may want to make a map of the garden with an overlying grid so he can keep track of exactly where he's spotted different bugs. Gathering information is a great time to practice using numbers, tables, and graphs. After scientists record their data, they look it over, think about it, and try to make sense of the information they've collected.

DRAWING A CONCLUSION

After analyzing the data, your child can practice coming up with a conclusion—a statement that sums up what he's learned. The conclusion should be about the question he started out to answer. Urge him to consider all possible explanations for the results he got. Which one seems the most likely? Do the data support or reject his hypothesis?

Teach your child to be honest and careful about what he's observed—not just to look for the results he expected. This is critical in scientific inquiry. Good scientific explanations are based on honest evidence collected during honest investigations.

If the initial results seem to support his hypothesis, you may want to ask your child: Is there still another way we can test it? Repeated testing is common practice in scientific investigation. It's also good practice to ask: Does this conclusion raise any new questions? (Many times, in science, it does!)

Scientists usually make the results of their investigations public, so being able to communicate findings clearly is important. Ask your child to recount his investigation to you, describe his observations, and explain exactly how he arrived at his conclusion.

Not all investigations yield the "right" answer. Sometimes results aren't at all what you expected. Sometimes the data seem confused. Sometimes the experiments simply don't work. Children often have a hard time dealing with these realities of scientific inquiry. Teach your child to deal constructively with setbacks. Again, we can learn from Edison. He once conducted experiment after experiment without finding the answer he needed. A friend said he was sorry the tests were failing. "We haven't failed," Edison said with a smile. "Now we know a hundred things that won't work, so we're that much closer to finding what will." Instill that kind of perseverance in your child, and you'll have a better science student on your hands.

Science at Home and Beyond

"Backyards and basements are great labs for children, but most parents just don't use them," a Tennessee science teacher says. "The ones that do—their kids are always my most eager students." Here are some ways to enrich learning at home.

- **Initiate investigations.** Don't wait for the school science fair. It's easy and lots of fun to get science projects going around the house. Put up a bird feeder, buy a field guide, and keep a list of birds visiting your backyard. Get a star chart and go star gazing with your child. Set up your own weather station with a thermometer, barometer, rain gauge, and wind vane.

  At your library or bookstore you'll find many good books chockfull of projects, experiments, and science "tricks" to do at home. Make your own volcano, or a shoe box camera, or electricity with a lemon. You'll be amazed at all the neat stuff you and your child can do together.

- **Keep a notebook for science observations.** Having a "nature notebook" or "science log" will encourage your child to keep a record of his investigations. He can practice writing down observations and also sketching things he sees.

- **Take your own science field trips.** Visit local zoos, museums, and nature centers. Parks often conduct naturalist-led hikes for young people. Look around—there may be a planetarium, aquarium, or

botanical garden within driving distance. Even if those kinds of resources aren't immediately available, with a little effort you should
be able to arrange eye-opening trips. Schedule a tour of a nearby
weather station, hospital lab, rock quarry, fish hatchery, a factory
that uses robotics—these are all great places for your child to witness
science in action.

- **Practice looking things up.** Almost every science investigation involves looking in books or other sources to see what's already
known. When your child has questions, help him track down answers with reference material—an encyclopedia, a science book at
the library, or on the Internet. When exploring nature, field guides
are particularly good reference tools.

- **Use the kitchen as a lab.** The kitchen is a great place for measuring,
timing, mixing, and watching physical and chemical changes. If you
can cook, you can teach all sorts of science. Which dissolves faster, a
whole sugar cube, or a crushed one? In warm water or cold? Challenge your child to guess, and then find out. Exactly what is that
coming out of the teakettle? Hold a metal pie pan above the spout
(watch out—it will get hot!) and catch some steam. How did those
drops of water get there?

- **Make household repairs together.** When something around the
house needs fixing—an old lamp, a latch on a cabinet door, a loose
step on the back porch—invite children to help you figure out how
to repair it. This is an excellent way to develop problem-solving
skills and teach some basic physics and mechanics. You can also
hunt at junk shops for cheap clocks and other gadgets your child can
tinker with. Urge him to take them apart and try putting them back
together.

- **Encourage collections.** Take a couple of zip-lock bags on outdoor
hikes to collect rocks, leaves, or shells. Practically any kind of collection—stamps, coins, baseball cards, even key chains—helps primary grade children practice basic science skills like observing,
comparing, measuring, classifying, and describing items.

- **Raise some plants or an animal.** Turn those garden chores into
botany lessons. Get some books to learn all about the flowers and

vegetables you grow together—their different parts, what they need to thrive, their different uses. For a first-rate zoology course, get a pet. There's no better way to teach youngsters about animal behavior. Your child will learn something about responsibility, too.

- **Build models together.** Encourage the creative putting together of models—Lego projects, model rockets, vehicles with moving parts, etc. Working with models helps develop mechanical sense and the ability to carry out projects.

- **Use math and measuring.** Mathematics is vital to scientific inquiry. Look for ways to incorporate it into your child's explorations. For example, if you've got a leaky faucet, he might see how long it takes to fill one eight-ounce cup. From that, ask your child to calculate how much water drips in a day. A week?

- **Watch science shows on TV.** This is an area where selective viewing pays off. Look for good series like *Nature* and *Nova,* and those aimed specifically at kids, like *Bill Nye the Science Guy.* And keep an eye out for science articles in newspapers and magazines that you can share with your child.

- **Look for clubs and programs to join.** Science groups abound—everything from amateur astronomy to computer clubs. You and your child may be able to join some of them together. There are probably some after-school, weekend, or summer science programs for students in your area. Find them by checking with your school's science teacher, the public librarian, a local museum, or nearby college science department.

- **Find a science mentor.** If your child really likes science, by the time he hits junior high his knowledge may outstrip yours. This is also the age when science gets a "nerdy" reputation with school kids. At that stage, you may want to find an adult who really knows the field your child is most interested in—either a professional or good amateur scientist—and who would be willing to offer encouragement. A science teacher or guidance counselor at school should be able to help you locate a good mentor.

At-Home Science Supplies

Children don't need a whole lot of fancy equipment to learn science, but a few supplies do wonders for their will to explore. One or two items for a kid's home lab might make a great birthday gift. Here are some ideas:

magnifying glass
magnets
compass
tweezers
eyedroppers
beakers, bottles, jars, plastic containers
spoons
thermometer
measuring sticks and tape
simple balance scale
stopwatch
binoculars
insect net
insulated wire, batteries, light bulb, simple switch
flashlight
pH paper
prism, lenses, small mirrors
sketch pad and quality pencils
field guides

You can find equipment in toy stores, hobby shops, hardware stores, and specialty shops (like electronics and nature stores). There are also mail-order supply houses that sell all sorts of science stuff ranging from dissection kits and chemistry sets to microscopes and telescopes. Two of the largest selections available by catalogue are from Edmund Scientific at 101 East Gloucester Pike, Barrington, NJ 08007 (www.edsci.com) and Carolina Biological Supply Co., 2700 York Road, Burlington, NC 27215 (www.carolina.com).

Resources That Help Your Child Learn Science

Here are some books, magazines, and other resources that can help your child learn science. Your child's teacher may have more suggestions.

Books

101 Things Every Kid Should Know About Science, Samantha Beres and Arthur Friedman (Lowell House, 1998)—A source for reference, browsing, and fun. Grades 4–7.

Bill Nye the Science Guy's Big Blast of Science, Bill Nye (Addison-Wesley, 1993)—A whirlwind tour of the science world. Grades 5–8.

DK Science Encyclopedia (DK Publishing, 1998)—Science facts from A to Z, presented in a well-organized, interesting manner. Ages 9–12.

Janice VanCleave's 200 Gooey, Slippery, Slimy, Weird & Fun Experiments, Janice Pratt VanCleave (John Wiley & Sons, Inc., 1993)—Full of great around-the-house experiments.

The New Way Things Work, David Macaulay and Neil Ardley (Houghton Mifflin, 1998)—A book of scientific explanations, everything from zippers and plows to dentist drills and windmills.

Magazines

National Geographic World (National Geographic Society)—A colorful monthly publication about geography, adventure, wildlife, and science. Ages 8 to 4.

Odyssey (Kalmbach Publishing)—Science magazine for kids. Ages 10 to 16.

Ranger Rick (National Wildlife Federation)—Introduces kids to the world of nature.

Scientific American Explorations—A magazine designed to introduce the whole family to science. Lots of ideas for parents.

Web Sites

Ask Dr. Universe (www.wsu.edu/druniverse)—Stocked with interesting answers to science questions.

Discover Online (www.discover.com)—An excellent site for advanced middle school and high school students. *Discover Online* targets kids and adults looking for serious discussion of current science issues.

FamilyPC Software Reviews (www.zdnet.com/familypc/filters/fpc.software.html)—A list of the "50 Best Software Programs" for kids, plus reviews of the latest educational software.

MAD Scientist Network (www.madsci.org)—Type in a science question and the answer appears. Perfect for the inquisitive child.

National Geographic for Kids (www.nationalgeographic.com/kids)—A broad site designed for children of all ages as an introduction to the world of science.

Smithsonian Magazine's Kids' Castle (www.kidscastle.si.edu)—Answers to basic science questions in an easy to use, child-friendly format.

techlearning.com (www.techlearning.com)—Hundreds of software reviews in science and other subjects.

PART III

MAKING
IT
WORK

THE SCHOOL CURRICULUM IS THE ENGINE OF AN ELEMENTARY education, but an engine alone does not make for a safe and comfortable ride. Part III examines some of the nuts, bolts, and assorted parts you'll need to make your child's K–8 education a dependable vehicle that will transport him as far as the high school doorway.

Chapter 10 reviews some key skills that contribute to a child's success in school, such as good study techniques and homework habits. It discusses two subjects of keen interest to students and parents alike: tests and grades. All of these areas require some monitoring by you. We offer reminders of your duties at home and pointers about how to stay involved at school.

Each parent has a slightly different set of education responsibilities. Those with youngsters who are disabled or gifted often face extra challenges. Chapter 11 gives an overview of steps that parents can take to help such children prosper, and lists some resources they can consult for further guidance.

Chapter 12 addresses problems that most parents encounter at some point in a child's academic career. Many U.S. schools suffer from low standards and expectations. Some are plagued by poor discipline that can pull down not only children's grades but also their attitudes and behavior. At some point, you may face the prospect of your child spending a year in a classroom with a mediocre teacher. We offer some tips for dealing with these problems and finding solutions before they damage your child's education.

Nothing is more important to a good education than character training. Schools must make deliberate efforts to help parents teach children about virtues such as perseverance, honesty, and responsibility—particularly in the elementary school years, when habits and dispositions are being formed. Chapter 13 takes up character education, as well as health and physical education and extracurricular activities.

Chapter 14 discusses three of the most ominous threats to children's education and general well-being: drug and alcohol use, premature sexual activity, and excessive television viewing. Elementary school students are very vulnerable to these temptations and troubles. They need your protection and guidance. We remind you of steps you must take and outline efforts that good schools make to keep their students safe.

Chapter 15 looks at an array of education fads and disputes. You may have read about some of them in the paper or heard about them on the news and thought to yourself: "That's just a lot of arguing among educators, academics, special interests, and politicians. It doesn't really affect my child." You might be wrong. These issues frequently inflict themselves upon schools. They affect what is taught and what kids learn. The discussions in this chapter will help you spot questionable policies and practices in your child's school.

Chapter 16 gives a tour of the education reform landscape, along with some suggestions about how you can help bring about needed change if it turns out that your school is afflicted by some of those troubles or fads. Sometimes that means tackling the education system. You'll need to know your way around, so we provide a road map and warning signs about the twists and turns you'll likely encounter.

You may not want to travel quite that far. The system, after all, is very large and much of what happens (or fails to happen) in it may seem distant. That's your option. As a parent, however, seeing to the education of *your* child is not optional. The main purpose of this book is to help you carry out that duty. Accordingly, we open this part of the book with a short list of absolute musts.

WHAT PARENTS MUST DO

You are your child's first and most important teacher. Here are ten steps you must take to strengthen his chances for a good education.

1. **Tell your child: education comes first.** A parent's example, attitude, and expectations can make all the difference.

2. **Read to and with your child.** Start in the pre-kindergarten years and never stop.

3. **Find out what your school is teaching.** Make sure it has high standards centered on the academic basics. Help your child meet those standards.

4. **Pay attention to character at home and at school.** Virtues such as hard work, responsibility, and respect are essential to academic success.

5. **Find out how the school expects its pupils to behave.** Read the code of conduct. If the school is not a disciplined place, little learning will occur.

6. **Keep in close touch with teachers.** Meet with them, phone and write them, heed their messages. Lend them a hand.

7. **Pay attention to homework.** Make sure your child does it and takes it seriously.

8. **Look after your child's health.** See that he gets a good night's sleep and eats a decent breakfast. Talk to him about the dangers of drugs and alcohol.

9. **Control the TV.** Mostly, turn it off.

10. **Make sure your child is in the right school.** Many schools are mediocre. Some are awful. Others are terrific. You have options. Find one that works well for your child.

CHAPTER 10

Helping Your Child Succeed in School

WHEN MONICA JONES'S STUDENTS RECEIVED SOME OF THE highest achievement test scores in Washington, D.C., the seventh grade teacher got a call from the deputy superintendent. He wanted to know her secret.

"I told him it was the involvement of parents," says Jones. "I could have taken credit, I suppose. I could have told him about my lesson plans, how often we go to the library, how I have them write essays, or even how the students inspire me. But really, I know in my heart, if I did not have the support of parents, my students would not do so well."[1]

If there is one thing educators can agree on, it's this: children do better in school when their parents get involved in their learning. They tend to get higher grades and have fewer behavior problems. They like school more and hold higher aspirations. They're more likely to go on to college. These effects cut across socioeconomic lines. All evidence points toward parents' support as one of the most important factors in a child's academic success.

Unfortunately, many moms and dads aren't as attentive as they should be. In overwhelming numbers, teachers claim that students are less motivated academically today than they were ten to twenty years ago, largely because of low parental involvement and supervision. They say that many parents spend less time with their children, place fewer demands on them, and are less in touch with their school lives. These trends leave teachers in a tough position. Even an excellent school cannot provide a good education without help from home.

This chapter outlines some of your key responsibilities and suggests some things you can do to foster academic success. We discuss building good study and homework habits. We go over some ways that schools measure pupil achievement, and some strategies you can use to help your child measure up. We address how to play an active role at school and build sound teacher relations. We outline how to determine whether your school really values parents' participation. There are few secrets here, but you will find solid, time-tested ways to stay involved with your loved one's education. It can make all the difference.

TEACHING YOUR CHILD GOOD STUDY HABITS

The key to success is a willingness to work hard. It's true in every aspect of life: in marriage, in parenthood, in friendships, on the job. It's crucial for success in school, too. Effort matters. There is a direct relationship between the amount of work that goes into studies and the amount that children learn.

Despite the continuing vitality of the American work ethic, we sometimes resist this truth when it comes to education. We're apt to place faith in innate intelligence as the secret of school achievement. The "smart" kids go to the front of the class while "slow" kids get left behind. When their child does poorly in school, parents often conclude that she "just isn't cut out for the classroom," or "she doesn't test well." Or that it's the school's fault, or that too many demands are being placed on kids these days, or any of a number of other excuses. It's a convenient philosophy, one that gets many parents off the hook, at least in their own minds.

In other parts of the world, different beliefs are at work. The distinguished psychologist Harold Stevenson has studied the attitudes of parents and students toward school success in the U.S. and several Asian countries where students outscore ours in international tests. He has found that Asian parents don't put as much stock in innate intelligence. Rather, they associate educational success with hard work. They believe that time invested in studying will lead to mastery of academic curricula. Effort counts.

This conviction is continually conveyed to children. It is portrayed, for example, in a tale about the ancient poet Li Po, which is retold in Chinese elementary school readers. One day, Li was walking beside a stream when he saw an old woman sitting beside a rock, grinding a hunk of iron. He asked her what she was doing. "Making a needle," she answered. Puzzled, Li Po asked her how such a large piece of iron could be ground into a needle. "All you need is perseverance," the old woman told him. "If you have the will and do not fear hardship, a piece of iron can be ground into a needle." Li Po walked on, but the old woman's words would not leave his mind. He realized that he would never make progress if he did not study hard. From that day he was a diligent student.

The credo that academic achievement comes through steady, devoted work is widespread in Asia. To be sure, there as here, some students don't learn as quickly as others. They have to study longer and harder. As the Chinese proverb says, "The slow bird must start out early." Even though they may fly at different speeds, through continued effort all children can learn, and most children can reach basic academic goals.[2]

It is essential that you foster in your own home that same faith that hard work is the key to school success. It is one of your most solemn responsibilities as a parent. As your child grows, let her know that studying is a top priority. There will be much joy in learning, but at the same time there needs to be determined effort. Make your child understand that studying must take precedence over practically everything else: watching TV, playing with toys, talking with friends, sports. Cultivate such an ethos in your home by the ideals you express, the rules you set, the behavior you model, the encouragement you give.

Another critical task is helping your child learn *how* to study. It takes certain skills. Children aren't born with them. They have to be developed, which means adults must take the time and responsibility to show youngsters the way. When students routinely sit down the night before a test, stare at their books, go to school the next day, and fail ("I tried, but I just can't learn this stuff!), often the problem is that no one has really taught them the art of studying well.

At this point you may be thinking: Isn't the school taking care of these things? Perhaps it is, but don't count on it. Today's parents cannot assume that their schools will train children in good study skills. Even if your school does, teachers still need you to reinforce their efforts at home. Studying conscientiously takes practice. It takes a desire to work hard. These things do not come naturally to most children. They must be nurtured by patient parents and teachers alike.

Study Tips and Techniques

Here are some study skills your child should learn. You may want to pick out one or two she needs to work on, and spend a little time practicing them together. You'll also find some reminders about how to keep your youngster on the right track. Most are obvious, but you'd be surprised how many parents and students violate these commonsense rules. They call for self-discipline on the part of all family members.

- **Set up a study area.** Make sure there is a place in your home that is designated for study—a quiet, well-lit area. It can be anywhere—your child's room, the kitchen table, or a corner of the family room if that works best. If you have space and means to provide your child with a personal desk, by all means do so. Whatever the arrangement, just make sure this cardinal rule goes into effect: during study time, the area is sacrosanct. It is off-limits to other activities and shielded from interruption.

- **Get rid of distractions.** It is astounding how many parents let their kids "study" in front of the television set. When someone is watching a sitcom out of the corner of her eye, flipping the dial on a blaring radio, or listening to others talk a few feet away, it is not possible to concentrate on academics. Precisely because study is work, you've got to make certain that more entertaining options are not available at the same time. No social phone calls. No computer games. Lay out the rules clearly, explain why they are important, enforce them, and make sure your child is not diverted while hitting the books.

- **Schedule study time.** Children respond well to structure. If the family routine includes designated study time on school nights, you are apt to encounter less resistance—and your child is more likely to get serious work done.

  Some parents find it useful to sit down with their kids and actually write out a study schedule. Whatever plan you come up with, stick to it. If you designate time for study and then regularly exempt kids from actually doing it, you will foster bad habits—like procrastination, laziness, and irresponsibility—that may plague your child for years.

- **Find the right amount.** Talk with your child (and the teacher, if necessary) about how much time is needed each day for homework and study. This will vary from child to child, from grade to grade, and, sometimes, from month to month. When setting up a study schedule, remember that small children have shorter attention spans than older children—especially when doing something alone.

- **Get the incentives right.** Getting good grades and doing well in school may be sufficient reward for some children, but others need more immediate carrots and sticks. Plan a favorite activity to do together after study time—playing catch or a board game. Bring out a snack. Let your child know that if she doesn't study, there will be consequences. She will not get to do some things she enjoys.

- **Spread it out.** Children are more apt to learn material well by concentrating on it during several shorter sessions spaced out over several days, rather than trying to stuff their brains with a bunch of unfamiliar ideas and facts immediately before a test. Don't buy into the myth of successful cramming.

- **Study regularly.** In elementary school, many lessons build on what has come before. Next week's assignments will probably require the base of knowledge and skills being constructed this week. If a child goes for extended periods of time without cracking a book, she may miss important building blocks, and will have a tough time understanding new readings and problems.

   Make sure your child brings her books home every day. Good students keep up with school lessons. If they miss school because of illness or other reasons, they methodically catch up on the content they missed so it can become part of the foundation for the next cluster of lessons.

- **Monitor understanding.** Some youngsters fall into the habit of reading page after page, their eyes just following the words, without fully absorbing the content. ("I studied it, but I don't remember anything!") It is important to train your child to pause frequently—perhaps at the end of each paragraph or page—and ask herself: "Do I understand what I've just read? What's the main idea here?" The point isn't to memorize every single fact, but rather to make sure she's grasped key concepts. (For more strategies that help build understanding while studying, see "Teaching Your Child to Study Actively," page 415.)

- **Practice taking notes.** Successful students know how to take good classroom notes. Unsuccessful students are often careless or incomplete about it. They write almost nothing down, or take notes only when the teacher tells them exactly what to record. Grade five or six is a good time to start working on this vital study skill. Encourage your child to listen carefully to the teacher and write down significant ideas as quickly and neatly as possible. She should also practice writing down important information the teacher puts on the blackboard (such as key equations and diagrams in math and science).

  During study sessions at home, your child should reread her notes while the lessons are fresh in her memory. She can clean them up where necessary and fill in any missing information that's important. Rewriting notes often helps solidify understanding. She should make sure they won't be unintelligible when she looks at them again days or weeks from now. This habit takes self-discipline and, in the beginning, help and guidance from you.

- **Review frequently.** Here is a strategy that most good students know and use: they go back over new material soon after learning it, whether it be a reading assignment from a textbook or notes taken in class. People tend to retain much more information and develop greater understanding if they review soon after learning it for the first time. By taking a few minutes then, they move a higher percentage of the material into their memory banks. Students who wait weeks to review a lesson usually find that they've forgotten most of it, and end up struggling to reconstruct what they thought they'd learned.

- **Learn to study with others.** Studying is mostly a private act, and studying alone is a discipline to be learned. Some lessons and projects, however, are tackled more efficiently with a pal or parent on hand, sharing the work, going over results, maybe even racing to see who can figure something out first.

  Do not assume your child will be able to study well with peers without some practice and initial supervision. She must learn the rules of good teamwork: concentrating on the task at hand; trading ideas; dividing work; speaking respectfully and quietly to others. To study together, children have to develop enough self-discipline to keep it from deteriorating into playtime or gab sessions. You will need to keep tabs on study groups until members demonstrate that they take the work seriously.

Most of these strategies call for practice and dedication on the part of children. In all likelihood, they are not going to happen without your attention. Good students usually have parents (or some other responsible adult) who have put in time teaching them proper study habits. They act as coaches, trainers, cheerleaders, and, at times, referees.

Good students have parents who show interest in their studies, who ask questions such as: What are you working on now? Have you learned that vocabulary list yet? Is there anything I can do to help, like call out any words or go over those history questions? Although those parents often get perfunctory answers—especially from older students—their sons and daughters know that their interest is an expression of love. In the end, that's the best incentive in the world for children to study hard.

Teaching Your Child to Study Actively

"Active" studying means intellectually engaging the information that's passing before your eyes—staying alert to the material, asking yourself questions about it, thinking about it as you go along. The more involved you are with the text, the more you'll learn from it. Here are several techniques that good students use for active studying. Teachers should coach your child in similar strategies, but they need to be put into practice at home. Help your child figure out which ones work best for her.

- *Identify main ideas and facts.* After reading a paragraph or page, stop and identify the key ideas in that section. Highlight or underline the most important words and sentences.

- *Make notes.* Write down main concepts, important dates, names, and terms, etc. Write a quick sentence or two summarizing the gist of what you've just read. Use those notes to review the lesson.

- *Make an outline of the text.* For example, after reading a story, write down the setting, main characters, sequence of action, main conflict, resolution, and theme.

- *Make a chart or diagram.* Categorize new terms or ideas. Make a time line to organize a history lesson. Draw a quick picture to represent what you're learning, if that helps.

- *Explain it to a parent or friend.* Teaching someone else firms up your own understanding. Talking about what you've learned can also bring up interesting points you may not have focused on at first.

- *Explain it to yourself.* Get instant review by telling yourself in your own words what you've just learned. Some students also find that reciting key ideas aloud bolsters their memory and understanding.

- *Connect new material with what you already know.* Think about how to-day's lesson relates to previous ones. If reading about the planet Jupiter, ask: How does it compare to Mars, which we read about yesterday?

- *Use lots of examples.* Often the best way to understand general principles is to look at specific examples. If learning about the associative property of multiplication, for example, make up your own equations that illustrate the principle.

HELPING YOUR CHILD WITH HOMEWORK

Homework is an indispensable ingredient in the recipe for school success. Student achievement rises significantly when teachers regularly assign it and children conscientiously do it. Unfortunately, many U.S. youngsters don't do much homework, either because their schools aren't giving it, or because no one at home is making sure it gets done. In some places assigning it is out of fashion. In other places, assignments are ignored or given only passing attention. The majority of U.S. public elementary school teachers report that their students do less than an hour of homework *per week.* This compares with about twenty-two hours per week of television watching. That ratio is poison for many kids' educations. Seeing that children do enough homework, and do it well, is a basic parental responsibility. You have to stay on top of this part of your child's schooling.

Teachers assign homework for a host of good reasons, perhaps the most important being that time on task predicts what students will learn. If they spend time on math, they will learn math; if they spend time on video games, they will learn video games. Homework gives children an opportunity to review, reinforce, and practice their lessons. It allows them to assimilate new information into the body of knowledge they already possess and to explore subjects in more detail than the teacher may have had time to cover at school. It helps them prepare for the next day's class and study for tests. It helps teachers gauge whether lessons are being absorbed, which areas a child is learning well, and which parts need extra attention.

Homework builds several habits necessary for academic success. It teaches children to follow directions, get themselves organized, and budget their time. It gives practice at research skills, such as using the library or Internet. It teaches students to work responsibly. Homework is also a vital strand in the line of communication between parents and school. It helps attentive moms and dads know what their children are learning, how demanding the curriculum is, and what teaching methods the school is using.

Despite clear benefits, some education experts downplay homework these days. "Homework Doesn't Help" a 1998 *Newsweek* article announced. Parents are told that those dreaded nightly lessons are pointless for young children. They only frustrate and anger students, convince them that school is painful, and lead toward academic dread. The education establishment reserves particular scorn for homework that involves practice or memorization. Assignments that help children "explore" or "discover" their own knowledge—such as students "determining the ecological effects of a neighborhood business" or "expressing their feelings" about the atom bomb—are generally given the stamp of approval. But exercises that involve actually mastering information and skills—whether it be practicing rules of grammar, filling in the state capitals on a U.S. map, memorizing a poem, or working a dozen long division problems—may be derided as useless "drill and kill" that suppresses creativity and chokes off kids' desire to learn.

That is a bunch of rot—as most good parents, teachers, principals, and coaches well know. "Nothing flies more in the face of the last twenty years of research than the assertion that practice is bad," say Professors John Anderson, Lynne Reder, and Herbert Simon of Carnegie-Mellon University. As they point out, the evidence "indicates that real competence only comes with extensive practice. By denying the critical role of practice, one is denying children the very thing they need to achieve competence."[3] If someone from your school makes light of homework assignments aimed at training children in important lessons and skills, trust your common sense: good practice does help make perfect.

How much homework should children get? There is no hard and fast rule. The amount a student receives will vary with age, the teaching methods being used, material being covered, and the child herself— some children need more time than others to finish assignments. One good rule of thumb is to expect at least ten minutes of homework per school night per grade level. First graders get about ten minutes per night; second graders about twenty minutes per night; third graders about thirty minutes per night; and so on. By eighth grade, students should expect to put in at least an hour and twenty minutes of homework per night.

These guidelines are not rigid, but if your child is spending significantly less time than this on homework, you need to ask a few questions. Keep in mind also that in just about any classroom, you'll probably find some parents who think their child isn't getting enough homework and others who think she's getting too much. In the end, you and the teachers have to be the judges. You need to satisfy yourself that your child is learning steadily but isn't overwhelmed.

It doesn't matter how much homework is given if it's trivial or dumb. Quality counts as much as quantity. Here are a few signs of good homework assignments. They should require your child to think. If kids constantly get busywork—for example, sixth graders making lots of posters for English class rather than doing much writing—then little learning will take place. Assignments should be directly related to classroom lessons. They should be carefully explained, either by written instructions or through discussions with the students (rather than the teacher hurriedly jotting the assignment on the board as the bell rings).

You cannot control the quality of homework assignments, but you can use them to appraise the school and teacher. Banal homework is a symptom of low academic standards.

You should see indications that homework is being promptly evaluated by teachers so that students understand their mistakes, are praised for good work, and have their errors noted. Assignments are nearly useless without feedback. Homework should count for something. At least some of the time, it should figure into your child's grade, so that she knows there are consequences for neglecting it.

For your child's part, remember that homework is worthwhile only when tackled with diligence. She may not be able to answer every problem or get each question right, but she must learn to give it her best shot. When youngsters make halfhearted, sloppy attempts, or turn to assignments when they're already weary from extracurricular activities, don't expect much learning to result. Homework raises achievement only when taken seriously.

There is something else we know about homework: it is more effective when moms and dads are involved. An overwhelming majority of high-achieving students say their parents pay attention to homework and even assist at times. Unfortunately, it's a different story in many American households. Only 10 percent of public school educators believe that their students' parents check to make sure homework is done, and done well. "Mom and Dad are just not sitting together at the kitchen table helping their child with homework anymore," says a

Michigan teacher. "Junior is on his own, and they're off on their own."[4] Former North Carolina teacher Jay Niver tells how he and his colleagues were called into the principal's office because so many pupils were failing. Niver unraveled a printout showing, among other things, that children often failed to turn in their homework. "The answer, I was advised, was to do homework in class. Now there's an oxymoron."[5] It is a sad state of affairs when schools give up on sending children home with work because they feel no one is there to make sure it gets done.

Homework is one of the best chances you have to share in your child's education. Approached in the right spirit, it provides a regular opportunity to show that you are keenly interested in what she's doing. Although sometimes frustrating for both child and parent, it is well worth the effort.

Staying on Top of Homework

Here are some reminders about parental responsibilities when it comes to helping your child with assignments. You needn't do all of these things every day, but this list may help you identify ways to stay productively involved.

Bear in mind that your participation will change as your child grows. When you first teach a youngster to brush her teeth, wash behind her ears, and comb her hair, you take an active part in the process. After she learns how, you check to make sure she's doing it properly and remind her when she forgets. Helping with homework is similar. Eventually, if you do your job right, tackling assignments will become second nature. At that point, what she'll need from you is evidence of interest, encouragement, and some occasional aid. But to get to that stage, you need to start molding good habits early in her academic career. The sooner you begin, the less likely homework is to become a source of misery in your household. (See "Teaching Your Child Good Study Habits," page 410, for more tips that will help with homework.)

- **Set priorities and make your expectations clear.** Talk to your child about the value of homework. Let her know that it's got to take priority over other activities, and that doing it isn't something she can negotiate. Set clear rules about getting it finished every day—and longer-term assignments tackled well in advance—and then stick to them.

Sometimes parents complain, "My kid's getting too much homework." In some schools that may be true, but the opposite problem is far more common. When it feels like there's too much homework, it could be because afternoons and evenings are overloaded with extracurricular activities.

- **Get control of the TV.** Six out of ten eighth graders say their parents rarely or never limit television watching. When the TV is on, homework will not get the attention it deserves. You must lay down the law, whether it's no TV on school nights, or no TV until homework is done.

- **Find the best time.** Many youngsters need a little downtime after school—a chance to have a snack or run around outside or just talk with you—before hitting the books. It varies from student to student. One child may work most efficiently in the late afternoon, another right after dinner. Help your child find the best homework time for her, then set as regular a schedule as possible. Remember that waiting until right before bedtime is most likely not a good idea. Kids are tired then, and putting homework last may teach your child to procrastinate. It may also lead to sleep deprivation—and get in the way of other valuable before-bed rituals such as reading together for fun.

- **Ask at school about the homework policy.** Teachers' expectations differ, so talk to them at the beginning of the year or semester. Ask questions such as: What sort of assignments will you be giving? Will there be homework every night? What is the best way to know what you are assigning? In general, how much time do you expect children to spend on homework? How much does homework count toward the total grade? As the year progresses, keep in touch and make sure the teacher is satisfied with the work your child is handing in.

- **Ask the teacher how she would like you to be involved.** How much help should you give your child? Should you call attention to mistakes so that they get corrected before the homework is handed in, or would the teacher prefer to see them herself? How far should you go in helping your child put that science project together?

- **Help your child keep track of assignments.** Teach her to write them down as she gets them. Many students find it helps to keep an assignment book for this purpose. Your child may prefer to keep a list on the computer or write on a calendar. Begin this important routine as soon as she starts getting homework. It will teach her to be careful about knowing what's due and when. Get into the habit of checking the assignment book regularly. There is no better way for you to stay on top of homework and find out what's going on in class.

- **Look over completed assignments.** Check homework every day when your child is young. Make sure it's complete, neat, and that effort went into it. (Some teachers will ask parents to sign and date homework so they'll know it's being monitored at home.) For junior high students who are conscientious about their assignments, you may only need to spot-check every few days. Even if your child finishes her homework at school, insist that she show it to you. It is important for her to realize that you sincerely want to see what she's learning.

- **Be available.** Help your child if she has problems or needs guidance, but remember that it's her homework, not yours. Doing it for her doesn't do her any good. (Some teachers say they get a fair amount of homework in parents' handwriting!) The main thing is to make yourself available—if not while she's actually doing the homework, then later in the day when you can talk with her about it and lend a hand if necessary. Children need to know that caring adults are there for them.

- **Check homework again after the teacher returns it.** Read her comments regularly to see whether she's satisfied with your child's work. You'll find out what your child has learned well and which areas need extra attention. You may detect patterns of recurring difficulty that will enable you to help your child—or that may warrant a conversation with the teacher. (If the teacher seldom returns homework with comments or grades, ask her what is happening to it.)

- **Help organize for long-range assignments.** Left to their own devices, most youngsters will procrastinate and leave big projects (term papers, science reports, novels they have to read) until the last minute. Teach your child that some types of homework can't be done all at once. Help her learn to break big jobs into smaller tasks. Planning a complex project is itself an extremely valuable skill that has to be learned. Encourage her to estimate how much time each step will take. Write down a schedule and help her stick to it.

- **Try a division of labor.** Busy parents often need to share homework supervision. For example, mom might be in charge of seeing that science and English homework gets done, while dad takes history and math. Single parents, if you are struggling to oversee homework all by yourself, get help. Explain to those who care about your children—grandparents, older siblings, friends, neighbors—how important this is. Consider forming a cooperative with other parents to take turns with homework duties.

- **Find a tutor if necessary.** There may be times when you need someone else to coach your child through her homework—perhaps because she needs a good bit of help, or because you no longer understand the math assignments, or simply because you think your parent-averse junior high student will work better with somebody else. There is nothing embarrassing about needing a tutor, and you shouldn't be afraid to inquire.

  Your first step should be to talk with the teacher. See if she thinks it's a good idea, and if she can recommend someone she trusts. She may put you in touch with an older student at the high school or a local college. Or she may refer you to a professional tutoring service. Talk to the tutor about what you will keep doing at home and how you can reinforce each other's efforts.

- **No homework? Talk with the teacher!** If your youngster comes home day after day and announces, "I did all my homework at school" or "I didn't have any today" you need to investigate. Call the teacher and find out whether your child is really doing all her assignments. If it turns out that the school gives little homework, or if it's always quick and easy, let the teacher know that you think it's important for your child to be working on challenging lessons at home. You may want to ask for additional assignments. If that doesn't work, you may want to have your child review classwork in the evenings, and find extra books for her to read.

- **Keep old homework.** Make sure your child holds on to her assignments for at least a few months after the teacher has returned them. They will be invaluable when it comes time to study for tests. Looking through them periodically is an excellent way for you to check for steady progress in learning.

- **Take a look at the books.** Look through your child's books every once in a while when she's not using them. The more familiar you are with her lessons, the better able you'll be to help out with homework, gauge how she's doing, and judge how demanding your school is.

Don't stint on praise when your child deserves it. Show off her good work. Set good examples. If you're in the den, working quietly and purposefully on the contents of that briefcase you brought home from work, or at your computer keyboard outlining the next day's presentation, your child will probably be more inspired to study.

Warning Signs of a Weak Homework Regimen

Be on the lookout for the following clues that something is wrong at your school:

- Students get little or no homework.
- Students aren't required to do their homework, or it doesn't count.
- Teachers don't regularly correct homework or give feedback.
- Much homework consists of easy projects or repetitive drills that require little thinking.
- Teachers tell you that homework does not do much good.
- Class time is used for children to do their homework before they go home.

TESTS AND TESTING

Few people are fond of school tests. Most teachers don't enjoy giving (or grading) them any more than students like taking them. The fact remains, however, that they are the surest means for you and your child to obtain feedback on whether she's really learning what she should. They are powerful incentives for children to put forth effort. Well-crafted tests, combined with the reviews that lead up to them, are worthwhile learning experiences in their own right. Taken as a whole, tests are friends of good education, good students, and education-minded parents.

Your child will face all sorts of tests in school. Some important decisions will be based on how she fares. It is your duty to help her learn how to prepare for and take them. It is your responsibility to monitor results.

Types of Tests

Here is a quick primer on different kinds of tests your child may encounter during the K–8 years.

TEACHER-MADE TESTS

These are the most familiar. Each teacher usually devises her own (sometimes borrowing from textbooks, workbooks, or teacher guides) and gives them on a daily or weekly basis to find out whether her pupils are learning. They are usually designed to check for specific knowledge and skills. They can be as simple as a twenty-word spelling test as complex as an essay-style take-home exam. The teacher grades them herself, and they usually come back with either a number (e.g., seventeen of twenty words correctly spelled) or a letter grade on them.

STANDARDIZED TESTS

Many districts, states, and private schools buy standardized tests from commercial test publishers and administer them every year, sometimes to all their students, sometimes only to those in selected grades. Such tests generally carry well-known names such as the Stanford 9, Metropolitan Achievement Test, or Iowa Test of Basic Skills. They are called "standardized" because they're administered in the same way with the same directions to all children taking them. Most follow the multiple-choice format.

Scores give parents and teachers information about how individual pupils are doing in various subjects and skills. In some cases, they are used to help decide whether a student should be assigned to advanced classes or remedial education. They may factor into decisions about whether to let a student skip a grade or hold her back for a year. Administrators and board members also use standardized test results to gauge how well the school district is doing as a whole.

Parents usually receive a computer printout of their child's test scores. If your school doesn't send test results home, talk with the teacher or principal. If the scores become part of your child's school record, then you are entitled by law to see them. Good schools want you to see them and are likely to have them signed and returned.

The results may or may not be clear to you. They may be expressed in a perplexing maze of numbers and terms; often they give your child's performance in "percentiles," "deciles," even "stanines." An explanation may be enclosed, but if you still feel like you need a degree in statistics to figure it all out, you're not alone. When in doubt, do not hesitate to talk with the teacher or school counselor and get her to explain exactly what the scores mean. Ask her to tell you how the results of the test might be used, if at all, in decisions regarding your child's academic future. Bear in mind that standardized test results can be good general indicators of how students are doing, but they also can be overused. They should never be the only reason for making important education decisions.

What Are the "Standards" in Standardized Tests?

One of the most confusing things about commercial achievement tests is that what the test-makers mean by "standardized" actually has nothing to do with "standards" in the ordinary sense. You might suppose that using "standards" means setting a level of achievement for specific skills and knowledge that children at a certain grade level *ought* to reach. The reality is that, for the most part, there are no "oughts" in the world of standardized testing. There are, in fact, no real standards. What happens, instead, is that the test-maker tries out the test on a "norming sample"—a representative group of youngsters, such as a large sample of children found in fourth grade classrooms around the country. Wherever their average score on the test falls is then defined as "fourth grade level work."

Keep this in mind when you're told that 60 percent of the fourth graders in your school are performing "at or above grade level." All it means is that three out of five of them are doing at least as well as the average fourth grader in the norming sample. The kids in that sample may actually be achieving far below students in other countries, perhaps far below what most children in fourth grade were achieving fifty years ago, and perhaps far below goals that the president, governors, and business leaders have said they would like children to meet.

Standardized tests can be useful instruments, but take their results in context. They are not necessarily evaluating whether your child knows what a well-educated pupil at her grade level ought to know, but rather how she compares to other pupils who've taken the same test. If real standards across the country are slipping from year to year, then comparing your child to a lower-achieving norming sample may not tell you whether your child is getting the kind of education she deserves and you want her to have.

DISTRICT AND STATE ASSESSMENTS

More and more states are developing their own academic standards and devising tests (often called "assessments") based on them. Some districts have embarked on this course for themselves—and sometimes the state and local standards do not perfectly coincide, or the test does not faithfully mirror the state's academic goals. Such assessments frequently depart from the multiple-choice format and make use of open-ended or "free-response" items where the student answers in her own words or shows her work, and where there may not be a "right answer." In some places the format is even more ambitious, relying on "portfolios" and "performances" by students rather than more conventional models for exams.

These assessments are used mainly to supply information for policymakers about how the school system as a whole is working. In such cases, they have little direct effect on individual children. Sometimes, however, they are used to determine which students are ready to be promoted to the next grade, or graduated from high school. (You may hear these tests referred to as "minimum competency tests," "state proficiency tests," or some comparable term.) In that case, they obviously make a big difference in people's lives. Talk with the teachers or principal to see whether your district or state gives such assessments, when they're given, and exactly how their results are used.

TESTS USED FOR DIAGNOSIS AND PLACEMENT

If the teacher or principal says something like "We might want to get your child tested," she is probably talking about individualized, diagnostic tests that may reveal the presence of a learning disability, giftedness, or other special circumstance that could affect your youngster's education. Obviously, this is very important, even life-shaping, for your child. You'll want to be extremely careful in how these test results are interpreted and what course of action the school (and its specialists) suggests. You may want to get your own independent evaluation of the results and, perhaps, of your child. Be aware that these are *not* the kind of tests that one prepares for and not the kind that we're focusing on in this book.

PRIVATE TESTS USED FOR ADMISSIONS

You are probably acquainted with the Scholastic Assessment (formerly Aptitude) Test or SAT, which is used by many selective colleges for admissions, and perhaps with its sibling, the PSAT. (In some parts of the country, the American College Testing program, or ACT, is more commonly used.) Though these are normally taken during high school, your child might encounter them as early as sixth or seventh grade, where they're sometimes used to select youngsters for special summer programs conducted on college campuses. Should you find yourself considering admission to private schools—especially the more elite kind known as "independent schools"—you will also likely encounter the Secondary School Admission Test (SSAT), which many such institutions require as part of the application process. Other tests of this type turn up from time to time, often used for limited purposes such as entry into specialized schools. These are all voluntary; your child's elementary school is not apt to require them for anything. If you happen upon them, it's probably because you are considering a change in your child's education arrangements.

Preparing for Tests

In the words of Hamlet, readiness is all. Nowhere is this more true than in education. Youngsters need to be taught how to prepare for tests. Since much of that preparation takes place at home, it's a process you'll need to practice with your child. How well you teach these habits and skills can make the difference between good and poor results. Much of it is simply a matter of instilling the self-discipline it takes to get organized and put in adequate study.

Generally speaking, the following tips are most pertinent when preparing for teacher-made tests. (Schools often work at getting students ready to take standardized achievement tests, but children seldom study for them in the sense described here.) Remember that it takes practice for youngsters to get some of these techniques under their belts, so be patient.

- **Know when the test is coming.** As soon as the teacher schedules a test, good students write it down in their assignment book or calendar. This allows both parents and child to budget preparation time.

- **Know what the test will cover.** Many students create problems for themselves by not clearly understanding what they need to study. For example, will the test cover just what's in the textbook, or handouts and classroom discussions, too? Which chapters will be covered? Which word lists or math operations?

Train your child to write down exactly which topics the teacher says the test will cover (e.g., the muscular system, skeletal system, and nervous system). Encourage her to find out as much as possible about what form the test will take—dictation, short-answer, multiple-choice, essay, etc. How many questions will there be? How much time will be allowed? Not knowing what to expect leads to unnecessary stress and wasted study time.

- **Review and practice on a regular basis.** A concert pianist doesn't wait until the night before a performance to start learning the score. Cramming may provide an occasional short-term success, but overall it doesn't work. Teach your child to spread the review sessions over several days, if necessary. Regular, paced study is the key to getting ready. Slow and steady wins the race.

  This rule applies to you, too. If your child can use your help preparing, don't wait until the eve of the test. You may need to set aside fifteen minutes every night for a week, but it is time well spent together and the results will please you both.

- **Be thorough about review.** Studying for a test usually involves more than reading back through the textbook, although that may be a big part of it. Your child may also need to review notes made in class or taken from other books. If she's already had quizzes covering this material, she should look back over them to make sure she knows how to answer everything. It's a good idea to go through old homework assignments; they often provide a road map to what will be on a test. There may have been classroom handouts. Does your child still have them?

  Much test-taking success is due to organizational skills, and much is due to perseverance. Train your child to keep track of all the material she'll need to get ready; once assembled, help her learn the stick-to-it spirit that it takes to review until she's prepared to display what she knows.

- **Make use of review sections in the textbook.** Many schoolbooks have summaries at the end of each chapter. They often highlight information that students are expected to know on a test. Many textbooks also contain practice questions. Run through these with your child and make sure she can answer them.

- **Take classroom review seriously.** Teachers often send signals about what is most important to know for a test—questions they repeat, sections of the book they go back over, information they write on the board to sum up a lesson. Sometimes they review material in class just after they've finished preparing the test, and therefore may give similar problems or questions. Good students learn to pick up on these cues. Your child should not, however, fall into the trap of assuming that a topic will not be on a test just because it was not mentioned during classroom review.

- **Anticipate test questions.** This is an important study skill that can really make a difference. As they review (or better yet, as they routinely do homework assignments), good students try to anticipate questions the teacher might ask on a test. When reading about the Constitutional Convention, for example: What was wrong with the old Articles of Confederation? What were some of the main debates at the convention? When you help your child study, teach her to get in the habit of thinking up and writing down possible questions, and then going over the answers before test time.

- **Don't be afraid of drill.** There are educators who pooh-pooh it, but for acquiring some kinds of knowledge, nothing beats repetition. Good students are usually those who practice at home—often with their parents' help. Call out vocabulary words, spelling words, or math facts to your child. Make flash cards with questions on the front and answers on the back: important terms, key ideas from textbooks, formulae your child must know. Practice doing several long division problems every night if that's what the test will cover. Rehearsal brings greater familiarity, which brings greater understanding and confidence about the material.

- **Take some practice tests.** It may help your child to take a mock test or two at home before the real thing. These can be as simple as asking a few questions about the story she's read, or giving some dictation, or asking her to explain those poetry terms. It may mean your reading through the section on earthquakes in the science book and quizzing her on the material. You may even want to write up a practice test using questions and problems from past homework assignments.

- **Spend extra time on trouble spots.** Children naturally avoid areas they find difficult (adding those pesky fractions, using commas correctly, etc.). Working a little harder to smooth out the rough spots now, when you have a chance to resolve them, pays off handsomely when test time rolls around. Work with your child on learning to recognize persistent errors and gaps. If necessary, help her take a closer look at her mistakes so she can understand what she's doing wrong. Often, a little more practice solves the problem.

Finally, help your child get physically and emotionally prepared for the test experience. It's not just an old wives' tale: children really do perform better in school when they get a good night's sleep and eat a nourishing breakfast. Emotional preparation means helping her find the right balance between apathy and panic. Help her understand that tests are to be taken seriously—they keep coming to us in various forms throughout our lives—but that they don't warrant nervous breakdowns. Serious-but-calm is the demeanor to aim for. Of course, the better prepared one is academically, the more in control of the material, the less one is apt to be stressed out.

Test-Taking Tips

Here are some important strategies for taking tests. Help your child find those that work best for her. Practice them at home, if necessary.

- As soon as you get the test, quickly jot down from memory—in the margins or on a scrap of paper—any key information you expect to need: formulae, rules, names, dates, etc. You won't have to worry about drawing a blank on it once you plunge into the test.

- Read the directions carefully. Many children skip this step! If need be, underline important direction words such as *compare* or *choose two*.

- Scan the whole test. Take a look at the types of questions so you'll know what you're facing.

- As you work, read each question carefully, word for word. Underline or circle key words. Stop and think for a second before you start to answer each question. Do you know what it's really asking?

- Skip over questions or problems that look like they might pose trouble. Come back to them after you've answered the rest. (Some students like to warm up to the difficult questions by answering the easier ones first, hard ones last.)

- Budget your time. Note which questions are worth more points, and leave time to answer them. Don't get too bogged down on any one question or problem.

- On essay questions, jot down your ideas and a brief outline before you begin to answer. Refer to these notes as you write. Then you'll know where you're going.

- On math and science tests, show your work. Write each step as neatly as you can. Even if you get the answer wrong, you may get partial credit for what you do know.

- If you have extra time, double-check your answers! This is a cardinal rule of test taking, and sometimes sets the "A" students apart from the rest. Watch for careless mistakes. Rework calculations and proofread essay answers. Look back to make sure you have provided all the information each question asked for.

When the corrected test comes back, don't just look at your child's grade and then put it aside. The main purpose of giving it in the first place is to see what she already knows well and where she needs more work. Marked-up tests are guideposts to higher achievement. Praise your youngster for right answers and good work, but also carefully review incorrect answers together. Have her work her way through those questions again so she can see what she did wrong. Save old quizzes. They make excellent study guides for the final exam.

The Anti-Test Bias

In some schools and some quarters of the education establishment, there is an aversion to giving students tests. More specifically, there is an ongoing campaign against any tests in which students must give answers that are either right or wrong—whether they be multiple-choice tests, short-answer, fill-in-the-blank, true/false, or another form. Tests that aim to zero in on how well students have mastered specific knowledge (such as the names of the Great Lakes) or certain skills (such as long division) are disparaged as old-fashioned. Exercises such as spelling bees, vocabulary tests, and grammar quizzes are eschewed. Exams meant to determine whether students have met specified learning goals are scorned. A Massachusetts middle school principal summed up the philosophy: "Good schools create the opportunity to learn rather than chain students to a standard."

Those who oppose testing make all sorts of arguments. They contend that teachers just "teach to the test"; that is, teach kids only what they'll need to know to pass the exam. This not only narrows the curriculum, it ignores individual students' interests and talents. Paper-and-pencil tests, it is said, devalue higher-order thinking skills like problem solving, reading for comprehension, analyzing, and thinking creatively. They encourage rote memorization of trivial facts. They give children the misleading impression that there is a single right answer for every problem. When everyone is forced to take the same test, some children are bound to do less well than others, and that damages their self-esteem. Critics argue that kids don't like tests in which they have to sit down at their desk and plow through ten or fifteen questions in a certain amount of time. It stresses them and turns them off to learning.

None of these arguments holds up under scrutiny. There is nothing wrong with "teaching to the test" if the test is demanding, the standards it is based on are high, and students must know an assignment or subject thoroughly in order to do well. (It's true that no one wants to see "teaching to the test" in the sense that students are taught *only* what is going to be on a test. The fault in these cases, however, is poor teaching, not the fact that a test is being given.) Furthermore, no one has ever demonstrated that asking a question which requires a child to demonstrate a command of specific knowledge or skills rules out the use of analytic or creative thinking. In fact, all you have to do is look at some multiple-choice or fill-in-the-blank questions on good tests to realize that these often involve lots of "higher-order" thinking skills. They may also require children to know some facts. That is good. There are some facts that everyone should know. Learning them is one mark of a good education.

Any time you give a test, you must expect that some kids won't score as well as others. It is a misguided notion, however, that we should bolster students' self-esteem by removing challenges, rather than working harder to make sure they can meet them. It's true that most children don't like to take tests, but life isn't one grand entertainment. We shouldn't be educating students to believe that they can simply avoid unpleasant tasks. The truth is that there *are* many questions, problems, and assignments in life in which solutions are either correct or incorrect. To pretend otherwise is to shortchange our children.

The real reason that tests are scorned by some educators and schools is that they do not want to be held responsible. Tests hold students *and* educators accountable, because they indicate the expectations that a school (or teacher or state) maintains for children and how well the children are doing vis-à-vis those expectations. Many U.S. schools do not teach demanding academic curricula. They do not do a good job of transmitting core knowledge and basic skills. So naturally, there is reluctance to give tests that would reveal those shortcomings. Rather than own up to the problem—which is slipping standards and ineffective schools—they disparage tests themselves. They would shoot the messenger.

No single test or testing method is perfect. Still, regular tests are good for students and schools. They get pupils to put forth greater effort. They give parents and educators vital feedback on children's progress. They give teachers information about the kind of job they're doing. When given on large scale, they help administrators and policymakers know how schools and districts are faring. Schools that are slack about giving tests or reporting their results may well have something to hide.

It varies from school to school just when children will enter the world of testing. Many teachers do little testing of kindergartners and first graders. They may prefer to use other kinds of assessments (classroom participation, writing and drawing samples, work on group projects) while youngsters get used to learning in a formal setting. At some point during the primary years (K–3), however, you should see low-pressure, short quizzes gradually become part of children's activities. By the intermediate grades (4–6), students should be used to the idea of being responsible for regular tests. In good elementary schools, teachers aren't obsessive about testing, but they know it's important, and they convey that to students.

"Authentic Assessment"

In some places educators are using, as an alternative to traditional tests, what is known as "authentic assessment" or "performance assessment." The idea is to judge kids through their performance of various tasks— writing a poem, putting on a play with classmates, or coming up with a way to solve a math problem.

Often students keep portfolios as part of this process (you may hear the term "portfolio assessment" used). A portfolio is basically a big scrapbook, a selection of a student's work over the course of a semester or year. It can contain just about anything that demonstrates what she can do—essays, math assignments, drawings, letters, descriptions of science projects, audio recordings, lists of books the student has read. Sometimes the teacher chooses work to go in the portfolio, sometimes the child chooses, and sometimes teacher and child choose together. The student and her classmates may be involved in evaluating portfolio material with the teacher. Proponents of portfolios and authentic assessment claim these are better ways to gauge each child's unique capabilities.

Authentic assessment has some advantages. It often requires kids to pull together the knowledge and skills they've learned and put them into action. Portfolios can be a good source of information for teachers and parents about a child's progress, and a great way for students to showcase their work. Although some talk as if all this were a modern educational breakthrough, it's not really new. Good teachers have always taken classroom performance and products into account in appraising their pupils.

What is new is the push to make authentic assessment the primary means by which students are evaluated in school. Supporters claim that teachers, if properly trained, can use portfolios to come up with objective, reliable grades that accurately describe how much students have learned. In reality, however, it's not easy to rely on a collection of poems, journal entries, and descriptions of how a child tried to solve a problem to determine whether she's meeting a set of academic standards.

Grading by portfolio is a notoriously inconsistent process. When different teachers are asked to judge the same portfolio (even when given the same scoring instructions), often they do not agree on what grade to give it. Various studies of portfolio assessment programs have used terms like "seriously flawed," "unreliable," and "large margins of error." Peter Berger, a Vermont middle school English teacher, describes how teachers were asked to score portfolio writing samples "objectively" in areas such as *Details, Organization,* and *Voice* using categories such as *Extensively, Frequently, Sometimes,* and *Rarely*: "Suppose you're trying to rate a piece's *Details*. If you think the details are 'explicit,' you score it an *Extensively*. If they're only 'elaborated,' of course, then you just give it a *Frequently*. Rating *Organization* requires that you distinguish between problems that 'affect unity or coherence'—a *Sometimes*—and those that 'make writing difficult to follow'—a *Rarely*. Scoring *Voice* is even easier. All you have to do is detect the difference between a 'distinctive' tone, an 'effective' tone, an 'attempt' at an 'appropriate' tone, and an 'appropriate' tone that's 'not evident.' . . . This is 'objective'?"[6]

Subjectivity plays a big part in evaluating many types of tests (such as essay exams). That certainly doesn't mean they're worthless. But portfolios alone ought not be relied on for consistent grading. It makes sense to treat them as part of the overall assessment process, not the mainstay. Most good schools and teachers use a variety of tools to grade their students—including traditional tests and quizzes.

If your school tells you it's jumped on the "authentic assessment" bandwagon, and that, instead of paper-and-pencil tests, your child will henceforth be judged on classroom activities and her portfolio, find out exactly how the teacher will arrive at the grade. Ask to see what standards your child will be expected to meet. If they seem vague, or the grading process sounds convoluted, you may not get reliable feedback about what your child is learning. You'll almost certainly get little good feedback about what she is *not* learning. While a portfolio may be able to demonstrate what your child can do, it's far less useful in pinpointing the important knowledge and skills she should have mastered but has not.

Warning Signs of Weak Testing Methods

Be on the lookout for the following signals that something is wrong at your school:

- Few tests given; competitive exercises such as spelling bees derided.
- Tests seem easy; students usually allowed to use open books.
- Grades based mainly on projects and activities (few paper-and-pencil tests).
- Tests seldom require students to recall specific knowledge or answer questions for which there are correct answers.
- Essay tests rarely given (in upper grades).
- Tests not promptly corrected by teacher and returned with comments.
- Students erratically tested on the knowledge and skills identified in curriculum standards.

GRADES AND REPORT CARDS

Grades and report cards are, of course, crucial ways for parents to find out how their children are doing. They serve several purposes. They tell whether students have mastered the learning goals set by the school. They indicate whether youngsters are ready to move on to the next set of goals or grade level. They help track the progress that students are making from period to period. Grades tell whether individual children are keeping up with their classmates. They signal areas where students excel, and therefore may need more challenge, as well as areas where they can use extra help. They motivate children to study, and they can give parents a good idea of the school's expectations.

Grades can do these things when they are clear and honest, when they really judge students' performance and incorporate meaningful standards. In many schools, however, grades are vague, inflated, or inconsistent. Report cards aren't trustworthy indicators of academic achievement. Such marks are worthless to parents and students alike. Not only do you need to pay attention to your child's grades, you must find out what they mean at your school.

Different schools use different methods to report student progress. Many stick with traditional letter (A to F) or numerical grades (0 to 100). In the primary years, it's common for children to receive an O (outstanding), S (satisfactory), N (needs improvement), or something along those lines. Some schools use a checklist of academic and social skills (such as "writes all letters of the alphabet" or "gets along well with classmates"). Teachers often supplement marks with written comments. Some schools use portfolios of student work and anecdotal records about classroom activities to show parents how their children are doing. You may see a combination of these approaches.

Parents often don't know how to interpret the marks their children receive. What does a C mean these days—average or low-quality work? Exactly what does it take to be "outstanding" as opposed to "satisfactory"? And what does "needs improvement" mean—that my child could use a little more work in that area, or that she's seriously falling behind?

You should realize that different teachers (sometimes even within the same school) have different ways of figuring grades. Some grade on the curve, so that a certain percentage of kids will get 'A's—whether or not they've really done 'A' work. Some teachers grade children strictly according to whether they've met stated goals (which may or may not be demanding). Others base grades on how hard pupils have tried, how far they've come in the last few weeks, and how much they participate in class. Thus a child in the slowest reading group and a child in the fastest group might both receive 'B's, even though one can read far better than the other.

Given these ambiguities, it is very important to communicate clearly and often with the teacher. As a rule, every report card should become the subject of a parent-teacher conversation. Ask about the grading policy. Get the teacher to explain how she arrives at a final grade that goes onto a report card. You may need to ask questions such as: Do you consider effort, improvement, and class participation in deciding on a grade—or just achievement? Exactly what do students have to know and do to get an 'A'? What does a 'C' signify? How much does homework count toward the final grade? How much do quizzes and exams count? How is my child performing compared to the rest of the class? Do you grade on the curve?

You may conclude that the grades coming out of your school are accurate appraisals. Or you may come to suspect that you cannot rely on them as measures of achievement. In that case, it's not a bad idea to monitor your child's progress yourself. Ask the teacher for a list of the skills, concepts, and knowledge that she expects her students to master during the semester. It should give you an idea of the standards and expectations against which your child will be graded. Keep an eye on your child's work to see if she's making steady progress toward meeting those proficiencies.

Grades are important, but don't obsess over them. This is an obvious point that some parents have a hard time remembering. Moms and dads must learn the fine art of letting their kids know that grades are to be taken seriously while not turning them into the be-all and end-all of education. Celebrate and praise good grades. Reward favorable report cards. When less satisfactory ones come, talk with your child and her teacher about the causes. Is it that she's not working enough? Is she not studying for tests, or handing in all her homework? Are the assignments too difficult? Is she bored in class? If necessary, ask the teacher to help you and your child work out a plan to pull those marks up. Chances are good that it will involve resetting some priorities and making extra efforts at home.

Grade Inflation

A frustrated mom wrote to a suburban Texas school system about the gap between her new stepdaughter's grades and actual attainment. For years, the girl had moved through the system as an honor roll student. She received the highest possible marks and most favorable comments on her report cards, which usually came punctuated with "smiley" faces. Now the child had hit high school, and trouble was brewing; "This 'A' math student asked her father and me just a year ago what the lines meant on a ruler. She also was puzzled by fractions. 'Isn't ¼ bigger than ⅓,' she asked, 'since 4 is bigger than 3?' This 'A' history student had never heard of the Holocaust, Prohibition, or the Salem Witch Trials. Just a few weeks ago, she struggled to answer, 'Who was Thomas Jefferson?' only to finally reply: 'Didn't he invent electricity or the telephone?' . . . Then I started reading some of her 'A' English papers and realized there was little connection between the work and the reward. I found errors in grammar and spelling left uncorrected; faulty logic and argument; no original analysis; inability to support a thesis; and a clear indication that the books discussed were not only not understood, but probably not even read." Yet this young lady had been moved up to an Advanced Placement English class.[7]

Grade inflation is widespread in American education. For example, among those students taking the SATs, the percentage with an 'A' average has been going up even as their combined math and verbal scores have been dropping. Colleges complain that many kids who graduate from high school with honors grades nevertheless have to go into remedial math or English classes during their freshman year.

This trend is one more sign of watered-down curricula and flagging academic expectations, a symptom of a system that has come to believe that many students simply cannot or will not meet demanding goals. Well-meaning educators who want kids to feel good about their performance hand out ever higher grades even as they lower the bar. Administrators put pressure on teachers to raise marks so their schools will look good to the public. "I am at a loss as to what to do," moans Maryland math teacher Laura Goetz, frustrated at having a poor grade changed by a school official who wants to keep failure rates down. "If I give a student what he deserves and the grade is changed in spite of me, I've done all I can do. When you lower standards like this, kids are lowering themselves."[8]

Teachers say that when they give out low marks, they also get no end of grief from parents. A 'C' can trigger an angry phone call or hurried trip to the principal's office by a couple convinced that their child's Ivy League prospects just went down the drain. Sadly, many parents have taken up the self-esteem cry, claiming that if their loved ones get low grades, their desire to learn will be quashed.

The drive to pump up rewards dilutes the meaning of achievement. It hampers an important means by which parents and schools uphold standards and demand accountability. It chips away at the notion that we succeed through hard work. ("How do you convince your child that he or she should be reading more, studying more, and working harder when the school system is giving that same student its highest rewards?" that discouraged Texas mom asks.) Everyone is lulled into thinking that their child is doing fine and that their school is better than it may be. America becomes the land of the self-satisfied where prizes are easily won, a Lake Wobegon where "all the children are above average." In the meantime, youngsters from other industrial nations are beating the pants off our students in international tests.

If grades have been inflating in your school, too, there is a good chance that your child is not really learning as much as her report card would lead you to believe—and probably not as much as similar grades signaled when you were in school. There is little you can do about grade inflation except speak out against it. In spite of the system, keep up your own commitment to high standards. Sometimes that's difficult. After all, everyone wants their children to get great marks, especially when so many others are getting them. In the long run, however, making things too easy on a student is unfair.

Don't ask teachers to hand your child better grades than she deserves. If she gets a low mark, take an honest look before you complain. If the teacher is assessing fairly and the grade is deserved, don't make a fuss at school. Make a fuss at home. Work harder with your child so she can do better next time. Remember that a good report card is a fine goal, but a good education is an even better one.

Grade Aversion

A passion against judging students runs deep in the education establishment. Experts write about how "rewards and punishments" are just ways to get students to "comply with adults' demands" and "manipulate someone's behavior." Grades are "bribes and threats" that foster "mindless obedience." Professional organizations urge elementary schools to de-emphasize letter grades and stop comparing students with one another. The faculty members of teacher colleges dislike the practice of singling out good students with academic prizes. Only one third of them consider recognitions such as honor rolls to be valuable incentives to learning. "When you have a system of doing for rewards, I react very viscerally," says a Chicago education professor. "I don't like hearing about a kid who's high-achieving [and] doing things in the classroom for stars."[9]

The anti-grade crowd makes the usual arguments. Grades are bad because they are a sorting device. They set up a ranking system, thereby violating the principle that all youngsters are equally worthy; who, after all, can really set a value on one child's unique talents over another's? They are gatekeepers, holding back some students by labeling them "losers" and destroying their self-esteem. As mere artificial incentives, they do nothing to inspire children to want to learn for learning's sake. It is said that they dampen creativity and diminish the enjoyment of learning. They offend the notion of self-guided learning, forcing students to study what teachers want them to learn, rather than helping children develop their own criteria for successful learning.

Perhaps worst of all, critics say, grades foster an environment in which children compete instead of work together to build a caring, co-operative community. Alfie Kohn, a well-known opponent of school rewards who is often asked to speak at educators' conferences, argues that the people who vigorously defend the idea of grades are elitist parents more interested in "academic one-upmanship" than in real education. These selfish mothers and insensitive fathers are "in effect sacrificing other children to their own. It's not about success but victory, not about responding to a competitive environment but creating one." The psychology of these parents, according to the critics, is "that it's not enough for their kids to win; others must lose—and they must lose conspicuously."[10]

This kind of disparaging of grades and rewards has had its effects. Across the country, many schools have eliminated class rankings and distinctions such as valedictorian. They've done away with honor rolls. Competing for academic recognition is out; teachers are encouraged to stop giving gold stars and other prizes that denote high-achieving students. Grades are often based on group performance rather than individual effort.

Some schools are de-emphasizing report cards in favor of "authentic assessment" techniques that make it harder to compare one student with another. Many have replaced letter grades with appraisals such as "substantial progress" and "moderate progress" that concentrate on children's development since the last report, rather than comparing their work to a defined set of standards. They use broad classifications that blur the lines between good, average, and poor performances. A grandfather in California notes that his fourth grade granddaughter received six "Fluents" and one "Transitional-plus" on her report card. "I can't really tell if this was good or bad, but when the other 'assessment options' are 'Emerging,' 'Beginning,' and 'Developing,' I think I should be proud," he decides.[11]

Despite some educators' antipathy toward grades, here is the bottom line: research and experience both show that they contribute strongly to effective teaching and learning. The evidence agrees with common sense. Most students study harder and learn more when they know that they're going to be held accountable through the marks they receive. The notion that grades damage creativity, true learning, and children's capacity for compassion is nonsense. Millions of Americans (and people all over the world) have grown up with grades and turned out just fine.

No grading system is perfect. Some, in fact, are quite imperfect. As we pointed out earlier, the marks students receive can sometimes be baffling. Sometimes they are inflated. Grading policies differ by school and by teacher. That is why it is so important for parents to communicate directly with teachers about grades and make sure they know exactly what the various letters, numbers, and phrases signify. What is abundantly clear is that when grades have stable meaning, they are an invaluable tool for motivating and informing students, parents, and teachers. For most students and schools, honest grades are a definite plus for the learning environment.

Exactly what form a report card takes—whether it's full of letters or numbers or checklists or written comments—is not the most important consideration. The crucial thing is that you get clear, consistent feedback that tells you whether your child is measuring up to standards the school has. If you are not getting that kind of information, you are going to have a tough time knowing how much your child really knows and how well she is really doing in the lifelong quest to become an educated person.

Warning Signs of Weak Grading

Be on the lookout for the following clues that something is wrong at your school:

- Unclear report cards.

- Teachers unable to explain standards for A-level work, B-level work, etc.

- Grades not linked to attaining clear learning goals (i.e., specific knowledge and skills).

- Lots of students get As; no one seems to get low grades.

- Little recognition for high-achieving students (e.g., no honor roll).

- Grades disparaged as "bribes and punishments" or destroyers of self-esteem.

- Grades heavily based on group performance rather than individual effort.

WHAT IF MY CHILD ISN'T PROMOTED?

The end of the school year approaches, and you get news that makes your heart sink: there is a serious problem with your child's progress, and the principal wants to talk with you about having her repeat a grade. All kinds of pent-up emotions boil over. You're frustrated and embarrassed. You're angry at the school and maybe at your child. At the same time, you blame yourself. But now you have some weighty decisions to make. You must focus on how to set things right.

Be aware that most school systems take parents' judgments and preferences seriously when considering "grade retention" (educationese for holding kids back). Some schools will not keep a child back without the parents' assent. Others have firm cutoffs: all children failing a certain number of subjects must repeat a year of school or do remedial work. Your school system (or state) may require students to pass proficiency exams before advancing to the next grade. Since the rules differ so much from place to place, you should request a copy of your school's promotion/retention policy and get to know it.

Educators disagree on the pros and cons of retention. (See "Social Promotion," page 610.) Each decision should be made on a case-by-case basis, weighing the abilities and needs of the individual student.

- **First, find out what went wrong.** Ask the teachers and principal to identify the standards your child has failed to meet. Is she not measuring up in one subject, or several? What skills and knowledge does she lack? Insist on specifics. Don't accept generalizations such as "She's behind her classmates" or "She's below grade level." Go over samples of your child's work with the teachers and figure out exactly what is wrong.

Once you've identified the shortcomings, try to determine the cause. Some children get into academic trouble because they've missed a lot of class. Sometimes out-of-school matters (puberty, trouble at home) get in the way of in-school success. Is a learning disability masquerading as low test scores? Is there a physical problem? Could it be that your child is not hearing the teacher or seeing the blackboard clearly? Perhaps she does not relate to the teacher's methods. Maybe it is the school's fault—your child may have been poorly taught, or she may have had a parade of substitutes instead of a steady teacher. Often there is a combination of problems.

- **Assess your alternatives.** You and the school staff may be able to figure out a better solution than repeating a grade. Could summer school help your child catch up? If the school doesn't offer that option, you may be able to arrange for private tutoring during the vacation. The school may agree to test her again, after she's had a summer of tutoring, and then make a final decision about retention.

Some schools have multigrade classrooms in which students spend more than one year. These can be particularly well suited for a youngster who is doing fine in some subjects but moving slowly in others. In a "two-three" classroom, for example, some children may be reading at the third grade level while doing math at the second grade level. Another possibility is partial promotion, so that your child remains with her age-mates in some subject areas but repeats coursework (or gets remedial help) in others.

- **Weigh the possible benefits and costs of repeating a grade.** There may be some unwanted side effects. Your child will undoubtedly feel discouraged. She may feel out of step socially with younger classmates. Some educators believe that staying back is such a blow to a child's self-esteem that it actually decreases the chances of academic recovery. They retain a student only as a last resort.

On the other hand, repeating a grade may be just what your child needs. Some youngsters require an extra year to mature emotionally or socially. Others need more time on core academic subjects. They aren't ready to tackle some topics and assignments until they get a bit older or have more practice. You do your child no service to push her on to the next grade if she hasn't learned what it will expect of her. You may launch a cycle of spiraling academic failure.

- **Don't make the same mistakes twice.** Be wary if the school suggests that what your child needs is a second year of exactly the same things that didn't work the first time. Another year in the same classroom can, with the right teacher, be terrific. It can also be a deadly dull and deeply frustrating repetition of failure.

  Your child is apt to be better served by something different, even while repeating a grade. Maybe she could use a different teacher or a different mix of classes and textbooks. You may also need to ask yourself: Would she be better off in a different school? The at-home regimen may need to change—stricter study hours and perhaps more supervision from you. Don't expect better results without some thoughtful changes.

- **Repeating a grade isn't the end of the world.** Nowhere is it written in concrete that every seven-year-old must be in second grade, every twelve-year-old in seventh. Millions of kids have stayed back a year along the way and then gone on to successful lives and careers.

  Sometimes moms and dads ask that their child be allowed to repeat a grade. One of the authors' children repeated first grade at his parents' request. It turned out to be a great decision.

- **Stay deeply involved.** Monitor your child's progress and study habits closely. Keep in regular touch with her teachers. Do not assume that repeating a grade will itself solve the problem. Do not leave it to the school to fix things. Helping your child catch up is your responsibility. Her chances depend on your aid and encouragement.

As usual, prevention is the best medicine. If year-end news that your child is being held back comes as a total shock, it may be a sign that you weren't paying enough attention as problems cropped up months earlier. It's also a sign that the school was not doing a very good job of communicating with you and sending home progress reports on a timely basis.

Be on the lookout for indications of trouble. If a problem develops, try to nip it in the bud. Talk to the teacher and come up with a strategy to help your child—whether it be tutoring, weekend programs, special homework assignments, or extra time studying with you at her side. Early diagnosis and intervention are the best ways to assure success.

Warning Signs of Academic Trouble Ahead

Parents must stay vigilant. Low test scores and bad report cards are obvious indicators. Here are some other early-warning signs that may portend problems at school. Your child:

- keeps forgetting her homework, says she doesn't have any, or doesn't complete it.
- doesn't know when assignments are due or tests are coming up.
- doesn't want to go to school in the morning.
- frequently complains of various aches and pains in the morning.
- talks about how she doesn't like school, or doesn't want to talk about school.
- makes excuses for not showing you her schoolwork.
- starts losing self-confidence.
- acts nervous and depressed.
- develops behavior problems.
- begins to show a lack of interest in studies.
- doesn't like to read, or has trouble reading.

GETTING INVOLVED AT SCHOOL

This section addresses the responsibility of mothers and fathers to get involved with the school itself. When parents take part in the life of the school, good things follow. Kids tend to get better grades and have fewer behavior problems. They often have happier relationships with their parents. They see that mom and dad seriously value education.

Involvement helps parents understand how the school works and what teachers' jobs are really like. It assists them in knowing what their children are being taught. Occasionally being visible at school gives parents more credibility in the eyes of teachers and principals—and therefore a stronger voice in the shaping of school policy and their own child's experience there.

Despite these benefits, many parents have bad track records when it comes to school involvement. They rarely get to know the teachers or attend school functions. They often say they don't have time or fear they have little to contribute. Sometimes they feel intimidated by the system or unwelcome in the classroom. No doubt these are real concerns, but the fact remains: by absenting themselves from school, they may be hampering their children's academic chances. Parents should do everything they can to make a little time, get over their anxieties, and take part. You should expect teachers and principals to put out the welcome mat. But they can't make you get involved. In the end, it's your duty, and it's your initiative that makes the difference.

Many dads, in particular, need to do a better job of participating at school. Often their attitude seems to be that it's "Mom's responsibility" to talk with teachers and attend back-to-school night. In two-parent families, mothers are twice as likely as fathers to be highly involved. This is a shame. Research shows that children are more apt to get 'A's and enjoy learning when their fathers take part in school activities.

None of this means that you have to turn up at school once a week, or that you must spend most of your spare time there. But you may have to rearrange your schedule occasionally to be there for your child.

Many schools are good about supporting parental involvement. In some places, the trend is to give mothers and fathers more of a say in how their schools are run. For example, you may hear the term "school-based management" or "site-based management." This approach shifts some decision-making authority from district bureaucracies to individual schools; it usually encourages administrators, teachers, and parents to share in decisions about curriculum, hiring of staff, budget priorities, and other matters.

Then there are schools that pay lip service to the idea of involving parents, but are skittish about anyone getting too close or gaining real leverage. They are all for "parental involvement" when it means showing up for fund-raisers and athletic events and agreeing with what administrators propose. They quickly cool to the idea, though, if it means giving parents any real say about issues such as what children should learn. "There is a clear line at school," says one mom in the Chicago area. "'If you like what we're doing, the door is always open. But if you don't, then it's your problem.'" Elaine K. McEwan, a former teacher and principal, observes that parents often feel like they get the cold shoulder when they raise concerns. "Whether you live in an urban neighborhood or an affluent suburb, the perception is that when parents ask tough questions, educators immediately circle the wagons, or throw educational jargon at you," she says.[12]

The specter of anxious moms and dads invading their turf, micromanaging teachers, and quarreling with each other about lesson plans puts some schools on the defensive. In fact, those things can happen if parents aren't respectful of educators' tough jobs and mindful that the whole school cannot revolve around their child.

Still, good schools manage to engage parents in nontrivial ways. They welcome them in many roles and practically any time. In good schools, you'll see parents showing up for sundry purposes, whether it be raising money, sitting on decision-making committees, or simply observing their children learn. In places where such participation is discouraged, something may well be wrong—something they don't want you to see.

If the school resists your involvement, be polite but persistent. Let teachers and administrators know you want to be their ally. Keep asking how you can help. Don't let anyone put you off. When you see a problem, find the right occasion to speak up. Offer a solution if you see one. Find other parents who want to have an influence and approach the school together. Tell teachers and administrators your expectations regarding your children. Remember, it's *your* school. It's paid for in part with *your* money, and *your* children are spending a big chunk of their lives there. You have both a responsibility and a right to be involved in its affairs.

Pledging Your Involvement

Some schools now ask parents to sign a "contract" in which they promise to remain involved in their child's education and the life of the school. The following excellent example comes from South Boston Harbor Academy, a charter school in Massachusetts. Students, parents, teachers, and the principal sign and date the contract. This has the effect of uniting all those involved in a common project and creating a sense of mutual responsibility. In good schools, parents do more than just put their names on such pledges. They do their best to live up to them.

South Boston Harbor Academy Contract of Mutual Responsibilities

Student

As a student at the South Boston Harbor Academy Charter School, I agree to:

1. Make the school a safe and orderly environment in which my fellow students and I improve our academic achievement.

2. Arrive at school on time and attend all my classes prepared to work.

3. Participate in class discussions and school activities on a regular basis.

4. Seek help when I do not understand what is taught or what is required of me.

5. Complete my homework assignments thoroughly and on time.

6. Behave appropriately in school by being respectful and courteous to my teachers and my fellow students.

7. Support the school community by setting an example of good citizenship for myself and encouraging my fellow students to do the same.

8. Read, sign, and abide by the guidelines and regulations listed in the student code of conduct and student handbook.

9. Recognize that as a Founding Student at the school, it is my work and actions that will make this school a success now and in the future.

10. Be held accountable as a student at the school by accepting responsibility for my actions.

Signature _____

Parent

As a parent at the South Boston Harbor Academy Charter School, I agree to:

1. Make the school a safe and orderly environment in which my child and his/her classmates improve their academic achievement.

2. Make sure my child arrives at school on time and attends all of his/her classes prepared to work.

3. Take an active role in my child's education by helping with his/her schoolwork and ensuring that it is completed thoroughly and on time.

4. Maintain high standards of academic excellence and expectations for my child and communicate them to my child on a regular basis.

5. Communicate regularly with my child's teachers regarding my child's academic and behavioral performance.

6. Be an active partner with the school in my child's education by participating in school activities.

7. Partner with the school in instilling in my child a lifelong understanding of the importance of education.

8. Read, sign, and abide by the guidelines and regulations listed in the parent handbook.

9. Recognized that as a Founding Parent at the school, it is my work and actions that will make this school a success now and in the future.

10. Be held accountable as a parent at the school by accepting responsibility for my actions.

Signature _____

Teacher

As a teacher at the South Boston Harbor Academy Charter School, I agree to:

1. Make the school a safe and orderly environment in which all of my students improve their academic achievements.

2. Arrive at school on time and prepared to teach.

3. Make the South Boston Harbor Academy an academically rigorous, college preparatory learning environment.

4. Convey the love and knowledge I have for my subject to my students on a regular basis.

5. Assess regularly, fairly, and constructively the efforts and work of my students.

6. Challenge and motivate students both inside and outside the classroom.

7. Communicate regularly with the parents of my students regarding their behavioral and academic performance.

8. Serve as a role model for students by conveying to them a lifelong understanding of the importance of education.

9. Recognize that as a Founding Teacher at the school, it is my work and actions that will make this school a success now and in the future.

10. Be held accountable as a teacher at the school by accepting responsibility for my actions.

Signature _____

Great Ways to Get Involved

Here are some ways to become engaged with your child's school. If you're like most parents, you won't have time to do all of these things every semester, but this list may help you identify a few paths to participaton.

- **Get to know your child's teachers.** Don't wait for them to approach you. Introduce yourself as soon as school begins. Talk about how to stay in touch during the year. *Getting to know the teachers and communicating with them on a regular basis is perhaps the most important way to be involved in your child's school.* (See "Good Teacher Relations," page 455.)

- **Learn who's who in your child's education.** In addition to getting to know the teachers, it's always a good idea to meet others on the school staff. Introduce yourself to the principal, assistant principals, librarian, guidance counselor, school secretary, nurse, coaches, and other adults who have contact with your child. If you're not sure what someone's job entails, ask. The better you get to know school officials, the more comfortable you'll feel going to them with questions, problems, and ideas. You'll also be better able to talk to your child about school and relate to her experiences.

- **Get to know other parents.** In particular, you'll want to meet some mothers and fathers of your child's classmates and pals. Talking with them is an invaluable means of gleaning news about the school, its teachers, its programs, and any problems it may face.

- **Join a parent-teacher group.** This can be an excellent starting point for involvement. Parent-teacher groups do everything from running school fairs to sponsoring parent workshops to weighing in on policy decisions.

    There is probably a PTA (parent-teacher association) or PTO (parent-teacher organization) at your school. Local PTAs are members of the national PTA (officially called the National Congress of Parents and Teachers). PTOs are usually grassroots, locally based groups with no affiliation with a state or national organization.

    Be aware that the national PTA has a strong political agenda that makes many parents uncomfortable and (in our view) opposes some sensible ideas for needed education reforms. State-level PTAs play similar roles in the politics and policies of a number of states. Some local PTAs take their cues from the national organization's agenda and end up toeing the line for the education establishment even when schools are slipshod. There are also fine local PTAs full of devoted members who do exemplary work on behalf of particular schools. You'll need to find out if your objectives are in line with the aims of your school's parent-teacher group.

- **Read the school handbook.** This is one of your first steps in getting to know your school—one that many parents never get around to taking! Your school should give you printed material outlining such matters as its discipline code, dress code, and grading policies. Sit down and familiarize yourself with this information. Some good tests of a school are: Does it have clear policies in these areas? Does it actually follow the rules and procedures set down in its handbook? Do parents take them seriously?

    If your child is in public school, there may also be a district policy manual that spells out system-wide rules (attendance standards, suspension and expulsion guidelines, etc.). You may want to review it. Ask at the principal's office how you can see a copy.

- **Attend school functions.** It is important to your child that you attend events in which she takes part—school plays or concerts, athletic contests, science fairs, and so on. Your school will also host activities for parents, such as open house, parents' night, and back-to-school night. Go to as many as you can. These are obvious chances to get to know teachers, administrators, and other parents; to learn the physical setup of the school (what the library is like, what kind of equipment the gym has, etc.); to gauge the atmosphere (whether the hallways are neat, the teachers cheerful, the principal dynamic); and to find out about school policies, curricula, and teaching methods in general. Lengthy discussions about your own child should wait for a private parent-teacher conference.

- **Visit your child's classroom.** This is probably the best way to get a firsthand look at your child's school experience. You may want to sit in on her classes one semester for a couple of hours or half a day. Don't show up unannounced; call the teacher and arrange a time in advance. Most good schools and teachers will be happy to honor your request. Some may be reluctant if they think you're coming to snoop. Explain that you want to get to know your school as well as possible. Be persistent.

Sit quietly and observe while you're there. Remember that what you see will be somewhat out of the ordinary. Your child will behave differently with you present. The teacher may vary her routine. Still, after a couple of hours you should get a pretty good idea of how disciplined the classroom is, whether or not the children are engaged, and what kind of rapport the teacher has with the students.

- **Volunteer some of your time.** Some parents are able to lend a hand almost daily. For others, once or twice a semester is the right amount. Schools need mothers and fathers to help carry the load. Doing even the smallest of jobs usually wins the staff's appreciation. There are all sorts of tasks you might perform—from being a class parent to helping the teacher locate materials she needs to driving on a class outing. If education is important to you, chances are you can occasionally find a way to pitch in and help. If you can't do much of this yourself, perhaps another family member can. Sometimes older siblings, grandparents, and others with more flexible time at their disposal can do some volunteer work.

- **Serve on a decision-making committee.** Many schools and districts have advisory committees or decision-making teams on which parent representatives sit. How much influence these boards have varies. In good schools, they often deal with significant issues such as textbooks and academic standards.

  If you have the time to serve, ask a parent leader or someone in the principal's office to tell you how you can take part. If your schedule keeps you from sitting on a committee, it's still a good idea to get to know the parents who are members. They can keep you posted on important decisions. In turn, you can probably find a way to lend an occasional hand, even if it means simply watching their kids in your home while they go to a meeting.

- **Attend a school board meeting.** This is a good way to get wind of proposals you may like or dislike before they make their way into the classroom. Call the superintendent's office to get a schedule of meetings. The agenda is usually posted in advance, and may even be on the Internet. You may want to form a network of parents who can take turns attending and then briefing one another on what happened. Make sure you vote in school board elections. The people who sit on that body may have a more direct impact on your child's life than any other elected officials in the land.

- **Keep up with news about your school.** Don't put aside those notices that teachers and administrators send home—read them! They can tell you a lot about what's going on. Your school may also have a newsletter it regularly sends home to parents, or perhaps a phone number you can call to get a recorded message about what's happening that week.

  Ask if your school or district has a home page on the Internet; this may be an excellent place to find out about schedules, upcoming meetings, policy changes, even lunch menus. Read articles about local schools in your newspaper. Remember that the more you communicate with teachers and other parents, the more news you're going to get about your child's school.

- **Don't overdo it.** Being "involved" does not mean voicing your opinion on every single issue with which you are not in total harmony with the school, or becoming so shrill that you destroy your relationship with the staff. It does not mean showing up at school again and again only to plead on behalf of your own child. Keep in mind that teachers have other youngsters to worry about, too.

  "Those parents who are all over teachers for every little thing become a real burden," says one educator. "This growing sense of 'entitlement,' particularly among upper-middle-class professional families in suburban public and private schools, drives more and more good teachers out of the field of education." The most effective parents are active on behalf of their own kids but also work for the benefit of the school as a whole.

Your participation in school affairs will probably need to evolve with your child's age. By around sixth grade, for example, many kids are appalled by the prospect of a parent sitting in their classroom, so you may decide that's no longer prudent. (One of the authors' sons, for fear of embarrassment, asked his mom to use only her first name when she came to his seventh grade class to give a talk!) But don't give up on school involvement as children hit the preteen years. When parents withdraw, grades often begin to slip. Keep up the effort, even though it may mean changing the ways you contribute.

Volunteering at School

If you are interested in giving some of your time, talk with the principal, the librarian, or your child's teacher. They should be able to offer suggestions or put you in touch with a staff member or parent who coordinates volunteer activities. If you aren't available during the school day, there are still ways you can help. Here are a few of the many useful tasks that parents can perform:

- Organize a classroom visit by a guest speaker.
- Coordinate a field trip or offer to drive.
- Tutor a student who needs extra help.
- Sponsor an after-school club (e.g., chess, art, computer club).
- Help coach or manage an athletic team.
- Help set up a science display.
- Be a hall or playground monitor once a month.
- Supervise a study hall session.
- Assist in the library or lunchroom.
- Help put on a program to honor good teachers.
- Make costumes or scenery for a school play.
- Help with a fund-raising project (e.g., book fair, auction).
- Take pictures or videotape at a school event.
- Prepare food for a class party.
- Give a talk about your profession, hobby, or trip.
- Help plan the school's annual carnival.
- Work in the school office (filing, copying, answering phones).
- Help clean up the school grounds or make repairs to buildings.
- Assist a teacher in the classroom.

Signs of Schools That Welcome Parents

Here are some characteristics you might see in a school that is serious about parental involvement:

- Keeps parents up-to-date (via a bulletin board, Web site, hot line, or newsletter) about upcoming school events, personnel changes, volunteer opportunities, etc.
- Informs parents about important changes under consideration *before* putting them into effect.

- Encourages parent-staff committees to weigh in on decisions that significantly affect the school (e.g., budget, curriculum, teacher hiring).

- Holds frequent events (such as open-house nights) where parents and teachers can meet, talk, and swap information.

- Provides phone numbers or e-mail addresses where parents can reach teachers.

- Supports an active parent-teacher group (PTA or PTO).

- Invites parents to observe children's classes.

- Greets mothers and fathers warmly; treats them in a courteous manner when they ask questions.

- Invites parents to make suggestions and evaluate the job that the school is doing, through surveys or direct communication with staff.

- Provides clear written information about school rules and procedures.

- Explains things to parents in everyday English, not jargon you can't understand.

GOOD TEACHER RELATIONS

Ask adults to name the individuals who have influenced their lives the most, and they usually include a teacher, principal, or coach. Most of the time, it was someone from the early years. As Lee Iacocca, former chairman of Chrysler Corporation, wrote in his autobiography, "If you ask me the name of my professors in college or graduate school, I'd have trouble coming up with more than three or four. But I still remember the teachers who molded me in elementary and high school."

When all is said and done, the faculty is the heart and soul of the educational enterprise that we call a school. We place our children in teachers' care with boundless hopes and high expectations. We ask that they nourish our loved ones' abilities so that each can live up to her potential. We want them to transmit the most important things to know. And we ask that they help shape the character of our young.

In return, we should be willing to give educators who accomplish these tasks our admiration and respect. Given the tough and important job that they do, they deserve as much thanks and honor as any profession in our society. Generally speaking, however, good teachers in this country don't get the recognition they deserve. Parents are sometimes quick to criticize but slow to praise. Educators often note with chagrin that they don't hear from many moms and dads until they have a complaint or a problem. "When I went to school, teachers demanded respect and used to get it," a New Jersey parent observes. "If I had a problem with a teacher, the first thing my mother said was, 'What did you do?' Now the teacher is always wrong."[13] When teachers fall short, they should be held accountable, but it's only fair that they be given our gratitude when they do their jobs well.

There are all sorts of ways to show your appreciation. Begin with honoring teachers in your child's presence. Tell youngsters that their teachers have an important job and must be shown respect and obedience at all times. Refrain from criticizing or second-guessing teachers in front of your child, or you will undermine their authority. Support their decisions and directions (including any punishment handed out for bad behavior) unless they are really unreasonable. Don't make excuses by blaming the teacher when the problem is really something your child has done or failed to do.

Bolster teachers' efforts by staying involved. The sincerest form of respect for a teacher is to help her do her job. Remember to say "thank you" to good teachers. Pick up the phone once a semester to say "nice going," or write a note expressing your appreciation. Send a letter of commendation to the principal. You might even write a letter to the editor of your newspaper, praising an excellent teacher by name and mentioning the good things she's done. Consider baking cookies or a cake for teachers on their birthdays or holidays, or having young children make a present (a bookmark, greeting card, etc.). Some parents invite teachers to their home for lunch or dinner once a year. These simple gestures are all much appreciated by educators.

The aim is not to butter teachers up, but rather to treat them as friends and allies who share an interest in the well-being of your child. These are people who do what they do because they love children. Some are sacrificing the prospects of higher pay in other jobs to be in the classroom. Think carefully about how you treat these stewards of your child's learning. Your youngster is more likely to do better in school when she learns from you that good teachers deserve esteem and attention.

In his great play *A Man for All Seasons*, Robert Bolt portrays an exchange between Sir Thomas More and a bright, ambitious young man named Richard Rich, who approaches More for advice on prospective careers. Sir Thomas asks: Why not be a teacher? "You'd be a fine teacher," he says, "perhaps even a great one." "If I was," asks Rich, "who would know it?" Sir Thomas replies, "You, your pupils, your friends, and God. Not a bad public, that." Indeed, that isn't a bad public for teachers in this or any age. We suggest that you make yourself part of it. We urge that you make respect and gratitude fundamental to your relationship with fine teachers at your school. When they ask themselves, "Who knows that I do a good job?" they should be able to answer without hesitation, "I, my pupils, *their parents*, and God."

Staying in Touch

Keeping an open line of communication with the school is one of your top responsibilities. Unfortunately, too many parents fall down on the job. "You send notices home, there's no response," says a Cleveland teacher. "You ask parents to come to conferences, they don't come. You send homework home, you can see that parents aren't paying attention to it."[14] Another problem is that some teachers aren't trained well in the art of communicating with parents. "I think the most important thing that many of us as teachers have to remember is that we do have to listen to the parents," says a second grade teacher in Rhode Island. "That's important. But, on the other hand, I think they have to listen to us, too. It definitely has to be a give and take."[15]

Here are some things to keep in mind about staying in touch:

- **Meet your child's teachers as soon as possible.** Take the initiative. Introduce yourself at the beginning of the school year—on back-to-school night, or sometime during the week before school begins (when the teacher is likely to be at school). Or just say a quick hello when you come to pick up your child. This is a simple but important step. An early face-to-face introduction can signal to the teacher that you are a parent who cares what happens in her classroom.

- **Trade some information at the start of the year.** As soon as possible, give the teacher a little information about your child (interests she has, books she's reading at home, activities you do together). You may want to ask for a brief get-acquainted meeting sometime during the first few weeks of school. Because the start of the year is a very busy time for educators, a phone call or exchange of e-mails may be more practical. The important thing is to establish contact, the sooner the better. "The parent understands the teacher's expectations, the teacher understands the family environment, and the child sees a united front," says Sharon Draper, 1997 National Teacher of the Year.[16]

- **Attend parent-teacher conferences.** Most schools schedule two or three parent-teacher conferences per year. They typically last twenty to thirty minutes, during which time the teacher should review your child's progress and show you some of her work. You should have time to ask questions. It is very important to attend these meetings faithfully and promptly, as the teacher may have scheduled several that day, one right after the other. (Teachers often express dismay at the percentage of parents who are late for conferences, or simply fail to show up.)

- **Schedule additional meetings if needed.** One half-hour session per semester with the teacher may not be sufficient. If you feel the need, do not hesitate to request an additional get-together. As long as you offer to work around her schedule, the teacher should be willing to accommodate you. If the school shows resistance ("We prefer that parents wait until the spring conference—it's just a month away") it may be a sign that it isn't really that interested in a partnership with parents.

- **Exchange notes.** Japanese and Chinese schools employ a technique that is quite effective in fostering close cooperation: each student carries a small notebook between home and school. Parents write about any problems or events at home that the teacher should know about, and teachers communicate about assignments, tests, classroom behavior, and other concerns.

  This is a nice model. In fact, notes or e-mails go back and forth between teachers and parents all the time at many good U.S. schools. Writing may be the quickest and easiest way to ask the teacher a question about the curriculum, send praise for a recent accomplishment, or let her know that your child doesn't understand a particular math lesson. Make it a priority to follow up on messages that the teacher sends home.

- **Keep in touch by phone.** A quick call every few weeks is, for many parents and teachers, the best way to touch base and give each other updates. Most good teachers give parents a phone number at which they can be reached. They may suggest the best hours to phone them. Some schools have installed voice mail for teachers so that moms and dads can leave messages. Some teachers even have Web pages where parents and kids can obtain homework assignments. Ask the teacher about the best way and time to get in touch with her.

Staying in touch gets tougher in the upper grades, when your child may have a half-dozen different teachers and they have scores of students. At that point, many schools stop scheduling regular one-on-one parent-teacher conferences. But keeping up the communication is still important. Make sure you meet all your child's instructors, however briefly. Often a parents' night at school consists of following your child's daily schedule, spending perhaps fifteen minutes with each of her teachers, and at least having the opportunity to say hello, hear a little about the curriculum, and pose any burning questions.

Finally, don't get carried away. You'll end up irritating a teacher if you call her every other day about each little problem that comes along. Keep in mind that she's got a raft of kids and parents to deal with. The best approach is to talk with her at the beginning of the year about how to communicate and settle on a system that works for both of you.

The Parent-Teacher Conference

The parent-teacher conference is your chance to check up on your child's progress, find out the teacher's expectations, make sure you share the same goals, and let her know what's going on at home. Time will be limited, so think about what you want to say and ask ahead of time. "I always ask parents to write down their questions before conferences," says Virginia teacher Linda Hoekstra. If a report card has recently come out, bring it with you.

You may want to pick a few of these questions to ask:

- How is my child progressing? How is she doing compared to her classmates?

- What are her best subjects? Her worst ones? Does she seem to have any special talents? Gaps that concern you?

- Does my child work hard at school? Should I be doing anything to improve her work habits?

- How is her behavior? Does she pay attention? Does she get along with her classmates?

- Is she on time for class?

- Does she participate in discussions and activities? Does she work well independently?

- Is she having any particular problems during the school day that I should know about?

- What will my child be learning in the coming weeks? Are there any major assignments coming up?

- How much homework should I expect to see my child do every night? Is she doing her homework well? Is she turning it in on time?

- How often do you give tests? What kinds of tests do you give? What can we expect by way of district and state tests?

- How do you determine grades?

- How should we communicate between conferences? With notes to each other? By telephone? By e-mail?

- What else should I be doing at home to help my child get a good education?

Working Out Problems with the Teacher

Sooner or later, there is apt to be some sort of problem to take up with a teacher. Here are some pointers about how to proceed:

- **Gather the facts.** Your first assumptions may be wrong. Remain open-minded. The problem may lie with the teacher or school. But it could also be your child's fault. It may even be something you are doing, or haven't been doing. Talk to your child carefully. Watch her behavior. Examine her work closely. You may want to sit in on a class. Talk with other parents to see if their children are encountering similar problems.

- **Call the teacher.** Minor glitches often can be fixed with a phone call or note. In other cases, you may need to schedule a face-to-face meeting with the teacher. Let her know ahead of time what you want to discuss so she'll be prepared.

- **Approach the teacher as a professional and an ally.** Avoid a confrontational attitude—a cooperative spirit will get you further. Until she gives you reason to do otherwise, treat any educator as a well-trained professional who intends the best for your child. Avoid personal criticism if possible. Focus instead on the curriculum, class materials, school policy, your child's needs, and so forth. Lay out the problem as you see it, and let her explain her view. Ask her to suggest a solution.

Give the teacher time to fix things, keeping in mind that she has other problems to worry about. Make sure you follow through on her suggestions. If you've seen no progress after a couple of weeks, or if you flat-out disagree, you may need to take your case to the next level.

- **Follow the chain of command.** Your school probably has a policy about resolving parent-teacher disagreements. Find out what it is. It may be spelled out in the parent handbook, or you may need to ask at the principal's office. Your next step will likely be to meet with a counselor or administrator, and after that, the principal.

  Be aware that, in going to the principal, you are crossing a line. Your relationship with that teacher may not be the same afterward. That should not stop you, but do your best to resolve matters with the teacher directly before going over her head.

  If you aren't satisfied with the response of the principal's office, you may need to keep going—possibly to the district superintendent's office, even to a school board member. Be polite but persevering.

Your chances of solving a problem vary. You can fix many troubles by simply having a word with the teacher. In other cases, success will depend partly on how long and hard you are willing to push. You also have to face the reality that you may not be able to resolve some issues to your satisfaction, particularly if you're dealing with a school system practiced in the art of preserving the status quo. There is always strength in numbers, however. Schools are much more likely to listen to groups of parents sharing a concern than to a lone voice crying in the wilderness.

Your Principal and Your School

It is hard to find an excellent school without an excellent principal. More than any other person, she is responsible for the school's character. A good principal is a CEO, general, cheerleader, and, above all, education leader. She has a vision of what a good school is, and she does whatever it takes to get students and teachers working toward those goals.

This is a job that comes with an amazing array of duties. A good principal not only manages the business of the school but also directs the learning process. She works with teachers to develop the curriculum. She evaluates and motivates instructors, and makes sure they have the resources they need. Because a good school maintains order, she knows that strong discipline and superior academics are two sides of a coin. She helps make up the budget and work out schedules. She treats parents as a kind of adjunct faculty and acts as liaison to the community. She comforts unhappy children and leads school assemblies.

Every good principal develops her own version of leadership, but *all good principals put academics first*. They focus on children's mastery of basic knowledge and skills in core subjects. If academics do not get top billing at school, the wrong person is in charge. A good principal protects the school as a temple of learning. Academic improvement is her constant theme, and she does everything in her power to make it happen. She stands up for high expectations and sees that school time is spent on learning, not squandered on peripheral distractions.

Much of a principal's work takes place behind the scenes, but a good education leader is also highly visible. She makes her presence known, monitoring corridors, visiting classrooms, lunching with children and staff. She spends time talking with teachers to get input and to spot problems before they become serious. She knows many of the kids by name. She's out there giving them pats on the back, asking them how things are going, reminding them of their goals, letting them know she cares. It's not unusual for a good elementary school principal to be standing at the front door in the morning, greeting her arriving students.

All of this is more than show. It helps establish order and brings a sense of common enterprise. A good principal knows what is going on in her school and who is doing what. She makes time for teachers, students, and parents who come by with questions. "In September a few years back, when I asked to meet with the principal to discuss the school's curriculum, I was told I would be able to talk with her in February," one mother reports. Something is wrong in such a school. If the education leader spends most of her time walled off from parents and their concerns, she is probably ineffective—no matter how busy she may appear.

Unfortunately, the public education system often makes it more difficult than it should be for principals to run their own schools. Sometimes their hands are tied by red tape, government regulations, court orders, and union rules. They must jump through hoops to deal with troublemaking students. Firing bad teachers is virtually impossible. The final say on the school budget is dictated from the district office. The most effective principals are often mavericks who make end runs around the bureaucracy, inventing ingenious ways to get what their schools need despite silly rules, rigid procedures, and empty coffers. That says much about the need for systematic reform.

Make an effort to introduce yourself to the principal. Get to know her a little, find out what kind of person she is, and watch her in action. Ask her: What is your vision for this school? What are your academic priorities? What are your plans to make sure they're accomplished? What are your expectations of students? Of parents? How can I help?

Getting to Know the Principal

- Is the principal focused on academics?
- Does she run an orderly, disciplined school?
- Does she inspire confidence and loyalty among teachers?
- Does she know many students and parents by name?
- Is she visible around school, and accessible to parents?
- Will she fight to get the best for her kids? (Or does she avoid rocking the boat?)
- Is she full of the energy it takes to run a good school?

Being a principal is a tough job full of long hours and headaches—and one of the most important jobs in our society. If you have a good principal at your school, you have much to be thankful for. Let her know that you appreciate her, and do whatever you can to support her efforts. If leadership at your school is weak, however, watch out. Problems almost certainly loom. Without a strong principal at the helm, most schools drift into the academic doldrums. Good schools are *led*.

Grading Your Involvement

How well do you stay involved in your child's education at home and at school?

- Does your child get a good night's rest and nourishing breakfast before school?
- Have you set a regular time for homework every day?
- Does your child have a quiet place to study?
- Do you check to make sure she's doing her homework?
- Have you taught her to keep track of assignments by writing them down?
- Do you look at her textbooks periodically?
- Do you read the teacher's comments on returned tests and assignments?
- Do you ever help your child prepare for tests by calling out questions or reviewing material with her?
- How often do you attend school functions such as parent-teacher conferences, open-house nights, and PTA/PTO meetings?
- Have you introduced yourself to teachers, the principal, and other members of the school staff?
- Have you read the school handbook to make sure you understand its rules and policies?
- Have you gotten to know the parents of some of your child's classmates?
- Have you observed a class?
- Do you ever volunteer at school?
- Do you keep in touch with the teacher through meetings, phone calls, or notes?
- Have you done something to thank or honor your child's teacher?

CHAPTER 11

Special Needs
and
Special Gifts

EVERY CHILD IS UNIQUE. ONE OF PARENTS' RESPONSIBILITIES is to recognize and protect the distinctive qualities of their children. A terrific education for one youngster will differ at least a little from an equally fine education for another, even within the same family. While all children must aspire to the general expectations, standards, and curriculum of the school, seeing to it that the education process addresses your child's singularities is part of your job. If you are fortunate, the school will see this as part of its job as well.

Some children, however, are exceptional in ways that call for even greater effort on the part of their parents and schools. Getting them the best possible education brings extra challenges for the adults who love and teach them. It can also bring extra rewards. We refer to girls and boys with disabilities, those with uncommon intellectual gifts—and to those children who have both at once. This chapter is meant especially for their parents. The first portion addresses the education of disabled youngsters, critically examines some of the issues in this field, and points parents toward additional resources. In the latter part of the chapter, we turn to the education of gifted children.

CHILDREN WITH DISABILITIES

All parents have solemn responsibilities for the education of their young, but nowhere are such duties weightier or more difficult than when a child has a disability. If yours does, or if you have observed a worrisome delay in his development, you are surely upset and at least a little bit confused. Some parents in this situation also find themselves feeling angry, guilty, and beleaguered. Here is how Patricia McGill Smith, director of the National Parent Council on Disabilities, describes these reactions:

> When parents learn about any difficulty or problem in their child's development, this information comes as a tremendous blow. The day my child was diagnosed as having a disability, I was devastated—and so confused that I recall little else about those first days other than the heartbreak. . . . Another parent describes the trauma as "having a knife stuck" in her heart.[1]

Do not despair. You are in a difficult situation, one you did not seek or expect to be in, but much can be done. There are many sources of information and help. Millions of other parents who have trod this rocky road ahead of you are glad to offer guidance, encouragement, and assistance.

The next few pages will introduce you to this complex topic. Educating children with disabilities spans a host of issues, however, and we are able only to touch on a few key points. The additional resources listed later in this section will provide more in-depth coverage.

We begin with three general guidelines:

- **Start early.** If your child does turn out to have a disability, the sooner you begin to deal with it, the brighter will be his prospects for a successful education and fulfilling life. Start early, both with the evaluation and diagnosis process and with the development and implementation of an education plan. Every state is supposed to provide early-intervention services for infants, toddlers, and preschoolers with disabilities. These include evaluation and, if your child is found eligible, the development (with you) of an individual plan for services for your child and your family.

- **Get help.** Don't be ashamed to seek it, and don't be too busy to accept it. You may be dealing with a complicated assortment of medical, psychological, educational, and emotional factors. It's not unusual for technology to play a role, too. There are people who have expertise in these various areas. Make use of them.

- **Take charge.** You may not think there are many pluses to being the parent of a disabled child, but here is some good news: under today's laws and policies in the United States, you have more to say about the education of your child—more rights, more involvement, more decision-making authority, and, yes, more responsibility—than do the parents of youngsters without disabilities. Expect to find yourself dealing with many different specialists, many divergent opinions, many conflicting regulations, and a lot of bureaucracy. Make yourself captain of this ship. Take control, think positively, and steel yourself for a long voyage.

What Is "Special Education"?

The term "special education" means individualized instruction designed to meet the unique needs of students with physical, mental, emotional, behavioral, or learning-related disabilities. In other words, it is education for youngsters who have some sort of problem that hinders their ability to learn successfully in a regular classroom using conventional teaching approaches. There was a time in this country when children with disabilities did not get a good shot at a proper education. That began to change in 1975 (earlier in some states) with passage of federal legislation now known as the Individuals with Disabilities Education Act, or IDEA. This law requires school districts to provide "free appropriate public education" to children with disabilities and learning problems.

According to the U.S. Department of Education, about five and a half million children—approximately twelve out of every 100 students—are presently classified as disabled. For example, youngsters who have difficulty seeing, hearing, or walking might be categorized as having an educational disability. So might children with mental retardation, chronic illness, emotional disturbance, brain or spinal cord injury, genetic conditions such as Down syndrome, or serious social maladjustment. The key is that the child's condition must interfere with his ability to learn.

"Disabilities" come in many different categories, often in combinations. Every youngster is a unique collection of capabilities and limitations. The idea of modern special education is to tailor an education program to the specific needs of a particular child, maximizing his strengths, compensating for (and where possible circumnavigating) his weaknesses. To the greatest degree appropriate to the child, he must be given access to the standard curriculum, helped to attain the academic standards of his school or state, and included in the life and activities of his school.

This can take some doing. If a child has a disability that affects his learning, placing him in a conventional classroom staffed only by a regular teacher may not work well. More is often needed. That may mean speech or occupational therapy, special tutoring, or medical assistance. It may involve physical accommodation (e.g., wheelchair access), special learning tools (e.g., Braille books and computers), or extra help (e.g., a nurse or classroom aide).

All this and more is possible in U.S. schools. Indeed, if your disabled child needs it for his education to succeed, he has a legal right to it, and you have the right to be involved in making these decisions.

Special ed is complicated and fraught with challenges. It is often controversial. (Those extra services, people, and equipment make a dent in the school system's budget, and the federal and state dollars supplied for these purposes are rarely sufficient to cover the full costs.) From the parent's standpoint, however, your job is to get the best education you can for your child. And that begins with an accurate evaluation of his situation.

Identification and Evaluation

Public school systems are supposed to have "child-find" strategies for locating disabled or handicapped children starting at birth. The system is obliged under federal law to provide special education services even for preschoolers. That's because of the educational value of starting early. In some states, health departments, social service agencies, and other organizations participate in these child-find activities.

Unfortunately, it doesn't always work the way it's supposed to. School systems are bureaucracies. Their budgets are not infinite. They are primarily concerned with the youngsters already enrolled in their schools. They are seldom fully reimbursed by federal or state programs, and therefore every additional disabled child whom they "identify" is likely to add to their fiscal burdens. So don't wait for the system to come seeking your child. If you, a preschool teacher, a pediatrician, or day care provider suspects that your child has a developmental delay or other disability, make it your business to look into it.

Do not panic. Just as a new parent is apt to assume that a baby's sniffle must mean pneumonia, so you may hastily conclude from the fact that your child is not walking or talking as soon as you think he should that something terrible is wrong. Please keep in mind that little children develop in different ways and at different rates, and they acquire various abilities at different ages. The fact that a new talker is hard to understand does not necessarily mean he has a speech impediment. It may just mean he hasn't yet had much practice.

While resisting panic, don't hesitate to convey your concern to your doctor or seek a consultation with a child development specialist. You may also contact your local school system and your state's early-intervention program for infants and toddlers. These agencies can help you decide whether your child needs evaluation. If they recommend some tests, it's probably a good idea. If your child has a physical disability, injury, birth defect, or genetic condition, you probably already know it. If the issue is a developmental delay or possible learning disability, however, some sophisticated tests may be needed to find out what's going on.

What if your child is already in school? Either parents or school may begin the process of determining whether a disability is contributing to a learning problem. Often it's moms and dads who first raise a red flag; they, after all, are most closely attuned to their child's welfare. If you think your youngster might have a disability that is interfering with his learning, talk with the teacher, principal, or school psychologist. Ask that your child be referred for a formal evaluation. Do not let school officials put you off while they wait to "see how he does."

If the teacher first suspects a problem, the school will probably get in touch with you and schedule a meeting. The staff will explain why they think your child should be referred for an evaluation, what procedures are involved, and what your rights are. They should give you this information in writing. They will ask for your written consent to conduct an evaluation and should explain how you can participate in the process. Since 1997, under federal law, you have the right to take part throughout, including decisions about what tests and other diagnostic procedures will be undertaken with your child.

No matter what the disability—even an obvious physical handicap—before a child can qualify for special education and related services, he needs a formal evaluation. (Indeed, under federal law he must be reevaluated at least every three years in case his condition changes. A vision problem, for example, might get more severe. A developmental problem might ease.) Think of this as a diagnostic process that must precede the development of an individualized education program (IEP) for your child. The school system will certainly be involved with it, but you may have to ask for it, or get a referral from your pediatrician or other expert.

Be prepared for a number of tests by a team of professionals, probably including teachers, a school psychologist, a learning disabilities specialist, a physician, and perhaps a school social worker. This team will look closely at factors such as your child's physical health, reasoning abilities, reading skills, emotional state, and social adjustment. The assessment must be provided by public schools at no cost to parents.

After these tests, the evaluation team reviews the results and recommends whether or not special education is appropriate. It will also suggest any "related services" that might benefit your child. These can include such things as physical therapy, social work and counseling, occupational therapy, help with speech or language, mobility and transportation aid, and medical-type procedures that may be necessary for the youngster to take full advantage of his educational opportunities.

If you're not sure of the school system's diagnosis or have doubts about the recommendations, seek a second opinion. You may wish to have your child tested by a doctor or psychologist who does not work for the school system. (Under certain circumstances, the school system will even pay for such an evaluation—and it is supposed to give you that information.) Or you may wish to take a copy of the school's test results to an outside specialist to get another analysis of the data and another set of recommendations. Be aware that differing diagnoses and conflicting opinions are not uncommon, especially in the area of learning disabilities. Be aware, too, that the school's recommendations may be colored by what resources it has available.

If you decide to have private testing done, look for a specialist experienced with children who have disabilities similar to your child's. Often, the best way to start is with a private agency that specializes in the education of all manner of disabled children and either has many different specialists on staff or has lists of them at hand for referrals.

If your child is under three years of age, and has a disability or developmental delay, educational services should be provided by your state's early-intervention system. The requirements for this program resemble those for school-age children. Depending on your state, it may be located in the education system or health, social services, or other human services agencies. You can check with the governor's office to find out how to locate it.

Learning Disabilities

If your child has a physical or emotional handicap or significant retardation, it is likely that you knew this well before he reached school age. That is why a huge fraction of the initial diagnoses that take place among youngsters who are already in school involve the knotty area called "learning disabilities" or "learning disorders." Indeed, these now account for more than half of all special education students.

There is, unfortunately, no commonly accepted definition of the term "learning disability." It's a nebulous label that is often—some say too often—applied to intelligent children who for some reason have problems learning in the same ways or at the same rate as other children but who apparently do not have more "traditional" disabilities such as physical and emotional handicaps.

Learning disabilities are generally believed to result from some neurological dysfunction within the child. They take several forms with names such as hyperactivity, dyslexia, minimal brain damage, and perceptual impairment. An extremely bright child who struggles with reading, no matter how much time he spends with books, might be classified as learning disabled. So might a child who is a good reader but has trouble writing words on paper. Other examples of students who may have a learning disability are those with very weak verbal skills for their age, those who can't seem to remember information that they hear, and those with difficulty concentrating on a given task.

The fact that there is no concise definition of "learning disability" is a clue that this is a complicated, contentious, and somewhat murky area. It's gotten even murkier as the number of diagnoses has soared in recent years. Some people now estimate that up to 20 percent of Americans may be learning disabled. That would mean that one out of every five schoolchildren is a candidate for special education. Such numbers naturally generate controversy. They make us wonder: Is there really something out of the ordinary with that many children? Why is their number rising so fast?

Skeptics argue that there is no proof of neurological defects in some students who have been identified as learning disabled. They point out that no one can say exactly what causes some children to have learning disabilities, and that there is no consistent set of symptoms. Diagnoses may be based more on judgment, opinion, and preference than medical evidence. A child who is characterized as "disobedient" and "argumentative" in one school might be described as having "oppositional defiant disorder" in another.

Some educators and doctors worry that we're going too far in "medicalizing" children's education problems, some of which might be successfully dealt with through the right mix of early academic help, expert teaching, good discipline, perseverance, and adult attention. The term "learning disability," they say, has become a handy management option for schools, an easy rationale for a teacher or principal to direct a child toward special education when in reality the school isn't doing a very good job of teaching him. It is also unfortunate but true that some administrators of special education programs are eager to maximize the number of children in their domains because bigger numbers bring larger budgets and greater prestige. (The flip side, many angry parents attest, is that, since special education can be costly for the school system as a whole, other officials build bureaucratic barriers that make it hard for disabled children to get the help they need.)

Policy arguments aside, be aware that the broad phrase "learning disability" does not itself constitute a legal category that qualifies a youngster for special education. Instead, it's an umbrella term covering many different conditions. Only if your child is found to have one (or more) of those conditions—a "specific learning disability" is the official term—is he a candidate for special education.

Be aware, too, that for all the talk of "attention deficit disorder" (ADD) and "attention deficit hyperactive disorder" (ADHD), this is not a "specific learning disability" in its own right. It is not unusual, however, for ADD to appear together with a specific disability that causes the youngster affected by it to qualify for special education. In that case, dealing with the interplay between the specific disability and the ADD problem becomes part of the child's individualized education program.

ADD and Ritalin

Millions of American schoolchildren have been diagnosed with attention deficit disorder (ADD) or attention deficit hyperactive disorder (ADHD), conditions marked by symptoms such as failure to pay attention, inability to concentrate, fidgety behavior, and forgetfulness. A common treatment is a pill called Ritalin, which is a trade name for the drug methylphenidate. By some estimates, the number of schoolchildren taking such pills is approaching four million.

To some parents, Ritalin is a miracle drug for kids who once seemed unteachable—girls and boys who were always squirming and disrupting the class, couldn't manage to wait their turn, never could remember assignments or listen to what others were saying. Ritalin and similar medications have helped many such students stay calm enough to pay attention to the teacher and focused enough to finish their assignments.

In the minds of others, however, Ritalin has become an easy chemical alternative to good teaching and parenting. Critics say that harried educators have learned to recommend it for rambunctious children as a quick way to make them more tractable in class.

Teachers, meanwhile, observe that often it is anxious *parents* who inquire about a diagnosis of ADD/ADHD when their daughters and sons don't live up to their hopes. Since 1990, Ritalin production has increased 700 percent, and 50 percent more children are taking the drug. Has something happened to American schoolchildren that so many now need medication in order to behave and learn? Or is it that, at the dawn of the twenty-first century, we now find it rather cumbersome to train children to good behavior, but expedient to medicate them into it?

There are other unanswered questions about Ritalin and similar drugs. No one knows exactly how it acts on the brain or how it helps children with ADD/ADHD to focus. In the short run, taking it appears to be safe, but researchers point out that we know little about the risks and benefits of its long-term use. Experts say that there is not enough communication among doctors, teachers, and parents about the drug. There are concerns about Ritalin abuse among teenagers; the Drug Enforcement Agency says that methylphenidate "ranks in the top ten most frequently reported pharmaceutical drugs diverted from licensed handlers."[3]

Our advice is to be cautious about putting your child on Ritalin (or any other drug that may affect his learning and behavior). Be sure to get a comprehensive assessment of your child's behavior and learning needs *before* trying any behavior-modifying medication. Examine alternative approaches. If a doctor prescribes Ritalin or similar medication, get a second opinion from a trained specialist who is experienced with a wide range of children and behavioral problems. Try to get a sense of how many children are taking Ritalin at your school. If lots of kids have been diagnosed with ADD/ADHD, you may wonder if the school might be a little too eager to medicate.

If you do decide to try Ritalin for your child, remember that it is no magic bullet. Although it seems to benefit some youngsters, it is no substitute for good teaching at school and at home. It needs to be accompanied by careful strategies for dealing with the child's behavior in both settings. Medication alone has *not* been found to improve the long-term prognosis for kids with ADD/ADHD. It may sometimes set the stage, but all children need lots of guidance from adults in learning how to behave and how to study.

Developing a Plan

If the evaluation process suggests that your child does, in fact, have a disability affecting his education, he is a candidate for "special" education.

Some parents resist this conclusion. Some feel ashamed or want to deny the problem. Others resist because they have heard troubling things about special ed, about how it's a vast bureaucracy, an endless maze, a cul-de-sac from which few children emerge with a good education. Others suspect—sometimes with good reason—that the teacher or school claims to have found a "disability" in their child when a more accurate statement of the problem is that educators haven't done a good job of teaching him basic skills.

Especially if the diagnosis is "mild learning disability," you may want to explore some options before boarding the special education ship. You may want to see whether a different teacher, extra tutoring, and some additional help from you at home can boost your youngster back onto a successful trajectory. Some parents change schools because they believe their children's special learning needs can be better met in a different setting, or because they have misgivings about the local school system's approach to special education. This is a fairly frequent reason for choosing charter schools, for example, many of which are designed especially for disabled youngsters.

It pays to be cautious and to examine alternatives. Special ed referrals are not always warranted. Some school systems have weak special ed programs that do not serve the youngsters in them well. Others have outstanding programs that do a terrific job. Most common is something in between, the sort of program that ends up being pretty much what you make of it.

But don't be so cautious that you serve your child badly. Many disabled children do benefit from appropriate specialized instruction and extra help. Your first thought should be to get the problem diagnosed and then apply the appropriate remedy. A good special ed program may be just what your child needs to reach his greatest potential. Your foremost responsibility is to ensure that he succeeds. Don't hold back for reasons of shame or guilt. We've seen situations where, for example, parents keep shifting their youngster from one school to another— sometimes after just a few weeks or months—in a desperate quest to avoid recognizing that the problem isn't just the school and that the child actually has a disability that would benefit from being acknowledged and addressed.

Such parents are anguished and upset. This is not an easy situation. We suggest trying to adopt an attitude like this: My child and I are going to take advantage of every bit of available help, and the process of getting and shaping that help is going to yield real benefit in terms of his learning. But that doesn't mean just handing my child over to experts. I must remain the captain of this ship. And if I conclude, after a fair test, that we're on the wrong vessel, we can move to another one.

The guiding force in any child's experience with special education is his IEP, his individualized education program. Think of writing this document as seizing the opportunity to mold his education to his needs and abilities, an opportunity that U.S. public education—wrongly, in our view—does not routinely make available to other parents and children.

The IEP spells out the details of your child's education program and daily instruction, as well as related services that are deemed necessary to making a successful education possible for him. This important document (which must be reviewed and renewed at least annually) serves as the blueprint for the school's handling of your child's education. You should take part—with the team of educators, experts, and specialists whose responsibility this is—in developing the IEP. It cannot be put into operation without your signature, but it is apt to be a much better plan if you play an active role in its construction.

Some wise veterans of the special ed world advise you to bear in mind that "special education is a service, not a place." The heart of an IEP is not only deciding *where* your child will be instructed—in the regular classroom, a "resource room," or other setting—but also what the contents of that education will be. Under federal law, a child in special education must have access to the school's regular curriculum. This means that, in addition to whatever specialized learning objectives a youngster may need, the eventual goal is for him to learn what other students are learning. Yes, it may require suitable modifications of instructional strategy and pace. It may also require extra help. All these should be calibrated to the child's own strengths and weaknesses. But whereas special education once focused on ensuring that a disabled youngster simply received "education services," in recent years the emphasis has properly shifted to the content of what that child is learning, the education outcomes that he will attain, the quality of his school experience, and accountability for its results. Figuring all that out should be the core of an IEP.

Not every school system has successfully navigated this change of emphasis, however, so it's important that you remain vigilant. As you help design the education program for your child, keep these questions in mind: Where does it lead? Are its goals closely aligned with the general curriculum and the school's standards? How will we know if it's succeeding? What will be the benchmarks and measures of progress? Who is responsible for its results? What is their track record? When are our opportunities for mid-course corrections?

Deciding on the Placement

Closely tied to these vital decisions about the IEP's content and direction are key judgments about the child's proper "placement"—that is, selection of the appropriate education setting (or settings) in which the plan will be put into effect. Special ed may not be a place, but at any given moment this service has to be provided somewhere.

There are many ways to design special education placements. Lots of combinations and variations are possible, and they may evolve in light of a child's experience and accomplishment.

Most children receive the greater part of their education in the regular classroom. Some remain there full-time, while others leave periodically to work with a special ed teacher in a "resource room" or other setting. Youngsters with more serious disabilities may be in a special ed classroom for much or even all of the day. Depending on the disability, a child may attend classes at a school that specializes in programs tailored to needs such as his. Some disabled youngsters even attend private schools because their parents, often with the help of attorneys, successfully argue that the child's needs cannot be satisfactorily met by the local public school system. (This is a complex and controversial topic but you should be aware that, under federal law and some state laws, publicly financed private schooling is an option for disabled youngsters in circumstances where the public school is unable to provide an appropriate education.)

By law, a disabled student must be educated in the "least restrictive environment," which ordinarily means including him to the maximum possible extent in regular schools and classrooms while recognizing that this placement may mean modifying what happens in those classrooms. The teacher, for example, may need additional training or assistance. The child may also need help in order to succeed in the regular classroom setting. Such help can be fairly straightforward—a desk at the front of the room, for example, or a technological device that assists him to see or hear or get around. (There have been remarkable advances on this front. If your child has a physical disability, make sure you explore the ever-growing array of hardware and software resources.) The help your child requires may also mean additional personnel in school: an instructional aide who joins him in class for part of the day, for example, occasionally even a full-time attendant. If your child is under three, services must be provided in a "natural environment" that's suited to the youngster's needs. (Natural environments mean places like home and child care where children of this age usually spend their days.)

Most special education experts and parents of disabled children feel strongly that the greatest possible inclusion is best. They point out that disabled youngsters benefit from positive interaction with their peers, from having role models and friends, and from the sense that they have not been segregated, isolated, or shunted aside. They note that segregating such children is both unfair and educationally damaging, that teachers may lower their expectations when all their students have disabilities, and that separate special ed classes can mean inferior education for children who are treated, in effect, as second-class students. Mainstreaming, in this view, offers the chance for higher expectations and more challenging studies. It builds confidence and social skills, helps remove the stigma of being a "special ed student," and fosters understanding among nondisabled peers.

At the same time, inclusion or mainstreaming remains controversial. Critics say that researchers have not yet proven that it leads to improved academic outcomes, and that disabled students are more likely to get necessary help in a smaller class that's specifically geared to them. They say it is wrong to place a child in a regular classroom where the teacher is not trained to deal with disabilities and may lack essential help. They say this leads to classroom disruption and can result in inferior education for everyone. A child who is mainstreamed most of the day but occasionally leaves for specialized instruction may miss important lessons while he is away and fall further behind in his regular studies. Mainstreaming, critics maintain, is often little more than an attempt by school systems to save money at the expense of needy students.

That's the controversy. As a parent, you are probably less interested in policy debates than in ensuring that your child has the right placement. You know that what works well for one student may be less successful for another. That's why you must watch carefully to see if your child's needs are being met, wherever it is taking place. Remain focused on the quality of the academic program. What is most important is that he be in a setting where the curriculum is solid, expectations are appropriately high, and he can get the instruction and services that he needs to meet them.

Special education shares with other spheres of American education the problem of underchallenging many students. Parents often go along, either because they aren't aware of how little is actually being expected or because they want their kids to earn good grades, be happy, and avoid stress. This is misguided. What disabled children need most from their schooling is the chance to compensate for and cope with their disabilities, and succeed to the greatest possible extent in spite of them. Education for a disabled youngster should not be primarily about accommodation, social acceptance, or self-esteem, although these are important. It should be about preparing to live successfully in the same world as others. Toward that end, you want your child in a program where he will be called upon to work hard and live up to his full potential.

Looking Out for Your Child

Gather information—and then keep gathering more at every step along the way. Don't settle for just one expert opinion. There are plenty of information sources available. Read. Ask questions. Form your own judgments. Join organizations that have years of experience with the education of disabled children.

Try to find other parents of children with disabilities and seek their assistance. They can advise you about questions to ask school officials and about strategies that have worked for them. They may also provide some welcome emotional support. In fact, you may want to join a parent support group. (A good source is the National Information Center for Children and Youth with Disabilities. See "Where to Get Help and Information," below.)

Parents sometimes find that school systems try to skimp on services for disabled youngsters. You may encounter bureaucratic obstacles. Make sure you are familiar with the pertinent laws and procedures for your school system. Ask the person who oversees special education at your school to explain anything you don't understand. Ask someone who's been through the process before to help you.

As we noted earlier, disabled children and their parents enjoy special legal rights and opportunities. The legal side of special education is its own labyrinth, and it is possible to fall under the sway of an overeager attorney who loves to litigate (and who bills accordingly). Don't rush to put your child's education in the hands of a lawyer. But do recognize, especially if you find that the school system is failing your child and its bureaucracy is balking, that you have options under the law, perhaps most importantly including the right to exercise a very large say in your child's education.

Vigilance is needed. You may work things out satisfactorily one year only to watch them come unglued the next because the school system, the teacher, or your child's needs have changed. That's why the IEP's annual update is valuable, as is the requirement of a periodic reevaluation of your child's condition.

All parents should monitor their children's education closely, but special ed parents doubly so. It's best to view yourself as your child's "case manager." Be prepared not only to participate in the planning of his education, but also, on many occasions, to take the lead. You may have to request conferences with school personnel, tutors, therapists, and psychologists. Do not assume that the specialists will regularly communicate with each other or with the classroom teacher. Do not assume that a carefully devised plan will be carried out with equal care, or that you will be notified of what's not working.

Find out exactly what the teacher is doing and why. Check on the providers of related services and extra help. Watch your child's progress and speak up if he does not make gains. Ask yourself: Is this program really giving him what he needs? No one knows your child like you do. No one else has his interests so much at heart. Be prepared to be an advocate for your child to see that he gets the chances he deserves.

Where to Get Help and Information

Special education is a big territory. There are many different disabilities and many sources of help. The foregoing discussion only begins to explore this landscape. Here are some resources that can help you learn more.

Books

Negotiating the Special Education Maze: A Guide for Parents and Teachers, Winifred Anderson, Stephen Chitwood, and Deidre Hayden (Woodbine House, 1997).

ADHD: Questions and Answers for Parents, Gregory S. Greenberg and Wade F. Horn (Research Press, 1991).

Magazines

Exceptional Parent
P.O. Box 2079
Marion, OH 43301
877-372-7368
www.eparent.com

Exceptional Parent is a general magazine for parents of disabled children. Many of the following organizations, which concentrate on specific disabilities, publish their own newsletters or magazines.

Disability Solutions
9220 SW Barbur Blvd.
#119-179
Portland, OR 97219
www.disabilitysolutions.org

Disability Solutions brings current research, medical information, education strategies, and practical suggestions to readers in language that is easily understood.

Organizations

National Information Center for Children and Youth with Disabilities
P.O. Box 1492
Washington, DC 20013
800-695-0285
www.nichcy.org

National Parent Network on Disabilities
1130 17th Street NW, Suite 400
Washington, DC 20036
202-463-2299
www.npnd.org

Parent Training and Information Centers and
Community Groups in the United States
This is a network of centers that offer training and information to parents
of children with disabilities and the professionals who work with them. To
locate a parent center in your state, you can contact:
Alliance Coordinating Office
PACER Center
4826 Chicago Avenue South
Minneapolis, MN 55417-1098
888-248-0822
www.taalliance.org

The Beach Center on Families and Disability
University of Kansas
3111 Haworth
Lawrence, KS 66045
785-864-7600
www.lsi.ukans.edu/beach

The Council for Exceptional Children
1920 Association Drive
Reston, VA 20191-1589
888-CEC-SPED
www.cec.sped.org

If your child is very young, contact the Council for Exceptional Children's
Division for Early Childhood
1380 Lawrence Street, Suite 650
Denver, CO 80204
303-556-3328
www.dec@ceo.cudenver.edu

U.S. Department of Education
Office of Special Education and Rehabilitative Services
www.ed.gov/offices/OSERS

Federation of Families for Children's Mental Health
1021 Prince Street
Alexandria, VA 22314
703-684-7710
www.ffcmh.org

National Association of Private Schools for Exceptional Children
1522 K Street NW, Suite 1032
Washington, DC 20005
202-408-3338
www.napsec.com

TASH (formerly The Association for Persons with Severe Handicaps)
29 West Susquehanna Avenue, Suite 210
Baltimore, MD 21204
410-828-8274
www.tash.org

Learning Disabilities Association of America
4156 Library Road
Pittsburgh, PA 15234-1349
412-341-1515
www.ldanatl.org

National Attention Deficit Disorder Association
P.O. Box 1303
Northbrook, IL 60065-1303
www.add.org

The International Dyslexia Association
Chester Building, Suite 382
8600 LaSalle Road
Baltimore, MD 21286-2044
410-296-0232
www.interdys.org

National Easter Seal Society
230 West Monroe Street
Suite 1800
Chicago, IL 60606
800-221-6827
www.easter-seals.org

American Council of the Blind
1155 15th Street NW, Suite 720
Washington, DC 20005
800-424-8666
www.acb.org

American Foundation for the Blind
11 Penn Plaza, Suite 300
New York, NY 10001
1-800-AFB-LINE
www.afb.org

National Association of the Deaf
814 Thayer Avenue
Silver Spring, MD 20910
301-587-1788
www.nad.org

Autism Society of America
7910 Woodmont Avenue, Suite 300
Bethesda, MD 20814
301-657-0881
www.autism-society.org

Brain Injury Association
105 North Alfred Street
Alexandria, VA 22314
703-236-6000
www.biausa.org

National Down Syndrome Society
666 Broadway
New York, NY 10012
800-221-4602
www.ndss.org

GIFTED CHILDREN

Having a gifted child is a blessing that carries unique responsibilities for parents. Special talents must be nurtured if they are to bloom. Regrettably, schools do not always recognize unusual potential in a youngster. Most schools are geared to the average or typical student. That means moms and dads must take the lead in making sure that gifted youngsters get the education they deserve.

There is no single set of criteria to identify "giftedness" in children. The term can mean students who excel academically, either in all subjects or in a specific area. Some children, for example, might be average students in English and history, while possessing a terrific aptitude for science. Children can also have gifts in nonacademic areas. Yours may be no great mathematician but a fine musician or athlete. He may, in fact, have a disability together with extra intellectual talents. Special needs and special gifts coexist more often than you might suppose.

Gifted children (particularly those who are gifted intellectually) often exhibit many of the following traits:

- Show a burning curiosity and thirst for knowledge.
- Grasp concepts quickly and get impatient with repetition.
- Are creative thinkers and problem solvers.
- Are keenly observant.
- Possess a great store of information about a variety of topics.
- Look for and welcome challenging tasks.
- Become deeply absorbed in work that interests them.
- Want their work to be perfect.
- Enjoy games that involve thought, reasoning, and playing with ideas.
- Have an expansive vocabulary.
- Learn faster than other children.
- Can do schoolwork well beyond their grade level.
- Get easily bored with schoolwork that's not challenging enough.

Many children show some of these signs on occasion, but gifted youngsters possess several such traits to an unusual extent, and frequently exhibit them.

Gifted children are not always easy to recognize in school. Sometimes, as you would expect, a gifted child is a "model" pupil, the extremely bright, articulate kid at the head of the class who breezes through assignments and always has his hand in the air to offer the right answer. Sometimes, though, it's just the opposite: the youngster who gets into trouble, doesn't bother to do homework, and doesn't pay attention in class. (In the latter case, giftedness is only one possible explanation for this pattern of behavior. It may also arise from problems such as lack of discipline, insufficient supervision at home, a learning disability, or emotional troubles.)

Sometimes parents discover that their child already knows most of the curriculum that's being taught to him. This is a clear sign that something is out of alignment. In all likelihood, one of two things is going on.

On the one hand, the teacher or school may have low expectations—an all too common tendency in American education. "We recently did a study in which we tested a local school's third graders on a math unit the teacher was about to start," reports Phyllis Aldrich, a gifted education specialist in upstate New York. "Before the teacher had even begun the unit, we found that 60 percent of the students knew 90 percent of the material. This was an average, heterogeneous group of kids. This is a far more prevalent problem than we had ever imagined ten years ago." Talk to the parents of your child's classmates. Do a significant number say that their children are rarely challenged? If so, you need to seek an arrangement that offers higher standards for all. (See "Low Standards and Expectations," page 492.)

On the other hand, if your child is the only one in his class, or one of a handful, who regularly seems to know most of the material ahead of time, he may indeed be intellectually gifted. You'll want to take steps to ensure that he's learning at a level appropriate to his ability and attainments. Keep in mind, though, that there is no single right approach for educating such youngsters. The key is to find a setting in which the child is stretched but not overwhelmed. "All children learn best when they are challenged to a moderate degree," says Aldrich. "If schoolwork is too easy, they tune out, learn to underachieve, and don't develop intellectual muscle. If the work is too hard, they also tune out."

Options for Gifted Students

If your child possesses a special talent, a teacher may spot it and approach you. Often, however, it is parents who first identify giftedness. Mothers and fathers, after all, are most aware of their children's abilities.

If you think your child shows unusual promise in a certain area, it is a good idea to keep a portfolio or record of behavior. Make it as specific as possible so that when you approach the school, you will have evidence. Simply saying "I think my child is really good at math" is not particularly persuasive. It's much better if you can point out that "my second grader has invented a fraction system and applied it to measuring gas on our family trip."

Make an appointment with the teacher and find out whether she believes your child has special abilities. The teacher, principal, or guidance counselor should be able to give you information about what sorts of school programs are available for gifted children. If you think one of these may be best for your child, ask that he be considered for it.

Your child may have to take some tests to qualify for a gifted and talented program. Sometimes the school administers an intelligence test, as well as tests to measure achievement and creativity. Teacher recommendations, grades, and samples of student work also may be considered. The procedure differs from place to place. If the school turns your child down for a gifted program, you might want to have him tested by a private psychologist. (Ask your pediatrician to help you locate a good one.) Sometimes an independent evaluation helps convince a school that a student's talents need extra nurturing.

Here are some of the approaches that schools take in teaching gifted students. Some schools have an "enrichment specialist" who can be helpful in suggesting a good path for a particular youngster.

- **Pull-out program.** A child is removed from his regular class every so often (perhaps an hour a day, maybe just an hour a week) to work in a small group of talented students. A teacher provides special instruction and activities.

    Be sure to inquire about the activities that occur in such a pull-out program. They may lack intellectual rigor. Some schools adopt them merely as a way to placate parents who are dissatisfied with the regular curriculum. The content itself isn't significantly different.

- **Ability grouping within a class.** A teacher may segment a heterogeneous class into smaller instructional groups of similar ability or achievement for part of the day. For example, students who are reading at a level well ahead of their classmates might be brought together to talk about the more advanced book they are tackling.

- **Tracking.** Some schools organize their classrooms according to students' speed or prior achievement. Sometimes this is done for a few selected subjects, sometimes for the entire curriculum.

- **"Gifted and talented" or "honors" program.** In some schools, a certain number of children attend special classes designed for gifted and talented students. The curriculum in these classes is accelerated and enriched. Sometimes they are linked to intellectually challenging high school programs such as the International Baccalaureate.

- **Content acceleration.** Teachers match individual children with more challenging materials so they can pursue studies at a faster pace and greater depth. A gifted student may go to a learning center with more advanced material in a corner of the regular classroom, or he may go to a room across the hall where three other children join him for acceleration in a specific subject such as math or reading.

- **Advancing a grade.** Sometimes parents and teachers decide that the best way to help a gifted child is for him to skip a grade. He might move to a higher grade for just one or two subjects, or for all subjects. Parents must weigh the possible social and emotional impact that such a move might have. While some kids do fine moving ahead, for others it turns out to be an unhappy experience. They miss their friends and feel out of place.

- **Special schools.** In some communities, you'll find whole schools that serve gifted and talented children. These may be magnet schools for pupils who show talent in certain areas such as science or the humanities. (Such schools more often serve high school and middle school students than primary school pupils.) Today, the options may also include charter schools with particular curricular or pedagogical specialties.

The school may wish for a gifted child to remain in his regular classroom while receiving special instruction and extra assignments. Note, though, that this ought not mean simply giving him a larger dose of the same work the class is doing. The goal is to challenge his abilities, rouse his curiosity, and exercise his creativity, not just do more worksheets. He needs to be able to look deeply into topics of interest and most likely pursue independent projects. It takes skill to orchestrate and oversee a gifted student's activities within the regular classroom setting. You may need to seek out teachers known for their ability to provide extra challenges to their quicker pupils.

Opportunities for gifted children are by no means limited to school. You may want to find a tutor or mentor who is expert in the area your child excels in. Check with local colleges. They often sponsor terrific enrichment programs for gifted youngsters, usually beginning around seventh grade. Some summer camps specialize in serving very able children.

Look for after-school and weekend activities (e.g., computer clubs, art classes) that cater to your child's special talent or interest. Make extra trips to the library, visit places of cultural interest, help your child find challenging books and software. A gifted and talented program at school is great, but it's not absolutely necessary—or sufficient—to stimulate a child's potential. Much depends on your efforts.

Being an Advocate for Your Gifted Child

Some schools do a good job teaching youngsters with exceptional abilities. Many do not. Most teachers are not specially trained to work with gifted youngsters. They may even see such children as bothersome because they ask endless questions, are restless, or just don't fit in. This is nothing new. Even Albert Einstein was considered a "slow learner" as a kid. Most school curricula are set up to educate groups of "ordinary" students. The individual who is somehow out of step—even if it's because he's brilliant—may get lost in the shuffle.

Politics enter this topic, too. Some educators and parents harbor a bias against special treatment for gifted children. Those kids are already fortunate, they say, and don't need extra help. They can make it on their own. In some circles, the whole notion that some children are "gifted" and others not is deemed inequitable or politically incorrect. Programs for gifted students are viewed as bestowing special privileges on a select few.

Public education in the U.S. today is hypersensitive to such charges of elitism. More often than not, therefore, schools end up neglecting their intellectually gifted pupils on "equity" grounds. State standards may also cause school systems to concentrate their resources on youngsters who lag behind rather than those who can easily clear the bar. It has become fashionable in many school systems today to abolish all forms of tracking and ability grouping. (See "Tracking," page 612.)

Though we don't like some forms of tracking, the fact is that few teachers can do justice to children of widely varying abilities and achievement levels in the same classroom at the same time. In such situations, they tend to focus on students in the middle and devote any leftover attention to those who need help to catch up. Gifted youngsters may be left to fend for themselves. This is wrong. Schools should provide the best possible education to every student, the swift as well as the slow, the eager as much as the reluctant. If they are not challenged, gifted children may come to associate school with boredom. If neglected, there is a chance that a youngster's unusual talent will wither or his lively interest wane.

If you are like most parents, you care less about the need to have your child labeled "gifted" and more about the reality of the challenges confronting him in his daily work. Do not automatically assume that the school will do a good job in supplying that challenge. In fact, you can count on few schools doing as good a job as you may wish. That's why you must take charge. Be prepared to advocate for your child and do whatever is necessary to augment (and perhaps alter) what the school supplies.

One strategy you might use in approaching administrators is to ask for equal opportunity for your child to have access to a challenging curriculum. Base your request on the need for "equity." Make clear that you are not asking for something extra or special (which could be interpreted as "elitism"). Simply state that you want for your gifted child the exact same situation that parents of other children want, i.e., an optimal match between the curriculum and the child's abilities. In other words, you are asking that your child have the chance to work just as hard as the average child. When administrators see that parents are not seeking a special break but rather an equal opportunity, they may find the request more palatable.

If there is no gifted and talented program at your school, look around—there may be one nearby. Talk with the principal and even school board members if you must. Don't be obnoxious, but make your expectations clear. It's not out of the question that your school can be persuaded to create a gifted/talented program of some kind, or that a teacher might agree to do some extra work with able youngsters. Contact one of the organizations listed below, which give advice to parents striving to get the best educations for their children. If there is someone in the superintendent's office who oversees gifted programs, get in touch with him. Make sure you rally other sympathetic parents to your side. In many places, programs for gifted students have come about largely because parents banded together to lobby for them.

A word of caution is also in order. In your desire to obtain the best possible education for your child, you may place excessive pressure on him. There is a difference between making sure he is challenged and making him feel overwhelmed and badgered. Even gifted children need to be children—need time to play and relax and hang out with other kids. It's also worth noting that many parents *want* their young ones to be gifted, sometimes more gifted (or gifted in different ways) than they actually are. By all means help your child be all that he can, but don't press him so hard that he feels like a failure when his achievements don't match your dreams.

Where to Get Help and Information

Here are some good books, periodicals, and organizations where parents can get more information about educating gifted children.

Books

Guiding the Gifted, J. T. Webb, E. A. Meckstroth, and S. S. Tolan (Gifted Psychology Press, 1994).

Your Gifted Child: How to Recognize and Develop the Special Talents in Your Special Child from Birth to Age Seven, J. F. Smutny, K. Veenker, and S. Veenker (Ballantine Books, 1989).

Teaching Gifted Kids in the Regular Classroom, S. Winebrenner (Free Spirit Publishing, 1992).

Magazines

Understanding Our Gifted, Open Space Communications, Boulder, Colorado, 800-494-6178

Gifted Child Today, Waco, Texas, 800-998-2208, www.prufrock.com

Organizations

The Center for Talented Youth
Institute for the Advancement of Youth
Johns Hopkins University
3400 North Charles Street
Baltimore, MD 21218
410-516-0337
www.jhu.edu/gifted

Hoagie's Gifted Education Page
www.hoagiesgifted.org

The National Association for Gifted Children
1707 L Street NW, Suite 550
Washington, DC 20036
202-785-4268
www.nagc.org

The National Research Center on the Gifted and Talented
University of Connecticut
362 Fairfield Road, U-7
Storrs, CT 06269-2007
860-486-4676
www.gifted.uconn.edu

CHAPTER 12

School Problems

THE COURSE OF EDUCATION DOES NOT ALWAYS RUN SMOOTH.
For most children, there are at least a few bumps along the way, sometimes caused by problems associated with the school itself. Things can
go awry even in schools that enjoy a good reputation. In bad schools,
they go awry much of the time. This chapter takes a look at three of the
most worrisome troubles you may encounter: low standards, bad teaching, and poor discipline.

Keep your eyes open for the symptoms described here. If you spot
them at your school, focus some energy on addressing them. Don't wait
for someone else to tackle the problem. It may be tempting to ignore it,
to tell yourself it's not really so bad, or to believe those who assure you
that "everything is fine." Turning a blind eye is likely to have consequences, though. If these school problems are left unattended, they can
do serious damage to your child's education.

LOW STANDARDS AND EXPECTATIONS

Low academic standards plague many elementary and secondary schools.
Signs of the dumbing down of American education abound. High school
graduates show up at college struggling with basic skills, stumped by adverbs and bewildered by fractions. Nationwide, about three in ten college freshmen are enrolled in some sort of remedial class.

Nearly two out of three high schoolers say they do not try very hard
to succeed in class, and half report that teachers do not insist on high
academic standards. "I didn't do one piece of homework last year in

math," says a California teenager. "I just took the tests. I'd get A's on the tests, not do the homework, and I got a B in class. There's just lots of ways to get around it."[1] Another student observes: "They practically hand you the diploma. If you had to work harder for it, then you would be actually learning something, rather than just staying in school for 180 days."[2]

Low expectations often begin long before high school. Students grow accustomed to losing no points for improper spelling or misused words. They take social studies classes that serve up lightweight treatments of history. ("The unit on the Revolutionary War culminated with an assignment to draw a picture of what 'revolution' means to you," says the suburban mom of an eighth grader.) They're measured by standards that put less emphasis on knowing scientific information and give decreased attention to memorizing math rules.

Grades rise as expectations fall. "In my class, if the students make even half an effort, they'll get an A or a B," says veteran English teacher Gail Reynolds. "These kids would have had to work very hard for a C twenty years ago. We're accepting less and less."[3]

The education establishment supports in principle the idea of expecting more from students. Then it balks when anyone actually tries to uphold or enforce meaningful standards. High expectations run counter to several dominant philosophies in the schools. Children must be allowed to develop at their own pace, it is said. Imposing others' expectations on them violates that process. Since every child is unique, his or her own standards for work must be respected. "Experts" assert that grade school children aren't ready for challenging lessons. Asking them to learn something that is "developmentally inappropriate" may harm them intellectually or emotionally. A rigorous curriculum may bruise their self-esteem and dampen their interest in learning.

Saddest of all is the view that high expectations are unfair because many students—particularly disadvantaged students—simply cannot meet them. A New York education school professor puts it this way: "Standards can sometimes be used to punish individuals. . . . [It] becomes a hammer to hit those people who did not make it. And that is not what you want education to be about."[4] This is a tragically damaging attitude, because disadvantaged children, like all youngsters, do better when adults expect a lot of them. Nonetheless, the "solution" is often to lower schools' expectations for those students, thereby dooming them to a bad education. Some schools drop their standards for everyone and then proclaim "success for all." It's like lowering the basketball hoop to make it *look* like everyone's a great player.

Do not automatically blame your child's instructors. Some may expect too little, but as a whole, no group is more frustrated with declining standards than teachers. Many are troubled by having to face classrooms in which significant numbers of children are not prepared at home to put forth their best efforts. They are frustrated at having to fight off administrators and parents who claim they want higher expectations, but whose first reaction when children don't meet them is: give these kids a break. "What happens in reality is that when several students fail, the principal hears from their parents," says one veteran Texas teacher. "The students and their parents make wild claims about the unfairness of the teacher. Instead of supporting the teacher's high standards, the principal runs to the teacher and requires him to 'dumb down' his course. When teachers are not supported by administrators, there is no possible way for us to keep our standards high."

Parents and educators all need to recognize the critical link between expectations and achievement. The attitudes adults have about what students can learn often become self-fulfilling prophecies. Those who communicate high expectations get greater academic performance from children. Those who set low standards get little in return.

Too often in American education, we forget that attaining high standards means doing *hard work*. We place too much emphasis on making learning fun. We all want school to be interesting and pleasant for children, but the aim should not be to satisfy a child's appetite for recreation. In some places, it seems as if there are no such things as "studies" and "assignments" anymore, just "activities" and "projects" that kids will find entertaining. As John Henry Cardinal Newman reminded us, "Do not say that people must be educated when, after all, you only mean amused, refreshed, soothed, put into good spirits and good humor, or kept from vicious excesses." Such occupations of the mind have their place, but they are not education.

Almost nothing of lasting value comes easy or free, and the continued pretense in many schools that learning is possible without persistent effort has had devastating consequences. The work ethic is at the core of the American tradition. It needs to be reinvigorated in American education.

Parents should expect educators to offer youngsters really good books, significant lessons, and challenging problems. Why? Because when offered with enthusiasm, such studies engage children. And be-

cause what students read and talk about in school will—one hopes—
profoundly influence their lives. We must influence them with the best
we have to offer. As the essayist John Ruskin said, education is the leading of human souls to what is best. There are many fine books, ideas,
and lessons worth our youngsters' time and attention. The list is long,
so there is no point in settling for mediocre fare. Schools should compete for the attention of the mind and heart by offering a quality product. Cheaper goods are available elsewhere.

Living up to solid standards is harder for some students than others.
After all, children come to school with different abilities and backgrounds. For some, it will take more time on task. It may take different
teaching strategies. But all students deserve a chance at rich and fulfilling learning. The late Albert Shanker, president of the American Federation of Teachers, told of asking a class of average and less than
average students: What should we give you to read? After a pause, one
student raised his hand and asked: Mr. Shanker, what do the smart kids
read? "If we adjust class content up or down to the differences students
come to us with, we will perpetuate those differences," Shanker reminded us. "If we expect all students to master a rich common core curriculum, there will still be differences, but they will be narrower."

The essential point is that virtually all students can meet solid standards if they know what is expected of them, work hard, and receive encouragement from caring adults. Requiring any less is selling children
short. A teacher in a Virginia school summed up her approach this way:
"Every time I set a really high expectation, the students have risen to
the challenge." That is the philosophy you want to see at work in your
child's school.

A Fifth Grader Asks Her Own Questions

A fifth grader wrote this letter to the editor of her hometown newspaper.
Does it remind you of your school?

I'm having fun in fifth grade in District 41.

In social studies my whole class made Indian shields, deerskins, and
villages, and 3-D caravel models. We also made collages from gold-
colored magazine cutouts and we colored and pasted sea serpent window
pictures.

In math we did worksheets with mazes and decoding of secret words
and sentences. We interviewed twenty people and made a picture of a
wolf for graphing. We've practiced about forty math problems. . . .

In reading we read the book *Lizard Music* out loud. If we lost our place, we had to do something silly, like skip around the room and sing "Happy Birthday" or say the Barney Song out an open window. . . .

For the last half hour each day we play games like Scattergories. We also make up our own gameboards, like "What would you do." Some kids actually stuck their faces in whipped cream and other kids sprayed Silly String on their clothes.

The question I have is why is fifth grade so easy? Why do some third grade kids at day care have harder work and more homework than I do? Why are some school projects like day care projects?

I'm going to middle school next year and I'm scared. My teachers don't believe in assigning homework, so I won't be ready for sixth grade. . . .

When I was eight, I swam more than 100 lengths a night on swim team. It wasn't fun, but it takes hard work to get good at something. In gymnastics I have to practice a lot to learn new skills. How do I get good at school, if we do mostly art projects, plays, and games? Shouldn't school be different from day care?

P.S. My mom helped me with this letter. She said real writers write for a reason about something that matters to them and for an audience.

Are Your Child's Textbooks Challenging?

One of the surest signs of decaying standards is the dumbing down of schoolbooks. The gradual simplification of student reading material has been going on for decades. James Michener, who once worked as a textbook editor, testified to the decline: "What I had once helped write as a suitable book for students in the sixth grade gradually became a book intended for grades seven through eight. Texts originally for middle grades began to be certified as being appropriate for high school students, and what used to be a high school text appeared as a college text. The entire educational process was watered down, level by level."[5] You can verify the trend yourself. The next time you're in a good used book store or library, try to lay your hands on a school reader from several decades ago. Compare it to one of today's texts. You'll almost certainly find that the old reader contains richer language and selections that encourage more sophisticated thinking.

Today, textbooks are designed according to the theory that modern kids have short attention spans and learn best when amused. More and more pictures fill the pages. "Text is a slow medium of gaining information; a picture is a very quick way," says a designer of children's books.

"By spending more time with the picture and less with the text, which we place right next to the image, kids absorb a lot more information quickly."[6] With that kind of fatuous recipe, no wonder reading skills of American youngsters aren't what they should be. "There's no question that every time we have to adopt a textbook, the reading level of the book is lower than the last," says John E. Stone, a Tennessee education professor. Research has found that schoolbooks for students beyond third grade have been simplified to their lowest level ever in this country.

Not surprisingly, research also indicates that more challenging books—those that are written at or just above the student's level—lead to better reading achievement. Reading expert Jeanne S. Chall and others have found that students who use more demanding textbooks tend to score higher on their SATs. Books used in the first few years of school seem to make the greatest difference.[7]

Clearly, parents of elementary school students should open their children's textbooks to find out just how challenging, or dumbed down, they are. If they strike you as simplistic or juvenile, talk with the teacher. Perhaps a change can be made. If not, you can surely supplement the school's choice of books with some better ones from a library or bookstore—or possibly from the teacher herself.

How to Gauge Your School's Expectations

Don't assume that your school's academic standards are high. Even institutions that enjoy good reputations in their communities may have low expectations. Here are some ways to find out how your school measures up.

- **Look at the school's standards of learning.** Academic goals should be written down for every grade, and should be readily available. Do they seem reasonably demanding? Are they clearly communicated to students and parents? (See "Checking On Your School's Standards of Learning," page 94.)

   Is the school actually teaching what it claims to be? Is it sticking to its written academic standards? Some schools show parents a blueprint of a good education, but don't really hold students accountable for those learning goals.

- **Look at textbooks, other instructional materials, and students' work.** Are your child's books and assignments sufficiently demanding, or is he bored by them? Try to look at other pupils' work, too—

displays in the classrooms and hallways, science fair exhibits, art show entries, writing in the school newspaper. Do assignments and projects seem appropriate for the students' grade level? Is serious learning the rule or the exception?

- **Ask to see examples of good work.** Ask the teacher to show you samples of papers or tests that received 'A's. These will be a good indication of her academic expectations.

  If necessary, look at samples of student work from other schools with strong reputations. (Your best bet may be to get in touch with parents of children at those schools.) How does it compare with the work your child is being asked to do? Does your child seem to be learning as much?

- **Find out how students at your school do on state and national tests.** Ask for information about where your school ranks or how many of its students do well on tests given throughout the state or district. The principal's office should be able to get you such data, although of course they will not tell you the grades or scores of individual students. Ask also for information about attendance rates and grade retention rates at your school.

  Some states now issue "report cards" on individual public schools. Often, though, parents must push to get answers—and then wade through cryptic numbers to find meaningful information. If your school is not used to parents asking for a clear explanation of its performance (or if officials have a poor record to hide), you may encounter resistance. Explain patiently that you need some way to judge your school's strong and weak points. If you don't understand the information you're given, ask someone at school to go over it with you. If that doesn't work, track down an education expert or activist in your community, or surf the Internet for one of the many lively parent discussion groups.

- **Visit your child's classes and watch teachers in action.** Set up occasional appointments to sit in the back of the room and observe. Are important lessons being taught? Are they challenging? Do teachers tell children what they must learn?

  Good teachers expect a lot from kids. They send the message: "I won't settle for less than your best efforts." They have a "can do" attitude, and they foster that same outlook among children. They teach students that, if they try hard, they can succeed beyond their own expectations.

- **Talk with other parents.** Ask them if their youngsters are being challenged. Are they satisfied with the school's academic goals? What do they see as its strengths and weaknesses?

- **Talk with your child.** Does he find the work challenging and interesting? Or does he consider most assignments easy and get through them quickly, even casually? Does he find many activities silly, or complain that the class is studying the same lessons covered last year?

- **Talk with the principal.** Good schools have principals who are fierce advocates of high standards. A good principal can spell out an academic vision for the school. She can tell you what she expects of children, and how she knows whether or not students are reaching those goals.

- **Visit a school with a good reputation in your area.** Call the principal's office and ask if you can sit in on a class or two—preferably at your child's grade level. Look at samples of student work on display. By visiting one or two nearby schools, you'll get a better feel for how your own stacks up.

- **Take notice of academic contests.** Does the school ever enter its students in competitions or exhibitions with other schools—essay contests, geography bees, math olympics, science fairs, art shows? If so, how do children from your school fare in such events? Or does your school shun all forms of academic competition and comparison?

- **See if your school prepares students well for high school.** Good high schools are often a mirror of good elementary schools. Ask the superintendent's office to give you information on SAT or ACT scores, average daily student attendance, and the dropout rate for high schools in your district. What percentage of students go to college? How many go to selective colleges? You might also talk to high school teachers about whether your elementary school is sending them well-educated students.

Press your school to set solid academic goals. In surveys, the American public supports the idea of high standards. In practice, it's often a different story. Parents frequently hold low academic expectations for their own children and schools. Accordingly, U.S. students have less motivation to study hard, and schools have little incentive to offer a quality education. A study by the research organization Public Agenda illustrates part of the problem. It found that only 36 percent of parents think that a person who knows virtually nothing about America's history or Founding Fathers might have trouble being a good citizen. Just 58 percent of parents say it is essential that schools teach kids that a representative government is the best system for Americans. "The schools should concentrate more on things that everybody uses in their daily life, rather than on who the president was," says a Birmingham woman. "Sure, I think history is important, but I think they should concentrate more on how to go out and get a job, more than the history."[8] No wonder so many American schools neglect academic basics.

Let the principal and teachers know that you support rigorous standards and are serious about academics. Stand behind good educators who get grief from parents for "expecting too much." Don't join the crowd that says "history and literature aren't practical, anyway," the group that looks the other way when schools lower the bar. There is always a side of human nature that tends toward the easy route. But that way teaches only lack of desire to strive for what is worth knowing and having. It is the more strenuous path, the one on which parents and teachers bring youngsters up to high standards, that leads to a good education. That's the one you want for your child.

Warning Signs of Low Expectations

Here are some signs that your school's academic standards are low:

- Expectations are not clearly communicated to students and parents.
- Relatively little time is spent on core academic subjects.
- Students are passed along from grade to grade even if academic goals are not reached.
- Books and handouts are simple.
- Tests and assignments are usually easy.
- Teachers give little or no homework.
- Discipline is poor.
- Good grades are given for mediocre work.
- Standardized test scores are low.
- Attendance rates are poor.
- Many students are bored by the pace of learning.

Fighting Low Expectations

If you sense that your child isn't learning enough, first try to diagnose the problem. You may be facing a single slack teacher or two within an otherwise sound school. In that case, the chances of improving your child's situation are relatively good. (See "Bad Teaching," page 505.)

If the problem goes beyond one or two teachers, the remedy becomes more difficult. Some schools have "gifted and talented" or "enrichment" programs for children who need greater challenges. Talk with the principal about options for students who are ready to move forward at a quicker pace. Be aware, though, that in poor schools, programs with high-minded titles can still have low expectations.

If mediocre standards are limited to just one subject, you may be surprised to discover how much ground you can make up at home. Get some books on that subject and make sure your child studies them. Look for summer and weekend programs he can attend for supplementary learning. Pay frequent visits to libraries and bookstores. Plan your own field trips to museums and historic sites. Devise special projects and assignments for your child. You may need to engage a tutor, perhaps a college student or retired teacher.

Unfortunately, the problem of low standards may be so pervasive in your school that supplementing at home isn't sufficient. If the situation is bad enough, get your child out of it. Find another school. The education system in this country sometimes makes that difficult for parents, but you'll probably find at least one or two options if you are willing to do some extra legwork—and perhaps some extra driving. Here are five possibilities:

- **Explore other public schools.** You may be able to avail yourself of a district or state "open enrollment" policy. A number of states now permit children to attend essentially any public school in the state, no matter what district it's located in. Some districts permit some or all children to choose schools within the district. Some have reciprocity agreements with adjoining districts, under which they accept each other's students. Even where these plans are not in place, it's often possible for parents to petition for their own child to change schools.

  To be sure, changing public schools can be a policy maze and a political dogfight, and the school system may try to foil you at every turn. You may need to find an outside advocacy organization, perhaps even an attorney. But chances are decent that, if you present yourself at the superintendent's office and say "Our present school is completely unacceptable and if necessary we will move out of this district to escape it. What are our options short of moving?" you will at least get a whiff of other possibilities in and around the public system.

- **Look for a public charter school.** Charter schools are independent public schools created by parents, teachers, or community groups. They operate free of many state and local regulations, and, in return, promise to meet the achievement goals stated in their charters. These schools do not yet exist everywhere, but every year more communities have some. If you consider one, check it out carefully, as you would any school. Most charter schools pursue distinctive education philosophies. You may not find yourself in agreement, but you may also find one that suits you well. Charter schools do not charge tuition. They are funded with tax dollars. (See "More About Charter Schools," page 504.)

- **Look into magnet schools.** Magnet schools are public schools that specialize in a particular subject area (such as math and science, or the arts) or stress a particular teaching approach. Some are established for gifted students, others for children who've had academic troubles. Sometimes they were founded to encourage voluntary racial integration by attracting youngsters from different backgrounds to attend school together. Whatever their specialty, the idea is that they will draw students from all over the district—hence their name.

  Ask at the superintendent's office if there are magnet schools within your school system and how to gain entrance. Bear in mind that the district may be required to keep a certain racial balance in each school or to take a certain number of youngsters from each neighborhood. Good magnet schools often have to turn applicants away.

- **Consider a private school.** Though the label "private" doesn't guarantee educational excellence, private schools are the long-established alternative to public schools. The U.S. has more than 25,000 of them, including some in every state and almost every sizable community.

  Private schools charge tuition, but they're not all super-pricey. The costliest are usually the "independent" schools, while "parochial" schools with religious ties of various sorts are often priced below $3,000 per year. Financial aid is frequently available. A number of parochial schools welcome youngsters who do not follow the school's faith. Parents should be aware, however, that they may try to teach all their students the tenets of that faith.

- **Teach your own child.** Between one-half million and two million U.S. children are home-schooled, at least for part of their education, and the number is growing. It's not unusual to encounter a youngster who was home-schooled for a few years, in public schools for a few years, possibly also in private or charter schools for a time. Some parents find that home schooling is something they can realistically undertake for part but not all of their child's education. A parent who is home with a new baby or toddler anyway may also be able to teach the seven-year-old. Some public (and charter) schools are willing to help home schoolers gain access to instructional materials; a few actually operate part-time schools so that a child may, for example, be home-schooled in the three Rs and history but come to school for science, art, and band. (See "More About Home Schooling," below.)

No matter where your child is schooled, maintaining your own high expectations is crucial. Talk to your child about the importance of trying his hardest. Set rules about doing homework, studying for tests, and completing assignments thoroughly. Nothing inspires endeavor more than a parent urging a child forward. When youngsters do not hear that call, they may quickly get into academic trouble. Remember: *It is extremely difficult—nearly impossible—for teachers at school to make up for low expectations at home.*

More About Home Schooling

Here are some good resources for parents interested in learning more about home schooling.

Books

The Basic Steps to Successful Homeschooling, Vicki Brady (Vital Issues Press, 1996)—Nuts and bolts guide to setting up a home-study program.
Family Matters: Why Homeschooling Makes Sense, David Guterson (Harvest Books, 1993)—A broad overview of the philosophical and political arguments for (and against) home schooling.

Homeschooling: A Patchwork of Days, Nancy Lande (WindyCreek, 1996)—Covers the experiences of 30 families who have home-schooled. Provides examples of daily schedules.

The Homeschooling Handbook: From Preschool to High School, A Parents' Guide, Mary Griffith (Prima Publishing, 1999)—Includes helpful examples of lesson plans and activities.

Should I Home School?: How to Decide What's Right for You and Your Child, Elizabeth and Dan Hamilton (Intervarsity Press, 1997)—Offers an introduction to many of the specifics involved with homeschooling.

The Successful Homeschool Family Handbook: A Creative and Stress-Free Approach to Homeschooling, Raymond and Dorothy Moore (Thomas Nelson, 1994)—Provides a good general introduction to homeschooling.

Web Sites

Homeschooling Resources for Parents and Students (www.accesseric.org/resources/parent/homesc2.html) Highlights magazines, newspapers, electronic sources, and books useful to parents who teach their children at home.

Home Schooling Legal Defense Association (www.hslda.org)—This advocacy organization's Web site gives a good introduction to home schooling issues and news.

More About Charter Schools

Here are some good resources for parents interested in finding out more about charter schools. Some focus on particular states, but all parents are apt to find them informative about this fast-changing domain of U.S. education.

California Network of Educational Charters (CANEC)
1139 San Carlos Ave, #304
San Carlos, CA 94070
650-654-6003
www.canec.org
Although California-focused, this site also provides national charter links.

Center for Education Reform
1001 Connecticut Ave., NW, Suite 204
Washington, DC 20036
800-521-2118
www.edreform.com
A comprehensive site with news and resources on charter schools.

Charter Schools Development Center
Institute for Education Reform, California State University
6000 J Street
Sacramento, CA 95819-6018
916-278-6069
www.csus.edu/ier/charter/charter.html
Provides technical assistance and resources to charter school developers,
operators, and charter-granting agencies in California and nationally. Also
gives information on how to order Eric Premack's *The Charter School Development Guide*, a useful guide to starting a charter school.

Massachusetts Charter School Handbook
The Pioneer Institute
85 Devonshire Street, 8th Floor
Boston, MA 02109
617-723-2277
www.pioneerinstitute.org/csrc/cshand.htm
A useful handbook from one of the best state-based charter school technical assistance centers.

U.S. Charter Schools
c/o WestEd
730 Harrison Street
San Francisco, CA 94107
415-565-3000
www.uscharterschools.org
Contains an overview of charter schools with resources and links to research sites.

BAD TEACHING

When all is said and done, the teacher is the single most significant factor in how much learning takes place at school. Nothing matters more to academic success than good teachers. Their influence is enormous. Your child may well spend more time listening to, talking with, and taking cues from teachers than any other adult outside the home. Fortunately for U.S. parents, this country is blessed with many fine educators. They deserve admiration and thanks.

Unfortunately, not all teachers are good at what they do. Like any profession, this one includes people of varying degrees of ability. Not only are there excellent teachers, there are also a fair number of ordinary to mediocre ones out there. And in nearly every school system, there are a few teachers who do not belong in any classroom.

Sometimes you can avoid bad teachers by asking ahead of time that your child be placed in the classroom of someone you think will do right by him. The best way to find out who the good teachers are is to talk to other moms and dads. No information travels faster along the grapevine. A few schools also provide classroom-by-classroom data, such as achievement test scores, that help parents make objective determinations. Teachers unions have lobbied successfully in most places to suppress publication of that sort of analysis, however, which means school-wide data are apt to be the best you can get. Nonetheless, which instructors are good and which are bad is rarely a secret within a school. Sometimes even other teachers will tell you.

Most schools have a general policy of not granting parents' requests for specific teachers. The reason is simple. If parents could select their kids' teachers, everyone would choose the best ones. Some teachers would end up with too many students, and others with too few. If you ask, you may be treated to the principal's standard spiel about how schedules are drawn up and children assigned to classrooms by some mysterious process over which no one seems to have any control.

Nevertheless, sometimes parents are pleasantly surprised to find they *can* influence the selection of their child's teachers, if they politely assert themselves. The principal is usually the person to ask. Make your request in the spring (i.e., before the placement process begins). It's often a good idea to put it in writing. Give a specific reason as to why you believe your child would flourish with a particular teacher—preferably a reason that gives the principal something plausible to cite but that doesn't criticize other teachers. For example, you might say, "Tashira is extremely interested in science, and I know that Ms. Young is particularly effective with science-minded students." Or "I believe that Joshua needs the kind of structured environment that Ms. Barnett's classroom offers."

Good administrators are interested in matching students with instructors who are most apt to succeed with them. So you may get the teacher you want. Your chances are probably better, by the way, if you've been involved at school. If the principal knows you've volunteered as a playground monitor, or remembers that you built a rabbit hutch for the kindergarten class, she may be more inclined to bend the normal procedures and grant your request. She is more apt to see you as an asset to the school and less like a self-interested pain in the backside.

Despite your efforts, however, there will likely be times when your child ends up with instructors you're not thrilled with. Mediocrity, rather than outright incompetence, is the problem you're most apt to encounter. For example, your child may end up with someone who is burned out or dull. In some cases, there may be one or two foibles you're not happy about—perhaps you feel she doesn't give enough math homework, or doesn't allow enough time to complete assignments. Often, you can talk with a teacher and figure out a way to resolve issues of this kind. (See "Working Out Problems with the Teacher," page 460.)

You may come to the conclusion that, even though you and your child aren't enthralled by a particular teacher, it's best to grin and bear it. After all, young people need to learn that dealing with flawed situations and uninspiring people is part of life. With supplemention at home, and possibly some outside tutoring or a summer program, your child's education can survive a weak teacher. But weak teachers should not be the norm in your school—or your child doesn't belong there.

A truly bad instructor is another matter altogether. There are some people who have no business being in any classroom. You may run into someone who lacks fundamental skills (like the ability to write a grammatically correct sentence) or isn't willing to put much effort into the job, someone who is surly and discourteous to children, even someone who is putting ideas you don't like into your child's head. An awful teacher can be a nightmare for a child, particularly a young one. She can destroy self-confidence, eviscerate the desire to learn, dampen achievement, and leave emotional scars. In the worst cases, it can take months or years to repair the damage done to a student's education. No child should be subjected to an incompetent teacher. If that's the situation you face, you need to take action.

Warning Signs of Bad Teaching

Parents must keep their radar tuned to detect bad teachers. Take action if you see some of these characteristics in an instructor:

- Shows little knowledge of the subject matter she's supposed to be teaching.
- Lacks basic academic skills (e.g., sends home notes containing spelling errors).
- Holds low expectations for students.
- Makes little effort to maintain discipline.

- Doesn't focus on academic goals.
- Can't communicate knowledge in an interesting way.
- Gives disorganized lessons and vague, careless assignments.
- Does not assign homework on a regular basis.
- Is not aware of your child's strengths, weaknesses, and interests.
- Shows little enthusiasm for her work.
- Belittles children's efforts.
- Shows no interest in communicating with parents.
- Exhibits unsound character or unprofessional behavior.

Saving Your Child from Bad Teaching

In many schools, the system protects bad teaching. It is very difficult for a public school to fire a mediocre or incompetent teacher once she's been in the classroom a few years. Technically, it may be possible, but in practice it is so arduous, time-consuming, and costly that it rarely happens. A vast bureaucracy defends bad teachers with an arsenal of weapons: laws and regulations, labor union contracts, confusing jargon, and an endless capacity to delay. Make-no-waves administrators worsen the problem. This does not mean you are powerless to save your child from poor teaching. There are things you can and should do, but you will need patience, determination, and backbone. Here are some steps you may need to take:

- **Find out what the problem is.** Make sure your complaint is justified. It might not be the teacher's fault. She may have been saddled with a terrible curriculum. Perhaps her teaching style is a bad fit for your child. Listen carefully to what your child says about the situation. Visit the classroom. Talk with other parents. Are they also concerned about this teacher's performance?

- **Meet with the teacher.** Describe the problem as you see it, and listen to what she has to say. Good teachers will try to work with you to fix things. Bad teachers will more likely blame your child, tell you the problem doesn't really exist, or promise to make a change that never comes. Be determined: you may need to meet two or even three times. Even if you're not getting anywhere, it is important to go on record as having tried. In many schools, the principal will not want to talk to you about a problem until you've first attempted to work it out with the teacher.

- **Take it to the next level.** If the teacher proves unresponsive, it's time to try elsewhere. Ask at the front office about whom to talk with next. Depending on the school's size, the next stop may be a school counselor or assistant principal. Eventually, you'll probably need to speak with the principal.

  Before you take this step, consider the ramifications. The teacher, of course, will not be happy that you are going over her head. A bad teacher, who is probably defensive to begin with, may consider it an attack on her reputation. She may thereafter harbor a grudge against you and may even take it out on your child. If, like many teachers, she has a "tenured" job, it will be difficult for the principal to do much, even if she agrees with you. Do not let that stop you. Proceed with your eyes open, though, and carefully consider what is best for your child.

- **Prepare your case.** When you meet with the principal, be ready to describe the problem and its specific effects on your child. It may help to put your concerns in writing. It is important to provide documentation if possible. For example, you might say, "I do not think Roberto is learning to write well, partly because Mrs. Altman never corrects his work. Here are the papers he has written and gotten back this semester, and there are no corrections or comments anywhere." Such documentation will demonstrate that you've examined the problem carefully. It will also send a message that you have evidence and plan to be persistent.

  Let the principal know you have tried to work things out with the teacher. Describe any remedies you've already tried. Tell her that your child's education is being hindered. Politely suggest the solution you think is best.

- **Don't be surprised if the wheels turn slowly.** It is possible the principal will spring into action and solve the problem. It is also possible little or nothing will happen right away. In your state, a formal complaint to the principal may trigger a complex, lengthy legal process that involves all sorts of district policies and union rules.

  Some principals are experts at defending their staff no matter what the merits of the complaint against them. They don't want to rock the boat or do anything to make their teachers unhappy. There are any number of ways a principal can stall. She may say your criticism is unfounded, or that she needs to gather more information. Or she may make a token effort to right things, and hope you will go away. Your perseverance may be tested.

- **Ask for a transfer to another teacher if necessary.** This is rarely easy, although it's usually more realistic than having something done about the unsatisfactory teacher herself. The principal knows that if she moves one child out of a bad teacher's classroom, other parents will want the same treatment. If you ask for a change early in the year, she may tell you to give the teacher another chance. Then, later in the year, she may say it's too late to do anything, and that you should just ride it out. The principal herself is probably handicapped by district rules about class size, student assignment procedures, and so on. But if you are persistent and can make a convincing case that a change in teachers would be best for your child, the principal may figure out a way.

- **Talk to the superintendent's office.** If the principal is no help, try your luck at the district level. Understand, however, that the superintendent's job is to manage an entire school system. You may be told that he does not get involved in the problems of individual students. The district office will be reluctant to do anything that undermines a principal's authority. In that sense, the odds are against you. On the other hand, you may find someone there with a receptive ear who is willing to help you find a solution to your problem.

- **Talk to a school board member.** Ordinarily it is not a board member's job to get involved in personnel issues or problems between individual students and teachers. She may be wary of interfering in the day-to-day operations of schools. But if you can convince her that a teacher is posing a real problem (especially if that person is affecting several students), and that you've tried other channels, she may make a phone call on your behalf. Sometimes a call from a school board member causes a few rusty gears in the district bureaucracy to start turning.

- **Keep your cool.** Make a fuss if necessary, but make a civil and responsible fuss. Honey is apt to attract more bees than vinegar, and the principal (or guidance counselor, department head, assistant superintendent) is more likely to try to solve a problem that is presented in a reasonable, courteous fashion. You may be frustrated at times, but angry outbursts will only brand you as a troublemaker or malcontent and give school officials an excuse not to deal with you.

- **Don't lose your backbone.** You may run up against the condescending attitude of "we are the experts about teaching and you're not qualified to judge what we're doing." Remember that they may know more about teaching, but you are *the* expert about your child, and therefore your opinion should not be taken lightly.

  Sometimes parents get confused by terms that educators employ (such as "developmentally appropriate" or "critical thinking skills"). If someone at school starts using jargon you don't understand, ask her to stop and explain. If she can't do so in clear, everyday language, then her educationese is probably a way to shield the school from accountability. Don't ever let anyone make you feel like the enterprise of educating your child is beyond your understanding. Good teaching is based on common sense, not on mysterious precepts known only to a professional elite.

- **Get other parents' help.** Find out if they're having problems with the same teacher. If so, unite. Here is an important rule to remember whenever you want to make a change at school: the powers that be are much more likely to respond when faced with a group of unhappy and determined parents.

- **Be mindful of your child's anxiety.** He may resist your intervention. He may shudder at the thought of having attention called to him, and worry about retribution from the teacher. Listen carefully to his concerns and be prepared to reassure him.

If you proceed in a calm but resolute manner, your chances of finding some sort of remedy are decent, even though it may not be a perfect solution. After all, the great majority of educators and administrators have children's best interests at heart. Sometimes, however, parents find themselves up against a system dedicated to protecting the status quo. No matter how hard you plead, no one is both able and willing to do anything about a bad teacher. There is nothing worse than knowing your loved one is sitting in a class where little learning takes place. If you find yourself banging your head against the wall while your child languishes, it's probably time to look for a different school.

POOR DISCIPLINE

In survey after survey, Americans complain that too many schools are disorderly, undisciplined places. "I sent my child to school hoping he would learn about good books and fractions and such," parents say. "He isn't learning those things well. But it's not just that; his behavior is worse, too. He comes home and uses language we never expected to hear coming out of his mouth." Teachers, meanwhile, complain that fewer and fewer kids arrive at school showing common courtesy and respect for authority—and that many display outright insolence. The worst-behaved students end up getting the most attention, and precious instruction time is squandered trying to get order. "It seemed like weeks before I heard 'please' or 'thank you' anywhere in the room," says one former teacher. "Every day, someone would simply ignore my direct request to pay attention or stop talking, although I stood just an arm's length away. . . . Something is happening between kindergarten and high school—and we're to blame because there is no accountability."[9]

Many schools are indeed reluctant to hold students accountable for their actions. Too often, the mind-set of the education establishment overemphasizes "encouraging individual choices" and letting children "work out" their behavior problems, while warning teachers that they'll only be placing themselves in an "adversarial role" if they emphasize rules, reward good conduct, and punish bad behavior. (Two of the authors visited a school where students had recently graffitied a wall. The principal explained that the children had felt a need to express their opinions.) Nevertheless, it is clearly wrong to lay all the blame for discipline problems on schools and school authorities. In many places, educators know that if they discipline the way they'd like, they will immediately be criticized by a parent or sued by a special interest group.

A community of adults surrounds every school, and all of those adults have responsibility for how students behave. The lion's share of that duty falls to mothers and fathers. Parents have a right to expect that children will be safe and secure while at school, and that the atmosphere will be conducive to learning. By the same token, educators have every right to expect that parents will do their part. Children need grown-ups to guide their conduct both at home and at school. Most kids don't do well with part-time discipline.

What Good Schools Do

It is hard to find a successful school that lacks firm discipline. Numerous studies show that good behavior and academic success go hand in hand. When schools are places of proper conduct, regular attendance, and respect for teachers, students are more likely to learn effectively and get better grades.

Good schools set high standards. They recognize that proper conduct is a habit molded through rules, routines, and examples. Students understand that they are there to learn. The teachers and principal act with authority to preserve order. These are things we have always known, if not always heeded. A book called *Classroom Management*, published in 1907, says: "There is no explicit formula that will cover each specific case, but one general suggestion may be given: *Get order*. Drop everything else, if necessary, until order is secured." That advice is no less true today. We are not talking about repression or mindless authoritarianism. We *are* talking about nurturing authority, about letting children know you care. We are talking about a place where adults understand that there can be little learning without discipline.

The origins of the word "discipline" lie in the Latin word *disciplina*, which means "teaching" or "learning." In its broadest sense, to discipline is to instruct. Good schools are places where teachers and administrators know that discipline is necessary for moral growth. It is an indispensable tool in teaching virtues such as responsibility, hard work, perseverance, and honesty. It is central in learning how to succeed at everyday behavior and how to live a good life.

The ultimate goal of discipline is to help children become people who behave well on their own—not just under the gaze of parents or teachers—people who respect others' rights, treat them fairly, obey the laws of society, act with integrity, take responsibility for their own behavior, say yes to the right things and no to the wrong. If children are to become morally mature beings, they must learn self-control. The real goal of discipline is to impart *self*-discipline. In this respect, a school's climate of order, its ethos, is an integral part of character education.

Most successful schools share these traits:

- **The rules of conduct are clear.** Effective schools make sure that students and parents know what is expected. They have written rules that spell out acceptable behavior on the school grounds and, sometimes, around the clock. The code of conduct also states the consequences of breaking the rules. School officials give parents and teachers copies of the discipline policy. Often it is included in the school handbook, which should be sent to parents. In many cases, individual teachers have additional classroom rules which are also carefully explained to parents and students.

- **The rules are enforced.** Students are held accountable. Punishments are prompt, fair, and consistent. Good schools and teachers discipline students in a variety of ways: a time-out, loss of privileges, detention, etc. But the school's response is not quixotic, erratic, or discretionary. It is sure, predictable, almost automatic. A student who makes a mess is required to stay in at recess and clean it up. A child who won't stop whispering in class gets moved to a seat away from his chatty friends for the rest of the semester. The important thing is that students know there will be *real* consequences to inappropriate behavior—not just something that makes them say mockingly, "Big deal."

- **The teacher is the moral authority in the classroom.** That authority rests on the fact that it is her responsibility to maintain a suitable learning environment, teach children good character traits, and keep them out of harm's way. If she is to fulfill those missions, she must have leeway to tell students how to behave and the clout to enforce those norms. Parents and school officials must back her up and make it absolutely clear to children that they must respect the teacher's authority. Good teachers, in turn, win children's respect by being fair and consistent. They are not domineering tyrants. They let students know they care about their well-being.

- **Good behavior is recognized.** Experienced teachers know it's important to pay attention to students who conduct themselves well, not just those who misbehave. They use positive incentives—a pat on the back, a word of praise, a gold star, a complimentary note. Many schools have formal programs to recognize good behavior—a "character honor roll," "good manners awards," or certificates for students with good attendance.

- **The school keeps parents informed.** Teachers should be able to handle routine infractions, but parents need to know if their children are consistently breaking the rules and whenever there is a serious problem. For some students, the knowledge that their parents may be summoned to school will itself help deter misbehavior. Many schools keep parents up-to-date with grades for behavior on pupils' report cards.

- **High academic standards are maintained.** One of the best ways to keep kids out of trouble is to keep them focused on their studies. In disciplined schools, the first priority is on learning, and everyone understands that. Children know they are there to work hard. They know they are to aim for certain learning goals. An academic environment fosters discipline, and discipline nourishes academics.

- **Adults teach children the need for self-discipline.** Good teachers talk to students about why specific rules—such as "no cutting in line" or "you must take a seat when the bell rings"—are necessary. They patiently explain (and model) virtues such as responsibility and patience. Teachers may help two students who've had a fight work out their differences, talk about what went wrong, and figure out a way to keep it from happening again. These actions are all part of good discipline. They mold character.

- **Good manners are a must.** Standards for etiquette and language should be included in the school code. Good schools don't let youngsters walk down the hallways shoving each other and yelling profanities. They teach children to be polite. "If civility in society breaks down, then those problems considered to be much larger will absolutely explode," Indiana principal Larry Hensley-Marschand observes. "Students rise to the occasion. Raise the bar and they will adjust."[10]

- **Students take pride in their school's appearance.** When children see messy classrooms, dirty hallways, and littered playgrounds, they naturally conclude that "no one cares." That attitude can quickly start to infect the way they approach their studies. Good schools instill in students a sense of pride and shared ownership. As one principal put it, "I teach my children, this is your book, your chair, your bus, your school." A sensible dress code combats slovenliness; it sends the message that school is a place for serious work, and that children should dress and act accordingly.

- **The principal leads the way.** No-nonsense principals are important in establishing school discipline. They make it their business to enforce the rules and set a good personal example. Principals in orderly schools are usually highly visible, day in and day out; they engage in "management by walking around." They're out there greeting students and monitoring behavior. "Children have to see, hear, smell, and touch you, or else they start doing bad things," says an Ohio middle school principal. A good principal keeps in close touch with the teachers and makes sure they share her vision of an orderly school.

- **Chronically disruptive students are taken out of class.** No matter how high the standards or excellent the curriculum, teachers cannot teach if a student who seriously disturbs the class is allowed to remain there. It hurts the chances for other children to learn. Educators must have the authority to remove children who repeatedly break rules, show disrespect, endanger learning, or threaten safety. There are a number of ways to handle such students, including alternative schools, in-school suspension, and programs that give troubled youngsters the assistance they need.

- **Officials respond swiftly to safety problems.** There is relatively little overt violence in the K–8 grades. Tragically, however, there are some elementary schools where guns, gangs, and drug dealing endanger children. In the face of serious threats to safety, administrators should do whatever is necessary to secure order: call in local law enforcement officers, mount security cameras, close exits, patrol corridors, suspend troublemakers. Whatever it takes. Students can't learn and teachers can't teach when they are afraid or distracted. The first requisite of a sound education is a protected, tranquil environment. School should be a safe haven for children, a place of calm purposefulness.

None of this means that good schools are always quiet, or that the rules restrict children like straitjackets. Kids are noisy, energetic, sociable creatures and—depending on the school's philosophy—it's possible for much learning to occur amid a greater din than you might suppose. You must distinguish, however, between the clamor that sometimes accompanies learning and the kind that interferes with it. That difference will depend in part on how your child functions. If he needs tranquillity to study, find a school (or classroom) where calm prevails. If he thrives amid some hubbub, that's fine, too. Many children need a mix of the two environments. Sometimes the optimum ratio changes as the child matures. The important thing to remember is that all children need a certain amount of discipline to learn. Satisfy yourself that the school is providing the right dose for your child.

What Parents Can Do

The public is right to be concerned about the lack of discipline in many American schools. We need to remember, however, that students take to school the habits and attitudes they have learned at home. The truth is that many parents are not teaching their children to conduct themselves well. As the sociologist Amitai Etzioni has written, "A significant proportion of the children who enter American schools each year seem to be psychically underdeveloped. Their families have not helped them mature to the point where they can function effectively in a school, relate constructively to its rules, authorities, and 'work' discipline."

Today, many good teachers burn out and leave the profession because their students are rude, unruly, uncooperative, and spoiled—and because some parents explain away their children's failings rather than share responsibility for disciplining them. It is difficult to hold educators responsible for discipline problems when they are dealing with kids who are not used to firm limits. Mothers and fathers have a responsibility to send to school children who are respectful, self-disciplined, and prepared to work hard and learn. Parents must signal clearly that they expect a well-disciplined school, but they must also do their own jobs at home.

Here are some ways to help ensure your child is well behaved at school.

- **Set limits at home.** Give your child fair rules and consequences for breaking them. Draw a bright line between right and wrong behavior. Talk to him about the reasons for rules. Remember that most children *want* caring adults to set clear, reasonable boundaries for them. Consistent rules and structures supply a sense of security in young lives.

- **Teach respect for adults.** Work with your child on manners—for example, saying "Yes, Miss Johnson" and "No, sir" and listening attentively to elders. In particular, teach respect for teachers. Let him know that cheerful, prompt obedience is part of that respect.

- **Teach respect for school rules.** Go over the school's code of conduct with your child. Make sure he understands the rules he's to follow. Talk with him about why they are necessary. Let him know that you expect him to stick to them. Show your own respect for the norms. For example, if you drive your child to school, make sure you get him there on time.

Parents should look over the school's discipline policy carefully. Does it seem sufficient and reasonable? Is the school following its own plan?

- **Talk to your child about his day at school.** Sometimes children are embarrassed to talk about problems they're having at school (such as other kids bullying them). Get into the habit of discussing school with your youngster, so that he is comfortable confiding in you. Make sure he feels safe at school. Children need to know that their parents are interested in what happens to them during the day.

- **Pay attention to the behavior of your child's friends.** If he spends time with troublemakers, expect trouble. Every once in a while you may need to take a firm stand and say "I do not want you hanging out with that kid." Your child will probably resent this for a while. You cannot let that stop you, unless you are willing to cede influence to peers who set bad examples.

- **Keep in touch with the teacher and other parents.** The better your relationship with the teacher, the easier it will be for both of you to teach discipline in consistent ways. She can keep you informed about your child's behavior in class, and you can let her know of any home situations that may affect his school conduct. Building a network of other moms and dads with children at your school is important because often the parent grapevine is the best way to find out about serious discipline problems.

- **Get a firsthand look at school discipline.** Every once in a while, arrange to visit the classroom, cafeteria, gym, or schoolyard. Watch what goes on (although it is well to remember that children and teachers may behave differently when a parent is present). Occasional volunteering is a great way to stay informed *and* help make the school a safe, orderly place. You might offer to be a playground monitor or lend a hand in the library. These are both good places to see how children behave at school. Wait with youngsters at the bus stop, or volunteer to ride on the school bus. Assist at events such as dances or basketball games. You might ask to sit on a school discipline committee, and help write and enforce the rules.

If your own child is disturbing other kids or teachers, you must, of course, do something about it. First, find out exactly what he is doing wrong, and see if you can figure out why. Children misbehave in school for all sorts of reasons. Your youngster may be bored with the lessons. He may not understand the importance of certain rules. His behavior might be a reaction to academic difficulties, or to discord at home. He might just be trying to impress his friends. These are the kinds of problems you can work with the school to solve.

He may also have a problem within himself. He might, for example, have a bona fide learning disability or behavior disorder. Perhaps he's angry with you or a sibling. He might be upset by a recent development (e.g., divorcing parents, a seriously ill friend). He may need more structured supervision at home. These things happen. Some are more readily fixed than others, but all need attention.

Often you'll find that the problem is not a big deal. It's that your kid—or someone else's kid—is just seeing what he can get away with, acting like a kid. That calls for old-fashioned discipline. In some cases, you may need to meet with the school staff, hear what they have to say about the problem, and together come up with a remedy. The teacher or principal may ask you to bring your child to the conference so that he sees a united front. When a child has serious problems controlling behavior or focusing attention, professionals within the school—counselors and school psychologists—may be asked to help.

Many people stew over the proper punishment for schools to use with troublesome students. Time-out? Stand in the corner? After-school detention? Suspension? Our advice is to take a pragmatic view: whatever works. If the school staff can induce your child to change his behavior by using a solution that is reasonable and fair, more power to them. Give school officials latitude to maintain a healthy learning environment. Cooperate with them.

Some parents want to believe that their child is always a little angel and that any discipline problems must be someone else's fault. These are the moms and dads who show up at school with a "Why are you picking on my kid?" attitude, even when their son or daughter undoubtedly has broken the rules. "As one father told me, it's perfectly acceptable to allow his child to experiment," says a New York assistant principal who took flak after punishing students for making mischief on school computers. "After all, we didn't want to squash his curiosity, did we?"[11] Just about every principal has stories to tell about parents who took a school to court for "denying their children's rights" (e.g., kicking them off the football team for missing too many practices, or suspending them for smoking in the bathroom). Such pressures cripple schools and send terrible messages to young people about respecting rules. Granted, sometimes teachers make mistakes; if you believe a punishment is unjustified, then naturally you must talk with school officials and try to work out something else. In general, however, parents must back schools' efforts to maintain order.

If your child has been disciplined, it's useful to recall the Golden Rule. You want him to behave toward others in school the way you expect others to behave toward him.

If you're reasonably sure that other children are causing a problem, make prompt contact with the school. A perceptive teacher is apt to be able to help diagnose the trouble, although the principal may also need to become involved, especially if the problem centers outside the classroom. Since the solution is likely to involve discipline of someone else's child, be understanding. Again, keep the Golden Rule in mind. Be firm and persistent until the problem is solved.

What if you face serious, school-wide discipline problems? *A school where the adults are not in control is one of the worst things that can happen to that school and to your child's education.* You must take action. Join forces with other angry parents. Agitate for a new discipline policy, or a new principal. You may have to demand security guards or policemen on the premises. Haunt school board meetings. March in to see the superintendent. Get in touch with the local television and newspaper reporters who cover schools. If necessary, find a new school. Do whatever you must. As long as your child is in an undisciplined environment, he risks physical harm, a mediocre education, and the development of bad habits that may stick with him for a very long time.

Warning Signs of Discipline Trouble at School

Here are some signs that a school is not attending to how students conduct themselves:

- No clear, written discipline code.
- There is a code, but teachers and students are unfamiliar with it.
- The written rules are not enforced.
- Teachers complain about lack of authority to control their classrooms.
- School is messy and in poor repair.
- Chronically disruptive students are allowed to remain in class.

- Students talk back to teachers and use vulgar language at school.
- Kids wander the hallways and school grounds.
- Children are often late to class.
- Students and teachers are indifferent to proper dress.
- Good behavior is seldom recognized or rewarded.
- School fails to notify parents of serious infractions.
- Children come home with bad habits.
- Low academic standards are the norm.

CHAPTER 13

Along with Academics

ACADEMICS ARE NOT THE WHOLE OF A GOOD EDUCATION. A solid upbringing tends to the mind, heart, body, and soul. This chapter covers three broad areas of a complete education: character training; health and physical education; and activities beyond the classroom.

Adults must concern themselves deeply with the moral training of the young. Nothing is more important, and therefore schools should take part in this enterprise. Some do a good job helping parents teach virtue, but in other places you find only faltering efforts. You need to be able to recognize a school that really cares about the character of its students. And, of course, you must attend to vital character lessons yourself. This is not a curricular afterthought. In many respects, it is the heart of it all.

We want children to grow up to have healthy lives. Youngsters need reliable information about how to care for their bodies. They need exercise to keep those bodies fit and mature guidance about growing into adulthood. Health and physical education should be supportive of good character. It should help make children (as the Scout oath puts it) physically strong, mentally awake, and morally straight.

A good education also broadens. It calls upon young people to cultivate talents and find lifelong interests. It opens their eyes to the world. Much of this learning takes place outside the formal school setting. After all, your child spends a relatively small fraction of her time in the classroom. How she spends all those extracurricular hours says much about the kind of person she will turn out to be.

To you falls the duty of overseeing these areas of learning. You must be the chief coach, trainer, coordinator, and role model. As always, you are the most important teacher in raising a healthy, happy, well-educated child.

CHARACTER EDUCATION

"We must remember that intelligence is not enough. Intelligence plus character—that is the goal of true education," said the Reverend Martin Luther King, Jr. A child's family is the first and most important incubator of morality. Molding character must begin in the home in the earliest years, but after that, schools must help. Parents rightfully expect their schools to be allies in the moral education of the young.

Throughout most of our nation's history, schools conscientiously undertook this task. The Founders assumed that teachers would tend not only to students' abilities but also to their character. Jefferson wrote that one of the essential elements of a sound education was "the improvement of one's morals and faculties."

During the nineteenth century, teachers went about their jobs with confidence that they knew what good character was and how to instill it in children. Horace Mann, the father of the public school, wrote that "the highest and noblest office of education . . . pertains to our moral nature." Schools taught the difference between right and wrong through discipline, the examples of teachers, and explicit instruction. The old *McGuffey Readers*, full of stories about courage, honesty, hard work, and compassion, became the most widely used textbooks in the land. The vision of schools was by no means perfect—it often included some venomous prejudices of the times. Nonetheless, educators made a sincere effort to draw on commonly shared values to impart good moral and civic character to children.

As the twentieth century progressed, the consensus that schools should teach virtue slowly broke down. New notions invaded the cultural landscape. Morality began to be viewed as chiefly a matter of individual choice. Refrains such as "My values aren't the same as yours" and "Who are we to judge what others are doing?" began to echo through our public discourse. In the 1960s and 1970s, most American schools staged a full-fledged retreat from character education. Word came down from school administrators and education professors: teachers should no longer directly instruct children about matters of right and wrong. That was "indoctrination." Instead, lessons were to be "value-neutral." Many schools embraced "values clarification," an approach in which students were encouraged to identify and "clarify" their own beliefs. Teachers posed questions such as "Do you think cheating is wrong?" and "How do you feel about people who lie?" Getting kids to talk about their feelings and values was encouraged, but many educators were no longer willing to say, "No, you're wrong" to the youngster who concluded that "lying is okay for me."

Before long, moral relativism had displaced traditional virtue in America's schools. In 1985, for example, the *New York Times* ran an article quoting educators as explaining that "they deliberately avoid trying to tell students what is ethically right and wrong." It reported on one counseling session in which several pupils concluded that a fellow student had been foolish to return $1,000 she found in a purse at the school. When they asked the counselor's opinion, he told them that "he believed the girl had done the right thing, but that, of course, he would not try to force his values on them. 'If I come from the position of what is right and what is wrong," he explained, 'then I'm not their counselor.'" Once upon a time, a counselor was a person who offered counsel, and who understood that adults do not form character in the young by taking a neutral stance toward questions of right and wrong or by merely offering "options."

When families break down, when educators act as if schools can be value-free zones, and when the popular culture bombards children with messages that emphasize self-absorption and self-gratification over self-control ("rules are made to be broken" and "grab for all you can get"), the results are predictable. The behavior of the young is bound to be affected—and we have proven it in this country. Here is what we now face in some schools: much cheating, stealing, and, in the worst cases, violent crime; acceptance of foul language and talking back to teachers; tragic levels of drug and alcohol use; heartbreaking numbers of teenage pregnancies and abortions; administrators who are afraid to take a strong moral stand for fear of being sued; too many graduates who believe there is no such thing as universal moral standards; and more and more children with a cloudy sense of right and wrong. These are all signs of a society failing to provide for the moral development of its young.

The good news is that, in recent years, character education has been making something of a comeback. As the National School Boards Association has observed, "a consensus seems to be emerging that 'good

character' should regain its central, historical and rightful place in public education." Many educators have come to the realization that they
can't get out of the business of teaching morality. Parents are realizing
that they can't turn their children over to the schools for six hours a day
without paying attention to the values their kids pick up there. "Five
years ago parents were saying, 'You can't impose your values on my
child,'" says one teacher. "Now they're saying, 'Please impose some values on my child!'"

The bad news is that, even when schools' intentions are honorable,
the execution is often wrong. There is still much hesitancy when it
comes to taking up moral education in a direct fashion. The idea that
no one has any business telling others what matters in private conduct
is alive and well. "I gave a speech about character at a prestigious private school in New York, and the teachers there attacked me," says one
headmaster. "They believe there are no rights and wrongs—only the
process for reaching beliefs about rights or wrongs." Educators don't
want to "force their values" on anyone. They worry that strict adherence to a moral code will stifle individuality, destroy creativity, interfere
with a child's natural development, and trample self-esteem.

In some schools, character education is a token effort, limited to
putting up signs that read "Help others" or "Thanks for being kind today." In other places, it occurs mainly through games and activities,
such as making "friendship chains" or painting pictures that illustrate
respect and cooperation. In too many schools, it still means getting kids
to emote about their feelings and discover "what's right for them" while
the teacher "facilitates" the dialogue like a TV talk show host. But the
adult at the front of the room never says, "Look, children, there are
some difficult issues of right and wrong in life, but most of the time the
difference between right and wrong is very clear, and you should always
try to do what is right as best you can." After decades of neglect, character education is stymied because many schools have lost a sense of
moral authority. They appear clueless about how to go about teaching
right from wrong. When not clueless, they seem reluctant.

There is nothing wrong with putting up posters, playing games that
encourage good behavior, or getting students to discuss values. These
exercises can be great for reinforcing messages about good character.
But they are not enough. Simply because your school does these things
does not mean it is really working to impart good character. In elementary school, good character education means *cultivating virtues through
the formation of good habits*. It means training young people—leading

their hearts and minds toward the good. That idea is still out of fashion in some education circles. It is completely alien to the prevailing mindset and practices in many schools. Your school may be talking a decent game of character education. But is it really *doing* it?

Goals of Good Character Education

In elementary school, character education is about teaching the basics. There are fundamental virtues that we all want our children to have and that we want our schools to help develop—traits such as fairness, self-control, and responsibility. The argument "Whose values should we teach?" does not apply here. We all agree on the value of these things. People may disagree on specific cases, but we all recognize the importance of good character.

By character education, we do *not* mean taking up issues like abortion, same-sex marriage, or gun control in elementary school. The formation of character in young children is different from, and must precede, the discussion of thorny ethical controversies and heated political disputes. First things first. In morality—as in life's other arenas—we take one step at a time. You have to walk before you can run, and you ought to be able to run straight before you are asked to run an obstacle course. Moral fundamentals should be taught first. The tough issues can, if parents and teachers wish, be taken up later. In fact, young people who have a clear sense of basic morality will be much better equipped to reach a reasoned and ethically defensible position on those tough issues.

Children are not born with knowledge of the virtues. They must learn what they are. Schools should teach youngsters to recognize traits such as honesty and compassion (and vices such as deceit and cruelty), both in themselves and in others. Students should learn the different forms that virtues take, what they are like in practice, and why they deserve admiration and allegiance. Children who leave elementary school with fuzzy notions about these moral fundamentals are headed for trouble.

Adults must not only help children come to know virtue, but also to admire it. Elementary school educators should encourage an imaginative attachment to the good. "In their mind's eye, eight-year-olds should long to slay menacing dragons like St. George, risk death for liberty like William Tell, hunger to fight for heaven's will like Mother Teresa," says Mary Beth Klee, founder of Crossroads Academy in New

Hampshire. "We need to cultivate a child's love of the truly heroic, and from that the rest follows from the heart. True character education is about moral affinity, about awakening in children a love of the good."

Teachers should also help inculcate sound habits in students. As Aristotle told us long ago (and as psychologists confirm today), it is habit that develops good character. "It makes no small difference," Aristotle wrote, "whether we form habits of one kind or of another from our very youth; it makes a very great difference, or rather *all* the difference." By tackling their assignments diligently, for example, children grow into adults who take work seriously. Attaining virtue is like so much else in life: it takes lots of practice. By putting virtues into action over and over again, we help them take root. Eventually they become second nature—they become part of one's character.

These, then, are the fundamental missions of elementary school with regard to character education. Schools must teach moral literacy, so that children have clear, solidly grounded concepts of good and bad. They must help children come to care deeply about the good. They must see that students put virtues into action on a routine basis and thereby acquire the habits that make for good lives. Good schools accomplish these goals in several ways.

How Schools Teach Good Character

When it comes to teaching the basic virtues, educators must be willing to use the language of morality—to speak in terms of good and bad, honest and dishonest, right and wrong. Adults must explain to children how we want them to act and why. Teachers must praise some actions and show their disapproval of others. They can't remain silent out of fear that someone will call them insensitive or preachy. As Mary Warnock of Oxford University has written, "You cannot teach morality without being committed to morality yourself; and you cannot be committed to morality yourself without holding that some things are right and others wrong." This does not mean browbeating children. Rather, it means talking with intellectual honesty and ethical candor. It means recognizing that sometimes children need to hear someone older and wiser tell it like it is.

Good teachers try to model virtuous behavior. By their everyday actions, they show students how to live. They show it by being on time to class each day, by coming to work with a good attitude, by preparing their lessons, by dressing neatly, by speaking politely to students and colleagues alike, by spending a little extra time after school with a child who needs help. You do not need a schoolful of saints to teach your child. You simply need people of generally good character who know that their actions speak volumes. In the business of teaching character, nothing is more important than the quiet power of moral example.

Good schools also invite children to discern and be moved by the moral dimensions of stories, historical events, and famous lives. There are hundreds of wonderful stories about virtue and vice to be shared with students. Do we want them to know what honesty means? Then we can teach them about Abe Lincoln walking three miles to return six cents and, conversely, about Aesop's shepherd boy who cried wolf. Do we want them to know what courage means? We can teach them about Ernest Shackleton and the voyage of the *Endurance,* or the 54th Massachusetts Colored Infantry charging Fort Wagner during the Civil War. Such stories give students specific reference points. They provide moral beacons that help children not only know virtue, but love it as well.

English and history lessons are not the only opportunities to teach about good character. A math teacher encourages perseverance by telling students to stick with a problem until they get the right answer. A science teacher talks to children about intellectual honesty in gathering and presenting data. In good schools, virtues are taught in every classroom and every subject.

Academic expectations shape habits. By studying hard, children develop certain traits of good character. When they are challenged to work up a mental sweat, they learn about virtues such as industry and persistence. Very different lessons are learned when schools lower the academic bar. When students rarely get homework, when they aren't held accountable for mistakes in spelling or grammar or arithmetic, when they can put forth little effort but still earn high grades, schools foster laziness, carelessness, and irresponsibility. Low academic standards have no place in a regimen of healthy moral training.

Good schools also promote good character through the rules they honor. Fair, consistent standards of behavior are crucial to moral development. They give children goals to aim for and opportunities to do the right thing. Living up to a code of conduct provides experience in living well. Precepts such as wait your turn, raise your hand before talking, turn in assignments on time, and keep your locker clean give pupils practice in virtues such as self-control and diligence.

Orderliness *must* prevail in any school that seriously aspires to transmit good character. Only a school run in a disciplined manner can teach self-discipline. Only a school in which students are held responsible for their actions can teach responsibility. Schools that take morality seriously reward good behavior and punish bad conduct, precisely because they know that lifelong habits and attitudes are being formed. They may do this in any number of ways, using both carrot and stick. For example, some schools let those with excellent attendance go on a special field trip, and give detention to those who are consistently late. Good schools often give grades for deportment, hand out demerits for bad behavior, or name students to a character honor roll. They may give special recognition for good sportsmanship. However they do it, they get the job done.

Character education is also affected by the physical condition of a school. The premises set a moral tone. They are bound to affect the attitudes of teachers and students. The building need not be fancy or new, but it needs to be well kept. A school with broken windowpanes, graffitied walls, littered floors, and a trash-strewn yard is a school that has failed one of its own lessons. Plato tells us in the *Republic* that the stamp of baseness on a building will sink deep into the souls of those it surrounds.

All of these factors—exhortations, examples, rules, expectations, stories, physical surroundings—shape traits in young children. You must consider the whole picture in deciding whether or not your school is a good moral training ground. Character education is not a special course or a few hands-on activities. It resides in the school's own character, its ethos. From the classrooms to the hallways to the lunchroom to the playground, training the heart and mind toward the good must be infused into everything that children do. A good school is bound by a set of moral ideas. The adults there recognize that a central task—arguably *the* central task—of education is steadily guiding children toward virtue.

Signs of Good Character Education

Schools that teach good character are staffed by adults who:

- Try to teach basic virtues such as honesty, diligence, fairness, and loyalty.
- Are serious about training children in good habits—completing assignments, telling the truth, being on time, accepting the consequences of their actions, etc.
- Talk to children about basic morality and do not hesitate to explain the difference between right and wrong.

- Try to model good behavior in front of students on a daily basis.

- Make sure the school is a disciplined place.

- Reward good conduct (e.g., a character honor role) and punish bad behavior.

- Insist on good manners; correct (and punish when necessary) children who are rude or who swear.

- Maintain high academic expectations.

- Use stories to teach about virtue and to help children admire the good.

- Are clear with parents about the school's goals and methods in teaching morality.

- Keep the school grounds clean and in good repair.

- Honestly care about the character of their students, and do not hesitate to say so.

Working with Your School

Ask teachers and administrators to tell you about the character education program. You may find a statement of the school's values printed in the handbook. Some schools even have a written compact with parents which spells out virtues to be taught in the classroom and at home. In some places, the plan for teaching character is precise. It may include, for example, studying a different virtue each week or month and constructing a number of lessons and activities around it.

Ask your child how character is taught at school. If she doesn't have a clue, that says something. See whether character traits are assessed on report cards. If not, does the school really focus on character? Does it ever hold parent meetings to explain how it handles character education and to make sure that teachers, moms, and dads are working together?

Let the staff know your expectations. Schools need to hear parents say that character counts. Keep the teacher informed about lessons you've been stressing at home. (For a while, one of the authors and his wife had an ongoing correspondence with their child's teacher about some areas that needed extra work—basic deportment, taking responsibility, and speaking out of turn. The teacher kept a behavior chart every day, and mom and dad reviewed it nightly. The coordinated effort was very effective.)

Speak up if you think your child is acquiring bad habits at school. If discipline is slack, make that a top concern at your next parent-teacher conference, parents' night, or PTA meeting. Go see the principal if you must. Call your friendly local school board member. If the school is not attentive to teaching character, complain forcefully (preferably in league with other parents) just as you would if the academic program were weak. Conversely, offer approval and praise if the school is doing a good job in this area! The voices of parents *do* matter—they *must* matter—if schools are to reinforce rather than undermine the values of home and family.

Make sure you support teachers' efforts. Stand behind them when they try to drive home a lesson about character—including those times when your child has caused a problem. One reason educators shy away from teaching morality is that so many parents kick up a fuss when they're told their child has done something wrong. Reports a principal who suspended a third grade boy for throttling a girl in the lunchroom: "The indignant parents were in my office the next day, demanding to know why he had been suspended. 'Boys just express their anger physically,' they told me." Too often, parents seem more concerned about their children's "rights" and what goes on their records than about their virtues and responsibilities. "I have sat in numerous conferences where the parents said to their child, in effect, 'Your problem is you got caught!'" says another administrator. There is no way schools can effectively teach about right and wrong if moms and dads rush in to bail their kids out whenever they get in trouble. In the campaign for good character, parents and educators have to close ranks.

Does Your School Live by a Character Code?

Many schools have a written code that spells out its norms. At good schools, they are not just pieces of paper. They are part of the life of the school. Teachers discuss the code with students and parents. Children know the consequences of not abiding by it. They know the character code is serious business.

Here is the character code of Mater Dei School in Bethesda, Maryland, attended by one of the authors' children. While it comes from a Catholic school, every clause is appropriate for any school.

"As a member of the sixth, seventh, or eighth grade at Mater Dei, I, along with my parents, realize that I have a responsibility to act as a strong role model both for my classmates and for the younger students in the school.

"I understand that my teachers feel that being a good person is the most important element of being a successful Mater Dei student, more important than the grades I get or the sports that I play, and this is why I am being asked to take on the responsibility of being a strong role model.

"It is also clear to me that I cannot be a good person simply by behaving well while at school; rather, I know that this is a full-time job, one that I must do twenty-four hours a day. I am beginning to understand that to be a good person means having outstanding character, and that my character is particularly tested when nobody is watching me and when I am the only one who really knows what I have done or not done. I have been told that it is virtuous character, not outstanding academic success, that will lead to happiness and success here at Mater Dei and later on in my life.

"With these thoughts in mind, I know that my school, Mater Dei, has the expectation that I will not be involved in cheating on tests, quizzes, or homework; that I will not lie to my teachers; that I will not pick on other students either verbally or physically; that I will not steal from others; that I will not plagiarize or copy directly from encyclopedias or other research materials when working on papers; that I will not misbehave if I am at school either before or after teachers are here; that I will take the best possible care of the school's property and grounds; that I will try my best to show my strong character at all times. I also know that the school expects my best effort in these areas but that it does not expect perfection.

"I further appreciate that I am a representative of Mater Dei when I am off campus and that my actions or inactions reflect upon the school, either positively or negatively. Accordingly, I know that I have the obligation to avoid poor behavior—including smoking, drinking, drug use, stealing, prank calls, and making fun of others—when I am away from school and that I will be disciplined by the school if I am involved in these activities or any other inappropriate behavior.

"Finally, I realize that all of my teachers are behind me in my efforts to be a good person by following this Character Code, and that because this is so important to the school and to me and my parents, I agree to follow it this year in order to make my school, Mater Dei, the best possible place for me and my fellow students."

Teaching Character at Home

Your family is the first and most important school of morality. Home is where your child comes to know right and wrong through the nurturing and protective care of those who love her more than anyone else. Teachers should be allies in this endeavor, but they cannot be substitutes. Schools cannot replace parents in the crucial task of molding character in the young.

Many children in this country do not receive enough attention to character formation at home. Four out of five teachers say they have serious problems in the classroom because parents don't set limits, create structure, or hold their kids accountable. "Some parents don't care, but most just don't have the time that's needed to give to their kids," says a California teacher. "They're working two jobs. The kids are left to do what they want, and when they misbehave, the rules are not enforced. They're not home to make sure the kids are doing the punishment."[1] A New Jersey educator observes: "Children with a 'laissez faire' attitude at home are often indifferent to their school's efforts in character education. Several years ago, a student who had cheated on a test confided to me, 'My parents really don't care, as long as I get into a good college.'"

Some moms and dads have lost faith in their own moral authority. Teachers say they come to school with questions such as, "What should we do when all of our son's friends are going to R-rated movies and he wants to go, too?" Or they remark, "We experimented and acted up when we were young, too—how can we in good conscience tell our children not to do what we did?" "Parents are afraid of their kids—or afraid their kids may not like them," a principal notes. "One dad said to a parent group here, 'I can't look in my child's bureau drawers if I think there is the possibility of drugs. The drawers are his property. He'll be angry with me."

When mothers and fathers fall down on the job, it leaves schools in an impossible bind. When parents don't instill good character traits at home, children show up for class ill-prepared to participate mentally and morally. Then, when schools become showcases of mediocrity, we complain. We wonder why the stream is bitter, when we ourselves have helped poison the spring.

You cannot afford to be timid or heedless in shaping your loved one's morals. Education hinges on your efforts in this area. Students who come from homes that teach key virtues—such as responsibility, perseverance, and a belief in the value of hard work—are more likely to have high academic achievement. When it comes to doing well in school, *nothing* is more important than the ideals you promote and model.

Here are a few reminders about teaching morality at home.

- **Model good character.** The best way to encourage the virtues is to exhibit them in your everyday actions. Show your child what courage, respect, and compassion look like in practice. Often you will fall short, but *try* to be the kind of person you hope she will become. That is the most any of us can do.

  Call attention to people who possess admirable character traits—

neighbors, friends, teachers, coaches. Don't hesitate to say, "There goes a good woman, that Mrs. Jones. We should all try to be more like her."

- **Talk about good character.** Speaking about virtue is not just "sermonizing." It is your responsibility to tell your child the moral facts of life. Talk to her about the difference between acting bravely and recklessly, why honesty really is the best policy, and what the word "loyalty" means. Youngsters don't naturally know these things. Your child needs to hear about them from you. Remember: kids only think it's lame to talk about character when all the adults around them act as though it is.

  Just because you aren't perfect doesn't mean you can't speak with moral authority. Nowhere is it written that only those who have never made a mistake are qualified to teach the young. Presumably, you've learned from your past transgressions. It is from experience, after all, that adults must speak to children.

- **Talk about your own efforts.** Kids need to know that the moral journey is lifelong, and that we adults continue to work on the traits that are hard for us. Talk to your children about your efforts to become more charitable in speech, less quick to leap to conclusions, or more persevering in difficult tasks. She won't be so quick to imagine "hypocrisy" in what you do versus what you say if she hears candid acknowledgment of your attempts to do better.

- **Share stories that teach about virtue.** Never underestimate the power of literature to teach good character. Stories and poems can help children see what virtues and vices look like. They offer heroes to emulate. Their moral lessons lodge in the heart and stay there.

- **Set rules for your child to live by.** The rules and precepts you establish—no TV until the homework is done, put the bike in the garage when you're through riding it, keep mean thoughts to yourself—give your child practice at virtues such as diligence, responsibility, and kindness. Obedience to rules is part of learning to live the good life.

  As your child grows, explain the reasons for the rules you have set. Let her know they are not whimsical. She may not always like your explanations, but giving clear reasons helps her understand the benefits of living up to a moral code.

- **Use carrots and sticks.** Praise and reward children for good behavior. Punish when necessary. Loving, judicious discipline is a part of teaching good character. When youngsters know they can expect consequences for bad behavior—whether it's being sent to their room, a time-out, or even the occasional swat on the bottom—they're much more apt to take precepts seriously.

- **Offer controlled choices.** Being able to make some choices in matters of right and wrong helps youngsters learn responsibility and independence. It helps them understand morality and experience the consequences of choosing immoral actions.

  It is critical, however, that you set limits on choices and offer clear guidance. Talk to your child about her bad decisions, and hold her accountable for them. Children should not have to stumble blindly to virtue. Adults should be there to show them the way and keep them from wandering too far off the path.

- **Teach respect for elders.** This is part of good character in the young, and it also affects academic achievement. Children who have little regard for adults have little chance of learning from teachers, coaches, and counselors at school.

  "Respect for authority" is not a message that children commonly get from the popular culture. Rather, they are bombarded with exhortations to revere and indulge their own desires. On television, they often see images of parents and teachers as bungling and wrongheaded. They see portraits of smart-aleck children who supposedly possess superior wisdom. You are pulling against the current here. Begin at home with "Honor thy father and mother."

- **Teach good manners.** Politeness, courtesy, civility—the habits these words represent are underrated and underused in our time. Walk through any mall on a weekend, and you are likely to hear groups of young people casually using foul language, sometimes at the top of their lungs. There was a time when a grown-up, a stranger with a sense of responsibility, would have halted those children and said, "This is a public place. Behave." Today, people pass by and say nothing.

  Manners still matter, and it is important that children learn them at home. Common courtesies are "little virtues." They lay the groundwork for living together, teach us to act properly in everyday situations, and train us in the larger virtues.

- **Teach good study habits.** Homework is a tool for developing good character traits such as responsibility, perseverance, and diligence. Stay on top of homework: talk with your child about it, make sure it's done well, and be available to help when necessary. (See "Helping Your Child with Homework," page 416.)

- **Give your child a few chores.** It has been said that there is nothing so fatal to character as half-finished tasks. Making your child responsible for simple jobs—and making sure she does them well— teaches dependability, independence, thoroughness, and steadiness in work. These virtues carry over to school assignments. Teachers often say they can pick out the children who have been given responsibility for chores at home.

- **Teach neatness and cleanliness.** The size of your home will have no bearing on your child's character. Its appearance, on the other hand, will teach potent lessons. If it's a constant mess—if your desk is piled high with junk, if you rarely put things back in their place, if you never make your child clean up her room—look for sloppiness to show up in her habits and schoolwork. Children's conduct often reflects the orderliness, or lack thereof, in their surroundings.

- **Keep up your guard against the mass media.** Many parents feel overwhelmed by the questionable and often pernicious messages coming at their children from TVs, movies, computer screens, radios, stereos, magazines, and some books. Cultural sleaze *does* influence youngsters' attitudes, but so do loving, caring parents. Spend time with your child and teach her the difference between good and evil.

  Do not give in to the worst of the popular culture. Monitor what your child sees and hears. Take a stand when necessary. Exert your authority to say, "No, I don't want you watching that," or to explain why something she's heard is wrong. It takes guts to turn off a movie halfway through, but sometimes it must be done. You are the best and perhaps only line of defense. If you surrender, your child will be fully exposed to an army of crass and corrosive values.

- **Help your child choose her friends.** Good friends bring you up, bad friends bring you down. The habits and values of other youngsters will rub off on your child. You improve her chances for school success if you encourage association with kids who value hard work, responsibility, and self-discipline—particularly in the preteen years and beyond, when children are so susceptible to peer pressure.

Young people often indulge their worst streaks in each other's company. St. Augustine tells how, when he was young, being a daredevil was a badge of honor among his comrades. No one wished to appear pious and innocent. "Among my equals I was ashamed of being less shameless than others, when I heard them boast of their wickedness. . . . I made myself worse than I was, that I might not be reproached," he says. Youth has not changed much since St. Augustine wrote his confessions. Make sure that your child's friends are allies of her better nature. Help her resist temptation by letting her know it's all right to go against the crowd. Teach the courage to be good even when others are bad.

As children get older, they naturally want more independence. The closer your child gets to high school, the more room you will give her to make her own decisions and, at times, her own mistakes. There will probably be disagreements. There will surely be times when your child spurns your moral guidance, and criticizes you for offering it. Do not give in. When you abandon your post, you abandon your child. Teens and preteens may not know it, but they need direction from parents more than ever. "When I was a boy of fourteen, my father was so ignorant I could hardly stand to have the old man around," Mark Twain said. "But when I got to be twenty-one, I was astonished at how much he had learned in seven years." Teaching character—like so much else in parenting—is for the long haul.

Character-Building Books

Here are some good books to help parents and schools teach about virtue.

Books That Build Character: A Guide to Teaching Your Child Moral Values, William Kilpatrick and Gregory and Suzanne M. Wolfe (Touchstone Books, 1994)—A guide to more than 300 books that celebrate virtues.

Building Character in Schools: Practical Ways to Bring Moral Instruction to Life, Kevin Ryan and Karen Bohlin (Jossey-Bass Publishers, 1998)— A practical guide for parents and schools in the campaign to teach character.

Core Virtues: A K–6 Literature-Based Program in Character Education, Mary Beth Klee (Link Institute, 1996)—Although this is a complete character education program for schools, parents will profit from the extensive bibliography of children's literature illustrating various virtues.

Educating for Character: How Our Schools Can Teach Respect and Responsibility, Thomas Lickona (Bantam Books, 1992)—Practical strategies to help schools teach respect and responsibility ("the 4th and 5th R's") as well as other virtues.

Family New Media Guide, William Kilpatrick (Macmillan, 1997)—Reviews movies and videos with an eye toward moral excellence.

Where to Get Help and Information

Here are some effective organizations where you can get good information and advice about character education. Check with your church or synagogue as well.

Center for the Advancement of Ethics and Character
School of Education, Boston University
605 Commonwealth Avenue, Boston, MA 02215
617-353-3262
http://.education.bu.edu/charactered

Center for Youth Issues
P.O. Box 22185
Chattanooga, TN 37422
800-477-8277
www.cyi-stars.org

 Character Education Partnership
918 16th Street NW, Suite 501
Washington, DC 20006
800-988-8081
www.character.org

Josephson Institute of Ethics
4640 Admiralty Way, Suite 1001
Marina del Rey, CA 90292-6610
310-306-1868
www.josephsoninstitute.org

Link Institute
270 Redwood Shores Parkway, Suite 514
Redwood City, CA 94065
650-631-1066
www.linkinstitute.org

Character and Faith

For most Americans, religion is a vital part of character development. Belief in God anchors their sense of right and wrong. It supports virtue and furnishes a context in which morality makes sense. Faith promotes hard work, honesty, individual responsibility, and discipline. It is a call to kindness, decency, and forgiveness in our homes, our schools, and our communities. Faith lifts each person outside himself and inspires concern for others. It offers boys and girls—and adults, too—a larger sense of purpose and a frame of reference as they go about their daily affairs.

America's early public schools relied upon faith as a pillar of democracy and virtue. Education and religion were closely allied. Students read the Bible and recited prayers in class. Today, of course, public schools are not allowed to promote religion. Therefore some parents of faith choose to send their children to a school operated by a church, synagogue, or other religious institution.

Many of these schools not only teach character well, they also get the academic job done better than their public school counterparts. For example, parochial schools frequently have better graduation rates and fewer discipline problems. Their students often learn more and do better on tests, even though these schools almost always spend less per student than nearby public schools. They do it largely through time-tested, commonsense practices, practices that were once standard in public schools: real standards of behavior, high expectations, and a concentration on basic skills and knowledge. Parents get involved. They hold the school accountable and are held accountable by the school. "For schools operated by a religious community," wrote the late Professor James Coleman of the University of Chicago, "school is not regarded as an agent of the larger society or of the state, to free the child from the family. Rather, it is an agent of the religious community of which the family is an intrinsic part."

Perhaps most important, these schools give human life a transcendent meaning. Their teachers act as God's stewards. They teach that life is largely a moral and spiritual journey and they treat their charges as moral and spiritual beings. When this dimension is present, children's minds, spirits, and efforts are lifted. They are more apt to approach their studies and activities in the spirit recommended by St. Paul: "Whatever you do, work at it with all your heart as working for the Lord." Or, as the sign hanging outside a second grade classroom in

Our Lady Queen of Angels school in East Harlem read, in a child's handwriting: "Dear God, help us all to have a better life."

The point is not that you must place your child in a religious school in order for her to acquire good values and solid academic achievement. Fine public schools can also help you accomplish these goals. The point is to remind you that faith can make a big difference to children—to their character, their studies, and their lives.

If you are a religious person, nothing is more important to the formation of your child's character than helping her come to know your faith. Making God's wisdom a part of her education will help her find virtue in ways that cannot be duplicated by any other means. Make time for family devotions. Read scripture together. Pray together, as a family. Attend your place of worship. Celebrate your faith's important holy days. Take advantage of religious classes and activities for young people. Help your child find some friends who share your faith. Encourage her to do community work through your church or temple. Teach your child that God loves her, that God cares about what she does, that God has created her for goodness. Above all, try to model a life of faith in front of her. Make sincere efforts at these things, and your child will have a wellspring of virtues to draw from.

HEALTH AND PHYSICAL EDUCATION

Grade-school children are growing all the time. They need plenty of exercise. They also need instruction from adults about how to keep their growing bodies healthy, clean, and out of harm's way. An orderly program of health and physical education is important.

Numerous reports have documented the poor physical condition of many American youngsters. They run too slowly, their muscles are too weak, and they spend far too much time sitting around. One recent survey found that only a quarter of American children get even twenty minutes of vigorous exercise daily. According to the Centers for Disease Control, the percentage of overweight children and adolescents has more than doubled in the past thirty years. American kids may be in worse shape than ever.

Parents should not rely on schools to make their children healthy. That's a fundamental responsibility of moms and dads. Organized physical education in school can, however, do a lot to provide the knowledge, skills, and motivation that youngsters need for a lifetime of health and exercise. Children should learn about how their bodies function; what kinds of food to eat; how to avoid illness; some basic first aid and personal safety; the dangers of illegal drugs, tobacco, and alcohol; and— when and where appropriate—sex education. Teachers and coaches can remind students to treat the body as a temple. As that body grows, it is important to make use of willpower, self-discipline, and common sense.

The physical education program should go hand in hand with character education. Coaches and PE directors can help children learn about teamwork and the importance of playing fairly. They can teach students about winning gracefully and accepting defeat in good spirit. They can teach kids to give their all.

Unfortunately, schools sometimes send the wrong messages. "What are we teaching about character when we coach soccer players to fall on the ground and writhe in pain when an opposing player gets near them?" asks an administrator. "What are we teaching when a coach screams at the referees? When we allow hazing and cursing in the locker rooms?" We don't help children become good men and women by letting them be bad sports.

A good PE program can also contribute to academic achievement. Some research suggests that children learn better when they're physically fit; disciplined activity can sharpen both mental acuity and one's appetite for learning. This modern-day finding would come as no surprise to students in classical times, when physical education was a standard part of schooling, not a diversion from it. The ancient ideal of *mens sana in corpore sano* ("a sound mind in a sound body") was rooted in the view that the truly educated person has learned to manage his life physically, mentally, and morally. Training and maintaining the body is part of getting one's overall self into shape. It molds good habits and attitudes, and in doing so helps discipline the intellect.

The best school programs approach health and physical well-being in the context of training for a wholesome life. As Teddy Roosevelt reminded us, a child "cannot do good work if he is not strong and does not try with his whole heart and soul to count in any contest; and his strength will be a curse to himself and to everyone else if he does not have thorough command over himself and over his own evil passions, and if he does not use his strength on the side of decency, justice, and fair dealing. In short, in life, as in a football game, the principle to follow is: Hit the line hard. Don't foul and don't shrink, but hit the line hard."

Elementary schools typically have recess for a few minutes a day (sometimes twice a day) and PE or gym class once or twice a week. In some schools, physical education is really that—organized exercises, activities, and lessons that actually help keep kids fit and teach them about health. In other places, however, the program lacks structure and is determined by whatever kids are in the mood for that day, whether capture the flag or a pickup basketball game. In some schools, it amounts to little more than a loosely supervised period for socializing or last-minute catching up on homework.

Consequently, many parents and policymakers have decided that PE is basically fluff, and that the school's scarce time with children could be better spent on something else. As schools have been asked to take on more responsibilities, pressure to cut back on physical education has mounted. "There has been a substantial erosion of PE programs over the last ten to fifteen years," says University of Michigan professor Charles Kuntzleman.[2] Nearly one-fourth of youngsters in grades four through twelve attend *no* PE classes at all during the school week.

Some schools are trying to reinvigorate their programs with what's known as the "New PE." Gone are the days of jumping jacks, running laps, climbing ropes, and choosing up sides for team sports. Those activities bore kids, educators say, or cause undesirable competition, so they're being replaced with pursuits meant to catch kids' interests, get their limbs moving, and avoid the dread specter of winners and losers. The New PE classes are generally more health and safety conscious, and they give kids a chance to try a variety of activities—step aerobics, juggling, in-line skating, dancing, riding a mountain bike, taking a nature hike, even learning how to swing a golf club.

The jury is still out on this new approach. In some places, it seems to raise children's enthusiasm and animation. Skeptics worry, however, that giving kids little nibbles from a long buffet of activities has more to do with recreation than physical fitness. Sometimes it seems more like preparing for tomorrow's health club membership than getting healthy and learning the rules of the game today. Some educators also say that the New PE's emphasis on "cooperative activities" (as opposed to sports contests) is yet another instance of schools trying to eradicate all competition among students.

The bottom line is that the quality of health and physical education programs varies greatly. Don't ignore this area on parents' night. Take a few minutes to see what kinds of activities the school offers. Look to see what equipment it has—balance beams, tumbling mats, climbing towers. Talk to teachers about how much exercise students get and how they get it. What are the school's goals in physical education? What health lessons does it teach? What character lessons are involved? Do children receive grades for their efforts? Are there fitness standards that they should attain? Does your own child participate enthusiastically and get along on the playing field? Remember to occasionally ask your youngster what she does during recess and PE when you discuss her day at school.

What Good Schools Teach

Here is a brief description of what a good health and physical education curriculum might look like. (For more on the subjects of drugs and sex education, see Chapter 14.)

THE PRIMARY GRADES

In the primary grades (K–3), a chief aim is to help children learn to control and coordinate their movements. Activities give practice with rhythm, agility, balance, changing direction, building speed, and so on. They include simple sports skills (e.g., running, jumping, throwing, catching, kicking) and basic games and exercises (e.g., rope jumping, foot races, dances, simple gymnastics, stretching). Instruction should encourage fitness, respect for rules, sportsmanship, safety, and the proper use of equipment. Some children in the early grades are not ready for competitive contests, though a game of tag, kickball, or capture the flag is always fun.

Topics in health should include basic hygiene (e.g., washing hands and brushing teeth); nutrition (e.g., what kinds of foods are healthy); functions of different body parts (e.g., how muscles work); disease prevention (e.g., inoculations help ward off many illnesses); first aid and safety (e.g., washing and bandaging minor scrapes); the dangers of alcohol, tobacco, and drug abuse; and how rest and exercise help the body.

THE INTERMEDIATE GRADES

In the intermediate grades (4–6), children take the skills they've learned in earlier years and apply them to team sports (e.g., soccer, basketball, softball) and individual sports (e.g., tumbling, foot races). Good programs teach the rules of different games. Students should get plenty of noncompetitive activities such as gymnastic exercises and dances, but you'll also see some competitive game playing at this level.

Children need to learn what healthy competition is all about. They need to learn how to use it to strive their hardest. The athletic field is an excellent place to prepare for being good sports about winning and losing in other aspects of life. Winning can and should be a goal, but so should "how you play the game." We want our children to learn respect for rules and the principles they represent.

Topics in health should include hygiene (e.g., the importance of personal cleanliness); nutrition (e.g., how to read food labels); disease prevention (e.g., how bacterial and viral diseases spread); first aid (e.g., taking care of bruises or insect bites); and safety (e.g., when using electrical tools). Children should learn about individual responsibility and resisting peer pressure in connection with alcohol, tobacco, and illegal drugs. Lessons about sexual maturation—taught according to community standards and with parental involvement and approval—should provide basic information about changes associated with puberty; conception; pregnancy; childbirth; and the importance of the family.

JUNIOR HIGH

Junior high students (grades 7–8) should refine their understanding of rules and strategy, as well as their skills, in connection with team and individual sports. Children should take part in a wide range of activities, both competitive and noncompetitive—soccer, basketball, track, volleyball, gymnastic exercises, dances. Activities should build stamina, strength, and agility. Lessons should continue to emphasize fitness, respect for rules, sportsmanship, safety, and proper use of equipment.

Topics in health should include hygiene; nutrition; prevention of disease; first aid; and the dangers of alcohol, tobacco, and illegal drugs. Students should learn to monitor their own weight, blood pressure, energy level, and other indicators of general health. Sex education—again, taught according to community standards and with parental involvement and approval—should provide basic information about the biological "facts of life" in an open, serious, and moral context, emphasizing responsibility, awareness of emotional and medical considerations, and the importance of family.

Keeping an Eye on the Health Program

Health classes at school demand parental supervision. As you would expect, there will probably be lessons about nutrition, disease prevention, hygiene, sex education, and the dangers of smoking and drug abuse. But you may also find lessons that seem to stretch the definition of "health," such as learning about the environment, developing a caring community, or building self-esteem. This is an area of the curriculum that can turn out to be a real hodgepodge.

Lessons sometimes broach sensitive areas such as birth control, how HIV is spread, alternative lifestyles, students' feelings of depression or anger with their parents. When classes wade into political issues, teaching materials may take sides. Some environmental literature, for example, implies that Americans are greedy and evil because they cause pollution. Some textbooks (and teachers) dispense selective morality about health issues—such as giving instructions that under no circumstances should children smoke cigarettes, while being far less judgmental about smoking marijuana, or implying that it's okay to have sex so long as you don't get sick or pregnant.

Weak health education programs can dish out well-meaning messages that result in confusion. Unpleasant surprises are not uncommon. "One kindergartner I know of came home from school one day extremely agitated about his mother's and father's nightly glass of wine before dinner," relates one educator. "In his school the kids had been treated to a puppet show about an alcoholic moose father who was beating the baby moose. Now the rattled kindergartner wanted mom and dad to give up that glass of wine before he started getting beaten. Why don't schools tell parents they're planning this stuff? They are often very secretive about their agendas in health."

Stay informed and be alert. Among good lessons about keeping healthy and fit, there may lurk messages you don't want your child to hear. Review teaching materials. Talk to teachers about the lesson plans. Let them know your opinion if you see something you don't like. Don't set out to make mountains out of molehills. But don't stand for lessons that don't meet your approval. Good schools have an opt-out program available to parents. Be prepared to make use of it and pull your child out of certain sessions if necessary.

Physical Fitness and Health at Home

For generations, American parents have taken primary responsibility for the physical fitness and health of their children. There is no reason for that to change. Schools can help, but keeping your child healthy and encouraging an active lifestyle is mainly your job.

The reality is that the total amount of vigorous physical activity that takes place under school auspices is insignificant for many kids. Therefore moms and dads should not count on schools to make sure that children get enough exercise. If they are to be healthy and strong—and to enjoy physical activity and sports—most of the effort has to come during the 90 percent of their lives that are more directly under the influence of parents.

Make sure that some after-school and weekend time is active time. See to it that your child does not turn into a high-tech couch potato, always camped out in front of the TV or computer. Kids need to study, but they also need to run, jump, climb, swim, and play. They need fresh air. You don't have to haul them to a fancy health club. Much of children's exercise can be unstructured "playground" activity. You may simply need to tell them to "go outside and play." Most will find a way to burn off energy. You will need to supply some basic equipment—balls and gloves, a jump rope, a basketball hoop, a bicycle and helmet, a Frisbee, perhaps a racquet or two.

As your child grows, you'll want to guide her into some after-school and weekend activities. Introduce her to a range of sports—hiking, swimming, canoeing, roller skating. Encouraging her to try a team sport in your community (such as baseball, basketball, or soccer leagues) is a great idea, so long as parents and kids don't let it come to dominate their lives. Organized sports teach many important qualities, and all kids should get some of this experience, even if they're not gifted athletes.

Try to set a good example by making sure your child sees you enjoying physical activity on a regular basis. The best way is to get out there and do something with your kids. For many parents and children, some of their best time together is spent tossing a ball, hiking a trail, or swimming at the community pool.

Train your child to treat her growing body responsibly. Teach about good eating and bathroom habits; the dangers of smoking, drinking, and drugs; the facts of life and the problems that can come from teenage sex. Do not assume that the school will do this job for you! In the end, a parent and family physician (and, in many cases, a minister, priest, or rabbi) make the best team for keeping kids healthy—not school health classes and clinics.

EXTRACURRICULAR ACTIVITIES

A dazzling array of extracurricular activities and pastimes awaits most American children, from computer classes to music camps to hockey leagues. The avalanche of opportunities brings good and bad consequences.

The benefits are many. A good education takes place in all sorts of settings and includes many kinds of lessons, not just academic. The broader experiences that children get outside the classroom—whether school-sponsored or not—help develop lifelong interests. They provide cultural opportunities and expand on lessons that teachers have taught. If chosen with care, extracurricular activities can provide valuable time with sound adult role models.

Extracurricular activities often help to develop physical talents and teach character traits such as self-discipline and responsibility. They are another way for kids to learn about the incomparable satisfaction associated with doing something well. They are usually good chances to be with friends. Children can relax and have fun while they learn.

For most Americans, busy as they are, modern life has brought much leisure time. People need to know how to occupy themselves in their spare hours. Much unhappiness and trouble are caused by boredom, or by frittering away time and energy in trivial, empty pursuits. Getting your child involved in a handful of out-of-class activities helps her learn how to put leisure time to good use.

On the other hand, kids shouldn't be overprogrammed. Some American children are growing up with ridiculous schedules. Monday brings swimming lessons, Tuesday art class, Wednesday guitar, Thursday soccer practice, and weekends are spent driving from game to tournament to match to recital. That's not counting sleep-overs, Sunday school, and family activities.

This frenetic pattern often begins in the early grades and picks up speed in junior high. By high school, kids' lives are jam-packed. "I'm on the soccer team, I'm in the choir, I'm the class president, and I'm taking piano lessons and French 3 this year. I have no more room," says a Maryland sophomore. "You do homework during breakfast, lunch, and dinner," a Virginia student explains. "There's no getting away. You can't even take a deep breath."[3]

Often the hectic pace is set by well-meaning parents. They want to give their children every opportunity, make them well rounded, and fill their records with activities that will look good on college applications. Occasionally, parents' motives are more questionable; some seem to be trying to live through their children, or keep up with the Jones's kids, or get junior into that elite university that turned Dad down twenty-five years ago. The result may be a burned-out kid who is too tired to study or concentrate in class. Serendipity drains out of childhood as families with grim faces risk speeding tickets in their ceaseless race from one activity to the next.

Kids need downtime. There are Saturday afternoons when they just want to relax, hang out with their friends, toss a ball for the dog, or have fun with a video game. They need some unstructured time, in part because they need to learn how to entertain themselves and set their own priorities.

This takes some balancing on your part. Resist becoming a round-the-clock cruise director. Give your child room to come up with her own ideas for something interesting, useful, or just plain fun to do. At the same time, you may need to offer a suggestion when she says "I can't think of anything to do."

Moderation is the key to organized activities. That, and some rearranging when you make a bad choice. If there is no joy in those ballet classes, your child may be overbooked, or perhaps it's time to acknowledge that she wasn't cut out to become a ballerina. Parents need to construct an *ordo amoris*—an order of the loves—in devising schedules. Talk about what is most important for your child's well-being, and set priorities accordingly. You'll probably decide, for example, that studying should come first in terms of time spent, and that out-of-school activities must not interfere. If learning about your religious faith is also high on your list, you'll have to think about whether it's worth skipping church for those weekend soccer tournaments. If your child is in love with music, she may need to cut back on another activity so she can devote enough time to piano. Most parents find that the extracurricular schedule needs some fine-tuning and readjusting every few months.

Make sure you leave time for each other in the equation. You may need to schedule activities together—playing cards or charades or taking a walk in the woods. Don't let all those extra pastimes encroach on being a family.

Here are some reminders about the tantalizing array of activities available to youngsters these days. Your first job is to offer guidance in making sensible choices. Obviously, your child's interests and talents will be top considerations. Some kids are so entranced by all the possibilities that they want to try everything, so parents must winnow the options. Other children are reluctant to try new activities and need to be nudged. Sometimes parents simply have to say, "This will be good for you—we're signing you up." As long as you're not pushing too much on them, more often than not children end up having fun and learning a lot.

- **National organizations.** Some of the best extracurricular activities are offered by local affiliates of well-known groups such as the Girl Scouts, Boy Scouts, YW/MCA, 4-H Clubs, and Young Life. In addition to teaching about a broad area of interest like the outdoors or husbandry, these organizations are committed to building good character in youngsters. They teach virtues such as good citizenship, loyalty to comrades, hard work, and responsibility.

- **Museum programs.** If there is a local museum—science, history, art, it almost doesn't matter—call the education department to see if it runs programs for children and families: talks about paintings, history walks through the old parts of town, classes that teach about insects, and so on.

- **Park and zoo programs.** Many local parks run educational events for kids such as nature hikes or classes about small mammals. Zoos and aquariums frequently host activities—demonstrations of how the staff takes care of the elephants, or sessions where youngsters can pet the llamas. Some zoos have programs in which older children take on regular volunteer duties.

- **Library programs.** Reading is one of the best extracurricular activities of all, so help your child get to know the library. Check to see what programs it offers for children—summer reading lists, book clubs, storytelling, films, talks about various subjects.

- **Church or synagogue.** Don't overlook the youth program at your place of worship. It's often a good way for preteens and teens to socialize while learning about faith and good character.

- **Sports leagues.** Since few schools have formal team sports in the early grades, many children are interested in joining an organized league (e.g., soccer, baseball, basketball) or taking classes (e.g., swimming, gymnastics, tennis). Our advice is to avoid premature specialization and encourage your child to try her hand at different sports. At this age, the point should be to develop some all-around athletic skills, burn energy, keep fit, learn how to play games, and *have fun*—not be the best eight-year-old soccer forward the world has ever seen. Once she finds a sport or two that interests her especially, by all means within reason let her follow them where they lead, perhaps to high school and college teams.

- **Art lessons.** Community art centers, local colleges, and museums often give classes in drawing, painting, sculpting.

- **Performing arts.** Keep an eye open for plays, concerts, and dance performances. Orchestras put on occasional events for children. You might also encourage your child to take some music or dance lessons, or to try out for a part in a local play.

- **Volunteering.** This is a great way for families to take on a project together. Don't wait for the school to require community service. Adopt a friend at a senior center, work at an animal shelter, help clean up a local stream, or take meals to the homebound. Volunteering will nurture in your child virtues such as kindness, friendship, and compassion.

- **Summer jobs.** For older children, a summer job teaches about work and the value of a hard-earned dollar. Kids learn a little about entrepreneurship by thinking of ways to make money—mowing neighbors' lawns, baby-sitting, watering plants, taking care of pets.

- **Enrichment programs.** If your child has a strong interest in a particular academic area, consider a program that will allow her to pursue that subject in more depth. Enrichment programs offer activities in areas such as science, computers, music, art, and foreign languages. They usually meet after school or on weekends. Summer camps that focus on particular academic or cultural areas (such as math camp or drama camp) are popular. Programs may be sponsored by the school system, a community organization, a college, or a private outfit. The atmosphere is usually relaxed; children can develop skills and talents in an informal setting and meet kids with similar interests. Talk to the teacher about the availability of out-of-school enrichment programs.

- **School-sponsored activities.** At some point (perhaps in junior high), the school will probably offer chances to take part in programs such as a service club, student newspaper, basketball league, student government, or chess club. Encourage your child to pick one or two. It's a good way to have fun with classmates, get to know teachers better, and cultivate school loyalty.

Summer Learning and Fun

Just because school's out doesn't mean kids should stop learning. Think of summer as an extracurricular session in the "school of life." The trick is to find the blend of education and recreation that's right for your child.

In some places, education reform has meant adding more days to the school calendar, so summer break isn't as long as it once was. Some communities have gone to year-round schooling that schedules several shorter vacations at various points in the year. However long your child's break, you'll surely be thinking about how she'll spend her time.

Pupils who are behind in their studies may need to use the summer to catch up. That may mean remedial classes, hiring a tutor, or doing some extra instructing yourself. Talk to the teachers to find out what kind of help your child needs. Parents whose children do makeup work know that it's important to balance it with fun. All work and no play is not a good way to spend the summer.

Most children won't need formal remedial help, but parents should still keep their brains in gear. Most important is to *keep your child reading*. If your school doesn't provide a summer reading list, see if the local library offers one. Call up the best school in your area and ask whether they'll share their list. Help your child pick books to read. However you do it, keep her reading. You can also give casual practice in other subjects; you might hone math skills, for example, by having your seventh grader figure out tips when you eat together at restaurants.

Most children enjoy one or two enrichment programs (such as a music workshop or photography class) during the summer months. Summer can also be a great time for kids to spend a little time away from home. At camp, children can learn about all sorts of topics not ordinarily taken up in school—how to paddle a canoe, tie knots, or cook a meal over an open fire. They can learn to depend on themselves, not their parents, to get through a day.

Summer shouldn't become one big structured program. Those long, sun-drenched days are the best time of all for kids to explore in their own ways—to learn how to fish, ride a bike, or pitch a tent. It's a great time for children to be with their families. Grandparents, in particular, were invented for summer. June, July, and August are the time to do simple things together (picnic, swim, and read), have grand adventures (a trip to the beach or mountains or a national park), or start hobbies (growing a vegetable garden or making model boats). It's your child's big chance to get to know the world outside of school. And a splendid chance for you and your child to get to know each other better.

CHAPTER 14

Temptations
and
Troubles

THIS CHAPTER DEALS WITH PROTECTING CHILDREN FROM some of the most pernicious of today's threats to their well-being and school careers: drug and alcohol use; premature sexual activity; and excessive television viewing. Since the Internet is now a part of so many youngsters' study lives (and leisure time), we offer some guidelines about its use as well.

Drugs and sex are obvious sources of trouble for kids. That we place television in their company may come as a surprise. Once upon a time, people expected something very different from this promising new medium. TV's early promoters promised that it would be the best thing to happen to learning since the printing press. Instead, it has become the most prevalent enemy of many children's chances for a good education.

These problems are part of the dark side of American popular culture. It is not a pretty sight. It is anti-education. It is destructive of sound values. At times it is degrading to young people. Some say, "There isn't much you can do about it. You can't shield kids from the bad in the world." In our view, that is altogether the wrong attitude. It is a defeatist recipe and, for parents, a terribly misguided one. You *can* shield children. Not from all that is bad, no, but from much of it. There are steps you can and should take to protect your young. It is the job of adults to fend off harmful influences and, to the best of our abilities, raise children in the presence of what is good. If we fail at that task, our daughters and sons have little chance of growing up healthy, happy, and well-educated.

DRUGS AND ALCOHOL

The use of illegal drugs and alcohol by young people is an American nightmare. In poll after poll, parents, students, and educators consistently identify drug use as one of the most urgent problems facing children and schools. Consider a few statistics:

- More than half of our students have tried an illegal drug by the time they graduate from high school.

- Three quarters of teens say that drugs are used, sold, and kept on their school grounds.

- Seven out of ten teenagers say they have friends who use marijuana.

- Nearly one in five children age twelve to seventeen report drinking alcohol within the past month.

- American teens see drugs as their worst problem, and half see the school drug situation getting worse.

All types of students fall prey to illegal drugs and alcohol. (For children, of course, alcohol *is* an illegal drug.) This plague doesn't discriminate by skin color, family income, or neighborhood. It's all over the country—even in middle-class suburban communities where parents often work long hours, don't see their kids in the afternoons, and give them nice allowances without realizing where the money is going. "It is easier to get marijuana, LSD, and drugs like that than it is to get cigarettes," reports one youth counselor in Fairfax County, Virginia, an upscale suburb of Washington, D.C., and one of the nation's most affluent communities.[1]

If you think this is exclusively a high school issue, you're wrong. Drugs are spreading in the lower grades, and the age of initiation is getting younger and younger. Fifty percent of middle schoolers now say there are drugs in their schools. Children who use alcohol or smoke marijuana often start around age thirteen. By the time they finish eighth grade, *30 percent* of American children have tried drugs.

Social influences play a significant role. The first temptations often come when kids are trying to impress each other. Elementary school students say the main reason for using alcohol and marijuana is to "fit in" with the crowd and act "grown up." Enticements surround them. Television, radio, and magazines are today's "super-peers." They bombard kids with thousands of messages that say it's cool to smoke and drink and even do certain drugs. Our children are listening. One study, for example, found that eight- to twelve-year-olds could name more alcohol brands than presidents. Another survey found that children knew the Budweiser frog better than slogans from ads intended for them, such as Tony the Tiger or Smokey the Bear. As former Secretary of Health, Education and Welfare Joseph Califano says, this is a society that "tosses children into a sea of drugs, alcohol, and cigarettes, which floods their schools and saturates their TV, movies, and music."

The situation is made worse by the fact that many moms and dads are in denial about the extent of the threat. They believe there is a serious problem out there, but only with someone else's children and in other people's schools. Even worse, some parents have a slack, permissive attitude. They expect kids to "do a little drinking" and don't think there's much they can do about it. Many baby boomers who experimented with illegal drugs as they grew up expect their children to do the same. They don't consider it a big deal. Attitudes about marijuana are especially lax. "Thank God it's only pot," some moms and dads say. Naturally, children get the message. Only about one in five teenagers feels that smoking marijuana is risky.

This is a shameful signal to send to young people. There is no such thing as a "soft drug" that parents can be ambivalent about. Cannabis is harmful to developing bodies and minds. Many baby boomers are unaware that the marijuana sold on the streets today is *many* times stronger than the grass of the 1960s and 1970s. It can disrupt and harm children's lives before you know what's hit them. And sometimes it is just a first step. Students who turn to more potent drugs usually do so after first using cigarettes and alcohol, and then marijuana. The research is clear on this point: *The greater a student's involvement with marijuana, the more likely it is that he will begin to use other drugs.*

Alcohol and drug use undermines academic performance. It erodes the self-discipline and motivation needed for learning. It can interfere with the brain's ability to take in, sort, and remember information. Research tells us that students who use marijuana regularly are much more likely to average 'D's and 'F's in school. Drug use is closely tied with being truant and dropping out. Students on drugs create a climate of apathy and disrespect for others. They can disrupt a whole class, even an entire school, and destroy the safe and orderly atmosphere conducive to learning.

When children begin to drink or use drugs, their world becomes more hazardous. Girls are more likely to get involved in sexual activity. (One study of adolescents with unplanned pregnancies found that nearly 50 percent had been drinking or using drugs before having intercourse. Other studies indicate that alcohol is involved in most date rapes.) Boys under the influence are more inclined toward violence and vandalism. Judgments are impaired. Youngsters are more apt to take dangerous risks and get into accidents. Alcohol is a factor in half of all vehicle-related injuries and deaths involving young drivers. Drinking or drug use can destroy ties to family and friends. It can cause youngsters to abandon their interests, values, and goals. It can cause physical, emotional, and psychological dependence that can destroy a life.

In today's America, illegal drugs and alcohol may pose the single greatest threat to your child's education and well-being. Attention to this danger is not an option. You *must* take certain steps to keep your child safe.

What Parents Can Do

Take the lead in keeping your child away from drugs. Your school should help, but do not expect it to handle this job for you. Schools cannot assume the role of primary protector. Everything we know about drug education and prevention tells us that parents are the first and main line of defense. What you say and do will become the strongest inoculation against alcohol and illegal drug use.

Since use often starts in the middle school grades, begin your efforts well in advance. Start educating early. Then, by the time your child reaches adolescence and wants more independence, he'll know the dangers involved and be ready to take responsibility for his behavior. He'll feel armed with clear expectations and his parents' trust that he is up to the challenge.

Tragically, a deafening silence is coming from too many parents. They don't talk to their children about the dangers of drugs, or they do it only once or twice. "Think about it," says one drug counselor. "In some places, 95 percent of drug education goes on in the school and 5 percent goes on at home. There is something wrong with that ratio."

There sure is. Peggy Sapp, president of the National Family Partnership in Miami, observes: "There is a big problem with a lack of confidence on the part of some parents. They don't want to tell children what to do and what not to do. Their norms and expectations are not clear. They say things like, 'I know that at all of the parties my kid goes to, people are serving beer and alcohol, but if I keep him at home I'll ruin his social life, and I just can't do that.'" That sad and telling statement reveals much about the roots of this country's drug problem.

In our opinion, it is best to approach prevention as a moral issue. Educate your child about the mental and physical harm, but also talk to him about right and wrong. "Drug use is wrong because it is immoral, and it is immoral because it enslaves the mind and destroys the soul," says political scientist James Q. Wilson. Youngsters who get hooked neglect school, grades, homework, and everyday responsibilities. In the end, they will neglect God, family, friends, and character. When children use drugs and alcohol, they put at risk everything in their lives that is noble and worthwhile. If you arm children with that recognition, they stand a much better chance of holding firm against temptation.

This message is missing in many American homes. "I'm not sure today's parents understand words like 'duty,' 'moral,' and 'immoral,'" one drug education expert wrote to us. That's a rather shocking assessment. We believe parents do understand those words, but in today's culture, they are often reluctant to voice them. It is time to start using them and teaching them to children. If we do not, this terrible problem will get no better.

Here are some good prevention strategies:

- **Set a good personal example.** Obviously, that means keeping illegal drugs completely out of your life. And send a message with your actions that alcohol is only for adults who drink responsibly and moderately.

- **Talk about standards of right and wrong.** Don't badger or threaten. Talk to your child seriously and lovingly about his responsibilities. Let him know this is very, very important to you. Encourage him to stand by what is right when pressured to drink or use drugs.

    Here is what you might tell your child: 1) Illegal drugs and drinking are dangerous—they can make you very sick and can even kill you. 2) You can get into trouble with the law. Then you get a record, a ruined reputation, and your friends' parents will not want their children to associate with you. 3) You will disappoint your family, your school, and your friends who care about you. 4) You will disappoint God. This is no way to treat your body, which is His creation. 5) With drug use, you aid criminals and drug cartels, evil people, and enemies of your country.

- **Establish firm standards of behavior.** Young people are less apt to use drugs when parents set clear rules and punish when those rules are broken. Set a zero-tolerance code of conduct about tobacco use, drinking, and drugs. When your child gets old enough, set rules about dating, curfews, and unsupervised activities. (See "Supervising Older Kids," p. 562.)

- **Praise your child for good behavior.** Affirm his courage when he makes the decision to avoid a party or situation where drugs could be present, or when he decides not to hang out with friends who are drinking. Children need to know that their parents are proud of them when they make responsible decisions.

- **Help your child learn to handle his problems.** Often kids turn to drugs because they're looking for an "escape" from issues they feel they can't deal with. It is very important to talk to youngsters about their anxieties and about how to cope with difficulties. Let your child know that drugs only compound problems.

- **Listen to your child.** Talk with him about his interests and concerns. Make sure he feels comfortable coming to you with problems or questions. Be available: kids need to know that they have their parents' attention when they want to discuss something important.

- **Know who your child's friends are.** Invite them to your home. Talk with your child about friendship. Let him know that real friends don't ask each other to do things that are wrong.

- **Keep close track of where your child goes.** Some children in this country have too much freedom to go when and where they please. "Parents should be very careful about allowing their kids to attend concerts or parties," advises Peter Greer, headmaster of Montclair Kimberley Academy in New Jersey. "At some concerts, drugs and dealers are everywhere. That is their job—to sell dope to as many young kids as possible."

- **Communicate regularly with other parents.** Get to know the moms and dads of your child's friends so you can reinforce each other's efforts. Talk with them about the nature of the drug problem in your community and school. Let them know your expectations about behavior. As your child gets older, work with other parents to establish common rules about curfews, parties, and unchaperoned social outings. You'll probably find that some families have standards of conduct you don't particularly like; you need to think about how they may influence your child.

- **Give your child regular duties.** Hold him accountable for them. This will build individual responsibility and self-discipline. Children who possess these virtues are less likely to try drugs.

- **Keep your child on track academically.** Emphasize the importance of schoolwork. Kids who are doing their homework and studying for tests are less likely to get into drugs. When they're learning, they have more interesting things to occupy their minds.

- **Go to your church or synagogue.** Keep in mind that youngsters who have an active religious life are much less likely to use illegal drugs, alcohol, and tobacco.

- **Encourage your child to play sports.** Young people who need to be in top physical shape to compete in athletics are much less likely to use drugs and alcohol. Good coaches and the rules they set are very useful allies in this campaign.

- **Keep your eyes and ears open when it comes to mass media.** Don't assume that movie your seventh grader wants to see or the CD he wants to buy is benign. Some films, song lyrics, and even magazine advertisements portray the drug culture as chic and cool. As best you can, keep your child away from those messages. Talk to him about how some advertisers try to make drinking and smoking seem glamorous. Help him separate myths from realities.

- **Be knowledgeable about drugs and the signs of drug use.** Educate yourself about different kinds of drugs, drug paraphernalia, street names of drugs, what they look like, their effects, and so forth. The more you know, the better your defenses will be. It's much better for your child to get information from you than from other children or on the street. Your school should be able to help you obtain some educational material. Or get in touch with one of the organizations listed in "Where to Get Help and Information" on page 566. (See also "Signs of Drug Use," page 560.)

• **Work with the school.** Find out what its drug and alcohol policies are. Learn how it teaches about drugs. Make sure it is sending and enforcing a clear, no-use message. As one principal puts it, "If the school has a history of not dealing hard with drugs, you do not want that school." Do everything you can to support the staff's efforts.

Parents who suspect that their children are using drugs often have to deal with feelings of anger, resentment, guilt, and failure. Sometimes they don't want to admit that their child could have a problem of this kind. They deny the evidence and postpone dealing with the situation. If you think your child may be involved with drugs or alcohol, *don't wait.* Ignoring the situation is the worst thing you can do. If you and your child face the problem promptly, there is a good chance you can overcome it together.

Get a plan of action. You may want to discuss your suspicions with your child in a calm, objective manner. Do not do it when you are angry or agitated. Do not confront your child when he is under the influence of alcohol or other drugs. Wait until he is sober. If your child is really using drugs, be prepared to hear him lie to you about it. Let him know you love him, but be firm. Impose whatever disciplinary measures you deem necessary. Get him away from the people, places, and circumstances that are encouraging drug use. The words of actor Carroll O'Connor, who lost a son to drug use, say it all: "Get between your child and drugs any way you can."

You may need help, especially if your child has engaged in heavy use. It's a good idea to seek advice from your doctor, minister or rabbi, school officials, a drug treatment agency, and other parents. They can help you find a drug treatment professional, if necessary. You can also consult the references listed on page 566 for general advice. The more allies you have in this fight, the better your chances of winning it.

Signs of Drug Use

It is sometimes hard to know the difference between "normal" adolescent behavior and that caused by drugs or alcohol. Any of the following signals may indicate drug use; however, they may also apply to a child who is having other problems at school or at home. Watch for extreme changes in behavior. If you have any doubts, have a doctor examine your child. You may also want to consider purchasing a home drug testing kit. Some parents find that keeping one on the shelf ends lots of arguments and gets them accurate information quickly.

- *Behavioral symptoms include:* a sudden change of friends; evasion and lying; mood swings; inappropriate anger and hostility; overreaction to criticism; reduced motivation and self-discipline; anxiety expressed in jerky or jittery movements; compulsive behavior. Also, be aware of changes in sleep patterns; irregular hours; a sudden loss of interest in hobbies and favorite activities; an unexplained presence or absence of money.

- *Changes in school performance include:* a marked downturn in grades; assignments not completed; increased absenteeism or tardiness.

- *Signs of physical deterioration include:* unhealthy appearance; indifference to hygiene; sallow complexion; weight changes; fatigue; appetite changes; memory lapses; difficulty in concentration; bloodshot eyes, dilated pupils, or imprecise eye movements; poor coordination; slurred or incoherent speech.

- *Signs of drugs and identification with the drug culture include:* alcohol- or drug-related posters, magazines, or slogans on clothing; a fake ID or driver's license; drug-related paraphernalia (e.g., pipes, cigarette rolling papers, small medicine bottles, small butane lighters, small glass vials).

Teaching Your Child to Say No

Your child will have an easier time avoiding temptation if you help him practice ways to say no. Start when he's in the early grades. Make up situations in which he may be asked to try alcohol, drugs, or unfamiliar substances. Here are some steps you can practice with him. Tell your child to:

- **Ask questions.** If unknown substances are offered, ask, "What is it?" and "Where did you get it?" If a party or other gathering is proposed, ask, "Who else is coming?" "Where will it be?" "Will parents be there?"

- **Say no.** Don't argue, don't discuss. Say no and show that you mean it.

- **Give reasons.** "I'm doing something else that night" or "The coach says drugs will hurt my game" are examples of some reasons that youngsters can use. Also, don't forget the oldest reason: "My parents will kill me."

- **Suggest other things to do.** If a friend is offering alcohol or other drugs, saying no is tougher. Suggesting something else to do—going to a movie, playing a game, or working together on a project—shows that drugs are being rejected, not the friend.

- **Leave.** When all these steps have been tried, get out of the situation immediately. Go home, go to class, join a group of friends, or talk to someone else.

(*Reprinted from* Growing Up Drug Free: A Parent's Guide to Prevention,
U.S. Department of Education)

Supervising Older Kids

Here are some tips about supervising junior high school children:

- When your child goes out, know where he is going, what he'll be doing, and whom he'll be with. Make sure that he knows where you are.

- Don't permit last-minute changes in plans (such as deciding to see a different movie or go to a different friend's house) unless your child first checks with you.

- Establish a time to come home, and set a rule to phone first if that curfew must be broken.

- Be awake when your child gets home at night. Greet him and ask him what sort of time he had.

- Assure your child that he can call to be picked up, any place and any time. Stay reachable, or make sure he knows how to contact a responsible adult who is.

- For parties at your house, be visible. Do not let kids leave the premises and then return again without checking with you first.

- For parties at other houses, always check with the parents to make sure they will be present and supervising. Adult-free houses with teens in them are powder kegs waiting to explode.

What Good Schools Do

Parents must take the lead in protecting their children from alcohol and other drugs, but schools should be allies. You should be able to count on their support, and they should be able to count on yours.

Most elementary schools do make sincere efforts. They have drug education programs (some more effective than others) and, in general, they do not tolerate alcohol or other drugs on school grounds. During the 1990s, however, attention to this country's drug problem slipped. Some schools are no longer as vigorous about prevention. There are fewer exhortations to children and fewer efforts to attack this problem head-on. Society as a whole has become laxer and more complacent. After making substantial headway in this fight in the 1980s, we've seen drug use rise among young people in recent years.

Schools and parents can never let their guard down. The minute they do, drugs may sneak into kids' lives. Here are some characteristics of schools that are seriously engaged in this tough battle. Those schools:

- **Determine the extent of alcohol and illegal drug use.** In many places, administrators and teachers are unaware that students are using and selling drugs on school property. Schools that are serious about prevention actively monitor the situation. For example, they may take anonymous surveys of students and teachers, or conduct unannounced locker inspections. They train teachers to recognize indicators of drug use. They hold meetings of school personnel to pinpoint areas where drugs may be used or sold. Administrators stay in close touch with the local police about arrests in the neighborhood and the availability of drugs in the community. They meet with parents to find out what they know about the prevalence of drug use. Find out whether your school takes these kinds of steps.

  Good schools keep records on problems that have occurred (such as how many drug-related suspensions and expulsions there have been in the last five years). They don't try to sugarcoat the truth. Naturally, they need to preserve individual students' and families' rights to privacy, but they let the community know in clear language exactly what the situation is on their premises.

- **Establish clear rules and consequences.** Good schools send an unambiguous message: if you use drugs, there will be a price to pay. They aggressively promote the fact that they are a drug-free environment. Their policies state that drug use, possession, and sale on school grounds and at school functions will not be tolerated. They spell out what constitutes an alcohol or drug offense, the consequences for violating the policy, and the procedures for handling violations. Copies of this policy are given to all parents and students. (Some schools now have "24 hour, 365 day" drug policies. That is, they hold students accountable for their behavior off campus on evenings, weekends, and holidays.)

  In schools that are tough on drugs and alcohol, the consequences for breaking the rules usually look something like this: A first-time offender is called to a required meeting with his parents and school officials. The school may ask student and parents to sign a contract stating that they acknowledge the drug problem and that the student agrees to stop using. He must enroll in a drug intervention or private rehabilitation program. Depending on the severity of the infraction, he may be suspended, given detention, or assigned to an alternative school. In some cases, the police are notified. Subsequent infractions lead to suspension and possible expulsion from school. If a student is caught dealing drugs, he is turned over to the police and faces either suspension or expulsion.

- **Enforce the rules and ensure security.** Good schools do what they say they'll do when students are caught with alcohol or other drugs. They don't give in when the parents of an offending student complain or make excuses. They live up to the terms of their drug policy.

  Security is an essential part of enforcement. When children are at school, they should be out of harm's way. Administrators should do whatever is necessary to keep strangers and drug trafficking out. Enforcement policies vary according to the severity of a school's drug problem. In some places, for example, administrators may require students to carry hall passes. In others, they may ask a police officer to patrol the grounds.

- **Teach drug prevention in every grade.** Good elementary schools teach students how to recognize specific drugs, including alcohol, tobacco, marijuana, inhalants, and cocaine. They tell kids about the dangerous effects of use. They coach youngsters in ways to say no to drugs—and teachers let children know they expect them to say no.

  Effective anti-drug curricula have a strong moral component. They send a resounding message: using drugs is wrong. Kids are taught that it is wrong because it harms the user's body and mind, fosters other vices such as lying and stealing, and hurts other people, especially the user's family. They're taught that if they take drugs they are breaking the law, helping pushers and dealers, and adding to one of society's worst problems. Good schools do not hesitate to help raise children to a moral obligation to control themselves and keep themselves drug- and alcohol-free. Without such a call to personal responsibility, anti-drug education usually has little effect. Be aware also that most school programs don't work very well if parents aren't leading the effort at home.

- **Reach out to the community for support.** Principals and teachers know that they can't combat the drug problem alone. They may not even be able to keep drugs off school grounds by themselves. So they enlist the community's support. For example, they may ask law enforcement agencies to clear the neighborhood of dealers and provide information about drug problems outside the school. They call on local professionals, such as doctors and pharmacists, to talk to kids about drug use. They ask business leaders to sponsor drug-free activities for youngsters. They hold meetings where parents and teachers can share information about recent drug problems.

You can help your school. Tell your principal and school board that drug use must not be tolerated. Stand by administrators who are tough on drugs. If illegal drugs or alcohol are on the school grounds, round up other parents to help you make a lot of noise until the problem is solved.

Make sure you and your child know the school's drug policy. Stick to it. If your own child is caught with drugs or alcohol at school, accept appropriate responsibility and follow the rules. Some parents suddenly decide the school's policy is too tough. They blame the teachers or other students for their child's behavior. Think twice before you start pointing fingers. If your child needs help and discipline, make sure he gets it. The worst thing you can do for him and his school is to start making excuses.

Stay in touch with teachers and other parents about the drug situation at school. Occasionally donate some time: chaperone a school-sponsored drug-free activity, round up a volunteer (such as a policeman) to speak to a class, or get involved with a parent-teacher committee that works on drug prevention. Above all, make sure your child gets a consistent no-drugs message at home.

Despite the grim news and statistics, most youngsters don't use drugs. They don't want their friends using them or their schools wrecked by them. Elementary school children take their cues from parents and teachers. When they know that the adults they respect are serious about staying away from drugs and alcohol, they behave accordingly. If parents and schools are tough and unwavering about this problem, they have the upper hand.

Questions to Ask About Drugs and Your School

- Is the drug policy spelled out clearly and given to all parents (for example, in the school handbook)?

- Is it a tough, zero-tolerance policy?

- Is drug education a part of the curriculum? Is it taught in every grade?

- Does the curriculum teach students how to recognize drugs, what their effects are, and how to stay away from them?

- Does it send a clear, unmistakable message that it is wrong to use illegal drugs, and that it is wrong for children to use alcohol?

- Are there regular meetings for parents, teachers, and administrators to discuss drugs and alcohol? Do people show up for them?

- Are school officials proactive and forthright in telling parents about the drug situation at school? Do they keep statistics on drug-related incidents?

- How many students have been suspended or expelled for drugs?

- Are the school grounds secure so that strangers cannot easily approach children?

- Is the school run in a disciplined, orderly manner?

- Does it conduct locker inspections when there are signs of serious problems?

- Does it enlist the community's support (e.g., the police department, local businesses, civic groups) to make the anti-drug program work?

Where to Get Help and Information

Parents have allies. Here are some effective organizations you can turn to for information and advice about protecting your child from illegal drugs and alcohol.

Community Anti-Drug Coalitions of America
901 North Pitt Street, Suite 300
Alexandria, VA 22314
703-706-0560
www.cadca.org

National Center on Addiction and Substance
Abuse at Columbia University
152 West 57th Street
New York, NY 10019-3310
212-841-5200
www.casacolumbia.org

National Family Partnership
2490 Coral Way
Miami, FL 33145
800-705-8997
www.nfp.org

Parents' Resource Institute for Drug Education (PRIDE)
3610 Dekalb Technology Parkway, Suite 105
Atlanta, GA 30340
770-458-9900
www.prideusa.org

Partnership for a Drug-Free America
405 Lexington Avenue
New York, NY 10174
212-922-1560
www.drugfreeamerica.org

SEX AND SEX EDUCATION

No subject in the curriculum sparks more debate than sex education. When one considers what's happening in the lives of many American students, it's not hard to see why this topic is controversial.

There has been some good news lately. The number of teenage pregnancies has declined during the last few years. But there is bad news, too. A 1997 survey found that nearly one half of school-aged children had had sexual intercourse. That same year, there were nearly 200,000 births to girls between the ages of ten and seventeen. Almost 90 percent of these mothers were unmarried. In 1995, there were 275,000 abortions performed on teenagers. Nearly four in ten teenage pregnancies end in abortion. Every year, approximately one in four sexually active teens contracts a sexually transmitted disease.

Most Americans favor sex education in the schools. They realize that this is a subject in which parents should be the primary teachers, but they also find it reasonable for schools to provide another opportunity for students to learn about this important area of life. Parents' support for this part of the curriculum comes not from their assessment that the programs are effective, but rather from a deep-seated feeling that they want certain things for their children. First, they want children to be knowledgeable of basic physiological facts about puberty, conception, and pregnancy. Second, they want them to know the risks of pregnancy and sexually transmitted diseases such as HIV. Third, parents want children to be able to resist pressures and do the right thing.

A lot is riding on these goals. If a teenager begins sexual activity at the age of sixteen and continues until twenty, he or she runs a very high risk of becoming infected with a sexually transmitted disease during those years. If children start younger, the risks increase even more. This can result in sterility, cancer, lifelong health problems, even death. Furthermore, girls who get pregnant are much more likely to leave school and forfeit their education. Though sex education may seem to some like an elective, for many girls it can mean the difference between a good education and none at all.

Accordingly, most American schoolchildren receive some kind of formal sex education before they graduate. In many places, the process begins in elementary school under the rubric of "health education," "family life education," or a similar name. The quality of these programs varies enormously. Some schools do an admirable job. In other places, sex education classes are not particularly constructive. And in some instances, they are horrible. Occasionally, it seems like anything goes. Chagrined parents open their newspapers and read the stories: A Massachusetts school board votes to teach preschoolers about homosexual lifestyles. ("We are on a trailblazing path," the superintendent says proudly.) A program developed in New Jersey begins teaching kindergartners about birth control and masturbation. Guidelines used by the New York City Board of Education instruct first grade teachers to offer their students the false and deadly statement that "new treatments for HIV/AIDS act like Superman's/Superwoman's lead shield" to protect the immune system.[2]

You may run into such shockers at your school. But what you're more likely to find, if the program there is typical, is a pervasive attitude that goes something like this: Offer students technical information. Offer them facts about their bodies and their reproductive systems. Tell them that they have choices to make, and tell them what the consequences of those choices could be. But don't give advice. Don't moralize. Certainly do not tell them that it is wrong for schoolchildren to have sex. As one Virginia girl notes, "Everyone tells us how to protect ourselves, but no one says not to do it."

Weak sex education materials are typically loaded with language about encouraging students to "know their options," "identify alternatives," and "examine their own values." The goal is to "equip young people to make the right decision about what is right for them." Planned Parenthood says that the aim is to "help them acquire skills to make decisions now and in the future." According to one set of guidelines used in Massachusetts, sexually healthy adolescents should "decide what is personally 'right' and act on those values."

The problem with this kind of teaching is that it does not teach. It does not teach because, while speaking to a very important aspect of life, it displays a conscious aversion to making moral distinctions. Indeed, it insists on holding them in abeyance. The words of a rational, mature morality often seem to have been banished from sex education. It is tantamount to throwing up our hands and saying to young people, "We give up. We will forego teaching you right and wrong, or even what is healthy and not healthy. Instead, please take these facts, this information, and take your feelings, your options, and try to make the best decisions you can. But you're on your own. We can say no more." It is ironic that in the part of their lives where children may need adult guidance most, they often find an abdication of responsible moral authority.

Quality sex education has to do not only with how people treat each other and themselves, but also how they *should* treat each other and themselves. It is about character. A sex education course in which issues of right and wrong do not occupy center stage is evasive and irresponsible. Schools do have a role in helping teach "the facts of life." Youngsters should know where babies come from and how their bodies work. But educators should place this information in a moral context. Sexual behavior is governed by the values one holds, not by mere awareness of available options.

In elementary school, placing sex education in a moral context involves saying exactly what most American parents say at home: *Children should not engage in sexual relations*. There should be absolutely no question about this stance on the part of K–8 schools. After all, the vast majority of these youngsters are no more than fourteen years old. Is there anyone who seriously argues that it's fine for sixth or seventh or eighth graders to have sex?

When adults maintain a studiously value-neutral stance, the impression likely to be left is, in the words of one student, "No one says not to do it, and by default they're condoning it." A sex education curriculum that simply provides "options" is delivering the wrong message. If elementary schools are going to talk to their charges about sexual relations at all, they should have the courage, common sense, and decency to say that it is wrong for children to have sex, and explain why. This is simply ethical candor and adult responsibility. The overwhelming majority of American parents would gratefully welcome help in transmitting such values.

In recent years, many sex education programs (both in elementary schools and high school) have begun to include lessons on abstinence. Unfortunately, however, refraining from sexual intercourse is often presented as but one choice among many. In many programs, abstinence is not emphasized. The school presents it as just another lifestyle option. "The problem I have with sex ed is that there is one sentence on abstinence and ten sentences on how to use a condom," observes school nurse Esther Splaine.[3] Curricular material may say that abstinence is the smartest, safest choice, but all too often the primary message is still that children must decide what is most comfortable for them. It is as if being "comfortable" with one's decision is the sum and substance of the responsible life.

The attitude underlying typical instruction is that abstinence is a quaint and naive approach. Children are going to experiment sexually, it is taken for granted, and there is little adults can do to stop them. The "realistic" approach, then, is to offer knowledge of how contraceptives work so they can have "safe sex." Planned Parenthood's sex education guidelines, for example, suggest that nine- to thirteen-year-olds be taught about contraceptives so that they are "able to name some and how to obtain them."

In our opinion, that lesson is a bad one to teach young children. Elementary schools should *not* be showing their charges how to use condoms and other contraceptives. Some parents will disagree with us, but we maintain that such instruction is harmful. After all, we don't keep young children away from alcohol by saying, "We don't want you drinking, but if you do decide to drink, here's how to mix a martini."

In an attempt to avoid "preaching" and "moralizing," some programs suggest that having sexual intercourse with condoms is as safe as abstinence. "Those who espouse this form of education almost never give clarity about the enormous health risks of disease and pregnancy to young people even if they use contraceptives," says Dr. Joe McIlhaney of the Medical Institute for Sexual Health in Austin, Texas. "For example, essentially all studies show that condoms give almost no protection from human papillomavirus (HPV), which is the cause of more than 93 percent of all cervical cancer and precancerous Pap smears. Many sexuality educators say they want to give full information, yet they rarely mention such risks."

The truth is that most adolescent children do restrain themselves if adults level with them, teach them personal responsibility, hold high expectations, and provide the necessary moral support. There are good programs that prove it. One is Best Friends, operated in inner-city schools in the nation's capital and adopted in other schools around the country. Founded by Elayne Bennett (the wife of one of the authors),

Best Friends is a character development program for girls, with messages about abstinence from sex, drugs, and alcohol. Girls begin the curriculum in the fifth or sixth grade and continue through high school. Group discussions explore topics such as friendship, love, and dating. Girls learn skills for making good decisions and developing self-respect through the practice of self-restraint. Teacher mentors help girls learn the difference between love and infatuation. In one evaluation among District of Columbia participants, only 1 percent of Best Friends girls had become pregnant, compared to 26 percent of their classmates.

Best Friends and other good abstinence-only programs recognize a fundamental truth that most sex education curricula miss: there is much more to sexual activity than physically gratifying oneself while guarding against pregnancy and sexually transmitted disease. As every adult knows, sex is inextricably connected to the psyche and to the soul. It is no mere riot of the glands that occurs, ends, and is meaningless thereafter. Sexual intimacy changes things—it affects feelings, attitudes, self-image, and one's view of another person. It involves men and women in all their complexity—their emotions, desires, and often contradictory intentions they bring with them, whether they mean to or not. It is, in other words, a quintessentially moral activity.

Far from being value-neutral, sex may be the most value-laden of any human activity. It has complicated and profound repercussions. If schools are going to speak to children about it, they should acknowledge that it involves a person at the deepest level of his or her being. To deny that, to make it out to be something less special and powerful than it is, is a dodge and a lie. Schools do not serve students well by acting as if sex were an activity of no moral significance.

Principles to Look for in Sex Education

Here are five principles that we believe parents of elementary school children should look for in sex education:

- **Sexual behavior is in large part a matter of character.** School should not act as if it is mainly a matter of "choosing what's right for you." Lessons should teach children sexual restraint as a standard to uphold and follow.

- **Sex is not simply a physical act.** Children should be taught the truth: sex is tied to the deepest elements of the personality. It involves complicated feelings and emotions, some ennobling and some that can cheapen one's finer impulses—and cheapen others.

- **Children run enormous health risks when they engage in sexual intercourse.** Schools should be honest with students about these risks: they can damage children permanently and change the entire course of their futures.

- **Sex education should stand up for the family.** Courses should speak of sexual activity in the context of marriage as an institution. They should stress the fidelity, commitment, maturity, and love required of the partners in a successful marriage.

- **Sex education courses should engage parents as allies.** Parents should be informed of the content, welcomed in class, involved in the homework, and encouraged to talk to their children. Teachers should be able to depend on mothers and fathers for follow-up on lessons. Parents need to be integrated into the curriculum from the beginning.

Teachers of sex education should speak to children of virtues such as responsibility, respect for self, and respect for others. They need to talk to girls about readiness for motherhood and how to say "No." Girls need adults to help them learn how to resist the lines they will be fed by boys. Parents have every reason to expect that sex education courses will use words like "modesty," "virginity," and "self-restraint." They have a right to expect that schools will not undermine the values that still lead most girls to see sexual modesty as a good thing. Likewise, teachers should talk to boys about the responsibilities of being a father. They should make clear that readiness for fatherhood should precede the acts that might make them fathers.

If sex education courses are prepared to deal with these truths of the human condition, they will probably be welcomed by most parents. If instead, they distort or omit certain aspects of this extremely important realm of human life, they are misleading and perhaps harming children. If these courses do not help in the effort to provide an education in character, there is little point in having them in the schools.

What Parents Can Do

Be aware of what your school is doing before your child enters the sex education program. Acquaint yourself with what's being taught, how it is taught, who is teaching it, and the implicit and explicit messages that it transmits.

Call the teacher or principal and ask to see a copy of the grade-by-grade curriculum outline for sex education. Good schools are happy to provide it. Many schools send some information about the sex ed program home to parents, but you may ask to see the plan in more detail. It's also a good idea to examine some of the teaching material that will be used. Where did it come from? What sort of training do the teachers get, and who gives it? (Outside agencies and consultants often help develop and direct the curriculum.)

You may want to observe a sex education class. Since many youngsters don't want their parents present during sex ed, some teachers schedule a special session for parents in which they actually teach some of the lessons, so that moms and dads can get a feel for what's being presented. You can also talk to other parents whose children have been through the same program and get their assessment.

Pay attention to *who* is teaching your child about sex. Teachers are role models for young people, so it is crucial that sex education instructors offer examples of good character by the way they act, and by the ideals and convictions they articulate to students. Talk with the teacher about her approach. The same material can be used quite differently in the hands of two different instructors. Keep in mind that some teachers are considerably more dedicated than others to addressing questions of character and morality in the matter of sexual behavior.

This is not an easy subject to teach. The curriculum and reading material may look restrained and tactful, but sometimes the questions students ask are not! Talking about this topic to a classroom of inquisitive youngsters takes considerable finesse. Teachers who handle it well deserve parents' gratitude.

What if you do not like what you see? In many school districts, parents can opt to remove their children from the sex education program. (You may be given a form for that purpose at the beginning of the school year.) If your child is the only one not participating, you will have to weigh his potential embarrassment against the harm you believe may be caused by leaving him in the program. Talk to the teacher about what your child would do during sex ed lessons if you remove him. Will the school be sensitive to students who opt out? ("My daughter was sent to the hall to sit on the floor while the class was going on," reports one dismayed mom.)

If you discover that the sex education program is a problem, you may want to unite with other parents to try to change or get rid of it. With much determination, it can be done. A notable example of parent backlash was the 1993 removal of the "Children of the Rainbow" curriculum from the New York City public schools. That curriculum, which included the controversial books *Heather Has Two Mommies* and *Daddy's Roommate*, angered many mothers and fathers. Mary Cummins, the "Irish grandmother from Queens," led a group of citizens who were frustrated by a system that seemed blind to their concerns, and eventually managed to rid the city of both the curriculum and the school chancellor who was behind it.

Be prepared for the cold reality that, in some places, anyone who dares to criticize the sex education program may be called a naive, sexually repressed, right-wing prude. You may be ridiculed. "I asked why abstinence did not play a noticeable part in the material," one parent reports of a meeting to preview a new course in sexuality. "What happened next was shocking. There was a great deal of laugher, and someone suggested that if I thought abstinence had any merit, I should go back to burying my head in the sand."

This kind of response has a purpose: to make you keep quiet and go away. Do not let it stop you. If you are uncomfortable with the sex ed program, do something. Find moms and dads who share your concern. ("A single frustrated parent will rarely get anywhere," one principal we know candidly advises.) Gather information about alternative programs. If necessary, get your child out!

No matter what you think of your school's sex ed program, be sure to offer your own careful lessons at home. Many parents admit that they don't do enough to teach their children about sex—a big part of the reason that schools have stepped into this role. Take this age-old duty of mothers and fathers seriously. Your expectations and involvement are critical. In the words of one report from the University of Minnesota, *parents who give clear messages about delaying sex have children who are less likely to have early intercourse.* Parents can help protect children from sexual activity and pregnancy by communicating their disapproval of adolescent sex and adolescent use of contraception.[4] Do not be taken in by the "they're going to do it no matter what you say" argument. That attitude is an evasion of responsibility and a risk to your child. Young people *do* pay attention when parents offer loving, caring guidance.

Explain the "facts of life" to your child when the time is right. Tell children that sexual intercourse must be postponed, that marriage is the best setting for sex and raising children. Make sure they understand the beauty and pleasure of sex, as well as the considerable risks of teenage sex, from pregnancy, AIDS, and other sexually transmitted diseases, to broken hearts and shame.

Tell boys that being a real man has nothing to do with having sex. Talk to girls about how to say "No" to a boy without hurting his feelings. Tell them that if a guy says the only way to prove your love is to have sex, *it's a line and a lie!* Youngsters today grow up getting all sorts of cultural signals that sex with just about anyone under any circumstances is not only permissible, but expected. Take a stand and help your children develop the moral strength to oppose these messages.

Do not leave sex education up to your school, to "experts," curriculum planners, or anyone else. Attentive mothers and fathers are the best protection children have. The most effective sex education comes in that irreplaceable crucible of character: the home.

Where to Get Help and Information

Here are four organizations that do a good job in the field of sex education:

Best Friends Foundation
4455 Connecticut Avenue NW, Suite 310
Washington, DC 20008
202-237-8156

The Loving Well Project
School of Education, Boston University
605 Commonwealth Avenue
Boston, MA 02215
617-353-4088
www.bu.edu/SED/lovingwell

The Medical Institute for Sexual Health
P.O. Box 162306
Austin, TX 78716-2306
512-328-6268
www.medinstitute.org

True Love Waits
127 Ninth Avenue North
Nashville, TN 37234-0152
800-LUV-WAIT
www.truelovewaits.com
This is a faith-based program suited to home and private school use.

TELEVISION AND YOUR CHILD'S EDUCATION

Television has become one of the most potent and destructive influences on education in America. It is the atomic bomb of some youngsters' school careers. By controlling their time, attention, and habits, it virtually wrecks their chances for academic success. It is an incredibly persuasive teacher, and many of its lessons are the opposite of what children need to learn. *Too much TV will harm your child's education. It can harm her character.* We know of few good students whose parents do not control the television set.

Television eats up an enormous portion of many kids' lives. American children watch on average more than three hours every day. Some watch much more. In a great many households, the TV set is on almost constantly. By the time they graduate from high school, many students have spent more hours watching TV than doing homework, reading, or talking to their parents.

This is a medium which absorbs, at a conservative estimate, one third of the typical American's free time. That makes watching TV the dominant activity with which Americans fill their leisure hours—occupying more time than the next ten most popular leisure activities *combined*. In fact, it's safe to say that the act of watching television is the single greatest consumer of leisure time the human race has ever known.

Here are a few of the reasons you should be concerned about the amount of TV watched in your home:

- **Too much TV means bad grades.** Extensive viewing often goes hand in hand with poor academic performance. Sitting in front of the set hour after hour can translate into less learning and slower intellectual development.

- **Families and children lose opportunity time.** Too much TV is damaging because of the behavior it *prevents* and the opportunities it steals. A child who is staring at a screen is not reading or writing. He's not doing homework, at least not seriously. He's not having an attentive conversation with mom and dad. He's not getting exercise. Those are the kinds of activities that turn children into healthy, happy, smart students. Turning on the TV turns off such endeavors.

- **TV is too easy.** Most TV viewing involves less concentration and alertness than just about any other daily activity. That's one of its chief attractions—all you have to do is sit back and stare. Many teachers note that when children get hooked on passive entertainment, they have a harder time mustering the effort that study requires.

- **TV caters to short attention spans and immediate gratification.** Teachers also know that it's harder for children to concentrate for any length of time when they're programmed to expect TV's rapid-fire format and channel-surfing mind-set. Television teaches that if you don't like what you see, zap it and move on to something else. Don't stick with things that aren't immediately enjoyable.

- **Children receive harmful messages.** The average American child sees tens of thousands of acts of glamorized violence on TV before he has finished grade school. The American Academy of Pediatrics warns that "Significant exposure to media violence increases the risk of aggressive behavior in certain children and adolescents, desensitizes them to violence, and makes them believe that the world is a 'meaner and scarier' place than it is."

   The average young viewer is also exposed to 14,000 sexual references each year. Many programs treat children to a barrage of images signaling that promiscuity is not only chic but also largely free of risk and responsibility. Programs and commercials offer young people guiding principles such as: If you want to be happy, you have to make your own rules. Happiness can be bought. Grab for all you can get. Drinking beer helps you make friends.

- **Television makes moral education harder.** Given what's on the screen, excessive television watching not only threatens your child's intellect, it puts character training at risk. In a survey of 4,000 parochial school teachers, half stated that television and the media are the greatest obstacles to teaching morals to students.

- **Too much TV might make your child fat.** Studies indicate that the more television children watch, the more likely they are to be obese. Growing children need to spend time running, jumping, and playing hard—not lounging in front of the tube, eating the junk food they see advertised.

Most American mothers and fathers realize the dangers of too much TV. They know the tube is mostly awash with bilge. They know their kids are soaking a lot of it up. Yet all too often they ignore the risks. Many U.S. parents don't do much guiding of their youngsters' program selections and seldom discuss them. In one study, three out of five eighth graders said their parents rarely or never limited their TV watching.

Television has an alluring, almost addictive power. Children beg to watch it, and parents give in. If a child is cranky or at loose ends, if you've just walked in from the office and you want an hour of peace and quiet—steer the kids into the family room and turn on the electronic baby-sitter.

Try this thought exercise to gain some perspective on this practice: In order to keep the children entertained, you leave the front door wide open so that an endless parade of strangers can slip into your house, even when you're not there, so long as they promise to stay in one corner. There they stand and speak to your children. They can tell whatever stories come into their heads, and try to convince your children to buy whatever wares they happen to be selling. They can show your children how to talk, and how to behave. They can take off their clothes and prance around. They can have sex with people they're not married to. They can shoot or stab each other. They can use foul language. They can celebrate criminal behavior and make fun of "traditional values." They can persuade your children as to what kinds of goals they should set for themselves, what prizes they should crave. They can teach them whom to admire and honor. They can suggest to your children the kinds of ideals they should esteem, as well as those to be scorned. All this in your living room or den or family room. All this while your children watch eagerly.

It's a scene worth imagining, because when you leave a child unattended, unrestricted, and intellectually unarmed in the presence of a television set, that's pretty much what you're doing.

Parents would do well to remember that television programs and advertisements are among the most sophisticated, penetrating forms of communication ever invented. Their aim is not just to entertain, but to reshape people's desires, habits, and dispositions. Children are impressionable. Often they cannot morally appraise the different behaviors they witness. They cannot always filter right from wrong, useful from harmful, noble from base. They look to adults for these lessons. If the grown-ups they spend the most time with are the ones they observe on TV, then those on-screen adults become their teachers. The lessons they offer are the ones that youngsters learn. That makes for a pretty sorry education.

Establishing Good TV Habits

Television watching is like any other habit. The sooner you get into a proper routine, the better. It is possible, of course, to enlist technology as an ally in this campaign. Parents can now buy electronic locks that let only people with a password turn on the TV set. You can buy time-channel locks that allow you to preset the channels and times that children can watch. There is also the V-chip, a device installed in new television sets which reads a rating assigned to each program and, if so instructed, automatically blocks some shows. The problem with the V-chip, however, is that it relies on ratings assigned by none other than the industry which produces and broadcasts so much inane programming. It's a bit like asking the wolf to watch over the sheep.

The truth is that *you* are the only one who can really keep track of how much television your child watches. You are the only one who can satisfactorily determine what he sees. It is your responsibility to maintain control over that set and help him learn some self-discipline. Here are some guidelines to keep in mind:

- **Set rules.** First, establish clear limits on when and what your child watches. Boundaries must be set. The American Academy of Pediatrics suggests that families create "electronic media-free environments" in children's rooms. That's a great idea.

    During the school year, we recommend no TV on weekdays for elementary school children, and limited TV time (perhaps two to four hours) during the weekend. Some families use the rule "no television until homework and chores are finished." Other parents insist that TV time equal reading time. You might want to try a "no TV week" (or month) in your home. Your family will probably discover you don't need it as much as you thought you did.

- **Stick to those rules.** Setting limits does no good unless they're steadfastly enforced. If you need to, keep a written record of exactly how much time your child spends in front of the TV, and what he is watching. That way there will be no doubt about whether he's staying within the limits you have set.

There will be occasions, of course, when you'll need to bend the rules—perhaps when a child is sick, a special program is coming on, or an event of national significance is occurring. Those times should be few, and you should let your child know that you haven't thrown the rules away. You're making an exception.

- **Be selective about what your family watches.** Much of what's on TV is junk, but there is also some programming that can inform, educate, even uplift children's minds. (Consider *Touched by an Angel*, for example.) While he is very young, you need to pick his programs. When he's older, you can give him some voice in deciding what to watch. Let him choose from a list of shows you've approved. Involving him in that decision will help him develop a sense of responsibility about television viewing.

  Do not assume a program is safe for your child just because a TV critic gives it a good review, or because it's on a channel "just for kids." If you do, you'll probably be accepting low standards. You must be your child's TV guide. That means you may need to view some programs ahead of time, to see if they're suitable.

- **Be prepared to suggest alternatives.** Many parents fear turning off TV because they don't want to hear their children whining about not knowing what to do. You may indeed hear that for a while when you first put them on a TV diet. Most parents soon find that, once their children lose their television dependency, they become more resourceful at finding other ways to have fun. In fact, you're more apt to hear complaints of "I'm bored" from kids who watch lots of TV.

  If you're setting TV rules for the first time, it will help if you have some options ready. Stock up with a few new games and puzzles. Take a trip to the library to make sure you have lots of good books on hand. Spend some time reading together as a family. Get outside with the dog or the basketball. Encourage your child to start a new hobby or two.

- **Talk to your children about what they see on TV.** Despite your best efforts to filter out the junk, they'll surely be exposed to plenty of bad ideas, improper conduct, and rough language. When they see promiscuity or violence rewarded on screen, and hear messages like "If it feels good, do it," talk to them about what is right and wrong, and let them know that real life often brings unpleasant consequences for such behavior.

You don't want to harp on TV so much that it spoils viewing for the whole family. But sometimes you're going to have to do some serious critiquing. Nobody else will do it for you. When was the last time you saw a television sponsor or network executive interrupt a show to remind children, "You should not imitate what you are seeing here—this not how we want you to behave"?

- **Be a good model.** It's a good bet that many parents don't crack down on their kids' viewing habits because they know they'd have to lead the way by example, and they dread the thought of sacrificing much of their own TV time. There is no easy way around this one. If your children observe that television is a big part of your life, they'll surely tend to devote their own time to it. For the good of your child's education, limit yourself.

Video and computer games can cause similar problems, as can the Internet. Kids are transfixed by them. They can become video game hermits. Here, too, you must set limits. Take the same precautions as with television. Set and uphold clear rules. Make sure games and "surfing" don't interfere with schoolwork or more active leisure time. Monitor them for sexual content, violence, and bad language. Spend a little time at the console with your child so you'll know what he's playing and what he's seeing.

Gauging Your Family's TV Habits

- How much TV do *you* watch? (Keep track of your viewing habits for a week. Every time you watch a program, write it down. You might be surprised by how the hours add up.)

- How many TV sets are in your home? Where are they? In the family room? The kitchen? Your bedroom? Your child's bedroom?

- Do members of your family watch TV together, or scatter to different rooms to watch?

- How many hours per day do your children watch TV? Can you name the programs they watched yesterday? (Try keeping a written log.)

- Is the TV constantly on, even when nobody is really watching it? Is the TV on during mealtimes?

- Do you have any set rules in your house about watching TV? Any limits? Are they enforced?

- How many times in the last month did you talk with your children about the programs and commercials they've seen on TV?

Internet Safety Rules

The Internet is a fabulous learning tool, a far richer resource than TV. It's also loaded with stuff that's bad for kids. Spam e-mail full of foul language. Scams where crooks try to get your child to give them your credit card number. Cybersex chat rooms where children discuss explicit sex with adults. Porno sites galore. (One parent we know watched as her child typed the word *toys* into a search engine—and got back dozens of Web addresses advertising *sex toys*.) You can't afford to be complacent. Take precautions to shield your child from the worst of the online universe and help him access the best of it.

- **Lay down firm rules.** Just as you have rules about watching TV, going to movies, and listening to music, you need to set parameters for computer use. For example, tell your child never to give out his password to anyone, not even friends. Never share personal information (e.g., name, address, phone number) over the computer without your permission. Never respond to messages that contain dirty words. Tell your child he must never agree to a face-to-face meeting with someone he's met online without your approval and supervision. Be very clear about what kinds of sites and material are off-limits.

- **Monitor at-home Internet use.** Pay attention to the sites your child visits and the files he downloads. They may easily contain some images and messages you don't like—not to mention some nasty computer viruses. Consider putting the computer in a common space like the family room so you can keep an eye on the screen. Depending on your child's age and maturity, you may want to let him go online only when you are there to supervise, or only after he's let you know that he's signing on.

- **Learn how to navigate the Net yourself.** If your home is wired to the Internet, at least one parent should be computer literate. It does not take more than a few hours to learn the basics. You may not become as adept as your child, but you should have a notion of what the Internet is all about. With a little effort, you can learn a few valuable tricks. Some Internet service providers, for example, make it easy to see exactly where on the Net your child has been surfing lately.

- **Use electronic filters.** Technology can help you block at least some offensive material. Look into software that screens content on the Web. Also, many on-line providers offer parental control options that let you halt children's access to certain types of sites, chat rooms, and e-mail. Be aware that these filters are not foolproof, and that kids delight in figuring out ways to get around them. Electronic safeguards are no substitute for your vigilance.

- **Spend a little time on the computer together.** Make exploring the Internet a family activity. Invite your child to show you his favorite cyberspace hangouts. Get to know his online friends. Help him find some safe, fun, educational sites. You can also help him learn to assess the information he runs across. (Much online material is frivolous or cannot be trusted.) Your child may seem to know a lot about computers, but he needs adults to teach him how to evaluate the information he encounters on the Web.

• **Get to know the school's Internet use policy.** Does it have one? Does a teacher supervise when kids are online at school? What happens if students are caught sending online obscenities or downloading pornography? Does the school use electronic filters? It certainly should. Some library and school groups oppose filtering software. They say it can end up blocking students from educationally valid material. But what comes through unfiltered access to the Internet is probably more detrimental. Filters or no, check to see whether teachers carefully oversee Internet use at school. If not, it's a virtual certainty that kids are getting into areas where they should not be.

CHAPTER 15

Current Issues in Education

CONTROVERSIES ALWAYS RAGE AROUND EDUCATION AND never more so than today. Strong views, turf defense, intense political interests, and clashing philosophies are all at work. It is important for you as a parent to have some orientation on the hot-button disputes that you are most apt to encounter in the course of your child's education.

Perhaps you and your youngster will be lucky enough to bypass many of these controversies. Maybe your school is tranquil, stable, and largely sheltered from the waves that roil the education seas. Most schools are not so fortunate. They are battered and buffeted by storm after storm. You may find yourself at raucous parent or school board meetings where these issues are hotly disputed by people who appear to know what they're talking about—or at least to hold strong opinions. You may hear them argued out by candidates for governor, mayor, or school board. You may read about them in news accounts, editorials, and opinion pieces.

You'll want to understand these debates, not only so you can be an informed participant-observer but also so you will know what to watch for in your child's school. Some dubious practices slip into schools like stealth weapons, barely noticed (at least by parents) and unremarked on. Our purpose in this chapter is not to turn you into a vigilante or policy wonk. It is, rather, to orient you to some of the major issues in contemporary American education. Even if you do not agree with our point of view—and we certainly have one—you are better off knowing the arguments.

In each case, we give a brief explanation of the issue and outline the controversy. We also tell you what we think.

Outcomes-Based Education

"Outcomes-based education" (OBE) is a term that first surfaced in the late 1980s, and has been part of the lexicon of education debates ever since. The original idea was that, instead of judging schools by what goes *into* them ("inputs" such as money spent per pupil, teachers' university degrees, and class size), we should judge them by what comes *out* of them—namely, how much and how well their students learn.

This fundamental concept of holding schools, educators, and children accountable for results makes sense for an important reason: we know from decades of research that there is no reliable link between a school's resources and the results it gets. It's counterintuitive, but on the whole it's true. Some schools spend a lot of money and get poor results, while other schools with fewer resources give children fine educations. Hence the best strategy to measure education success is to focus on the end product.

Controversy about outcomes-based education has come from two directions. Some educators do not like being held accountable for school results. They note, for example, that children arrive in their classrooms with various strengths and weaknesses accumulated over the years. Given those differences, they argue, it is unfair to hold schools— and those working in them—responsible for making sure that all students meet certain standards.

A more serious problem arose when some states allowed trendy education thinkers to specify what the schools' "outcomes" ought to be. The original reformers had in mind basic skills and fundamental knowledge in subjects like English, math, science, and history (e.g., first graders should be able to find the Atlantic Ocean on a map, and fourth graders should know who Paul Revere was). But a funny thing happened on the way to the classroom. The education establishment began to set fuzzy, jargon-filled goals, such as that students should "apply principles, concepts, and strategies from various strands of mathematics to solve problems that originate within the discipline of mathematics or in the real world." States began framing many desired outcomes in terms of emotions, attitudes, and interpersonal relationships. In that vein, students were to meet criteria such as "appreciate their worth as unique and capable individuals" or "make environmentally sound decisions in their personal and civic lives."

Over time the whole OBE concept began to go off the tracks. A number of parents grew confused and irritated when they realized that the new goals were so vague they meant nothing at all. Conservative parents in particular were upset when they discovered that the full might of the state was going to be used to ensure that their child's school instilled certain politically correct attitudes. They didn't think this was the state's proper business. Nor do we.

In our view, outcomes-based education was a good idea that got hijacked. The problem is not the emphasis on school results. The problem is that there is a bias in the education community against concentrating on basic skills and important subject matter. In many places, therefore, the "experts" who were placed in charge of the process selected abstract, watered-down outcomes that seem bent on social engineering more than anything else. That kind of foolishness continues in many schools today. It's a great idea to hold students and educators responsible for results, but they must be quantifiable academic results, not propaganda or meaningless abstractions.

Education Standards

One of the most common education reforms is called "standards-based" reform. It argues that schoolchildren are apt to be better educated if those in charge are clear about just what it is that they're supposed to learn.

This is so self-evident that you may wonder why it's even called reform. Unfortunately, for years many U.S. schools had goals that were so nebulous that their academic objectives were often indecipherable. "Helping every child maximize his potential" and "preparing students for successful lives in our multicultural world" became typical. Increasingly, there was no way of really knowing just what skills and knowledge were to be acquired.

As a result, the past decade has seen most states, many local systems, and some individual schools busily setting new standards. With the standards usually come some form of test (often termed "assessments") and frequently an "accountability" system. Accountability is the notion that rewards of some kind should be attached to success in attaining standards, and sanctions or interventions should follow failure.

All of this is deeply controversial on several levels. First, there is the thorny question of what constitutes good standards and who ought to set them. Then there is the politically delicate matter of the consequences for students and schools that don't meet those standards. Many educators object to consequences in principle. A number of parents aren't too keen about them, either, at least not when applied to their own children.

Most states have done a mediocre job of setting standards. Often they have merely come up with more fuzzy goals that are thin on specific knowledge and skills that kids should master. (There are happy exceptions, however, such as Virginia's history standards, California's math standards, and Massachusetts's English standards.) The specified standards are often too high to suit some people and too low for others. Schools often feel constrained by the state's goals. And every sort of faction and interest group is bent on ensuring that the standards pay adequate heed to its particular concerns or enthusiasms.

As for consequences, the first time Virginia tested to see if students were meeting its new and much praised standards, 97 percent of all schools in the commonwealth had scores so low they cannot count on retaining their accreditation if their results don't improve in the coming years. What democratic government can survive the backlash of declaring that nearly all the state's public schools don't cut the mustard and may not remain accredited? How many elected officials can handle this kind of heat? (Virginia's results have already improved, though they still have a long way to go.)

Standards also have consequences for individual pupils who are told they may not be promoted to the next grade or graduate from high school unless they pass a certain test or get a specific grade point average. Immediately, we hear—often from parents as well as educators—that it isn't fair, that there must be something wrong with the test, that it's wrong to test students on material unless you can be certain that the school actually taught it, that this process discriminates against minorities and the disabled, and so on.

High-stakes tests—the kind whose results really do count toward important decisions like promotion and graduation—will inevitably cause debate on many fronts. They are necessary, however, for any serious accountability system that is keyed to academic standards and meant to make a difference. Standards that don't lead to changed behavior and results are not worth the paper they're printed on. Yet people are disinclined to change their ways. Schools are astonishingly conservative institutions, not in what they teach or the values they impart but in their organizational response to change.

We assume that you, as a parent, want your child to attend a school with demanding, sensible academic standards, and that you believe in real consequences for everyone concerned with her education, including you and your child. Good things should happen to those who meet standards. For those who do not, something must change or they'll continue not meeting those goals.

You'll want to look closely at the standards your school is following. Find out well in advance just what the consequences are, and on whose shoulders they fall. Please do not become one of those parents who believe in standards only so long as it's other people and other people's children who must change their ways in order to reach them.

Skills Versus Knowledge

Amazingly, today's fashionable education thinkers often scorn the idea that students must master important factual knowledge. Requiring children to learn "mere facts" is derided as "rote learning" that turns education into a game of Trivial Pursuit. The job of the educator, it is said, is to "teach the child, not the subject." Telling a youngster what is important to know is said to be oppressive. "Imposing" knowledge on her will stifle her creativity and her enthusiasm for learning. Besides, the argument goes, knowledge is changing so fast nowadays, there's no reason to memorize any of it.

This deep prejudice against facts is illustrated by an incident related by E. D. Hirsch of the Core Knowledge Foundation, who has labored long and hard to address this problem in the schools. In his excellent book *The Schools We Need*, Hirsch recalls addressing a group of administrators from around the country and being asked what sorts of things he thought first graders should know. He mentioned several examples, such as some fables of Aesop, some elements of geometry, and being able to identify the Atlantic and Pacific oceans and the seven continents. "Immediately, one of the participants asked me if I really thought it was of any use whatever to a first grader to learn the seven continents," Hirsch recounts. "No one at the meeting was willing to defend the idea of teaching such facts to young children. Even if some might have privately favored doing so, no one dared to speak out."[1]

To many in the education establishment, the mental process of searching for answers is far more important than mastering any particular body of knowledge. What matters most to them is "learning how to learn." Schools are enthusiastic about making sure students acquire "higher-order thinking skills." Learning goals typically call for teaching kids to "think critically" and "solve problems." Give children the skills to find information and reflect upon it, the argument goes, and they'll become "lifelong learners." There's no need to force them into demonstrating specific knowledge.

The problem with this rationale, of course, is that skills don't help students much without knowledge to apply them to. No child can think critically or conceptually about U.S. history, for example, if she doesn't know who George Washington was, or what took place at the Constitutional Convention. Without basic information, all you're left with is uninformed opinion. Knowledge is to skills as bricks are to mortar. You need both for sturdy intellect.

Modern education philosophy seems to have forgotten that knowledge makes you smarter. As Hirsch points out (and research by cognitive psychologists confirms), highly skilled intellectual competence comes *after*, not before, you know a lot of "mere facts." In order to be a critical, independent thinker, in order to firm up those higher-order thinking skills so beloved of education experts, you need a considerable amount of knowledge. The more you know, the better you're able to learn. For example, students grasp the meaning of what they're reading much better if they already have some background knowledge to apply to that material.

Furthermore, knowledge fosters—not stifles—creativity. People we think of as creative geniuses are "brilliant" in large part because they have devoted long years to mastering knowledge in a particular field; what they know has become second nature, and their minds are free to focus and invent. Leonardo da Vinci was able to create great paintings and sculpture in part because of the hours and hours he'd spent studying human anatomy. Edison was right: genius is 1 percent inspiration and 99 percent perspiration.[2]

Common sense tells us that some things *are* more important than others for American students to know. There is a solid core of fundamental knowledge that does not change much from year to year or even generation to generation. It is a core that includes essential rules of writing and speaking, great works of literature, operations of mathematics, basic laws of science, salient events of history, and principles of constitutional government.

The reluctance to articulate what is academically important and what we should expect students to know has weakened the foundations of American education. It is robbing elementary school children of the base of knowledge they need to be true "lifelong learners." No one argues for a curriculum of memorized facts and nothing but facts. Yet students cannot seriously question, analyze, and think critically without some intellectual goods. As George Eliot observed, empty sacks will never stand upright.

Multiculturalism

At its best, "multiculturalism" means helping children develop knowledge of a number of different cultures and a respect for other people's heritages. Schools have worked hard to broaden what they teach to include the histories and achievements of groups that once received scant attention. This effort is very important in a country where people trace their roots to every corner of the globe. Defined that way, multiculturalism is a good thing.

In some places, however, zeal for multiculturalism has gone over the top and is doing more harm than good. Some educators spend so much time stressing diversity that the focus becomes what makes us different from one another, rather than what Americans have in common. Identity is often reduced to race and ethnicity. For example, the teachers' guide to one reading series advises: "To help students begin to develop cultural awareness and understanding, they first need to learn who they are—their ethnicity, gender, and social class—and how they are viewed by society. . . . Both students and teachers have participated in relationships of domination, submission, oppression, and privilege which have helped to shape who they are and how they see the world."[3]

This is quite a burden to place on an elementary school classroom and a grave distortion of what education at that level is all about. People who think that way are really saying that the kind of politically correct "postmodern" thinking that has been taking over the university campuses should be inflicted on fourth graders as well. We could not disagree more.

Some proponents of multiculturalism insist that ethnicity largely determines how youngsters think and learn. Hence different curricula and pedagogies are better for certain groups. They say, for example, that Latino children learn more in "cooperative learning" settings. Others have argued that many African-American children actually speak a genetically based language called "African Language Systems" (also known as "Ebonics"), and that they should receive instruction in that tongue, not only to help them learn standard English but also to maintain their "primary language." The credibility of such claims aside, one must wonder just how much these approaches will bring us together as a nation or help the children they purport to speak for.

Another problem is that children can spend so much time in "diversity training" and "cultural awareness" activities that little time is left for teaching basic skills. Important topics tend to get crowded out of a curriculum that is based on ethnic representation rather than academic basics. Even mathematics is not immune. Math is math, you would think, but the field called "ethnomathematics" asserts that one culture's idea of math isn't the same as the next. Ethnomathematics teachers try to make the subject relevant to minority children through "math activities" from different cultures, such as ancient basket weaving techniques or sewing animal skins into clothing. Occasionally spicing up a lesson with such illustrations is one thing. But spend too much time on them, and kids may never get to decimals, geometry, and algebraic equations.

In some classrooms, a distinguishing feature of multiculturalism is its disdain for Western civilization. The idea of victims and victimizers becomes an organizing theme of the curriculum. The implicit message is: have respect for all cultures but be suspicious of anything European and white. Children spend a lot of time learning about white males as greedy, violent oppressors of women and minorities. As one Minnesota teacher told journalist Richard Bernstein: "The sentiment in my room is that [the students] don't like Christians and they don't like white people, because they saw what has been done in the name of Christianity and what the white people did to the Indians and the Africans." So what did she teach those children about George Washington? "That he was the first president, that he was a slave owner, that he was rich— not much," she says.[4]

At times, multiculturalism turns out to be just a cover for a left-leaning political agenda aimed at shaping students' opinions and transforming society. For example, a multicultural advocacy association holds seminars for teachers on "issues of power and privilege within dominant social groups" and "becoming an effective change agent." Teacher colleges, as part of their focus on diversity training, hold workshops on topics such as ways to "usurp the existing power structure." What kind of objective is that for an elementary or secondary school education?

If the aim of multiculturalism is really to teach children about different cultures, well and good. But if it interferes with the study of basic knowledge and skills, foists a political agenda on students, and encourages them to think of themselves and others primarily in terms of ethnicity, then it's a problem. Parents should look to see exactly what their children are being taught in school in the name of increased sensitivity.

Discovery Learning

This fine-sounding phrase hides a bushel of mischief. Very popular among trendy education thinkers and professors, the theory holds that children learn best by discovering knowledge for themselves through hands-on projects and problem solving, rather than reading something out of a textbook or taking down what a teacher says. The idea is that knowledge you acquire for yourself is more likely to be understood and retained than a piece of information handed to you by someone else.

This view of education is seductive. It sounds so natural, energetic, and ambitious. Taken in moderation, it makes sense. As we all know, the lessons we figure out for ourselves tend to sink in deepest and stick with us longest. It is also true that there are some topics, subjects, and assignments where discovery learning is important. A lab experiment in science, for example, is a form of discovery learning. So is making a map of the school grounds, and collecting and classifying leaves. A good education obviously includes such activities. Virtually no one believes that learning should consist only of listening to teachers and reading from textbooks.

But discovery learning has real limitations in practice when schools try to turn it into the main way children learn academic lessons. As we see it, there are three major drawbacks.

First, it is truly inefficient. Having children figure out mathematical operations, for example, by playing games and making things takes a lot of time. There are not enough hours in the school year for students to unearth all there is to know on their own. Furthermore, can we really expect most children to "discover" the Pythagorean theorem for themselves? The periodic table of the elements? The ten articles of the Bill of Rights? Of course not! A good education carefully and systematically imparts to children what many centuries of human intellect have already figured out—and then liberates them to find out more for themselves.

Second, unless the teacher is ready with corrections, a lot of things one "discovers" for oneself turn out to be wrong. To take a simple example, a child generalizing from the words deer, geese, and mice would end up with absurd notions about the plural form of most English words. Hard-core devotees of discovery learning, however, seem to harbor a bias against correcting mistakes. (One fourth grade math program, for example, tells educators "not to judge the rightness or wrongness of each student's answer.") It is said that raising children to be preoccupied with "right answers" will squelch their inquisitiveness, interfere with the discovery process, and violate the child's individual understanding of the world. This is an odd sort of education, one that relegates truth to second place.

Third, in some places discovery learning becomes a vehicle to reject the idea that there are important skills and information that all children should learn. What's more important, we're told, is developing lifelong learning habits. The implication is that we should not be alarmed if a child makes it all the way through school without learning where the Mississippi River is; it is simply because she spent much of her time learning how to explore ideas that truly interest her. That rationale may sound considerate and child-centered, but all too often it's just an excuse for not teaching fundamental lessons.

In its place—treated as a supplementary instructional method that enlivens and illuminates a curriculum directed by teachers—discovery learning can be valuable. Taken as an overriding education theory for the K–8 grades, it is apt to produce an inadequate education.

Teachers as Facilitators

Discovery learning is a close relative of a theory known in education circles as "constructivism"—the idea that learning is an active process in which students create their own knowledge rather than receive it from teachers. Modern education philosophy puts great stock in the notion that children must be free to construct their own understandings of the world, and should not have an adult tell them how or what to think. This approach has profound implications for the role of the teacher in the classroom.

Many educators say that their job is to be a "facilitator." Rather than transmit knowledge to students, they help them become "active seekers." Facilitators provide environments that encourage children to "learn how to learn." They try to make the classroom alive and exciting, a place where curiosity is piqued. It is said that teachers ought to function as a "guide on the side, not the sage on the stage." They should relinquish their domineering role as the "keeper of the right answer" and lead students to reach their own understandings.

Meanwhile, old-fashioned techniques like demonstrating how to solve a math problem and then assigning ten practice problems are derided as a "chalk and talk" or "jugs and mugs" approach to instruction—wherein knowledge is poured from teachers (jugs) into their pupils (mugs). That kind of instruction, we're assured, results only in passive listening, mindless recall, regurgitation of information, and dull, lower-order learning.

As we noted in connection with discovery learning, the teacher-as-facilitator approach has some merit. Often children do learn more when they are actively involved, rather than passive listeners. A good education is much more than memorizing and parroting what the teacher says. Yet even John Dewey, who fathered so much "progressive" education philosophy in the early twentieth century, warned against going too far in this line of thinking:

> There is a present tendency in so-called advanced schools of educational thought . . . to say, in effect, let us surround pupils with certain materials, tools, appliances, etc., and then let pupils respond to these things according to their own desires. Above all let us not suggest any end or plan to the students; let us not suggest to them what they shall do, for that is an unwarranted trespass upon their sacred intellectual individuality. . . .
>
> Now such a method is really stupid. . . . Since the teacher has presumably a greater background of experience, there is the same presumption of the right of a teacher to make suggestions as to what to do, as there is on the part of the head carpenter to suggest to apprentices something of what they are to do.

Many parents, teachers, and even students complain that facilitating just isn't enough. Time and again, the American public has seen the devastating effects of programs that rely on children to construct their own educations. We've seen it in whole-language reading programs that assume children will develop their own strategies to recognize words on a page. We've seen it in math classes that concentrate almost entirely on "problem-solving strategies" but rarely on learning the multiplication table, and in social studies classes that are basically a series of "projects" in which youngsters explore other cultures by cooking their foods or singing their songs. With all the exhortations about "facilitating" and admonitions against turning students into "passive recipients" of knowledge, some teachers end up dispensing—and holding students accountable for—too little information and too few skills. The result: students who don't read well, can't multiply, and don't know much about history and geography.

The alternative to constructivism in the classroom has various names, including "direct instruction," "mastery learning," "explicit teaching," and "precision teaching." The vital components of direct instruction are simple. They start with the assumption that the teacher knows something that children need to learn. She sets clear goals for her students, goals that are stated in precise terms of the skills and knowledge to be acquired. She presents organized assignments in a carefully planned sequence. She gives students clear, concise explanations and illustrations of subject matter. Direct instruction teachers ask students frequent questions to see if they understand the work. They require thorough practice of basic skills. They test to see whether their lessons have taken hold. Despite their unpopularity with modern education experts, direct instruction methods produce solid academic results.

Good teachers aren't rigid about the methods they use. They might spend the first half of a period talking to the whole class from the front of the room, and the second half giving low-key guidance to groups of pupils who are busy with hands-on projects. The goal is the same: to instruct the young in the knowledge and skills determined by adult society to be valuable. Such teachers recognize that students need older and wiser people to explain many lessons to them. They understand that there is nothing wrong with a grown-up running a classroom authoritatively; indeed, they take pride in the high degree of professionalism that enables them to do this well. They know that children are eager to learn from adults when those adults act like they have something important to teach. There is something wrong in a school where educators pretend otherwise.

Developmentalism

In education, "developmentalism" is the idea that each child develops in natural stages at her own pace, and that learning should never be forced on her lest she be harmed. According to this view, a youngster's intellectual growth is like the unfolding of a plant. Give it lots of time, space, and nurture, and it will thrive. Try to force it, and it will end up stunted and deformed. You may hear educators—especially in the preschool and primary grades—use the term "developmentally appropriate practice." What they mean is that a lesson is suitable for a child at her present stage of natural development. By "developmentally inappropriate," they generally mean a lesson that is being taught too soon, and will therefore be a waste of time, perhaps even detrimental to a child's intellectual health.

This view of education makes some sense, mostly when applied to the first few years of life. The earliest "lessons" children learn—like how to crawl and walk and talk—do follow a sequence determined largely by nature as their bodies develop. Even then, however, we all know that a child is more apt to walk when adults coax and praise her, and is more likely to speak real words and sentences when adults in her life are speaking to her. Even preschoolers tend to rise to expectations that grown-ups hold for them, and to follow examples set for them. By the time kindergarten and first grade come around, it's even more important that adults set the pace. Despite what some modern educators claim, there is no credible research to support the theory that each student is ready to learn academic subjects (such as how to convert fractions into percentages) according to a unique pace dictated by her inner nature.

To be sure, different students learn things at different speeds. Some master their sentence diagramming sooner than others, for example. Maturity surely plays a role, but after the age of six or so, how quickly and how well children learn their lessons is influenced mainly by factors such as how much they already know, how much practice they get, and how much effort they put into their schoolwork.[5]

Yet developmentalism is entrenched as a guiding philosophy in American elementary schools. In our opinion, it often ends up serving as a rationale for low standards and expectations, an excuse to assume that children cannot learn as much as they really can. If a youngster hasn't learned her basic math facts and is still counting on her fingers in the fourth grade, she's said to be "not ready" to do simple calculations in her head, and everyone feels better about this shortcoming. Teachers are discouraged from requiring hard work on grounds that it would put "pressure" on the kids. It's more important to help them feel interested and enthusiastic, it is said. Standards end up being whatever children are inclined to do. This approach leaves both schools and students conveniently unaccountable for making sure important lessons get learned.

Obviously, it is possible to push too hard, to expect too much at too young an age, and to present material that exceeds a child's comprehension. (We've never met a third grader who could handle the prose or content of Boswell's *Life of Johnson*.) Frankly, however, asking too much of students is a rare occurrence in U.S. schools. The more widespread problem is asking too little.

When it comes to academics, it is the job of adults to gently stretch children's minds. They should not go overboard. But neither should they aim too low in the name of developmentalism. When you hear the phrase "developmentally appropriate," your antennae should start to quiver. It may mean that your child, instead of being taken in hand and escorted speedily into the world of learning, will be encouraged to wander at her own pace. That may be the kind of education you want for her, but it's not the kind we think most youngsters need and deserve.

Multiple Intelligences

Harvard professor Howard Gardner has developed a theory that many educators love: that children possess various forms of intelligence. He thinks he's found eight so far, and only a couple of them resemble what has traditionally been thought of as intelligence. The others involve attributes such as spatial perception and social skills. Gardner describes, for example, a "musical intelligence" that gives someone unusual sensitivity to melody and rhythm, and a "bodily kinesthetic intelligence" that enables good athletes to use their bodies in extraordinary ways.

This multiple intelligences theory has won hordes of followers in American schools. Consultants rave about it. Educators hold seminars to discuss it. Hundreds of schools claim to be based at least in part on multiple-intelligences pedagogy. After all, it fits neatly with so many ideas that are at work in education today. It celebrates diversity, relativism, and egalitarianism: each child can be intelligent in his or her own way, and they're all equally valuable. It encourages self-esteem and downplays competition. If there are multiple intelligences, there are even more different learning styles, so teachers do best to act as facilitators and let each child explore the world in her own way. And of course some intelligences don't really lend themselves to objective measurement, so conventional tests must not be relied upon too much.

This is mostly nonsense. Intellectual intelligence of the traditional sort is surely not all that matters when it comes to getting a good education—hard work, for example, is also valuable. Certainly people's talents, interests, and capabilities differ; that's one of the wonderful things about humankind. It's also true that children may gain important skills and knowledge through different classroom approaches. That's why great primary-school teachers bring to bear a whole arsenal of methods for, say, teaching reading.

None of that, however, means that we need "a new definition of human beings, cognitively speaking," as Gardner says. Despite some educators' infatuation, the scientific community has found no evidence to support the idea that there are several different sorts of "intelligences." Most psychologists and others who study intelligence view this theory as opinion, not science.[6]

One must wonder if a theory backed by little or no scientific evidence should influence the way educators define a good education. If the staff at your school talk frequently about "multiple intelligences" and "different learning styles," and they say things like "working with other people is a form of intelligence," be on your guard. If your child isn't learning to read well and gets no math homework, but the teacher is telling you that "she cooperates well with others, so she has real interpersonal intelligence," loud alarm bells should go off. You may be getting a dressed-up excuse for a failure to teach important lessons, and a handy way to avoid accountability for academic achievement. That's not a school we'd want children to spend much time in.

Cooperative Learning

Recent years have seen a growing preference in many U.S. schools for group work rather than individual study. In "cooperative learning" (sometimes called "collaborative learning" or "group learning"), teachers divide a class into small groups of students who work on assignments together. For example, groups may be told to come up with a way to solve a math problem, or asked to make a poster showing how people depend on the land. Students may even write papers as a group (a practice known as "collaborative writing"), rather than individual essays. Projects often culminate in a group product or report. The group demonstrates what it has learned and everyone shares a single grade. In some classrooms, you may see four-student tables or "pods" of desks arranged in clusters to facilitate such cooperative learning.

Proponents of this method say that children often learn best when they can talk through their ideas with each other. Since teachers frequently form groups out of students of varied abilities, kids get the chance to help one another. Slower pupils get the benefit of more advanced students' knowledge and skills. More advanced students consolidate their own understanding by explaining things to their classmates.

Cooperative learning is said to improve children's social skills, such as the ability to get along. It supposedly raises their self-esteem. Supporters say it encourages learning through experimenting and discovering—and that it's more fun than listening to the teacher talk.

Your child may indeed receive some benefits from cooperative learning, but be aware that this method has real drawbacks. Without careful supervision, groups of children tend to wind up playing or quarreling. Nor is it uncommon for one or two students to end up doing most of the assignment, while others in the group coast along and copy answers. "Last week my daughter got an A on a team English assignment," one frustrated parent reports. "She was deliberately teamed with the weakest, never-do-anything student in the class. She did all the work. He got the same grade. She feels cheated, and he did not learn anything." It takes close monitoring and a teacher with considerable skill to ensure a real distribution of work and learning within a group.

The underlying problem with cooperative learning is that it can devalue individual achievement. Parents complain that, in some classrooms, students who strive to do the best work or go the extra mile are made to feel as though they are not "cooperating" with the group. Naturally, in such situations, the most industrious children are apt to grow bored and resentful. The elevation of cooperation and egalitarianism over competition and individual accomplishment is a strong current in American education today. You find it in all areas of the curriculum. "The notion of competing against one another for the best science project is absolutely the opposite of what we want to do," explains the principal of a Virginia science magnet school. "The notion should be, what can we learn from each other, and how can we work collaboratively to develop each other's ideas? How can we celebrate what we are learning and feel good about this process, rather than always have a winner and a loser?"[7]

Often overlooked is a simple fact of the human condition: thinking is ultimately an individual endeavor. Each child has just one mind to develop. Often the best way to exercise that mind is in solitude, by tackling tasks on one's own. Thinking, judging, knowing, and understanding—in the end, these are processes that each brain must carry out inside itself. Many of the critical skills we want children to gain in school, like solving math problems and writing, need lots of individual practice.

Teamwork is a fine thing, too. Youngsters should get used to working with others. If cooperative learning is used with restraint, it can be a great way to learn. It has not proven to be effective, however, as the principal means of teaching. Your child will be judged by the world according to her own abilities and accomplishments, or lack thereof. If your school is organized so that most assignments are collaborative efforts and students are routinely graded as groups rather than as individuals, you probably have grounds for concern.

Self-Esteem

From reading and writing to health class and the athletic field, one article of faith pervades the modern curriculum: the conviction that children cannot achieve unless they first form a positive self-image. Helping youngsters feel good about themselves seems to have become an overriding goal in American education. Examples abound: A kindergarten teacher invites youngsters to announce their self-admiration as a part of a course called "I Like Me" ("I like me because of my hair!" "I like me because I like my Yankees hat!")[8] A sex education course advises educators not to express shock at anything sixth graders say about their sex experiences for fear of hurting their feelings.[9] A puzzled mom reports that her daughter was awarded a certificate of recognition for *future* achievement. She was supposed to feel good about great things she hadn't even done yet!

The strange thing about all the emphasis on feelings and self-worth is that there is little evidence it actually helps children learn important things. After years of research, no one has been able to establish any causal link between higher self-esteem and greater academic achievement. On the contrary, some studies indicate that it's not uncommon for high self-esteem to be linked to *low* performance. Nor does there seem to be much connection between self-regard and behavior. As one recent study noted, bullies, gang members, and criminals often have inflated views of themselves.

Yet the cult of self-esteem flourishes in our education system. In order to raise students' self-regard, many schools have lowered standards, made classes easier, inflated grades (or made them meaningless), and eliminated the idea of failure. In the words of psychologist Roy Baumeister of Case Western Reserve University, "It makes everyone feel good, and it's certainly easier than doing your math homework."

This therapeutic approach has had predictable effects. In international tests, American high school students score at the bottom when it comes to math achievement, but rank number one when asked to rate how good they feel about their own math skills. More college freshmen than ever rate themselves as "above average" or "in the highest 10 percent" academically compared to their peers—even though many of these self-satisfied young people can't write a coherent essay or tell you who James Madison was. (Madison, incidentally, suffered from no excess of self-esteem as a young man. On the contrary, he didn't think he would amount to much. He worked very hard to achieve his standing. Sometimes a sense of incompleteness can be good for you.)

Schools are right to want to help kids build positive, can-do attitudes. Yet clearly that well-intentioned impulse often leads to putting the cart before the horse. Real self-respect is a by-product of effort and actual achievement—not an aim in itself. "We should set reasonable expectations for our students," says one Texas teacher. "Then when they truly reach whatever reasonable goal has been set for them, they will feel self-assured and confident; nothing can take that good feeling away from them because it is built on a solid work ethic." On the other hand, lowering standards while dispensing indiscriminate praise only sets young people up for a fall when they reach college or the job market and suddenly discover they aren't as terrific as they've been led to believe.

Unfortunately, many moms and dads have bought into the mind-set of affirming self-image no matter what. A Virginia teacher tells of a mother who showed up before the start of the school day to protest the B+ he'd given her son. "English is his forte; you are destroying his self-esteem," she complained.[10] When parents pressure teachers to drop expectations or reward students who haven't done the work, they do their children no favors. Rather than chasing cheap self-esteem, it's far better to concentrate on academics and teach that self-respect is something earned, usually with hard work.

Choice Among Schools

Should the superintendent's office assign children to schools? Or should families be able to pick the schools they like? This is perhaps the hottest of the hot-button issues in American education today.

Advocates of mandatory assignment say it makes for more precise planning and greater efficiency to know in advance how many children will be enrolled in each school. They say it's the surest way to ensure that all children get an equally good education, and that it's more democratic because it mixes different sorts of youngsters instead of letting them cluster according to their interests, their ethnicity, or their families' idiosyncrasies.

Proponents of school choice respond that mandatory assignment often confines children (especially low-income children) in bad schools. Holding a captive audience chokes off the kind of competition and marketplace discipline that might help unsatisfactory schools improve. Supporters of school choice also point out that children and schools differ, and that a school that works well for one youngster will not necessarily suit the next one. Better to encourage families to find the schools that best fit their daughters and sons, a process that causes both parents and children to become more "invested" in their school because, after all, they chose it.

We do not believe that bureaucrats should be in the business of assigning children to schools. Indeed, in our view it is wrong to make a child go to a bad school—or a school that she and her parents dislike— when there's one not far away that would suit her better. All families should have the right to select the schools their children attend. Wealthy families, as a rule, already do this either by settling in neighborhoods with good public schools or by paying for private schooling. It's the poor who most often find themselves with no exit.

One of most widely discussed proposals to foster school choice is the use of "vouchers." Under a voucher plan, rather than telling parents which school their child must attend, the state or local government gives each child's family a chit worth whatever amount of money that community would otherwise pay per pupil to operate its public schools. This voucher can be exchanged for an education at the school of the parents' choosing. This allows families the opportunity to enroll their children in the schools they think will do the best job of educating them.

Even among supporters of school choice, however, controversy rages over how extensive the choices should be. For example, should the state help families have the option of sending their children to private schools? How about religious schools?

Public opinion on this issue has been shifting. In 1998, for example, 51 percent of Americans favored vouchers that would permit the maximum degree of school choice (including attendance at private schools), up from 43 percent just two years earlier. Among public school parents, 56 percent supported vouchers in 1998, while 40 percent were opposed. Four years earlier, voucher opponents had held a slim lead.

The voucher movement is slowly spreading. In 1999, for example, low-income youngsters living in Milwaukee and Cleveland could obtain government-financed vouchers to attend private and parochial schools. About fifty communities also have privately funded voucher (or "scholarship") programs underwritten by philanthropists. Florida has enacted a program that will give vouchers to students stuck in schools judged by the state to be failing. A number of other state legislatures are weighing variations on the voucher idea.

The public school establishment has declared war against every sort of voucher, using scary rhetoric about the "demise of public education." A college of education dean recently went so far as to liken voucher programs to "ethnic cleansing." The two big teachers unions are particularly vehement on this issue, clearly recognizing that it threatens their near-monopoly control of education. The president of the National Education Association compared vouchers to "leeches" that would suck the blood from the public school system. School choice has become a major battleground between those that want to preserve an iron lock on education power and money, and those who want to disperse control to families and foster pluralism in schooling.

We belong to the latter camp. We favor school choice, and believe that the more of it the better. Choice among public schools is good; policies that include charter, private, and parochial schools are better. American parents should be able to select places where they know their children will learn. If the quality of the product they're getting is shoddy, they should be able to take their children elsewhere. If we really believe that parents are the first and most important teachers, we should be willing to trust them with this most basic of education decisions.

PUBLIC VERSUS PRIVATE SCHOOLS

Many parents who can afford the option believe their children are better off in a private school. Many low-income parents say that if they had the money, that is the choice they would make, too.

We are strong partisans of parents being able to choose schools, but we do not take for granted that a private school is always the right choice. "Private" does not automatically mean "good," any more than "public" means "below par." There are excellent public schools. There are very satisfactory hybrids, such as charter schools. There are also plenty of private schools that have succumbed to silly education fads.

On national assessment results, while there is nearly always a significant achievement gap between private and public schools, the margin of difference is narrower than one might suppose. On the 1998 NAEP reading assessment, for example, 27 percent of eighth graders in public schools achieved "proficiency," as did 48 percent of those attending private and parochial schools. That's a sizable gap, but the numbers still indicate that more than half the private school pupils were *not* proficient readers. Given that the gap between wealthy and poor children was nearly as wide, nobody can say with certainty that it's the superior education provided by private schooling that makes the difference in student achievement. A good portion of that difference may well be caused by factors such as family circumstance.

We're certainly not putting down private schools. Two of the authors have selected them for their own children. Private schools often do a fine job. They are nearly always safe, and often small and friendly. They can teach religion and reaffirm children's faith. They are relatively responsive to the concerns and priorities of parents. If you are considering private schools for your child, however, you must be a careful shopper, just as you are when weighing the merits of different public schools.

PUBLIC CHARTER SCHOOLS

Some families are turning to a new education option called "charter schools." These public schools are independently operated and freed from most regulation in return for a pledge to deliver superior results within a stated period of time (typically five years). If the charter school produces the results it promised, it gets its charter renewed and continues to operate independently. It can be closed down for failure to deliver—or by failing to attract and satisfy its customers. Since charter schools are public, they don't charge tuition.

In most states with charter laws (almost three-quarters of all states) these schools come in many flavors and forms: traditional and progressive, big and little, graded and ungraded, and so forth. Since the charter movement is relatively new, most of these schools have been operating for just a few years and cannot yet show definitive results. Their facilities are often unconventional and frequently minimalist. Sending your child to a charter school is thus a bit of a gamble. You'll want to spend some time there and talk with parents before settling on it. Several hundred thousand families have made this decision, however, often because they are desperately unhappy with the other education options available to them. Most families that have headed in this direction have been quite satisfied. (See "More About Charter Schools," page 504.)

HOME SCHOOLING

Home schooling is just what the name suggests: parents teaching their own daughters and sons at home instead of sending them to school. Estimates of the number of home-schooled youngsters in America range from a half million to as high as two million, and the number is growing. Some form of home schooling is now legal in every state, though the rules and regulations vary widely.

Not long ago, this was considered a fringe movement. The term "home schooler" conjured up the image of a mom and her kid hunched over the kitchen table with a twenty-year-old textbook and the shades drawn. Nowadays, that mom (or dad) is likely to be a member of a sophisticated network of parents who trade information via the Internet, newsletters, magazines, and associations. There are catalogues brimming with teaching materials designed just for them. As more and more people know friends who are taking over their kids' education, it has become socially acceptable again. (We say "again" because in the early days of this country, many children received at least part of their formal education at home.)

Parents decide to home-school for a wide variety of reasons. Many are people of deep faith who want to instill their own strongly held values in their children. Others are concerned that the local public schools are not safe, that discipline isn't what it should be, or that expectations are too low. Some home schoolers have children with disabilities or unusually gifted youngsters who need extra attention. Some believe strongly in the benefits of one-on-one instruction. The common thread is that, for one reason or another, all these parents believe they can do a better job teaching their kids than a conventional school can.

Critics warn that many home-schooled children may not get a good education. Advocates say that the evidence indicates just the opposite. They point to studies that show students schooled at home actually score higher on achievement tests than their counterparts in public and private schools.

Opponents also say that if home-schooled children are isolated from the community and lose the chance to grow up around lots of other kids, they won't develop good social skills, and therefore won't be good citizens. Yet the image of home schoolers as hermits has little basis. In fact, Christian Smith and David Sikkink of the University of North Carolina report that home-schooling families (as well as families that choose private and religious schools) are *more* consistently involved in their communities and affairs of public life than families of public school children. Most home-schooling parents go out of their way to engage their kids in social activities like Scouts, 4-H clubs, team sports, and art programs. They form cooperatives with other parents, take turns teaching different subjects, and get together for group projects. Some schools open their doors to home-schooled children on a part-time basis so that they can join field trips and extracurricular activities like soccer or band.

We have the greatest respect for home schoolers. Mothers and fathers who choose this route make a huge commitment. They should not have to do so because there are no good schools available. In America in the twenty-first century, no family should feel it has to educate at home to educate well. (See "More About Home Schooling," page 503.)

FOR-PROFIT SCHOOLS

Should people be able to operate schools for a profit? Or does that pose the risk of putting money first and kids' educations second?

This country actually has a long, albeit slender, tradition of profit-making private schools at the elementary and secondary school level. (At the college level, the for-profit sector is huge, including what is now America's largest private university, the University of Phoenix.) Sometimes parents don't even know whether the private school their children attend is a for-profit or nonprofit venture. It's often hard to tell the difference unless you know something about the institution's corporate structure.

There is also a long tradition of public schools purchasing goods and services from private firms that make a profit from the transaction. Familiar examples include things like food services and bus transportation, as well as supplies and equipment. You can be certain that those textbooks, chalkboards, and computers in the neighborhood public school were made and sold by for-profit companies.

What's newer—and to some quite controversial—is the use of profit-seeking firms to provide academic instruction and to operate entire public schools. Sometimes a public school system hires a private company to manage one or more schools. Sometimes charter schools are started by private firms. In other instances, a parent group or community organization obtains a charter and then "outsources" the school's management to a for-profit company. Several hundred U.S. schools now operate this way. (One of the authors, in fact, used to work for a firm that's now in the business of managing regular public schools as well as public charter schools.)

Some of the critics are simply anti-capitalist. They don't put much store in the free market and don't think an important "public" good should be tainted by commerce. Others worry that the fiscal bottom line will take precedence over the education bottom line. They fret that the school's owners must eventually be tempted to cut corners, to hold off hiring that extra science teacher in order to boost this year's profits, or to stockpile funds to open a school in another city. They cite the hucksters of shoddy goods that are all too prevalent in the for-profit sector of higher education.

Defenders of for-profit schooling reply that no school is apt to yield much of a financial profit over time unless it's a good school that people want to send their children to. Objective observers also note that it's far from clear that the firms now beginning to run schools will actually reap the kinds of profits that investors are looking for. To prosper and grow, for-profit schooling is going to have to yield both educational and financial returns. Today we cannot be sure that this will happen, but we believe it's worth trying.

Competition is healthy for K–12 education. It can come from many directions, including nonprofit as well as for-profit organizations. No matter who is running your school, you'll want to make sure that it isn't stinting on quality education, that its teachers and other personnel are first-rate, that supplies are adequate and books are ample, and that most of the money in the school's budget makes its way into actual instruction of children. So long as that is happening, it seems to us secondary whether management is the responsibility of a nonprofit organization or a money-making private firm.

Religion and Schools

In the 1960s, 1970s, and 1980s, American public schools expelled religion. The process began in 1962, when the Supreme Court ruled that school prayer is unconstitutional, a decision that confused many teachers and principals. They concluded that, if schools were not to encourage people to be members of one religion or another, then the whole question of faith was out of bounds. Suddenly religion was taboo in American classrooms. Students might be encouraged to talk about birth control, alternative lifestyles, even anger toward their parents—but not about God. Textbooks went to extraordinary lengths to avoid *any* reference to religion. One American history text, for example, defined pilgrims as "people who take long trips."

Some educators say the situation had improved a little by the 1990s. Public schools began to realize that, even though the courts had declared school-sponsored prayer unconstitutional, God need not be banned altogether. For example, a consensus emerged that it was all right for students to pray privately at school, and say grace to themselves at lunchtime. Many schools began allowing students to form religious clubs (such as Bible study groups or prayer groups) and meet on school grounds just like any other club. Publishers began paying a bit more attention to religion in social studies textbooks, even though the coverage was often spotty.

If there has been improvement, however, it has come in small doses. Educators say they still get mixed signals about what's permissible. A federal appeals court, for example, has ruled that limited prayer at school graduation ceremonies is okay, but student-led prayers at high school football games are unconstitutional. Fearing lawsuits, public schools bend over backward to avoid the subject of faith. In a Virginia school, fifth graders croon about the "Twelve Days of the Holidays" instead of the "Twelve Days of Christmas." In New Jersey, a first grader picks a story about Jacob and Esau from his book of Bible stories to read to the class, but is told "the Bible is not allowed"—even though the selection doesn't mention God. In a Tennessee school, a teacher approves ideas for papers on witchcraft, black magic, and the occult, but turns down a youngster who wants to write a paper on the life of Jesus Christ, explaining that it's "not an appropriate thing to do in a public school."

In most schoolbooks, the treatment of religion is still abysmal. The topic is most often presented as a minor detail of civilization, something that plays a small role in human life. The place of religion in the nation's founding is the best-kept secret in U.S. history class. Textbooks often portray it as a repressive or backward force in our past. Many high school students encounter religion only twice: when they study the Puritans and the Scopes trial. "In both cases," reports the American Textbook Council, "Christianity is likely to be presented as a negative phenomenon, something dark and superstitious, a cultural force leading to intolerance and witch hunts, or to irrational refutation of science and evolutionary theory."

Educators who wish to present a more complete and honest picture get little encouragement. "The easiest thing is to back away from the issue of religion altogether," says a veteran Massachusetts teacher. "There is no support system in place in the schools of education, in academic lounges, in the public schools themselves, anywhere, to help young teachers if they wished to tackle the subject of religion. . . . The topic can be dangerous for teachers: parental blow-back, special interest groups in the community."[11]

Public schools must not indoctrinate children, but that does not mean they should deny essential facts about religion. Here are four principles that we believe most American parents hold regarding the place of religion in their public schools:

- **Teaching *about* religion without advocating any one religion in particular.** America is one of the most religious countries in the world. Children should learn about the different faiths that are part of the fabric of U.S. society. Schools should acknowledge that religion is a vital part of our civics, literature, art, music, poetry, and politics. They should tell the whole truth: the history of religion is inseparable from the history of humankind. Children can learn about all sorts of faiths when they study the cultures of the Mayan and Aztec empires, the Egyptians and Babylonians, the ancient Chinese. They can learn about faith when they study Michelangelo's Sistine Chapel ceiling, or read the story of David and Goliath. An educated person does not have to be a believer, but she should understand something about religious traditions.

- **Presenting the Judeo-Christian ethic as a formative influence in American life.** It denies our shared heritage to pretend that American laws, ideals, and principles as a free people were developed in a moral vacuum. The story of America is impossible to fathom without understanding the religious roots from which our highest aspirations and accomplishments sprang. Teachers should tell children how the Puritans founded a "shining city on a hill," a place with a sacred mission: to be a beacon calling others to the New Jerusalem. They should explain that the Founders of this country were people of deep faith who believed that religion was an indispensable support for democracy. They should let students know that when the

Reverend Martin Luther King, Jr., carried the "gospel of freedom" to the mountaintop, he looked to Jesus as his guide. Honesty demands that schools acknowledge that the history and fate of this nation are intertwined with religion.

- **Recognition that many people consider themselves creatures of God.** For many students, parents, and teachers, faith is a living force. Their convictions should be respected. The real frustration of many religious people—Christians, in particular—is not that their creed is not affirmed by the schools, but that often it seems to be viewed with active suspicion. Public schools should act as though religion is something *good*, not something that needs to be warded off.

- **Appreciation that, for most people, faith is the anchor of morality.** Religious belief is transcendent. It helps children see life as something sacred, spiritual, and beyond the material. It is a central motive for studying hard and behaving well. Allowing children to draw on their beliefs will help restore a sense of moral seriousness to schools. Public institutions should force no one to pray—but neither should they erect confusing barriers that make it difficult for youngsters to seek God's guidance. They should encourage children to use their own faith to develop traits such as honesty, diligence, and responsibility. Schools should remember that religion can help girls and boys become good students and good citizens.

Parents who want religious formation to be an explicit and purposeful part of schooling should seek private or parochial schools. At the same time, public school parents should not have to feel like their schools are places where every trace of religion has been scrubbed away. For most people, that is not what life is about. It's not the kind of place America is.

Social Promotion

Should children have to repeat a grade if they fail to meet academic standards? Or does it do more harm to hold them back while their classmates move on? That's the crux of the "social promotion" debate.

Some educators argue that repeating a grade gives slow learners more time to master essential lessons. It gives other youngsters the extra time they need to mature emotionally and socially. For unmotivated students, the thought of having to "stay behind" is a powerful incentive to try harder. Sending children ahead without essential skills and knowledge just dooms them to failure in the coming years.

Other educators argue that holding kids back does nothing to help their academic achievement over the long run—in fact, they say, flunking students will dampen their interest in learning and increase the chance that they'll drop out. Branding them as failures is a sure way to crush their self-esteem. Combine the humiliation of having to repeat a grade with the awkwardness of being the biggest, oldest kid in class, and the child may turn into a discipline problem.

Most people agree that decisions about whether or not to promote should be made on a case-by-case basis, according to each youngster's difficulties and needs. (See "What If My Child Isn't Promoted?" page 442.) The problem is that the "case-by-case" principle often means, in reality, virtually abolishing failure. In some places, kids are passed along from one grade to the next regardless of how much they've learned. They're passed right through the system and handed a diploma even though they can barely read or write, let alone know much history or science. There has been lots of talk recently about ending social promotion in American public education, but the practice remains widespread.

It would be easy to lay all the blame on teachers, but the issue is more complicated. Many teachers say they feel pressure from administrators to pass kids no matter what, because high failure rates make schools look bad. "Teachers have told me they've stopped bothering recommending retention or summer school, because principals are not going to back them up," says Virginia educator Rick Nelson.[12] Administrators, meanwhile, feel heat from *parents* who throw fits and blame the school when their children don't meet required standards. Consequently, some schools have become failure-free zones, and educators do just about anything to pass students—give easy assignments, accept work long after it was due, hand out lots of extra credit, allow open-book tests, even replace tests with group projects.

Over time, this means that standards erode across the board. Lessons get watered down, grades are inflated, and education is cheapened for everyone. "When you socially promote large numbers of students, you pull down what you expect of all students," points out Frank Brogan, lieutenant governor and former education commissioner of Florida.[13] The message goes out to children: there is no need to work hard. You're going to pass anyway.

The same remedy does not fit all students, and requiring a child to repeat a grade is not always the surest way to strengthen her education.

But a couple of things are clear. A system that routinely fails to enforce its own standards in fact has no standards. And just passing kids along, unprepared for what awaits them, fixes nothing. An unofficial policy of wholesale social promotion, well intended though it may be, is in the end a cruel policy of neglect.

Tracking

Tracking—the practice of grouping students by ability and achievement—is a common feature of schools and one of the most hotly debated topics in American education. Middle schools and high schools often use tracking to group their pupils into "faster" and "slower" classes. For example, a student who is a great reader may take an honors English class, while one who struggles with reading may take a remedial class. Elementary schools frequently use a form of tracking called "ability grouping" or "homogeneous grouping" to organize students into groups within classes. You may remember this from your own childhood when, for example, different reading groups (perhaps dubbed "Redbirds" and "Bluebirds") worked with the second grade teacher at various times—and probably read different books—because they were reading at different levels.

Tracking is sometimes controversial among parents whose children are placed in "slower" groups, even as its abolition upsets parents who like the fact that theirs are in "faster" classes. It comes under fierce attack by many in the education establishment who see it as discriminatory. Critics say it is unfair and elitist to sort children on the basis of their academic prowess. It's even racist, some assert, because poor and minority students get shoved into low tracks where they're sentenced to impoverished educations.

In the last couple of decades, the message has gone out: tracking is a bad policy. Accordingly, many school systems have moved away from it in favor of something that educators call "heterogeneous grouping," which means mixing children of various levels of achievement and trying to teach them all in the same setting with the same teacher. This trend irks many parents who worry that, if their high-achieving child is grouped with slower youngsters, her own education will suffer.

You may hear it said that "research proves" tracking is ineffective, that it helps no one academically, and that heterogeneous grouping boosts achievement for all kids. Be wary. Extensive research has yielded mixed results, according to Tom Loveless of the Brookings Institution, who has carefully studied the issue. "Research comparing tracking and heterogeneous grouping cannot conclusively declare one or the other as the better way of organizing students," he reports. That's partly because tracking strategies differ so widely from school to school.

Tracking can be either a harmful or useful idea, depending on how it's done. The kind we deplore is the type that consigns some children to a low-track curriculum devoid of serious academic content. In some places, low-track children face banal assignments and paltry expectations. They practice menial skills, take vocational training, or basically do very little while a teacher baby-sits. This kind of sorting really is a caste system and it's wrong.

The kind of tracking that can be useful is the type that *treats all children to serious academic content*, regardless of the group they are in or the speed with which they're mastering the curriculum. Schools must deal with the reality that different children do learn at different speeds and can handle subjects in varying degrees of depth. Grouping by ability and achievement makes it easier for teachers to tailor instruction so that everyone is suitably challenged. Faster students aren't held back, and slower students aren't neglected. We find nothing wrong with such tracking, so long as the groups are not immutable and they all focus on important academic content. If that is the case, you probably want your child taught with others who are at approximately the same achievement level.

If your school does track, ask some careful questions: What sorts of tracks are there? How do you assign children to groups or tracks? What criteria do you use to make tracking decisions (e.g., grades, achievement test scores)? Do I have a say about where my child is placed? Once she's placed in a track, how often is that decision reviewed? Is it possible to be in one track for some subjects and a different track for others? How hard is it for children to move from a lower track to a higher one?

The governing principle should remain: all children deserve access to a rich curriculum, a common core of worthwhile knowledge, important skills, and sound ideals. That's the philosophy you want to see in your child's school. Good schools may vary the pace and pedagogy as appropriate, but they take pains to retain the content for all.

Class Size

It's an article of faith with many parents (and teachers) that children learn better in small classes and that one should pick schools accordingly. Enormous political energy and many tax dollars have recently poured into efforts to reduce class size, especially in the primary grades. There is no doubt that most teachers would rather teach small classes, and no doubt that *if the teacher knows what she is doing* it's possible to pay more attention to individual pupils when there aren't as many of them. Yet it is wrong to assume that a small class is always best.

The research on this issue is truly ambiguous. Most studies show little relationship between class size and student achievement—particularly when, as is often the case, the difference is between twenty-seven or twenty-eight kids per class and twenty-three or twenty-four. There is some evidence that very small classes (fewer than fifteen pupils) are more effective if teachers alter their approach and organize lessons to take advantage of the much-reduced class size. When the difference is between twenty-eight and twenty-four pupils, though, most teachers don't do anything different. They deliver the same lessons in the same way (though of course they have fewer term papers and tests to grade). The children don't learn significantly more.

California has begun an ambitious program to reduce class size in the primary grades. A 1999 evaluation of its first two years showed a minimal effect on test scores. Small gains in achievement came at a very high cost and with unwanted side effects, such as an increase in the number of inexperienced and poorly educated teachers and the exodus of many veteran teachers from inner city schools to the suburbs.

In the debate about class size reduction, the issue of teacher quality is often overlooked. To have smaller classes, schools must hire more teachers. Many parents assume that these will all be good teachers. That's not a safe bet. Qualified people aren't always available—especially if schools need to hire a lot of them at once in order to reduce class sizes across the board. Would you rather have three good teachers each with a classroom of twenty-five students, or add one bad teacher and divide the students four ways? How many parents would be happy with the nineteen-pupil classes if their child ended up in the room with the weak teacher?

Highly effective schools may also have very large classes, as we see in many Asian countries. Catholic schools in the United States also have somewhat larger classes than public schools. In years past, they often had classes of thirty or more students, yet were generally regarded as providing their pupils with a very good education.

Good teachers who organize their lesson plans to impart valuable skills and knowledge in an effective way can often work well with large classes. If you face the choice between a great teacher with a large class and a mediocre teacher with a small class, go with the great teacher, not the small class. Remember, too, that every day brings more ways of individualizing a child's learning experience, especially through technology—but also through tutoring, after-school programs, and the like.

Spending on Schools

As with small classes, many parents take it on faith that the more money their school has and spends per pupil, the better its education must be. Education reform would be far simpler than it is if money alone were the answer. But it's not so. Numerous studies have shown that more dollars do not guarantee better schools.

We've proven it many times over in the United States. Generally speaking, underfunding of schools is not a problem in this country. As a society, we invest immense sums in education, and expenditures keep climbing. Public schools now spend about $6,000 per year per pupil. That represents a tripling of expenditures, adjusted for inflation, since the 1950s. Yet few would argue that education got three times better in this country during that period—in fact, most indicators show that school performance deteriorated for many pupils. When compared to other economically advanced countries, U.S. schools are near the top of the list in terms of per-pupil expenditures, but at or near the bottom in terms of how much children learn from year to year.

You don't have to look at long-term trends or go abroad to see that money alone can't buy a good education. The proof is all around us. Today, many a low-spending U.S. school—public, private, parochial, charter, and so forth—delivers a first-rate education. Many a high-spending school system (especially in big cities, but also in suburbs and rural areas) produces shoddy results.

Running a school undeniably takes funds: to employ teachers, keep the building cooled and heated, buy desks, books, equipment, and necessary technology, and so forth. It is also true that some U.S. schools do not have sufficient resources. There are places without enough books to go around, places where devoted teachers must dig into their own pockets to purchase vital classroom supplies. Yet even in those cases, the problem may not be so much lack of funds as how they're spent.

All too often, here is what happens: as schools increase their budgets, additional resources go toward bureaucracy, new programs, across-the-board salary increases, and amenities that have little to do with academic basics. Ironically, as more money has been spent on American schools, the proportion of dollars actually devoted to classroom instruction has declined. The Organization for Economic Cooperation and Development reports that the United States is the only major industrial country where teachers comprise fewer than half the employees of public schools.

If a school spends additional money on more of the same kinds of inputs, you can expect essentially the same results. If instead it devotes funds to high-payoff projects—for example, developing a more challenging curriculum, hiring better teachers, or the imaginative use of technology—then it can make a positive difference. The key is to remember that the essence of a good school isn't money. Most of the problems plaguing schools in this country—low standards and expectations, not enough discipline, a lack of focus on academics—are largely unrelated to spending.

The question of how much funding your school receives is not trivial, but don't be fooled by politicians or administrators who would have you believe that the more money thrown at your child's education, the better it will be. It doesn't work that way. When examining your school, pay attention first and foremost to what comes out by way of results, not what goes in by way of money.

School Uniforms

Are school uniforms a good idea because they minimize clothing distractions, cut down on wardrobe competition between kids, and create an orderly, workmanlike atmosphere? Or do they rob youngsters of individuality and threaten their freedom of expression?

Across the country there is a trend toward uniforms. Many educators say they help improve discipline, attendance, and achievement. "Kids get more serious when wearing nice pants, ties, and a sport jacket," says a Washington, D.C., area principal. On days when students get to wear whatever they want, he adds, "There's a different tone in school—looser. Their attention span gets shorter. There's more pushing and shoving in the corridors. They're more in a party mentality than a business mentality."[14] Uniforms encourage students to focus on what school is about rather than how they look. Many parents feel that they simplify all sorts of other things, from morning agonies about what to wear that day to department store tantrums (and spending sprees) when it's time to buy the back-to-school wardrobe.

Educators say it's tougher to teach when kids are surrounded by T-shirts emblazoned with beer ads, sexual slogans, even gang insignia, or when girls show up for class sporting the "Lolita look." It's high school students who push the clothing envelope the furthest to grab their peers' attention and get a rise out of adults, but the younger kids always want what the older ones wear. The latest teen fashions quickly trickle down to the middle schools and even primary grades.

These displays are distracting to children. They can affect one's sense of self. Sloppy dress promotes sloppy thinking and sloppy behavior. A school uniform is a symbol that young people are expected to behave in an orderly way, be on time, and act with courtesy while they're at school. Dressing for academic success sends a message that school is a serious place, meant for people who are diligent about their studies. It promotes pride in school. Uniforms also encourage kids to express themselves and notice each other's individuality in more significant ways than shoes and shirts.

In general, we find that schools with uniforms or dress codes—provided they are enforced—are places that are more serious about learning. You may not agree. Certainly, we have seen (and in some cases raised) academically successful children who never went near a uniform. But almost every good school places some limits on clothing, jewelry, hairstyles, and the like. Many good schools have also found that a simple, tidy uniform of some kind is conducive to serious learning.

Year-Round Schooling

Here and there around the country, schools are experimenting with something called "year-round education" (YRE). Despite the name, it usually does not mean that students are in class all year. Rather, it's a term for calendars that do away with the long summer vacation and have shorter, more frequent breaks instead. For example, students might get three-week breaks in October, January, April, and July.

In most YRE arrangements, the number of days each student attends class remains the same as in the traditional school calendar. Why make a change, then? Economics often has a lot to do with it. By dividing its students into three or four groups, each with different vacation times, a school can stagger its schedule so that one group is always on vacation. This means more kids can be taught under the same roof during the course of a year. That relieves overcrowding and lets communities put off having to build new school buildings. It may save you some tax dollars, but whether or not it does your child any good is another question.

YRE supporters claim that it does in fact boost academic achievement by minimizing "summer learning loss." The shorter breaks mean kids don't forget as much of what they learned the previous year, and teachers don't have to spend so much time reviewing in the fall. This is a particular problem for disadvantaged youngsters and others whose summers contain little intellectual stimulation. Supporters also say that the standard school calendar is an outmoded construct that dates back to agrarian times when families needed the kids to help harvest fields in July and August (and when air conditioning did not exist). Three or four weeks of vacation at a time is enough nowadays—after that, kids are bored and ready to start back to school. Some working parents like YRE because they don't have to arrange day care for the long summer months.

Critics remain skeptical of claims of improved school performance. They say there is no reliable evidence that the new schedules have any real effect on test scores one way or another. For many families, however, the main bone of contention is loss of the beloved summer vacation. They believe that the long break in the warm months gives kids a chance to grow, explore, and learn in important ways that schools just can't provide. Perhaps most important, it gives them time to be with their families. "Kids are already spending so much time in scheduled activities—whether it's day care, after-school programs, or school itself—that they're stressed out and over-regimented," says Heather Tepe, a Maryland homemaker who helped defeat a YRE proposal for schools in her area. "They need some downtime—time to be kids."[15]

In some places, schools are actually lengthening the academic year for their students, either through YRE schedules or simply by shrinking the traditional summer break. America's 180-day school year is indeed short compared to other industrialized countries. Japanese students, for instance, go to school nearly 240 days a year. That discrepancy may help explain why foreign students have been whipping American youngsters on international tests. Skeptics note, though, that more class time doesn't assure more learning. The real problem, they say, is that many U.S. schools are dishing up a mediocre education to begin with. How is offering an extra month of a watered-down curriculum and low expectations going to help students? You don't fix a lousy two-egg omelet by adding a third egg—that just gets you a bigger omelet that also tastes bad.

Since changes in the school schedule can affect every member of the family, people have strong opinions on this subject. Not everyone wants the same thing. The authors, in fact, are split on this one. That's just one more reason parents ought to be able to decide where their children

get their education. This is a big country, with room enough for schools with all sorts of calendars. Give people plenty of choices among lots of good schools, we say, and let parents decide what's best for their families and children.

Computers in the Classroom

When you hear the next pitch about cyber-enriching your child's education, keep one thing in mind: so far, there is no good evidence that most uses of computers significantly improve learning.

Across the country, schools are spending millions of dollars getting computers into classrooms and wired to the Internet. Most educators are excited about the new high-tech possibilities. Students can suddenly e-mail boys and girls in foreign lands. They can publish their own writings electronically. They can conduct all sorts of virtual science projects, such as "dissecting" on-screen frogs. Computers offer instant, relatively inexpensive access to worlds of information—everything from maps to electronic encyclopedias to programs that can help youngsters trace their own family trees.

We do not doubt that computers (and other new technologies) will continue to bring significant changes to U.S. classrooms, just as they're changing the way many of us go about our jobs. But generally speaking, studies haven't shown computers to be any more effective than pencils and paper in teaching children reading, writing, adding, subtracting, and other basic lessons.[16] Some educators say that, if not used properly, computers can actually deter learning.

Critics point to several problems. Many software programs are little more than glorified video games, loaded with glitzy flashing images and random noises that do a far better job of seducing students than encouraging concentration and thinking. Ninety-nine percent of so-called educational programs are "terrible, really terrible," says Harvard education professor Judah Schwartz, who also notes that the most mindless use of computers seems to be at the elementary school level.

Some educators worry that computers stifle the imagination by stuffing kids' minds with "canned" images. Others say that too much virtual learning comes at the cost of valuable real-world learning activities, like looking at insects through a magnifying glass or having a thoughtful conversation. Some teachers and parents watch in alarm as administrators cut back in other areas of the curriculum (such as art and music classes) to buy computers and wire schools. When teachers aren't

trained to teach differently with the help of that equipment, all too often they end up forfeiting its latent benefits and allowing their students to play games or roam the Web.

Keep in mind also that, although "learning to use a computer" sounds sophisticated, in truth learning to point-and-click or surf the Net doesn't take much skill. (Many kids know how to do those things before they get to school.) The more important and time-consuming task for schools is stocking children's minds with valuable knowledge and helping them develop critical skills so they can put those computers to good use. They need, for example, the discernment to separate worthwhile information from the garbage in cyberspace. "What good is a multimedia Internet feed to a child who can't pay attention in class?" asks computer pioneer Clifford Stoll. "To a kid who will not read more than one paragraph? To a student who is unable to write analytically?"[17]

Children need to learn how to use and be comfortable with computers, but not at the expense of learning core knowledge and skills such as reading, writing, thinking, and listening. Computers can't compensate for inadequate or incomplete lessons. They can't substitute for a strong curriculum, solid standards, and high expectations. They can't replace good books. They certainly can't replace a good teacher—or time spent learning with a parent at home. The computer can be an important *tool* for teaching and learning, but for most elementary school students, it is not a fundamental subject in itself.

Teacher Training and Certification

In 1998, the state of Massachusetts decided to give basic competency tests to people applying to be public school teachers. Nearly 60 percent of these would-be educators, all of them college graduates, failed. Many performed at fifth- or sixth-grade levels in reading and writing. Misspellings ("diferant," "improbally," "integraty") were rife. Describing the drafting of the Constitution, one candidate wrote: "In the convention, delegats had to debat and compermise." Others defined the word "abolish" as "a law about something" and a preposition as "a description of what is taking place in a sentence." In Virginia, meanwhile, one third of would-be teachers flunked a national test of basic reading, writing, and mathematics. In a New York school district, three quarters of the teacher applicants flunked a reading comprehension test pegged to the level of high school seniors.

Are some U.S. teachers unqualified? This is a sensitive subject. Teach-

ing is one of our most honorable professions. It's also one of the toughest jobs in America. Thousands of wonderful, capable women and men serve in our schools. Most are not especially well paid. Yet they approach their work with a great sense of duty and enthusiasm. Still, honesty compels us to tell you that some teachers are not properly prepared to do their jobs.

Why do we have this problem? Begin with the fact that many future teachers are themselves victims of a weak elementary and secondary education. They're subjected to years of dumbed-down curricula and low expectations, then graduate from high school without having learned the very fundamentals they hope to teach others someday. "They are afraid of math; they are afraid of arithmetic; I'm not saying anything about geometry," says a Brooklyn college professor. "If they carry this attitude to the classroom, you will maybe have kids who don't know geometry."[18] Sheila Schwartz, a retired professor of English education, laments: "Many had writing skills that ranged from depressing to horrifying, especially when we remember that these same people eventually went on to teach writing to high school students. A disturbing number could not write a lucid sentence or paragraph."[19]

Once in college (or graduate school), these young people enroll in teacher education programs that have notoriously low standards and expectations. It is no secret that, at many universities, an education major produces one of the easiest degrees. Unfortunately, that means schools of education attract some applicants who are among the least academically accomplished in their classes. Future teachers spend relatively little time mastering the subjects they'll be teaching, but lots of time on classroom methods, the history and philosophy of education, and various theories of child development. Instead of learning more mathematics, in other words, they learn how to talk to fourth graders about mathematics.

Most colleges of education and graduate schools of education are staffed by professors who transmit and defend the silliest ideas, worst-conceived fads, and most dysfunctional practices in primary and secondary education. Only 12 percent of education professors, for example, say that it is absolutely essential that teachers expect students to be neat, on time, and polite. A mere 19 percent say it's essential for teachers to stress correct spelling, grammar, and punctuation.[20]

At education schools, future teachers learn to use jargon like "constructing one's own knowledge," and "getting students to develop the subtext of what they're doing." They listen to professors say things like, "So writing gave you permission to think on paper about what's there," and discuss deep questions such as, "What was it like to listen to each other's responses?"[21] They're often treated to heavy doses of political correctness in classes like "Diversity and Change," "Classism," "Sexism," and "Oppression and Education."[22] This is not to say that all schools of education are awful. There are a handful of strong programs and some excellent professors out there. But frankly, many of these institutions are an embarrassment.

People who want to teach enroll in these programs because it's hard to get a teaching job otherwise. Public schools ordinarily employ only "state-certified" teachers. To get one of those certificates, one must usually submit to a conventional teacher-training program. For the most part, states will certify anyone with the right combination of education school courses, even if they don't know much about the subject they expect to teach. Critics observe that most states pay more attention to the qualifications of veterinarians treating America's cats and dogs than those of the people educating children.

Fortunately, there are exceptions. A number of states permit public schools to hire teachers with "alternate certification," which usually means a fast track into the classroom without a lengthy detour through a college of education. (Sometimes, though, the "alternative" program amounts to little more than deferring the ed school experience; and some states only permit the hiring of such people in emergency situations.) Many state licensure systems also accept graduates of teacher training programs located within liberal arts colleges. These generally seem to do a better job than the education schools, partly because they have higher academic standards, and partly because the teacher preparation program is embedded in a liberal arts framework. We should also note that one of the virtues of private schools and (in most states) charter schools is that they're free to hire capable individuals who did not have to pass through education schools.

Finally, you should know that a worrisome number of teachers in American schools are teaching "out of field," which means they've been assigned to teach subjects in which they have little or no background. Neither teachers nor principals like this practice, but school officials say they often have no choice. They simply can't find enough qualified educators. It's mainly a problem in high schools, but it also affects middle schools. Obviously this is not good for students' learning, yet schools usually do not let parents know when they're doing it.

It bears repeating that most teachers are enthusiastic, devoted professionals who want the best for children. They deserve our gratitude and respect. But the reality is that just because an individual has graduated from an "approved" teacher training program and has been certified by a state does not guarantee that she is well qualified to teach your child. That's one reason parents should always keep an eye on schoolwork and get to know the teachers.

Teachers Unions

The overwhelming majority of U.S. public school teachers belong to unions, as do some private and charter school teachers. Nearly all belong to affiliates of the National Education Association (NEA), which has about 2.3 million members (not all of them teachers), or the American Federation of Teachers (AFT), which has about 900,000 members. Despite initial rejection of the idea by the NEA membership in 1998, these two groups are likely to merge into a single vast organization in the not-too-distant future.

The teachers unions wield enormous clout in the worlds of politics and education policy. They influence decision makers from the schoolhouse to the statehouse to the White House. That's too bad, because—with happy but rare exceptions—they have resisted serious efforts to reform and strengthen American education. These unions were started for legitimate reasons, but over time they have become almost completely self-serving in their actions and policy views. Partly because of them, many American schools have lost their focus, their confidence, and a clear sense of their mission.

You're most apt to see the leaders of the national unions on TV or quoted in the press, but it's actually their state and local affiliates that do most of the heavy lifting and make the most mischief. They've stood against testing teachers to make sure they're qualified, and have made it virtually impossible to fire incompetent teachers. They insist that all teachers be paid alike regardless of their specialty or whether they're really good in the classroom. Over the years, the major unions have tried to sabotage almost any kind of school choice idea, whether it be vouchers or charter schools or tuition tax credits. They've opposed efforts to hold schools accountable for meeting real academic standards. In short, the teachers unions have fiercely resisted any changes that would interfere with the public school system monopoly or tie consequences to its performance.

The NEA is the most entrenched and aggressive opponent of education reform. It's also a behemoth political action organization that routinely supports liberal political candidates and takes left-wing stands on many national and international affairs. As journalist Sol Stern has observed, "It would be an understatement to say that the NEA favors an expansion of the welfare state. Its economic program more closely resembles the most radical of the European socialist parties."[23] In recent years, for example, the NEA has gone on record in favor of contraceptives dispensed by school-based clinics, nationalized health care, D.C. statehood, and killing an anti-ballistic-missile defense system. Of course, reasonable people can disagree about these issues. The real question is: Why is the NEA concerning itself with such matters when so many American children aren't learning to read and write well?

Many teachers don't agree with the NEA's stances and feel that its politicization has done a tremendous disservice to their profession. A few have begun to ask that a portion of their dues be refunded if it is spent on political advocacy rather than collective bargaining. In some states and communities, teachers have formed their own independent professional organizations which provide them with some of the benefits of union membership (such as group liability insurance) without the political activities of the two major unions. Some educators predict that rising defections will force the big teachers unions to reform. That remains to be seen.

You may be lucky enough to live in a community with a relatively enlightened teachers union local, or in a state whose laws don't give the teachers unions much clout. But if your child attends a public school, chances are that the NEA and AFT influence is strong. Unfortunately, that may weaken the quality of her education and the prospects of making badly needed reforms.

Bilingual Education

To be a citizen is to share in something common—in common principles, common memories, a common language in which to discuss our affairs. The common language of the United States is English. Our schools' common task is to ensure that immigrant children who don't speak English learn it as quickly as possible so they can enjoy all the opportunities of American society.

Immersion methods (sometimes called "English as a second language" instruction) are generally the fastest, surest way to accomplish that task. Under this approach, students may spend one or two hours a day in classes where their native language is spoken, but for most of the day they attend regular English-speaking classes. Through "immersion" in an English-rich environment, they hear, speak, read, and write the language as much as possible—and thereby learn it as quickly as possible. This approach is especially important if a child's outside-of-school environment does not include much English conversation.

Many schools, however, use a method called "transitional bilingual education," which usually isn't "transitional" at all, but rather a politically inspired semi-hoax perpetrated on millions of immigrant children. It claims to teach youngsters English while simultaneously letting them learn other subjects (e.g. math, science, social studies) in their original language. It routinely consigns the English-teaching part of the day to a brief period and treats English as if it were a foreign language. Too often, the main point of bilingual education turns out to be preserving a child's original language and culture, rather than helping her adapt to new ones. For many students, it slows rather than expedites their evolution into young Americans who are comfortable, fluent, and successful in English.

Despite billions of dollars in federal support, this program has proven to be a dismal failure. "I have relatives who have been in bilingual education ten years and they still are not fluent in English or in Spanish," notes a California high schooler who had the good fortune to be educated in English-immersion classes. "I think that's very sad. They don't even have a chance to go to college."[24]

Survey after survey and election after election make clear that most immigrant parents are keen for their children to learn English quickly. They know that the common language is the key to success in this country. In a 1996 survey, four out of five Hispanic parents indicated that they wanted their children to be taught their academic courses in English, not Spanish. Two years later, many Latino voters in California favored Proposition 227, which passed with 61 percent and which undertook to virtually end the "transitional" approach to bilingual education. As veteran education journalist James Traub summarizes the evidence, "Very few immigrants care about multiculturalism or bilingualism; they want their children to learn English as fast as possible in order to make it into the American mainstream, where good jobs are available—and they take the common-sense position that the best way to learn English is by, well, learning English."[25]

It is a wonderful thing for children to know more than one language. Many U.S. children do not, and that is a shame. We favor foreign language instruction, beginning in the elementary years. But the national priority must remain ensuring that every child in an American school who does not already know English learns it as fast as possible. Until she is fluent, everything else ought to take second place.

CHAPTER 16

Parents and Education Reform

THIS CHAPTER IS FOR PARENTS WHO ARE INTERESTED IN education reform—those who want to help transform "the system." That may not be high on your list of priorities. You may have your hands full looking after your own child's education. You may feel that you don't have the time or energy to fight larger battles. That's okay. Our purpose is not to turn you into a crusader. Being a good parent is a consuming enterprise all by itself.

Nevertheless, you may discover, as have many parents before you, that your efforts to do right by your child will lead you up against regulatory rigidities, bureaucratic frustrations, and interest groups pressing in the opposite direction. The issue at hand may be as simple as trying to get a different teacher for your child. It may be your exasperation with the way reading is taught in first grade, or the vacuousness of the sixth grade social studies curriculum. It could be any of a thousand things. While your goal is simply to fix a problem affecting your child, you are apt to find out that the solution keeps eluding you because of some system-wide or state-wide policy, or even a national trend. You may also find that other parents share your discontent and frustration. Practically before you know it, you find yourself evolving into someone who is trying to make your school a better place. If that happens, we say welcome to the world of education reform.

You probably will not be surprised to learn that reform is largely about politics. We don't necessarily mean Democrats and Republicans,

626

though they certainly get involved. We mean politics in the broadest sense. Plato, it has been said, understood that the most fundamental political question is: Who gets to teach the children? Those who shape the minds and dispositions of the rising generation have much to do with the course of society. In some ways, education reform is a battle of ideals and visions as well as politicians and interest groups.

In the contemporary politics of America, much education reform can also be likened to a great tug of war between "producers" and "consumers," i.e., between those who run the public education system and those parents and students who depend on their schools. For whose benefit does the system operate? Consumers, of course, you say. Yet today's sad reality is that it often operates more for the benefit of the producers. Trying to change that reality is what reformers end up doing.

Machiavelli wrote in *The Prince* that "There is nothing more difficult to carry out, nor more doubtful of success, nor more dangerous to handle than a new order of things." Take that warning to heart. The public school establishment is one of the most stubbornly intransigent forces on the planet. It is full of people and organizations dedicated to protecting established programs and keeping things just the way they are. Administrators talk of reform even as they are circling the wagons to fend off change, or preparing to outflank your innovation. Reform debates often take place in a highly charged atmosphere. "I was screamed at by adults and students at meetings, in phone calls, and when I was simply walking downtown," says a New Jersey parent who joined the local school board and tried to make changes.[1] Before you join the fight, know that it can easily become an all-consuming, hair-pulling endeavor. It is worth it, though, because the stakes are so high.

THE EDUCATION ESTABLISHMENT: THE BLOB

To understand many of the problems besetting U.S. schools, it is necessary to know something about the education establishment—once christened "the blob" by one of the authors. The first thing you should understand is that, to a large degree, the governance of American public education is separate from the regular elected government of the community or state. Mayors, city councils, governors, and legislatures do not operate the schools. That's not to say they don't fervently delve into education issues, particularly those concerning budgets, but they do not run the public schools the way they run the highway department, fire department, or welfare department.

Instead, the schools are run by a parallel government, usually consisting of local and state school boards—sometimes appointed, often elected—which employ professional educators known as superintendents, commissioners, or chancellors. Those senior officials, in turn, manage local school systems and state education agencies. This was all set up in the late nineteenth century to insulate education from politics. It was thought to be the best way to keep patronage-minded mayors and aldermen from interfering with schools, and to engage civic leaders in the governance of education. Sometimes it still works that way, especially in small towns and suburbs. For the most part, however, it has led to an insular and fortified political arena of its own, hard to penetrate and change whether one is an aggrieved parent or a reform-minded governor.

The Local Blob

School systems, also known as school districts, are, strictly speaking, creatures of the state, but they also tap into the American affection for local control. Every state except Hawaii has created these local systems to administer its public schools. There are about 16,000 of them in all, ranging from tiny districts with just a handful of pupils to vast metropolitan systems with (in New York City's case) more than a million students. A school district may serve a specific town or an entire county. In rural areas, there are "regional" and "consolidated" systems that cover vast territories.

Almost every system has a school board, sometimes called the school committee or board of education. This part-time lay group exercises control over the district. It is responsible for such matters as adopting budgets, selecting textbooks, setting curricular guidelines, and hiring the superintendent.

Board members are supposed to be responsive to consumer concerns and voter priorities. Sometimes that turns out to be true. Be cautioned, though, that with increasing and lamentable frequency, U.S. school boards are being populated by people with a political agenda, by agents of the teachers unions, by aggrieved former employees of the school system (often with a grudge to settle), and by single-interest representatives whose top priority is to visit their particular enthusiasm on all the community's children.

Even when a board avoids such special interests in terms of its own membership, moreover, it may be pushed around by "experts" pursuing dubious ends of their own. Professionals—especially those on the school system's own staff—sometimes take advantage of board members' lack of credentials and unfamiliarity with the jargon, achieving their ends by drowning the board in arcane analyses and otherwise exploiting its amateur status. Parents need to understand that the board may have been co-opted. They should keep pushing and questioning board members about their policies and the system's actions. Gentle reminders about who is employed by whom may help!

Boards don't always have the last word. Their hands are often tied by great tangles of state and federal regulations. Sometimes they are so splintered that little needed change can occur. In 1999, Los Angeles school board members got so tired of their own internal squabbling and dysfunction, they voted to spend $30,000 of the taxpayers' money on group therapy for themselves.

The superintendent of schools is, in effect, the district CEO. He or she usually works for the school board and is in charge of running the system's day-to-day operations. Superintendents spend much time wrangling over budget, personnel, and curriculum matters. In larger districts, they oversee a bureaucracy of assistant superintendents, department heads, and other administrators. A good superintendent is a skillful organizer and helps set a tone of academic excellence in every school in the district. A bad superintendent in a poorly managed system can quickly ruin morale among principals and teachers.

Your school also has a little government of its own. The principal is usually the boss, a person chosen by the local superintendent (and approved by the school board) to direct the affairs of that particular school. Some principals do a terrific job, while others are mostly concerned, like the rest of the blob, with preserving the status quo. The sad fact is that today's principals often lack the power to fix many serious problems in their own schools. They take their orders from higher-ups in the superintendent's office, and have all sorts of restrictions imposed on them by government regulation.

Other local entities are involved in different aspects of school governance. The fire inspector keeps watch over building safety, the police may be involved with school security, and sundry health and social services agencies may be on hand to look after the non-education needs of students and families. The local janitors union may have much to say about when the school can be open. The list of school "stakeholders" quickly gets a mile long. They may do a fine job for your school. Be aware, though, that each stakeholder is often more concerned with its bit of power or piece of the budget than with the educational effectiveness of the school as a whole.

The State Blob

No matter what you may hear out of Washington and notwithstanding all the talk of "local control," constitutional responsibility for education in the U.S. rests with the states, which also supply about half the money to pay for public school budgets. Every single state constitution gives the state the job of furnishing education to its citizens, and every state has enacted a compulsory attendance law which requires children to attend school. Most states have also taken direct responsibility for certifying teachers and other public school personnel, for establishing (often slipshod) statewide academic standards, and for setting specific high school graduation requirements. The state level is where most crucial decisions are made about such reforms as charter schools and school choice programs, and where issues are fought out concerning the regulation of private schools and home schooling. Decisions made in your state capital are at least as consequential for your child's school as actions at the local level.

Public education has its own bureaucracy at the state level. It consists of a state department of education, which is usually guided by a "chief state school officer" (who may go by the title of commissioner, superintendent, or secretary of education) and a state board of education. The state department of education writes regulations that affect schools, makes sure local districts follow state laws, and exercises great influence over education policy throughout the state. It is invariably a complex maze of administrators and entrenched programs. The state commissioner, board, governor, and legislature often quarrel over reforms and fight over turf.

Since the mid-1980s, a number of governors of both political parties have plunged into education reform, often with good results. But governors and, more particularly, state legislators are often vulnerable to lobbying from teachers unions and other established stakeholders trying to fend off changes. So education reform at the state level has had mixed results.

The Federal Blob

Notwithstanding the fact that the U.S. Constitution never mentions the word "education" and the related fact that the Tenth Amendment reserves to the states those powers not explicitly given to the federal government, Washington wields influence over K–12 education that is out of proportion to the 7 percent or so of the public school budget that it provides. That influence takes three major forms.

First, Washington establishes federal programs that give money to schools for certain limited purposes. These grants are made to induce schools to do something that Congress has decided is desirable, whether it be drug abuse prevention programs, reducing class size, or ensuring gender equity in junior high school science curricula.

Second, Washington issues regulations and mandates, usually in the name of civil rights enforcement, that go far beyond the availability of federal money for specific purposes. Thirty years ago, racial desegregation was the big issue in this area. Now the regulatory (and judicial) hand is more often felt in rules for educating and accommodating disabled children.

Third, the president and U.S. secretary of education use the bully pulpit to make pronouncements about what is good in American education, what is bad, and what needs to change. As education has become potent politically, school issues are more and more in the Washington spotlight, discussed in speeches, radio broadcasts, and Sunday television interview shows.

Washington makes a lot of noise about education, and the more the federal education bureaucracy grows, the greater its ability to interfere in schools. Nonetheless, as a parent-reformer you are likely to find that the majority of your concerns really involve decisions made at state and local levels. You're all but certain to find that those are the places where your efforts have greater impact.

Special Interest Groups

The blob also contains literally hundreds of education interest groups. The biggest, wealthiest, and most powerful are the two teachers unions, the National Education Association (NEA) and American Federation of Teachers (AFT). Examples of other major groups are the National Association of Elementary School Principals, the National Association of Secondary School Principals, the American Association of School

Administrators, the National School Boards Association, and the Association for Supervision and Curriculum Development. There are also smaller and more specialized outfits such as the National Association of School Psychologists and the National School Public Relations Association.

Many of these groups have affiliates at the state and local levels. This ever-expanding, interlocking directorate of interests makes up the education establishment. The members of these organizations may be fine, dedicated people, but you must recognize that the chief *political* function of these groups is to block changes that don't serve their interests and to push policies that serve their ends.

Unfortunately, the one group you might expect to have parents' interests front and center on its agenda, the parent-teacher association, has been largely co-opted by the establishment. Your local PTA may be just fine, but do not expect much help—especially from the national PTA and its state affiliates—in reform efforts such as allowing greater school choice for families. You're more likely to find them campaigning arm in arm with the teachers unions to maintain the status quo. "I don't mind people being political at all, but I do mind it if they don't allow others to express dissimilar views or if they only tell one side," says a Virginia father who attended a state PTA convention and heard nothing but attacks on reform initiatives.[2] Alas, there's much truth in the quip that the PTA has become "too much T and not enough P."

The Anti-Blob

The good news is that some groups are more apt to have consumer interests in mind and also wield some clout of their own. The National Governors Association and the Business Roundtable are examples of organizations that have pressed for real reform. Dissident groups have even begun to emerge from the education establishment. For example, in addition to the Council of Chief State School Officers (the traditional organization for state superintendents), there is now a group called the Education Leaders Council, which advocates very different policies and whose existence belies the CCSSO's claim to speak for all the states. A number of teachers who don't agree with the two big unions have launched their own professional associations. In some schools, as alternatives to a PTA, parents have started parent-teacher organizations (PTOs), which send no dues to a state or national organization.

Several groups provide informal support for reform-minded parents, teachers, and officials. For example, the Educational Excellence Network has for years functioned as an information clearinghouse for education scholars who don't follow the conventional wisdom. (You can consult its Web site at www.edexcellence.net.) Local reform activists often turn to the Center for Education Reform for advice and information. (Its Web site is www.edreform.com.) Change-minded parents locate kindred spirits through the Education Consumers ClearingHouse (www.education-consumers.com), a grassroots group that serves parents, policymakers, taxpayers, and others with a consumer's perspective on public education.

Such anti-blob groups can trigger real improvements. A now famous example of grassroots reform is the saga of Mathematically Correct (www.mathematicallycorrect.com), an organization born in the fall of 1995 when four California families, each concerned about the new New Math lessons being offered in their schools, found each other and began to press for change. They were told that no other families had complained and that such matters are best left to education professionals. They were ignored, placated, even insulted, but they refused to go away. They established an Internet site and took their case to teachers, administrators, legislators, the media, and professional mathematicians. They found allies in parents scattered across the country. Battles were waged in cyberspace, meetings, hearings, and newspaper columns.

The result? People began to wake up and pay attention. Mathematically Correct was able to play a significant role in rewriting California's math standards, which had been mediocre but are now among the best in the land. As goes California in education, so goes much of the nation. Those four families and the hundreds of allies who joined them played a key role in transforming the national debate about math education. The more such constructive, dissident groups, the better.

WAYS TO BRING ABOUT CHANGE

If you find yourself entering the school reform wars, realize from the outset that this is no kids' game. Back in the 1950s, Admiral Hyman Rickover, father of the nuclear submarine, compared education reform to "moving a graveyard." The celebrated businessman-politician Ross Perot, after a year involved in education reform in Texas in the early 1980s, termed it the "meanest, bloodiest, and most difficult thing I've ever been into." It hasn't gotten any easier. The forces of inertia remain strong. The blob is huge, shrewd, and utterly tireless when it comes to clinging to control. Yet it's by no means hopeless, as Mathematically Correct and other parents groups across the country have illustrated.

As you head down this path, keep in mind three rules of thumb. First, there is power (and greater safety) in numbers. The more people you muster to share your concern, the more likely you are to get the attention of decision makers and the less likely to be dismissed as someone pursuing a self-serving interest. Second, sunlight is a pretty good disinfectant. A lot of changes are easier to make after the problem has been exposed to public view. You may find that the media are useful allies. Third, be ready for a long siege. These wheels turn slowly and almost every one is connected to others that must also turn. The blob will try to outlast you. That's one of its most effective tactics for combating change: it stonewalls and dithers, hoping you'll give up and go away. If you run out of patience, the reform you seek won't happen.

Here are a few basic ideas and suggestions to guide you. For more detailed advice, a good resource to consult is *The School Reform Handbook* by Jeanne Allen and Angela Dale, published by the Center for Education Reform in Washingon, D.C.

Join or form a parent organization. You need not act alone. Find allies and band together. When parents act as a group, they are taken *much* more seriously by the education establishment. Making common cause with others will allow you to strategize and share valuable information. It's also comforting to have others to commiserate with.

The kind of organization you seek may already exist. Join your school's PTA or PTO and see whether anyone is working on the issues you're concerned about. Perhaps some other community association is already tackling school reform. In that case, your job is to locate it and plunge in. If necessary, you and some like-minded parents may opt to start your own group to press for specific changes at school.

This can be easier than you may suppose, and you ought not shy away from the challenge. Beginning with twelve parents in southeastern Wisconsin, a group called PRESS (Parents Raising Educational Standards in Schools) grew to over 1,000 members statewide in less than a year because parents rallied around one particular issue: the state's vaguely worded "academic outcomes."

- **Master the facts.** You can be sure that members of the education establishment will have all sorts of facts and figures ready to support their position. They will portray themselves as the experts who know all about how to educate children, as opposed to you, the misguided amateur. You must be ready to bolster your own arguments and, at times, call their bluff. There is nothing like having facts at your fingertips and being able to point to specific examples of policies that have either failed or worked out for the better in other schools.

  Begin your basic research by getting into the habit of reading about education issues in newspapers and magazines. Learn who's who in your school and district hierarchies. Get to know your school, district, and state policies. Bone up on the specific issues you're interested in. It is amazing how much education research can be done via the Internet. Build a list of valuable Web sites and newsgroups. Do old-fashioned legwork: visit that terrific school you've read about and see firsthand how they do it. Perhaps above all, swap information with other concerned parents. Before you know it, you'll be an "education expert" on one or two issues, and will have just as many facts in your arsenal as your opponents, maybe more!

- **Get attention for your issue.** You cannot afford to be meek if you want to be a reformer. The blob finds it easy to rebuff timid parents. Squeaky wheels are the most likely to get oiled. If you have a complaint or an idea that isn't getting proper attention, you probably need to make some noise about it—without becoming an insufferable annoyance. If you don't get satisfaction within the school itself, you and your group can escalate your concern up the hierarchy: head for the superintendent's office, and phone school board members.

  Start a Web site or newsletter for parents at your school. Write letters to the editor of your newspaper or pen an opinion editorial. Talk to the newspaper about conducting a survey of parents in your community. Local civic groups such as Rotary or Lions clubs are often great forums for spreading the word; you might be able to speak at their luncheons, write short pieces for their newsletters, or convince them to sponsor a town forum. If it's a state policy you want to change, organize a drive to collect 25,000 signatures. Send your petition to the governor and legislature, and tell the media about it.

  Sometimes you can really hold the establishment's feet to the fire by getting news coverage through your local paper, radio, or TV station. Your group will need to cultivate good relationships with reporters who cover education issues so that they know they can rely on you for good information, lively opinion, and other kinds of assistance.

Don't shy away from talk radio. Get to know the local hosts. Send them materials pertaining to troubling education developments in your community. This can be an efficient way to catch the attention of many other parents and citizens and to acquaint them with concerns previously unfamiliar to them.

- **Enlist influential allies.** Your group will be more successful if it musters aid from other quarters. Every organization that you have anything to do with—the company where you work, your service club, your church—can become active in education reform. Collectively, you can force superintendents, school boards, even the legislature to address your issues.

  Seek out groups in your community that may be sympathetic to your position: the chamber of commerce, professional societies, veterans groups, and so on. Get acquainted with local citizens groups; they often include retirees with an interest in quality education and the time to help with mailings and events. Find out where community leaders stand on reform, and what they're willing to do to support your efforts. Talk to prominent businessmen, local politicians, your U.S. congressman, editorial writers, ministers and rabbis, teachers and principals.

  In addition to state and local groups, make use of national reform organizations, think tanks, and research foundations concerned with education reform. These places can send you information and put you in touch with others around the country who are working on similar issues. (See "Good Web Sites for Parent-Reformers," page 643.)

- **Attend school board meetings.** This is an excellent way to find out what's going on in your district and be alerted to coming changes before it's too late. You can buttonhole board members (a friendly member can be a great asset to your reform efforts) and chat up the newspaper reporters who cover these events. Introduce yourself to other parents who have testified about similar concerns. If necessary, build a network of moms and dads who take turns going to sessions. Most school board meetings are attended by very few people, so parents who show up as an organized force can make a real impression.

Usually there is a time in the meeting when citizens have a chance to address the board. Get on the agenda and present your case. If your group does not speak up, board members may never even know there is a problem, or another side to the issue. If you stand up, speak the truth, and show evidence that you represent the interests of many parents, you can move a school board in your direction.

- **Meet with legislators.** Many proposed state laws have immense potential to influence what occurs in the classroom. (State academic standards and testing methods are important examples.) Get to know your representatives and senators, especially those who represent your community and those who serve on the legislature's education committees. These people are heavily lobbied by the teachers unions and other establishment groups and they may not hear from constituents who hold a different position on these issues.

In 1995, the Wisconsin parents' group PRESS thwarted a legislative effort to introduce a costly and unproven testing methodology into the state's classrooms. Concerned parents across the state contacted legislators who were unaware of the bill's impact. Representatives weighing a controversial issue often need political protection from powerful special interest groups such as the teachers unions. It can be very helpful for them to be able to explain that "I've been hearing from dozens of parents in my district who are concerned about this proposal, and I'm afraid I won't be able to support it."

- **Take part in elections.** School board elections, in particular, are often held on days when no other contests are on the ballot. That makes for small voter turnouts, which means elections are easily influenced by teachers unions and other blob interests. It also means that, if your group can get out the vote, it can make the difference.

Find out exactly where candidates stand. Hold a candidate forum. Most districts offer free use of school conference rooms or auditoriums that are suited to this purpose. This will give your group of parents greater visibility and legitimacy and may well boost your numbers. See that your group queries the candidates about specific issues that concern you. Politely insist on specific answers. Pick one or two ways to support candidates who share your concerns—

distribute campaign literature, round up endorsements, make campaign contributions, write letters to the editor.

If you really want to earn your halo, run for the school board yourself. You'll end up putting in many long and usually thankless hours of work. School boards (and state legislatures) need good, reform-minded people. Education today has suffered because parents and citizens have abandoned the field to "experts" and special interests.

- **Volunteer at school.** Most schools offer parents several ways to get involved, from chaperoning field trips to tutoring students. (See "Getting Involved at School," page 445.) By pitching in and earning your spurs, you gain credibility as a parent who cares about education, not just someone who complains. You'll come to understand more about what's going on at school, the kinds of problems teachers face, the regulations that may tie the staff's hands, who the decision makers are in the district, and which issues get people stirred up.

  Many schools have building-level councils to suggest and review policies. These usually consist of parent and teacher volunteers. You may find a whole range of such councils in your school, from a "Nutrition Committee" that examines the lunch menu to committees that review textbooks or recommend budget priorities. Sometimes these groups have real power, although most are advisory. (In private and charter schools they are more apt to function as true governing boards.) Nonetheless, joining one can be an excellent way to gain some influence and get a look at school governance.

  Be aware that, in many schools, the parents on these councils are hand-picked by the school administration because they sympathize with its agenda. They are sometimes a way of muting dissidents. If you have been vocal on a particular issue, you may be asked to participate in order to rein you in. This is done through the group process known as "consensus building." Be prepared to provide an alternative point of view during council meetings. If necessary, write a letter of dissent at the end of the process and insist on being listed as a dissenter on any policy reports that are issued at the conclusion of your group's deliberations.

- **Supply the solution yourself.** Sometimes the best way to ameliorate problems is to step in and supplement what the school is already doing. For example, if the school needs a knowledgeable music teacher, it may be easier to raise funds to hire one than to haggle with the superintendent's office over the budget. (In some communities, parents have started foundations that raise money to address shortcomings.) If you're concerned that your school doesn't pay enough heed to children's classics, you might be able to work with an enthusiastic teacher to start your own "great books" reading group. If you're worried about a lack of order and security, organize a brigade of parents who take turns volunteering as hall monitors.

Sometimes the surest way to achieve the reform you seek is to switch to a school that's already doing things right. In fact, sometimes that's the only way. Your greatest leverage—both over your own child's education and over the system as a whole—is the ability to vote with your feet. When schools know that they don't have a captive audience, they pay more attention to parents' concerns. Marketplace forces not only benefit the families that switch schools, but also have a catalytic effect on schools themselves. It's important to be aware of the alternatives available in your community—whether that means a different public school, a charter school, a private or parochial school, or even home schooling.

If there are no suitable options, you can always think about joining with other parents and starting your own school. This is a grueling project, but hundreds of moms and dads have done it. Not so many years back, organizing a school of your own meant starting a private school, and that's still a viable option. Today, however, founding a public charter school is also possible in many jurisdictions. This movement is relatively new, but parent and student satisfaction levels are sky-high in most of these schools, and waiting lists are common. (See "More About Charter Schools," page 504.)

Tips and Warnings

Here are several points to keep in mind as you tread the path of education reform:

- **Focus on one or two problems.** Don't take on everything at once. You stand a much better chance in battling entrenched interests if you concentrate your efforts on a single issue at a time. Be clear about what problem you are bent on solving, then zero in on where its solution is most apt to lie, whether at the school, district, or state level.

- **Work from the bottom up.** It's almost always best to start as close to the problem as possible, not way up the establishment ladder. You may want to speak with the teacher first (although she will probably lack power to change school policy), then the principal, then the superintendent, then a school board member, and on up. Remember that a school system is a bureaucracy. You may alienate people if they discover you've gone over their heads without first consulting them. Besides, you may pick up some valuable advice and allies on your way up the chain of command.

- **Get sympathetic teachers involved.** This is important. Most teachers are eager to find solutions to their schools' shortcomings. Some will be reluctant to buck the system, but others will join you. You will benefit from their help. Good teachers know what really works in the classroom and what does not. Their support also gives your group greater credibility in the eyes of the establishment.

- **Don't be deterred.** Some schools and systems treat citizen-reformers like invaders. The door is open until you try to make a needed change. "I spent hours getting together the right information, but when I brought it to the school board I was ignored," says a North Carolina mom worried about her school's lack of attention to history. The establishment hopes you will tire and go away. Without perseverance, you cannot win.

- **Be on guard against buck passing.** You will run into administrators and policymakers who say, "Gee, I'd love to help but that one's out of my hands." Get that person to tell you exactly *whose* hands it's in. Problems in schools can often be ameliorated if parents are persistent and politely insist that someone shoulder responsibility.

- **Don't be confused by jargon.** The education establishment uses fancy-sounding terms (like "authentic assessment" or "higher-order thinking skills") which usually stand for simple ideas. Jargon is often a cover for foolish fads. If someone uses "ed speak" you don't understand, ask them to explain themselves in plain English.

- **Don't automatically accept claims of "research says."** Our schools are constantly subjected to silly, untested ideas by people who will tell you that their methods are backed by proven theories. The truth is that the field of education research is littered with shoddy, slanted reports that often prove nothing at all. If someone tells you that research backs their position, ask them to show it to you. Take a close look (if they can even come up with it). It may be bunk. If it conflicts with common sense, it's probably wrong.

- **Listen carefully.** Don't let the heated politics of school reform turn you into a closed-minded crusader. Always take time to study the other side's arguments and find out if they have any merit. Remember that educators—particularly veteran teachers—often do have solid ideas about how to make schools better.

- **Keep your cool.** Be firm but polite. This isn't always easy when you feel that your child's welfare is at stake. Tempers sometimes fly in the education reform arena. You probably won't get very far if you are hostile, though. You'll just force officials into a more defensive position.

- **Be prepared to be called names.** Just because you are courteous does not mean others will be. A favorite tactic of the education establishment is to attack reformers as "right-wing extremists" who are trying to impose their views on everyone else. If you criticize anything at all about public education, you may be painted as a mean-spirited elitist who doesn't care about others' children. This business is not for the faint of heart!

- **Use the Internet.** It has become a valuable tool for transmitting and receiving news about education reform, communicating with other parents who are fighting the same battles, and circumventing entrenched interests. "The education establishment still wants to know how we did it," says Larry Gipson of Mathematically Correct, the group that played such a big role in reforming California's math standards. "Now they are starting to understand the power of the Internet, because they got hit very hard with this."

- **Support and respect good teachers.** Educators say that some parents storm in with the attitude that the schools must be saved from the teachers. "They make you feel like you don't know as much as you do," says a California teacher. Do your best not to trigger that kind of tension. Support good teachers while going about the task of reform.

Education reform is tough work, but a few determined parents and teachers banded together can eventually make a difference. Although changes are hard to come by, the rewards are immense. The campaign for reform immerses you in the community. It teaches firsthand lessons of what democracy is all about. It shows children that parents care deeply about their learning. Says Philadelphia father Robert Hall: "When my daughters see me going to school and writing letters to make their schools better, they see that Dad is really concerned about their education."[3]

Good Books About Education Reform

Here are some worthy books for parents interested in education reform. Those with asterisks are good ones to start with.

*Beyond the Classroom: Why School Reform Has Failed and What Parents Need to Do, Laurence Steinberg (Simon & Schuster, 1996).

Break These Chains: The Battle for School Choice, Daniel McGroarty (Prima Publishing, 1996).

Charter Schools: Creating Hope and Opportunity for American Education, Joe Nathan (Jossey-Bass Publishers, 1996).

Dictatorship of Virtue: Multiculturalism and the Battle for America's Future, Richard Bernstein (Knopf, 1994).

Dumbing Down Our Kids, Charles Sykes (St. Martin's Press, 1995).

High School Achievement: Public, Catholic, and Private Schools Compared, James S. Coleman, Thomas Hoffer, and Sally Kilgore (Basic Books, 1982).

Improving Your Child's Education: A Parent's Handbook for Working with Schools, Chrys Dougherty (Omni Publishers, 1997).

Inside American Education: The Decline, The Deception, The Dogmas, Thomas Sowell (Free Press, 1993).

Is There a Public for Public Schools?, David Matthews (Kettering Foundation Press, 1996).

*The Learning Gap, Harold W. Stevenson and James W. Stigler (Touchstone Books, 1994).

Losing Our Language: How Multicultural Classroom Instruction Is Undermining Our Children's Ability to Read, Write, and Reason, Sandra Stotsky (Free Press, 1999).

Market Education: The Unknown History, Andrew J. Coulson (Transaction Publishing, 1999).

*New Schools for a New Century, Diane Ravitch and Joseph P. Viteritti, eds. (Yale University Press, 1997).

The Political Dynamics of American Education, Frederick M. Wirt and Michael W. Kirst (McCutchan Publishing Co., 1997).

Politics, Markets, and America's Schools, John E. Chubb and Terry M. Moe (Brookings Institution, 1990).

Public Education: An Autopsy, Myron Lieberman (Harvard University Press, 1993).

Reinventing Public Education: How Contracting Can Transform America's Schools, Paul T. Hill, Lawrence C. Pierce, and James W. Guthrie (University of Chicago Press, 1997).

The School Reform Handbook: How to Improve Your Schools, Jeanne Allen with Angela Dale (The Center for Education Reform, 1995, with 1999 supplement).

The Schools We Need & Why We Don't Have Them, E. D. Hirsch, Jr. (Doubleday, 1996).

The Troubled Crusade: American Education, 1945-1980, Diane Ravitch (Basic Books, 1983).

We Must Take Charge: Our Schools and Our Future, Chester E. Finn, Jr. (Free Press, 1991).

Why Our Children Can't Read and What We Can Do About It, Diane McGuinness (Free Press, 1997).

Winning the Brain Race: A Bold Plan to Make Our Schools Competitive, David T. Kearns and Denis P. Doyle (ICS Press, 1988).

Good Web Sites for Parent-Reformers

Here are some good Internet addresses for parents interested in education reform.

Alliance for Parental Involvement in Education
www.croton.com/allpie
A nonprofit group that fosters parental involvement in education and supports those interested in home schooling. Offers a newsletter, conferences, workshops, and materials.

The Center for Education Reform
www.edreform.com
An active broker in school reform nationwide. Promotes school choice and charter schools, and does much grassroots work with schools and parents.

CEO America
www.childrenfirstamerica.org
A national clearinghouse of privately funded K–12 scholarship programs.

Core Knowledge Foundation
www.coreknowledge.org
Advocates a model curriculum that provides a solid, coherent foundation of learning for students.

Council for Basic Education
www.c-b-e.org
Promotes a curriculum strong in the basic subjects.

Education Consumers ClearingHouse
www.education-consumers.com
A grassroots networking and information site for parents, policy makers, and taxpayers.

Educational Excellence Network
www.edexcellence.net
A project of the Thomas B. Fordham Foundation, in connection with the Manhattan Institute. Led by author Chester E. Finn, Jr., it contains information on many education issues and links to numerous other sites.

Educational Resources for Busy Parents and Educators
www.elainemcewan.com
A Web site based on the work of Elaine McEwan. Provides resources for parents on issues such as ADHD, school leadership, and reading.

Kids Web
www.kidsvista.com/index.html
Provides child-focused access to the Web. Contains information targeted at the K–12 level.

Mathematically Correct
www.mathematicallycorrect.com
A grassroots group of parents and educators fighting the ills of "new New Math" in California and beyond.

National Assessment Governing Board
www.nagb.org
Provides information on what American students know and can do in reading, math, and a range of academic subjects both nationally and state-by-state.

National Center for Education Statistics
www.nces.ed.gov
Tons of hard data from the principal federal education statistics agency.

National Right to Read Foundation
www.nrrf.org
Provides parents with research on various approaches to reading and information about home-based reading programs.

Policy.com
www.policy.com
A mega-site that links think tanks, advocacy groups and other policy organizations.

PRESS (Parents Raising Educational Standards in Schools)
www.execpc.com/~presswis
An organization of concerned citizens in Wisconsin committed to raising academic standards. This site has lots of good education hyperlinks.

Public Agenda
www.publicagenda.org
Conducts public opinion surveys on important social issues, including education.

Saxon Publishers
www.saxonpub.com
Contains materials on the Saxon math curriculum, which has gained nationwide fame as a reliable "back to basics" series.

School Wise Press
www.schoolwisepress.com
A consumer-friendly Web site that provides rankings and information on California schools. Could serve as a model for other states and communities.

techlearning.com
www.techlearning.com
Excellent source of consumer information about education software for the elementary and secondary years, meant primarily for educators but fully accessible to parents.

Town Hall
www.townhall.com
A one-stop shopping center of conservative think tanks and advocacy groups.

U.S. Department of Education
www.ed.gov
News, statistics, publications, and more from the Department of Education in Washington, D. C.

Notes

Introduction

1. *Playing Their Parts: Parents and Teachers Talk About Parental Involvement in Public Schools* (New York: Public Agenda, 1999).

Chapter 1: Fostering a Love of Learning

1. David Elkind, *The Hurried Child* (Reading, Massachusetts: Addison-Wesley, 1989), p. 130.

2. *Playing Their Parts: Parents and Teachers Talk about Parental Involvement in Public Schools* (New York: Public Agenda, 1999), p. 25.

Introduction to Part II: The Core Curriculum

1. E. D. Hirsch, Jr., and John Holdren, *Books to Build On* (New York: Delta, 1996), p. 12.

2. Ibid., p. 17.

Chapter 5: English

1. Carol Innerst, "High School Grads Missing Basic Skills," *Washington Times*, January 8, 1998, p. A6.

2. Nanci Hellmich, "Invented Spelling: Creative or Crippling to Kids?" *USA Today*, June 5, 1996, p. D7.

3. Edward E. Ericson, "They Can't Write!" *American Enterprise* (American Enterprise Institute, Washington, D.C.), September/October 1996, p. 14.

4. Leslie Wakulich, "Computers in Class Threaten Penmanship," *Washington Times*, January 6, 1997, p. A2.

5. Herbert R. Kohl, *Should We Burn Babar?* (New York: New Press, 1995).

6. Sandra Stotsky, *State English Standards: An Appraisal of English Language-Arts/Reading Standards in Twenty-Eight States* (Thomas B. Fordham Foundation, Washington, D.C.), July 1997, pp. 27–28.

7. Heather Mac Donald, "Why Johnny's Teacher Can't Teach," *City Journal* (Manhattan Institute, New York), spring 1998.

8. DeNeen Brown, "A Word on Good Grammar," *Washington Post*, March 16, 1998, p. A1.

9. Sol Stern, "My Public School Lesson," *City Journal*, autumn 1997, p. 15.

10. DeNeen Brown, "A Word on Good Grammar."

11. Paula Gray Hunker, "Reading Together," *Washington Times*, April 21, 1998, p. E1.

Chapter 6: History and Geography

1. Walter A. McDougall "The Three Reasons to Teach History," *Middle States Council for the Social Sciences, 1998 Yearbook* (University Park: Pennsylvania State University, Middle States Council for the Social Studies), p. 112.

2. *Guidelines for Geographic Education: Elementary and Secondary School* (Washington, D.C.: Joint Committee on Geographic Education of the National Council for Geographic Education and the Association of American Geographers, 1984), p. 2.

3. Richard Halliburton, *Richard Halliburton's Complete Book of Marvels* (Indianapolis: Bobbs-Merrill, 1960), p. 7.

4. Joy Hakim, "Reading, Writing, and . . . History," *History Matters!* online edition, National Council for History Education, Westlake, Ohio, May 1996.

5. Mark Clayton, "Textbook Size Expands to Include Extras," *Christian Science Monitor*, online edition, December 1, 1997.

6. Bernard DeVoto, *The Year of Decision: 1846* (Boston: Houghton Mifflin, 1943), p. xix.

7. Diane Ravitch, "Tot Sociology: What Happened to History in the Grade Schools," *The Key Reporter* (Phi Beta Kappa Society), autumn 1987, p. 1.

8. "Core Knowledge Schools Take Root Across the Country," *American Educator* (American Federation of Teachers), winter 1996–97, p. 4.

9. Jay Mathews, "Teaching History as a Matter of Fact," *Washington Post*, March 11, 1997, p. A1.

10. Steve Farkas, *Different Drummers: How Teachers of Teachers View Public Education* (New York: Public Agenda, 1997), p. 22.

11. Ibid., p. 20.

12. David Warren Saxe, "The History Standards: Still an Outrage," *Weekly Standard*, March 10, 1997, p. 23.

13. Alexander Stille, "The Betrayal of History," *New York Review of Books*, June 11, 1998.

14. Mark Clayton, "A Page Out of the History-Text Debate," *Christian Science Monitor*, online edition, December 1, 1997.

15. Alexander Stille, "The Betrayal of History."

16. Ibid.

17. Ken Ringle, "Historian on the March," *Washington Post*, December 20, 1997, p. F1.

18. *A New Generation of History Textbooks* (New York: American Textbook Council, 1998), p. 6.

19. Pam Belluck, "Pilgrims Wear Different Hats in Recast Thanksgiving Tales," *New York Times*, November 23, 1995, p. A1.

20. Sol Stern, "My Public School Lesson," *City Journal* autumn 1997, p. 15.

21. Lynne Cheney, "The End of History," *Wall Street Journal*, October 20, 1994.

22. Alexander Stille, "The Betrayal of History."

23. Stephen Henn, "Arlington Student Tops State in Knowledge of Geography," *Northern Virginia Sun Weekly*, April 10, 1997, p. 1.

Chapter 8: Mathematics

1. Victoria Benning, "Math Teachers' Modern Ways Don't Add Up for Everyone," *Washington Post*, November 2, 1997, p. A1.

2. Richard Lee Colvin, "Formulas for Math Problems," *Los Angeles Times*, January 5, 1997.

3. Romesh Ratnesar, "This Is Math?" *Time*, August 25, 1997.

4. Steve Farkas, *Different Drummers: How Teachers of Teachers View Public Education* (New York: Public Agenda, 1997), p. 11.

5. Victoria Benning, "Math Teachers' Modern Ways Don't Add Up for Everyone."

6. Donna Horowitz, "'Touchy-Feely' Math Arouses Parents' Ire," *Washington Times*, November 18, 1996, p. A2.

7. *Curriculum and Evaluation Standards for School Mathematics* (Reston, Virginia: National Council of Teachers of Mathematics, 1989), p. 95.

8. *Everybody Counts: A Report to the Nation on the Future of Mathematics Education* (Washington, D.C.: National Research Council, 1989), p. 62.

9. Richard Lee Colvin, "Formulas for Math Problems."

10. Lynne Cheney, "Exam Scam," *Weekly Standard*, August 4, 1997, p. 25.

11. E. D. Hirsch, Jr., and John Holdren, *Books to Build On* (New York: Delta, 1996), p. 305.

12. Sol Stern, "My Public School Lesson," *City Journal* autumn 1997, p. 15.

13. Lynne Cheney, "Exam Scam."

Chapter 9: Science

1. William Souder, "Evidence Grows, Suspects Elusive in Frogs' Disappearance," *Washington Post*, July 6, 1998, p. A3.

2. Debra Saunders, "Science Snoots Wage War on Real Standards," *San Francisco Chronicle*, October 2, 1998.

3. *The Bayer Facts of Science: Education III: A U.S. Student Report Card on Science Excellence*, Executive Summary, Bayer Corporation, 1997, p. 7.

4. Millicent Lawton, "Evolution Debate Accents Deeper Science Disquiet," *Education Week*, online edition, May 6, 1998.

5. Steve Farkas, *Different Drummers: How Teachers of Teachers View Public Education* (New York: Public Agenda, 1997), p. 11.

6. *Are We Building Environmental Literacy?* Independent Commission on Environmental Education, George C. Marshall Institute, Washington, D.C., 1997.

Chapter 10: Helping Your Child Succeed in School

1. Betty Holcomb, "Why You Should Be in Your Child's School," *Good Housekeeping*, September 1998, p. 174.

2. Harold W. Stevenson and James W. Stigler, *The Learning Gap: Why Our Schools Are Failing and What We Can Learn from Japanese and Chinese Education* (New York: Simon & Schuster, 1992), p. 94.

3. Matthew Robinson, "Does Good Practice Make Perfect?" *Investor's Business Daily*, April 24, 1998.

4. *Playing Their Parts: Parents and Teachers Talk about Parental Involvement in Public Schools* (New York: Public Agenda, 1999), p. 32.

5. Jay Niver, "Too Many Students Don't Bother to Study," *Wilmington Star-News*, June 23, 1996, p. E6.

6. Peter N. Berger, "Portfolio Folly," *Education Week*, online edition, January 14, 1998.

7. "A Parent's Perspective," *Network News and Views* (Educational Excellence Network, Washington, D.C.), October 1995, p. 120.

8. Paige Bowers, "State's Math, Science Standards Graded," *Washington Times*, March 11, 1998, p. A12.

9. Steve Farkas, *Different Drummers: How Teachers of Teachers View Public Education* (New York: Public Agenda, 1997), p. 13.

10. Alfie Kohn, "How Privileged Parents Undermine School Reform," *Phi Delta Kappan*, April 1998.

11. "Gaye LeBaron's Notebook," *The Press Democrat* (Santa Rosa, California), June 16, 1998.

12. Bonnie Miller Rubin, "Academic Partnership an Elusive Goal," *Chicago Tribune*, October 4, 1998.

13. *Time to Move On: African-American and White Parents Set an Agenda for Public Schools* (New York: Public Agenda, 1998).

14. Lynn Balster Liontos, *Involving the Families of At-Risk Youth in the Educational*

Process (University of Oregon, Eugene: ERIC Clearinghouse on Educational Management, 1991), p. 1.

15. Lynn Olson, "An A for Effort," *Teacher Magazine*, online edition, August 1995.

16. Beth Levine, "Tips from Top Teachers," *Reader's Digest*, September 1998, p. 146.

Chapter 11: Special Needs and Gifts

1. Patricia McGill Smith, "You Are Not Alone: For Parents When They Learn That Their Child Has a Disability," essay on Web site www.npnd.org/notalone.htm.

2. Nancy Gibbs, "The Age of Ritalin," *Time*, November 30, 1998, p. 86.

3. Mary Eberstadt, "Why Ritalin Rules," *Policy Review*, April/May 1999, p. 24.

Chapter 12: School Problems

1. Rene Sanchez, "Teens Tell Researchers High School Is Too Easy," *Washington Post*, February 11, 1997, p. A22.

2. "Dumbing Down the Schools," *Washington Times*, November 27, 1997, p. A16.

3. Kent Fisher, "Promoting Failure," *St. Petersburg Times*, May 17, 1998.

4. Steve Farkas, *Different Drummers: How Teachers of Teachers View Public Education* (New York: Public Agenda, 1997), p. 21.

5. Alexander Stille, "The Betrayal of History," *New York Review of Books*, June 11, 1998.

6. *A New Generation of History Textbooks* (New York: American Textbook Council, 1998), p. 4.

7. Jeanne S. Chall, "What Students Were Reading 100 Years Ago," *American Educator*, summer 1994, p. 26.

8. *A Lot to Be Thankful For: What Parents Want Children to Learn About America* (New York: Public Agenda, 1998), p. 15.

9. Jay Niver, "Too Many Students Don't Bother to Study," *Wilmington Star-News*, June 23, 1996, p. E6.

10. Kim Asch, "Indiana High School Swears Off Profanity," *Washington Times*, January 4, 1999, p. A1.

11. "Schools Discover Internet Access Can Weave an Extremely Tangled Web" (Associated Press), *Washington Times*, September 1, 1998, p. A3.

Chapter 13: Along with Academics

1. *Playing Their Parts: Parents and Teachers Talk About Parental Involvement in Public Schools* (New York: Public Agenda, 1999), p. 25.

2. Kathleen Kennedy Manzo, "As Some Skate Forward, Others Dodge PE," *Education Week*, online edition, April 2, 1997.

3. Eric L. Wee, "Students Go Extracurricular Mile for Admission to Elite Colleges," *Washington Post*, May 7, 1996, p. A1.

Chapter 14: Temptations and Troubles

1. Patricia Davis and Pierre Thomas, "Youth Users and Sellers Abound in Affluent Suburbs," *Washington Post*, December 14, 1997, p. A20.

2. Wendy Shalit, "Sex Ed's Dead End," *City Journal* spring 1998.

3. Marilyn Gardner, "Shifts in Sex Ed—Talking Abstinence," *Christian Science Monitor*, August 11, 1998.

4. Robert W. Blum and Peggy M. Rinehart, *Reducing the Risk: Connections That Make a Difference in the Lives of Youth*, Division of General Pediatrics and Adolescent Health, University of Minnesota, Minneapolis, 1997.

Chapter 15: Current Issues in Education

1. E. D. Hirsch, Jr., *The Schools We Need* (New York: Doubleday, 1996), p. 55.

2. "Why General Knowledge Should Be a Goal of Education in a Democracy,"

speech by E. D. Hirsch to the Core Knowledge National Conference, Atlanta, March 14, 1998.

3. Andrew Hazlett, "See Spot Run Multiculturally," *Wall Street Journal*, February 22, 1999.

4. Richard Bernstein, "Dictatorship of Virtue: Multiculturalism in Elementary and Secondary Schools," *American Experiment Quarterly*, summer 1998.

5. E. D. Hirsch, *The Schools We Need*, p. 249.

6. James Traub, "Multiple Intelligence Disorder," *The New Republic*, October 26, 1998, p. 20.

7. Jay Mathews, "Forget Einstein. Think Team!" *Washington Post*, August 20, 1997, p. A1.

8. Jessica Portner, "Today's Lesson: Self-Esteem," *Education Week*, December 7, 1998, p. 25.

9. Matthew Robinson, "Education Theory Stresses Emotions Over Skills," *Investor's Business Daily*, National Issue, June 10, 1996.

10. Karl Zinsmeister, "Doing Bad and Feeling Good," *The American Enterprise* (American Enterprise Institute, Washington, D.C.), September/October 1996, p. 46.

11. Gilbert T. Sewall, *Learning about Religion, Learning from Religion* (New York: American Textbook Council, 1998).

12. Victoria Benning and Amy Argetsinger, "Schools Pressured on 'Social Promotion,'" *Washington Post*, February 26, 1999, p. B1.

13. Kent Fisher, "Promoting Failure," *St. Petersburg Times*, May 17, 1998.

14. Ken Adelman, "Dressing Better for Improved Education," *Washington Times*, January 31, 1996.

15. "Year-Round Schools: Do They Improve Academic Performance?" *CQ Researcher* (Congressional Quarterly Inc.), May 17, 1996.

16. Todd Oppenheimer, "The Computer Delusion," *The Atlantic Monthly*, July 1997, p. 45.

17. A. McKenzie, "Internet Pioneer Reverses Course, Calling Computers Mostly a Waste," *Dallas Morning News*, August 4, 1998.

18. Randal C. Archibold, "Getting Tough on Teachers," *New York Times*, November 1, 1998.

19. Sheila Schwartz, "Teaching's Unlettered Future," *New York Times*, August 6, 1998.

20. Steve Farkas, *Different Drummers: How Teachers of Teachers View Public Education* (New York: Public Agenda, 1997), p. 9.

21. Heather Mac Donald, "Why Johnny's Teacher Can't Teach," *City Journal*, spring 1998.

22. John Leo, "Dumbing Down Teachers," *U.S. News & World Report*, August 3, 1998.

23. Sol Stern, "How Teachers' Unions Handcuff Schools," *City Journal*, spring 1997, p. 35.

24. Richard K. Munro, "Bilingual Miseducation," *Selected Readings on School Reform* (Thomas B. Fordham Foundation, Washington, D.C.), fall 1998, p. 153.

25. James Traub, "The Bilingual Barrier," *New York Times Magazine*, January 31, 1999, p. 34.

Chapter 16: Parents and Education Reform

1. Lee M. Silver, "My Lesson in School Politics," *New York Times*, September 10, 1997.

2. David Nakamura, "PTA Alternative Embodies a Shift in School Activism," *Washington Post*, September 28, 1997.

3. Betty Holcomb, "Why You Should Be in Your Child's School, *Good Housekeeping*, September 1998, p. 174.

Index